Professional
SharePoint® 2007
₋₋₋₋pment

Professional
SharePoint® 2007
Development

John Holliday, John Alexander,
Jeff Julian, Eli Robillard,
Brendon Schwartz, Matt Ranlett,
J. Dan Attis, Adam Buenz,
and Tom Rizzo

Wiley Publishing, Inc.

Professional SharePoint® 2007 Development

Published by
Wiley Publishing, Inc.
10475 Crosspoint Boulevard
Indianapolis, IN 46256
www.wiley.com

Copyright © 2007 by Wiley Publishing, Inc., Indianapolis, Indiana

Published simultaneously in Canada

ISBN: 978-0-470-11756-9

Manufactured in the United States of America

10 9 8 7 6 5 4 3 2 1

Library of Congress Cataloging-in-Publication Data is available from the publisher.

For general information on our other products and services please contact our Customer Care Department within the United States at (800) 762-2974, outside the United States at (317) 572-3993 or fax (317) 572-4002.

Trademarks: Wiley, the Wiley logo, Wrox, the Wrox logo, Programmer to Programmer, and related trade dress are trademarks or registered trademarks of John Wiley & Sons, Inc. and/or its affiliates, in the United States and other countries, and may not be used without written permission. Microsoft and Excel are registered trademarks of Microsoft Corporation in the United States and/or other countries. All other trademarks are the property of their respective owners. Wiley Publishing, Inc., is not associ-ated with any product or vendor mentioned in this book.

Wiley also publishes its books in a variety of electronic formats. Some content that appears in print may not be available in electronic books.

To my beautiful wife, Alice, for her steadfast encouragement and never-ending support; to my amazing mother, Frances, whose courage and gentle nobility continues to inspire the best in me, and to His Holiness Sri Sri Ravi Shankar, the fountain of knowledge at the center of my universe.

— *John Holliday*

To my wonderful and devoted wife, Heidi, for her unending support and encouragement; without you this would not have been possible; and to my loving parents for always believing in me.

— *Brendon Schwartz*

Eli Robillard would like to dedicate his chapters to the two girls who have always provided constant support and inspiration: his mother, Ruth, and his daughter, Irina.

— *Eli Robillard*

About the Authors

Consultant, author, and coach **John Alexander** is a recognized Microsoft Certified Trainer (MCT), Microsoft Certified Solution Developer (MCSD) and has served as the Microsoft regional director for the Kansas City region for the last nine years. Experienced in the delivery of scalable, stable, and open enterprise-level .NET Web applications, John is an industry-recognized trainer, consultant, speaker, and writer on the Microsoft .NET vision and implementation at both the technical and business decision-maker level. He has also coached several teams of developers, including one that was directly responsible for placing their organization on *CIO* magazine's Agile 100 list. You can reach John at john@alexanderjulian.net. John is a principal with Alexander & Julian Inc, a Microsoft Partner specializing in Microsoft SharePoint Server 2007 and custom .NET development. Known for excellence in software delivery, Alexander & Julian prides itself on solving business challenges with innovative solutions.

Aside from being very passionate and somewhat obsessed with the latest and greatest Microsoft technologies that regularly come out of Redmond, **J. Dan Attis** has been heavily involved in the local Atlanta user group community since 2003, where he landed after completing his degree in applied mathematics at the University of Western Ontario, a hardcore technology program at The Information Technology Institute (ITI), and a short contract in North Carolina. In addition to being an occasional speaker at both the VB.NET and the C#.NET user groups, he helped create the Free Training 1,2,3! series (www.freetraining123.com) to help developers learn Microsoft technologies. Dan created and presented material at the first SharePoint 1,2,3! event (www.sharepoint123.com) along with the other leaders of the Atlanta Microsoft Professionals user group. Dan is also on the team responsible for the highly successful Atlanta Code Camps that run every year, as well as being a speaker. Today, Dan works as a senior consultant for Intellinet, working primarily with cutting-edge SharePoint and .NET technologies, creating innovative technology solutions that achieve measurable business improvements for their clients. He resides in Roswell, Georgia, with his wonderful wife, Jody, and their beautiful daughter, Lily.

Adam Buenz, MVP, CCSP, MCP, is an enterprise software architect for ARB Security Solutions specializing in knowledge management, collaboration strategies, and business process automation. In 2006, Adam was awarded the Microsoft Most Valuable Professional (MVP) citation for Windows SharePoint Services for his contributions to the SharePoint community. Adam is currently completing his Masters degree in mathematics. Adam blogs at www.sharepointsecurity.com/blog and can be contacted at adam@sharepointsecurity.com.

John Holliday is an independent consultant and Microsoft MVP for Office SharePoint Server and has over 25 years of professional software development and consulting experience. John has been involved in a broad spectrum of commercial software development projects ranging from retail products to enterprise information systems for the Fortune 100.

After receiving his bachelor's degree in applied mathematics from Harvard College and a J.D. from the University of Michigan, John developed a specialized computing language for constructing legal expert systems. His expertise includes all aspects of distributed systems development, with a special emphasis on document automation, collaboration, and enterprise content management.

In addition to his professional career, John is actively engaged in humanitarian activities through Works of Wonder International, a nonprofit organization he cofounded with his wife, Alice, and the Art of Living Foundation, an international service organization devoted to uplifting human values throughout the world.

Jeff Julian is a principal consultant with Alexander & Julian Inc, a Kansas City–based Microsoft partner and software consulting firm. His ability to resolve business challenges and passion for the software community was evident when Microsoft awarded him the Most Valuable Professional award in the area of XML for four years in a row. Jeff is also the founder of the largest blogging site of Microsoft professionals, named Geekswithblogs.net. You can contact Jeff by email at jeff@alexanderjulian.net.

Matt Ranlett, a SQL Server MVP, has been a fixture of the Atlanta .NET developer community for many years. A founding member of the Atlanta Dot Net Regular Guys (www.devcow.com), Matt has formed and leads several area user groups. Despite spending dozens of hours after work on local and national community activities such as the SharePoint 1, 2, 3! series (www.sharepoint123.com), organizing three Atlanta Code Camps, working on the INETA board of directors as the vice president of technology, and appearing in several podcasts such as .Net Rocks and the ASP.NET Podcast, Matt recently found the time to get married to a wonderful woman named Kim, whom he helps to raise three monstrous dogs. Matt currently works as a senior consultant with Intellinet and is part of the team committed to helping people succeed by delivering innovative solutions that create business value.

Eli Robillard is a frequent speaker at user groups and conferences, a technical editor, a Microsoft Office SharePoint Server MVP, the founder of the Toronto SharePoint Users Group, a member of the Microsoft Canada Speakers Bureau, and a founding member and past chair of a group of high-profile industry influencers and early adopters known as the ASPInsiders. As the principal architect in the Technology Architecture Group at Infusion Development Corporation, Eli designs SharePoint solutions for Wall Street, Bay Street, and large organizations worldwide. He lives in Toronto, Ontario, Canada, where he plays music and goes on adventures with his 10-year old daughter.

Brendon Schwartz actively participates in the Atlanta area user groups and is known as one of the Atlanta .NET Regular Guys (www.devcow.com), of which he is also one of the cofounders. He is currently on the INETA board of directors as the vice president of technology, working to solve the technology problems of a large nonprofit organization using SharePoint and ASP.NET. Brendon currently works for Wintellect, solving real-world business problems through the use of Microsoft technologies such as SharePoint, .NET, Office, and VSTS. In addition to presenting at local user groups, he created the Free Training 1,2,3! series to help developers learn Microsoft technologies. As a .NET community leader in Atlanta, Brendon coauthored and presented the training material for SharePoint 1,2,3! (www.sharepoint123.com). He also writes technical articles for Microsoft, as well as other magazine publications on the topics of SharePoint and business intelligence. Brendon has worked on the leadership teams of five different user groups and has been interviewed for his community efforts on podcasts, including the ASP.NET Podcast, .NET Rocks!, and The SharePoint Show podcast. Brendon serves as the co-chairman of the Atlanta Code Camps (www.atlantacodecamp.com), at which he also regularly presents.

Credits

Senior Acquisitions Editor
Jim Minatel

Development Editors
Ami Frank Sullivan
Sara Shlaer
Sydney Jones

Technical Editors
Dave Schmitt
Phred Menyhert

Production Editor
Debra Banninger

Copy Editor
Foxxe Editorial Services

Editorial Manager
Mary Beth Wakefield

Production Manager
Tim Tate

Vice President and Executive Group Publisher
Richard Swadley

Vice President and Executive Publisher
Joseph B. Wikert

Compositor
Laurie Stewart, Happenstance Type-O-Rama

Proofreader
Nancy Carrasco

Indexer
Melanie Belkin

Anniversary Logo Design
Richard Pacifico

Foreword

After three years, the time is here. Microsoft Office SharePoint Server 2007 has shipped with great fanfare and lots of accolades from customers, partners, and the press.

It's humbling to be part of the team that helped bring this monstrous release to market. When I worked on SharePoint Portal Server 2001 (codenamed Tahoe back then), Microsoft was making its first official foray into the portal market with document management added in for good measure. For those of you who worked with SharePoint in those days, the 2001 version was a good first attempt to enter into a new market for Microsoft even with some of the limitations we knew the product had. With the 2007 release, I can definitely say that we have worked hard to make sure SharePoint meets the needs of diverse sets of customers from the smallest business to the largest enterprise.

So, why should you care about SharePoint and this book?

Well, if you look at the 2007 release, we've extended the surface area of SharePoint twofold. The previous version of SharePoint was a great collaboration, portal, and enterprise search tool. We've enhanced each of those capabilities, while at the same time adding enterprise content management, business process management and e-forms, and finally business intelligence capabilities to the product. That's a lot of new technology, information, APIs, and best practices that you need to learn. You'll need a great teacher and this book is that teacher.

The authors cover the breadth of SharePoint without sacrificing the depth you need to understand how to build complete and robust SharePoint solutions. In fact, you will find yourself consistently reaching for this book on your bookshelf, earmarking pages that have the tips and tricks you need to get your job done, and this book will quickly become an indispensable part of your SharePoint reference set.

After reading this book, you will become a sought-after SharePoint expert ready to tackle the problems that your users throw at you. I know I learned a number of new things about SharePoint after reading this book. I think you will, too.

Tom Rizzo
Redmond, WA
March 2007

Contents

Contents

Contents

Contents

Contents

Contents

Contents

Contents

Introduction

If you're a .NET or Microsoft Office developer, this book will give you the tools and the techniques you need to build great solutions for the SharePoint platform. It offers practical insights that will help you take advantage of this powerful new integrated suite of server-based collaboration software tools along with specific examples that show you how to implement your own custom solutions. You'll then be able to apply this information to create collaborative web-based applications that enhance user productivity and deliver rich user experiences.

You'll start by building a strong foundation based on a thorough understanding of the technologies that come with the SharePoint platform, while also drilling into specific implementation areas. Next, you'll dive into seven key SharePoint development areas: the base collaboration platform, portal and composite application frameworks, enterprise search, ECM, business process automation and workflow, electronic forms, and business intelligence.

Who This Book Is For

This book is for ASP.NET developers who want to add collaboration support to their existing applications, Windows/Office client developers who want to move their solutions from the desktop to the web, and experienced SharePoint version 2.0 developers who want to take advantage of the new capabilities available in Windows SharePoint Services 3.0.

What This Book Covers

You will learn all about Windows SharePoint Services and MOSS 2007, including the following:

- ❑ Ways to enhance collaboration using calendars, tasks, issues, and email alerts
- ❑ Techniques for developing applications with integrated RSS, blogs, and Wikis
- ❑ How to build, configure, and manage portal solutions
- ❑ Strategies for using enterprise search, XML, and XSLT
- ❑ Methods for improving enterprise content management and business intelligence
- ❑ Ways to take advantage of built-in support for regulatory compliance and web publishing
- ❑ How to create custom workflows and integrate them into your solutions

Conventions

To help you get the most from the text and keep track of what's happening, we've used a number of conventions throughout the book.

- ❑ We *highlight* new terms and important words when we introduce them.

- ❑ We show keyboard strokes like this: Ctrl+A.

- ❑ We show file names, URLs, and code, within the text like this: `persistence.properties`.

- ❑ We present code in two different ways:

```
In code examples we highlight new and important code with a gray background.
The gray highlighting is not used for code that's less important in the present
context, or has been shown before.
```

Source Code

As you work through the examples in this book, you may choose either to type in all the code manually or to use the source code files that accompany the book. All of the source code used in this book is available for downloading at `www.wrox.com`. Once at the site, simply locate the book's title (either by using the Search box or by using one of the title lists) and click the Download Code link on the book's detail page to obtain all the source code for the book.

> *Because many books have similar titles, you may find it easiest to search by ISBN; this book's ISBN is 978-0-470-11756-9.*

Once you download the code, just decompress it with your favorite compression tool. Alternately, you can go to the main Wrox code download page at `www.wrox.com/dynamic/books/download.aspx` to see the code available for this book and all other Wrox books.

Errata

We make every effort to ensure that there are no errors in the text or in the code. However, no one is perfect, and mistakes do occur. If you find an error in one of our books, such as a spelling mistake or faulty piece of code, we would be very grateful for your feedback. By sending in errata you may save another reader hours of frustration and at the same time you will be helping us provide even higher-quality information.

To find the errata page for this book, go to `www.wrox.com` and locate the title using the Search box or one of the title lists. Then, on the book details page, click the Book Errata link. On this page you can view all errata that has been submitted for this book and posted by Wrox editors. A complete book list, including links to each book's errata is also available at `www.wrox.com/misc-pages/booklist.shtml`.

If you don't spot "your" error on the Book Errata page, go to `www.wrox.com/contact/techsupport .shtml` and complete the form there to send us the error you have found. We'll check the information and, if appropriate, post a message to the book's errata page and fix the problem in subsequent editions of the book.

p2p.wrox.com

For author and peer discussion, join the P2P forums at p2p.wrox.com. The forums are a web-based system for you to post messages relating to Wrox books and related technologies and interact with other readers and technology users. The forums offer a subscription feature to email you topics of interest of your choosing when new posts are made to the forums. Wrox authors, editors, other industry experts, and your fellow readers are present on these forums.

At http://p2p.wrox.com you will find a number of different forums that will help you not only as you read this book but also as you develop your own applications. To join the forums, just follow these steps:

1. Go to p2p.wrox.com and click the Register link.
2. Read the terms of use and click Agree.
3. Complete the required information to join, as well as any optional information you wish to provide, and click Submit.
4. You will receive an email with information describing how to verify your account and complete the joining process.

> *You can read messages in the forums without joining P2P, but in order to post your own messages, you must join.*

Once you join, you can post new messages and respond to messages other users post. You can read messages at any time on the web. If you would like to have new messages from a particular forum emailed to you, click the Subscribe to This Forum icon by the forum's name in the forum listing.

For more information about how to use the Wrox P2P, be sure to read the P2P FAQs for answers to questions about how the forum software works as well as many common questions specific to P2P and Wrox books. To read the FAQs, click the FAQ link on any P2P page.

1

The Microsoft Application Platform and SharePoint

By Eli Robillard

An *application platform* is the foundation upon which developers build the software that people use from day to day. After an introduction to SharePoint, this chapter takes a look at application platforms, with particular attention to the Microsoft Application Platform. Finally, the starring roles of Windows SharePoint Services 3.0 and Microsoft Office SharePoint Server 2007 are explained in a way that may change the way you think about enterprise applications.

SharePoint Products and Technologies

SharePoint is a set of products and technologies with informative and collaborative web-based capabilities that help people create, organize, distribute, and maintain stored knowledge. SharePoint web sites and pages are commonly used to build intranet and extranet portals and team sites, as well as public-facing Internet sites. SharePoint is a great platform upon which to build applications and provides many key services in the greater story of the Microsoft Application Platform.

SharePoint shows great maturity in terms of its user interface, database design, and workflow and communication features. It provides a standard interface with standard navigation, enabling users to focus on tools and information, not on learning how to navigate new menu controls. SharePoint helps resolve database and business logic issues by providing a powerful complement to structured data — that is, a managed environment to store unstructured data that gets the information and business rules onto the network and out of local Excel files. SharePoint takes advantage of the first workflow platform built into an operating system and makes it easy for developers and power users to use Windows Workflow Foundation (WF) to automate business processes.

SharePoint integrates with IM and email, though you will still want Office Communications Server (OCS, formerly LCS) to audit and manage IM messaging as effectively as you manage email. SharePoint reduces the load on email by providing effective alternatives: appropriate, organic team sites for teams to share information, where teams can use document libraries with versioning, apply enforced "checkout" for editing, and provide links to documents rather than create versioning nightmares by emailing attachments to the whole team for review.

The set of SharePoint Products and Technologies includes two platforms: Windows SharePoint Services (WSS) and Microsoft Office SharePoint Server (MOSS). In a nutshell, WSS is used to create web sites for team collaboration on a common project. MOSS builds on WSS with capabilities for portal publishing, enterprise search, enterprise content management (ECM), business process automation, and business intelligence (BI) reporting and analysis tools. While WSS will serve well the needs of small companies and individual departments, MOSS is designed to be an "enterprise-class" platform to manage and control a company's diverse knowledge assets.

Windows SharePoint Services

Windows SharePoint Services (WSS) is a technology provided as an extension to Microsoft Windows Server 2003 (and above). WSS is free, and if it was not provided as an option when you installed Windows Server, you can download and install it from the Microsoft Downloads site (http://msdn2.microsoft.com/en-us/downloads/default.aspx) at any time. According to the Product Team, WSS "provides a platform for collaboration applications, offering a common framework for document management and a common repository for storing documents of all types."

WSS includes *Site Templates* for Team Sites, Document Workspaces, Meeting Workspaces, blogs, and Wikis. Since any site can be saved as a template, it is easy to create your own library of templates for reuse. Microsoft makes a collection available for downloading, and still more templates are available on the web.

Each WSS site may include document libraries, form libraries, calendars, announcements, task lists, issues lists, and custom lists. Each of these is simply a special instance of a list, and each list contains items or rows. What makes each distinct are the columns stored, and the views provided. For example, a calendar contains columns for the event name, start and end dates, and a description. It provides calendar views that you can switch from Daily, to Weekly, to Monthly. But whatever the columns and views, a calendar is simply a collection of items in a list.

WSS 3.0 reintroduced the concept of the *content type*. Companies work with many different types of content — expense reports, presentations, proposals, memos and more — and each of these types might have its own template and metadata fields. Content types let you define and consistently apply the rules for each type, for any page, library, or list in which you've allowed a type to be stored.

Content types can also be inherited, so you might have a base "Presentation" type with fields to store Product, Intended Audience, Duration, and Status (Draft or Final). This type may in turn be inherited by "Internal Presentation," which sets a base PowerPoint template, and "External Presentation," which sets both a document template and additional fields for Event Name and Event Date.

Microsoft Office SharePoint Server

Microsoft Office SharePoint Server (MOSS or OSS) comes in two versions: Standard Edition and Enterprise Edition. Standard Edition is a Microsoft product built upon WSS. MOSS extends WSS with functionality for web content management (WCM), records management (RM), integrated digital rights management (DRM), workflows, Single Sign-On (SSO), document retention and auditing policies, expanded search including People Search, and site variations to ease the maintenance of multilingual sites. MOSS also provides a My Site for each user, with both a private view for storing personal information and a public view to share photos, personal information, and more.

In MOSS, content types can also be associated with workflow and lifecycle policies. For example, you might have a base `Presentation` type, which sets a policy to "review or delete six months after last update." This type may in turn be inherited by `Internal Presentation`, which sets a base PowerPoint template, and `External Presentation`, which sets both a document template and a workflow so that all external presentations first obtain the approval of the marketing and legal departments.

Among the WCM features of OSS is the *Page Layout*. In MOSS, a Master Page may contain a Page Layout, which in turn contains HTML and fields. Page Layouts are great for organizing the body of a page. Each Page Layout is associated with a content type, and the content is stored in the type's fields. For example, you could have a Page Layout for products with a two-column display and a photo in the top left, and another for news items with a banner and a three-column layout. You can associate either of these with a Site Template, for example the Publishing Site, to provide multiple layouts without having to create a new Site Template. In WSS the Site Template and Master Page control page layout. In MOSS, Page Layouts provide many more combinations.

Microsoft Office SharePoint Server: Enterprise Edition contains the features of Standard Edition plus the following: a Forms Server to publish browser-based forms from InfoPath, an Excel Server for spreadsheet publishing, the Business Data Catalog to ease the displaying and searching of external data stores, and data visualization features for reporting and business intelligence.

Both WSS 3.0 and MOSS 2007 are .NET 2.0 applications with XML web service interaction layers and ASP.NET presentation layers (described in depth in Chapter 2).

SharePoint is a secure, reliable, scalable platform for developing enterprise web applications. This book shows you how to accomplish just that.

The Microsoft Application Platform

An application platform is a reliable, reusable set of products and technologies on which to develop and host applications that may span disparate environments and technologies. Each component in an application platform provides a *service*, which may be used by any application in an enterprise. An application, in turn, simulates or provides *business capabilities* to the people who use it. An application platform has a service-oriented architecture (SOA), meaning that each component provides a standard service which may be replaced with an equivalent provider of that service. Figure 1-1 illustrates the general structure of an application platform.

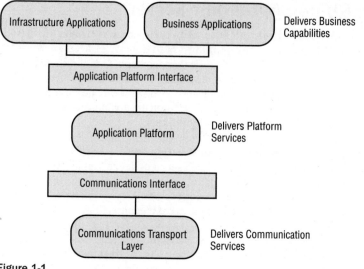

Figure 1-1

SOA has evolved to describe mainly XML web-service-based architectures, but in the context of an application platform a service is simply a platform service and not necessarily an XML web service. An application platform interface may provide access to platform services via a variety of methods. However, the application platform interface does not necessarily act as a broker for service consumers to discover or be matched to service providers. Instead, it is up to the application platform architect to identify and install appropriate service providers to meet the needs of the enterprise.

The *Microsoft Application Platform* (MAP) is a consistent, reusable platform upon which to standardize the development, deployment, operation, and administration of enterprise applications. The potential benefits include lower costs for server hosting, administration, software development, and training, and more efficient processes for the architecture, design, construction, deployment, and monitoring of applications.

To this end, common tools are used throughout the MAP stack:

- ❑ *Windows Server* provides a common server platform.
- ❑ The *Microsoft Management Console* (MMC) provides a common server management interface.
- ❑ The *.NET Framework* and the underlying *Common Language Runtime* (CLR) provide a common language layer for both client and server applications written in a variety of languages.
- ❑ *Visual Studio* (VS) provides a common integrated developer environment. *SQL Server* provides a common structured data store.
- ❑ And *Windows Workflow Foundation* (WF) provides a common business process engine.

The wonderful thing about common tools is that once you understand how each works, you can venture anywhere in the MAP and reuse that knowledge. And then there is SharePoint. While several technologies anchor the platform, the centerpiece of the MAP undoubtedly is SharePoint. SharePoint is an incredibly rich

ASP.NET application with a powerful object model for implementing applications as web sites. SharePoint can be used to build public web sites, intranets, extranets, and collaborative team sites. It provides the web front end for a growing set of Microsoft products, including Team Foundation Server and Project Server. You can often use SharePoint to build your own enterprise applications without writing a line of code.

It helps to understand how Microsoft describes and positions its application platform. In the aptly titled whitepaper, "What Is an Application Platform?" the opening bars go something like this:

> *The Microsoft Application Platform is a portfolio of technology capabilities, core products, and best practice guidance focused on helping IT departments to partner with the business to maximize opportunity by increasing their ability to drive the right efficiencies, customer connections, and value added services for business growth.*

You may have heard or read this before, whether recently from Microsoft or 20 years ago in the brochure of some other technology. The difference now is that Microsoft has evolved to the point of simplicity and commoditization where it is finally possible to realize the dream.

Microsoft divides its platform into five categories: Data Management, Workflow, Communications, Lifecycle Management, and User Experience. The following sections detail each of these categories.

Data Management

Data management includes all elements of the data chain, from the storage of raw bits and bytes right up to the manipulation and analysis provided by database and file systems. At the application level, data rendered into lists, items, reports, and graphic visualizations is now a reliable, predictable commodity.

Storage

Applications work with many data types, each with unique storage requirements. *SQL Server* is a relational database that is good at storing data, which may be described as a set of entities and their relationships. The *NT File System (NTFS)* is excellent at storing files: executable files, server configuration files, files to be transferred over FTP, files to be served over HTTP, and large files that are not practical to store in a database. *Windows SharePoint Services* is great at storing files used by information workers: Word and other text documents, Excel spreadsheets, PowerPoint decks, MS-Project files, images, and anything else you might find in a typical user's My Documents folder. SharePoint is also great at storing lists: Contacts, Tasks, Issues, Announcements, News, Events, or anything else you like, from your CD collection to "Things to bring to my party."

Reporting

SQL Server Reporting Services is the key reporting tool in the MAP. It provides the web-based Report Manager and produces reports over web services in a variety of formats, including HTML, Excel, and PDF. Reporting Services also provides SharePoint Web Parts to select, configure, and display reports

Analysis

SQL Server Analysis Services allows the powerful analysis of data stored in SQL Server and the construction of data cubes used for OLAP analysis, scorecard analysis, and data mining.

Visualization and Business Intelligence

Data visualization is about building graphs, charts, and other images that represent your data. *Business intelligence (BI)* is what you provide to business decision makers to help them make decisions. Or, as one might say, "When provided with enough knowledge no decision remains. There is only what is to be done."

The MAP provides BI features in *Office SharePoint Server* for building lists of Key Performance Indicators (KPIs) and for the surfacing of these KPIs in BI Web Parts. Microsoft offers *Proclarity* and *Business Scorecard Manager* to allow the construction of more complex business analysis and data-mining visualizations, which may be surfaced in a variety of formats.

Workflow

Windows Workflow Foundation (WF) is ostensibly a developer platform for creating state management systems that implement or support business processes with code. The Office vision for WF integration is to "facilitate human processes by attaching business logic to items and documents in SharePoint, while providing context and tracking progress."

While WF is appropriate for workflow in documents and lists, *BizTalk* is the appropriate platform for multistep transactions on structured data, or the orchestration of data flow and business processes among several enterprise systems.

Communications

A network is quiet without communications. Communication protocols provide reliable messaging features on a network including translation or marshaling across boundaries, and message queuing. On a human level, communication services facilitate conversations.

Office Communications Server (OCS, previously known as "Live Communications Server") hosts real-time messaging services. OCS provides PC-to-PC Voice over IP (VoIP) calls, PC-to-phone calls, instant messaging (IM) services, video, and conferencing services. OCS provides encryption services between Office Communicator clients, and capabilities to archive and audit IM conversations. Most companies have this control with e-mail, and one would expect all will eventually want the same for IM conversations.

IM client applications include Office Communicator (the preferred client) and Windows Live Messenger. OCS allows communication with "foreign" IM networks including Yahoo, AOL and the public Microsoft Live Messenger network.

OCS is also an IP PBX which means that it can act as a company's VoIP phone switch, or it can communicate with an existing IP PBX or TDM switch. This allows integration among OCS transports, an enterprise's phone system (VoIP or traditional), and public phone networks. For example, if you're leaving the office for a meeting, you can forward all calls dialed to your desktop PC or desk phone to your cellular phone, or if you don't respond to a request for a PC-to-PC IM session, the caller could opt to send a message to your cellular phone via SMS. The capability of providing high-quality PC-to-PC voice calls over a WAN instead of incurring toll charges between offices often motivates companies to move to OCS or an OCS-VoIP hybrid.

OCS includes *LiveMeeting,* a web conferencing host ideal for online meetings, whiteboarding, and webcasts. Live Meeting sessions can be recorded for later playback. Live Meeting is also available separately as a hosted service.

Service-Oriented Architecture (SOA)

In an SOA, BizTalk provides a service bus and advanced messaging, enabling any application with a service bus adapter to talk to any other application on the service bus, reducing the development effort for application-to-application communications by an order of magnitude. Both free and commercial adapters exist for a variety of common platforms, including SAP, JD Edwards, and PeopleSoft.

Office Live Server is a hub for real-time conversations between people that combines the previous Live Communication Server (LCS), Communicator, and Live Meeting products. LCS provides secure instant messaging, IP telephony, and Voice over IP (VoIP) services. Communicator is the supercharged client that provides the user interface on the desktop; LiveMeeting is a web-conferencing host which is great for online meetings, whiteboarding, and webcasts. Live Meeting sessions can be recorded for later play-back. Live Meeting is also available separately as a hosted service.

In recent times, any application which makes available its functionality through XML web services might be said to adhere to a service-oriented architecture. Though it is beneficial to keep presentation and application layers loosely-coupled, this particular trait is not what was originally meant by "SOA." Instead, the focus of SOA is on standardizing the interfaces of many applications to the point that one application in a category can be substituted for another.

Lifecycle Management

Lifecycle management tools for applications support the development, deployment, and operational management of software.

Development

Visual Studio (VS) is an integrated development environment (IDE) that supports custom development across the MAP. *Visual Studio extensions for Windows SharePoint Services* (VSeWSS) support the development of SharePoint workflow, Web Parts, site definitions, solutions, and more. *Visual Studio Tools for Office* assist in the development of functional extensions to Microsoft Office client applications (e.g., Word, Excel, and Outlook). VSTO supports creation of new ribbon items and document actions, and provides programmatic access to the new event model and XML document formats of the Office 2007 suite.

ASP.NET, Windows SharePoint Services, and Office SharePoint Server all offer powerful APIs and design-time tools for application development.

Visual Studio Team System is a set of Visual Studio editions designed specifically for application architects, developers, and testers. VSTS integrates with Team Foundation Server (TFS) to provide a seamless end-to-end experience for agile software development and software project management. While the default process is based upon the Microsoft Solution Foundation (MSF) v4 methodology, VSTS and TFS can be used with nearly any methodology. Services provided by TFS include scheduling, task assignment, source code control, and bug tracking.

Deployment

Visual Studio creates *installation packages* and *SharePoint Solutions* that facilitate the provisioning of solutions.

MSBuild is a build engine which supports full configuration of the build process. Capabilities include the scripting of pre- and post-build events, and the build-time modification of files (e.g. `web.config`) to automate the generation of packages for differing environments. The Visual Studio *Web Deployment Projects* (WDP) extension provides an interface for creating MSBuild configuration files.

Operational Management

Microsoft Operations Manager (MOM) provides monitoring, auditing, and alert services across the MAP.

User Experience

.NET *WebForms* (ASP.NET) and *WinForms* provide a presentation layer for the MAP. Each provides a standard set of controls for constructing user interfaces, one for the web and the other for desktop applications.

Windows SharePoint Services builds on ASP.NET to provide a more powerful and consistent user experience than ASP.NET alone. Beyond the consistent set of controls found in ASP.NET, WSS supports the creation and configuration of the pages and sites themselves, allowing the no-code construction and deployment of collaborative web sites. This is a simplified description that unfolds in the next chapter.

A recent development in .NET is the Windows Presentation Foundation (WPF) which is a performing cross-platform alternative to Macromedia Flash.

A Service-Oriented View of the Microsoft Application Platform

The Open Group is a consortium that mainly deals with open standards and interoperability among technologies that originated on UNIX or Linux systems, for example, LDAP. It does a good job of describing the standard services found in an application platform, and it is an interesting exercise to map the Open Group model to the Microsoft stack. According to the Open Group, an application platform consists of the following standard service categories: Data Interchange Services, Data Management Services, Graphics and Imaging Services, International Operation Services, Location and Directory Services, Network Services, Operating System Services, Software Engineering Services, Transaction Processing Services, User Interface Services, Security Services, and System and Network Management Services. Figure 1-2 shows both the Open Group Service Map (left) and the Microsoft Application Platform Service Map (right).

It is convenient to replace *Graphics and Imaging Systems* with the more general *Media Services* category. This new category then contains Graphics and Imaging Services, Animation Services, and Audio and Video Services. Also, *Transaction Processing Services* are omitted and described instead as a feature of *Data Management Services*.

In addition, the Open Group defines standard *infrastructure applications*, which are built on and extend the capabilities of the application platform. While the capabilities of infrastructure applications are also well standardized and somewhat generic in the industry, the key differentiator is that these applications do provide (or simulate) business capabilities rather than platform services, and are typically designed with user interaction in mind.

The Open Group classified Workflow Services, Publish and Subscription Services, Payment and Funds Transfer Services, Calendar and Scheduling Services, System Management and Monitoring Services, and

Web Browsing Services as infrastructure applications. This implies that more than one implementation of each might exist for a given enterprise platform. We now know this implication is not necessary.

It is possible that the Open Group classified these as infrastructure applications rather than as platform services for a couple of reasons. For one, these services can be built using the application platform and so are "a level above," or derivative of the platform. Or, it could be because until recently these scenarios were typically built as one-off applications rather than as generic platform services; a typical development project would be to construct a Capital Requisition workflow application, not a Workflow Framework. The fact that the Open Group chose to include International Operations as a platform service lends strength to this argument. In the Microsoft stack shown on the right-hand side of Figure 1-2, you can see that several of these are now first-class platform services upon which applications are built, and not simply tacked-on instances.

The categories used by the Open Group are convenient to describe application platform services, though the definitions described here will differ from the official Open Group specification.

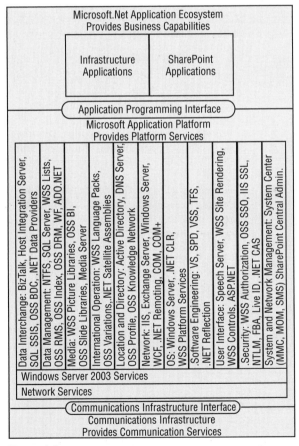

Figure 1-2

Data Interchange Services

Data Interchange Services support the exchange of information between the application platform and external systems. Examples include importing data from a DB2 database hosted on an external AS/400 server into SQL Server, the translation of an invoice from a supplier's XML format to your own in an electronic data interchange (EDI) system, the conversion of an incoming fax into a TIFF file that can then be stored in a file system, or the encoding of video into a computer-playable format.

The following table lists the Microsoft technologies that provide Data Interchange Services and describes the specific services and framework features provided by the technologies:

Microsoft Technology	Data Interchange Services and Features
BizTalk	*Data Mapping Services* provide interoperability among data storage systems by clearly identifying data sources, destinations, and transformations.
	Data Orchestration provides workflow for business systems by describing the orchestration of business processes involving more than one system.
Host Integration Server	*Data Adapter Services* include TCP/IP and SNA services, which allow connectivity to data stored on hosts, including IBM mainframes and AS/400s. A common scenario is to interoperate with an IBM DB2 database.
SQL Server	*Integration Services (SSIS)* provides data integration with external systems. SSIS supports the movement and optional transformation of data into or out of a SQL database.
Office SharePoint Server	*Business Data Catalog (BDC) Services* allow for the definition of connections to external data stores including web services, SQL Server stored procedures, and ODBC sources. The BDC offers a common object model and user interface components (Web Parts).
	Document Conversion Services allow the automatic conversion of documents. Built-in converters include Word-to-HTML and Word-to-PDF converters.
.NET Framework	*Data Providers* provide a common interface for "plugging in" connectivity to database platforms. This creates a loosely coupled relationship between connecting to the data and subsequent manipulation. Standard .NET data providers include SQL Server, Oracle, and ODBC.

Data Management Services

Data Management Services support the storage, manipulation, and retrieval of data, and optionally support transaction management as a guarantee of data integrity. Query processing, data-reporting, and analysis services once existed mainly as applications distinct from data management service providers (e.g., Crystal Reports and Cognos Business Intelligence), but these capabilities are now commonly integrated into the data management layer.

The following table lists the Microsoft technologies that provide Data Management Services and describes the specific services and framework features provided by the technologies:

Microsoft Technology	Data Management Services and Features
NTFS	*File System Services* allow for the discovery, storage, and retrieval of files, which may hold data, configuration, or executable instructions.
SQL Server	*Relational Database Management System (RDBMS) Services* provide for the structural definition, storage, retrieval, querying, and manipulation of relational data.
	Reporting Services support the definition, management, calculation, and rendering of reports.
	Analysis Services support data-mining capabilities, including the definition, management, calculation, and rendering of data cubes.
	Transaction Services guarantee that multistep operations will succeed or fail as a single unit, and not partially.
	Replication Services facilitate the replication of data from server to server, optionally with a witness service to guarantee transactional integrity.
Windows SharePoint Services	*Database Services* provide for the structural definition, storage, retrieval, and filtering of lists and list items.
	Index Services enable the indexing and subsequent querying of SharePoint objects and their metadata.
Office SharePoint Server	*Document Lifecycle Management Services* provide for the definition and enforcement of policies per document type (a.k.a. "content type"). Processes and rules in the definition may include major and minor versioning, rules for retention, associated workflow processes, and rules for authorization (i.e., digital rights management).
	Records Management Services provide a managed repository for the secure storage, controlled access, and enforced auditing of data declared as a "record."
	Index Services in OSS gain capabilities beyond WSS, including the indexing of data stored external to SharePoint such as imported Active Directory profiles and data described by the Business Data Catalog.
	Digital Rights Management Services ensures that rights assigned in a document library travel along with documents as they are opened or downloaded from the library.

Continued

Microsoft Technology	Data Management Services and Features
Windows Workflow Foundation (WF)	*Workflow Services* provide a common execution engine for the management of states and transitions as information moves through a process involving one or more applications.
.NET Framework	The *ADO.NET* programming model allows the in-memory representation, manipulation, and querying of relational data. The *XML* object model provided by .NET allows the in-memory management of hierarchical data.

Media Services

Media Services support the creation, manipulation, and distribution of media assets, including images, animation, video, and audio. Creation includes automatic generation or rendering, for example, the rendering of objects, skins, and textures in a video game. Manipulation includes the use or modification of existing artifacts, for example adding an echo effect to an audio sample, or adding titles to a video sequence. Distribution includes the broadcast or streaming of audio or audio-video files. The Open Group specification also includes the storage and retrieval, but even a digital asset management system is more appropriately considered a form of data management service, and this layer operates independently of the media being stored and retrieved.

Examples include Data Visualization Services, Flash Server, the graphics subsystem of any operating system or video game console, and Windows Media Server. The following table lists the Microsoft technologies that provide Media Services and describes the specific services and framework features provided by the technologies:

Microsoft Technology	Media Services and Features
Windows SharePoint Services (WSS)	*Picture Library Services* provide a user interface and basic data structure for the browsing and management of images.
Office SharePoint Server	*Business Intelligence Visualization Services* (delivered as Web Parts) provide a user interface for Analysis Services and Business Intelligence Services.
	Slide Library Services provide a user interface and smart client (PowerPoint) integration for the storage and management of presentation slides.
SQL Server Reporting Services	*Reporting Services* (delivered as web services) render reports in a variety of formats including HTML, Excel, and PDF.
Microsoft Media Services	*Media Services* provide for the creation, digital rights management (DRM), and streaming or broadcast of audio, video, and television content.
.NET Framework	The *.NET Framework* provides classes and methods for rendering images at runtime.

International Operation Services

International Operation Services provide a means to build applications independently of the language or locale in which they will be presented or operated and allow extending an application to support additional language or culture-specific interfaces. To enable the construction of culturally distinct applications, International Operation Services provide a means of storing and rendering information about: character sets, data representation (e.g., numbers, dates, and currency), and media resources including on-screen text, graphics and associated audio. Content stored in an application is in the realm of Data Management Services, but if services related to a specific structure or schema are provided by the platform to aid in the storage and retrieval of multi-cultural content, that aspect is an International Operation Service.

The following table lists the Microsoft technologies that provide International Operation Services and describes the specific services and framework features provided by the technologies:

Microsoft Technology	International Operations Services and Features
Windows SharePoint Services	*Language Packs* install language-specific Site Templates for SharePoint.
Office SharePoint Server	*Content Management Services* provide the Site Variation feature which allows designation of one primary site branch (e.g., http://myserver/en/default.aspx) and one or more tertiary site branches (e.g., http://myserver/fr/default.aspx). New sites in the primary branch are automatically distributed to the tertiary branches for translation.
.NET Framework	The *Resource File* and *Satellite Assembly* model allow a UI to contain placeholders for text and graphics, which are replaced at runtime by mappings defined in a culture-specific Resource File. Resource Files are packaged and distributed as Satellite Assemblies.

Location and Directory Services

Location and Directory Services support the naming, registration, search, and retrieval of metadata of resources, primarily to identify the names and addresses used to locate resources on a network. With respect to authentication, a Directory Service may act as a credential store and group membership service, but Security Services are responsible for challenging a consumer to provide credentials and controlling access to resources.

Examples include Lightweight Directory Access Protocol (LDAP), Active Directory (AD), Domain Name System (DNS) services, and Universal Description, Discovery and Integration (UDDI) services. The following table lists the Microsoft technologies that provide Location and Directory Services and describes the specific services provided by the technologies:

Microsoft Technology	Location and Directory Services and Features
Active Directory (AD)	*Directory Services* of AD allow Users and Computers in a security zone to be managed in a directory tree, as well as the definition of Groups, and the association of Users with Groups. Attributes of the User schema are extensible. For authorized entities, AD also supports queries to list members or to verify group membership.
	Authentication Services provide credential management and positive identification of entities (users or agents) upon request.
	AD is designed to comply with the IETF *Lightweight Directory Access Protocol (LDAP)*.
Domain Name System (DNS) Server	Directory Services provided by DNS Server translate domain and computer host names into IP addresses.

Network Services

Network Services define the services and protocols available to distributed applications where components that compose the application or resources used by the application exist at different logical or physical locations on a network. Examples include Hypertext Transport Protocol (HTTP), electronic mail services (SMTP and POP3), network time services (NTP), remote print services, file replication services, voice over IP services (VoIP), remote process invocation (e.g., RPC), videoconferencing services (e.g., H.323), and text messaging services (e.g., SMS).

The following table lists the Microsoft technologies that provide Network Services and describes the specific services or framework features provided by the technologies:

Microsoft Technology	Network Services and Features
Internet Information Server (IIS)	*Hypertext Transport Protocol (HTTP) Services* implemented by IIS enable the hosting of web applications and web services (see *Operating System Services*).
	File Transport Protocol (FTP) Services implemented by IIS enable remote File Management Services.
Exchange Server	*Electronic Mail Services* allow the receipt and transmission of electronic mail.
	Shared Calendar Services support the central storage and management of event calendars.

Microsoft Technology	Network Services and Features
Windows Server	*Network TCP/IP Services* allow communication among the services hosted both within a server and external to a server.
	Replication Services facilitate the distribution or "mirroring" of files stored in NTFS from a primary server to alternate servers.
Windows Communication Foundation (WCF)	*Communication Services* provided by the WCF provide a secure, reliable mechanism for applications to communicate via HTTP web services.
.NET Framework	*Remoting Services* provide a mechanism for applications to communicate over any TCP/IP channel.
	The .NET Framework provides integration with Component Object Model (COM) Services, COM+ and related technologies to enable communication with COM-based services. COM-based services include Microsoft Message Queuing (MSMQ), Active Directory (AD), and Windows Management and Instrumentation (WMI).

Operating System Services

Operating System Services support loose coupling between the description of applications as programming language instructions, and the hardware that executes those instructions. Subcategories include operating systems and virtual machines. Examples include the Windows application programming interface (API), the .NET Common Language Runtime (CLR), and the Java Virtual Machine (JVM). Virtualization Services such as Virtual Server and VMWare are not included in this category as their existence should be completely irrelevant to applications.

Note that this definition is a general version of the Open Group specification, which defines OS Services solely as the layer between an application and physical hardware, and does not include the further abstraction made possible by virtual machines.

The following table lists the Microsoft technologies that provide Operating System Services and describes the specific services and API features provided by the technologies:

Microsoft Technology	OS Services and Features
Windows SharePoint Services	*Collaboration Services* are provided by Windows SharePoint Services (WSS), which is a free component of Windows Server executed on an instance of the .NET CLR hosted inside an IIS web application.

Continued

Microsoft Technology	OS Services and Features
.NET Common Language Runtime (CLR)	*Virtual Machine Services* of the CLR provide a common execution language for Microsoft .NET languages. The only criteria for .NET languages are that they comply with the Common Language Infrastructure (CLI) specification and compile to MSIL, which is the language executed by the CLR.
Windows Server	Windows Server provides Web Application Hosting Services implemented by Internet Information Services (IIS). The Windows application programming interface (API) provides access to server resources not managed by the CLR.

Software Engineering Services

Software Engineering Services support the design and construction of applications. Examples include Visual Studio, SharePoint Designer, Team Foundation Server, Visual Source Safe, SourceGear Vault, language compilers (e.g., C#, VB.NET, IronPython and Ruby), script interpreters (e.g., Classic ASP) and build management services (e.g., MSBuild).

The following table lists the Microsoft technologies that provide Software Engineering Services and describes the specific services and framework features provided by the technologies:

Microsoft Technology	Software Engineering Services and Features
Visual Studio (VS)	VS is an *integrated developer environment (IDE)* which supports the design, construction, compilation, and testing of applications on the Microsoft Application Platform.
SharePoint Designer (SPD)	SPD is an IDE for SharePoint. SPD supports the management, extension, and modification of sites, data structures, and workflows.
Visual SourceSafe (VSS)	*Source Code Management Services* allow the controlled storage and management of applications' source code.
Team Foundation Server (TFS)	TFS provides *Project Management Services* specific to team software development projects with features supporting the architecture, development, testing, and bug tracking of applications.

Microsoft Technology	Software Engineering Services and Features
.NET Reflection	Reflection allows .NET code to inspect or emit .NET code. Reflection can infer information about assemblies, modules, types, parameters, and other .NET objects by examining their metadata. Reflection emits code by dynamically generating Microsoft Intermediate Language (MSIL) opcodes; for example, to create dynamic types or their instances, or to invoke methods.

User Interface Services

User Interface Services define how users interact with an application. Examples include Web Browser Services, Speech Recognition Services, Text-to-Speech services, Print Services, and Computer-Based Training Services (e.g., SCORM servers).

The following table lists the Microsoft technologies that provide user Interface Services and describes the specific services and framework features provided by the technologies:

Microsoft Technology	UI Services and Features
Speech Server	*Speech Recognition Services* support user interfaces controlled by voice or phone keypad rather than by keyboard or mouse.
Windows SharePoint Services (WSS)	*Content Management Services* in WSS start with an HTTPModule that interprets each requested URL and composes the output with that URL's configured Asp.NET Master Page, SharePoint Page Layout, SharePoint Configuration, SharePoint Personalization, and SharePoint Content.
	WSS includes a *Web Part Zone* object, which hosts Web Parts on SharePoint-hosted pages. The SharePoint Web Part Zone differs from the ASP.NET Web Part in that it provides backward compatibility with WSS 2.0 Web Parts, while the ASP.NET version supports the hosting of user controls (.ascx).
	Aside from this exception, the WSS user interface is almost entirely implemented with ASP.NET.

Continued

17

Microsoft Technology	UI Services and Features
ASP.NET	*User Interface Services* provide a programming model and runtime browser utilities (e.g., JavaScript code) for the construction, rendering, and configuration of cross-platform HTML, DHTML, and CSS. *Personalization Services* allow users to personalize Web Part configuration in any given ASP.NET or SharePoint page.
.NET Framework	The .NET Framework provides a development platform for Desktop Applications (a.k.a. "WebForms") and Web Applications (a.k.a. "WinForms").

Security Services

Security Services secure application resources so that only authorized entities have access to them. Therefore a Security Service is responsible for authenticating the identity of one who requests access to a resource (AuthN), confirming that the identity is authorized to access the resource (AuthZ), ensuring that credentials are kept confidential in transit, and ensuring the appropriate protection of the application resource both as it is stored and transmitted. Security Services often rely upon secure credential stores provided by a Directory Service and access control lists stored with a secure Data Management Service.

Security categories include: Authentication Services, Authorization Services, Security Auditing Services, Trusted Communication Services (e.g., SSL), Cryptographic Key Management Services, Encryption Services, and Single Sign-On (SSO) Services.

The following table lists the Microsoft technologies that provide Security Services and describes the specific services and framework features provided by the technologies:

Microsoft Technology	Security Services and Features
Windows SharePoint Services	*Authorization Services* provide management of Access Control Lists (ACLs) at the levels of Farm, Site, List, and List Item. ACL entries pair AD Users, AD Groups, and custom site groups with site roles. Site roles are associated with permission levels, which may be customized or extended. *Permissions assigned in a site* are inherited by child sites and contained lists, and *permissions assigned in a list* are inherited by contained list items unless the inheritance is explicitly broken. Whenever inheritance is broken, a new ACL is created for the object.

Microsoft Technology	Security Services and Features
Office SharePoint Server	*Single Sign-On (SSO) Services* in SharePoint provide a credential store to associate authenticated Share-Point users and service accounts with additional credentials required to access external resources.
	Information Rights Management Services bind a user's document library permissions with document permissions, which are applied to the document whenever a document is opened or downloaded from SharePoint. The document is encrypted locally for offline protection.
Internet Information Server	*Trusted Communication Services* implemented by the Secure Sockets Layer (SSL) transport to provide encryption for HTTP conversations between two machines.
	Configuration Services allow the selection of Anonymous, NTLM, or certificate-based authentication.
.NET Framework	The Membership Provider model allows for the loose coupling of an authentication model and presentation-layer features, including login, logout, and change password controls. Out-of-box providers include NTLM Authentication, Forms-based Authentication (FBA), and Windows Live (aka Passport) Authentication.
	The Code Access Security (CAS) model requires that running code be provided with explicit permissions to access resources.
	Encryption services provide standard libraries for the encryption and decryption of data.

System and Network Management Services

System and Network Management Services support the deployment, configuration, monitoring, and fault management of applications and the network resources that serve applications. Examples in this category include configuration management (CM) services for all component resources, performance monitors and indicators, fault detection monitors with response escalation, accounting management services to calculate chargebacks on usage, capacity management services to monitor resources and proactively plan expansion, and specific management tools for Print Services, Storage Array Services, and other network appliances.

This is a two-way street — your applications should include services that allow for their programmatic configuration, monitoring, and administration by System and Network Management Services. When it comes time to build test harnesses, to populate your application with data, or to plug your application into a continuous monitoring tool like Microsoft Operations Manager (MOM), you will likely discover that a little extra attention in this oft-neglected area provides great returns.

The following table lists the Microsoft technologies that provide System and Network Management Services and describes the specific services and framework features provided by the technologies:

Microsoft Technology	System and Network Management Services and Features
Microsoft Operations Manager (MOM)	*Monitoring Services* provided by MOM allow the real-time monitoring and logging of servers, applications, and network appliances on a network. *Publish and Subscribe Services* allow people and processes to subscribe to and presumably act upon events raised by MOM.
Systems Management Server (SMS)	*Deployment Services* provided by SMS facilitate the automatic installation and upgrade of software installed to machines within a physical or logical zone.
Windows SharePoint Services	*Configuration Management Services* allow the assignment of servers to roles in a SharePoint farm.

Summary

This chapter provided you with a solid foundation on which to expand your SharePoint knowledge. By now, you should have a firm grasp on the difference between SharePoint Services and SharePoint Server, and be familiar enough with the Microsoft Application Platform to use it effectively. This chapter touched on data management, lifecycle management, workflow, and communications, before delving more deeply into a service-oriented view of the Microsoft Application Platform. The next chapter covers what you need to know related to the development platform specifically, and walks you through setting up your development environment.

MOSS 2007 Overview
for Developers

By Eli Robillard

To become a master SharePoint developer, one must understand what SharePoint is, and how it works. "To be" is to be related, so to explain what SharePoint is, this chapter will describe precisely how it is related to other components in the Microsoft stack. The flow of communication among these components describes how SharePoint works. When you understand these things, you have the knowledge both to change the way SharePoint works and to use it as a platform on which to build your own solutions. This chapter describes the architecture of SharePoint, and then moves on to help you build a development environment in which to create SharePoint applications.

Architectural Overview of SharePoint

SharePoint is a three-tiered application (see Figure 2-1). The presentation layer lives in the file system as an ASP.NET application, the logic lives in .NET assemblies, and the data resides in a SQL Server database. On the surface, Windows SharePoint Services is a web application platform that provides a collection of services accessed through SharePoint web pages, XML web services, and a .NET application programming interface (API). SharePoint's core functionality is provided by an infrastructure of .NET assemblies and Windows Services. SharePoint stores all content and configuration in SQL Server databases. These databases contain stored procedures and other potential points of interaction, but they should never be directly accessed or modified. Microsoft Office SharePoint Server (MOSS) augments WSS with features for portals (Chapter 8), search (Chapter 9), content management (Chapters 10 though 13), business processes (Chapter 14 and 15), and business intelligence (Chapter 16).

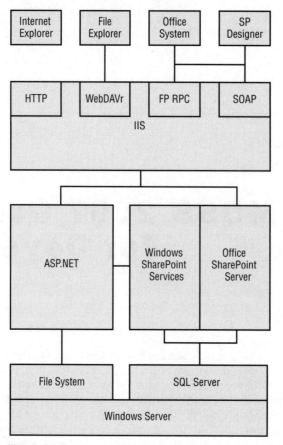

Figure 2-1

Upon installation, SharePoint requires a SQL database server and an IIS web server. The first database created is the configuration database. SharePoint is installed into a subtree popularly called the "12 hive" which defaults to the following location:

```
C:\Program Files\Common Files\Microsoft Shared\web server extensions\12
```

The 12 hive contains SharePoint's utilities, assemblies, resources, and the web services and web applications that compose its interface. SharePoint's next requirement is an IIS Virtual Server, also called a web site or web application. The first is the SharePoint Central Administration (SCA) site, which is created automatically on a random port of the server. You can think of this web application as an interface for the configuration database. Once SharePoint is configured, you can create sites.

Installing SharePoint to a web application is known as **extending** the web application. This modifies the web.config to include the SharePoint HTTPHandler, and to mark SharePoint objects as safe. For each SharePoint web application a content database is created, though it is also possible to connect a new web site to an existing content database in order to share data between front-end sites.

SharePoint's Scopes of Configuration

The scopes important to SharePoint for the configuration of the platform and its features are: the farm, the web application, the site (a.k.a. the site collection), and the web (formerly called the site in previous versions of SharePoint).

The **farm** is the server or set of servers that host SharePoint. Upon installation, roles are assigned to each server in the farm, and services are bound to servers based on roles and expected traffic patterns. The farm is also defined by its connectivity with external services, including Active Directory and Exchange Server. There is one configuration database per farm, and it is administered by any instance of the Share-Point Central Administration web application within the farm.

The **web application** is the IIS entity where an application pool context is set for SharePoint, and an address (URL) is defined by IP address, port, and/or host header so that each instance of SharePoint can be located with a web browser or mapped to a DNS common name. The web application has a physical web.config file to configure authentication and to mark components as safe, and virtual folders mapped to physical folders that contain ASP.NET files. These physical files are shared among all SharePoint web applications hosted in the farm. Web applications are discussed further in Chapter 3.

A SharePoint site (SPSite) is an object which contains webs (SPWeb). Developers refer to SPSites as "site collections." SPWebs are often referred to as "sites," especially within SharePoint's user interface (e.g., "Create Sites and Workspaces"). The top-level web, or RootWeb of an SPSite is usually positioned at the first folder in a SharePoint path (e.g., /personal or /sites), with the web application's root being an exceptional case of SPSite. Each SPSite contains resources available to all of the SPWebs it contains, including SharePoint features and special document libraries called galleries. Galleries exist to hold content types, site columns, Site Templates, List Templates, Web Parts, workflows, and master pages. Each of these is discussed in detail in Chapter 3.

An SPWeb is a web within a site collection, and each web may contain its own set of child webs. The RootWeb of a site collection provides an interface to manage the resources (e.g., the galleries) of the site collection. As noted previously, the nomenclature is falling back to the "old ways" of calling an SPWeb either a "site" or a "web site," and these terms are still used in the Site Settings and Create pages. Once a Feature is installed in a site collection, it is available to activate (or deactivate) in a web. Similarly, once a content type is installed in a site collection, it is available for assigning to libraries or publishing sites within individual webs.

Figure 2-2 depicts a MOSS site and two child webs that form one site collection, and a top-level site with two more webs that form another site collection.

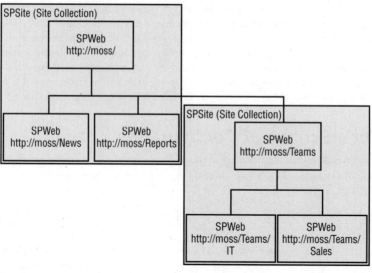

Figure 2-2

SharePoint Farm Server Roles

Several server roles combine to make up the SharePoint small, medium, and large farm configurations. The three principal roles in a MOSS Farm are: Web Front-End, Application Server, and Database. A collection of servers assigned to a single role may be referred to as a node.

Web Front-End (WFE)

The web front-end node hosts the presentation layer of a SharePoint deployment. The WFE is either a single server or a set of network load balanced (NLB) servers that host SharePoint web sites and the Central Administration web site.

Application (App) or Shared Services Provider (SSP)

The application node hosts the logical layer of a SharePoint deployment, and contains more Shared Service Providers. A SSP provides a central point for MOSS services, including: the Index Service, the Query Service, profile import and management, audience management, content management logic, the Business Data Catalog, Excel Services, Forms Services, job scheduling, and usage reporting. Each SharePoint web application can have its own SSP (but not more than one), and multiple SharePoint Applications can share the same SSP.

Index

An Index server is configured to scan the content of SharePoint sites, external web sites, and Business Data Catalog data stores, capturing information used to build indices that facilitate high-speed searching from within SharePoint applications. This scanning process is called "content crawling." When there is more than one WFE, the Index role should either be installed on its own server (the SSP) or on the database server. The Index role creates one index per SSP and may provide this service for several SSPs though their indices can not be aggregated. Since the Index role manages just one index per SSP, a separate Index server can exist for each SSP.

The index is propagated to all Query servers unless the Query and Index Services reside on the same physical machine. Therefore, in a farm it is best for the WFE and Query roles to be paired on a machine, for a single machine to host shared services, including Search and Index, or for Index Services to be hosted on its own server in what might be called a shared services farm. However, the Index role cannot be made redundant; it cannot be clustered. If an Index server goes down, each Query server may continue to use a propagated index until the role is restored.

Query/Search

The Search server returns search results to the WFE or web service that calls it. Search may be installed on the same machine as the WFE role, the same machine as the Index role, or on its own server. It should not be installed to two servers where one is a WFE and the other is an Index server. In this scenario the index would not propagate from the Query/Index server to the Query/WFE service because (as described earlier) the index is not propagated if it resides on the same machine as the Query Service. WFE and Search roles are often combined for performance; in effect, the index is cached on the WFE and the separate Index server does not affect WFE performance.

WSS 3.0 Search and Index

If MOSS is not installed, Search and Index must reside on the same server.

Excel Calculation Server

Excel Server is responsible for rendering Excel and business intelligence (BI) data inside MOSS sites. It can be made redundant by assigning the role to all WFE servers, or to all Application servers. It is often paired with the WFE role for performance, even before the Query role is paired with WFEs. Excel Server requires MOSS Enterprise Edition.

Forms Server

Forms Server is responsible for rendering InfoPath forms published for web use. It can be made redundant by assigning the role to all WFE machines, or to all Application servers. Forms Server requires MOSS Enterprise Edition.

Database Server (SQL)

The database server stores SharePoint configuration, site content, personalization, and user profiles. Either SQL Server 2000 or 2005 will work, though MOSS is optimized for SQL 2005. Different editions of SQL Server 2005 allow different configurations. Express Edition may only be used in a SharePoint stand-alone configuration. Standard, Developer, or Enterprise Edition may be used for small and medium farms. Either Developer or Enterprise Edition is required to cluster the SQL Server role in a medium or large farm. Developer Edition may be used in development and testing environments, but Standard or Enterprise licenses must be obtained for each live production environment. The following table indicates which SQL Server Editions may be used in each environment:

SQL Version	Single SQL Server	SQL Cluster	Dev	Test	Production
WMSDE	Yes		Yes		
SQL Express	Yes		Yes		
SQL Developer	Yes	Yes	Yes	Yes	
SQL Standard	Yes		Yes	Yes	Yes
SQL Enterprise	Yes	Yes	Yes	Yes	Yes

SharePoint Farm Configurations

Depending upon the number of servers available and your need for performance or redundancy, there are several recommended configurations from which to choose. SharePoint roles and components are modular, with the intent that when the performance of any single machine is overwhelmed by traffic, the extra load can be handled by intelligent expansion of the farm.

Stand-Alone: One Server

All SharePoint and database server roles are installed to a single server. See Figure 2-3.

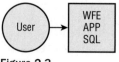

Figure 2-3

Small Farm: Two Servers

All SharePoint roles are provided by one server, and the Database role is provided by another. See Figure 2-4.

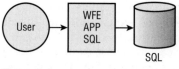

Figure 2-4

Medium Farm: Three to Five Servers

In a medium farm, the WFE and APP roles are hosted on separate servers. The WFE role may be filled by two or more load-balanced servers, and the Database role may be filled by two or more clustered SQL servers. Note that if you have six or more servers you can technically build a medium farm (e.g., 3 WFE/1 App/2 SQL), but a large farm is likely to be a preferable configuration (2/2/2).

Two medium server farms are shown in Figures 2-5 and 2-6. The key similarities are that the WFE and APP roles are on separate servers, and APP remains on a single server. Although the APP server may be hosting MOSS Enterprise features as well (e.g., BDC, Forms Server, Excel Server), these are not detailed in the diagram.

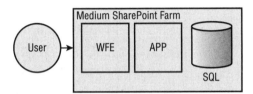

Figure 2-5

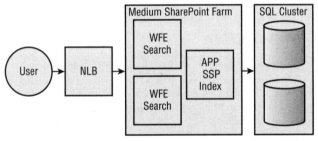

Figure 2-6

Large Farm: Four or More Servers

A large farm has the WFE and database characteristics of a medium farm (with a three-machine mini-mum), and the services provided by the APP node are divided among several machines. For example, the APP layer may include one or more redundant Query servers, one or more Index servers (one per SSP), an Excel server, and a Forms server. Given the trend towards modular applications, it would be conceivable to host other non-SharePoint services in this layer, including Project Server, third-party applications, or an in-house application. Note that if you have four or five servers, a medium farm is more likely the preferable configuration.

A large farm is depicted in Figure 2-7. In this case, one WFE includes Search and two do not. This might be optimal if the load-balancing and routing hardware sets the affinity for a particular SharePoint URL to a single machine (perhaps with its own SSP), while requests to other SharePoint web sites are served by the remaining machines (perhaps configured with another SSP). Since the Index role remains separate from the Search role, this will work. In this case, the two Application and Index servers are likely each configured for a particular SSP as well. In addition, one (and optionally more) servers are each allocated to Excel Calculation and Forms.

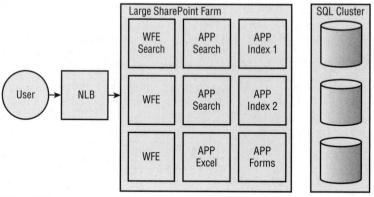

Figure 2-7

SharePoint Composition

While understanding how to compose an intranet or extranet is not the focus of this book, it is useful to see how a well-structured MOSS site is arranged. The top-level intranet, public web site, extranet, and Team Sites in Figure 2-8 would each be created in distinct web sites (registered in DNS), each with its own content database. Personal My Site sites are a feature of the SSP and are optionally stored in a separate content database.

In SPS 2003 terms, the intranet corresponds to portal areas, Team Sites stay roughly the same, the public web site could be a Microsoft CMS web site in the DMZ, and the extranet would be hosted on a separate SharePoint deployment in the DMZ.

Note that the major Intranet site headings in Figure 2-8 (Products, News, Document Repository, Search Center, Report Center, etc.) for this business unit are not named according to organization chart boundaries (e.g., Sales and Marketing). The goal of an intranet is the same as for a web site: Everything is available within three clicks, and headings make it obvious what lies beneath. If you build an intranet site for each and every department, send a photographer around to take smiling pictures of teams in funny poses, and post "why we're the best department at Floobar" teasers, no one will visit any of these. Each site will be outdated in one month, and stagnant in two. Instead, build Team Sites and get individuals involved within their teams. Organizational charts and groupings of cross-department teams (e.g., committees, projects, or management) drive the hierarchy of Team Sites. Discovery of information drives the design of intranet portal sites.

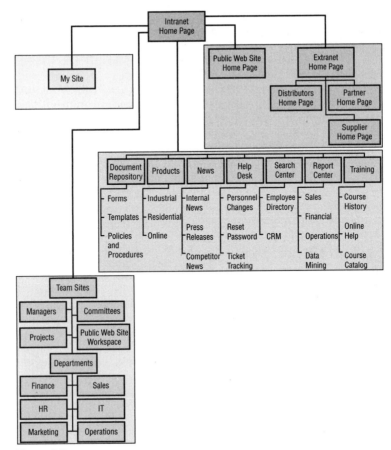

Figure 2-8

SharePoint and ASP.NET

As you learned in the first chapter, SharePoint is composed of logical services. People do not directly use services. People need interfaces that provide pleasant and efficient user experiences. ASP.NET provides the human interface layer — or presentation layer — for SharePoint. ASP.NET web pages are a combination of static HTML (e.g., text and images) and dynamic controls whose contents or "rendering" are determined at runtime. For example, controls exist to display lists of data (e.g., the ListView control), tables of data (e.g., DataGrid and GridView controls), and form elements (e.g., DropDownList and Button controls).

While designing SharePoint 2007 (and that's what it really was before any decisions were made to make this feature part of the WSS 3.0 base or that feature part of MOSS Standard or MOSS Enterprise), the ASP.NET team was working on "Whidbey," which became ASP.NET 2.0 and Visual Studio 2005. Someone came up with the great idea to turn products like SharePoint and Content Management Server (CMS is a popular ASP.NET platform for building and publishing public web sites) into pure service platforms, and to move their presentation layer features into ASP.NET.

With this decision, ASP.NET 2.0 gained features like master pages (from CMS) and Web Parts (from SharePoint), as well as features that can be used as standards across platforms, including: form fields, the Authentication Provider model, and Site Maps. For example, the Authentication Provider model describes a consistent interface for credential stores (e.g., Active Directory, user names and passwords kept in a database, or MS Live, formerly Passport). When the interface is consistent, standard ASP.NET 2.0 controls for logging in, signing out, and changing passwords can be reused no matter which provider is present. WSS publishes Site Maps as an XML web service which ASP.NET `Breadcrumb` and `Tree View` controls consume to provide navigation on SharePoint pages.

Now that these elements are part of ASP.NET, a developer who understands the ASP.NET providers and related controls already understands most of what it takes to create a SharePoint page.

Elements of a SharePoint Page

A SharePoint page is a web page (`*.aspx`) which refers to a master page (`*.master`), and a style sheet (`*.css`). A *master page* often contains a standard page header with a company logo, a footer with links to copyright and privacy policies, plus `asp:ContentPlaceHolder` controls that determine where content will go. Each page that uses a particular master will contain `asp:Content` tags matched to the placeholders of the master. Unlike a standard ASP.NET page, a master page file and CSS file specified through the WSS user interface (specifically the Site Settings Menu) can override those set within the physical `.aspx` file stored on disk. Figure 2-9 provides a visual description of WSS page structure.

The processes and elements for building custom pages and master pages are described in Chapter 3.

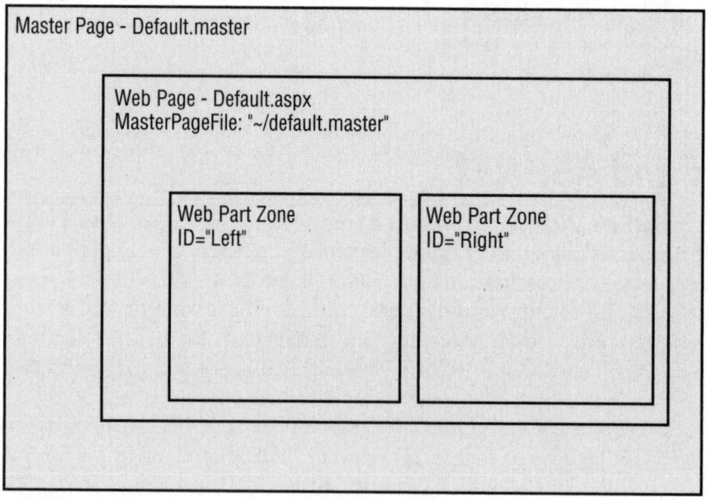

```
Master Page - Default.master

    Web Page - Default.aspx
    MasterPageFile: "~/default.master"

        Web Part Zone          Web Part Zone
        ID="Left"              ID="Right"
```

Figure 2-9

Elements of a MOSS Publishing Page

The Publishing site is a Site Definition available in MOSS designed expressly for creating and deploying web content. It differs from other SharePoint web pages in that instead of creating a physical file and describing content (and Web Part zones) within `asp:Content` tags, this information is stored in the database as a Page Layout. Figure 2-10 depicts the composition of a Publishing Page.

Before creating a Publishing Page, a content type must be created in the site collection. This content type describes the fields that will contain the content on the page, typically text and images. A Page Layout is then created in the SharePoint Designer in which the fields of the content type are dragged into the layout. More than one Page Layout can be created for a content type. This too is published to the site collection. When a Publishing Page is created, the Page Layout is selected. Since the layout is by design bound to the content type, all the creator needs to do next is fill in the content fields for the new page. Like all SharePoint content, versioning and workflows are available, and beyond this a publishing schedule can be defined or assigned.

Web content management is further described in Chapter 13.

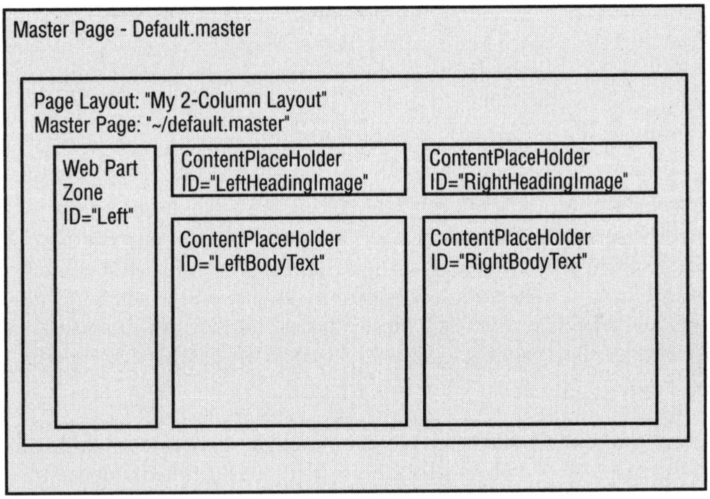

Figure 2-10

Site Templates and Site Definitions

When you extend a SharePoint server you select a Site Template. Templates exist for publishing sites, news sites, Team Sites, Meeting Workspaces, blog sites, Wiki sites and more. You can also save the sites you create as templates so that you can reuse formats over and over again. The default out-of-box templates are stored in the `12\TEMPLATE\SiteTemplates` path, and each template has its own subfolder. Developers call these templates **Site Definitions.** Each Site Definition contains ASP.NET page files (e.g., `default.aspx` and `default.master`), and the `ONET.XML` file that describes the navigation bars, features enabled, lists available for users to create, and document templates available to create new libraries. The Configurations section of `ONET.XML` allows the site definition to specify several configurations, each with specific features, lists, and Web Parts as well as their positions in the Web Part zones. For example, the STS Site Definition defines configurations not only for the Team Site, but also for the Blank Site and Document Workspaces.

When you select Save as template from the Site Settings menu, you are not saving a new site definition into the file system. Instead your template is saved in the content database and will then appear in the site collection's **site template gallery**. To be reused in another server's site collection, the Site Definition from which the Site Template was created must be present on the target server as well. The Site Template actually describes the deltas, or changes, which were applied to the Site Definition in order to arrive at the Site Template.

When you create a new SharePoint site based on a Site Definition, part of the configuration process is to note which definition was used, and this cannot be subsequently changed. In a similar manner, the configuration of each "live" site is also a collection of deltas applied by a site administrator. If personalization is enabled, then this second set of deltas is applied per user as well (where they exist).

One Site Definition that is new to SharePoint 2007 deserves mention: the Global template. This template is always provisioned before any other template and contains base lists, definitions for the galleries (the Site Template, List Template, master page, and Web Part galleries), and default master page.

To learn more about ONET.XML, *custom Site Definitions and Custom List Definitions, refer to Chapter 4.*

The SharePoint Page Request Lifecycle

To recap: When you create a site, you select a Site Template. What is described as a Site Template in the UI might actually be either a pure Site Definition or a template stored in the Site Template gallery that is based on a Site Definition. Wherever it comes from, the template includes pages like `default.aspx`, `default.master`, and a CSS file, although these physical files are not copied from the file system into the content database. Rather, their original location is noted in the database along with the location URL of the new site.

For example, when you create a new site with the Team Site template called MyTeamSite at the URL `http://moss/myteamsite/`, no physical site is created, but document entries are created in the content database based on the names of ASPX files found in the template. When `http://moss/myteamsite/default.aspx` is requested, IIS will hand control to the SharePoint `HTTPHandler`. SharePoint does a lookup in the content database, discovers that MyTeamSite is based on the Team Site Definition, and commences loading the `default.aspx` page from that base template. Any reconfiguration of the site is reapplied, then per-user personalization. When it comes time to render the MyTeamSite-specific content, this content is also rendered by SharePoint. Finally, the page is served by IIS in fulfillment of the request.

Your Development Environment

Before you can build, you need a foundation. Subsequent chapters in this book assume that you will be developing on a stand-alone SharePoint server with Visual Studio and that your developer tools are installed on the same machine. You can build that environment in a virtual machine with the steps described in this chapter.

However, for "real-world" development, experience has shown that keeping your development tools off of the server is a good practice. Depending upon your situation, it may not always be the best practice, and it does require remote debugging so that it is also not the "easiest practice." But this configuration brings both discipline and the benefits of loose coupling to SharePoint development. By interacting with the server as a SharePoint user would, you avoid all the inconsistencies that come with running browser sessions on locked-down web servers, you don't fill your server's GAC with quite as much junk, and you develop better development habits.

Read each section once through to understand what to watch for before building the environment. This is especially true when building the server. The local machine is also called the *host*, and the virtual machine (VM) that contains the server is also called the *guest*. Like a hotel, a host can have many guests.

Developer Tools

The two main factors determining the speed of your SharePoint development environment are RAM and hard drive speed. If you do a lot of development, you will also want plenty of disk space to hold all those VMs.

First, give your virtual machines as much RAM as possible. The minimum RAM recommended for a live MOSS server is 2 GB, though you can survive on less. If you have 4 GB, give the VM 2 GB. If you have 3 GB, give the VM either 1.5 GB or 2 GB. If you have 2 GB or less, buy more RAM or host your server elsewhere. Seriously, at 1 GB or less, you may experience issues during installation.

If you need Exchange Server in your lab for any reason (another 2 GB recommended), you've grown out of laptop labs and should build this on a Virtual Server (or VMWare) host if you want some hair left over when you're done. To build medium or large farms in a virtual environment, Microsoft Virtual Server running on a 64-bit Windows 2003 Server R2 machine can address up to 1024 GB. A 64-bit Vista machine provides the same expandability with Virtual PC or VMWare, although many laptops in this book's life-time will have a hard limit as low as 4 GB.

To optimize available memory, wouldn't it be great if you could share a base server image among several machines in a virtual farm and have each VM use a separate hard disk file that represented the delta from the base image? You can do this with both VMWare and VirtualPC. Some versions of VMWare have the ability to intelligently share read-only memory pages across VM images, which can be a great way to reduce the amount of real memory consumed by multiple VM's running at the same time. This also reduces swapping. This capability in Virtual PC is called a Differencing Disk. The "big three" factors of hard drive performance are rotation speed, transfer rate, and isolation. Put another way: You want a big fast external drive. Your guest server will run faster if it doesn't need to share cycles with your host's operating system, so put it on an external drive.

Then assume that the virtual hard drives (VHD files) of SharePoint virtual servers will range from 5 GB to 20 GB, with the median around 10 GB. You will have three or four base (or "Do Not Touch") images, and a copy perhaps for every customer, or every production server you support. After a few mental calculations, you will likely find that a 7200 RPM SATA drive in the 200GB to 500GB range is a good place to start.

Your bottleneck will be transfer rate, so get a hard drive enclosure with a FireWire or eSATA interface. If you don't have FireWire or eSATA on your host machine, you'll need an adapter for ISA, CardBus (PCM-CIA II), or ExpressCard, whichever your machine supports. If you use a desktop with SATA support, the straight-through adapter for your backplane is sometimes included with the enclosure.

Why not USB 2.0? Because it's slow. FireWire is 33% to 70% faster than USB, depending on the operation. eSATA is about five times faster than USB 2.0. Check out the stats in the following table:

Hard Drive Interface	Transfer Rate (Mbits per second)
USB 2.0	480
FireWire 800	786
eSATA	1500 to 2400

Can you build a virtual machine and develop SharePoint components on a computer with 2 GB RAM and 10 GB free on the hard disk? Yes. Is the experience rewarding? The answer depends upon both your brilliance and your patience.

Host System Software

A minimal list of software required for SharePoint development on the host is:

❑ The .NET Framework version 3.0

❑ Visual Studio and/or SharePoint Designer

❑ Virtual PC or VMWare to host a SharePoint virtual machine, unless a physical machine is available

Beyond a web browser and these, everything in the following list is optional, but each will improve development time or reduce aggravation, depending on the task at hand. An online search for the title will locate the download; in some cases a shorter search phrase is provided. All items are free downloads except those marked [$], and free evaluation versions are available for each of these, too. The list is arranged roughly in the order of installation.

Title	Description
.NET Framework 2.0	This is ostensibly included in .NET 3.0, but for completeness you should have a copy of the .NET 2.0 redistributable on hand and ready to install separately from 3.0.
.NET Framework 3.0	Includes Windows Presentation Foundation (WPF), Windows Communication Foundation (WCF), and essential to SharePoint: Workflow Foundation (WF).
Internet Explorer Developer Toolbar	Inspect HTML source, style usage, IFrame content, image locations, and more.
Fiddler HTTP Debugger	Inspect and manipulate HTTP traffic between your browser and the server.

Title	Description
Lutz Roeder's .NET Reflector	A class browser, explorer, analyzer, and documentation viewer for .NET. that enables you to view, navigate, search, decompile, and analyze .NET assemblies in C#, Visual Basic, and IL.
PowerShell	Write scripts to automate administration and configuration tasks. Search online for *PowerShell SharePoint Provider* to locate excellent scripts.
Office System Professional Plus Edition [$]	The Professional Plus Edition includes Word, Excel, Outlook, and PowerPoint, plus Access, Publisher, and InfoPath. There is also an Enterprise Edition, which includes OneNote and Groove.
SharePoint Designer (SPD) [$]	SPD is an increasingly essential tool for creating SharePoint master pages, workflows, data views, and more.
Visual Studio 2005 (VS) [$]	VS is the most powerful IDE for building solutions anywhere on the Microsoft Application platform.
Visual Studio 2005 Extensions for Windows SharePoint Services 3.0 (VSeWSS)	Build Web Parts, field controls, List Definitions, Site Definitions, and content types. Also includes the SharePoint Solution Generator (SPSolGen) which converts lists and sites "Saved as Template" into List and Site Definitions. Search online for *VSeWSS*.
Visual Studio 2005 Extensions for .NET Framework 3.0 (Workflow Foundation)	Design Windows Workflow Foundation solutions for SharePoint and other .NET applications.
Visual Studio 2005 Tools for the 2007 Microsoft Office System (VSTO)	VSTO is used to build: Office System (Word, Excel, etc.) add-ins and ribbon elements, Outlook forms, and InfoPath templates. Search online for *VSTO*.
BDC Metadata Manager [$]	Generate BDC XML from SQL data sources. The commercial version also builds definitions for web services. Search online for *BDCMetaMan*.
Windows SharePoint Services (WSS) 3.0 Software Development Kit (SDK)	The SDK contains the entire WSS object model and sample code in help format (CHM), and can either be downloaded or read online. Search online for *WSS 3.0 SDK*.
Microsoft Office SharePoint Server 2007 SDK	The SDK contains the entire OSS object model in help format (CHM), and can either be downloaded or read online. Search online for *MOSS 2007 SDK*.

Continued

Title	Description
Virtual PC 2007	VPC is required unless you have spare servers available to host your development lab. VMWare is a popular alternative. Both are free.
SQL Server Express Edition	You may want a small local SQL server if you develop more than SharePoint and need a handy data store. If not, SQL Express is built into the SharePoint stand-alone install so you do *not* need to download or install it separately. This is the successor to MSDE.
SQL Server 2005 Developer Edition [$]	A robust alternative to SQL Express, Developer Edition is a version of SQL Server Enterprise Edition licensed only for development, testing, and demos; it includes the popular SQL Server Management Studio.

There are other great developer tools out there, and many more will be released in this book's life. As of today, deep familiarity with the items listed above will enable you to become a skilled SharePoint developer.

Building the Host Machine

You already know how to install software, so instead this section will help you configure your local machine to develop against a SharePoint server running in Virtual PC. Building a host machine involves selecting an IP address, and installing and configuring a Loopback Adapter.

First select an IP address range to use for your development lab. This should be in a private address range and somewhat random so as not to conflict with other networks you connect with. The available private ranges of IP addresses are listed in the following table:

IP Range
10.0.0.0 to 10.255.255.255
172.16.0.0 to 172.31.255.255
192.168.0.0 to 192.168.255.255

The subnet mask of machines in your lab will be 255.255.255.0 unless you have a reason for choosing otherwise. This will provide addresses for 256 machines. A wider subnet mask would increase the risk of overlap with networks to which you connect.

What Is a Subnet Mask Anyway?

An IP address is made up of four numbers, or octets, ranging from 0 to 255. The subnet mask along with an IP address indicates the lower and upper range of your network by placing 255 (or binary 11111111) in octets, which do not vary, and a 0 (or binary 00000000) in octets that are free to vary. A logical AND of the binary mask against a machine's IP address indicates which other machines will be in the same subnet. For subnet mask 255.255.0.0 the first two octets are fixed, and the last two are free to contain numbers from 0 to 255. If you select the address 10.11.12.13 at random from the table above, and a subnet mask of 255.255.255.0, then the subnet address range is 10.11.12.0 to 10.11.12.255.

Once you have selected an IP address range and a subnet mask, begin the installation and configuration of the Loopback Adapter.

Install the Microsoft Loopback Adapter on the Host Machine

An instance of the Microsoft Loopback Adapter on the host machine will be used to host a local network that includes the virtual machines. The host machine will be able to connect to the guest server, browse its web sites, and debug its processes over this local network. Follow these steps to install the Loopback Adapter:

1. Click Start and Control Panel, and open the Add Hardware Wizard.

2. Click Next. Wait a moment while the wizard scans for hardware.

3. Select Yes, I have already connected the hardware, then click Next.

4. Scroll to the bottom of the list and select Add a new hardware device. Click Next.

5. Select Install the hardware that I manually select from a list (Advanced). Click Next.

6. Select Network adapters, Microsoft, Microsoft Loopback Adapter.

7. Click Next. Click Next again. Wait a moment. Click Finish.

Configure the Loopback Adapter on the Host Machine

Once the Loopback Adapter is installed, it must be configured to use an IP address in your selected range.

1. Click Start, Control Panel, and open the Network Connections utility.

2. Right-click the Microsoft Loopback Adapter connection and select Properties.

3. Double-click Internet Protocol (TCP/IP).

4. Set an IP address for this adapter:

   ❑ Select Use the following address

   ❑ IP Address: 10.50.50.1

❑   Subnet mask: 255.255.255.0

❑   Default gateway: Leave this blank.

5.   You can ignore DNS. Click OK. Click OK again.

If you have not done so already, install your developer tools now, including Virtual PC. You have built your host machine and set it up for the development environment; now it's time to build the server. The upcoming sections include steps to build either a WSS 3.0 or a MOSS 2007 server.

Building the Server

Building a SharePoint server is an experience that no developer should miss. Building servers efficiently is a skill that no developer should be without. This section contains several parts: building the base Windows Server, installing an Active Directory domain controller, installing IIS, installing WSS, and installing MOSS.

Task: Create a Windows Server 2003 Base Image

This process includes creating a new VM definition, adjusting the settings, and installing the operating system (OS) and .NET Framework. Then the OS is activated and Windows Update is run to install all available service packs and patches. Once the base image is in a reliable, pristine state, it is backed up for reuse. You should plan about three hours for this process.

Create a New Virtual Machine

Follow the following steps to create a virtual machine in Virtual PC:

1.   From the Start, Programs menu, start Virtual PC.

2.   Click New. Click Next.

3.   Select Create a new virtual machine. Click Next.

4.   Type the name and location. The default is My Documents\My Virtual Machines. To create the VM on your external drive, enter the location and a name. In this case, you're creating a VM in F:\VMS called WindowsServer2003Base. Click Next.

5.   Select an operating system. You will select Windows Server 2003 unless Windows Vista Server (Longhorn) is available. Click Next.

6.   Adjust the RAM. For this base image 1 GB or 1024 MB will suffice. Click Next.

7.   For the virtual hard disk options, select A new virtual hard disk. Click Next.

8.   Create the hard disk in the same location that you selected in step 4. Adjust the virtual hard disk size to a reasonable size. 4 GB or 4096 MB is a good start. You can resize the disk at any time. Click Next.

9.   The wizard is complete. You can use the Back button to review your choices. When you are satisfied that everything is correct, return to this panel and click Finish. Your new machine is now displayed in the Virtual PC console.

Configure Virtual Machine Settings

Once the machine is created, add it to the virtual network by connecting a second network adapter on the virtual machine to your host machine's Loopback Adapter.

1. Click Settings.

2. Click Networking.

3. Change the setting Number of network adapters to 2.

4. Change the setting Adapter 2 to Microsoft Loopback Adapter.

5. Click OK.

Install the Operating System

Now that the VM is fully configured in Virtual PC, install an operating system:

1. In Virtual PC, click Start to power up your virtual machine.

2. If you have a Windows Server 2003 Standard SP2 CD or DVD, insert it in your host machine now. If you have a Windows Server 2003 SP2 ISO file (e.g., from MSDN), on the menu bar, click CD, then Capture an ISO Image, and browse to the location of your Windows Server 2003 SP2 ISO image. Open the image.

3. Follow the on-screen instructions to install the server operating system. Unless you are using an evaluation version, a license key will be required.

    If a Virtual Machine Additions window opens, click OK to close it. If your mouse is "trapped" within the window, you can free it by pressing the right-side Alt key.

When you get to Network Settings, you will configure an IP address for the second network adapter.

1. Choose Custom settings. Click Next. The primary networking device will come up first (even if #2 is shown in the label). You pegged this to your host's network card in step 2. Leave it with its default settings, and it should be able to use the same DHCP service as your host machine to connect to the Internet.

2. Click Next. The second card will come up.

3. Select Internet Protocol (TCP/IP), and click Properties.

4. Enter a private IP address that is different from, but in the same subnet as, the one you used for your host machine's Microsoft Loopback Adapter. Enter the same subnet mask that you used for the Loopback Adapter. Ignore gateway and DNS.

    ❑   IP address: e.g., `10.50.50.4` or `192.168.50.4`

    ❑   Subnet mask: `255.255.255.0`

    ❑   Default gateway: Leave this blank.

5. Leave DNS entries blank. You will create a HOSTS file on your host machine for resolving addresses. Click OK.

6. Back on the Windows Setup Networking Components panel, click Next.

7. Allow this machine to be a member of WORKGROUP, unless you have a reason for joining it to an existing domain. Click Next.

8. Wait for 15 to 25 minutes as files are copied. Once the process is complete, Windows will start.

9. Press the right-side Alt and Del keys together to log in to your virtual machine. The Administrator password was configured during substep 3. Now is a good time to create a text file (e.g., readme.txt) in the virtual machine folder that contains the password.

Edit the HOSTS File on the Local Machine

The virtual network will not be served by the same DNS server used by the host machine. Therefore, to locate a virtual machine by name rather than IP address, an entry must be added to the HOSTS file of the host machine.

1. Open File Explorer and navigate to C:\WINDOWS\system32\drivers\etc.

2. Right-click the HOSTS file and select Open. In the pop-up, select Notepad. Click OK.

3. Add the IP address and machine name of your virtual machine on a blank line.

4. Close the Window, and click Yes when prompted to save the changes.

Activate Windows

Until the operating system is activated, an expiration date is set. The server will not operate beyond the expiration date. This set of steps removes the expiration date:

1. Click the keys in the desktop tray to open the Let's Activate Windows Wizard.

2. Select Yes, let's activate Windows over the Internet now, and click Next.

3. Select No, I don't want to register now, let's just activate Windows, and click Next.

4. The Checking for connectivity. . . page will open, then Configure your network settings. If your local network does not require proxy settings, click Next.

5. Thank You! will be displayed. Click OK. If activation is unsuccessful, verify that the network settings from previous steps are complete.

6. Run Windows Update to ensure that the latest service packs and updates are installed.

Install Virtual Machine Additions

Virtual Machine Additions will allow you to access folders on your local machine, and to move the mouse freely in and out of the Virtual PC window.

1. If you connected to an ISO image to install the OS, you can disconnect it now.

2. Click Action on the Virtual PC's menu bar, and select Install or Update Virtual Machine Additions.

3. A message is displayed, click Continue. Once the image is mounted, click Next.

4. Click Finish. Click Yes to restart your virtual machine.

5. Log in again and close the Manage Your Computer panel.

Install ASP.NET 3.0 on the VM

ASP.NET 3.0 includes ASP.NET 2.0 and Windows Workflow Foundation (WF). Both are required by SharePoint. Follow these steps to install ASP.NET 3.0:

1. If you have a folder containing the .NET setup (version 3.0 or above) on your local machine, open File Explorer on your local machine and drag the folder onto the little folder icon on the bottom of your Virtual PC window. This makes the folder available from within your VM, starting with drive Z: and working backward.

2. Open File Explorer inside the VM and run the setup for the .NET Framework.

3. If prompted to Run, Open, or Cancel, click Run or Open. Prerequisites will be checked and files will be copied.

4. If you agree with the terms, accept the license and click Install. Clicking on the balloon in the lower right will show the progress in detail.

5. When installation is complete, click Exit.

Back Up Your Base Image

You have now created a reusable base image. At this point, it is prudent to make a backup of this image to save time when creating servers in the future.

1. Click Start and Shut down your VM. Enter a reason of "Base Image Complete."

2. Copy the folders containing the VHD and VMC files (set during step 1) into a folder named Do Not Touch.

3. Once the files are backed up, you can create a new machine by moving or copying the VHD into another folder, renaming it according to purpose (e.g., WSSBaseImage.vhd or MOSSBaseImage.vhd) and using Virtual PC to create a new virtual machine configuration (VMC) in the same folder. This is how subsequent instructions will begin to prepare a virtual machine for SharePoint.

Use SYSPREP to Create Server Farms

Though not required for a development environment, you may want to build a virtual SharePoint farm. Each machine in your farm will need a unique security identifier (SID), which is generated with a SYSPREP script which also initializes a machine image and (optionally) joins it to a domain. While the SysInternals utility called NewSID will also reset the SID, issues with the resulting images will not be supported by Microsoft, and there is a known issue with installing SharePoint on such a machine.

Note that this task is not required for the environment used in the remainder of this book.

Copy a VM to Use for the Windows Server SYSPREP Image

To create virtual server farms now or in the future, follow these steps to create a SYSPREP image:

1. Remember the Do Not Touch folder you created to back up your first image? Create a subfolder there called WindowsServerSysprep and copy your Windows Server 2003 Base virtual machine's hard drive (VHD) into it (e.g., F:\vms\DoNotTouch\WindowsServerSysprep\). Rename the VHD to match the folder name (e.g., WindowsServerSysprep Hard Disk.vhd). Create a new virtual machine configuration (VMC) in Virtual PC, also with the same name, and be sure to browse to the same folder. Rather than create a new VHD, select An existing hard disk, and browse to your new VHD. Do not click Enable undo disks.

2. Add a second network adapter and configure it as you did for your Windows Server Base image.

3. Start your VM and log in.

Copy the Deployment Utilities and Run Setupmgr.exe

Before running SYSPREP, you run SETUPMGR to define the default settings for new servers. Follow these steps to define your server settings:

1. Copy the files from your Windows Server media located in the ...\support\tools folder to a new folder inside the VM named C:\deploy. You can alternately locate and download these files from Microsoft Downloads by searching for your server name and "Deployment Tools." For example, search online for *Windows Server 2003 SP1 Deployment Tools*.

2. Download the wsname utility, and copy the wsname.exe executable to the C:\deploy folder. To locate this file, search online for *David Clarke wsname*.

3. Open Windows Explorer, navigate to C:\deploy and run setupmgr.exe. Click Next.

4. Select Create new. Click Next.

5. Select Sysprep setup. Click Next.

6. Select your version of Windows 2003 Server (Standard or Enterprise). Click Next.

7. Select Yes, fully automate the installation. Click Next.

8. The next window allows you to set answers for unattended setup. If you leave any entries blank, the user will be prompted for answers during installation. The following items should be set:

   - ❑ Name and Organization
   - ❑ Time Zone
   - ❑ Product Key should be set if you subscribe to Microsoft Licensing.
   - ❑ Computer Name. A utility will be used to rename the machine. For now, either select Automatically generate . . . or select Use the following . . . and provide a default name (e.g., SPSERVER).
   - ❑ Administrator Password. Optionally check the box to Encrypt the Administrator password in the answer file.
   - ❑ Regional Settings. Select your region.

❑ On the Run Once page, type `c:\deploy\wsname.exe`, and click Add.

❑ Identification String may be left blank. On this page click Finish. Then click Cancel to close the wizard.

9. Add a subfolder to `C:\deploy` to save your answer file: `C:\deploy\sysprep\sysprep.inf` and click OK. The utility generates your answer file and makes a copy in `C:\sysprep`.

10. Copy the files `sysprep.exe` and `setupcl.exe` into the `C:\sysprep` folder.

Run Sysprep.exe

Once your machine definition is configured with `SETUPMGR`, `SYSPREP` will seal the image and force it to invoke your configuration steps the next time it is opened.

1. Get your virtual machine into a clean state. Close any running applications and make any final adjustments. This is your last chance!

2. Click Start, then Run; type `c:\sysprep\sysprep.exe`, and click OK.

3. Click OK.

4. Check the box labeled Don't reset grace period for activation. Click Reseal.

5. Click OK. This will force the generation of a unique SID when you launch your new machine. A unique SID will be required to avoid conflicts in the virtual server farm.

`Sysprep` will then do its thing and shut the machine down.

Prepare and Test the SYSPREP Image

The virtual machine you prepared will now automatically run a series of tasks when started. You don't want this to happen until you are actually ready to build a farm. Next, you will remove the virtual machine from Virtual PC, move it to a safe location, copy it to a trial location, and test it to make sure it works.

1. Open the Virtual PC Console.

2. Select the `WindowsServerSysprep` virtual machine, and click Remove. Click Yes to confirm this.

3. Copy your VHD to a new location where you can test it. For example, `F:\vms\SharePointFarm-DC\`. Rename the VHD file to match the folder name.

4. Create a new Virtual PC machine with the same name. When naming the machine, browse to your new folder so that the VMC is stored there with the VHD (New, Next, Create, Next, `SharePointFarm-DC`, Browse, Save, Next, Windows Server, Next, 256 MB, Next, An existing virtual hard disk, Next, browse to the VHD and Open, Next, Finish).[ED: Is the list in parentheses okay, or should the series of steps be spelled out in detail?]

5. Open Settings, configure a second network adapter, and assign it to the Microsoft Loopback Adapter as you did for your Windows Server Base image. Click OK.

6. Start the new virtual machine. Windows will be prepared. Click through any prompts or answer any questions unanswered during `SETUPMGR` configuration. It is normal to see an Error message regarding the Administrator password. The server will then automatically restart.

7. Log in as Administrator using the password supplied during setup.

8. You will be prompted to enter a machine name. Supply a unique name that this machine will use on your virtual network. For example, SPFARM-DC. Click Set Name. Click Yes to restart.

9. Log in and click Start ⇨ Control Panel ⇨ Network Connections ⇨ Local Area Connection 2. Click Properties.

10. Select Internet Protocol (TCP/IP), and click Properties.

11. Enter a private IP address which is different from, but in the same subnet as, the one you used for your host machine's Microsoft Loopback Adapter. Enter the same subnet mask that you used for the Loopback Adapter. Ignore the gateway and DNS.

   ❑ IP address: e.g., 10.50.50.2 or 192.168.50.2

   ❑ Subnet mask: 255.255.255.0

   ❑ Default gateway: Leave this blank.

   ❑ DNS Servers: Leave these blank.

   You will create a HOSTS file on your host machine for resolving addresses. Click OK. Click Close.

12. Your virtual machine is now configured.

Optionally, at this time you can install Active Directory and DNS on this virtual machine by following the instructions in the next section. You can further test this virtual machine by starting your Windows Server Base image (or a copy) in Virtual PC and joining it to your new domain. To join another virtual machine to the domain, configure the DNS for Adapter #2 with the SPFARM-DC IP address. Then click Start, right-click My Computer, and click Properties. Click on the Computer Name tab and then click Change to enter the name of your domain. If the two machines can coexist on your virtual network, you've succeeded.

Prepare the Virtual Machine for SharePoint

The preparation stage is identical for both WSS and MOSS. WSS and MOSS are composed of ASP.NET applications, and ASP.NET requires IIS server. SharePoint also needs access to an Active Directory domain controller (for authentication) and a DNS server (for machine name to IP resolution), though these are network services and in a production environment they would rarely be installed to SharePoint servers. In your development environment, they will coexist nicely with a stand-alone configuration. Plan on this taking you roughly one hour.

Copy a VM to Use for SharePoint

SharePoint will be installed to a copy of the base virtual server you created earlier. These steps describe the process for copying a virtual machine into a space where you can continue its preparation to be used as a SharePoint (WSS or MOSS) server.

1. Copy your Windows Server 2003 Base virtual machine's hard drive (VHD) into a folder named IIS6Base and rename the VHD to match the folder name (e.g., IIS6Base Hard Disk.vhd). Create a new virtual machine configuration (VMC) in Virtual PC also with the same name. Rather than create a new VHD, select An existing hard disk, and browse to your new VHD. If

you also check Enable undo disks, you will be able to roll back the state of your VM to the point of your last save, which is the end of the last VM session where you committed changes. For base images, you can skip undo disks; for live development machines, you may want to enable them.

2. Add a second network adapter and configure it as you did for your Windows Server Base image.

3. Start your VM and log in.

Install Active Directory and DNS on the Virtual Machine

AD and DNS only need to be installed once in any given subnet. If you are building a server for a farm where they already occur, you may skip this step.

You could follow these steps independently of the other tasks to create a server that provides only AD and DNS services. You might want this when recreating a production farm where AD and DNS pre-exist SharePoint and you want to keep the two separate in your development environment as well. Since AD and DNS services will be required for all SharePoint development, you can also install these on a separate server (with 256 MB or less RAM required) so that you only need to build it once, and then carry the same test accounts from project to project.

Note that after these steps have been run and a machine is a domain controller, you can no longer use the image with the SYSPREP utility to create new virtual machines; a machine must be SYSPREPed before it is either a domain controller or a member of a domain.

1. Click Start, Administrative Tools, and then Configure Your Server Wizard. Click Next, then Next again.

2. Select Typical Configuration for a first server.

   If this option is not available, select Domain Controller (Active Directory), click Next, confirm your choice, and click Next again, then follow the steps to install and configure Active Directory and DNS from step 4 forward. When complete, come back to step 3 here.

3. Type the full DNS name for the new domain. This is not a web domain, so you can give it an entirely different suffix to avoid confusion with web domains (e.g., dev.myCompany.local). Click Next.

4. Accept the default NetBIOS name (DEV if you used the above example). Click Next.

5. Review your options and click Next. Active Directory is configured. Read the message and click OK. Once the process begins, *never* click Cancel. To uninstall the program or make changes, it is better to let the process complete and start over.

6. Select the virtual card that connects you to the Internet. This will be Local Area Connection; the other will be the IP address you configured for Adapter #2. Leave checked the option to set up a Basic Firewall. Click Next. Click Finish.

7. If prompted to insert the Windows 2003 Server media, either insert the disk in the host machine or recapture your ISO image through the CD menu on the menu bar.

8. When complete, the VM will automatically restart. Log in to resume.

9. Review the Server Configuration Progress page, and click Next. Click Finish. The server is now configured.

Install Internet Information Server (IIS) on the Virtual Machine

IIS is required to host web applications. Follow these steps to install IIS on your virtual machine by assigning it to the Application Server role.

1. The Manage Your Server window will be displayed. Click Add or remove role. If you disabled the Manage Your Server window, click Start ⇨ Administrative Tools, and select the Configure Your Server Wizard.

2. Click Next, then Next again.

3. Select Application Server (IIS, ASP.NET), and click Next.

4. On the Application Server Options page, check the second box, Enable ASP.NET. Click Next. Click Next again. Installation will begin.

5. The wizard will declare This Server Is Now an Application Server. Click Finish.

Install and Enable ASP.NET 2.0 on the Virtual Machine

ASP.NET 2.0 was installed on your machine along with 3.0 during the preparation of Windows 2003, but IIS doesn't yet know about it. The following steps explicitly install ASP.NET 2.0 and mark it as Allowed in IIS Web Service Extensions:

1. Locate and execute the ASP.NET 2.0 setup.

2. Select Repair, and click Next. During the repair, ASP.NET is installed to IIS and marked as allowed.

3. When setup is complete, click Finish.

4. Confirm that ASP.NET 2.0 is installed and allowed:

❑ Open IIS Manager. Click Start ⇨ Administrative Tools, then Internet Information Services (IIS) Manager.

❑ Click the + by the server name to expand its node.

❑ Click the Web Service Extensions node. ASP.NET v2.0.50727 should be listed as Allow. If not, check your Event Viewer to locate any errors that occurred during installation.

5. If you will be creating more than one server in a farm, now is a good time to run Windows Update, and shut down your virtual machine and backup your VHD and VMC files for reuse. Note that once a machine is joined to a domain, you can no longer use SYSPREP to reuse it for subsequent images.

Create a Stand-Alone WSS 3.0 Virtual Machine

This process describes the installation of WSS 3.0 and assumes a Basic setup. If Advanced is selected, you also have the option of specifying a database server external to the local machine, which creates a small farm rather than the stand-alone configuration. You should plan on this process taking about 30 minutes.

Create a Virtual Machine for WSS

In the last section, you prepared a base image for SharePoint. From here you can install either WSS or MOSS. Follow these steps to create a virtual machine on which to build a WSS server:

1. Copy your SharePoint-prepped virtual machine's hard drive (VHD) into a folder marked WSS3Base and rename the VHD to match the folder name (e.g., `WSS3Base Hard Disk.vhd`). Create a new virtual machine configuration (VMC) in Virtual PC, also with the same name. Rather than create a new VHD, select An existing hard disk, and browse to your new VHD.

2. Add a second network adapter and configure it as you did for your base image.

3. Start your VM and log in.

Set Up WSS 3.0

Now that you have a virtual machine created, install WSS.

1. Locate and run setup.

2. If you agree to the terms of the agreement, check the box and click Continue.

3. Choose the installation to perform. Advanced allows you to select between Web Front End and Stand-alone, and to set the location of the Content Index file. Basic is fine unless you have a reason to change these options. Either click Basic or click Advanced, then click Install Now to proceed.

4. When the process is complete, leave the check box selected and click Close.

5. Now you're in the WSS Configuration Wizard. Click Next. Click Yes. After that, it may seem that the 10 tasks will never complete (particularly 2 and 8). Be patient.

6. Once configuration is complete, click Finish.

7. A web browser opens. Enter your Administrator credentials and click OK.

8. When the message box appears, click Add to include this server as a trusted site.

9. Uncheck the box: Require server verification (https:) for all sites in this zone. Click Add. Click Close.

10. If a message appears, check the box In the future, do not show this message, and click OK.

11. Congratulations! Welcome to Windows SharePoint Services 3.0.

12. Create a backup: Shut down this virtual machine, and copy the VHD and VMC to a safe location.

Create a Stand-Alone MOSS 2007 Virtual Machine

This process describes the automatic setup for MOSS 2007. The process should take you about 30 minutes. In a complete setup, you would also define service accounts and have the option of creating the SharePoint databases on an external SQL database. In the Basic setup described here, the SharePoint application pool will run with the identity of NETWORK SERVICE. While it is useful to understand how to correctly configure a domain service account, the purpose of this setup is to create a development environment.

Create a Virtual Machine for MOSS

Previously, you prepared a base image for SharePoint. From that image you can install either WSS or MOSS. Follow these steps to create a virtual machine on which to build a MOSS server.

1. Copy your Windows Server 2003 Base virtual machine's hard drive (VHD) into a folder marked MOSS2007Base and rename the VHD to match the folder name (e.g., MOSS2007Base Hard Disk.vhd). Create a new virtual machine configuration (VMC) in Virtual PC also with the same name. Rather than create a new VHD, select An existing hard disk, and browse to your new VHD.

2. Add a second network adapter and configure it as you did for your base image.

3. Start your VM and log in.

Install SQL Server Developer Edition (Optional)

If you want to use SQL Server Developer Edition on this server, install it now. Note that the primary benefit is SQL Server Management Studio, and this can also be installed (with SQL Server Client Tools) and run from your host machine.

Install MOSS

Now that your virtual machine is prepared for the purpose, install MOSS.

1. Locate and run setup for MOSS 2007.

2. Enter your Product Key (PID) and click Continue. Note that it is the PID that determines the version that is deployed (Evaluation, Standard, or Enterprise). The installation bits for all versions are identical. You can upgrade from Evaluation to either Standard or Enterprise, or from Standard up to Enterprise by entering a new PID. However, you cannot downgrade after deployment.

3. If you agree to the terms of the agreement, check the box and Continue.

4. Click either Basic or Advanced. Advanced will allow you to choose between Complete (can add servers to form a farm), Web Front End, or Stand-alone (cannot add server to create a farm). If you installed SQL Server Developer or Standard Edition, or another SQL Server is available, select Complete. Advanced will also let you set locations for Administration applications and the Content Index. Click Continue when you are satisfied. Installation will begin.

5. When it is complete, leave the check box selected, and click Close to run the Configuration Wizard.

6. This is the SharePoint Products and Technologies Configuration Wizard. Click Next. Click Yes. In time, the 10 tasks will complete.

7. When you see Configuration Successful, click Finish.

8. A web browser opens. Enter your Administrator credentials and click OK.

9. When the message box appears, click Add to include this server as a trusted site.

10. Uncheck the box Require server verification (https:) for all sites in this zone. Click Add. Click Close.

11. If a message appears, check the box In the future, do not show this message, and click OK.

12. Congratulations! Welcome to Microsoft Office SharePoint Server 2007.

13. Back up your virtual machine. Shut down this virtual machine, and copy the VHD and VMC to a safe location.

Install and Configure Active Directory and DNS

Active Directory server is an LDAP server that provides authentication services for SharePoint. The DNS server provides IP address translation services. Both are typical in a production intranet and will be required to create a development environment that simulates the production environment. The following steps are provided to create an AD/DNS server separately from a SharePoint server. If used to create these services on a SharePoint server, they must be followed before SharePoint (WSS or MOSS) is installed.

1. Click Start, then click Command Prompt.

2. Type **dcpromo** and press Enter.

3. Click Next, Click Next again.

4. Select Domain controller for a new domain. Click Next.

5. Select Domain in a new forest. Click Next.

6. Type the full DNS name for the new domain. This is not a web domain, so you can give it an entirely different suffix to avoid confusion with web domains (e.g., dev.myCompany.local). Click Next.

7. Accept the default NetBIOS name (DEV if you used the above example). Click Next.

8. Accept the default database and log folders unless you have a reason to use different locations. Click Next.

9. Ditto for this page: Accept the default location unless you have a motive to do otherwise, and click Next.

10. Select Install and configure the DNS server on this computer . . ., and click Next.

11. Select Permissions compatible only with Windows 2000 or Windows Server 2003 operating systems, and click Next.

12. Type a restore mode password. This can (and probably should) match your Administrator password. Click Next.

13. Review your options and click Next. Active Directory is configured. Once the process begins, *never* click Cancel. To uninstall it or make changes, it is better to let the process complete and start over.

14. If prompted to insert the Windows Server 2003 media, either put the disk in the local machine or use Virtual PC's CD menu to capture the ISO image you used when installing the OS. The DNS Service will be configured. Again, *never* click Skip DNS Installation.

15. When the process is complete, click Finish. The next message will ask you to restart the computer.

16. After logging in, a message may indicate say This Server Is Now a Domain Controller. Click Finish.

Configure Remote Debugging

The final task for creating a development environment is to configure remote debugging between the host and guest machines. These steps can also be applied to configure remote process debugging on any server. Prerequisites for remote debugging:

❑ Create a developer account (e.g. SPDeveloper) in the credential store used by your SharePoint server (either Active Directory or the server's user manager found in Administrative Tools, Computer Management, Local Users and Groups). This account name should match the account name you will use on the host machine during development, and the password must match as well. Add this account to the **Domain Admins** group in the development Active Directory, or the local **Administrators** group if creating a local account. An account with the same name must be listed in the **Logon as a service** policy list (Local Security Settings, Local Policies, User Rights Assignment).

❑ Visual Studio (2005 or above) is installed to the host operating system.

The following steps share the SharePoint DLLs and web folder so you may access them remotely, and install the remote debugging tools to the guest environment:

1. On the guest (SharePoint) machine, open Windows Explorer and navigate to the following location:

```
C:\Program Files\Common Files\Microsoft Shared\web server extensions\12\ISAPI
```

Right-click the ISAPI folder, select the **Sharing** tab, and enable **Share this folder**. It will ease navigation to change the **Share name** from ISAPI to a more descriptive name like **SPAssemblies**.

Click the **Permissions** button, **Add** your SPDeveloper user, click **Full Control**, then click **OK**.

Click the **Security** tab, **Add** your SPDeveloper user, click **Full Control**, then click **OK**.

2. Follow the above steps to share and provide read/write permissions to the default web root folder:

```
C:\Inetpub\wwwroot
```

3. Create a C:\debug folder inside the guest machine and copy into it the contents of the following folder on the host machine:

```
C:\Program Files\Microsoft Visual Studio 8\Common7\IDE\Remote Debugger\x86
```

Note that if you are creating a 64-bit server, you would instead copy the x64 folder. Note: You can make this folder available for copying into the guest OS by dragging the Remote Debugger folder onto the small folder icon at the bottom of your Virtual PC window.

4. On the host machine, run the **Visual Studio Remote Debugger Configuration Wizard** (Start, All Programs, Microsoft Visual Studio 2005. Visual Studio Tools).

Check the box to "Run the Visual Studio 2005 Remote Debugger" service. Enter your developer account credentials. Click **Next**.

Enable the switch to **Allow only computers on the local network (subnet)**. If debugging on another domain you may need to enable the **Allow any computer** option instead. This will open the ports on your development machine necessary for remote debugging.

You can now debug remotely. The following steps will configure remote debugging for a Visual Studio project.

1. Start the remote debugging monitor: right-click `c:\debug\msvsmon.exe`, select **Run as** and enter your developer account credentials.

Click **Tools**, **Options** and copy the server name to the clipboard.

2. Create a new Visual Studio project on the host machine. For example, create a new C# SharePoint Web Part project. Configure the guest server as your build location by changing your project properties: xxxxxxxxx.

3. Right-click References, select **Add Reference**. Click **Browse** and type the name of your server's SPAssembly share. For example: `\\10.50.50.1\SPAssemblies`

Upon connection to the share you will need to authenticate to the server using your developer account credentials.

Double-click **Microsoft.SharePoint.DLL** to create the reference.

4. Click **Debug**, then click **Attach to Process**. Paste the server name you copied in step 1. Select the **w3wp.exe** process.

Summary

Now that you have completed this chapter, you should have a thorough understanding of SharePoint architecture, including the different SharePoint Farm Server configurations and roles, and how Share-Point works with ASP.NET. You've learned all about publishing MOSS pages and site templates. Finally, assuming you've followed the comprehensive steps included in the second half of the chapter, you now have a development environment up and running. You've built a host machine and a server, and created two standalone virtual machines with all the necessary programs installed. You are ready to embark on some professional-level SharePoint development.

3

The SharePoint User Experience

By Brendon Schwartz

Windows SharePoint Services v3 (WSS) provides tremendous functionality right out of the box. When many developers and end users think about performing custom development, they tend to think about having to write code. Because Windows SharePoint Services is a framework, and Microsoft has already written a user interface layer, you can make many development changes without writing any code. This chapter looks at some of the basic functionality that is provided when you install WSS v3. Keep in mind that you will also have this functionality in Office Share-Point Server 2007 because Office SharePoint Server simply builds more functionality on top of the core functionality provided by WSS v3.

WSSv3 provides enhanced lists and libraries that you can use to create a fully functional site. The improvements made to lists give you more control over the performance of the list. For example, lists now contain easier ways to stay connected with users, such as the new RSS feature, but lists still offer you the ability to notify users with email. Lists are useful, but what really makes them powerful is the ability to add metadata that describes the columns included in a list. I start the discussion by looking at a basic list, created by using Site Columns. After that, I discuss Content Types and how you can use them to create more flexible and useful lists with a lot of distinct data in them.

In previous versions of SharePoint, it was difficult to change the overall appearance of a site and to support variations in the site navigation user interface (UI). Now the 2007 version greatly simplifies these tasks by using master pages and site navigation controls borrowed from ASP.NET 2.0, which is the foundation of SharePoint 2007. A master page can provide a common look and feel for all pages in the site, and changes you make to the master page automatically propagate to all dependent pages. Site navigation controls make it easy to display only the links that are relevant to the user.

Finally, this chapter talks about how SharePoint 2007 takes advantage of many other ASP.NET 2.0 features. For instance, SharePoint sites are now compatible with a broad range of browsers and can even be configured for use from mobile devices. In addition, web developers will be happy to learn that SharePoint no longer contains its own page rendering engine but rather uses the one built into ASP.NET. This means that you can build ASP.NET web pages and blend them into a SharePoint site without a lot of rework. In this chapter you take a look at:

❑   The standard features of Windows SharePoint Services v3, including lists and document libraries

❑   The columns of lists, including the Site Columns and Content Types

❑   Enhancements to the user interface and how to modify the site look and feel

❑   The addition of Mobile Development to Windows SharePoint Services v3

Site Design Starts with Web Applications

Every site has a web application at its core. The web application is the central location for many of the features of SharePoint and is physically located on a web server using Internet Information Server (IIS). Creating a web application also allows for some key decisions about the application such as the definition of an authentication method. It is here that you will be deciding on the content database for SharePoint. To begin making a site in Microsoft Windows SharePoint Services 3.0, you start by creating a web application that creates a new content database: When creating a new application for the SharePoint 2007, a site designer will need to decide on the type of authentication method for that site. In addition, each web application will use a database to store the data from the site.

> Web application is the new name for what was known as a "Virtual Server" in Windows SharePoint Server v2. The term Virtual Server confused new developers and end users because Microsoft also has a product known as Microsoft Virtual Server. To help resolve the confusion, the SharePoint team now calls the sites that are created in IIS, web applications.

1.   Navigate to the Central Administration page, click the Application Management tab.

2.   Under SharePoint Web Application Management, click the Create or Extend Web Application. This is where you can decide if you want to use an existing site already created in IIS or if you want to create a new web site.

3.   To create a new web application click on Create New Web Application.

> Keep in mind that you must have permission to create a new web application in IIS. This will also set up the authentication of the application in IIS also.

4.   The next page shows the settings for the web application being created. On the left side of the page are descriptions of the settings. On the right side of the page is where the settings can either be accepted as the defaults or changed to be custom values. See Figure 3-1. When you are done, click on OK. SharePoint will then create the new web application.

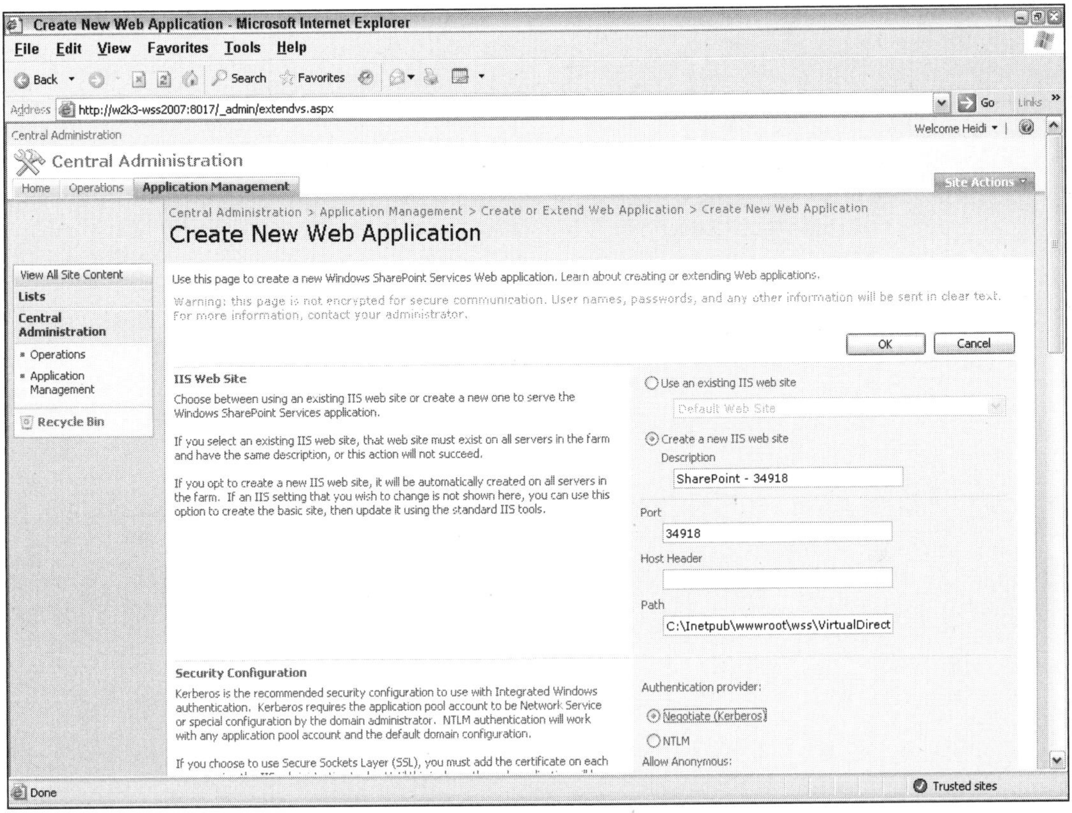

Figure 3-1

Content Is Stored in a Site Collection

Even though a web site has been created, a site collection needs to be added to have a place to store the content of the site. The site collection is a top-level site that will contain all of the other pages in the site. It is the parent to all the child sites that can be created. Once the site collection has been created, the site can be viewed. When a new SharePoint web application is created, a site collection is not automatically created by SharePoint. Therefore, when you are finished creating a new web application, SharePoint will prompt you to create a site collection. To create a site collection navigate to the Application Created page, click on the Create Site Collection link.

Another way to access the site collections page is from the Application Management tab, under Share-Point Site Management by clicking on Create Site Collection.

The Create Site Collection page allows the first customization of the site you are creating. It is here that a title, description, and URL can be provided (see Figure 3-2). A template needs to be selected, depending on the needs of the site. A primary and secondary site collection administrator can be named here, as well as a predefined quota template, used to limit resources used for this site collection. After filling in all of the information, click OK and the top-level site will be created!

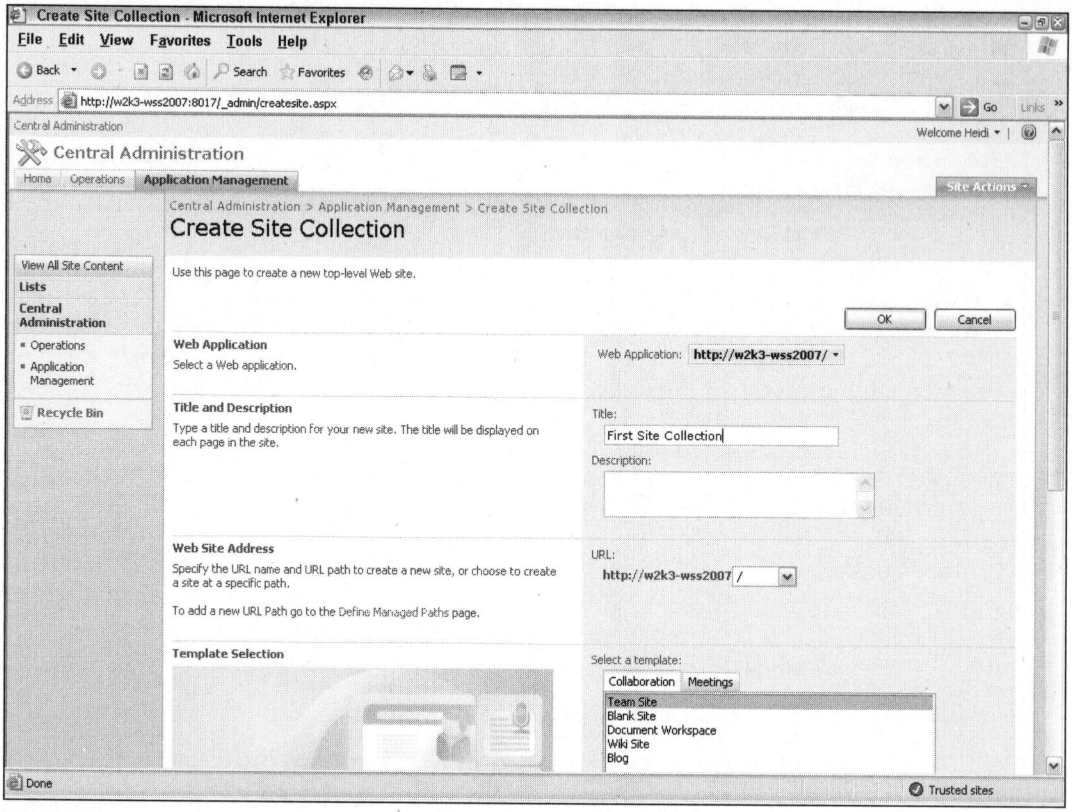

Figure 3-2

SharePoint provides a link to the URL so that the site can be opened in a new browser, while providing an OK button that will return you to SharePoint Central Administration. At this point, the rest of the changes will be done in the site collection, so follow the URL to the new site, instead of going back to the Central Administration page. The SharePoint site has been set up and is now ready for customization. Figure 3-3 shows a simple team site that has been selected as the template for the site collection.

Using SharePoint Lists and Libraries

SharePoint is made up of content and data. The content in SharePoint is the user interface and information stored in Web Parts, while the data is information that SharePoint stores in the database and can be versioned. The lists and libraries of SharePoint are the core to store data in SharePoint. Lists and libraries are web pages in Windows Services SharePoint 2007 where information can be stored and organized. Many types are available and are covered in the following sections. A list is simply that — a set of data that lists information that is helpful to the users. The lists can be set up and customized by a site designer or authorized user to contain any number of fields required for list data. A library is where a collection of files, as well as associated data, can be stored and managed. SharePoint makes it very easy to store and manage information in a way that is most useful to the end user. Every list is defined in a file called

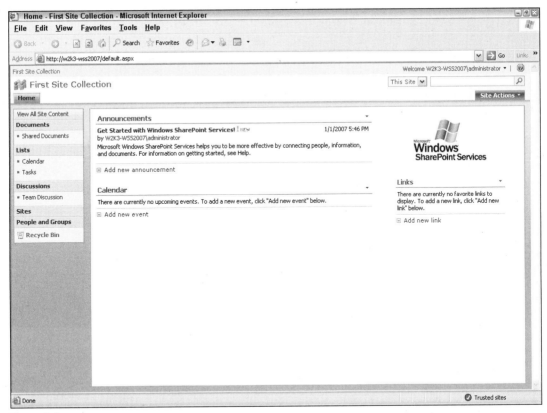

Figure 3-3

Onet.xml that is stored in the site definition. Following is a table that describes some of the standard lists you will find in some of the Onet.xml file, as well as the number that represents the list internally. This value is used in many of the configuration files to reference the list as well as when programming with lists. Keep in mind you might not have all list types for every site.

Value	Available on Default Team Site	Description
100	Yes	Generic list
101	Yes	Document library
102	Yes	Survey
103	Yes	Links list
104	Yes	Announcements list

Continued

Value	Available on Default Team Site	Description
105	Yes	Contacts list
106	Yes	Events list (Calendar)
107	Yes	Tasks list
108	Yes	Discussion board
109	Yes	Picture library
110	No	Data sources
111	No	Site template gallery
113	No	Web Part gallery
114	No	List template gallery
115	Yes	XML Form library
119	Yes	Wiki Page library
120	Yes	Custom grid for a list
150	Yes	Project Tasks
200	No	Meeting Series list
201	No	Meeting Agenda list
202	No	Meeting Attendees list
204	No	Meeting Decisions list
207	No	Meeting Objectives list
210	No	Meeting text box
211	No	Meeting Things to Bring list
212	No	Meeting Workspace Pages list

Value	Available on Default Team Site	Description
300	No	Portal Sites list
1100	Yes	Issue tracking
2002	No	Personal document library
2003	No	Private document library

Using Pages to Display Lists

To provide end users with a way to get to lists SharePoint allows you to create pages to display information. A SharePoint site allows you as the site designer to organize and store the lists and documents you create all in one place. To start with, you need to have a page that allows you to add the content and lists. To create such a page, click Site Actions on the Site Settings page, then select Create. The Create page is where you can select any type of content to add to a SharePoint site. These items are managed by categories that can be created, including: lists, document libraries, discussion boards, surveys, and pages. Once the page is created, you can then place any number of lists or content items on the page. The following table shows each type of page that you can create with in SharePoint 2007.

Name	Description
Basic Page	Creates a simple web page that can be modified by using a web browser to add text, pictures, and tables. This is a simple page that can be created if you are unsure of what you need, and it can be modified later as needs arise.
Web Part Page	Can be used to create a page that will be used to share many different items. A Web Part page can show many different Web Parts on the same page. Each Web Part can be used to show various items, including lists, libraries, links, and other types of information. This type of page is very versatile and can be used when many different types of lists need to be shown on one page.
Sites and Workspaces	An entirely new site or workspace can be created to serve as a new place for collaboration, communication, or content storage. Sites can be created in order to hold all of the lists and libraries that are created and used. A new site can be created for all the different teams that might need one, or all the different uses that may be needed for one team. Each site serves as a place where the team can come together and share information and work together on different things. A work team can create their own site, or a company division may have a site of their own.

Storing Data with Lists and Libraries

Data that is stored in SharePoint is stored in one of two ways:

❑ **Lists** — These contain data elements that define what data is contained in SharePoint. Some common examples are a list of links, a list of announcements, or a list of custom data elements.

❑ **Libraries** — Libraries are a special type of list that has built-in capabilities to handle storing files. This includes version and new file template features.

Site designers will use either libraries or lists to store the data. Even though a library is a specialized type of list, it is discussed separately because it has features that set it apart from a standard list.

Adding Lists to the Site

You can customize lists as needed, but there are a number of prebuilt lists that SharePoint provides to help you create sites quickly. When one of these items is created, it can be placed on your top-level site and accessed by many users. The built-in lists are described in the following table.

Each predefined list is shown to the user in the user interface in different categories. The first set of lists is the types of lists that are used in the communications category to communicate with other users in a SharePoint site. Each communication list is in the following table.

Name	Description
Announcements	A list that can be used to share short bits of information, such as announcements, news, status updates, and the like. This is a good page to use as a company's intranet home page to keep employees up to date with any changes or news about the company that needs to be shared.
Contacts	Can be used as an online address book. This list makes it easy to manage information about all of your different contacts, such as customers, partners, and employees. Information can be shared between this list and other WSS-compatible contacts programs. Contacts are very important in any type of business, so a central storage area of contacts can be very powerful to help in day-to-day business. Sales forces, in particular, would also rely heavily on contacts pages that could store information about the customer, such as personal information, order history, and any other information that could be helpful in making the sale.
Discussion Board	Used as a place for people to read and post in a discussion-style format. A discussion board also provides features to help manage the discussion threads and to control the content, such as restricting posts from unauthorized people. This could be used as a central area to have brainstorming sessions, especially if there are people all over the world who can't meet because of geography or time schedules.

In addition to the lists in the Communications category, you can also use the tracking lists described in the following table.

Name	Description
Links	Lists URL links to web pages and other resources that need to be kept on hand and shared among people. This is good both for keeping commonly used links all in one place and for rarely used links, so they are kept in one central place and not lost.
Calendar	Used to view upcoming events in a calendar-based list. A company team can share a calendar to keep track of deadlines, meetings, rollouts, and the like. Also, information can be shared between the calendar list and a WSS-compatible events program.
Tasks	Keeps track of the assignment and completion of tasks that need to be done. All people on a team can see how the project is coming along and what tasks still need to be completed to make deadlines.
Project Tasks	Similar to the tasks list, the project tasks list provides a graphical view in the form of a Gantt chart. A group of work items that need to be done can be tracked by the entire team on the project. This list can also be opened in WSS-compatible programs.
Issue Tracking	Can be used to manage issues by assigning them to a person or team, creating a priority order, and tracking the progress of the issue. An issue-tracking list is ideal for a customer service department that is responsible for dealing with customer issues and making sure that they are followed through to resolution.
Survey	Helpful when trying to poll, or survey, a group of people on certain issues. You can create questions for users, and create the answers that they must choose from. This is a great tool to get feedback from customers that use your site, and since they simply choose from prewritten answers, the time it takes them to complete the survey can be kept to a minimum.
Sites and Workspaces	An entirely new site or workspace can be created to serve as a new place for collaboration, communication, or content storage. Sites can be created in order to hold all of the lists and libraries that are created and used. A new site can be created for all the different teams that might need one, or all the different uses that may be needed for one team. Each site serves as a place where the team can come together and share information and work together on different things. A work team can create their own site, or a company division may have a site of their own.

Creating a Standard Link List

A common list that many sites have created is the link list, which can be used to share web pages' links with other users of the site. To create the link list, follow these steps:

1. Click Site Settings and then Create.

2. On the Create page, click on Links under the Tracking heading. All lists have a name and description field you can fill out.

3. The only required field is the name field, but a description will help your users know what the list is about. Enter a name and description for the links list; you can use information like "Real Estate Links," and the description will be "Web sites for real estate services." The option to display the list in the Quick Launch bar is set to Yes by default. This will display the new list on the Quick Launch bar, which is the default setting for Navigation.

4. Click on the Create button, and the Real Estate Links page is displayed as shown in Figure 3-4.

Notice that the new Real Estate Links list page is shown under Lists on the Quick Launch bar. However, the new list does not exist on the other sites that have been created such as child sites. When a new list is created, a default page is created that displays the list that was just produced. In this example, the page that is created manages the links and has a default view of the links. This list can be added to one of the content pages with a set view of the data.

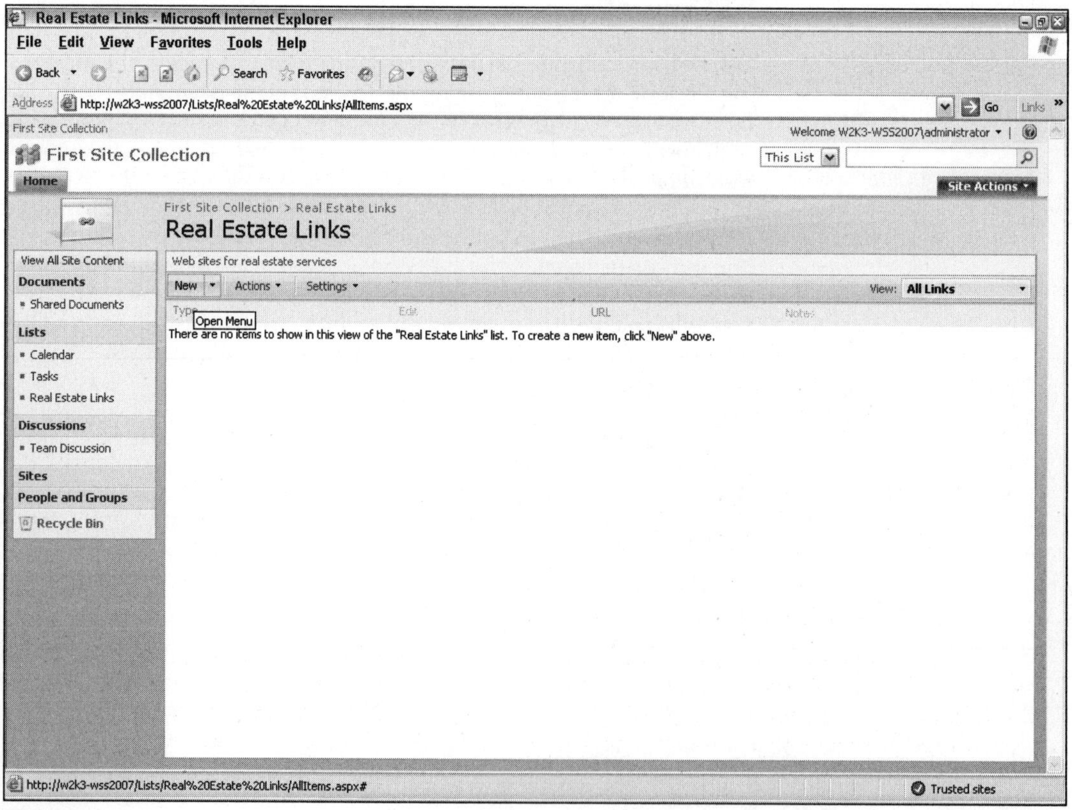

Figure 3-4

Managing Lists

Lists are one of the central concepts of SharePoint and how data is stored within SharePoint. Most lists are updated with data on a regular basis and are not static. Some common actions that you can perform on lists are adding items, removing items, and modifying the list settings. These actions can be performed either through the web user interface, through the object model, or through web services. In the following sections, you learn how to use the user interface to perform such tasks and more.

Adding Items to Lists

To add items to lists, you must have the correct permissions or you will not be able to access the create list item pages. Here are the steps required to add a link to the new list you just created:

1. Click on New at the top left of the page. Each list will have a different set of fields to enter for the data. The links list has a URL and description that are required fields and a notes field, which is not required.

2. Type the URL for the new link in the first space, and then add a description.

3. Click OK, and the link will be shown at the top of the link list page. The description is shown under URL to let users know what the link is, and the notes are shown. If the description is clicked, it takes the user to the web site. Each list can be used in the same way but will require different fields. You will find the correct use of each list as the functionality is required on the site.

> The links page is ideal for links that are used often, so they are ready at hand. Alternatively, it is great for links that are not used very often, so they can always be found in one centralized place.

At the top of the links section of the page, there are a couple of buttons that should be discussed. These buttons are labeled New, Actions, and Settings. Each set of buttons provides functionality that allows the user to manage, display, and update the list.

The New button can create a new item or a new folder. The lists have folders turned on by default to allow users to store data in the familiar folder structure.

Taking Action on the List Items

The Actions menu provides the ability to work with the items in lists as data exporting data, and setting up interaction with the list. In addition, the Actions menu allows users to export the data to other tools such as Microsoft Access and Microsoft Excel. This allows end users to use the most common tools they use every day to work with the list items. Finally, users can use the Actions menu to provide notifications about events that happen on a list such as adding new items.

Changing List Settings

The Settings button displays a menu that enables you to create a column, create a view, or manage list settings. Each different list or document library page will have buttons similar to these, which allow the user to customize the list as needed. The customization of the data and information is one of the strengths of SharePoint that makes it so powerful and useful for both the developer and the end users.

Creating Custom Lists

When none of the lists that are provided by SharePoint meets your needs, a custom list can be created. To create a custom list, you must specify the columns that are needed, and then a web page is created that allows for adding or editing each of the items.

To create a custom list, follow these steps:

1. Click the Create link from Site Actions.

2. Select Custom List, and then give the new list a name and a description.

3. Click on Create and the new list is created. Once the new list is created, you will need to add your own columns to the list. I talk about columns shortly.

Adding items to a custom list is the same as with any other list type. The column fields that will need to be filled out depend on what columns have been added to the custom list. The only field that the list item needs by default is the Title field. To add items to the list, click on New and then type the title for the item, and click OK. A list can be created for any need that cannot be met by using any of the existing lists.

Creating Custom Lists in Datasheet View

When a custom list is needed, and the best format for the list would be a spreadsheet, you can create a custom list in datasheet view. When created, this list opens in a spreadsheet-like environment so that the user can easily add, edit, and format data. This makes it easy to work on lists that have a lot of data that needs to be organized in a format that can support using a lot of columns and rows. Columns and items can be added in the same way as when using a custom list. However, it is important to remember that a custom list in datasheet view does require a WSS-compatible list datasheet control and ActiveX control support.

Importing Data from Spreadsheets

A new list can be created by using an existing list that has the same columns and contents as you would like to have in the new one. However, to import a spreadsheet, you must have a WSS-compatible spreadsheet application. When importing the spreadsheet, simply type the name and description, and then browse to select the file location of the spreadsheet you would like to import. Once the imported spreadsheet is created, it can be modified in the same way as custom lists.

Adding Document Libraries to Sites

A document library is created in much the same way as a list. Just as with lists there are document libraries that you can create from the Create page. Each one of the libraries can hold specific types of files and is designed to help provide the necessary document management functions of SharePoint. These libraries are discussed in the following table.

Name	Description
Document Library	Used when there are many documents that need to be shared among many people. Various actions can be done with document libraries such as using folders, having different versions (versioning), and using the file checkout feature. This can be very helpful when there are many developers working on different parts of a web site, all using various documents that contain code.

Name	Description
Form Library	Can be used to store XML-based documents. An XML editor is required to use a form library, such as Microsoft Office InfoPath. However, this library is very useful to manage business forms that are based on XML.
Wiki Page Library	Can store an interconnected collection of Wiki pages, and it is also able to support storing pictures, tables, Wiki linking, and hyperlinks. This opens the library up to many different uses because it supports such a large variety of media. Wiki pages are commonly used to share authoritative information on many different subjects.
Picture Library	Used for storing and sharing pictures. The picture library makes it easy to manage and display pictures by offering features such as thumbnail photos, different options for downloading, and the use of a slide show. An auto insurance company could use a picture library for accident claims. Picture libraries are also very popular for personal use as well as the different business uses that could arise.

Creating a Standard Document Library

One common type of list is a document library. A document library contains a column type of file where you can store documents. Once you create a document library you can then have the system display the documents it contains on other pages as well as perform searches within the documents.

1. From the top-level page, click on the Site Actions tab, and select Create.

2. Choose the Document Library link under Libraries. Type in a name and description for the document library on the New page.

Because a document library is just a type of list, the same structure as in other lists, such as name and description, will be found in libraries.

For example, you could type in Standard Offers with a description of Standard Offers for types of listings. To display the document library on the Quick Launch bar leave the Navigation button on Yes. To enable versioning on a document, you can select the option to have a version kept for each document that you check in. The Document Version History button will determine if the version history is kept or not. The versioning of documents can be very helpful when trying to keep track of changes in documents.

> **Every time a new version is created the database size will grow. Make sure to store the version only if it is required for a document library.**

Finally a document template can be selected for the library. The document template will be the default file type for all new files that are created in this document library. For this particular example, choose Microsoft Office Word 97-2003 document, as shown in Figure 3-5. Click Create, and the document library is created.

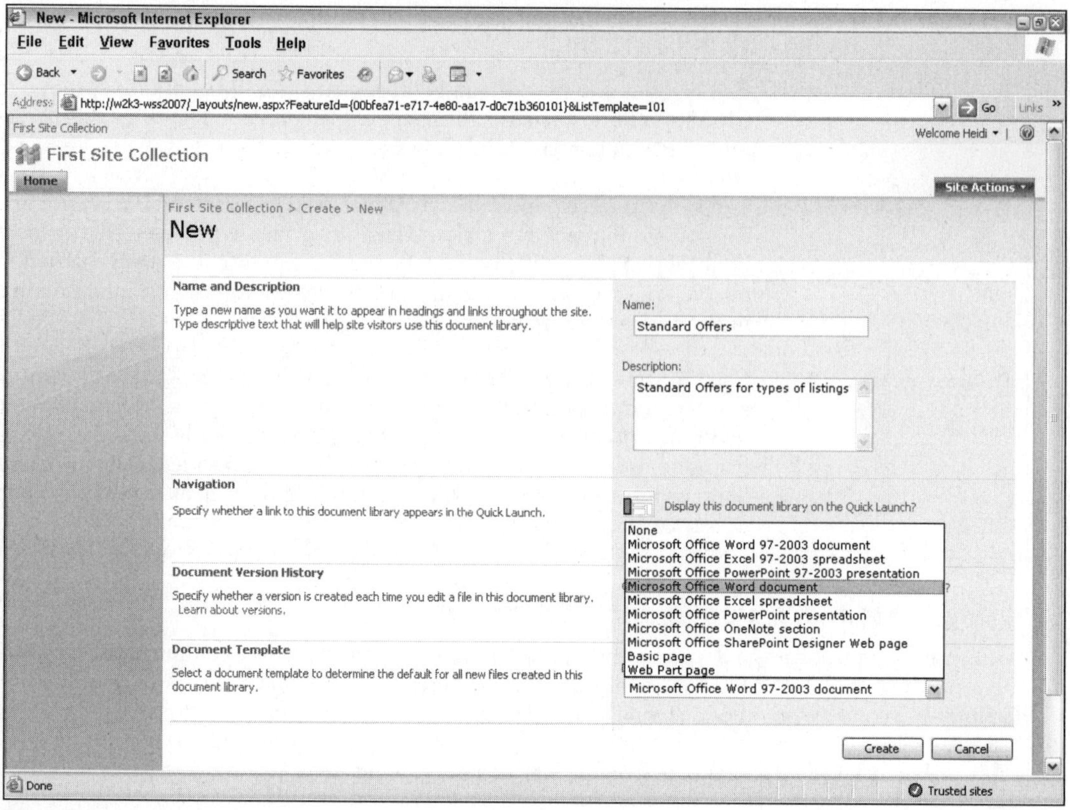

Figure 3-5

Once the library is created, end users can create a new file or they can upload the file. Because Microsoft Office is fully integrated with SharePoint, the document opens directly in the application selected as the file type.

Deleting a List or Document Library

Lists are stored in the database, and they are not always shown in the Quick Launch bar. To see all the lists that are available on the site, simply click the View All Site Content on the Quick Launch bar, and you will see all of the lists that have been created on the site. You will notice that they are again displayed in categories to make them easy to find. To completely delete a list or a document library, navigate to the page you want to delete, then follow these steps:

1. Click on the Setting button on the top-left menu of the list or library page, and select List Settings or Document Library Settings, depending on what you are deleting.

2. The middle heading, Permissions and Management, has a top link, labeled Delete this list or Delete this document library. Once you click on the link, a message pops up to make you confirm your selection.

3. The list or library that you have chosen to delete will be removed, and all of the files associated with it will be deleted. Confirm that you are sure you want to delete the list or library by clicking on OK. SharePoint will then go to the All Site Content page, which shows all of the existing pages for the site.

Using the Recycle Bin

One of the biggest problems in previous versions of SharePoint was not being able to restore documents or items that end users accidentally deleted. SharePoint 2007 now has the ability to easily restore these items from a two-stage recycle bin. On the Quick Launch bar, the bottom link is for the Recycle Bin. Whenever a list or library is deleted, it is removed from the site and stored in the site's Recycle Bin. An item's document type, name, original location, created by, deleted date, and size are all shown on this page. These items can be restored to the site, or they can be "emptied," which would delete the items, sending them to the site collection administrator's recycle bin. It is important to note that after 30 days, a deleted item will automatically be emptied from the Recycle Bin. Items that have been deleted from the entire site collection can be managed from the Site Collection Recycle Bin, for which a link is provided.

Customizing List Columns

Customizing columns in a list is quick way to add more meaning and value to the data you store in SharePoint. To customize a list, follow these steps:

1. Click the Quick Launch link for a list, such as the Real Estate Links page created earlier. The default columns are shown, which include Type, Edit, URL, and Notes for a links list. Perhaps a new column is needed, to show who added the link.

2. On the page menu, click Settings and then Create Column. The Create Column page is shown. Here, you specify settings for the new column. The name of the column is what the end users will see.

3. Set the value to Added By, and then select the single line of text. Make sure to always add a meaningful description for the users who will navigate through the site.

4. Add the description **Agent that added the link**.

5. You have the option at this point to require information to be added to the column or not. For this case, information will be required, so change the button to Yes. In addition to the settings for all columns, there are type-specific settings that appear once you select a list type — for instance, the maximum number of characters and the default value. In this case, limit the number of characters to 25 and don't set a default value to limit space used for this list.

6. Click on OK, and the Real Estate Links page is shown, but now there is a new column that is shown on the right — the Added By column.

Adding Items with Custom Columns

Now, whenever a new link is created, there is a new column that must be filled out. Click on the New button at the top of the page. The New Item page is shown, with the items that can be filled out. The URL information section is required, which is shown by the red asterisk that is next to URL. The Notes section does not require any information. The new Added By column is shown next, with an asterisk next to it. This information must now be included anytime a new link is added.

Modifying Items with Custom Columns

Any previous links that were added before this column was added won't include your new information. Therefore, if you edit an existing link, you must add the new information before changes can be saved. If you edit the item, but don't add information for the newly required column, SharePoint doesn't save it, and displays a message box requesting that a value be specified for the required field.

Setting Permissions

Permissions can also be set for a list from the list page. Keeping with the previous example, hover the mouse over the URL in the list, and an arrow appears on the right for a drop-down menu. Click the arrow, and the menu appears, with options that include View Item, Edit Item, Manage Permissions, Delete Item, and Alert Me. Click Manage Permissions, and the permission for this particular list item (the link) are shown. Three types of users/groups are set by default: Members, Owners, and Visitors. The Owners of the group are allowed full control. Members of the group, or member users, are allowed to contribute to the site. Visitors, however, are only allowed to read information on the site; they are not allowed to change anything. These permissions are inherited from the parent folder or list.

There is only one button on this page, which is the Actions menu button. This button allows you to manage the permissions of the parent or to edit permissions. If you choose Manage Permissions of Parent, the Permissions page for the entire site is pulled up. Changes you make to these permissions are then passed down to the list being edited, through inheritance. Here, you can create new users/groups and set their permissions, as well as edit or remove the current users/groups' permissions. However, if you choose Edit Permissions from the list on the Permissions page, the original permissions are copied from the parent and then changed. Once these changes are made, the list will stop inheriting changes from the parent. This ensures that any changes you make aren't overwritten by changes made to the parent permissions.

Understanding SharePoint List Views

The way each site is viewed can be changed to allow for optimal viewing by users, depending on their individual needs. SharePoint allows for the creation of different types of views, among which users can choose according to their needs. Views allow users to see the items on a list sorted in a particular order or by the most current modified date or by any other view that may be needed. Views can also be created that allow users to see only certain items of a whole list, depending on matching criteria and how the view was set up. Once a view is created, it is always there for users to choose as their current view. Each type of list may come with a predefined set of views. Some of the most common lists are shown in the table below with the default views.

List Type	View Name
Document Library	All Documents (Default View)
	Explorer View
Calendar	Calendar (Default View)
	All Events
	Current Events
Task	All Tasks (Default View)
	My Tasks
	Due Today
	Active Tasks
	By Assigned To
	By My Groups

Managing Existing Views

Each site is created with a default view. From the list or library page, click on the Settings button, and select List Settings. This brings up the Customize page for the site. This page has all of the list information, along with ways to manage the general settings, permissions, communications, columns, and views. At the bottom of the page is the section that shows the different views. There should be a list of the views that are available for this list. The default view is All Links, which shows all of the links, sorted in the order they were created.

Creating a New View

A new view can be created from the Customization page, as follows:

1. Click Create View at the bottom of the page. Alternatively, click the Settings button on the list page, and then click Create View. A new view can be created to select columns, filters, and other display settings that would be more helpful and productive to the users.

2. The Create View page comes up. Click Choose a view format in the first section to create an entirely new view. Or, choose Start from an existing view to begin building your view from one that already exists.

Using the Start from an existing view section to create a new view can be helpful when creating a view that has many of the same settings as a view that has already been created but is slightly different. The existing view can be chosen, and then slightly modified and saved as an entirely different and new view.

Choosing a View Format

To create a completely new view, select one of the views under Choose a view format. You can choose from the following views as your starting point:

❑ **Standard View** — Shows data on a basic web page that can be customized.

❑ **Calendar View** — Shows information in a daily, weekly, or monthly calendar format.

❑ **Datasheet View** — Gives the ability to view the data in a spreadsheet that can be edited. This allows for easy editing of large amounts of data and also for quick and easy customizing.

❑ **Gantt View** — Is a visual representation of the data in a graph view. It is used to show how a team's tasks relate over time.

A standard view is the most common type of view and should work well in most cases. Choose a view name that is intuitive and descriptive, so that when users are choosing a view they know what this one will show. An example of a name to use for a links list is "Sort by URL" because that list will sort the links by the URL description.

Selecting the Audience for the View

When creating your views, there are two options for the type of audience that the view can be created for:

❑ **Personal View** — Allows the view to be viewed only by the owner of the site.

❑ **Public View** — Can be used by anyone using the site.

This audience will come in handy when you need to have a specific view for just yourself but don't need to create the view for everyone else to see, such as a list task for one user.

Choosing Columns to Display

In the Columns section, you determine which columns to include in a view. If a column is not checked, the information isn't shown. If the column is checked, the information is displayed. To the right of all of the columns, are drop-down boxes where you can set the order in which the columns should be displayed. All of the columns that have been created for this list appear as valid selection items, but you may not want to show all of the items in the view.

Sorting and Filtering Items in a View

Organizing the data is the primary use of views. To accomplish this, the sorting and filtering of the data is used to create a very specific list for the end users. Sorting is a good way to provide a detailed list of information with the most important items at the top of the list. This option allows columns to be sorted alphabetically or numerically, depending on the type of information in the column. When you are building the view, you can sort the items by the column, either in ascending or descending order. The items can be sorted by one or two columns.

Filters allow the view to show only certain items that meet the set criteria. The option of not using a filter is available, and in that case all items in the view will be shown to the user. If the view does require filtering, you can enter criteria that allow only certain items to be shown. For instance, the view can be set to only contain items that have been created by a certain user. The number of filters can be extended by clicking the Show More Columns... link. The filters allow you to compare the data or use the And/Or operators with each filter. Each filter can use a column field and compare it to a set of data using predefined operators:

- ❑ Is equal to
- ❑ Is not equal to
- ❑ Is greater than
- ❑ Is less than
- ❑ Is greater than or equal to
- ❑ Is less than or equal to
- ❑ Begins with
- ❑ Contains

Other options can be set for the new view being created. Columns can be displayed in groups, columns can be totaled, and the style of the view can be changed. The view can be set up so that users have to navigate through folders to view items or so that they can view all of the items at one time. The number of items returned can be limited, and the view can be made a mobile view, as well. When all of the settings have been selected, click on OK and the view is created.

Choosing a View

Now that there are multiple views to choose from, your users can select a view other than the default view. From the list or library page, there is a drop-down menu at the top right of the page labeled View. Click on the arrow on the right, and the different options that can be chosen are shown. The view can be set to All Links or any of the other views that have been created. Options in this All Links drop-down menu enable you to modify a view or create a new view.

Adding and Removing Lists and Libraries

The functionality and the look of a site can be changed by moving the Web Parts around for optimal placement. From the main page, you can modify the home page to contain any of the lists or libraries that you have created:

1. Click on the top-right tab, labeled Site Actions, and select Edit Page. This allows you to add, remove, or update Web Parts on the page. When clicked, the page comes up in Edit Mode, allowing easy manipulation of the Web Parts.

2. At the center of the top of the page is a link labeled Add a Web Part. Click it to open a window that allows for the addition of any or all of the types of Web Parts that are available. Notice that any new lists or libraries that have been created are also available in this selection.

3. Select what to add, such as a links Web Part, and click Add at the bottom of the screen. At the top the page shows the Links Web Part that was just added. Now, the different sections of the page can be used to sort various types of links.

Deleting a list or library is similar to adding one:

1. Under the Site Actions menu, select Edit Page. The page will be switched to the Edit Mode, where the different Web Parts can be managed separately.

2. At the top right of each Web Part, there is an Edit menu with a small arrow. Simply click the Edit menu and select Delete from the menu options.

List Notifications

SharePoint has the ability to send notifications when certain events happen. By default, SharePoint exposes the change `type` and `alert changes` events. The change type can be all changes as well as just adding, editing, or deleting items, whereas the alert changes can be any change as well as someone else changing documents, depending on whether you choose "filter by me" or not. These notifications can occur in two different ways: RSS feeds, and email alerts. The user subscribes to an RSS feed, and the information is pushed out whenever new information is added. An email alert, on the other hand, is triggered by an event and is sent out when the event occurs.

RSS Feeds

RSS feeds allow for new information to be pulled to users when they request it.

1. Navigate to the list from which you would like to provide an RSS feed, and simply click Actions.

2. Select View RSS Feed. A page will come up confirming that you would like to subscribe to this RSS feed.

3. Click on the link that says Subscribe to this feed. A message box pops up so that the RSS feed can be named whatever you want, and it allows you to save the feed in the proper place.

4. Click on Subscribe, and a confirmation page will be shown.

Whenever information is updated on the site, the information will be pulled down to your computer when the RSS application makes a request.

> **To receive notifications through an RSS feed, the user must have an RSS reader set up and must subscribe to the feed. Internet Explorer 7 and Outlook 2007 both include RSS readers.**

Alerts

Another way of being notified when information is changed is to set up an alert. Alerts notify the user via email whenever changes are made to the list.

1. From the list page, click on Actions and select Alert Me.

2. The New Alert page comes up, where the alert settings can be selected.

3. Enter an alert title you want to use in the email, which will be included in the subject of the notification email that is sent.

4. Next, names or email addresses must be entered to show where the alerts should be sent.

5. Select the type of changes that you want to be alerted to, along with setting filters for specific criteria that should be met for an alert to be sent.

6. Finally, you can also choose the frequency of the alerts — either an immediate email when changes are made, a daily summary email, or a weekly summary. If you choose a daily or weekly summary alert, the exact day and time of the email can be set from this page as well.

7. Click on OK when all settings are made, and the alert is set.

Content Management Improvements

Lists and libraries are the primary data sources and storage locations for SharePoint sites. Because of this, there have been some enhancements to lists that allow for better collaboration and better management of documents. These new features are completely integrated with Microsoft Office 2007 and allow users to perform the actions from within the Office application of their choice.

Customizing the Home Page

SharePoint makes it easy to customize a site:

1. From the top-level site, click on the Site Actions tab located on the right. Select Site Settings, and you will see five menus across the top of the page, with options listed below them.

2. Under Look and Feel, click on Title, description, and icon.

3. On the page that comes up there are places to change the title and description, and to insert an image as a logo or icon for the pages. Also under Look and Feel is a link to change the site's theme. SharePoint provides many different-colored themes to personalize the site. These are simply ways to change the look and feel of the site without having to spend a lot of time on the process. End users will quickly know what site they are on and will notice that all of the pages do not look the same.

Site Navigation

Navigating through a SharePoint site is very intuitive. The menu on the left of the screen can be used to visit different pages that are added, including lists, calendars, and so on. This menu is called the Quick Launch bar. Alternatively, the main team site itself can be used as a portal for access to all the different pages by using Web Parts. Also, under the Look and Feel menu options on the Site Settings page, the view for the site can be changed to a tree view, allowing for the site's content to be shown in a physical representation. This changes the Quick Launch bar on the top-level site by also showing a site hierarchy, which may be more helpful for some users. Figure 3.6 shows the tree view of menu options once it has been enabled under Site Hierarchy.

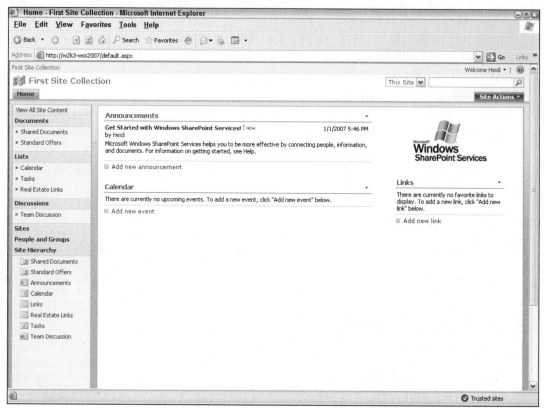

Figure 3-6

Versioning

Many users have data that is constantly changing and need a way to keep track of these changes. Share-Point provides this ability through the use of versioning. *Versioning* is when a copy of the old data is kept in storage while the new data is shown in a list. With SharePoint 2007, you have the ability to maintain a number of versions of data as well as restore and compare different versions of that data.

The ability to use versioning has been added to all lists. This is a great improvement over the previous version of SharePoint, which only allowed versioning on document libraries. In addition to having versions for all lists, the ability to add content approval for items has also been added as a feature. This allows for draft items to be created and also to be stored in any type of list.

> Keep in mind that when you use versioning on a list, a new database record will be created for each item that is created or edited. This can become a problem for the size of the database over time, so make sure to limit the number of versions or to have a plan to maintain the database.

There are two types of versioning that can be used within SharePoint. SharePoint lists maintain versioning by creating a new copy of the row every time one is created or edited Document libraries have the ability to create major versions of the document (for example 1, 2, 3, 4) or major and minor versions of documents (for example 1.0, 1.1, 1.2, 2.0).

Required Check Out

In previous versions of SharePoint, users had the option of checking out files from a document library, but this did not occur very often. You now have the ability to require that the document be checked out prior to modifications, in order to prevent two users from making simultaneous changes to the same document. A notification message is displayed to the user, notifying them that they must check the file out before modifying it. The user can then select to check the file out and make changes, or not perform the operation and leave the document as it was.

Improved Storage with Lists

There are several techniques using lists that make storage easier or more functional for your needs. The following sections cover using folders, cross-list queries, and indexing.

Using Folders on All Lists Option

In the past, users could organize document libraries by using folders inside of the list, but this could only be done with document libraries in Windows SharePoint Services 2003. It is now possible to have folders on all list types simply by activating the option.

1. Start by going to the Settings of the list.

2. Select the Advanced Settings option.

3. Under the List Advanced Settings, you will find the Folders section. To enable folders on the document library, select Yes under the Folders section. This will add the ability to have the New Folder option under the New menu of the list.

Indexing Lists

SharePoint now enables you to create an index on a list in order to improve performance when retrieving list items. In previous versions of SharePoint, it could be difficult to store large lists without having an impact on the performance of the site itself. Even though 2000 items per folder was large for some lists, it was not enough to use the lists as a real storage source for some external applications that needed much larger lists.

To solve this problem, SharePoint now allows lists to be indexed, allowing for the storage and use of much larger lists. To activate a column as an indexed column, navigate to the Settings page of the list and then select the Indexed columns from the Columns selection area.

Once you are on the Indexed Columns page, select the column that should be indexed. Keep in mind that a few resources will be used for every column that is being indexed, so try to keep it reasonable.

Using Cross-List Queries

A Cross-List query is a way to query a list that could be in the same site or another site and get back the meta data related to that list. This can come in useful when you need to display information about a list that is located in another site such as an HR department displaying information about a list in accounting. To make the retrieval of list data easier across multiple lists, the SPSiteDataQuery object can be used to bring back a collection of items. To perform the same operation in previous versions of SharePoint required the creation of custom code to bring back all of the list items individually from each list. To perform the query, the SPWeb object is used with a method called GetSiteData that passes in the SPSiteDataQuery object and returns a DataTable with the list items selected.

Follow these steps to enable the user to use cross-queries:

1. To begin, create an SPSiteDataQuery object and create an SPWeb to search through:

```
SPWeb site = SPContext.Current.Web;
SPSiteDataQuery query = new SPSiteDataQuery();

DataTable dtResults = site.GetSiteData(query);
```

2. Using the CAML markup language set the list types that will be searched through. Every list has a numeric value that is used to define the list.

```
SPWeb site = SPContext.Current.Web;
SPSiteDataQuery query = new SPSiteDataQuery();
query.Lists = "<Lists ServerTemplate=\"107\" />";
DataTable dtResults = site.GetSiteData(query);
```

3. To define a query that will return the list items requested, first create a query in CAML.

> To help create CAML statements, community members have created a CAML Builder at www.u2u.info/SharePoint/U2U%20Community%20Tools/Forms/AllItems.aspx and a CAML viewer at www.codeplex.com/SPCamlViewer.

```
SPWeb site = SPContext.Current.Web;
SPSiteDataQuery query = new SPSiteDataQuery();

query.Lists = "<Lists ServerTemplate=\"107\" />";
query.Query = "<Where>" +
                "<Eq>" +
                  "<FieldRef Name=\"Status\" />" +
                  "<Value Type=\"Choice\">Not Started</Value>" +
                "</Eq>" +
              "</Where>";
DataTable dtResults = site.GetSiteData(query);
```

4. Because you are searching the entire site for information, the list data could be very large. The
    RowLimit property helps limit the size of data that is returned to you.

```
SPWeb site = SPContext.Current.Web;
SPSiteDataQuery query = new SPSiteDataQuery();

query.Lists = "<Lists ServerTemplate=\"107\" />";
query.Query = "<Where>" +
                  "<Eq>" +
                    "<FieldRef Name=\"Status\" />" +
                    "<Value Type=\"Choice\">Not Started</Value>" +
                  "</Eq>" +
                "</Where>";
query.RowLimit = 10;
DataTable dtResults = site.GetSiteData(query);
```

5. The ViewFields property allows you to specify the fields that will be part of the list of items
    returned. This way, only the fields that are important are returned, without all of the other
    columns that don't matter. This also helps limit the amount of data returned to the user.

```
 SPWeb site = SPContext.Current.Web;
SPSiteDataQuery query = new SPSiteDataQuery();

query.Lists = "<Lists ServerTemplate=\"107\" />";
query.Query = "<Where>" +
                  "<Eq>" +
                    "<FieldRef Name=\"Status\" />" +
                    "<Value Type=\"Choice\">Not Started</Value>" +
                  "</Eq>" +
                "</Where>";
query.RowLimit = 10;
query.ViewFields = "<FieldRef Name=\"Title\" />";
DataTable dtResults = site.GetSiteData(query);
```

6. The Webs property allows you to manage the scope in which the query executes. The query
    is set to the current web site when created, but can be changed based on the Webs property.
    The current web site is determined from the method GetSiteData of the current SPWeb object.
    There are two possible values that can be used with this option: recursive and SiteCollection.

    ❑   **Recursive** — Instructs the query to search all web sites below the current web site object.

    ❑   **SiteCollection** — The query will search all locations that are in the same site collection
        as the web site object.

The following code demonstrates how you can limit the scope of your query just to the SiteCollection.
This allows you to get data only from the locations that are required.

```
SPWeb site = SPContext.Current.Web;
SPSiteDataQuery query = new SPSiteDataQuery();
```

```
query.Lists = "<Lists ServerTemplate=\"107\" />";
query.Query = "<Where>" +
                "<Eq>" +
                  "<FieldRef Name=\"Status\" />" +
                  "<Value Type=\"Choice\">Not Started</Value>" +
                "</Eq>" +
              "</Where>";
query.RowLimit = 10;
query.ViewFields = "<FieldRef Name=\"Title\" />";
qry.Webs = "<Webs Scope='SiteCollection' />";
DataTable dtResults = site.GetSiteData(query);
```

Working with Site Columns

The data that is stored in SharePoint lists are described by site columns. These columns can be defined at a site level and describe the data that users will enter when they add new rows in the list. Many times you will create new columns or add columns from a predefined global list of columns.

Creating Site Columns

There are two different ways to add a column to a list. You can add a column from a list of existing columns or can create an entirely new column. SharePoint has a list of existing columns that are commonly used, such as address, city, date, and the like. However, if none of these commonly used columns is what you need, then you can add a new column that you create.

Adding an Existing Column

To add an existing column, follow these steps:

1. In the Settings page of a list or library, click the option to Add from existing site columns.

2. Once clicked, this link takes you to an Add Columns from the Site Columns page, where you can select and add columns from the already available columns. You can add any of the following columns from the existing groups to a list: Address, City, Date Created, and Status. There are many more columns, and each is listed in a category to help you find the columns quickly. The columns will be added in the order that you select them.

Creating New Columns

If none of the existing site columns matches what is needed, a custom column can be created:

1. On the Settings page of the list, simply click Create column or use the Settings menu of the list.

2. Select the column name along with the type of information that will be stored in it. If currency is being stored, options would include the minimum and/or maximum value allowed, the number of decimals, and the currency format. If date and time information is being stored in the column, the options include showing the date only versus the date and time, the default date and time you want shown, and the ability to set a calculated value. There are many default types that data can be stored as. See the following table.

Type	Description
Single line of text	Used for text that will fit in a single line of text. Usually for text lengths with 255 characters or less.
Multiple lines of text	Contains more than one line of text. The number of lines can be set in the column definition.
Choice	Provides a number of items to select from. Options include Drop-Down menu, Radio buttons, and Checkboxes.
Number	Standard numbers such as 1, 1.0, 100. The minimum and maximum can be specified as well as the number of decimal places.
Currency	Display a number as the selected currency type. Holds the same properties as a number with the addition of the currency type.
Date and Time	Ability to use the date and time as the value of the field with the option include Date only or Date and Time. A default value is available for the current date or a specified date.
Lookup	Uses information already on the site to display in another list. This is useful for reusing data already on the site.
Yes/No	A simple check box that provides the list with Yes/No ability. A default value can be supplied and is set to Yes in the menu options.
Person or Group	Use this column to use information about the users and groups in the site. You can select from People or People and Groups and display selected information about them.
Hyperlink or Picture	Display a link or hyperlink to another resource. The format URL can be selected as Picture or HyperLink
Calculated	Displays a calculated value that is based on other columns in the list. A subset of types is available to display the information once it is calculated.

Changing Column Order

Sometimes the column order can be important to the end users. The order can affect the way the data appears in a view. For this reason, SharePoint provides the ability to place the columns in the order that is best for your application.

1. Navigate to a list on the site, then in the list Settings page, select Column ordering, which allows you to use the Change Field Order option.

2. The columns can be set in any order from this page simply by setting the number order of each column. Notice that when you change the columns on the page, they actually move to the new position. When you change a column to a higher-order number, all numbers below that position are bumped down one.

3. Change the column in position 7 to position 1. Each field name changes the number that is associated with it, for example position one becomes position 2, position 2 becomes position 3, and so on. Conversely, if a number is moved down in position, all numbers below it are moved up one.

4. Change position 4 to position 7, then you can see that position 5 becomes position 4, position 6 becomes position 5, and position 7 becomes position 6.

Using Site-Level Columns

To allow for the reusability of columns, you can create columns at the site level or the list level. If you want to reuse a column across many different lists, the best approach is to create a site-level column. The command for this action is in the Site Settings menu under Site Actions. When you are on the Site Settings page look under the Galleries category and there is a listing for the Site Columns. Changing the column at the site level will change the value for all of the lists using the column. If a list needs to keep the column information no matter what the rest of the site has make the column a list-level column. A new or existing group must be assigned to the column being created, with the default group being custom columns. This group assignment will be used when selecting the column in a list. Additional column settings such as a description of the column can be provided, along with other options that are dependent on the type of information the column will store.

Modifying a Column

Columns can be modified after they have been created. On the list Settings page, click on the name of the column you want to change. For the example columns created above, click on Address. When the column is selected, a page shows the column name, its source, and the type of information stored in the column. It also allows the column to be a required column. Making a column a required column means that there must always be information stored in the column. If you modify the column from the site-level columns, you will also have an option to update all of the list columns based on that site column.

Understanding Content Types

SharePoint gives you the ability to organize and store data through the use of content types. Content types are what make it possible to store different types of content in the same list or document library. Basically, content types are a collection of settings that you can define and apply to your data. In SharePoint 2.0, when a list was created, you would define a set of columns that defined all data contained in that list. Every column was set up to track data for all items on that list, and all of the items had to fit into the schema defined by that list, and were ultimately contained by that location.

In SharePoint 3.0, the items in a list do not have to have metadata that fits into every column defined in the list. Metadata is the columns that have information that describe the information you are storing. For instance, you might store a document in a library, and the metadata would be items such as title, modified, and modified by. You can now take two different items that have different categories of information, and put them in the same list or document library. For example, if you needed to store information about houses that you are selling as a real estate agent, you might store the listing contract and offers. Each set of documents might have a different set of metadata, but they need to be stored together in the same list. This allows you to store data in a more centralized, organized manner. The different content types would each have their own defined columns that would allow them to store different information, but the content types would still coexist in the same list or document library. These different content types can also have different workflows or custom attributes assigned to them, allowing different courses of action to be taken.

Using File Formats for Content Types

Content types allow data to no longer be bound to a single location. This new structure allows content types to be made available across multiple sites. They are no longer defined by a list or document library, as they were in SharePoint 2.0. The content types can now be defined, stored, and managed through the site collection. Additionally, content types are not bound by file format, either. When you create a new document of a certain content type, SharePoint will automatically create the document using the template that has been set up. However, you have the ability to upload a file to the document library, defined as the same content type, and the type of file does not matter. Content types can also be assigned to list items and folders, which have no file format.

> Content types made for lists can only be used for lists, and ones made for document libraries can only be used for document libraries. However, content types made for folders can be used for either.

Look at this example. A real estate agent may have many listings to manage. She also gets offers on those listings — some that are acceptable, and some that are not. The agent may want to store listing documents and offer documents in the same document library, but the columns defined for each are going to be different. In this example, two content types could be defined — call them Listings and Offers. The Listings content type will define columns that are associated with a listing, such as: listing date, listing price, seller name, and seller phone number. However, the Offer content type would have a different set of defined columns, such as: offer date, offer price, closing date. Each of these content types has different metadata, but they can both be stored in a central document library.

You can view the entire list of site content types by following these steps:

1. Navigate to the site collections main page.

2. From a publishing page, click Site Actions, then Site Settings, and then Modify Site Settings, or from a standard page select Site Actions, then Site Settings.

3. Under the Galleries section, select Site content types, which lists all of the content types in the site collection.

Creating Content Types

Many times companies will have their own definition of what describes data. In that case, you will want to create your own content types that can be part of the site collection. To create your own content type, use the following steps:

1. Click on the Site Settings page

2. Then under Galleries, click on the link that takes you to Site content types. Here, you will find all of the content types that you can use on the current site and its subsites.

3. Click on the button available at the top left labeled Create to create a new content type.

4. Enter a meaningful name and description, then select the parent type of List Content Types and the parent content type Item.

5. Keep the group as Custom Content Type, and press OK.

The content type of Item is the most basic type of content type. The Item content type only contains a field called Title. When a new content type is being created, the default settings are copied from the parent content type. Also, when the parent content type is changed in the future, the changes can also be pushed down to the child content types. This makes inheriting and changing a content type much easier than having to change every item that has used the content type. Being able to inherit types allows for a much more meaningful use of data and enables you to easily build more complex sets of data.

On the New Site Content Type page, specify the name and description of the new content type. In the example shown in Figure 3-7, the name of the new content type is Offers Made. Next, select a parent content type from the drop-down list, and then select the actual parent content type. Again, remember that a content type created for lists can only be used for lists, and one made for a document library can only be used for a document library, but a content type made for a folder can be used for either. In the example, the parent content type is set to Document Content Types and the Parent Content Type chosen is Document. Next, choose a new or existing group to put the content type into, and then click OK. Because a new content type is being created, Custom Content Types was chosen for the group.

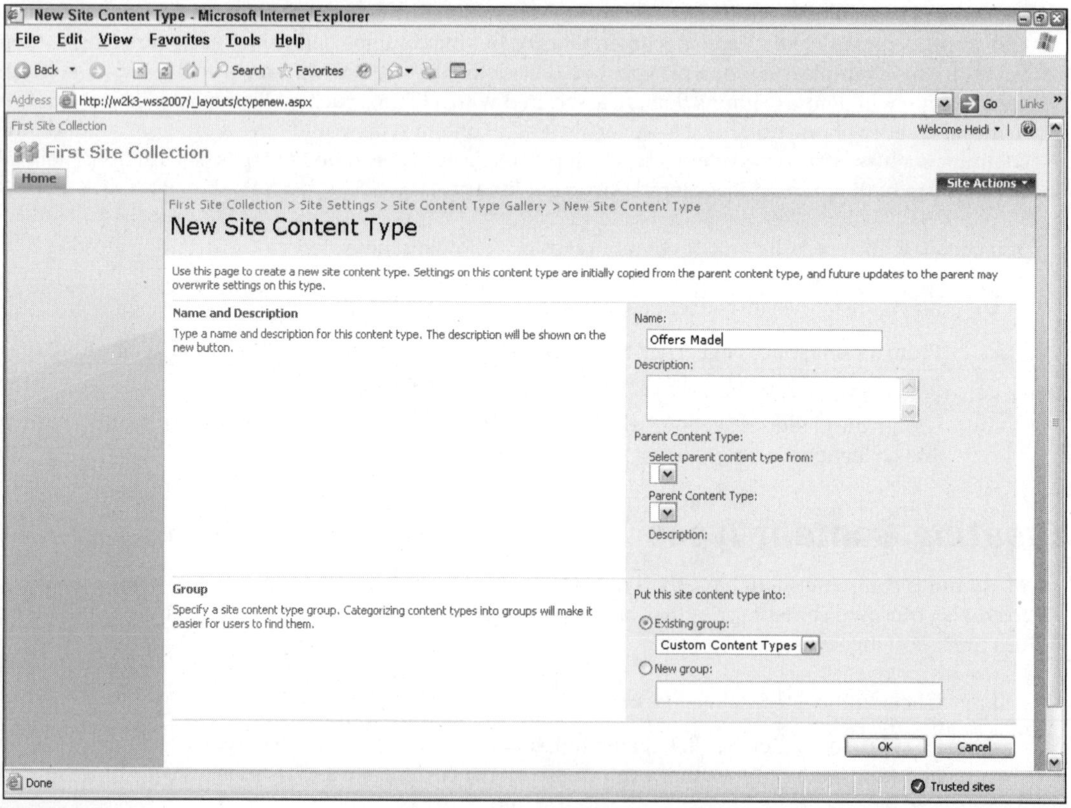

![New Site Content Type Internet Explorer window showing the New Site Content Type page with Name "Offers Made", Parent Content Type section, and Group set to Custom Content Types]

Figure 3-7

Assigning Settings to Content Types

Content types have many attributes that need to be set when they are created. When the new content type is created, SharePoint brings up the Site Content Type page for that new content type. It is here that you can assign all of the settings to your new content type. A content type can include information such as properties, workflows, document templates, custom forms, and custom information that is stored in XML.

Under the first heading, Settings, there is a link to change the name, description, and group. Since all of these settings were just set when the content type was created, they are okay for now. The next link is for advanced settings. Because this content type is a document content type, this link allows for the assigning of a document template. Whenever a new document is created using the Offers Made content type, SharePoint automatically uses this assigned document template.

The advanced setting page is also where the content type can be set to read-only. If the content type is not read-only, it can be modified later by users through the user interface in SharePoint. Below the Read Only option is the Update Sites and Lists section that sets inheritance for the updates of the content type to all of the child sites and list content types that inherit from it. Back at the Site Content Type page, the link Workflow settings is used to view or make changes to the workflow settings for the new content type. The link Delete this site content type is used to delete the new site content type.

Windows SharePoint Services Pages

WSS 3.0 has two types of pages, called administrative pages and user pages. Both are ASP.NET 2.0 pages, but they were designed to use different master pages. Every page can contain a master page file using the `MasterPageFile` attribute of the `@Page` directive.

- ❑ **Administrative pages** — These pages are used to provide management features such as list settings and web pages under Site Settings. This would include the administration pages, as well as the page that uses the `application.master` page. These pages can be shared across many sites.

- ❑ **User pages** — These pages are the pages generated by the end user and the basic pages required to display information to the user.

Administrative Pages

Administrative pages provide end users with management ability through the user interface. These pages do not contain dynamic content such as Web Parts, and they use a different master page than the content pages. These pages use the master page `~/_layouts/application.master`. These pages are also known as application pages because they inherit their functionality from the administration context.

User Pages

User pages are created by the end user or are used to display information to the user. Each page has the value of `~masterurl/default.master` as the default master page, which allows the site designer to make a modification to a single page for the entire site. Keep in mind that this only affects the pages that have the value of `~masterurl/default.master`.

Master Pages

Master pages are not a new concept to the programming world. They are a common solution used for ASP.NET 2.0 pages. Prior to master pages, developers used server-side includes, scripts, and user controls to help them provide a consistent look and feel across the entire site. Master pages were designed to allow developers to create a single version of the common elements of a page and then create content areas that each page could define. Master pages are another set of technology that SharePoint gives developers to use and implement due to the fact that it is built upon ASP.NET 2.0 functionality. The master page in SharePoint allows a site creator to define the common look and feel of a site in a single location. It also allows for the end user to modify the master page for designers such as SharePoint Designer 2007.

default.master

The main master page for the content pages is `default.master`. This page is located on each front-end web server. The `default.master` page contains many content placeholders to display the correct data from content pages. Any custom master page must contain the same set of the content placeholders or the page may not be rendered correctly. Whenever a new page is created, the `default.master` page will be added to the `@Page` directive. See Figure 3-8. Some of the common placeholders are for the navigation bars and main content area.

Each site can use a different master page, but each master page must be defined within a site collection.

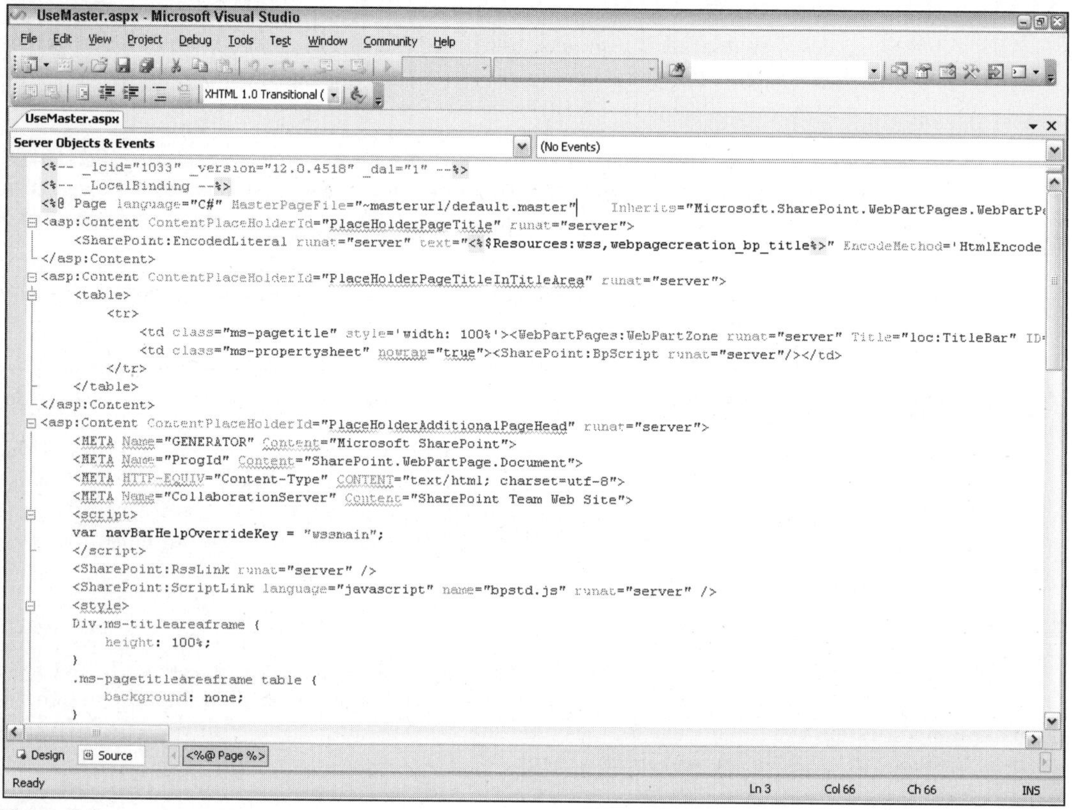

Figure 3-8

To correctly display the Web Parts, the `default.master` page will contain one `WebPartManager` control which in SharePoint is the `SPWebPartManager` and one `WebPartZone` control that will be contained in the content pages. The `WebPartManager` class maintains the Web Parts, location, and personalization that a content page contains.

> *The `WebPartManager` control must be declared before any of the `WebPartZone` controls to provide the web part zone elements shown on the page.*

What about Ghosting/Unghosting

One major topic with SharePoint 2003 was a concept known as ghosting and unghosting. A page would be known as ghosted if it had not been customized. The problem was that if you modified a page (unghosted), especially with Front Page 2003, the page would be saved into the database, and you would lose the enhanced performance of using the file off of the disk. The other problem was that once you unghosted a page in SharePoint, there was no supported way from the user interface to re-ghost the page back to the original look, and even if you did re-ghost it back, all of the work for that page would be lost.

Some of the problems facing unghosting a page were:

❑ A small performance loss from getting the cached version directly from the physical disk drive. This occurred because there were more trips to the database to get multiple sets of information.

❑ Changes to the site templates did not affect the pages that were unghosted. This could sometimes be a big problem if there were many pages, say for a corporate portal that was customized with FrontPage 2003.

With SharePoint 2007 the problem does not disappear, but does become less of a problem. There are few reasons why this is not as much of a problem, such as:

❑ ASP.NET 2.0 allows providers in many areas of the ASP.NET framework. One such area is the Virtual Path Providers. SharePoint implements a custom Virtual Path Provider that allows pages to be retrieved from the SQL Server database and then sent to the ASP.NET 2.0 page parser.

❑ SharePoint now uses ASP.NET 2.0 to parse and compile the web pages, which provides much needed extensibility and all of the functions of ASP.NET.

❑ Many page designers found it difficult to revert pages back to the original state. Now, with SharePoint Designer 2007, you can simply click on the page to allow you to revert back to the original file.

As you can see, there are really no problems in creating customizations with pages in SharePoint 2007. The content will still be stored in the database, but the ASP.NET team made sure to provide all of the required functionality to SharePoint inside of the ASP.NET architecture. Also, to help users understand the difference between the two scenarios, SharePoint now calls the action of changing the pages "Customized" and "Uncustomized."

Editing SharePoint Master Pages

To edit a master page in Windows SharePoint Services, Microsoft recommends two options. The first option is to make a local copy of the `default.master` file simply by using the copy-and-paste functionality in Windows Explorer. Or, you can use a tool like SharePoint Designer 2007 to make the changes. If you are making major changes to the master page, I would recommend taking the time to evaluate using SharePoint Designer 2007 with its integration abilities for SharePoint 2007. Even if you make a change in SharePoint Designer 2007, you can still download the master page that you created or save it into a source control system. Office SharePoint Designer 2007 will provide more functionality than just editing a master page, but it is one of the only products on the market today that allows you to edit the master page in a WYSIWYG manner.

> Microsoft recommends that you do not edit the `default.master` file that is shipped with Windows SharePoint Services. This file can be changed by upgrades or service packs, unless it is edited.

Creating New Content Pages

As discussed earlier, the master page associated with pages is the `default.master` file. There are situations in which you might want various pages to reference different master pages. With ASP.NET 2.0, you can simply reference a master page with the following `@Page` directive. Many companies will want to have a different layout than the default master page that is provided with SharePoint. You can easily make your own master page for all of your pages to have the same look and feel across those pages.

```
<%@ Page MasterPageFile="my.master"%>
```

The `MasterPageFile` directive tells ASP.NET 2.0 to look on the local file system for a file called `my.master`. This works for basic web applications, but SharePoint 2007 needs the ability to make the page use master pages that are designed for the correct site. To accomplish this, Microsoft has created a library just to hold master pages, called the master page gallery. This allows users to create as many master pages as the site requires and upload them locally to the site collection. To navigate to the master page gallery go to the site's settings page and use the Master pages and page layouts link to show the page in Figure 3-9.

Master Page Locations

In order to easily reference master pages from the content pages, SharePoint 2007 provides tokens that can be used to direct the content page to the right location. There are two types of tokens that you can use when designing the content pages: dynamic tokens and static tokens.

- ❑ **Dynamic tokens** — These tokens allow developers to modify variables in code that can change the location of the master page.

- ❑ **Static tokens** — These tokens allow you the ability to create a scope of the page and the master page location.

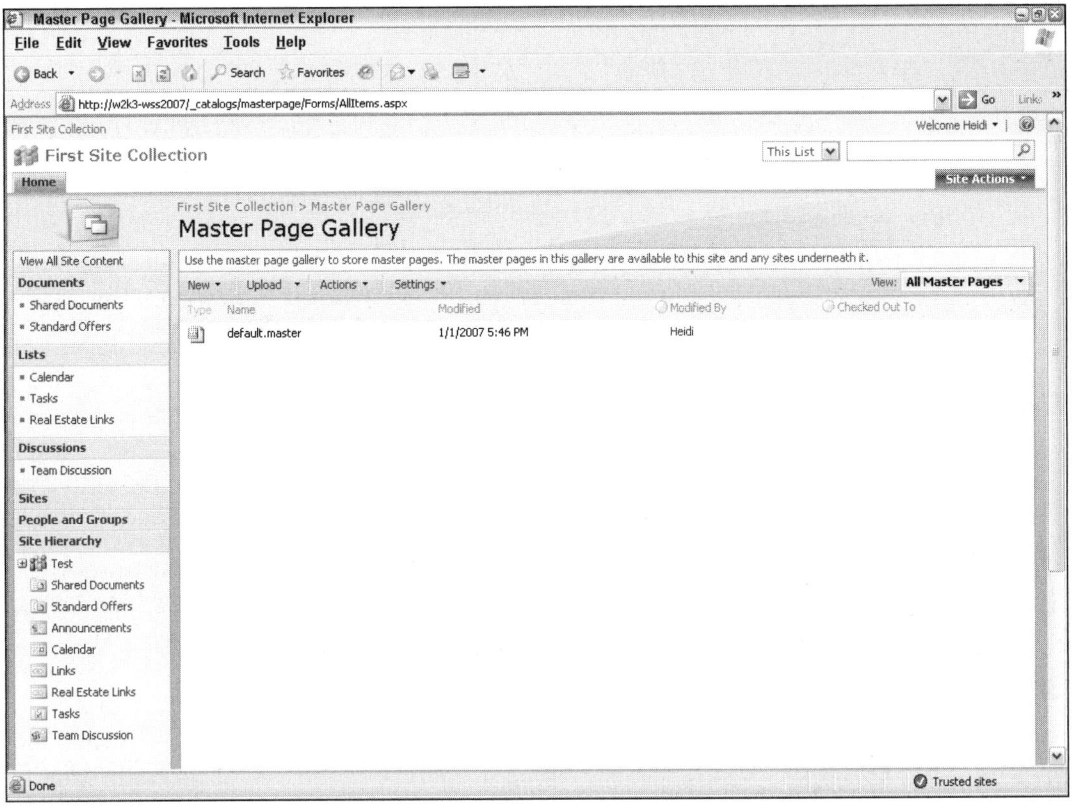

Figure 3-9

These tokens are specific to SharePoint 2007 and are only used within SharePoint 2007. An error will be thrown in applications that only use standard ASP.NET 2.0.

SharePoint provides the following dynamic tokens to use when developing pages.

Token	Location
~masterurl/default.master	The entire token must be used and is replaced by the value in MasterURL, set to /catalogs/masterpage/default.master by default.
~masterurl/custom.master	The entire token must be used and is replaced by the value in CustomMasterUrl, set to /catalogs/masterpage/default.master by default.

The following table describes the static tokens you can use to develop pages in SharePoint.

Token	Location
~site/<master page>	The master page is located in the site-level master page gallery. The token will be replaced by the site URL location and the master page will remain.
~sitecollection/<master page>	The master page is located in the site collection–level master page gallery. The token will be replaced by the site collection URL location, and the master page will remain.

Dynamic Tokens

There are only two dynamic tokens that are used within SharePoint. These tokens allow the you to define a token name that can be changed without having to change each page that has been created. This can be very useful when trying to build many pages for a site or importing pages from another site that you have already created. When you use the dynamic tokens, the entire token is replaced by the value of either `MasterUrl` or `CustomMasterUrl` by SharePoint. When SharePoint is installed, both `MasterUrl` and `CustomMasterUrl` point to the same location, which is the local site level master page gallery located at `/_catalogs/masterpage/default.master`.

Static Tokens

To allow you to keep the master pages scoped to the local site or site collection, SharePoint provides two static tokens that can be used with master pages. This allows you the ability to select a master page in the site collection master page gallery by using the `~sitecollection/<master page>`. To use the local site master page gallery you simply use `~site/<master page>`.

Windows SharePoint Services Mobility

With the large adoption of SharePoint in many organizations, the need to be able to view data from many locations has become critical. This is especially true for organizations that have employees on the move such as a sales force or mobile workers. The big question becomes how to keep your employees connected to the data in SharePoint. One solution is to simply provide the lists using mobile views. I have already talked about what a view is, but now you will look at how to add mobile views as well as develop your own view for the mobile pages.

Defining a List as a Mobile List

To define a list as a mobile list, set the mobile options of the list settings through the user interface or configure the list through XML. To set the list as a mobile list through the user interface, first navigate to the site and list that you want to display as a mobile list, then navigate to the lists' settings page. There are two major settings that can be used to provide a page with mobile settings. These settings are part of the list XML definition file. When the list is configured through the user interface, the URL for the mobile view of the home page, as well as a direct link to the mobile list, is located below the options for setting a list to a mobile list.

❑ **MobileView attribute** — If this attribute is set to true, the list will appear in the mobile pages as a valid mobile list.

❑ **MobileDefaultView attribute** — When a list is a valid mobile list, setting this value to true will make the list the default list that appears to the user. You can only have one default mobile view per list.

A mobile list is just a standard SharePoint list that is marked with mobile attributes. The mobile list will still show up in the selection of lists on all device types, including a regular browser.

Mobile Pages

To view a list as a mobile list, start by providing the list with a mobile view and then navigate to a site that has a mobile list. Navigating to a mobile page has been simplified by having Windows SharePoint Services perform a redirect to the mobile page. To view a site in a mobile-rendered format, Microsoft has provided the ability to simply place /m at the end of the site's URL location, as follows:

```
http://<server name>/<site path>/m
```

Open either your mobile browser or Internet Explorer, and navigate to `http://localhost/m`.

> You can view the mobile pages in a regular browser such as Internet Explorer to make sure that the pages are working, before trying them on a mobile device. This can help when trying to resolve some issues and determine if the problem is with the Windows SharePoint Server or with the mobile device itself.

The built-in mobile pages are located at `C:\Program Files\Common Files\Microsoft Shared\web server extensions\12\TEMPLATE\LAYOUTS\MOBILE`. In addition to the list of pages, there is also a `web.config` file that has mobile-specific settings for the site. These settings are shown in the following tables.

The following table lists the common mobile pages used on a standard site.

Page Name	Description
default.aspx	The default page used for redirecting the mobile pages to the correct site home page
mblerror.aspx	The mobile page used to display all errors to the user
mbllogin.aspx	The login page for handheld mobile devices
mbllogout.aspx	The logout page used to complete a session

The following table lists the mobile pages that are commonly used on the team site.

Page Name	Description
dispform.aspx	Displays a single item from the list item with the valid mobile fields that can be displayed
editform.aspx	Provides the ability to edit a single item selected from the list of items
mbllists.aspx	The default page for team sites used to make the mobile available lists viewable
newform.aspx	Create a new list item from the mobile device using the mobile template fields
view.aspx	Used to display the list of items for the document library of lists selected with a mobile view

The following table lists the mobile pages that are used in the blog sites.

Page Name	Description
bloghome.aspx	The default page for blog sites used to make the blogs mobile available
delete.aspx	Deletes the current blog post with a confirmation about the deletion that will send the item to the Recycle Bin
mbllists.aspx	Displays all of the lists available on the blog site
newcomment.aspx	Creates a new comment for the blog post with the required mobile fields
newpost.aspx	Provides the ability to enter a new blog post from a mobile device using the standard ASP.NET mobile controls to enter data
viewcomment.aspx	Allows the mobile device the ability to show the comments from the blog post

Mobile web.config Settings

The web.config file contains many settings that are specific to mobile pages and can be modified by editing the file or through code. If you have more than one front-end web server, each server will contain its own copy of web.config file, so you'll have to propagate any changes to all servers.

Page Redirection

To allow the user to navigate to the right page, Microsoft uses something called the bi-level redirection feature. This feature lets all users navigate to the same page, which is the entry point, and then be redirected to the correct default page of the site. When you navigate to a standard mobile page, you will be redirected to the correct mobile list for that page. There are two standard default views for mobile pages:

❑ **mblists.aspx** — This is the default mobile page layout for the Team Site Mobile pages. This page only displays the lists that have enabled a mobile view.

```
http://<servername>/<site path>/_layouts/mobile/mbllists.aspx
```

❑ **bloghome.aspx** — This is the default mobile page layout for the Blog Site Mobile pages. The view type determines which set of blogs are displayed. If `ViewType` is set to 2, then the blogs of the current user will be displayed; otherwise, all blogs will be displayed.

```
http://<servername>/<sitepath>/Blog/_layouts/mobile/bloghome.aspx?ViewType=Integer
```

> Microsoft recommends not modifying the default pages that are shipped with Windows SharePoint Services because your changes could be overridden by an upgrade or a patch. Be sure to make a copy of the default page and create your own page based on that copy instead of changing the default file.

Displaying the Default Pages

Every list can contain a mobile page. When you set up the mobile list, you can have multiple views of the data but only one default view. The default view is the one selected first on the mobile drop-down list control (see Figure 3-10).

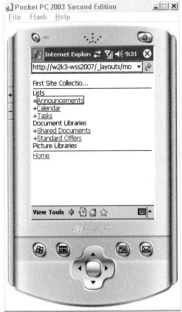

Figure 3-10

Displaying Columns on the Mobile Page

The browser can display very complex types of columns in a full browser, but the mobile device has some limitations on what it can display. The bandwidth and screen size of the mobile device being used can have an impact on what is displayed. At times, you have to develop pages that can be displayed on a variety of different devices, all with different views. The following table lists the columns that display on a mobile device, and the ones that can be edited by using the mobile pages.

SharePoint Field Type	Control in Read-Only Mode	Control in Edit Mode
Single line of text	Label	TextBox
Multiple lines of text	TextView	TextBox
Choice (menu to chose from)	Label	SelectionList
Number (1,1.0,100)	Label	TextBox
Currency ($, ¥, €)	Label	TextBox
Date and Time	Label	TextBox
Lookup (information already on this site)	Label	SelectionList
Yes/No (check box)	Label	SelectionList
Hyperlink or Picture	Link	TextBox
Calculated	Label	N/A

Mobile User Control Templates

To extend pages, you need to create control templates that Windows SharePoint Services can consume. These templates are made up of basic ASP.NET control files and are stored in files with the extension of .ascx. Microsoft stores all of the default templates in the control template folder in a file named MobileDefaultTemplates.ascx. In order for SharePoint to find and load the file, it must be stored in a location where SharePoint knows to look for it. That location is under the SharePoint directory.

Defining Browsers

To allow for multiple types of browsers, ASP.NET provides a configuration file where new mobile browsers can be defined. This is very useful with the number of mobile devices that are released each year. And, as the wireless industry adds more capability to connect through phones, this number is bound to increase even more. To add your own browser, look in the ASP.NET 2.0 folder App_Browser on your local front-end web servers. Inside of that folder is a file called compat.browser. Defining a new mobile browser is outside the scope of this book, but look at the ASP.NET 2.0 documentation on the browser element for more information at http://msdn2.microsoft.com/en-us/library/ms228122.aspx.

State Management of Mobile Pages

Most mobile browsers do not have the ability to store state in cookies like full-fledged browsers do. You might have already noticed that when you select a page, any data that must be sent back to the server is stored in the Address bar of the browser.

Displaying on a Small Device

Due to the screen limitations of mobile devices, all of the lists and all of the text may not fit onto the device. When this situation occurs, Windows SharePoint Server uses a preconfigured length to determine where to stop displaying the text that is too wide for the device. Instead of just cutting the text off at that point, SharePoint adds three dots called an ellipsis to notify the user that there is more information that could not be displayed on that screen. The default settings are stored in the mobile `web.config` file in the application settings. If the key is set to zero or if the key does not in appear in the `web.config` file, the ellipsis will not be displayed. Any changes to the values made in code will overwrite the default values from the `web.config` file.

Working with Large Lists

When the page has too many items to display on a single mobile page, the page displays only a set number of list items. It then allows the user to navigate to other pages. This navigation on the mobile device is known as pagination, and there are a number of pages that already provide this functionality. These pages are the home pages and the viewing pages. To provide this pagination functionality, SharePoint relies on the underlying ASP.NET 2.0 framework and the ASP.NET 2.0 mobile controls for pagination.

Creating Custom Mobile Pages

When developing custom mobile pages, you use a new set of mobile controls in the `Microsoft.SharePoint.MobileControls` namespace. Keep in mind that all of SharePoint is built on Microsoft ASP.NET 2.0 and that the mobile controls in Windows SharePoint Services are built on top of the ASP.NET 2.0 mobile controls.

> **It is easy to use mobile pages, but it can be difficult to update mobile pages for an entire portal and not just a single site.**

Creating Mobile Pages

When designing mobile pages for SharePoint, you can use a template that contains the mobile controls on the page. To define a template, create a SharePoint mobile page that is made up of a header, content, and footer section. First create a template, and then place it in the directory where SharePoint loads all of the mobile templates.

1. Open the following folder: `\Program Files\Common Files\Microsoft Shared\web server extensions\12\TEMPLATE\CONTROLTEMPLATES`.

2. Create a new file named `CustomMobileTemplates.ascx`.

3. Add the following imports and directives:

```
<%@ Control Language="C#"   %>
<%@ Assembly Name="Microsoft.SharePoint, Version=12.0.0.0, Culture=neutral,
PublicKeyToken=71e9bce111e9429c" %>
<%@ Register TagPrefix="mobile" Namespace="System.Web.UI.MobileControls"
Assembly="System.Web.Mobile, Version=1.0.3300.0, Culture=neutral,
PublicKeyToken=b03f5f7f11d50a3a" %>
<%@ Register TagPrefix="SharePoint" Namespace="Microsoft.SharePoint.WebControls"
Assembly="Microsoft.SharePoint, Version=12.0.0.0, Culture=neutral,
PublicKeyToken=71e9bce111e9429c" %>
<%@ Register TagPrefix="SPMobile" Namespace="Microsoft.SharePoint.MobileControls"
Assembly="Microsoft.SharePoint, Version=12.0.0.0, Culture=neutral,
PublicKeyToken=71e9bce111e9429c" %>
<%@ Import Namespace="Microsoft.SharePoint" %>
```

4. You can add either the header, contents, or footer template in the custom control. This code adds one of each:

```
<SharePoint:RenderingTemplate RunAt="Server" ID="Mobile_STS_HomePage_Title">
  <Template>
    <mobile:Label RunAt="Server" Text="Team Site Custom Mobile" Font-Size="Large"
Font-Bold="True" />
  </Template>
</SharePoint:RenderingTemplate>
<SharePoint:RenderingTemplate RunAt="Server" ID="Mobile_STS_HomePage_Contents">
  <Template>
    <mobile:Label RunAt="Server" Text="Custom Mobile Control" />
    <mobile:Label RunAt="Server" Text="" BreakAfter="true" />
    <SPMobile:SPMobileListIterator RunAt="Server">
      <SPMobile:SPMobileList RunAt="Server"
        BaseType="DocumentLibrary"/>
    </SPMobile:SPMobileListIterator>
  </Template>
</SharePoint:RenderingTemplate>
<SharePoint:RenderingTemplate RunAt="Server" ID="Mobile_STS_HomePage_Navigation">
  <Template>
    <mobile:Link RunAt="Server" Text="Wrox" NavigateUrl="http://www.wrox.com/" />
    <SPMobile:SPMobileComponent RunAt="Server" TemplateName=
"Mobile_Default_HomePage_Navigation" />
  </Template>
</SharePoint:RenderingTemplate>
```

5. Save the file and the new changes.

6. Click the Start button, then select Run and type **IISRESET**.

7. Navigate to the home page to see the changes.

The following list covers the available templates:

❑ **Header Template** — The header part of the template can be used in a section to display information that will not change based on the information in the list. This could include such items as a company name, list title, or even the date the list was requested.

❑ **Contents** — The contents area is usually where the list items are located. Depending on the screen, this could be a list of items, some input areas for data, or even just useful information about an item. To display the contents, use the SPMobilePageContents control.

❑ **Footer Template** — The footer can contain the actions that need to be performed on the items. There is no reason that these actions could not also be in the header if the list of items were too long on such a small device. The way an action is usually rendered in the mobile device is through a URL.

Summary

This chapter introduced you to the out-of-the-box features SharePoint provides. You looked at how to use these features to "develop" a site from within the user interface as well as how to add to code like CAML to the other user interface elements.

You learned to create web applications and modify them according to the needs of your organization by:

❑ Creating the standard web applications and site collections

❑ Storing data on the server with SharePoint predefined lists and libraries

❑ Modifying the look of the site by adding user interface elements

❑ Creating new content types to store data

❑ Implementing your own set of mobile controls or using the predefined ones

As you can see, there are many changes that you make to SharePoint using the existing framework. Some of these options only require you to add code to the user interface elements without updating or using compiled code.

Now you should be ready to open up your development environment and create the components that make up SharePoint, such as WebParts. In the following chapters, you will see how all of the elements that you have seen through the user interface can also be created, added, and removed through code.

WSS v3 Platform Services

By Dan Attis

Windows SharePoint Services version 3.0 (WSS v3) offers developers an immense set of features that can be leveraged to customize and extend its out-of-the-box functionality. This chapter explores how you can use these features to create customized solutions to solve complex problems while adding tremendous business value to some of the out-of-the-box functionality discussed in other chapters.

Throughout the course of this chapter, you will become familiar with the following concepts:

- ❏ Site Definitions
- ❏ Custom field types
- ❏ Features
- ❏ Solutions
- ❏ Web Parts

To help explain why all of these seemingly disparate topics are discussed in the same chapter, imagine the following scenario. Suppose that you created a Custom Field Type to be used on a list of your choosing, had a custom Web Part that talked to an external system, and needed a custom Site Definition to ease the creation of your custom sites by placing the appropriate Web Parts on the home page among other things. All three of these could be packaged into a Feature and deployed via a Solution. This is by no means an exhaustive list of the possibilities and is only meant to demonstrate how these five topics may end up being related in your custom solution. Each of them could be created and deployed independently as well, if that was desired.

All of the examples and demonstrations in this chapter utilize what can be referred to as a manual approach to development and deployment. With respect to development, a set of templates known as the Visual Studio Extensions for Windows SharePoint Services v3 are currently in development. Rather than include code and templates that are subject to change, this chapter steps through the fundamentals manually without using the templates, and I refer you to Appendix A on the Visual Studio Extenions for an overview of the templates in their current state. With respect to deployment, all of the examples aside from the Feature example created in this chapter, are deployed in the old-school way (file copy and/or command line). The "right" way to deploy the examples in this chapter is through the Solution Framework. Because that is introduced and discussed later in this chapter, we will only use it for the example immediately preceding it, in this case, the Feature example.

Many aspects of the WSS development process involve the creation and maintenance of XML files. Editing an XML file without an intimate knowledge of the underlying schema file (XSD) is quite difficult. Doing so in an environment that supports IntelliSense and not having IntelliSense available to you while editing your XML files can be very disappointing. WSS v3 does in fact ship with an XSD file that you can attach to your environment. The following steps outline this process and we highly recommend that you walk through it before beginning any of the hands-on examples in this chapter.

1. Open Windows Explorer and navigate to [*Visual Studio 2005 Installation Directory*]\Xml\Schemas.

2. Create a new XML file, and insert the following snippet into it:

```
<SchemaCatalog xmlns="http://schemas.microsoft.com/xsd/catalog">
  <Schema
    href="file://C:/Program Files/Common Files/Microsoft Shared/web server
extensions/12/TEMPLATE/XML/wss.xsd"
    targetNamespace="http://schemas.microsoft.com/sharepoint/"/>
</SchemaCatalog>
```

3. Save the file and give it a meaningful name, such as wsscatalog.xml.

4. Open Visual Studio 2005 and create a new XML file.

5. Create a WSS v3 XML file root node such as <Feature>, add the xmlns attribute and choose the SharePoint namespace from the list provided to you by IntelliSense.

From this point forward, you will have IntelliSense available to you as you edit this file for all elements and attributes. This will certainly make your life much easier as you begin to create, edit, and maintain all of the different types of XML files you will encounter during your WSS v3 development experiences.

In addition, all references to the SDK are referring to the Windows SharePoint Services 3.0 SDK located at the following URL (http://msdn2.microsoft.com/en-us/sharepoint/default.aspx).

It's now time to dive into some WSS v3 development and begin by creating a custom Site Definition.

Site Definitions

A Site Definition is used to determine the initial look and feel as well as contain the core functionality of a site when it is provisioned. A Site Definition is defined as a collection of files that reside in a subdirectory located in the [WSS]\TEMPLATE\SiteTemplates folder on each of the front-end web servers. The WSS v3 installer currently places this folder deep in the Program Files area, with the typical address of

`C:\Program Files\Common Files\Microsoft Shared\web server extensions\12\`. The rest of this chapter uses the notation `[WSS]` to represent this folder path.

The out-of-the-box Site Definitions supplied with WSS v3 are listed in the following table. Multiple Site Definitions within the same folder location are defined as individual configurations within Onet.xml (discussed soon). All of these are visible any time a user chooses to create a new site by clicking on the Sites and Workspaces link on the Create page accessed via the Site Actions menu. Custom Site Definitions appear here as well as WSS v3 is made aware of them. The process to create and deploy a Site Definition is demonstrated later in the chapter.

Template Name	Template Category	Location
Team Site	Collaboration	`[WSS]\TEMPLATE\SiteTemplates\sts`
Blank Site	Collaboration	`[WSS]\TEMPLATE\SiteTemplates\sts`
Document Workspace	Collaboration	`[WSS]\TEMPLATE\SiteTemplates\sts`
Wiki Site	Collaboration	`[WSS]\TEMPLATE\SiteTemplates\Wiki`
Blog	Collaboration	`[WSS]\TEMPLATE\SiteTemplates\Blog`
Basic Meeting Workspace	Meetings	`[WSS]\TEMPLATE\SiteTemplates\MPS`
Blank Meeting Workspace	Meetings	`[WSS]\TEMPLATE\SiteTemplates\MPS`
Decision Meeting Workspace	Meetings	`[WSS]\TEMPLATE\SiteTemplates\MPS`
Social Meeting Workspace	Meetings	`[WSS]\TEMPLATE\SiteTemplates\MPS`
Multipage Meeting Workspace	Meetings	`[WSS]\TEMPLATE\SiteTemplates\MPS`

Office SharePoint Server 2007 includes additional Site Definitions (shown in the following table) that are used to assist in providing some of the added built-in functionality used by features such as publishing, records management, reporting, personalization, and searching.

Template Name	Template Category
Document Center	Enterprise
Records Center	Enterprise
Personalization Site	Enterprise
Site Directory	Enterprise

Continued

Template Name	Template Category
Report Center	Enterprise
Search Center with Tabs	Enterprise
Search Center	Enterprise
Publishing Site	Publishing
Publishing Site with Workflow	Publishing
News Site	Publishing

It is very important to understand that Site Definitions are different than Site Templates. A custom Site Template is a collection of customizations applied to a site by an end user or developer that are all placed into a file with an .stp extension and stored in the Site Template gallery of the top-level site in a site collection so that they are available for use in all subsites subsequently created in that site collection. A custom Site Template consists of the differences or the "delta" between the underlying Site Definition from which the site was created and the state of the site when the custom Site Template is generated. From this definition, you can see that a custom Site Template is tethered to its underlying Site Definition; therefore, if the Site Definition is not present, the custom Site Template will not function.

> **When trying to decide between using a Site Definition or a Site Template, the general rule of thumb is that if the customizations are simple and few, use a custom Site Template. If the customizations are complex and many and include items such as content types, site columns, workflows, and the like, use a custom Site Definition.**

Site Definitions improve performance and scalability, as they are cached in memory on the web server on startup, reduce round trips to the content database, and can be reused across multiple sites. Information is subsequently pulled from the web server's cache at runtime. Pages as well as list schema information are read from the cached files, but to the user, appear to be actual files within the physical web site. SharePoint's process of rendering a page from cache is sometimes referred to as viewing a "ghosted" (WSS v2 term) or "uncustomized" (WSS v3 term) page. The key thing to note is that the actual content of an uncustomized page resides on the file system. The row referring to an uncustomized page in the content database contains a column whose value points to the physical location of the page on the disk within the Site Definition folder on the web server.

When a page is customized, it becomes "unghosted" (WSS v2 term) or "customized" (WSS v3 term) and the changes made to the page are stored in the content database. This is a vast improvement over how "unghosted" pages were handled in WSS v2. In WSS v2, the entire page, not just the differences or delta, was stored in the content database. Subsequent requests for an "unghosted" page were served from the content database thereby resulting in a slight performance hit when compared to serving them directly from the web server's cache. This process in WSS v2 led to maintenance headaches in many cases because it was not easy, at times not possible, to revert back to the original "ghosted" or "uncustomized" page. In WSS v3, Microsoft has provided a link (see Figure 4-1) on the Site Settings page to revert a page or an entire site to its original state before any customizations were applied. Using this link simply deletes the changes that were stored in the database for that particular page or site. This is a substantial improvement over how WSS v2 handled page customization. It's now time to discuss a number of the files needed to create and support a custom Site Definition.

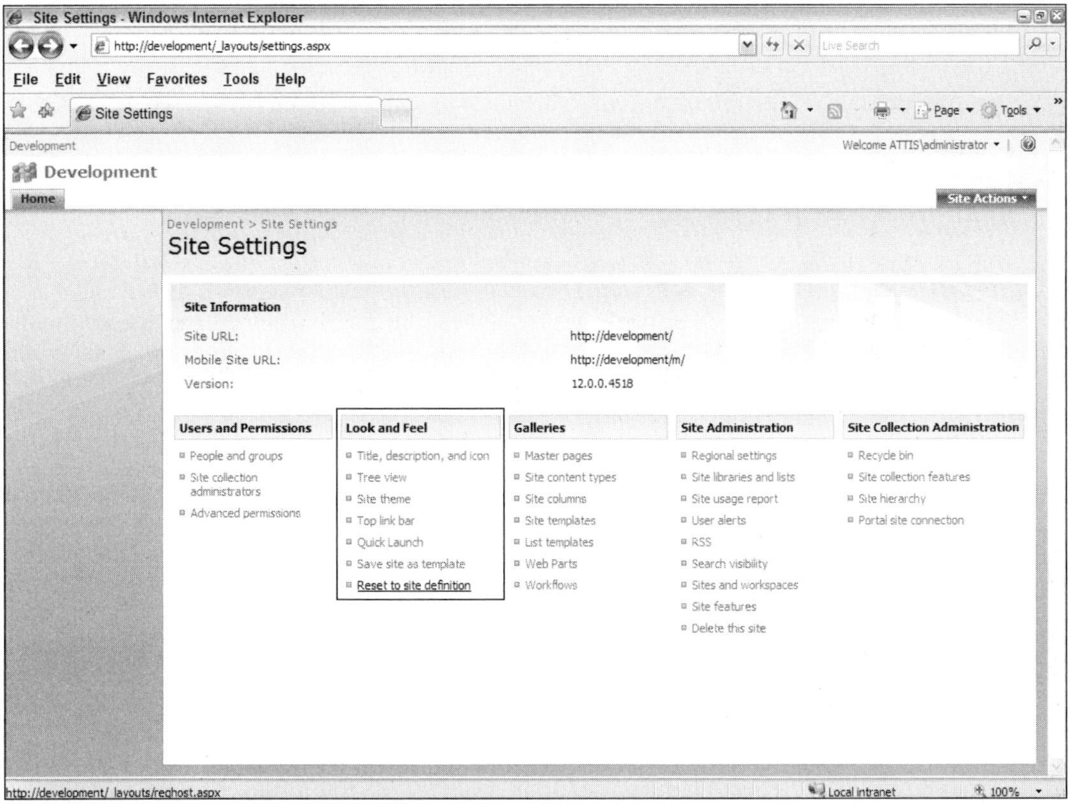

Figure 4-1

Site Definition Files

Many files can make up the structure of a Site Definition, including XML, ASPX, ASCX, and master page files as well as document template files and content files. A Site Definition must reside in an appropriately named folder in the `[WSS]\TEMPLATE\SiteTemplates` folder. In addition to the preceding folder and files, a file by the name of `WebTemp*.xml` must also exist in the `[WSS]\TEMPLATE\1033\XML` folder, where "*" should be replaced with the name of your custom Site Definition. This file specifies the configuration(s) for your custom Site Definition templates. It is read once and cached by the web application on startup.

The heart and soul of a Site Definition is the `Onet.xml` file. This file exists for each and every Site Definition in a SharePoint installation, and you can find it in the XML subfolder of the Site Definition folder. The main functions of this file (as described in the SDK) are listed here:

❑ Define the top and side navigation areas that appear on the home page and in list views.

❑ Specify the list definitions that are used in the Site Definition and whether they are available for creating lists on the Create page.

❑ Specify document templates that are available for creating document library lists on the New page, and specify the files used in the document templates.

❑ Define the base list types from which default WSS v3 lists are derived. Used only in the Global `Onet.xml` file (discussed later in this chapter).

❑ Specify the configurations of lists and modules that are used within Site Definitions.

❑ Specify WSS v3 components.

❑ Define the footer section used in server email.

By creating a custom Site Definition, you can tailor the available functionality used to cater to your particular business needs. Some of the possible customizations you can include in our custom Site Definition include the following:

❑ Specify an alternate Cascading Style Sheet (CSS) file, JavaScript file, or ASPX header file for a Site Definition.

❑ Modify navigation areas for the home page and list pages.

❑ Add a list definition as an option to the Create page.

❑ Add a document template for creating document libraries.

❑ Define a configuration for a Site Definition, specifying the lists, modules, files, and Web Parts that are included when a site is provisioned (provisioning a site is synonymous with creating a site).

We cannot stress how important it is to not modify any of the files owned by WSS v3. The only supported method of creating Site Definitions is to start from scratch by building out the `Onet.xml` file and other supporting files manually, or preferably (and much easier), by making a copy of one of the packaged site definitions that most closely matches your needs and modifying the copy. This method essentially guarantees that your site definition will not break any existing sites nor will it be overwritten by a service pack in the future.

The `Onet.xml` file contains a number of elements that together all work in tandem to provision a site as it is defined within this file. The top-level element in the `Onet.xml` file is the `Project` element, which is described in more detail in the following table.

Attribute	Description
`Title`	Required `Text`. Specifies a default name for a SharePoint site.
`Revision`	Optional `Integer`.

Attribute	Description
ListDir	Required Text. Specifies the directory to implement in new lists.
AlternateCSS	Optional Text. Used in an Onet.xml file to specify the name of an alternate cascading style sheets (CSS) file located in the [WSS]\TEMPLATE\LAYOUTS\1033\STYLES directory that defines styles to use in the site definition.
CustomJSUrl	Optional Text. Alternate JavaScript file for custom scripts.
AlternateURL	Optional Text.
AlternateHeader	Optional Text. ASPX file for alternate header
DisableWebDesignFeatures	Optional Text. Blocks specific editing features that are used in Microsoft Office SharePoint Designer 2007. Possible values include the following, which can be delimited using semicolons: wdfbackup wdfrestore wdfpackageimport wdfpackageexport wdfthemeweb wdfthemepage wdfnavigationbars wdfnavigationview wdfpublishview wdfpublishselectedfile wdfopensite wdfnewsubsite

The Project element in turn contains the following elements:

- ❑ NavBars
- ❑ ListTemplates
- ❑ DocumentTemplates
- ❑ Configurations
- ❑ Modules

NavBars

Definitions for the top navigation area and the side navigation area are both contained in the `NavBars` element. The `NavBars` element can contain multiple `NavBar` elements, which the following table describes in more detail. A `NavBar` element is a header level link. When looking at the Quick Launch navigation bar on the left-hand side of the screen, this equates to the Documents, Lists, Discussions, Sites, and People and Groups links that appear in the navigation after creating a Team Site.

NavBar Attribute	Description
Body	Required `Text`. Contains the body of the definition for the navigation bar.
ID	Required `Integer`. Specifies the ID of the navigation bar.
Name	Required `Text`. Contains the name of the navigation bar.
Prefix	Optional `Text`. Contains the opening tag for the table that contains the navigation bar.
Separator	Optional `Text`. Specifies the separator to use between items in the navigation bar.
Suffix	Optional `Text`. Contains the closing tag for the table that contains the navigation bar.
Url	Optional `Text`.

Links can be added by including any number of `NavBarLink` elements within any of the `NavBar` elements. Table 4-5, from the SDK, outlines the attributes of the `NavBarLink` element. These links will appear under the `NavBar` elements defined above. For example, you could add a link to a Status Reports document library under the Documents header defined by its `NavBar` element by adding a `NavBarLink` element within it in the XML. This, of course, assumes that you are including a Status Report document library in your Site Definition; otherwise, the link would not be very helpful!

NavBarLink Attribute	Description
Name	Required `Text`. Contains the text displayed for the hyperlink.
Url	Required `Text`. Contains the URL for the hyperlink.

ListTemplates

List Definitions that are part of your custom Site Definition are contained within the `ListTemplates` element. The details surrounding the `schema.xml` file that is used to define a List Definition is beyond the scope of this book but can be researched at http://msdn2.microsoft.com/en-us/library/ms459356.aspx. The following table outlines the attributes of the `ListTemplate` element. Only `BaseType`, `DisplayName`, and `Name` are required attributes; the remaining ones are all optional. Many of the attributes that you see here you also see when viewing a list's settings through the SharePoint user interface.

ListTemplate Attribute	Description
AllowDeletion	Optional `Boolean`. `TRUE` to specify that lists created through the list definition cannot be deleted; otherwise, `FALSE`.
AllowEveryoneViewItems	Optional `Boolean`. `TRUE` to allow any user to view items in the library. The `AllowEveryoneViewItems` attribute is used, for example, in the Master Page gallery to give all users access to master pages.
AlwaysIncludeContent	Optional `Boolean`. `TRUE` to specify that list content be included by default when lists created through the list definition are saved as list templates in the user interface; otherwise, `FALSE`.
BaseType	Required `Integer`. Specifies the base type, or default schema, for lists created from the definition.
CacheSchema	Optional `Boolean`. `TRUE` to enable schema caching of the list when provisioning a site. The `CacheSchema` attribute is used, for example, in the global Onet.xml file to enable caching of the user list for the current site collection.
Catalog	Optional `Boolean`. `TRUE` to specify that the list definition is for a site gallery, a list gallery, or a Web Part gallery.
Category	Optional `Text`. Specifies the category with which to associate lists created through the list definition. Possible values include Libraries, Communication, Tracking and Custom Lists.
Default	Optional `Boolean`. `TRUE` to specify that new SharePoint sites will include this list.
Description	Optional `Text`. Provides a description of the list definition.
DisableAttachments	Optional `Boolean`. `TRUE` to specify that users can attach files to items in lists created through the list definition; otherwise, `FALSE`.
DisallowContentTypes	Optional `Boolean`. `TRUE` to specify that content types can be managed on lists created through the list definition; otherwise, `FALSE`.
DisplayName	Required `Text`. Specifies the display name of the list definition.
DocumentTemplate	Optional `Integer`. Currently unused. This is only valid in a `ListTemplate` element whose `BaseType` is set to 1 (document libraries). For future compatibility, this should either be left blank or correspond to the `Type` attribute of a `DocumentTemplate` element in the `DocumentTemplates` enumeration. This attribute has been deprecated in WSS v3.

Continued

ListTemplate Attribute	Description
DontSaveInTemplate	Optional `Boolean`. `TRUE` to exclude the content of the list when the list is saved as a custom list template or when the site to which the list belongs is saved as a custom site template through the user interface.
EditPage	Optional `Text`. Specifies the name of a custom form to use as the page for editing items in lists created through the list definition.
EnableModeration	Optional `Boolean`. `TRUE` to specify that content approval is enabled by default in lists created through the list definition; otherwise, `FALSE`.
FeatureId	Optional `Text`. Specifies the GUID that identifies the Feature with which the list definition is associated.
FolderCreation	Optional `Boolean`. `TRUE` to enable folder creation within the list and to specify that the New Folder command appears on the New menu in list views; otherwise, `FALSE`.
Hidden	Optional `Boolean`. `TRUE` to specify that the list definition is not available on the Create page for creating lists.
HiddenList	Optional `Boolean`. `TRUE` to specify that a list created from the list definition is hidden.
Image	Optional `URL`. Specifies a URL to an icon used to represent a list.
MultipleMtgDataList	Optional `Boolean`. If `MultipleMtgDataList="TRUE"` is specified, the list within a Meeting Workspace site contains data for multiple meeting instances within the site.
MustSaveRootFiles	Optional `Boolean`. `TRUE` to save the pages contained within a special document library that is used internally for a Meeting Workspace site when the list template is saved without content. This attribute is not intended for public use.
Name	Required `Text`. Specifies the internal name of the list definition. No spaces or special characters can be used. This name is also used to find the folder that contains the `Schema.xml` file that defines the schema in use.
NewPage	Optional `Text`. Specifies the name of a custom form to use as the page for creating items in lists created through the list definition.
NoCrawl	Optional `Boolean`. `TRUE` to specify that the list not be visible in search results; otherwise, `FALSE`.

ListTemplate Attribute	Description
OnQuickLaunch	Optional `Boolean`. TRUE to display lists created from the list definition on the Quick Launch bar.
Path	Optional `Text`. Specifies the name of the site definition that contains the list definition, for example, `STS`. This path is assumed to be relative to the `12\TEMPLATE` directory. The path can be directed at a features schema, for example, `Features\Announcements`. This attribute has been deprecated in Windows SharePoint Services 3.0.
RootWebOnly	Optional `Boolean`. TRUE to specify that the list created from the definition exists only in the root web site of a site collection. This attribute has been deprecated in Windows SharePoint Services 3.0.
SecurityBits	Optional `Text`. Defines read, write, and schema design security. Each digit in the string corresponds to the three security settings contained in the List of Lists database table. This attribute does not apply to document libraries.
Sequence	Optional `Integer`. Specifies the ordering priority to use for the list definition on the Create page. If `Sequence` is not set, the list definition shows up last in arbitrary order with any other list definitions that also lack a `Sequence` value. Two list definitions that specify the same sequence are sorted together in an arbitrary order.
SetupPath	Optional `Text`. Specifies the path to a folder in the Windows SharePoint Services setup directory (`\\Program Files\Common Files\Microsoft Shared\web server extensions\12\TEMPLATE`) that contains a file to be included in the list definition.
SyncType	Optional `Boolean`. TRUE to override the default client list type associated with a Windows SharePoint Services base template.
Type	Optional `Integer`. Provides a unique identifier for the list definition. This identifier must be unique within the feature, but need not be unique across all feature definitions or site definitions. This attribute corresponds to the `Type` attribute of the `List` element.
Unique	Optional `Boolean`. TRUE to specify that the list definition or list template can only be used to create a list during site creation and cannot be used to create a list through the object model or user interface after the site template or definition is applied. Setting this attribute to TRUE has the effect of making the list hidden so that it does not appear as an option on the Create page or on the Documents and Lists page.

Continued

ListTemplate Attribute	Description
UseRootFolderForNavigation	Optional Boolean. TRUE to specify that a link to the list that is displayed in Quick Launch points to the root folder so that users go to a custom welcome page, instead of to the default list view page.
VersioningEnabled	Optional Boolean. TRUE to specify that versioning is enabled by default in lists created through the list definition; otherwise, FALSE.

Note that a ListTemplate element contains two separate attributes for type; Type and BaseType. The Type attribute is used to specify a unique identifier for the list definition itself while the BaseType attribute is used to identify the base list type for the List Definition that corresponds to the Type value of one of the base list types defined in the Global Site Definition's Onet.xml file located at [WSS]\TEMPLATE\ GLOBAL\XML. Within the Global Site Definition, discussed later, you will see that there are five List-Templates defined.

- ❑ Master Page Gallery
- ❑ Users
- ❑ Site Template Gallery
- ❑ List Template Gallery
- ❑ Web Part Gallery

All of the above (with the exception of the Master Page Gallery) are only available on the root web. The ListTemplate definition for the Web Part Gallery looks like the following snippet. You can see that the RootWebOnly attribute is set to true, thereby limiting this list template to use on a top-level site.

```
<ListTemplate
  Name="wplib"
  DisplayName="$Resources:core,webpartgalleryList;"
  Description="$Resources:core,webpartgalleryList_Desc;"
  SetupPath="global\lists\wplib"
  Type="113"
  BaseType="1"
  Hidden="TRUE"
  HiddenList="TRUE"
  NoCrawl="TRUE"
  FolderCreation="FALSE"
  Unique="TRUE"
  RootWebOnly="TRUE"
  Catalog="TRUE"
  OnQuickLaunch="FALSE"
  SecurityBits="11"
  AllowDeletion="FALSE"
  Image="/_layouts/images/itdl.gif"
  DontSaveInTemplate="TRUE"
  DocumentTemplate="100" />
```

The following table lists the default list types. This list is handy when you are creating your own List Definitions, Site Definitions, or even event handlers which are discussed in Chapter 5.

Value	Description
100	Generic list
101	Document library
102	Survey
103	Links list
104	Announcements list
105	Contacts list
106	Events list
107	Tasks list
108	Discussion board
109	Picture library
110	Data sources
111	Site template gallery
113	Web Part gallery
114	List template gallery
115	XML Form library
120	Custom grid for a list
200	Meeting Series list
201	Meeting Agenda list
202	Meeting Attendees list
204	Meeting Decisions list
207	Meeting Objectives list
210	Meeting text box
211	Meeting Things To Bring list

Continued

Value	Description
212	Meeting Workspace Pages list
300	Portal Sites list
1100	Issue tracking
2002	Personal document library
2003	Private document library

It's interesting to note the lack of numbering. For example, you may notice that the number 112 is mysteriously missing from the list. While developing on this platform and writing this book, we have had plenty of time to snoop around the WSS v3 Framework. If you were to browse to any site, go to Site Settings under Site Actions and click on People and groups, you would arrive at a page representing of list of users in a particular group. If this is a new site, the group you are looking at is most likely <site> Members, *where* <site> *can be replaced with the name of the site when it was provisioned. If you view the HTML source code of this particular page and scroll down toward the bottom, you will observer that there is a* listTemplate *hidden field that contains a value of 112. We leave it up to you to explore this "phenomenon" further, if it has in fact stirred your interest.*

Document Templates

The DocumentTemplate element is used to define the document templates that are available on the New page when creating a document library. These templates are listed in the Document Template drop-down on the New Document Library page (see Figure 4-2). Table 4-8 outlines the attributes of the DocumentTemplate element. Only DisplayName and Type are required. You could use this section of the Site Definition to define a standard status report template that all projects in your organization might be required to use.

DocumentTemplate Attribute	Description
Default	Optional Boolean. TRUE if the template is the default choice in the Template Type drop-down list box of the New Document Library page.
Description	Optional Text. A description of the template.
DisplayName	Required Text. The display name of the template.

DocumentTemplate Attribute	Description
Name	Optional `Text`. The internal name of the template.
Path	Optional `Text`. The name of the site template to which the document template belongs.
Type	Required `Integer`. A unique ID for the template.
XMLForm	Optional `Boolean`. `TRUE` if the document template applies to a form library.

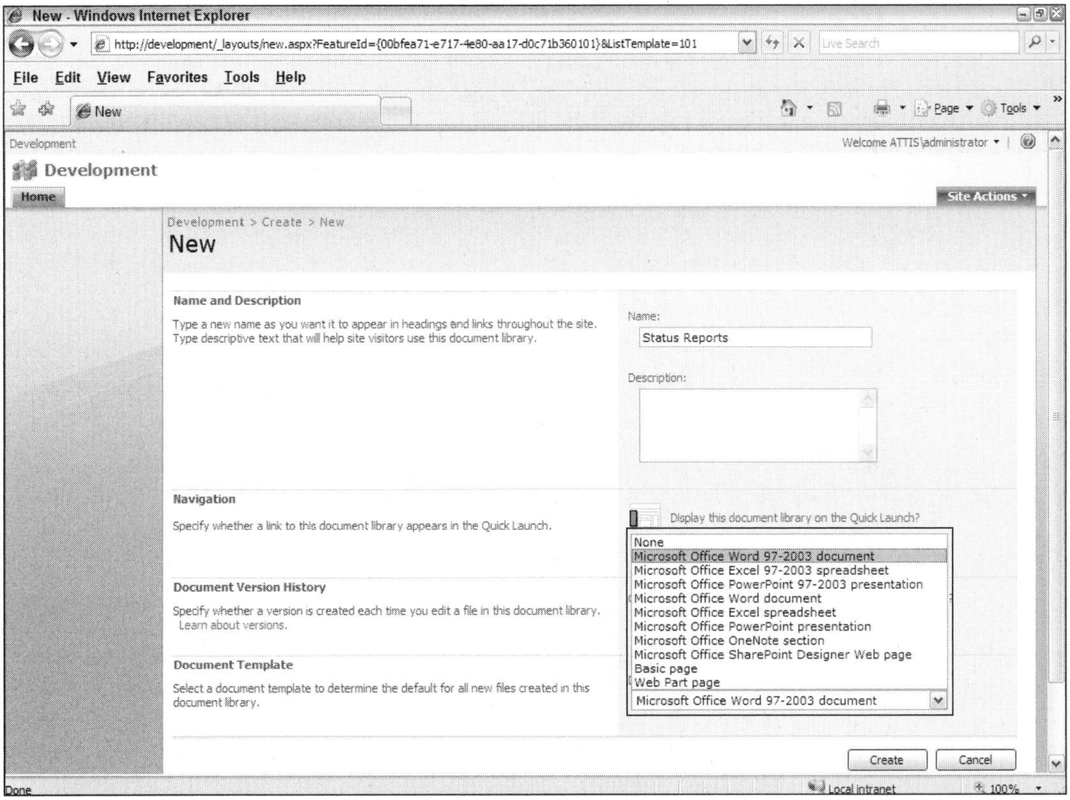

Figure 4-2

Each of the `DocumentTemplate` elements may contain a `DocumentTemplateFiles` element which in turn may contain a collection of files that are part of a multi-file document template. Each of these files is contained in a `DocumentTemplateFile` element that contains a reference to a file that is used within a document template. The following table outlines the attributes of the `DocumentTemplateFile` element.

DocumentTemplateFile Attribute	Description
`Default`	Optional `Boolean`. `TRUE` to specify that the template file is the default file.
`Name`	Required `Text`. The full path to the template file.
`TargetName`	Required `Text`. The full path to the target.

The following snippet illustrates how you could include a new document template in your Site Definition. Document template files are stored in subfolders within the `[WSS]\TEMPLATE\1033\STS\DOCTEMP` folder. Storing them using a file structure that includes a locale allows you to have localized templates in different languages if necessary.

```
<DocumentTemplate
  Path="STS"
  DisplayName="Status Report"
  Type="10001"
  Description="Use this template for a project status report.">
  <DocumentTemplateFiles>
    <DocumentTemplateFile
      Name="doctemp\word\statusreport.dotx"
      TargetName="Forms/statusreport.dotx"
      Default="TRUE" />
  </DocumentTemplateFiles>
</DocumentTemplate>
```

Configurations

The `Configurations` element contains individual `Configuration` elements that are used to define the Lists, Modules, Site Features and Web Features that are created by default when a site is provisioned using a Site Definition. Each Configuration can also contain an `ExecuteUrl` element that can be used to specify a URL that is called immediately after a site is provisioned, perhaps to enable some postprocessing. The `ExecuteUrl` element could be used to simulate a `SiteCreated` event, which does not currently exist within the WSS v3 object model. Configurations also allow a developer to reuse existing list definitions and modules already defined in the `Onet.xml` file. The value of the `ID` attribute for each `Configuration` element within the `Configurations` element in the `Onet.xml` file corresponds to the ID specified in the `WebTemp*.xml` file containing the configurations for a particular Site Definition. The following table outlines the attributes of the `Configuration` element.

The `Configuration` *element is used in both the* `Onet.xml` *file of a Site Definition and the* `WebTemp.xml` *file. In* `Onet.xml`, *it is used define configurations as described in the previous paragraph. In* `WebTemp.xml`, *it is used to define the specific configurations that are contained within a Site Definition.*

Configuration Attribute	Description
AllowGlobalFeatureAssociations	Optional `Boolean`. Specifies whether global Feature associations are allowed on the template.
CustomMasterUrl	Optional `Text`. Specifies the URL for a custom `.master` page to implement in web sites created through the site definition.
Description	Optional `Text`. Contains the description of the site configuration that appears on the Template Selection page.
DisplayCategory	Optional `Text`. Specifies a category for the site definition, for example, `Collaboration` or `Meetings`.
Hidden	Optional `Boolean`. Specifies whether the site configuration appears as an option on the Template Selection page.
ID	Required `Integer`. Specifies a unique ID for the configuration.
ImageUrl	Optional `Text`. Contains the URL for the preview image displayed on the Template Selection page.
MasterUrl	Optional `Text`. Specifies the master page to use for web sites created through the site definition.
Name	Optional `Text`. Contains the name of the configuration.
RootWebOnly	Optional `Boolean`. TRUE to specify that the site created from the definition exists only as the root web site in a site collection.
SubWebOnly	Optional `Boolean`. TRUE to specify that the site created from the definition exists only as a subsite within a site collection.
Title	Optional `Text`. Contains the title of the configuration that is displayed on the Template Selection page.
Type	Optional `Text`. Identifies the configuration with a specific site definition.
VisibilityFeatureDependency	Optional `Text`. Used in a `WebTemp*.xml` file to hide the site definition based on the activation state of the specified Feature. When a site definition contains Features that depend upon another Feature, setting this attribute prevents the site definition from appearing as an option on the New SharePoint Site page if the specified Feature is not installed or activated. This attribute is not supported for Features with the web application scope.

The Configuration element contains the following subelements.

❏ ExecuteUrl — As mentioned before, this element is used to specify a URL that is called imme-diately after a site is provisioned, perhaps to enable some postprocessing.

❏ Lists — This element contains the collection of List instances as well as their default data for a particular configuration.

❏ Modules — This element contains the collection of Modules for a particular configuration.

❏ SiteFeatures — This element contains the collection of site collection Features to activate for a particular configuration when a site is provisioned through the Site Definition.

❏ WebFeatures — This element contains the collection of site Features to activate for a particular configuration when a site is provisioned through the Site Definition.

Perhaps the most useful attributes of the Configuration element is the CustomMasterUrl attribute. Using this attribute allows you to include an additional master page in your site definition that you will be able to use without customizing your pages using SharePoint Designer and consequently storing them in the content database. Essentially, you will be able to provide a custom master page that can be referenced via a simple change in the file system (uncustomized) version of your Site Definition page template file(s). This concept is demonstrated in the walkthrough that begins a little later in this chapter.

As noted in the SDK, WSS v3 activates features specified within the Onet.xml file in the order that they are listed. Consequently, you must specify Features that are depended upon before Features that depend upon them.

Modules

The Modules element specifies the modules that are available to all configurations. A module is defined as a file or collection of files as well as a location where the files are installed during site provisioning. Additionally, if one of the files is a Web Part page, the module can specify which Web Parts should be included on the page. The following table outlines the attributes of the Module element.

Module Attribute	Description
IncludeFolders	Optional Text.
List	Optional **Integer**. Specifies the type of list, which is defined within Onet.xml.
Name	Required Text. Contains the name of the file set.
Path	Optional Text. Contains the URL for the file set. Use only low-order ASCII characters, and no spaces, for Feature folder and file names.
RootWebOnly	Optional Boolean. TRUE if the files specified in the module are installed only in the top-level web site of the site collection.

Module Attribute	Description
SetupPath	Optional Text. Specifies the path to a folder in the Windows SharePoint Services setup directory ([WSS]\TEMPLATE) that contains a file to include in the module.
Url	Optional Text. Specifies the URL of the folder in which to place the files when a site is instantiated. Use only low-order ASCII characters, and no spaces, for the Feature folder and file names.

Take a quick look at the module included with every Team Site created using the built-in Team Site Site Definition. You can immediately see that the URL for the file (page in this case) is defined as default .aspx. As you move down through the XML code, you can see that this page contains a number of list view Web Parts as well as an image Web Part (contents omitted for space). You will also see an announcements list view Web Part, a calendar list view Web Part, an image Web Part, and a links list view Web Part.

```
<Module
  Name="Default"
  Url="" Path="">
  <File
    Url="default.aspx"
    NavBarHome="True">
    <View
      List="$Resources:core,lists_Folder;/$Resources:core,announce_Folder;"
      BaseViewID="0"
      WebPartZoneID="Left" />
    <View
      List="$Resources:core,lists_Folder;/$Resources:core,calendar_Folder;"
      BaseViewID="0"
      RecurrenceRowset="TRUE"
      WebPartZoneID="Left"
      WebPartOrder="2" />
    <AllUsersWebPart WebPartZoneID="Right" WebPartOrder="1">
      <![CDATA[<WebPart
        xmlns="http://schemas.microsoft.com/WebPart/v2"
        xmlns:iwp="http://schemas.microsoft.com/WebPart/v2/Image">
        ...
        remainder omitted for space
        ...
      </WebPart>]]>
    </AllUsersWebPart>
    <View
      List="$Resources:core,lists_Folder;/$Resources:core,links_Folder;"
      BaseViewID="0"
      WebPartZoneID="Right"
      WebPartOrder="2" />
    <NavBarPage Name="$Resources:core,nav_Home;" ID="1002" Position="Start" />
    <NavBarPage Name="$Resources:core,nav_Home;" ID="0" Position="Start" />
  </File>
</Module>
```

A more complete examination of the child elements of the `Module` element is beyond the scope of this book. The following link tells you everything you need to know: `http://msdn2.microsoft.com/ en-us/library/ms460356.aspx`. Alternatively you could search the SDK for "Module Element (Site)" and be brought to the appropriate location.

Global Site Definition

The Global Site Definition is a new and very special Site Definition found at `[WSS]\12\TEMPLATE\ GLOBAL`. This Site Definition contains the elements required by the framework in order for it to function at the most basic levels, including all of the base types. By isolating as much of the common functionality for each site into the Global Site Definition as possible, custom Site Definitions need only contain the elements that are needed to make the Global Site Definition unique to the business problems that it is being designed to address.

The Global Site Definition is used in the provisioning process of each and every site.

> **As noted in the SDK, do not modify the contents of the** `Global Onet.xml` **file located at** `[WSS]\TEMPLATE\GLOBAL\XML`. **Doing so is not supported and may break your installation. Base list types cannot be added.**

Creating a Custom Site Definition

The following section outlines the steps necessary to create a custom Site Definition by copying one of the existing ones and modifying it to suit your needs. For this exercise you will use the **Team Site** (sts) Site Definition as a starting point. Keep in mind that best practice dictates that you copy one of the existing Site Definitions that most closely meets your needs and develop from it.

You will be using **Visual Studio 2005** to develop your custom Site Definition. By using Visual Studio 2005, you will enjoy the benefits of a full-featured development environment that includes, among other things, color-coding, post-build scripting (to move files around if needed), as well as XML schema validation. Keep in mind that this type of development should only be done in a development environment, never in production. Site Definitions should eventually be deployed using the WSS v3 Solution Framework discussed later in this chapter. The process used here makes it easy to work on Site Definitions, as changes can be seen immediately, since all of the files will be in the correct place on the file system and usable after you build your project.

1. Create a new project by clicking Project under the New option from the File menu.
2. Under Project types, select the Class Library template under Windows in the language of your choice.

   .NET code is not a requirement for a Site Definition, so the choice of language is not significant. We are using a Class Library project type, so that you will always get a project that compiles, thus enabling you to run post-build scripts.

3. In the Location text box browse to `[WSS]\TEMPLATE\SiteTemplates` and click Open. By placing the project here, most files will already be where they need to be for the Site Definition to function. You will use a post-build script to move any files that need to be located elsewhere to their final location.

4. Uncheck the Create directory for solution check box.

5. Give your Site Definition a meaningful name such as **MySiteDefinition**, and click OK.

In WSS v2, this folder name had to be all uppercase. Upon glancing at the out-of-the-box Site Definitions provided with WSS v3, you can see that this is no longer a requirement; for example, sts.

6. Delete the `Class1.cs` or `Class1.vb` file. It is not needed.

7. Create an XML folder by right-clicking on the project node and selecting New Folder from the Add context menu.

8. Add an existing `Onet.xml` file by right-clicking on the XML folder and selecting Existing Item from the Add context menu. Navigate to the XML folder within the sts Site Definition (`[WSS]\TEMPLATE\SiteTemplates\sts\xml`). Be sure to select All Files (*.*) in the Files of type drop-down list. Select `ONET.xml`, and click Add. This process creates a copy of Onet.xml in your project.

9. Make the following edits to `Onet.xml`.

   ❑ Delete the `Blank` and `DWS` Configuration elements (see Figure 4-3).

   ❑ Delete the `DefaultBlank` and `DWS` Module elements (see Figure 4-4).

10. Add an existing `WebTemp.xml` file to the root of the project by right-clicking the project node and selecting Existing Item from the Add context menu. Navigate to the XML folder within the 1033 folder (`[WSS]\TEMPLATE\1033\XML`). Select `WEBTEMP.XML` and click Add.

11. Rename the file in the preceding step to **WEBTEMPMySiteDefinition.XML**.

12. Make the following edits to `WEBTEMPMySiteDefinition.XML`, as shown in Figure 4-5.

   ❑ Delete all Template elements except for `GLOBAL` and `STS`.

   ❑ Change the `Name attribute of the STS` element to **MySiteDefinition**.

   ❑ Change the ID attribute to **10001**.

   ❑ Delete the `Blank Site and Document Workspace Configuration elements`.

   ❑ Change the Title to **My Custom Site**. This change and the two that follow are to be made to the Team Site configuration.

   ❑ Change the Description to **My Custom Site Description**.

   ❑ Change the DisplayCategory to Custom so that this Site Definition appears under its own tab in the Template Selection section of the Create new site page.

The `Name` attribute must be the same name that you gave the folder containing this Site Definition. Also, the `ID` attribute must be a unique value greater than 10,000. Values up to and including 10,000 have been reserved for use by WSS v3.

```
MySiteDefinition - Microsoft Visual Studio
File  Edit  View  Project  Build  Debug  XML  Data  Tools  Window  Community  Help

ONET.XML
   1   <?xml version="1.0" encoding="utf-8"?>
   2   <Project
   3       Title="$Resources:onet_TeamWebSite;"
   4       Revision="2"
   5       ListDir="$Resources:core,lists_Folder;"
   6       xmlns:ows="Microsoft SharePoint"><!-- _locID@Title="camlidonet1" _locComment="{StringCategory=HTX}" -->
   7     <NavBars>...
  15     <ListTemplates>...
  17     <DocumentTemplates>...
  75     <Configurations>
  76       <Configuration ID="-1" Name="NewWeb" />
  77       <Configuration ID="0" Name="Default">...
 112       <Configuration ID="1" Name="Blank">...
 130       <Configuration ID="2" Name="DWS">...
 165     </Configurations>
 166     <Modules>...
 223     <ServerEmailFooter>$Resources:ServerEmailFooter;</ServerEmailFooter>
 224   </Project>
```

Figure 4-3

```
MySiteDefinition - Microsoft Visual Studio
File  Edit  View  Project  Build  Debug  XML  Data  Tools  Window  Community  Help

ONET.XML
   1   <?xml version="1.0" encoding="utf-8"?>
   2   <Project
   3       Title="$Resources:onet_TeamWebSite;"
   4       Revision="2"
   5       ListDir="$Resources:core,lists_Folder;"
   6       xmlns:ows="Microsoft SharePoint"><!-- _locID@Title="camlidonet1" _locComment="{StringCategory=HTX}" -->
   7     <NavBars>...
  15     <ListTemplates>...
  17     <DocumentTemplates>...
  75     <Configurations>...
 166     <Modules>
 167       <Module Name="Default" Url="" Path="">...
 186       <Module Name="DefaultBlank" Url="" Path="">...
 202       <Module Name="DWS" Url="">...
 222     </Modules>
 223     <ServerEmailFooter>$Resources:ServerEmailFooter;</ServerEmailFooter>
 224   </Project>
```

Figure 4-4

13. Add an existing `default.aspx` file to the root of the project by right-clicking the project node and selecting Existing Item from the Add context menu. Navigate to the sts Site Definition folder ([WSS]\TEMPLATE\SiteTemplates\sts). Select `default.aspx` and click Add.

14. Add an existing `default.master` file to the root of the project by right-clicking the project node and selecting Existing Item from the Add context menu. Navigate to the Global Site Definition folder ([WSS]\TEMPLATE\GLOBAL). Select `default.master` and click Add.

15. Rename the file in the preceding step to **MySiteDefinition.master**.

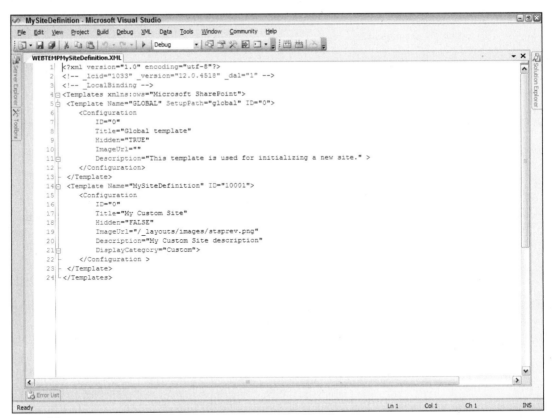

Figure 4-5

16. Add a `Module` element to the `Modules` section of `Onet.xml` to instruct SharePoint to place the `MySiteDefinition.master` file into the master page gallery. Note the `List` attribute of 116. This can be obtained by viewing the HTML source of any master page gallery on any site. You will discover that there is a plethora of hidden fields and values toward the bottom of most pages that are quite useful.

```
<Module
  Name="MySiteDefinitionMasterPage"
  List="116"
  Url="_catalogs/masterpage"
  RootWebOnly="FALSE">
  <File
    Url="MySiteDefinition.master"
      Type="GhostableInLibrary" />
</Module>
```

17. Add a `Module` element to the `Modules` element within the `Default Configuration` element.

```
<Module Name="MySiteDefinitionMasterPage" />
```

18. Add a `CustomMasterUrl` attribute to the `Default Configuration` element to tell it to use the custom master page.

```
<Configuration ID="0"
  Name="Default"
  CustomMasterUrl="_catalogs/masterpage/MySiteDefinition.master">
```

19. Change the `MasterPageFile` attribute in the `default.aspx` page from the `~masterurl/default.master` token to the `~masterurl/custom.master` token. This tells the `default.aspx` page to use the `CustomMasterUrl` defined in the previous step.

20. Right-click on the project node and select Properties from the context menu.

21. Click on the Build Events tab.

22. Enter the following command in the "Post-build event command line" text box to copy the `WebTemp.xml` file to the correct location. Be sure that the entire command is on a single line.

```
xcopy ..\..\WEBTEMPMySiteDefinition.XML "C:\Program Files\Common
Files\Microsoft Shared\web server extensions\12\TEMPLATE\1033\XML\" /y
```

23. Save your changes, and build the project by right-clicking on the project node and selecting Build.

24. Reset Internet Information Services (IIS) or recycle the application pool of the web application in which you will be testing your Site Definition.

25. Open a browser to any WSS v3 site within the preceding web application. Choose Create from the Site Actions menu and choose Sites and Workspaces. Your custom Site Definition will appear under the Custom tab in the Template Selection section of the New SharePoint Site page, as shown in Figure 4-6.

At this point, your custom Site Definition is ready to be used to provision a site. Creating a site now using your Site Definition would essentially give you a site identical to an out-of-the-box Team Site. Because the purpose of creating a custom Site Definition is to have a custom site, you'll want to make some changes.

Earlier in this chapter you saw that the `Project` element of the `Onet.xml` file defined an `AlternateCSS` attribute and a `CustomJSUrl` attribute. You are going to use these attributes to allow users of the custom Site Definition to have the ability to override the global styles and/or the default platform behavior (with respect to JavaScript). Now, create both a `core.css` file and a `core.js` file, tell your Site Definition where they are, and override a default style.

1. Navigate to the Layouts folder located at `[WSS]\TEMPLATE\LAYOUTS`.

2. Create a Custom folder.

3. Within the Custom folder you just created, create a MySiteDefinition folder to place the custom `.css`, `.js`, and image files you will use for your custom Site Definition created in the previous section.

4. Add a new `.css` file to the root of the project by right-clicking the project node and selecting New Item from the Add context menu. Select the Style Sheet template, name the file **core.css**, and click Add. The contents of this file should be empty.

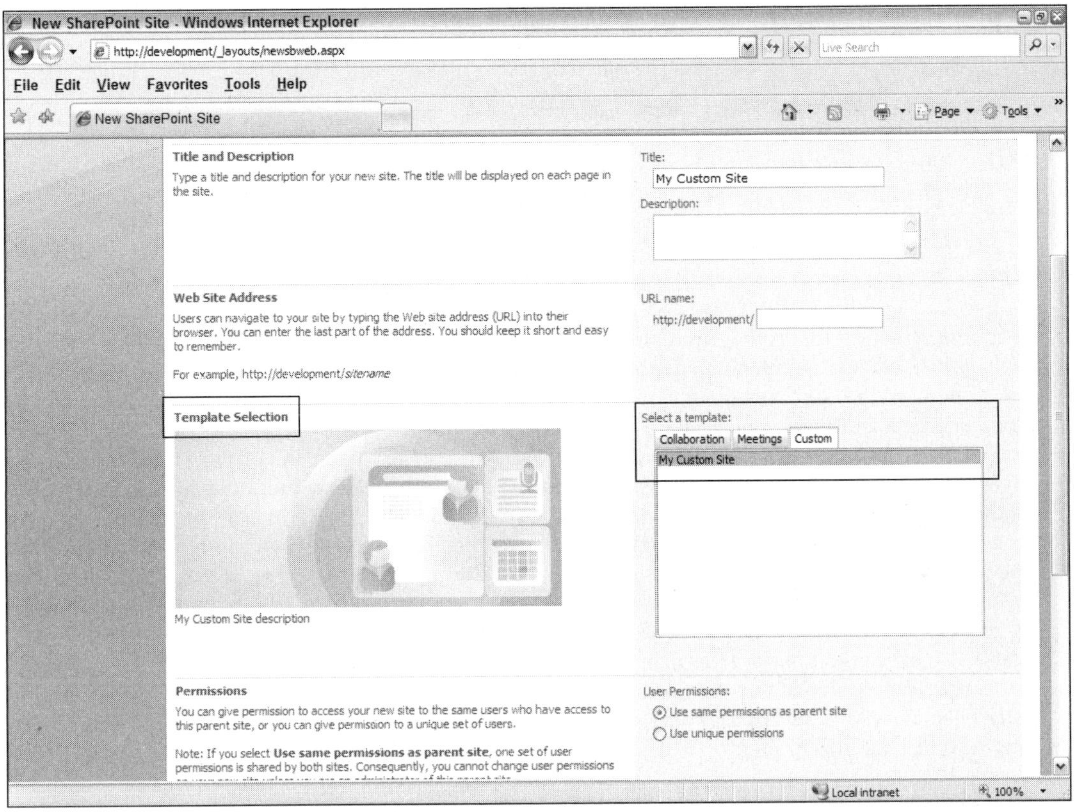

Figure 4-6

5. Enter the following command in the "Post-build event command line" text box to copy the
`core.css` file to the correct location. Be sure to not remove any commands that may have
been added in previous steps.

```
xcopy ..\..\core.css "C:\Program Files\Common Files\Microsoft Shared\web
server extensions\12\TEMPLATE\LAYOUTS\Custom\MySiteDefinition\" /y
```

6. Add a new `.js` file to the root of the project by right-clicking the project node and selecting New
Item from the Add context menu. Select the JScript File template, name the file **core.js**, and click
Add. The contents of this file should be empty.

7. Enter the following command in the "Post-build event command line" text box to copy the
`core.js` file to the correct location. Be sure to not remove any commands added in previous steps.

```
xcopy ..\..\core.js "C:\Program Files\Common Files\Microsoft Shared\web
server extensions\12\TEMPLATE\LAYOUTS\Custom\MySiteDefinition\" /y
```

8. Open the `Onet.xml` file in your `MySiteDefinition` project.

9. Add a root-relative `AlternateCSS` attribute to the `Project` element of your custom Site Definition:

```
AlternateCSS="/_layouts/Custom/MySiteDefinition/core.css"
```

10. Add a root-relative `CustomJSUrl` attribute to the `Project` element of your custom Site Definition:

```
CustomJSUrl="/_layouts/Custom/MySiteDefinition/core.js"
```

A common request that comes up with respect to the out-of-the-box look and feel of a SharePoint site is the Quick Navigation menu along the left-hand side of each page (see Figure 4-7). You can manipulate the contents of the Quick Navigation menu by going to Site Settings and clicking on Quick Launch under Look and Feel, but there is no easy way to hide *only* the header of this menu (the View All Site Content link). One approach is to add a Content Editor Web Part to every page on your site that contains the CSS style necessary to hide this element. This process is very tedious and would need to be done on all pages in the site. Additionally, not all of the pages allow you to add Web Parts. An example of such a page is the `viewlsts.aspx` page, which lists all of the lists of a specific base type. You can now see that the above process will not work for all of the pages on the site. If you had added the `AlternateCSS` attribute to your Site Definition before provisioning your site, you would now have the ability to override styles on pages that do not allow you to override them manually, using the above technique, among others. You could also have accomplished this using SharePoint Designer, but that approach would require you to customize each page that you wanted to apply the style to. Yet another way to accomplish this task would have been to remove the appropriate `NavBar` element from the `NavBars` section of `Onet.xml` representing the Quick Launch header.

The following set of steps outline how to add a CSS style to your custom `.css` file before or after your site has been created in order to inject new look-and-feel styles. This concept can also be applied to the custom JavaScript file.

1. Open the `core.css` file in your `MySiteDefinition` project.
2. Add the following style to `core.css`:

```
.ms-quicklaunchheader
{
   display:none;
}
```

3. Save your changes and build the project.
4. Open a browser to any SharePoint site within the preceding web application. Choose Create from the Site Actions menu and choose Sites and Workspaces. Create a site using the `MySiteDefiniton` Site Definition. You will see that the header on the Quick Launch menu is not visible (see Figure 4-8).

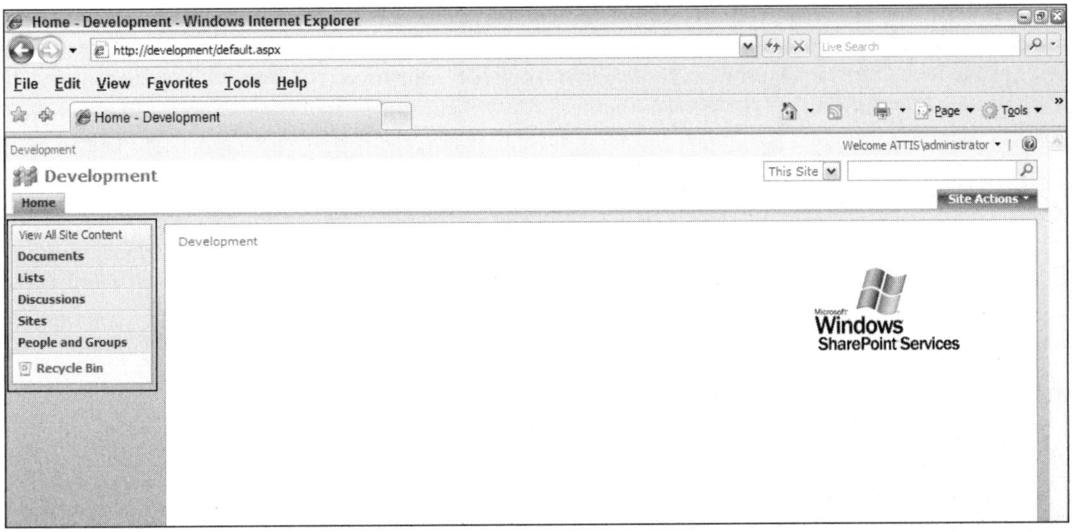

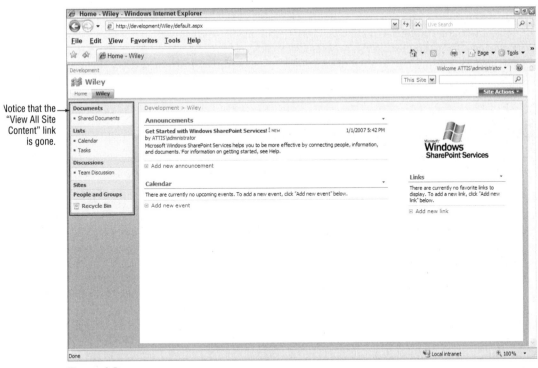

Figure 4-7

Notice that the "View All Site Content" link is gone.

Figure 4-8

This technique can be applied to any style. If there is an element on a page whose look you would like to change, simply view the HTML source of the page and search for the style that is applied to that element or its container. Override that style in your custom .css file. Remember, you own both of these custom files.

> *Remember that most browsers cache pages so that subsequent requests for the same page will appear faster to the end user. Since the above technique modifies an external .css or .js file and not code on the page itself, depending on your browser settings, your changes may not be visible or it may seem like they are not working at all since the link to the external file has not changed, thereby preventing your browser from requesting a newer version of the page. The easiest solution is to manually clear your browser's cache. If that does not "appear" to work, try using a new browser instance and/or resetting IIS.*

Custom Field Types

Although the out-of-the-box field types supplied with WSS v3 are numerous (see Figure 4-9), they may still be lacking in the sense that they cannot possibly support all of your data entry and validation needs. Surely, there will be a business need for a type of field type that is simply not provided by the WSS v3 framework. WSS v3 allows you to create your own custom fields to support your specific requirements and needs. You can control the custom field's properties and the field's rendering, as well as the field's validation requirements.

In order to create a custom field type, you first need to create a class that represents it. This class must inherit from one of the base field type classes. You must also create a field type definition file that contains the information that WSS v3 needs to correctly instantiate and run the field type. You can optionally include information that defines how WSS v3 should render the field type. This last task is beyond the scope of this book and will not be demonstrated; however, feel free to peruse the SDK and see how easy it is to accomplish.

Custom Field Type Classes

The process of creating a custom field class, as mentioned above, involves inheriting from either the SPField base class or one of the classes in the table showing field type classes supporting inheritance. Although it is possible to inherit from other field type classes not in this list, doing so is not supported. This class will control how your field data is retrieved from and inserted into the content database.

Here is how you would create a custom field to contain a Social Security number. The following class inherits from SPFieldText, which is the single line of text field. You go through this example in more detail at the end of this section.

```
using Microsoft.SharePoint;

public class SocialSecurityNumber : SPFieldText
{

}
```

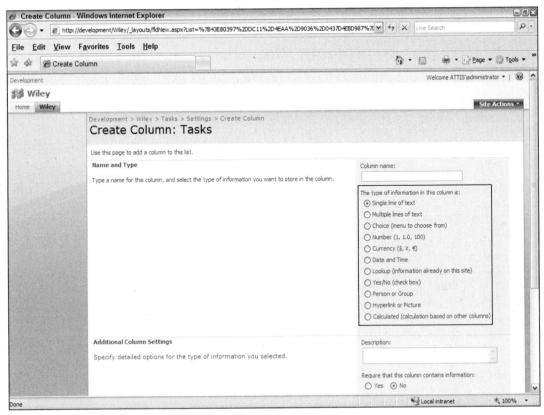

Figure 4-9

Class	Description
SPFieldBoolean	Represents a Boolean field type.
SPFieldChoice	Represents a choice field type.
SPFieldCurrency	Represents a currency field type.
SPFieldDateTime	Represents a date-time field type.
SPFieldLookup	Represents a lookup field type. The field value for the SPFieldLookup class is contained in the SPFieldLookupValue class.
SPFieldMultiChoice	Represents a multichoice field type. The field value for the PFieldMultiChoice class is contained in the SPFieldMultiChoiceValue class.
SPFieldMultiLineText	Represents a multiline text field type.

Continued

Class	Description
SPFieldNumber	Represents a number field type.
SPFieldRatingScale	Represents a ratings field type. The field value for the SPFieldRatingScale class is contained in the SPFieldRatingScaleValue class.
SPFieldText	Represents a single-line text field type.
SPFieldUrl	Represents a URL field type. The field value for SPFieldUrl is contained in the SPFieldUrlValue class.
SPFieldUser	Represents a Windows SharePoint Services user.
SPFieldMultiColumn	Represents a multicolumn field type. SPFieldMultiColumn is a field type that is hidden from the user interface and is accessible only through the object model. The field value for the SPFieldMultiColumn class is contained in the SPFieldMultiColumnValue class.

The WSS v3 framework provides an extensive set of overridable functions and properties when you choose to derive from either the SPField class or any of the classes listed above. This is extremely valuable because most of the properties and behaviors that will make your custom field type unique are going to be contained in your derived class. For example, the SPField base class contains the members listed in the following table from the SDK, whose implementations can be overridden if necessary for your custom field type should you choose to inherit from SPField.

Member	Description
FieldRenderingControl	Returns the field type control used to render the field. This control is used to render the field in display, edit, and new forms, the Data Form Web Part, and any pages that use field controls.
FieldRenderingMobileControl	Returns the field type control used to render the field in mobile applications.
GetFieldValueAsText	Returns the field data value as a string.
GetFieldValueAsHtml	Returns the field data value as a string, formatted as HTML. This HTML-formatted field value is most often used to render the field value directly on a page, the version history page, and other managed code rendering. However, this HTML-formatted field value is not used on the display form. Field rendering for the display form is the same as rendering for list views; that is, it is rendered from the Collaborative Application Markup Language (CAML) definition of the field type display pattern.

Member	Description
GetFieldValueForEdit	Returns the field value to be rendered in Edit Mode. This method is used for the Edit and New forms.
GetValidatedString	Returns the validated field value. Use this method for custom validation and data serialization logic. This method may, in turn, use the ToString method of the field value object to convert the field value object into a string.
GetFieldValue	Returns the field value as a field value object. Use this method when the field type requires a complex data type that is different from that of the parent field type.
FieldValueType	Returns the field value type. Use this method when the field type contains its own custom value type object.
PreviewValueTyped	Returns a preview value of field data, for a design time view of the field control in display and Edit Mode.
OnAdded	Use to specify custom field type logic after a field is added.
OnUpdated	Use to specify custom field type logic after a field is updated.
OnDeleting	Use to specify custom field type logic before a field is deleted.

Custom Field Value Classes

If you have a need for a custom field type whose data is stored in a format not supported by any of the built-in field types from which you have derived your custom field type, there is no need to worry. WSS v3 has provided you with a *custom field value class* that you can structure in such a way that you can store any type of data as long as you abide by a couple of simple rules noted here:

❑ It must be serializable. Each field value class must implement the ToString method to convert the field value to a format suitable for storage.

❑ It must implement two constructors that can simply call the constructors of the parent class.

If your custom field class requires a custom field value class, you will most likely need to override the two methods listed in the following table.

Method	Description
GetFieldValue	This method converts the specified string into a field type value object. Your custom field object should return the custom field value object when the SPField.GetFieldValue method is invoked. WSS v3 returns this field value object when the SPListItem.this["field name"] method is called.
GetValidatedString	This method converts the field type value object into a serialized string.

Custom Field Data Validation

One of the most compelling benefits to creating your own custom field types is that you can also include your own custom validation logic. This creates an invaluable potential increase in business value to any SharePoint list. One of the most common complaints heard in the field is that the supplied columns do not provide the necessary validation required by some specific business rules. The options available to you in implementing your custom validation include inheriting the validation from the parent field class that you are deriving from, overriding the parent's validation or a combination of the two. The GetValidatedString method is where you specify your custom validation logic.

```
public override string GetValidatedString(object value)
{
}
```

Data validation can be performed in many other places, including form controls. Any server-side data validation logic that you think you will need should be added to the GetValidatedString method. This method is invoked whenever data is stored in a SPField class or a derived class, that is, your custom field type, using any of the following methods:

- ❏ Through a form control
- ❏ Through the user interface
- ❏ Programmatically through the object model

As noted in the SDK, it is possible for users to update the data in a field that does not invoke the GetValidatedString method and therefore, any data validation logic contained in the method. This includes using unmanaged code or web service methods that do not invoke the SPListItem object to update the field data. For example, when a user updates list item data by using the datasheet view, the list items are updated without invoking the GetValidatedString method. It is very important that you remain aware of this and that you test your custom field type in all of the scenarios in which you envision it being used.

Your custom field type class can also use the GetValidatedString method to return string error messages to the calling application or form, allowing you to provide graceful display and handling of any data validation errors that may occur. End users like this type of behavior, so it's probably a good idea to take advantage of this feature. This code may appear in the body of the GetValidatedString function to return an error message that is stored in one of the field properties should the value of the field not be in the correct format.

```
throw new SPFieldValidationException
{
  GetCustomProperty("ExceptionMessage").ToString());
}
```

The SDK states that your field type should include validation logic that requires a specified value for the field, if the field is defined as required on a list. If you do not include such logic, users can submit the new or edit form without setting the field value. The Required property specifies whether a field is required.

Custom Field Type Definitions

Now that you have a good understanding of the code required for a custom field type as well as an understanding of the options available to you when creating your custom field types, let's discuss the contents of the field type definition file, the other required component for SharePoint to even be aware of all of the code you have written to support your custom field type. The SDK states that a field type definition file is an XML file that contains the following information.

❑   The strong-named assembly (with version number and public key) and class name for the field type

❑   The parent class of the field type class

❑   Display name and description of the field type

❑   Optionally, the schema for the field type properties, and rendering patterns for the field in the user interface

Field type definitions should be placed into an XML file named with the `fldtypes*.xml` format and placed in the same location as the out-of-the-box field type definition file (`[WSS]\TEMPLATE\XML\ FLDTYPES.XML`). The out-of-the-box field type definition file, `FLDTYPES.XML`, should not be modified, since it could be modified with a future service pack, thereby removing any customizations you may have made (even though you shouldn't have). When creating your field type definitions, we encourage you to look at this file for guidance because the built-in field types are defined here and will provide you with most, if not all, of the information, you will need to define yours. A field type definition file can contain definitions for multiple field types, although when creating your own, it is recommended that you place one per file. By having a separate file for each custom field type, many developers can be working on their own field type definitions simultaneously, if needed. Also, it is much clearer to a new team member what a file named `fldtypes_ssn.xml` is as opposed to a file named `fldtypes_ custom.xml`.

The outermost element in a field type definition is the `FieldTypes` element. It represents a collection of field types. The `FieldType` element represents a single field type definition. A `FieldType` element may contain multiple `Field` elements, each representing an attribute of a field type. It may also contain a `PropertySchema` element that represents the schema of the field type properties as well as up to two `RenderPattern` elements (`DisplayPattern` and/or `HeaderPattern`) that define the HTML and script that WSS v3 will use to render the field type in the user interface.

The `Field` element contains a single required attribute, `Name`, that represents the name of the specific aspect or property of the field type, which the `Field` element represents. The following table, from the SDK, summarizes the `Field` elements available for a given `FieldType`.

Value	Description
TypeName	Required `String`. Represents the name of the field type. `TypeName` should be a fixed, nonlocalizable string.
ParentType	Required `String`. Represents the name of the type from which the field class is derived.

Continued

129

Value	Description
TypeShortDescription	Required `String`. Represents the short description of the field type that is displayed in the user interface. `TypeShortDescription` should be a localizable string.
UserCreatable	Required `Boolean`. `TRUE` to enable users to add fields of this field type to lists. `FALSE` to allow use of the field type in list schemas, but to hide the field type from users.
FieldTypeClass	Required `String`. Represents the strong name of the field type class library. `FieldTypeClass` includes the class name and assembly name with `Version`, `Culture`, and `PublicKeyToken`.
ShowOnListAuthoringPages	Optional `Boolean`. The default is `TRUE`. Represents whether this field type is displayed for inclusion on lists. If set to `TRUE`, displays this field type on list authoring pages so that users can include the field type on their lists.
ShowOnDocumentLibrary-AuthoringPages	Optional `Boolean`. The default is `TRUE`. Represents whether this field type is displayed for inclusion in document libraries. If set to `TRUE`, displays this field type on document library authoring pages so that users can include the field type in their document libraries.
ShowOnSurveyAuthoringPages	Optional `Boolean`. The default is `TRUE`. Represents whether this field type is displayed for inclusion on surveys. If set to `TRUE`, displays this field type on survey authoring pages so that users can include the field type in their surveys.
ShowOnColumnTemplate-AuthoringPages	Optional `Boolean`. The default is `TRUE`. Represents whether this field type should be displayed as a column template field type. If set to `TRUE`, displays this field type on column template authoring pages so that users can select to create a column template of this field type.
AllowBaseTypeRendering	Optional `Boolean`. The default is `FALSE`. Represents whether a client application renders the field as its base type, if the client application cannot determine how to properly render the custom field type. If set to `TRUE`, and the client application cannot properly render the custom field type, the client application renders the field as the default Windows SharePoint Services parent field type from which it inherits. If this is set to `TRUE` for a field type, then in the field schema for a field of this field type, the Field element must include a `BaseRenderingType` attribute that specifies the default Windows SharePoint Services parent field type from which the field inherits.

The `PropertySchema` element represents the schema of the field type properties. The `PropertySchema` element contains a `Fields` element, which in turn contains a `Field` element for each field type property you want to define. You can use standard Collaborative Application Markup Language (CAML) within each `Field` element. If you define the field type properties in the `PropertySchema` element, the framework will render those properties based on that schema.

The rendering of our field type properties can also be defined using a field editor user control. By using the `PropertySchema` element to render your field properties, you are limited to the rendering options available using CAML and you will not be able to specify custom processing or validation handling of your field properties. Best practice dictates that you use this process for simple field type properties that do not require complicated processing or validation and to use a field editor control for field properties that require code to handle complicated property settings and interface rendering. The details of implementing field editor controls are beyond the scope of this book but, as always, are described in detail in the SDK. The two key points to implementing a field editor control are to inherit from the `UserControl` class (or a class derived from it), and implementing the `IFieldEditor` interface. This is how you might define a simple text property using a `PropertySchema` element within a field type definition.

```xml
<PropertySchema>
  <Fields>
    <Field
      Name="ExceptionMessage"
      DisplayName="Exception Message"
      MaxLength="255"
      DisplaySize="25"
      Type="Text">
      <Default>Invalid Social Security Number Format</Default>
    </Field>
  </Fields>
</PropertySchema>
```

The `RenderPattern` element defines the HTML and script that WSS v3 uses to render the field type in the user interface. It contains a single required attribute, `Name`, that may contain one of two possible values, `DisplayPattern` or `HeaderPattern`. These are the two possible render patterns that can be defined in this file. The patterns for rendering the field type on a New or Edit page are set through the use of form controls. If a particular render pattern in not specified for your custom field type, the field type will inherit the render pattern of its parent.

Deploying Custom Field Types

Custom field types are always deployed to an entire server farm. The WSS v3 Solution Framework should be used to deploy your custom field type and is discussed later in this chapter. At a high level, the steps required to manually deploy a custom field type include the following. They are looked at in greater detail in the following section.

❑ The field type class must be deployed as a strong-named assembly to the Global Assembly Cache (GAC).

❑ The field type definition XML file must be deployed to the same location as `fldtypes.xml`. That location is `[WSS]\TEMPLATE\XML\`. Each field type definition should be included in a file named `fldtypes*.xml`.

❑ If you have specified a custom field editor user control for the field type, it must be deployed to `[WSS]\TEMPLATE\CONTROLTEMPLATES`.

Creating a Custom Field Type

The following example demonstrates how to create a custom field type to support the entry and validation of a Social Security number. The functionality that exists after you complete your custom field type is such that when a list item is created or updated, if the value entered in a text box does not match the format of a Social Security number specified through the use of a regular expression, the list item will not be saved to the content database and you are notified with a friendly error message. Once created and deployed, your custom field type can be used like any of the built-in field types: as a site column, as well as in content types, document libraries and lists.

Create a Custom Field Type class

The following steps teach you how to create a custom field type class:

1. Create a new project by clicking Project under the New option on the File menu.

2. Under Project types, select the Class Library template under Windows in the language of your choice.

3. In the Location text box, browse to `C:\Documents and Settings\Administrator\My Documents\Visual Studio 2005\projects`, and click `Open`.

4. Uncheck the Create directory for solution check box.

5. Give your Custom Field Type project a meaningful name such as **CustomFieldType**, and click OK.

6. Add a reference to **System.Web**.

7. Add a reference to **Microsoft.SharePoint**. It is assumed that your development environment includes an installation of WSS. This particular assembly is listed as Windows SharePoint Services and is near the bottom of the list.

8. Delete the `Class1.cs` file.

9. Add a new class file, naming it **SocialSecurityNumber.cs**.

10. Add a public modifier to the `SocialSecurityNumber` class.

> Although the last step may not be necessary if the public modifier is, in fact, already there, it is important to confirm that the class you created is indeed public. If the class file is created differently for some reason, and this can happen depending on your environment, the modifier may not be added. In this case, it takes on the default value, which is protected. When this happens, the class will not be visible outside of the assembly, rendering it unusable by WSS.

11. Add `using` statements for both the `Microsoft.SharePoint` and `System.Text.RegularExpressions` namespaces.

12. Edit the class declaration to inherit from `SPFieldText`.

```
public class SocialSecurityNumber : SPFieldText
{
}
```

13. Implement the constructors of the `SPFieldText` base class.

```
public SocialSecurityNumber(SPFieldCollection fields,
   string fieldName)
   : base(fields, fieldName)
   {
   }

public SocialSecurityNumber(SPFieldCollection fields,
   string typeName,
   string displayName)
   : base(fields, typeName, displayName)
   {
   }
```

The project should compile at this point.

Sign the Assembly

Custom field type assemblies must be deployed to the Global Assembly Cache (GAC), so be sure to sign the assembly prior to building it. The following steps guide you through the process of signing your assembly.

1. Right-click on the project node, and select Properties from the context menu.

2. Click the Signing tab.

3. Check the Sign the assembly check box.

4. Select <New…> from the "Choose a strong name key file" drop-down list.

5. Enter **CustomFieldType** in the Key file name text box.

6. Uncheck the Protect my key file with a password check box.

7. Click OK.

8. Save your changes and build the project.

You informed the WSS v3 framework of your custom Site Definition earlier in this chapter; you must also inform it in a similar fashion of your custom field type. To do this, create an XML file prefixed with `fldtypes` and place it in the `[WSS]\TEMPLATE\XML` directory. The following steps guide you through this process.

Create a Field Type Definition

Now you create a field type definition.

1. Add an XML file to your project, and name it `fldtypes_SocialSecurityNumber.xml`.

2. Add the required `FieldType` element to make WSS v3 aware of your new custom field type. The resulting file should resemble the following code snippet:

```
<?xml version="1.0" encoding="utf-8" ?>
<FieldTypes>
  <FieldType>
```

```
      <Field Name="TypeName">SocialSecurityNumber</Field>
      <Field Name="ParentType">Text</Field>
      <Field Name="TypeDisplayName">Social Security Number</Field>
      <Field Name="TypeShortDescription">Social Security Number (123-45-6789)</Field>
      <Field Name="UserCreatable">TRUE</Field>
      <Field Name="ShowInListCreate">TRUE</Field>
      <Field Name="ShowInSurveyCreate">TRUE</Field>
      <Field Name="ShowInDocumentLibraryCreate">TRUE</Field>
      <Field Name="ShowInColumnTemplateCreate">TRUE</Field>
      <Field Name="Sortable">TRUE</Field>
      <Field Name="Filterable">TRUE</Field>
      <Field Name="FieldTypeClass">
        CustomFieldType.SocialSecurityNumber,
        CustomFieldType,
        Version=1.0.0.0,
        Culture=neutral,
        PublicKeyToken=77d0bef6f861f263
      </Field>
      <Field Name="SQLType">nvarchar</Field>
      <PropertySchema>
        <Fields>
          <Field Name="ExceptionMessage"
            DisplayName="Exception Message"
            MaxLength="255"
            DisplaySize="25"
            Type="Text">
            <Default>Invalid Social Security Number Format</Default>
          </Field>
        </Fields>
      </PropertySchema>
    </FieldType>
  </FieldTypes>
```

The public key token in the above code must match exactly the public key token of your compiled assembly.

Extract the Public Key

The following steps outline the process required to extract the public key token from the compiled assembly.

1. Open a Visual Studio 2005 Command Prompt window by clicking on Start ⇨ Programs ⇨ Microsoft Visual Studio 2005 ⇨ Visual Studio Tools ⇨ Visual Studio 2005 Command Prompt.

2. Type **sn -T <assembly>** where <assembly> is the complete path to the Field Type's assembly within your project. If this path contains spaces, place it within double quotation marks. The command window should look similar to Figure 4-10.

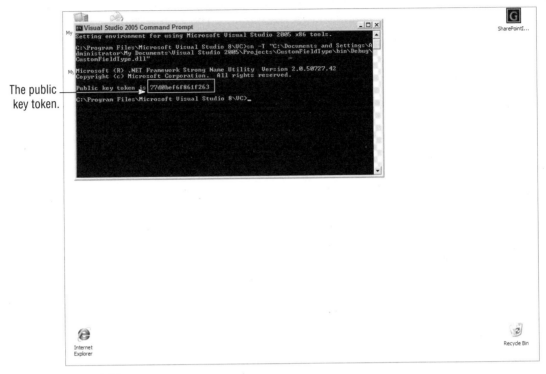

The public key token.

Figure 4-10

Before you dive into the implementation of the custom field class, it is worth noting that an emerging best practice when developing WSS v3 components is to build the component's frame, deploy it into development, and then add and test your code in an iterative fashion until you are satisfied with the result. This will reduce the time you spend debugging your deployment steps and allow you to concentrate more on the implementation of your custom business rules and other logic. Ideally, your custom field type should be deployed via a WSS v3 Solution, which is discussed later in this chapter. For the time being, you want to automate the deployment of your custom field type assembly to the Global Assembly Cache (GAC) and your `fldtypes_SocialSecurityNumber.xml` file to the correct location in your development environment's file system so that you can continue to work on it and more importantly view your changes as you go.

Automate Deployment

It's time to automate deployment, using the following steps:

1. Right-click on the project node, and select Properties from the context menu.

2. Click the Build Events tab.

3. Enter the following command in the "Post-build event command line" text box to copy the `FLDTYPES_SocialSecurityNumber.XML` file to the correct location:

```
xcopy ..\..\FLDTYPES_SocialSecurityNumber.XML "C:\Program Files\Common
Files\Microsoft Shared\web server extensions\12\TEMPLATE\XML\" /y
```

4. Enter the following command in the "Post-build event command line" text box to copy the compiled assembly to the GAC:

```
"C:\Program Files\Microsoft Visual Studio 8\SDK\v2.0\Bin\GacUtil.exe" /nologo /i
"$(TargetPath)" /f
```

5. Enter the following command in the "Post-build event command line" text box to recycle the application pool so that your changes will immediately be visible. Be sure to replace *MyApplicationPool* with the correct name of your application pool.

```
C:\WINDOWS\system32\cscript.exe C:\WINDOWS\system32\iisapp.vbs /a
"MyApplicationPool" /r
```

6. Save your changes and build the project.

At this point, you should be able to add your custom field to a list. Figure 4-11 illustrates what you will see at this point when adding your custom field to a Tasks list called Tasks.

There is your custom field type, in all its glory.

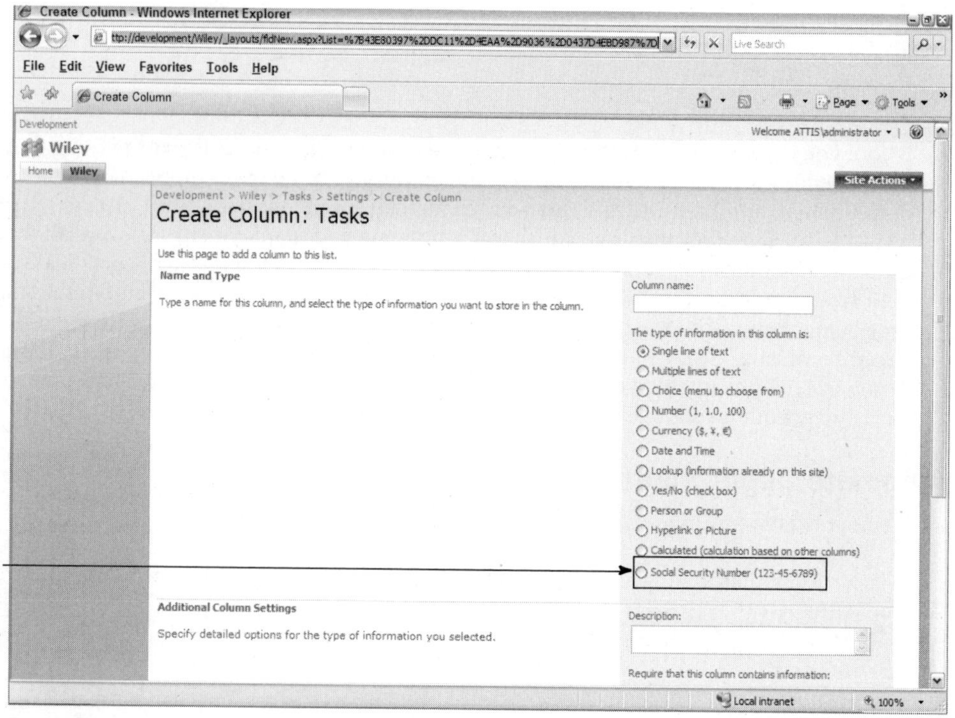

Figure 4-11

The SDK states that you must be aware that a custom field class does not inherit the field type property renderings specified in its parent class. For example, if you derive a custom field type from the SPFieldText *class, your new custom field type does not inherit the rendering information for any of the field properties of* SPFieldText, *such as* MaxLength. *To render any of the parent class's field type properties, you must specify your own renderings, using a field editor user control.*

Now that the framework for your custom field type is in place, and it has been successfully deployed, you can add the additional business rules and logic to the code so that it will actually do what it is supposed to do, which is to accept and validate a Social Security number. At this point, it is simply a SPFieldText column without any of the additional field rendering properties that you do not get through inheritance, as noted above.

Implement Custom Field Type Functionality

You will need to add functionality to your custom field type. To do so, follow the instructions here:

1. Override the GetValidatedString method by adding the following code to your custom field type class:

```
public override string GetValidatedString(object value)
{
    string _SSN = value.ToString();

    // only validate if a value was entered
    if (_SSN.Length > 0)
    {
        // Create a regular expression for a valid SSN
        Regex _Regex = new Regex(
          @"^\d{3}-\d{2}-\d{4}$",
          RegexOptions.IgnoreCase);

        // if the value entered does not match the Regex,
        // present the user with the custom exception message
        // supplied by one of the custom field properties
        if (!_Regex.IsMatch(_SSN))
        {
            throw new SPFieldValidationException(
              GetCustomProperty("ExceptionMessage").ToString());
        }
        else
        {
            return _SSN;
        }
    }
    else
    {
        return _SSN;
    }
}
```

2. Build the project.

You should now be able to add only list items whose value in the custom field matches that of your built-in Regex for a Social Security number. Perhaps a more robust solution would be to create a custom field type that has a custom property that is itself a regular expression string and have the GetValidatedString evaluate the match based on that custom property. You can try that on your own if you wish.

As you can see, custom field types can be very powerful and flexible. Although this example did not explore the rendering options at length, you should have a good enough idea of what is possible to enable you to build your own custom field types that solve your very own complex business problems. The extensibility of the platform has been provided for exactly that purpose.

Features

Features could be said to be the most ground-breaking addition to this version of WSS. A SharePoint *Feature* is a collection of SharePoint elements that can help a user accomplish a particular goal or task. Features can also be described as logical groups of elements that together serve a common purpose. How many times have you had a need to add a chunk of functionality to an existing server farm, web application, Site Collection, or site, such as an event handler, custom navigation, or maybe even a set of lists or document libraries all at once? An example is a set of lists and libraries combined with workflow and custom navigation that contain the functionality required to enable a certain business process to function within SharePoint. Features make it possible to activate or deactivate functionality in the course of a deployment, and administrators can easily transform the template or definition of a site simply by toggling a particular Feature on or off in the user interface. As noted in the SDK, Features provide the following capabilities:

❑ Scoping semantics for determining where custom code runs

❑ Pluggable behavior for installing or uninstalling Features within a deployment

❑ Pluggable behavior for activating or deactivating Features at a given scope

❑ A scoped property bag for storing data required by a Feature within its scope

❑ The basis of a unified framework for distributed deployment of WSS v3 solutions

A Feature is implemented by adding a subfolder containing a Feature definition file in the following folder ([WSS]\TEMPLATE\FEATURES). If you were to take a look at this folder after performing a default installation of Office SharePoint Server, you would see 137 Features installed with the product. It is very apparent that SharePoint itself leverages Features throughout its own implementation. Each Feature subfolder must include a Feature.xml file that defines the base properties of the Feature and lists the element manifests associated with it, which are XML files containing additional information about the functionality included in the Feature, along with any other supporting files that the Feature may require in order to function. After a Feature folder is created, you can install, activate, deactivate, and uninstall the Feature using the stsadm.exe command-line tool or through the object model. Features can also be activated and deactivated through the user interface.

When you install a Feature you make its definition known to all front-end web servers across the entire server farm, meaning the area to which the Feature is scoped now displays the Feature in its list of available Features to activate. When you activate a Feature, you make it available at the scope defined within the Feature definition.

The Feature element is used in `Feature.xml` to define a Feature and to inform SharePoint of the location of all the Feature's supporting files. Items that were previously contained within an extremely large Site Definition file have now been broken out as separate elements within various Features. An element can be described as an atomic unit of functionality within a Feature. A Feature may include any number of elements. Examples of elements, as previously mentioned, may include a custom menu item or an event handler among others. Each element on its own may not be very useful, but a combination of several elements together could make up a very powerful and versatile solution.

Feature Definition File

In a Feature definition file, the Feature element defines a Feature and specifies the location of assemblies, files, dependencies, or properties that support the Feature. `Feature.xml` contains a top-level Feature element, which in turn has three child elements, `ActivationDependencies`, `ElementManifests`, and `Properties`. The Feature element defines a Feature to activate or deactivate at a specified scope using the attributes in the following table, as noted in the SDK.

Attribute	Description
ActivateOnDefault	Optional `Boolean`. TRUE if the Feature is activated by default during installation or when a web application is created; FALSE if the Feature is not activated. This attribute equals TRUE by default. The `ActivateOnDefault` attribute does not apply to site collection (Site) or web site (Web) scoped Features.
AlwaysForceInstall	Optional `Boolean`. TRUE if the Feature is installed by force during installation even if the Feature is already installed. For example, if set to TRUE, Feature installation callouts will always fire anytime a user tries to install the Feature (even if it is already installed) by using either the `scanforfeatures` or `installfeature` command-line operation. This attribute equals FALSE by default. The `AlwaysForceInstall` attribute affects Features of all scopes.
AutoActivateInCentralAdmin	Optional `Boolean`. TRUE if the Feature is activated by default in the Administrative web site, site collection, or web application. This attribute equals FALSE by default. The `AutoActivateInCentralAdmin` attribute does not apply to Farm-scoped Features.
Creator	Optional `Text`.

Continued

Attribute	Description
DefaultResourceFile	Optional Text. Indicates a common resource file for retrieving Feature XML resources. If you specify a resource in the file, WSS v3 looks by default in \12\TEMPLATE\FEATURES\ FeatureName\Resources\Resources.<Culture>.resx. However, if you want to provide a shared core resource file for all the Features in your application, you can specify an alternate file through which to access resources by using DefaultResourceFile. For example, if you set DefaultResourceFile="MyFile", WSS v3 looks in \12\ Resources\MyFile.<Culture>.resx to retrieve localized resources for your Feature.
Description	Optional String. Returns a longer representation of what the Feature does.
Hidden	Optional Boolean. This attribute equals FALSE by default.
Id	Required Text. Contains the globally unique identifier (GUID) for the Feature.
ImageUrl	Optional Text. Contains the site-relative URL for an image to use to represent the feature in the user interface (UI).
ImageUrlAltText	Optional Text. Contains the alternate text for the image that represents the feature.
ReceiverAssembly	Optional Text. If set along with ReceiverClass, specifies the strong name of the signed assembly located in the Global Assembly Cache from which to load a receiver to handle Feature events.
ReceiverClass	Optional Text. If set along with ReceiverAssembly, specifies the class that implements the Feature event processor.
RequireResources	Optional Boolean. TRUE to specify that WSS v3 check whether resources exist for the Feature by verifying that the standard "sentinel" resource for the Feature is present for a particular culture. The resource file is named according to the format <FeatureDir>\Resources\Resources.xx-xx.resx, where xx-xx is the culture. The RequireResources attribute allows you to constrict the visibility of certain Features depending on whether resources exist in a particular language for the Feature.
Scope	Required Text. Can contain one of the following values: Farm (farm), WebApplication (web application), Site (site collection), Web (web site).

Attribute	Description
Scope	Required Text. Can contain one of the following values: Farm (farm), WebApplication (web application), Site (site collection), Web (web site).
SolutionId	Optional Text. Specifies the solution to which the Feature belongs.
Title	Optional Text. Returns the title of the Feature. Limited to 255 characters.
Version	Optional Text. Specifies a System.Version-compliant representation of the version of a Feature. This can be up to four numbers delimited by decimals that represent a version.

The ActivationDependencies element is used to specify a list of Features on which the activation of the current Feature depends. If the Feature on which the current Feature depends is hidden and inactive, it is activated automatically. Such a hidden Feature is deactivated when the last Feature depending on it is deactivated. If the Feature is visible, it is not activated automatically. A hidden Feature on its own cannot have any activation dependencies.

Here is an example of a very basic Feature definition. Note that the ElementManifests element is not required. All that is required is a Scope and an ID. A title is useful and recommended, but if not supplied, the system will generate one.

```
<Feature Title="My Feature"
  Scope="Web"
  Id="24A46E4D-7D86-47c4-A139-06F8B3E4B5AD"
  xmlns="http://schemas.microsoft.com/sharepoint/">
  <ElementManifests>
    <ElementManifest Location="Elements.xml" />
  </ElementManifests>
</Feature>
```

The ElementManifests element contains references to element manifests and element files that contain definitions for the Feature's elements.

The Properties element contains a list of the default values for Feature properties.

Feature Scope

A Feature is activated for a single scope, including farm (see Figure 4-12), web application (see Figure 4-13), site collection (see Figure 4-14) and site (see Figure 4-15). The Feature scope is set by the Scope attribute of the Feature element.

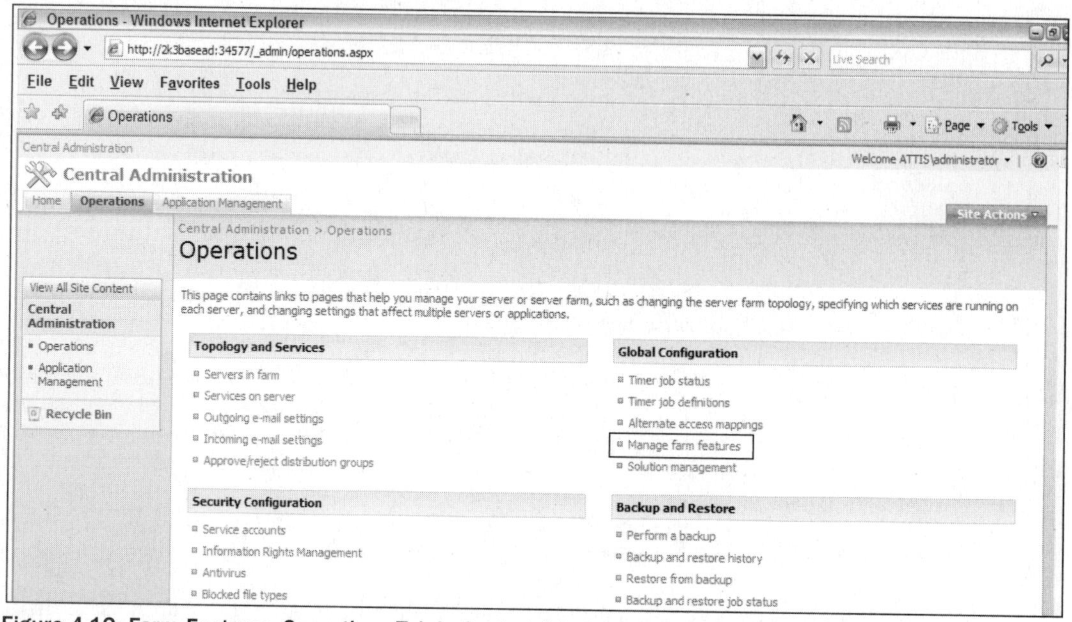

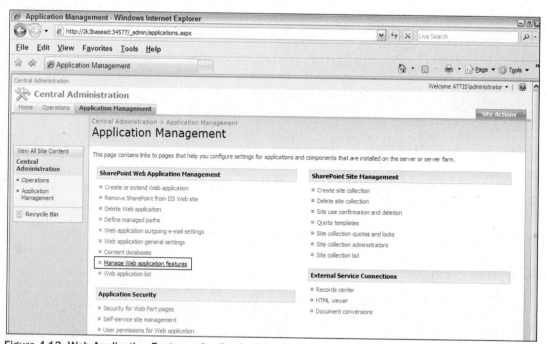

Figure 4-12: Farm Features, Operations Tab in Central Administration.

Figure 4-13: Web Application Features, Application Management Tab in Central Administration.

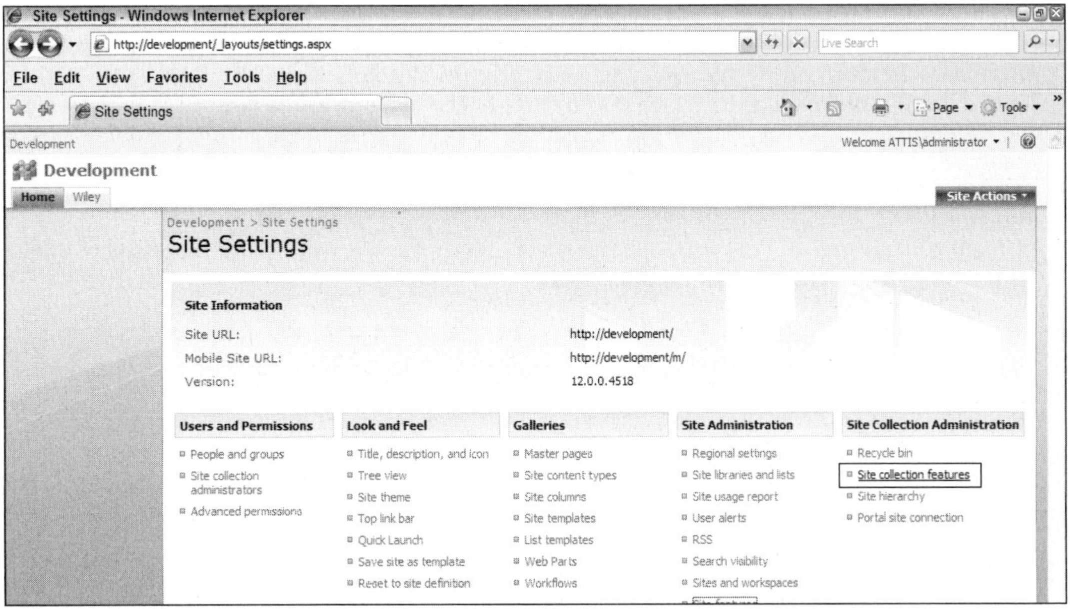

Figure 4-14: Site Collection Features, Site Setting of Top-Level Site.

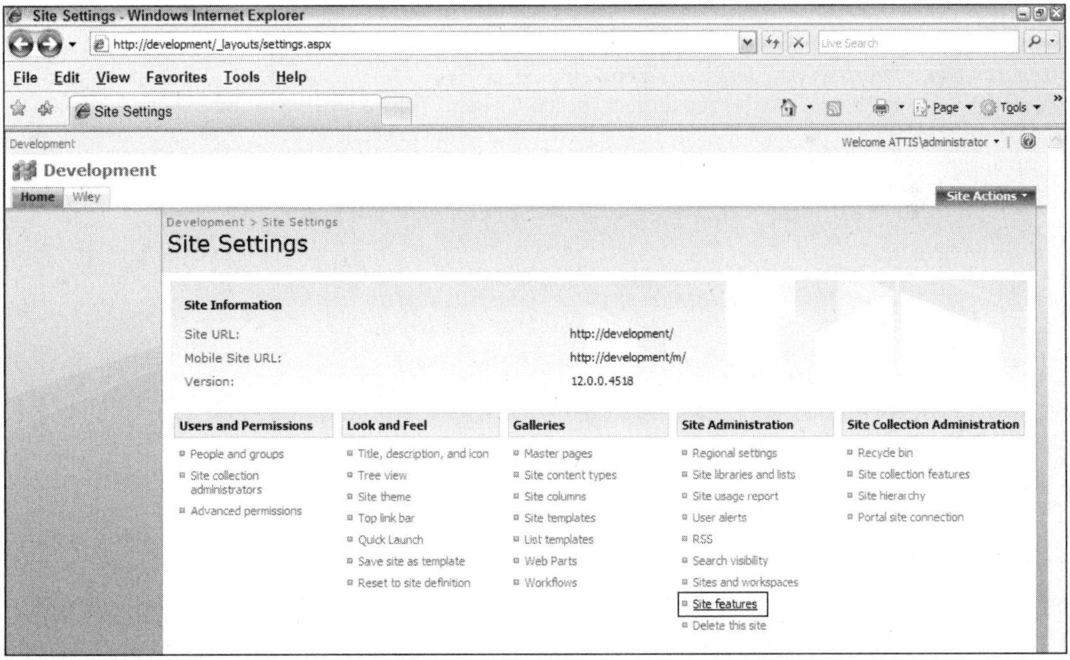

Figure 4-15: Site Features, Site Settings of Site.

While a site Feature is one that you scope at the individual site level, a site collection Feature contains items that apply to the entire site collection (for example, content types that are shared across the site collection), as well as items that can be activated on a per site basis. You also might deploy a custom Forms Based Authentication login screen that you would want to be available to all sites in a site collection, for example. Elements that can have either site collection or site scope include list definitions (templates and instances), modules (file sets), and item content type behaviors (per item custom menu options and per item events).

A Feature that is scoped at the web application level can contain elements for web application assemblies as well as web application administrative links.

A Feature that is scoped to the farm level can contain elements that can function anywhere in a SharePoint farm and can contain links to globally available pages, such as those in the _layouts folder.

Two types of resources can be implemented in Features to support files.

❑ Local resources stored in a subdirectory within the Features folder in the \Template\Features directory.

❑ Shared application Feature and Site Definition resources that are stored in \web server extensions \12\Resources and are designed to be used across Features and Site Definitions.

Activation Dependencies and Scope

A Feature activation dependency can be defined as a requirement in the relationship between two Features. You can define activation dependencies either for Features of the same scope or for Features across different scopes. A cross-scope activation dependency exists when a Feature at a particular scope has a dependency on another Feature that is at a different scope. Generally speaking, activation dependencies are used for either Feature groupings, as is demonstrated in the following code with the TeamCollab Feature, or to guarantee particular resources for a Feature.

```
<?xml version="1.0" encoding="utf-8"?>
<Feature
  Id="00BFEA71-4EA5-48D4-A4AD-7EA5C011ABE5"
  Title="$Resources:core,teamcollabFeatureTitle;"
  Description="$Resources:core,teamcollabFeatureDesc;"
  ImageUrl="WssTeamCollaborationFeature.gif"
  ImageUrlAltText=""
  Scope="Web"
  DefaultResourceFile="core"
  xmlns="http://schemas.microsoft.com/sharepoint/">
  <ActivationDependencies>
    <ActivationDependency FeatureId="00BFEA71-D1CE-42de-9C63-A44004CE0104"/>
    <!-- AnnouncementsList Feature -->
    <ActivationDependency FeatureId="00BFEA71-7E6D-4186-9BA8-C047AC750105"/>
    <!-- ContactsList Feature -->
    <ActivationDependency FeatureId="00BFEA71-DE22-43B2-A848-C05709900100"/>
    <!-- CustomList Feature -->
    <ActivationDependency FeatureId="00BFEA71-F381-423D-B9D1-DA7A54C50110"/>
    <!-- DataSourceLibrary Feature -->
    <ActivationDependency FeatureId="00BFEA71-6A49-43FA-B535-D15C05500108"/>
```

```
        <!-- DiscussionsList Feature -->
        <ActivationDependency FeatureId="00BFEA71-E717-4E80-AA17-D0C71B360101"/>
        <!-- DocumentLibrary Feature -->
        <ActivationDependency FeatureId="00BFEA71-EC85-4903-972D-EBE475780106"/>
        <!-- EventsList Feature -->
        <ActivationDependency FeatureId="00BFEA71-513D-4CA0-96C2-6A47775C0119"/>
        <!-- GanttTasksList Feature -->
        <ActivationDependency FeatureId="00BFEA71-3A1D-41D3-A0EE-651D11570120"/>
        <!-- GridList Feature -->
        <ActivationDependency FeatureId="00BFEA71-5932-4F9C-AD71-1557E5751100"/>
        <!-- IssuesList Feature -->
        <ActivationDependency FeatureId="00BFEA71-2062-426C-90BF-714C59600103"/>
        <!-- LinksList Feature -->
        <ActivationDependency FeatureId="00BFEA71-F600-43F6-A895-40C0DE7B0117"/>
        <!-- NoCodeWorkflowLibrary Feature -->
        <ActivationDependency FeatureId="00BFEA71-52D4-45B3-B544-B1C71B620109"/>
        <!-- PictureLibrary Feature -->
        <ActivationDependency FeatureId="00BFEA71-EB8A-40B1-80C7-506BE7590102"/>
        <!-- SurveysList Feature -->
        <ActivationDependency FeatureId="00BFEA71-A83E-497E-9BA0-7A5C597D0107"/>
        <!-- TasksList Feature -->
        <ActivationDependency FeatureId="00BFEA71-C796-4402-9F2F-0EB9A6E71B18"/>
        <!-- WebPageLibrary Feature -->
        <ActivationDependency FeatureId="00BFEA71-2D77-4A75-9FCA-76516689E21A"/>
        <!-- WorkflowProcessLibrary Feature -->
        <ActivationDependency FeatureId="00BFEA71-4EA5-48D4-A4AD-305CF7030140"/>
        <!-- WorkflowHistoryList Feature -->
        <ActivationDependency FeatureId="00BFEA71-1E1D-4562-B56A-F05371BB0115"/>
        <!-- XmlFormLibrary Feature -->
    </ActivationDependencies>
</Feature>
```

Recalling the Site Definition you created earlier in this chapter; you may have observed that it used a number of Features. Upon closer inspection, you would have noticed that the `TeamCollab` Feature defined in the Site Definition's `Onet.xml` file was actually a wrapper Feature that included a number of dependent Features, noted prior.

❑ A `BasicWebParts` Feature

❑ A Three-state Workflow Feature

❑ A `TeamCollab` Feature

❑ A `MobilityRedirect` Feature

The concept of Features containing Features and activation dependencies is immediately clear once you have a basic understanding of how Features work. Start from the most widely scoped Features and work your way down to the most narrowly scoped features in the `Onet.xml` file of the custom Site Definition.

The `MobilityRedirect` Feature is an example of a hidden feature that is scoped to the site level. It is installed to allow the site to be rendered seamlessly by mobile devices. If you did not need this Feature in the custom Site Definition you could have easily removed this Feature and not installed it. It is hidden to keep an administrator from inadvertently deactivating it.

The `TeamCollab` Feature is an example of a Feature that is not hidden, is scoped to the site level, and is activated in the `Onet.xml` of your custom Site Definition. By inspecting the `Feature.xml` file for the `TeamCollab` Feature, you can see that it contains 19 `ActivationDependency` elements. The `TeamCollab` Feature is essentially a wrapper feature that subsequently activates the following Features when it is itself activated.

- ❏ `AnnouncementsList` Feature
- ❏ `ContactsList` Feature
- ❏ `CustomList` Feature
- ❏ `DataSourceLibrary` Feature
- ❏ `DiscussionsList` Feature
- ❏ `DocumentLibrary` Feature
- ❏ `EventsList` Feature
- ❏ `GanttTasksList` Feature
- ❏ `GridList` Feature
- ❏ `IssuesList` Feature
- ❏ `LinksList` Feature
- ❏ `NoCodeWorkflowLibrary` Feature
- ❏ `PictureLibrary` Feature
- ❏ `SurveysList` Feature
- ❏ `TasksList` Feature
- ❏ `WebPageLibrary` Feature
- ❏ `WorkflowProcessLibrary` Feature
- ❏ `WorkflowHistoryList` Feature
- ❏ `XmlFormLibrary` Feature

As you can see, the Feature framework has completely encapsulated many of the items that used to be included in individual Site Definitions in the previous version of WSS. There is no longer a need to define a list or document library in a Site Definition, simply activate the `List Template` Feature (assuming that it is installed).

The `BasicWebParts` Feature is an example of a hidden Feature that is scoped to the site collection level. It makes the following familiar Web Parts available to an entire site collection and is activated in the `Onet.xml` of your custom Site Definition.

- ❏ Content Editor Web Part
- ❏ Page Viewer Web Part
- ❏ Image Web Part
- ❏ Site Users Web Part (`Members`)

❑   Form Web Part (`SimpleForm`)

❑   Relevant Documents Web Part (`UserDocs`)

❑   User Tasks Web Part

❑   XML Web Part

When creating activation dependencies there are certain rules you should keep in mind in order to avoid scenarios such as circular dependencies, performance limiting dependency chains, and so on. These rules, from the SDK, are grouped into three distinct categories: same-scope rules, cross-scope rules and general rules.

❑   Same-Scope Rules

    1. If a Feature is dependent on another Feature at the same scope, and the second Feature is not activated when the first one is activated, WSS v3 activates the second Feature.

    2. If a Feature is deactivated, WSS v3 deactivates a same-scope dependent hidden Feature when the last visible Feature that has an activation dependency on that hidden Feature is deactivated.

❑   Cross-Scope Rules

    1. Cross-scope activation dependencies are not supported if the Feature depended upon is at a more restrictive scope. For example, a site collection–scoped Feature cannot have an activation dependency on a web site–scoped Feature.

    2. Feature activation dependencies are not supported across scopes if the Feature that is depended upon is not visible. In other words, a web site–scoped feature cannot be dependent on a site collection–scoped Feature that is not visible in the user interface.

    3. If the Feature that is depended upon is not activated, activation of the depending Feature fails. For example, if a web site–scoped Feature depends on a site collection–scoped Feature that is not activated, provisioning of the web site Feature (or of a site definition that contains such a web site Feature) fails.

❑   General Rules

    1. Dependencies can work only one level deep. In other words, dependency chains are not supported. WSS v3 does not support more than one level in activation dependencies if the last Feature is visible; that is, if a visible Feature depends on a second visible Feature that, in turn, depends on a third visible Feature. However, WSS v3 does support more than one level in activation dependencies if a visible Feature depends on a second visible Feature that, in turn, depends on a hidden Feature.

    2. You can target an activation dependency against hidden or visible Features, but hidden Features cannot have activation dependencies. The Hidden attribute on the Feature element determines whether the Feature is displayed in the user interface.

    3. When more than one Feature has a dependency on a given Feature, keep in mind the danger of leaving one of the depending Features in a bad state. For example, assume that a visible, site collection–scoped Feature named Feature B depends on a hidden, site collection–scoped Feature named Feature A, and that a third visible, web site–scoped Feature named Feature C is also dependent on Feature A. Deactivating Feature B also deactivates Feature A, thus leaving Feature C in a bad state.

Feature Elements

As always, the best way to learn more about how Features are built is to look at the Features that are installed with the product. The following table from the SDK illustrates the various elements and their scoping options that you can include in your own hand-rolled custom Features.

Element	Scope	Description
Content Type	Site	Contains a schema definition you can reuse and apply to multiple list definitions.
Content Type Binding	Site	Content type binding enables you to provision a content type on a list defined in the Onet.xml schema. Lists defined in the Onet.xml schema cannot be modified directly.
Control	Farm, WebApplication, Site, Web	A delegate control contains a registration for a well-known control installed on a web page. This lets you replace existing controls, such as the WSS v3 search control, with another control.
Custom Action	Farm, WebApplication, Site, Web	You can define the following kinds of custom actions: ❑ Content type links for the content type settings page ❑ Drop-down menu actions for the drop-down menu that appears for an item ❑ Form toolbar buttons for New, Edit, or Display form toolbars ❑ Site Settings link for the Site Settings page
Custom Action Group	Farm, WebApplication, Site, Web	Defines a group of custom actions.
DocumentConverter	WebApplication	Contains the definition of a document converter. A document converter is a custom executable file that takes a document of one file type, and generates a copy of that file in another file type.
Feature/Site Template Association	Farm, WebApplication, Site	Binds a feature to a site definition or template so that created sites are provisioned with the feature.
Field	Site	Contains a field definition that can be reused among multiple lists.

Element	Scope	Description
Hide Custom Action	Farm, WebApplication, Site, Web	Hides a custom action that has been added through another custom action.
List Instance	Site, Web	Provisions a SharePoint site with a specific list of data.
List Template	Site, Web	Contains a list definition or template, which defines a list that can be provisioned in a SharePoint site.
Module	Site, Web	Contains a set of files with which to provision sites.
Receiver	Web	Contains an item event receiver registration.
Workflow	Site	Contains the definition for a workflow in a list.

The requirements for all of the preceding Feature elements vary, depending on the type of customization you are making. In most cases, a `Feature.xml` file contains a Feature element that uniquely identifies the Feature, specifies its scope, and points to an XML file whose top-level Elements element defines the elements composing the Feature. The following sections describe a selection of the above Feature element options in more detail. For details on all of the available Feature elements, consult the SDK by visiting `http://msdn2.microsoft.com/en-us/library/ms474383.aspx`. Alternatively, search the WSS SDK for "Element Types."

ListTemplate Element

A `ListTemplate` element defines a list definition in the `Schema.xml` file of a particular list type. A list template, once defined, can then be used to create instances of a list. The `Schema.xml` file for a list can be stored in a `ListTemplates` subdirectory of the Feature folder, or it can point to another directory. The meat and potatoes of list schemas are beyond the scope of this book, but if you are the curious type, take a look at the Features for each of the out-of-the-box lists because that is where their list schemas are now defined. Remember, they are no longer defined in the Site Definition `Onet.xml` but have been encapsulated into individual Features.

Imagine that your company has invested many hours in defining a list to use on a Team Site, perhaps for a development project site. This list may have many fields already defined that are required to be on every list instance when it is created. This particular Feature would most likely be scoped to a site collection so that content administrators of all sites in a site collection would be able to create this list simply by going to the Create page. As mentioned earlier, the team collaboration lists Feature is an example of a wrapper Feature that encapsulates many of the lists you see on the Create page. Many of these lists, on their own, are hidden `ListTemplate` Features. If you were to deactivate this Feature, you would see that you would not be able to create many of the lists normally included on the Create page.

List Instance Element

The `ListInstance` element defines the default data with which to provision a given list type. This element maps to the `List` element located within the `Configuration` element in `Onet.xml`, as discussed earlier in this chapter.

Perhaps your company does not want to burden its development project Team Site users with creating instances of certain predefined lists. They want to ensure that these lists are instantiated correctly, along with default data required that may be specific to each list instance. A list instance Feature could serve that purpose. By activating a list instance Feature, certain lists would be immediately created within a particular site, perhaps enabling standards to be better followed. This Feature becomes very valuable if you have a need to instantiate many lists at once, as this could take some time if done manually as well as be prone to user error.

Following is an example of a `List Instance` element that creates a Project Announcements list and adds it to the Quick Launch menu. Because this list instance is based on the existing announcements list that is installed with the product, you must reference that list using the `FeatureId` attribute as well as the `TemplateType` attribute. This list instance also defines a default item to place in the list.

```
<ListInstance
  Id="10002"
  Title="Project Announcements"
  FeatureId="00BFEA71-D1CE-42de-9C63-A44004CE0104"
  Description="All Project Announcements should be added to this list."
  TemplateType="104"
  Url="ProjectAnnouncements"
  OnQuickLaunch="TRUE">
  <Data>
    <Rows>
      <Row>
        <Field Name="Title">Welcome to the site!</Field>
      </Row>
    </Rows>
  </Data>
</ListInstance>
```

Custom Action Element

Custom actions can be used to include additional actions to menus of the user interface within WSS v3. They can define a new menu item in the administration menu, or perhaps a new link in the Site Actions drop-down menu. Custom actions can be added to a number of existing menus. To define a custom action for a particular menu, identify the menu by setting the `Location` attribute, and if needed, set the `GroupID` attribute to the specific location within that menu. The following table shows the available `Location` and `GroupId` values as defined in the WSS SDK.

Area	Location	GroupID
Display form toolbar	DisplayFormToolbar	n/a
Edit form toolbar	EditFormToolbar	n/a

Area	Location	GroupID
New form toolbar	`NewFormToolbar`	n/a
List view toolbar	`ViewToolbar`	n/a
Edit control block menu (per item)	`EditControlBlock`	n/a
New menu for list and document library view toolbars	`Microsoft.SharePoint.StandardMenu`	`NewMenu`
Actions menu for list and document library view toolbars	`Microsoft.SharePoint.StandardMenu`	`ActionsMenu`
Settings menu for list and document library view toolbars	`Microsoft.SharePoint.StandardMenu`	`SettingsMenu`
Upload documents menu for document libraries	`Microsoft.SharePoint.StandardMenu`	`UploadMenu`
Site Actions menu	`Microsoft.SharePoint.StandardMenu`	`SiteActions`
Site Settings Site Collection Administration links	`Microsoft.SharePoint.SiteSettings`	`SiteCollectionAdmin`
Site Settings Site Administration links	`Microsoft.SharePoint.SiteSettings`	`SiteAdministration`
Site Settings Galleries Links	`Microsoft.SharePoint.SiteSettings`	`Galleries`
Site Settings Look and Feel links	`Microsoft.SharePoint.SiteSettings`	`Customization`
Site Settings Users and Permissions links	`Microsoft.SharePoint.SiteSettings`	`UsersAndPermissions`
Site Actions menu for surveys	`Microsoft.SharePoint.StandardMenu`	`ActionsMenuForSurvey`
Site Settings links for surveys	`Microsoft.SharePoint.SiteSettings`	`SettingsMenuForSurvey`
Content Type Settings links	`Microsoft.SharePoint.ContentTypeSettings`	n/a

Continued

Area	Location	GroupID
Central Administration Operations page	`Microsoft.SharePoint .Administration.Operations`	n/a
Central Administration Application Management page	`Microsoft.SharePoint .Administration .ApplicationManagement`	n/a

In addition to specifying the `Location` and `GroupID` to have the custom action placed in the appropriate menu location, you also may need to specify the user permissions (Rights) required to perform the action or the placement (Sequence) of the custom action in relation to existing actions in the menu. The URL tokens in the following table are also available to you if needed when building a URL for your custom action:

Custom Action URL Token	Purpose
`~site`	Web site (`SPWeb`) relative link
`~sitecollection`	Site collection (`SPSite`) relative link
`{ItemId}`	Integer ID that represents the item within a list
`{ItemUrl}`	URL of the item being acted upon
`{ListId}`	GUID that represents the list
`{SiteUrl}`	URL of the web site (`SPWeb`)
`{RecurrenceId}`	Recurrence index

Additional Feature Features

There is a rich set of classes available in the object model that allows you to manipulate Features and their properties programmatically. The details on how to use these classes are beyond the scope of this book, but here is a list for reference:

- ❏ `Microsoft.SharePoint.SPFeature (SPFeatureCollection)`
- ❏ `Microsoft.SharePoint.SPFeatureProperty (SPFeaturePropertyCollection)`
- ❏ `Microsoft.SharePoint.SPFeatureScope`
- ❏ `Microsoft.SharePoint.Administration.SPFeatureDefinition (SPFeatureDefinitionCollection)`
- ❏ `Microsoft.SharePoint.SPFeatureDependency (SPFeatureDependencyCollection)`
- ❏ `Microsoft.SharePoint.Administration.SPElementDefinition (SPElementDefinitionCollection)`

The Feature framework also includes a set of classes for responding to Feature events. The following events are supported:

- ❏   `FeatureInstalled`
- ❏   `FeatureUninstalling`
- ❏   `FeatureActivated`
- ❏   `FeatureDeactivating`

Note that some of these events are post events, meaning that they fire after the respective behavior has been committed and the Feature definition is created in the collection of Feature definitions for the farm.

Installing and Activating Features

During development, Features can be installed and activated via the stsadm command-line administration tool. For production environments, deploying via a WSS v3 Solution, as discussed later in this chapter, is the recommended approach. The following table illustrates the `stsadm` commands used for Feature management. Regardless of the environment, a Feature must be installed and activated before it can be used. Features must be deactivated before uninstalling them unless they are `WebApplication`-scoped or `Farm`-scoped Features.

Feature stsadm Command	Description
`stsadm.exe -o installfeature`	`{-filename <relative path to Feature.xml> | -name <feature folder>}` `[-force]` `stsadm.exe -o uninstallfeature` `{-filename <relative path to Feature.xml> | -name <feature folder> | -id <feature Id>}` `[-force]`
`stsadm.exe -o activatefeature`	`{-filename <relative path to Feature.xml> | -name <feature folder> | -id <feature Id>}` `[-url <url>]` `[-force]`
`stsadm.exe -o deactivatefeature`	`{-filename <relative path to Feature.xml> | -name <feature folder> | -id <feature Id>}` `[-url <url>]` `[-force]`

Creating a Feature

The following example demonstrates how to create a Feature. Once created and installed, it can be activated and deactivated as needed within the scope specified in the `Feature.xml` file. You create two list instance Features as well as a custom action that provides a direct link to www.wiley.com from the Site Actions menu.

Create Feature.xml

Follow these steps to create a Feature:

1. Create a new project by clicking Project under the New option from the File menu.

2. Under Project types, select the Class Library template under Windows in the language of your choice.

3. In the Location text box, browse to `C:\Documents and Settings\Administrator\My Documents\Visual Studio 2005\projects` and click `Open`.

4. Uncheck the Create directory for solution check box.

5. Give your Feature project a meaningful name such as **WileyFeature**, and click OK.

6. Add a reference to **System.Web**.

7. Add a reference to **Microsoft.SharePoint**.

8. Delete the `Class1.cs` file.

9. Add a new `.xml` file to the root of the project by right-clicking the project node and selecting New Item from the Add context menu. Select the XML File template, name the file `Feature.xml`, and click Add.

10. Add the following code to your `Feature.xml` file to define your Feature. Be sure to give your Feature a unique GUID by using the Create Guid external tool on the Tools menu within Visual Studio. You will scope your Feature to Web so that it can be activated on a site-by-site basis.

```
<Feature Title="Wiley Feature"
  Scope="Web"
  Id="C4F991C4-4DA8-4af3-94C3-4F416EB76C0F"
  xmlns="http://schemas.microsoft.com/sharepoint/">
  <ElementManifests>
    <ElementManifest Location="Elements.xml" />
  </ElementManifests>
</Feature>
```

Create Elements.xml

Follow these steps to create an element:

1. Add a new `.xml` file to the root of the project by right-clicking the project node and selecting New Item from the Add context menu. Select the xml File template, name the file **Elements.xml** and click Add. Add the following code to your `Elements.xml` file to define the two `ListInstance` elements you want to include in your Feature.

```
<Elements xmlns="http://schemas.microsoft.com/sharepoint/">
  <ListInstance
    Id="10001"
    Title="Project Contacts"
    FeatureId="00BFEA71-7E6D-4186-9BA8-C047AC750105"
    Description="All Project Contacts should be added to this list."
    TemplateType="105"
    Url="ProjectContacts"
    OnQuickLaunch="TRUE">
    <Data>
      <Rows>
        <Row>
          <Field Name="Last Name">Gates</Field>
          <Field Name="First Name">Bill</Field>
        </Row>
        <Row>
          <Field Name="Last Name">Balmer</Field>
          <Field Name="First Name">Steve</Field>
        </Row>
      </Rows>
    </Data>
  </ListInstance>
  <ListInstance
    Id="10002"
    Title="Project Announcements"
    FeatureId="00BFEA71-D1CE-42de-9C63-A44004CE0104"
    Description="All Project Announcements should be added to this list."
    TemplateType="104"
    Url="ProjectAnnouncements"
    OnQuickLaunch="TRUE">
    <Data>
      <Rows>
        <Row>
          <Field Name="Title">Welcome to the site!</Field>
        </Row>
      </Rows>
    </Data>
  </ListInstance>
</Elements>
```

> Be sure to copy the above code exactly as it appears. The `FeatureId` for both the
> Contacts List instance and Announcements List instance must match the GUID of
> their respective Features if the list instance is being based off of an existing list (as
> they are in this particular case). If they do not, you won't be able to successfully acti-
> vate your Feature. It will however install. This particular requirement is very diffi-
> cult to troubleshoot, so pay very close attention.

*As an aside, take a closer look at the GUIDs for the out-of-the-box list template Features you are
using in this example. It is interesting to note that the last few characters in their respective GUIDs
(`Contacts List = 105`, `Anouncements List = 104`) match the list template ID of that
particular list in WSS v3.*

2. Add the following Custom Action Element to the Elements collection in your `Elements.xml` file.

```
<CustomAction
  Id="WileyLink"
  Title="Wiley.com"
  Description="Link directly to the Wiley Website"
  GroupId="SiteActions"
  Location="Microsoft.SharePoint.StandardMenu" >
  <UrlAction Url="http://www.wiley.com/" />
</CustomAction>
```

Deploy Feature

Follow these steps to put your Feature into action.

1. Enter the following command in the "Post-build event command line" text box to copy the `Feature.xml` file to the correct location:

```
xcopy ..\..\Feature.xml "C:\Program Files\Common Files\Microsoft Shared\web
server extensions\12\TEMPLATE\Features\WileyFeature\" /y
```

2. Enter the following command in the "Post-build event command line" text box to copy the `Elements.xml` file to the correct location.

```
xcopy ..\..\Elements.xml "C:\Program Files\Common Files\Microsoft Shared\web
server extensions\12\TEMPLATE\Features\WileyFeature\" /y
```

3. Save your changes and build the project.

Your Feature is now deployed to the appropriate location on the file system thanks to the post-build events you created above. SharePoint is not aware of the Feature, however, because it is not yet installed.

Install Feature

Installing the Feature can be done manually, as demonstrated in the following steps, or through a WSS v3 Solution. The next section returns to this example to demonstrate the use of a Solution to install a Feature, but for now, you will install the Feature manually. Then you will activate it and see the results!

1. Open a Visual Studio 2005 Command Prompt window by clicking on Start ➪ Programs ➪ Microsoft Visual Studio 2005 ➪ Visual Studio Tools ➪ Visual Studio 2005 Command Prompt.

2. Navigate to the bin directory of the 12 Hive by typing the following command, including the double quotation marks:

```
cd "C:\Program Files\Common Files\Microsoft Shared\web server
extensions\12\BIN"
```

3. Install your Feature by typing the following `stsadm` command:

```
stsadm -o installfeature -name WileyFeature
```

4. Activate your Feature by browsing to the Site Settings page of a site by clicking on Site Settings under Site Actions. Click on Site features under Site Administration. Click the Activate button next to your newly installed Feature.

5. Click on Home or the appropriate tab representing the current site's home page to return to the current site's home page.

Notice that you have two new links in the Quick Launch navigation, one for Project Contacts and one for Project Announcements (see Figure 4-16). If you mouse over one of the links, you will notice the URL in the status bar appears. The URL does not contain any spaces (%20) as was explicitly indicated in each of the list instance Feature elements defined earlier.

If you click on either of the two new list instances, you can see that our default items have also been added for you (see Figure 4-17). Clicking on Site Actions after activating your new Feature also reveals your new link to www.wiley.com (see Figure 4-18). Remember, you hard-coded your link right into your Feature's element definition. You could have, with a little bit of work, created a link that was populated from a database, or perhaps even opened in a new window. We'll leave that exercise up to you. A good starting point might be to look at the classes available to you in the `Microsoft.SharePoint.WebControls` namespace.

We have only touched on two of the element types available for implementing Features. We simply do not have the space in this book to demonstrate them all. We encourage you to peruse the SDK and look at the examples provided. Microsoft has done extensive work in the WSS SDK, and it certainly shows as you will be able to find an example of most Feature element types.

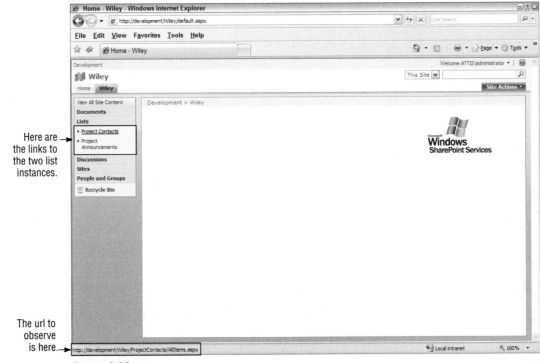

Figure 4-16

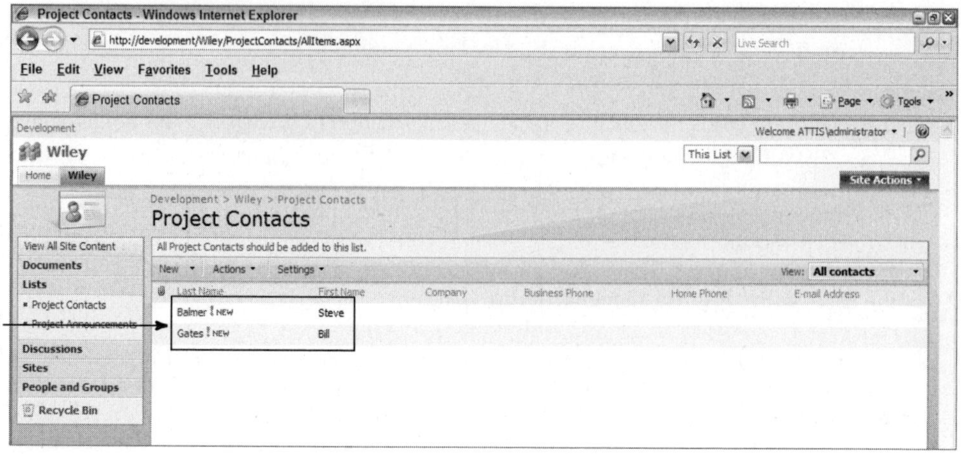

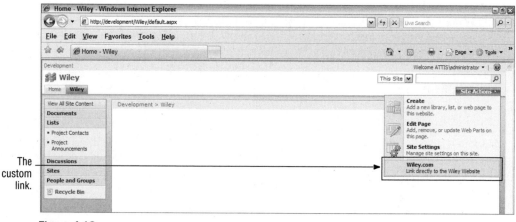

The default values.

Figure 4-17

The custom link.

Figure 4-18

Solutions

The WSS v3 Solution Framework is a most welcome addition to the WSS v3 framework. Solutions are used to package and deploy custom actions, site definitions, templates, Web Parts and assemblies, and other WSS v3 components. The WSS v3 Solution Framework provides you with a way to bundle the components of a particular customization into a new type of file, called a Solution file. A Solution file is simply a cabinet (.cab) file with a .wsp extension. Solutions not only allow you to deploy your customizations, but they also allow you to disable and upgrade them as well. Some of the benefits of and reasons for using the WSS v3 Solution Framework described in the SDK include the following. The more you work with the Solution Framework, the more you will ask yourself how you had managed to do SharePoint deployments in the past. Most of the time, it was a manual process, and considering that this is the SharePoint team's first stab at trying to ease the pain, they have done a pretty good job.

❑ **A unified infrastructure for deploying solutions** — For ease of functionality changes, sites should not be permanently bound to the Features and functionality of the site when it was first created. By using Features, you can easily enable and disable functionality at the site level, as well as convert sites from one type to another.

❑ **Integrated deployment** — Solutions enable developers and administrators to easily install files on the front-end web servers in a server farm. Windows SharePoint Services can package all of the Windows SharePoint Services entities into one file, add the file to the Solution Store, and deploy it to the front-end web servers. The Solution Framework allows you to do the following:

    ❑ Deploy new solutions and upgrade existing solutions across the farm.

    ❑ Synchronize a front-end web server so that its state is consistent with the state of other servers in the farm.

❑ **Unified localization** — There are central facilities for specifying localization settings, as well as ways to specify localizable token databases.

Solution Schema

A Solution manifest file is used to define the parts of a solution, including its files, assemblies, code access security, Web Parts, Features, site definitions, and other resources. The WSS v3 Solution Framework uses this file to determine where on the front-end servers to put the other files in the Solution package.

Solution Element

The `Solution` element (attributes shown in the following table) is the top-level element for a Solution manifest file. Of note is that because solutions can be scheduled to be deployed at a particular time by a SharePoint administrator, and some Features such as a Site Definition require an IIS reset to be visible in the user interface, you can choose to have the deployment perform an IIS reset, preferably at a time when usage would be minimal on the server(s).

Solution Element Attribute	Description
DeploymentServerType	Optional Text. Determines whether the solution is deployed to a front-end web server or to an application server. Possible values include `ApplicationServer` and `WebFrontEnd`.
ResetWebServer	Optional `Boolean`. `TRUE` to specify that the web server be reset through Microsoft Internet Information Services (IIS).
SolutionId	Optional `Text`. Contains the GUID for the solution.

The start of a Solution file may look like the following snippet:

```
<Solution
  xmlns="http://schemas.microsoft.com/sharepoint/"
```

```
        SolutionId="B1A9415C-D804-4877-8DE2-9A9EA2015B59"
        DeploymentServerType="WebFrontEnd">

    ...contents...

  </Solution>
```

Solution packages have a hierarchical structure. A manifest file is located at the root, while the directories for the various pieces of the solution described in the previous sections are stored in their respective subdirectories. It is important to note that the directory structure inside of the .wsp file determines the final directory structure on the server file system. For example, if the location attribute of a FeatureManifest element in a Solution manifest is set to MyFeature/Feature.xml, the Feature, along with any ElementManifest elements defined within its ElementsManifests element, are copied to a folder called MyFeature in the Features folder on each of the front-end web servers when the solution is deployed. Note that it is not necessary to specify the Features folder itself. The WSS v3 Solution Framework knows where to put the Features defined within the FeatureManifests element.

The Solution element may contain any combination of the following child elements depending on the components involved. They are all described in more detail throughout the following pages.

- ❑ ApplicationResourceFiles
- ❑ Assemblies
- ❑ CodeAccessSecurity
- ❑ DwpFiles
- ❑ FeatureManifests
- ❑ Resources
- ❑ SiteDefinitionManifests
- ❑ RootFiles
- ❑ TemplateFiles

ApplicationResourceFiles Element

The ApplicationResourcesFiles element is used to specify the application resource files to include in a solution. It can contain one to many ApplicationResourceFile child elements whose attributes are listed in the following table.

ApplicationResourceFile Element Attribute	Description
Location	Required Text. Specifies a relative location within the Solution that contains the application resource file.

Assemblies Element

The Assemblies element is used to specify the assemblies to include in a solution. It contains one to many Assembly child elements whose attributes are listed in the following table. Some Features such as a custom field, require that the assembly be placed in the Global Assembly Cache, whereas best practice dictates that a Web Part's assembly be placed in the web application's bin folder.

Assembly Element Attribute	Description
DeploymentTarget	Optional Text. The preferred target of deployment of the assembly. The assembly is copied to the target specified by the DeploymentTarget attribute (for a Web application) or the Global Assembly Cache (for a server farm). Possible values are GlobalAssemblyCache and WebApplication.
Location	Required Text. The relative file path of the assembly within the Solution.

An example of an Assembly Element would resemble the following snippet:

```
<Assemblies>
  <Assembly
    Location="MyAssembly.dll"
    DeploymentTarget="GlobalAssemblyCache">
  </Assembly>
</Assemblies>
```

The Assembly element may contain any combination of the following child elements, depending on the components involved.

- ❏ ClassResources
- ❏ SafeControls — In the case of a Web Part you would need to include this element.

ClassResources Element

The ClassResources element is used to specify the class resources of an assembly that is included in a Solution. It contains one to many ClassResource child elements whose attributes are listed in the following table.

ClassResource Element Attribute	Description
FileName	Optional Text. The name of the class resource file.
Location	Optional Text. The relative path of the class resource within the Solution.

SafeControls Element

The `SafeControls` element is used to specify the safe controls of an assembly that are included in a Solution. It contains one to many `SafeControl` child elements whose attributes are listed in the following table. The Solution Framework will handle adding and removing these entries to and from the appropriate `web.config` files as needed as you deploy and retract your Solutions. It will even create backups of your `web.config` files for you.

SafeControl Element Attribute	Description
Assembly	Optional `Text`. The name of the control assembly.
Namespace	Optional `Text`. The namespace associated with the assembly.
Safe	Optional `Boolean`. TRUE to add the control to the safe controls list; FALSE to remove it.
TypeName	Optional `Text`. The control type.

CodeAccessSecurity Element

The `CodeAccessSecurity` element is used to specify the code access security for the Solution. It contains one to many `PolicyItem` child elements. `PolicyItem` elements contain the following two child elements.

❏   `Assemblies`

❏   `PermissionSet`

Assemblies Element

The `Assemblies` element is used to specify the assemblies that are associated with a Solution's code access security policy. It contains one to many `Assembly` child elements whose attributes are listed in the following table.

Assembly Element Attribute	Description
Name	Optional `Text`. The name of the assembly.
PublicKeyBlob	Optional `Text`. The assembly's public key, in binary format.
Version	Optional `Text`. The version of the assembly.

PermissionSet Element

The `PermissionSet` element is used to specify the permissions for a Solution's code access security policy and contains the following attributes. It contains one to many `IPermission` child elements that are each used to specify an individual permission in a permission set. The attributes of an `IPermission` element are listed in the following table:

IPermission Element Attribute	Description
Class	Required `Text`. The name of the class associated with the permission set.
Description	Required `Text`. A description of the permission set.
Name	Optional `Text`. The name of the permission set.
Version	Optional `Text`. The version of the permission set.

DwpFiles Element

The `DwpFiles` element is used to specify the Web Part files (`.dwp` or `.webpart`) to include in a Solution. It contains one to many `DwpFile` child elements whose attributes are listed in the following table.

DwpFile Element Attribute	Description
FileName	Optional `Text`. The name of the Web Part file.

FeatureManifests Element

The `FeatureManifests` element is used to specify the Features to include in the Solution. It contains one to many `FeatureManifest` child elements whose attributes are listed in the following table. The Solution Framework will parse each `FeatureManifest` element and determine what other files to include in the Feature deployment such as `Element.xml` files and supporting resource files if any are needed.

An example of an `Assembly` element would resemble the following snippet:

```
<FeatureManifests>
  <FeatureManifest Location="WileyFeature\Feature.xml">
<FeatureManifests>
```

FeatureManifest Element Attribute	Description
Location	Required `Text`. Specifies a relative location within the Solution that contains the Feature description file.

Resources Element

The `Resources` element is used to specify the resources to include in the Solution. It contains one to many `Resource` child elements whose attributes are listed in the following table:

Resource Element Attribute	Description
`Location`	Required `Text`. Specifies a relative location within the Solution that contains the resource file.

SiteDefinitionManifests Element

The `SiteDefinitionManifests` element is used to specify the Site Definitions to include in the Solution. It contains one to many `SiteDefinitionManifest` child elements whose attributes are listed in the following table:

SiteDefinitionManifests Element Attribute	Description
`Location`	Required `Text`. The relative path of the root folder for a Site Definition.

Each `SiteDefinitionManifest` element should also contain a `WebTempFile` element that is used to specify a web template file that is associated with a Site Definition manifest. It contains the attribute noted in the following table:

WebTempFile Element Attribute	Description
`Location`	Required `Text`. Specifies a relative location within the Solution that contains the Web template file.

RootFiles

The `RootFiles` element is used to specify the root paths to which Solution files are copied. It contains one to many `RootFile` child elements whose attributes are listed in the following table:

RootFile Element Attribute	Description
`Location`	Required `Text`. The root path to which Solution files are copied.

TemplateFiles

The `TemplateFiles` element is used to specify the template files to include in the Solution. It contains one to many `TemplateFile` child elements whose attributes are listed in the following table:

TemplateFile Element Attribute	Description
`Location`	Required `Text`. Specifies a relative location within the Solution that contains the template file.

Deploying a Solution

Solution deployment is designed so that developers can essentially hand off a solution file to a SharePoint administrator who can then deploy it in a predefined, safe and consistent way. Solution deployment can be summarized as the process of distributing, unpacking and installing solution files to the SharePoint servers. The three main components of solution deployment, as explained in the SDK, are:

❑   **The solution store** — A centralized collection of all SharePoint solutions for the server farm. The first step in deploying a solution is to add the solution to the store.

❑   **Deployment** — Distribution, unpacking, and installation of the solution to the front-end web servers. After adding a solution, whether it is a new solution or an upgrade for an existing solution, to the server farm Solution Store, it must be deployed uniformly to the front-end web servers.

❑   **Synchronization** — Process of taking a new front-end web server, or a damaged or inconsistently performing front-end web server, and synchronizing its state to that of the other front-end web servers.

Solution Store

The Solution Store is an area in the WSS v3 configuration database that stores solutions and their files. Solutions can be added to the Solution Store in one of three ways.

❑   **Command line** — An administrator can add and remove solution files from the Solution Store using the `stsadm` command-line utility.

❑   **Central Administration** — An administrator can manage solutions by clicking on the Solution management link in the Global Configuration section of the Operations tab in Central Administration. Solutions can only be removed from the Solution Store this way, not added.

❑   **Object model** — As with almost all SharePoint functionality, solutions can also be added and removed via the object model.

Deployment

The first step in deploying a solution is to add it to the Solution Store. This process can be initiated from either the `stsadm` command-line tool by using the addsolution command (see the following table) or by using the object model. A Solution cannot be added to the Solution Store via the user interface in Central Administration. The following command is used to add a Solution to the Solution Store. This process also validates the Solution manifest file and ensures that all files referenced within it can be found in the Solution file.

Command	Description
`stsadm.exe -o addsolution`	`{-filename <Solution filename>}`
	`[-lcid <language>]`

A Solution is deployed locally, or by using a timer service irrespective of whether it is a new deployment or a deployment of a Solution upgrade (discussed later). Both local and timer-based deployments can be triggered by using command-line instructions or through the object model.

Local and Timer Service Deployment

The following descriptions from the SDK may come in handy as you're working through this chapter.

In a local deployment, Solution files are deployed only to the computer from which the deployment operation was initiated. Under this scenario, the Solution is not marked as "deployed" in the configuration database until the Solution files are deployed to all applicable servers in the server farm. Then, in the case of new Solution deployments, Solution features are registered, and schema and definition files are committed to the configuration store.

In deployments that use the timer service, the deployment creates a timer job. This timer job is picked up by the timer service on each web server in the server farm. The timer job uses the WSS v3 administrative web service to access appropriate privileges to deploy Solution files to each computer.

Initially, manifests and Feature manifests are parsed to find assembly and `_layouts` files, which are copied to the appropriate locations. All other files contained within a feature directory are copied to the feature directory. After Solution files are copied to the target computers, a configuration reset is scheduled for all front-end web servers; the reset then deploys the files and restarts IIS. For upgrades, the deployment has no impact on the end user experience. The new versions of the Solution files do not over-write the old files; therefore, if a computer is restarted or the upgrade process is aborted, the servers are synchronized with their other data files. Finally, for new Solution deployments, Solution features are registered, and schema and definition files are committed to the configuration store.

The `deploysolution` command is used to deploy a Solution that is present in the Solution Store. A Solution can also be deployed by navigating to and clicking on the Solution management link in the Global Configuration section of the Operations tab in SharePoint Central Administration (see Figure 4-19). This will display a list of Solutions added to the store by either of the two methods previously mentioned. Clicking on a Solution will take you to the Solution status screen. If the Solution is not deployed, the menu bar will present the user with both a Deploy Solution button and a Remove Solution button (see Figure 4-20). If the Solution is deployed, the menu bar will present the user with a Retract Solution button (see Figure 4-21). Clicking either Deploy Solution or Retract Solution will present the user with the option to perform the operation immediately or to schedule it for a more convenient time. Clicking Remove Solution will generate a confirmation dialog and remove the Solution immediately from the Solution Store if accepted.

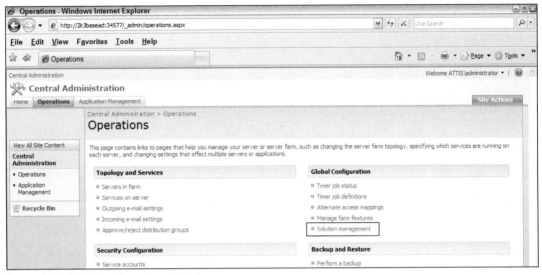

Figure 4-19: Solution Management Link.

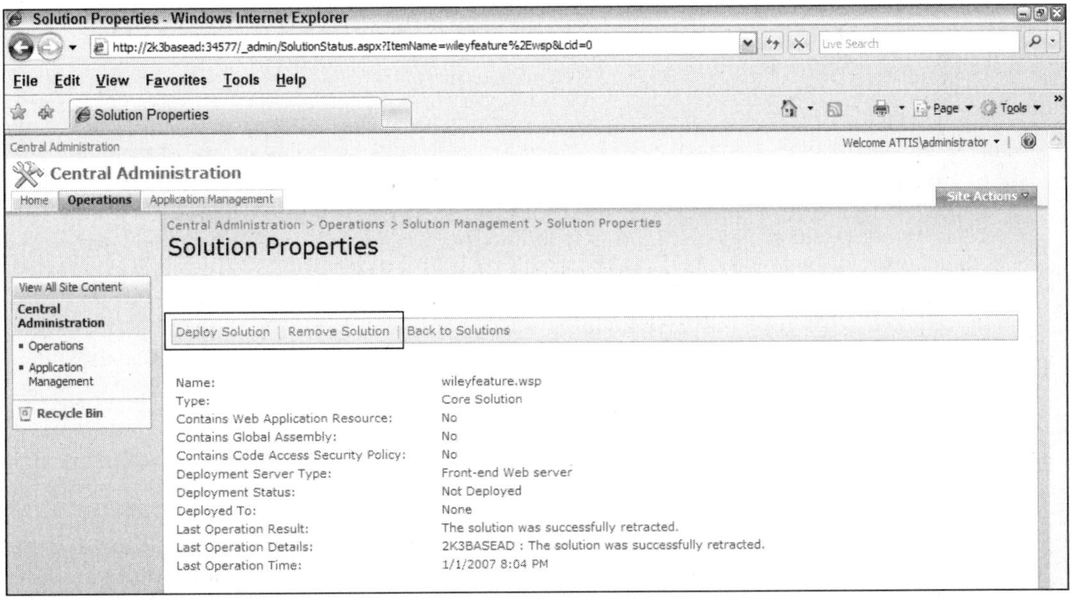

Figure 4-20: Deploy or Remove Solution.

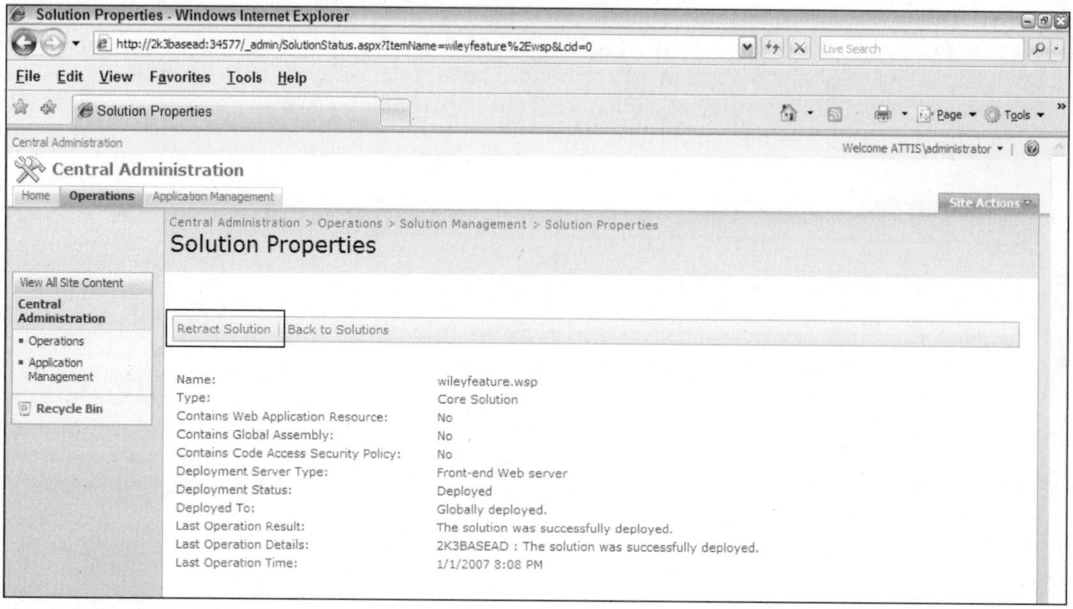

Figure 4-21: Retract Solution.

A number of things can occur that may cause a Solution deployment to fail. The timer service may not be activated on a front-end web server. In this case, the deployment will remain in a pending state until the timer service is started. In addition, the WSS v3 administrative service may not be activated on one of the servers, which will cause an administrative alert to be sent to an administrator with this information. Additionaly, the actual extraction of the solution package itself could fail on one of the servers or a file copy failure may also cause a solution deployment to fail. Whatever the case may be, the solution will not be marked as deployed.

A deployment can only be cancelled if the deployment timer job has not yet started running on any of the deployment target servers. If a deployment timer job begins running on any of the target servers, the deployment can no longer be canceled.

The contents of a Solution may change over time, and the SDK defines two fundamental types of changes that can happen to a Solution:

- **Makeup change** — Features or site definitions are added to a solution. A solution may have entire features added. If a newer version of a solution is defined (*solution versions* are different solution packages that share a GUID) that is missing features or site definitions, then those features and site definitions are removed.

- **Definition change** — Elements are added to or removed from Features or Site Definitions. As a result of definition changes, a Feature or a site template may add or lose files. As the Feature or site definition changes over time, files that are no longer defined in the Feature Definition are removed. This applies to assemblies as well. If a solution with global scope loses its assemblies, those assemblies are removed from the Global Assembly Cache. If a feature with web application scope loses its assemblies, those assemblies are removed from the local bin directory.

Synchronization

The synchronization process pulls solutions that the front-end web server does not have. These solutions are then redeployed onto the computer selected for synchronization. This process will help you immensely should you need to add a server to your farm.

Upgrading a Solution

Upgrading a Solution is possible using the WSS v3 Solution Framework. This may happen if you have a need to add or update one or more of the components of a Solution already stored in the Solution Store. The Solution Framework handles the backing up of existing Solution files (in the case of an exception), the removal of the old files and the delivery of the new file(s). Only certain types of Solution upgrade scenarios are supported. The following two lists illustrate those that are supported and those that are not.

> *The SDK states that in all cases where supported changes or additions are made to feature files (either feature .xml files or element .xml files), you must perform a reset (iisreset) of Microsoft Internet Information Services (IIS) to refresh the cache with the new .xml files. For existing feature activations, best practice is to reactivate the feature.*

Supported Upgrades

The following list from the SDK outlines the supported upgrade options available when choosing to upgrade a Solution. Essentially, you can add new functionality and update existing files and functionality.

- ❑ Adding new files in a solution upgrade and removing old versions of the files
- ❑ Adding new features in a solution upgrade
- ❑ Updating or changing the receiver assembly for existing features in a new version of a solution
- ❑ Adding or changing feature elements (element .xml files) in a new version of a solution
- ❑ Adding or changing feature properties in a new version of a solution

---

Unsupported Upgrades

The following list from the SDK outlines the unsupported upgrade options not available when choosing to upgrade a Solution. Essentially, you cannot remove existing functionality or change the scope of existing features.

- ❑ Removing old features in a new version of a solution
- ❑ Changing the ID or scope of old features in a new version of a solution
- ❑ Removing feature elements (element .xml files) in a new version of a solution
- ❑ Removing feature properties in a new version of a solution

---

The following table illustrates the syntax used to perform a Solution upgrade via the stsadm command-line utility. A Solution can also be upgraded via the object model.

Command	Description
stsadm.exe -o upgradesolution	{-name <Solution name>
	-filename <upgrade filename>}
	[-time <time to upgrade at>]
	[-immediate]
	[-local]
	[-allowgacdeployment]
	[-allowcaspolicies]
	[-lcid <language>]

There are a couple of things to keep in mind when performing Solution upgrades, the first being that the Solution must be in the Solution store. In addition to the requirement just mentioned, we need to be aware that at the time of an upgrade the Solution may be deployed or the Solution may not be deployed. If the Solution is not deployed, you should not use the -immediate or the -time flags in the upgrade-solution command (if deploying via command line). Doing so will cause an exception, as an upgrade cannot be scheduled if a Solution is not deployed. If the Solution is deployed, be sure to use either the -time or -immediate flags in the upgradesolution command, as a time must be specified to run an upgrade if the Solution is already deployed.

Retracting a Solution

Retracting a Solution can be viewed as the opposite of deploying a Solution. The process will remove assemblies, files, resources, safe control entries, and other Solution components from all of the servers to which they have been deployed. The process also uninstalls Features if necessary as part of a complete retraction. As with Solution deployment, a Solution can be retracted immediately using the context of the SharePoint administrator, or scheduled using the timer service and its context. As stated in the SDK, retracting a Solution involves the following concepts:

❑   Only one active retraction with one particular solution is supported in a given server in the farm at any particular time.

❑   A solution cannot be retracted unless all the language packs associated with it are retracted first.

❑   A solution cannot be removed from the Solution Store if the solution is deployed.

❑   When a solution is retracted, all files for that solution are retracted, even if another solution points to the same file. This can be avoided by ensuring that each solution points to a unique set of files. This last item is crucial. Sharing files across Solutions may result in a very bad end-user experience if one is retracted.

As with adding and deploying Solutions, Solutions can be retracted and deleted through the stsadm command line tool, the object model or the user interface within Central Administration. The `stsadm` commands to retract and delete a Solution are listed in the following table:

Command	Description
stsadm.exe -o retractsolution	{-name <Solution name>}
	[-url <virtual server url>]
	[-allcontenturls]
	[-time <time to remove at>]
	[-immediate]
	[-local]
	[-lcid <language>]
stsadm.exe -o deletesolution	{-name <Solution name>}
	[-override]
	[-lcid <language>]

Creating a Solution

A solution can be created, like almost everything else, in a variety of different ways. The method described in the following section is a robust, repeatable, and reliable process. For demonstration purposes, let's package up the Feature you built in the previous section into a WSS v3 Solution.

Create MakeCAB Directive File

You will use MakeCAB.exe to package the Solution file. MakeCAB.exe is a tool included with Windows 2000 or later. If you would like more information on MakeCAB.exe, you can download the Microsoft Cabinet Software Development Kit from http://msdn2.microsoft.com/en-us/library/ms974336.aspx.

1. Open up the WileyFeature project created in the Feature section earlier in this chapter.

2. Add a new .txt file to the root of the project by right-clicking the project node and selecting New Item from the Add context menu item. Select the Text File template, name the file wsp.ddf, and click Add. This file is known as a directive file for the MakeCAB.exe utility. It is used to instruct the utility where to place the files you specify within the CAB file that is outputted.

3. Add the following code to the wsp.ddf file, and click Save:

```
;***  MakeCAB Directive file");

.OPTION EXPLICIT
.Set CabinetNameTemplate=WileyFeature.wsp
```

```
.Set DiskDirectoryTemplate=c:\wsp
.Set CompressionType=MSZIP
.Set UniqueFiles=OFF
.Set Cabinet=on

;Files to place into the CAB Root
Manifest.xml

;Files to place into the CAB WileyFeature directory
.Set DestinationDir=WileyFeature
Feature.xml
Elements.xml
```

In examining the preceding code, you can see that you are setting some initial properties. You are instructing the utility to name the file `WileyFeature.wsp`. That is the file extension that the WSS v3 Framework is expecting. You are also instructing the utility to place the file into a certain directory, in your case `c:\wsp`. This is completely arbitrary, since in most cases you will be delivering the Solution file to an administrator. However, since you want to test your Solution deployment, it would be marginally easier to place it in a location that is easy to type. All file paths in a directive file are relative to the location of the `wsp.ddf` file, which in this case is the root of your project. In addition, ensure that the folder path you specify as the `DiskDirectoryTemplate` above exists or the utility will throw an exception. Remember, the only way to add a Solution to the solution store is to add it either through the object model or by using the `stsadm -o addsolution` command. You will be using the latter in this example.

Create Solution Manifest

Only three files need to be in this particular Solution. All WSS v3 Solutions need a manifest file. As discussed earlier, this file informs the WSS v3 Solution Framework of the various components of our Solution. The WSS v3 Solution Framework knows how to read and interpret this file. The only other files you need to include in this Solution are the `Feature.xml` and `Elements.xml` files.

1. Add a new `.xml` file to the root of the project by right-clicking the project node and selecting New Item from the Add context menu. Select the XML File template, name the file `Manifest.xml` and click Add.

2. Add the following code to the `Manifest.xml` file:

```
<?xml version="1.0" encoding="utf-8" ?>
<Solution
  xmlns="http://schemas.microsoft.com/sharepoint/"
  SolutionId="F8275F75-E503-4cf1-A6FC-A828592A3AF5"
  DeploymentServerType="WebFrontEnd">

  <!--list all features included in this solution-->
  <FeatureManifests>
    <FeatureManifest Location="WileyFeature\Feature.xml"/>
  </FeatureManifests>
</Solution>
```

In examining the preceding code, be sure to give your Solution a unique `SolutionId`. The `FeatureManifests` element lists the single Feature that you are deploying. Remember, a Solution can contain any number of Features, Site Definitions, Web Parts, and other SharePoint components. The schemas defined earlier should help guide you in including all of the necessary files that may be required by any particular Solution you may need to create.

Build the Solution File

Execute the following steps to build the Solution file:

1. Enter the following commands in the "Post-build event command line" text box to have the MakeCAB.exe utility generate the Solution file. The path in your environment to the MakeCAB.exe utility may be different. Remember to include the double quotation marks if your path includes spaces.

```
cd ..\..\
"C:\Program Files\Microsoft Cabinet SDK\bin\MakeCAB.exe" /f wsp.ddf
```

The first line moves the execution context to the root folder of the project. The second line calls into the MakeCAB.exe utility and reads in the wsp.ddf directive file you created to build your Solution file and place it into the appropriate location as defined within the directive file itself.

2. Save your changes and build the project.

3. Browse to the output folder you designated in your directive file, and you should see the WileyFeature.wsp file.

If you are curious, you can change the extension on the .wsp file to .cab and explore its contents. You will see that it has the folder structure you specified in the directive file designed above.

As discussed, the only way to add a Solution to the solution store is to do so via the object model or by using the stsadm command-line utility.

> **At this point, you need to do some house cleaning. Since you are deploying the same Feature you had created earlier in this chapter, you need to make sure that you remove it completely in order to successfully test your Solution. The Feature needs to be deactivated in all sites that it was activated in by using the user interface or the stsadm -deactivatefeature command. It also needs to be uninstalled by using the stsadm -o uninstallfeature command. Finally, you need to remove any files and folders that your Feature may have used from the file system. In this case this is the WileyFeature folder that is located in the [WSS]\TEMPLATE\ FEATURES folder. If you had any other files, safe control entries, assemblies, and the like that were part of your Feature, you would have to remove those as well.**

Add Solution to Solution Store

Now, add your Solution to the solution store using the stsadm command-line utility.

1. Open a Visual Studio 2005 Command Prompt window by clicking on Start ➪ Programs ➪ Microsoft Visual Studio 2005 ➪ Visual Studio Tools ➪ Visual Studio 2005 Command Prompt.

2. Navigate to the bin directory of the 12 Hive by typing the following command including the double quotation marks:

```
cd "C:\Program Files\Common Files\Microsoft Shared\web server
extensions\12\BIN"
```

3. Add your Solution to the solution store by typing the following stsadm command:

```
stsadm -o addsolution -filename c:\wsp\WileyFeature.wsp
```

4. Browse to the Solution Management screen in Central Administration by clicking on the Operations tab and then Solution management. You will see your Solution, as shown in Figure 4-22.

5. Click on the Solution name to access the Solution status screen, as shown in Figure 4-23.

6. Click on Deploy Solution, and choose to deploy the Solution immediately.

At this point, when deployment is complete, the items in the Solution are available for use. In this case, it means that your Feature will be available for activation. If you had deployed a Site Definition as part of your Solution, it would now be available as an option if you were to create a new site. If you had deployed a custom field as part of your Solution, it would now be available as an option when creating a new column in a list. The same applies to all of the other different components that you are able to deploy via a WSS v3 Solution.

In the case of your Solution, which contains a single Feature, when you browse to [WSS]\TEMPLATE\ FEATURES, you will see that a WileyFeature folder was created that contains your Feature.xml and Elements.xml files from when your Solution was deployed.

You can now upgrade your Solution if you want to by using the upgrade rules discussed earlier in this chapter. You could also retract your Solution as well as remove it if you wanted to at this point. We leave you to explore the Solution Framework some more on your own and explore how beneficial and welcome this process will be to the SharePoint administrator as well as to many IT departments. Developers, in theory, should no longer need to manually modify files on the SharePoint servers. Also, all of the changes made to the system are now stored in the content database as a Solution.

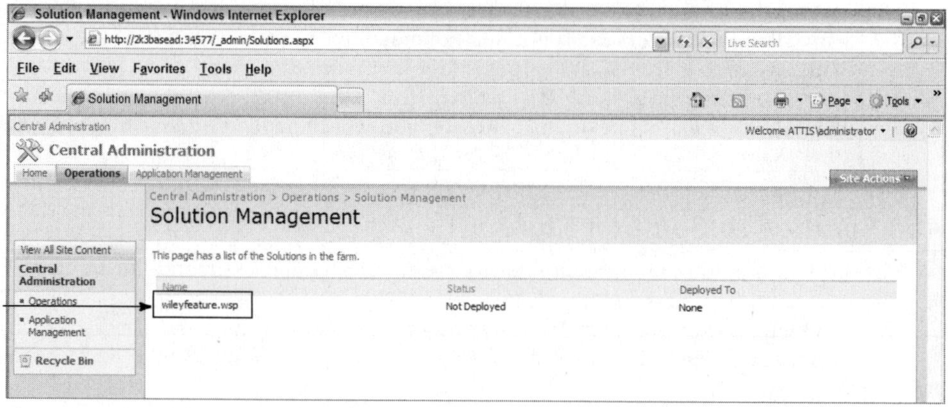

Figure 4-22: Solution Management.

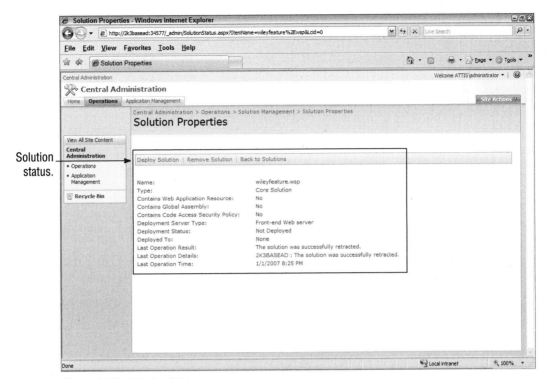

Figure 4-23: Solution Status.

Web Parts

A Web Part is a user interface component similar to the familiar controls we see on ordinary web pages, such as text boxes and buttons. However, in addition to providing "canned" UI functionality, Web Parts can also participate in SharePoint's personalization infrastructure. That is, individual users can add, remove, and configure their own custom view of a SharePoint site by manipulating the Web Parts available to them. Users, of course, have this privilege only if the SharePoint administrator grants it to them. Also, while web controls typically provide simple UI functionality such as text boxes, Web Parts are often complex UI elements that can connect to back-end data providers or business processes.

In WSS 3.0 the Web Part infrastructure is built entirely on top of the ASP.NET 2.0 Web Part classes. This means that with very little additional training, an ASP.NET developer can build Web Parts that will also run in the SharePoint environment. Web Parts can be used to perform a myriad of tasks. They can connect to a SQL Server database, connect to an Active Directory, or access SQL Server Reporting Services among other things. Almost anything you can do with custom code, you can do within a Web Part. Web Part development is relatively easy and is a powerful way to extend SharePoint and ASP.NET sites.

The following nonexhaustive list borrowed from the SDK, demonstrates some of the ways in which you can use custom Web Parts:

❑   Creating custom properties, you can display and modify in the user interface and access via the code in your Web Parts.

❑ Improving performance and scalability. A compiled custom Web Part runs faster than a script.

❑ Implementing proprietary code without disclosing the source code.

❑ Securing and controlling access to content within the Web Part. Built-in Web Parts allow any users with appropriate permissions to change content and alter Web Part functionality. With a custom Web Part, you can determine the content or properties to display to users, regardless of their permissions.

❑ Making your Web Part connectable, allowing Web Parts to provide or access data from other connectable Web Parts.

❑ Interacting with the object models that are exposed in WSS v3. For example, you can create a custom Web Part to save documents to a WSS document library.

❑ Controlling the cache for the Web Part by using built-in cache tools. For example, you can use these tools to specify when to read, write, or invalidate the Web Part cache.

❑ Benefiting from a rich development environment with debugging features that are provided by tools such as Visual Studio 2005.

❑ Creating a base class for other Web Parts to extend. For example, to create a collection of Web Parts with similar features and functionality, create a custom base class from which multiple Web Parts can inherit. This reduces the overall cost of developing and testing subsequent Web Parts.

❑ Controlling the implementation of the Web Part. For example, you can write a custom server-side Web Part that connects to a back-end database, or you can create a Web Part that is compatible with a broader range of Web browsers.

Web Part Infrastructure

The WSS 3.0 Web Part infrastructure is built on top of the Microsoft ASP.NET 2.0 Web Part infrastructure. This topic could span multiple chapters, but in the interest of space we are only going to scratch the surface and discuss the topics needed to design, deploy, and debug a simple WSS v3 Web Part. What follows is a crash course, if you will, on developing a simple WSS v3 Web Part. After reading the following section, you should be able to move forward and solve all kinds of different business problems you may have for which you think a custom Web Part would be able to provide a solution. Keep in mind that you will be working in a very familiar environment, Visual Studio 2005, and with very familiar languages, C# or VB.Net. Remember, aside from interacting with the WSS v3 object model (if necessary), most of the code required to create a Web Part is most likely code you are already very familiar with writing. The following sections cover some of the best practices for designing a Web Part, the steps needed to deploy a Web Part manually, and how to debug a Web Part.

ASP.NET Web Part Infrastructure

The ASP.NET Web Part infrastructure is based on a `WebPartManager` class that manages the lifetime of Web Part instances at runtime. Each ASP.NET web page that uses Web Part controls must contain the following two items, remembering that WSS v3 pages are just ASP.NET pages.

❑ Exactly one `WebPartManager` object that tracks which Web Parts have been added to each particular zone, and stores and retrieves data about how each Web Part has been customized and personalized.

❑ One or more `WebPartZone` objects, into which Web Parts are placed.

Web Parts that require dynamic characteristics (such as retaining customization and personalization data) must be created within Web Part zones — in ASP.NET, Web Parts cannot be placed outside of a Web Part zone.

WSS v3 Web Part Infrastructure

The WSS v3 Web Part infrastructure uses many of the controls in the ASP.NET Web Part control set and also introduced a number of its own controls that inherit from the ASP.NET base classes and provide some additional functionality.

WSS v3 SPWebPartManager Class vs. ASP.NET WebPartManagerClass

Instead of using the `WebPartManager` (`System.Web.UI.WebControls.WebParts.WebPartManager`) class, WSS v3 uses the `SPWebPartManager` (`Microsoft.SharePoint.WebPartPages.SPWebPartManager`) class, that inherits from the former. Any page in WSS v3 that contains Web Parts on it must have an instance of the `SPWebPartManager` class on the page to manage the Web Parts. This object is used to track which zone each of the Web Parts is in, connection information related to Web Parts, and personalization settings. The `SPWebPartManager` object is also responsible for raising the Web Part events that occur during a Web Parts lifetime.

The SDK tells us that the default master page that is provided with the Windows SharePoint Services technology includes an instance of `SPWebPartManager`, so this control is automatically included with all of your WSS v3 content pages, assuming that you are using the default master page.

WSS v3 WebPartZone Class vs. ASP.NET WebPartZone Class

The `WebPartZone` (`Microsoft.SharePoint.WebPartPages.WebPartZone`) class used by WSS v3 is not to be confused with the `WebPartZone` (`System.Web.UI.WebControls.WebParts.WebPartZone`) class used by the ASP.NET Web Part framework. The WSS v3 version inherits from the ASP.NET version and is primarily responsible for maintaining a consistent look and feel across Web Part controls. The `WebPartZone` and `SPWebPartManager` classes are the magic behind the persistence mechanism provided by Web Parts. Together, they handle the serialization of data associated with Web Parts into the appropriate WSS v3 content database.

WSS v3 WebPart Class vs. ASP.NET WebPart Class

Unlike the previous two classes, in which SharePoint-specific classes were created (`SPWebPartManager` and `WebPartZone`) that inherit from their ASP.NET counterparts, the `WebPart` class that is used in SharePoint is the same `WebPart` class that is used in ASP.NET. This is possible because WSS v3 is built directly on ASP.NET. Although it is still possible to build a Web Part and derive it from the `WebPart` class contained in the `Microsoft.SharePoint.WebPartPages` namespace or the `WebPart` class contained in the `System.Web.UI.WebControls.WebParts` namespace, Microsoft highly recommends inheriting from the `WebPart` class contained in the `System.Web.UI.WebControls.WebParts` namespace unless any of the following requirements are present:

- ❑ Cross-page connections

- ❑ Connections between Web Parts that are outside a Web Part zone

- ❑ Client-side connections

- ❑ Use of the data-caching infrastructure (provided by SharePoint, not ASP.NET)

- ❑ Multiple providers for a single consumer with respect to connectable Web Parts

Web Part Design

As with any other component you may choose to design, whether it be a user control in a web application or maybe even a custom server control, a good design in the beginning will most likely save you from a great number of potential problems down the road. Keep in mind that not everyone starts out as an expert Web Part developer. Web part design and development, although still classified as specialized by some, is by and large becoming more and more mainstream in today's development community. As the adoption rate for SharePoint increases, Web Part developers will no longer find themselves few and far between. On the contrary, with the entire Web Part platform being transformed into what is essentially a superset of the ASP.NET 2.0 platform, Web Part design and development not only becomes easier for the masses but also becomes more appealing and accessible.

Following some best practices will also make life a little easier for developers down the road, whether they are adding enhancements or possibly trying to fix a potential bug (yes, we all have bugs in our code). In addition to a plethora of best practices that carry over from the .NET development world, such as variable naming, spacing, casing, and many others, there are a few additional items to keep in mind when developing Web Parts. This list is by no means all inclusive and a more exhaustive list can be viewed at the following URL (http://msdn2.microsoft.com/en-us/library/ms916817.aspx) in the SDK. This list was originally created for WSS v2, but most of the concepts and ideas still apply.

- ❑ **Handle exceptions appropriately by making good use of try . . . catch blocks** — Catching exceptions and presenting the user with a clean message makes the user experience much better.

- ❑ **Check Permissions before rendering your Web Part** — For example, displaying a Save button to a user who does not have permission to save would not produce a very good user experience. Remember, you have access to all of the user's permissions when rendering the Web Part's user interface.

- ❑ **Validate properties before saving** — Since Web Part properties can be modified in a number of places, for example in the tool pane, in the .webpart or .dwp file among others, validation code should be called in the properties' Set accessor method. This is not commonly done; however, in most cases, this is the last chance you will have to validate its value.

- ❑ **Validate all user input** — All user input should be validated before performing any operations with that input. There are many reasons for this including preventing SQL injection, cross-site scripting, buffer overflow, and so on. The appropriate use of validators as well as server-side error handling is always a good practice and strongly encouraged.

- ❑ **HTMLEncode all user input rendered to the client** — Try not to emit HTML manually at all if possible. Make use of the rendering capabilities of the System.Web.UI.HtmlControls and System.Web.UI.WebControls namepaces. They exist to provide the correct markup to the many devices that access your SharePoint site. A label rendered in Internet Explorer will have very different HTML markup than a label rendered on a mobile phone.

The most important take away here is to be mindful of performance, error handling, and of course the end-user experience. If end users have a lousy experience, they will most likely not come back.

Creating and Deploying a Web Part

The process of creating a custom Web Part, although not terribly complex, does involve a series of steps that must be performed in order for the Web Part to function properly within the WSS v3 environment.

These steps may seem like a lot a first, but as you design and develop an increasingly large number of Web Parts, they will eventually become second nature. All of the code used to run a Web Part needs to be contained inside an assembly. Signing Web Part assemblies is not required, but it is most certainly a best practice and encouraged. Signing, however, is required if the assembly is to be deployed to the Global Assembly Cache (GAC). It also aids in enforcing code access security. Traditionally, this (GAC deployment) may not be something that a developer has much control over in production, so signing the assembly will allow this process to proceed if it is needed. The security policy that is being used by the site on which the Web Part is deployed must trust the Web Part's code. Having the trust level in the web.config set to Full is not recommended. Instead, the recommended best practice is to make a copy of the WSS_Minimal security policy and to add to it the appropriate permissions as new Web Parts are developed and added to the system. The complete detailed process of creating a custom code access security file is outside the bounds of this book; however, there are a few good examples online. Again, we remind you that the easiest way to learn how to do a lot of tasks outlined in this chapter in particular is to look at how Microsoft has done them within SharePoint. Go ahead and make a copy of the wss_minimaltrust.config security file located at [WSS]\CONFIG and take a look at it. In order for the Web Part to run within a WSS v3 site, a SafeControl entry must also exist in the site's web.config file. As mentioned, this process will become second nature as you develop more and more Web Parts. Most importantly, remember that security is a good thing.

Your custom Web Part is going to be very simple. Once you understand the fundamentals of creating and deploying a Web Part, you will be able to extend this example to perform many other tasks. It will accept a string from the user and return that string converted to the standard Pig Latin form as defined by Wikipedia (http://en.wikipedia.org/wiki/Pig_latin). It will contain a text box for the input, a button to initiate the conversion, and a literal control to display the result. You will also give the user the ability to bold the result by changing one of the Web Part's custom properties.

Create the Web Part Class

You begin Web Part creation by creating a WebPart class:

1. Create a new project by clicking Project under the New option from the File menu.

2. Under Project types, select the Class Library template under Windows in the language of your choice (C# is used in this example).

3. In the Location text box, browse to C:\Documents and Settings\Administrator\My Documents\Visual Studio 2005\projects and click **Open**.

4. Uncheck the Create directory for solution check box.

5. Give your Web Part project a meaningful name such as **PigLatin**, and click OK.

6. Add a reference to **System.Web**.

7. Delete the Class1.cs file.

8. Add a new class file, naming it **PigLatinWebPart.cs**.

At this point, you will have an empty class that essentially has no functionality, nor is it a Web Part. It needs to inherit from one of the two WebPart classes discussed earlier in this section. Since you don't need any of the functionality specific to the WSS v3 Web Part, you should have it inherit from the ASP.NET Web Part class.

9. Have it inherit from the System.Web.UI.WebControls.WebParts.WebPart class.

Since you are going to be creating a couple of user interface components for your Web Part you need to add a couple of `using` statements to your class to reduce the amount of code that you will have to type. You also will be using some ASP.NET attributes located in the `System.Web.UI.WebControls.WebParts` namespace; so add a `using` statement for that namespace as well.

10. Add `using` statements for the `System.Web.UI`, `System.Web.UI.HtmlControls`, `System.Web.UI.WebControls`, and `System.Web.UI.WebControls.WebParts` namespaces.

11. Build your project.

Add AllowPartiallyTrustedCallers Attribute To Assembly

Microsoft states that since the bin directory is a partial trust location, your Web Part does not automatically grant full trust code permissions when it is executed. Because the code that calls into your Web Part will be granted only partial trust permissions, your Web Part needs to have the **AllowPartialTrustedCallers** attribute set on it. You can set this attribute at the assembly level using the following steps:

1. Click the plus sign next to the Properties node in your project.

2. Open the AssemblyInfo.cs file and add the following attribute at the bottom of this file.

```
[assembly: System.Security.AllowPartiallyTrustedCallers()]
```

3. Build your project.

> The SDK states that marking an assembly as safe to AllowPartiallyTrustedCallers puts a lot of responsibility for safe implementation on the developers.

Create the Web Part User Interface Properties

It is time to decide how the Web Part will look. We determined earlier that your Web Part will consist of a text box for input, a button for initiating the conversion process, and a literal control to display the result. A common way to display these controls is to place them into a table.

It is generally accepted as a best practice to not emit HTML directly through your Web Part code but instead to let the .NET framework handle this process. It knows how to emit a button control on a variety of platforms. By leveraging this built-in capability provided by Microsoft, you drastically reduce the chances that your HTML will be rendered incorrectly across different browsers, as it might if you were to write it yourself. This concept will be demonstrated shortly.

Place the text box and the button in one row of the table, each in its own column, and place the literal control in the second row, spanning the two columns. Give the table a width of 100%.

1. Declare the protected member variables that will represent your user interface elements, both visible (text box, button) and nonvisible (table, rows, columns):

```
protected HtmlTable _MainTable = null;
protected HtmlTableRow _Row1 = null;
protected HtmlTableCell _Column11 = null;
protected HtmlTableCell _Column12 = null;
```

```
protected HtmlTableRow _Row2 = null;
protected HtmlTableCell _Column21 = null;
protected TextBox _InputTextBox = null;
protected Button _ConvertButton = null;
protected Literal _OutputLiteral = null;
```

2.   Declare a private Boolean field to determine whether or not to bold the result string.

3.   Add code for the public property and private member field that will be used to determine whether or not to bold the result string when it is rendered:

```
private bool _BoldResult = false;

[Personalizable(PersonalizationScope.Shared),
WebBrowsable(true),
System.ComponentModel.Category("User Interface"),
WebDisplayName("Bold Result"),
WebDescription("Check to bold the output.")]
public bool BoldResult
{
  get { return _BoldResult; }
  set { _BoldResult = value; }
}
```

There are a few things to note in the above property. Note that it is decorated with multiple attributes. The `Personalizable` attribute is used to determine if the property can be set on a user-by-user basis (`PersonalizationScope.User`) or on a shared basis (`PersonalizationScope.Shared`). The `Category` attribute specifies the name of the category in which to group this property when displayed in the tool pane. The `WebBrowsable` attribute is used to determine if this particular Web Part property is displayed in the tool pane when the properties of the Web Part are modified. The `WebDisplayName` defines the friendly name for this property, and the `WebDescription` attribute defines the string value to use as a tooltip for this property.

Render the Web Part User Interface Components

The next step is to override the `CreateChildControls` method of the `WebPart` base class. This method, as described in the SDK, is called by the ASP.NET page framework to notify server controls that use composition-based implementation to create any child controls they contain in preparation for posting back or rendering. It is here that you will create instances of your controls, including the table, rows, columns, text box, button, and literal controls; define any properties; and hook up any event handlers. You will include error handling in the form of a `try . . . catch` block. If an exception were to occur, it would simply clear out the controls collection of the Web Part and add a literal control to the table to display the error. You may want to change this before going to production to display a more user-friendly error, but for development purposes, this will suffice. Having this type of error handling in place now will be beneficial down the road as the user interface of your Web Part gets more and more complex and error prone.

1.   Override the `CreateChildControls` method in your class by adding the following code to it:

```
protected override void CreateChildControls()
{
  try
  {
```

```
// create the main table
_MainTable = new HtmlTable();
_MainTable.Style.Add(HtmlTextWriterStyle.Width, "100%");

// create row 1
_Row1 = new HtmlTableRow();

// create column 1
_Column11 = new HtmlTableCell();
_Column11.Style.Add(HtmlTextWriterStyle.Width, "70%");

// create the input textbox
_InputTextbox = new TextBox();
_InputTextbox.ID = "InputTextbox";

// add the textbox into column 1
_Column11.Controls.Add(_InputTextbox);

// add column 1 into row 1
_Row1.Controls.Add(_Column11);

// create column 2
_Column12 = new HtmlTableCell();
_Column12.Style.Add(HtmlTextWriterStyle.Width, "30%");

// create the button
_ConvertButton = new Button();
_ConvertButton.ID = "ConvertButton";
_ConvertButton.Text = "Convert";
_ConvertButton.Click += new EventHandler(ConvertButton_Click);

// add the button into column 2
_Column12.Controls.Add(_ConvertButton);

// add column 2 into row 1
_Row1.Controls.Add(_Column12);

// add row 1 into the main table
_MainTable.Controls.Add(_Row1);

// create row 2
_Row2 = new HtmlTableRow();

// create column 1
_Column21 = new HtmlTableCell();
_Column21.Attributes.Add("colspan", "2");

// create the output literal
_OutputLiteral = new Literal();
_OutputLiteral.ID = "OutputLiteral";

// add the literal into column 1
_Column21.Controls.Add(_OutputLiteral);
```

```
        // add column 1 into row 3
        _Row2.Controls.Add(_Column21);

        // add row 2 into the main table
        _MainTable.Controls.Add(_Row2);

        // add the table to this Web Part's control collection
        this.Controls.Add(_MainTable);
    }
    catch (Exception ex)
    {
        Literal _ErrorMessageLiteral = new Literal();
        _ErrorMessageLiteral.Text = ex.Message;

        this.Controls.Clear();
        this.Controls.Add(_ErrorMessageLiteral);
    }
}
```

If you try and build your project at this point, the build will fail. If you look closely at the above code, you will see that you have wired up an event handler but have yet to define it. Go ahead and stub out your event handler, so your code will compile.

2.   Add the following event handler code stub to your WebPart class:

```
protected void ConvertButton_Click(object sender, EventArgs e)
{
}
```

If you have followed the steps so far, the class you have created is not decorated with the public access modifier. In C#, the default class access modifier is internal; therefore, your Web Part will not be visible outside this assembly, nor will you be able to add it to a page.

3.   Add a public access modifier to the PigLatinWebPart class:

```
public PigLatinWebPart : System.Web.UI.WebParts.WebPart
{
    ...
}
```

4.   Build your project.

Sign the Assembly

As discussed earlier in this chapter, it would be a good idea to deploy your Web Part at this point. Once the Web Part is successfully deployed, you can then come back and implement the code necessary to convert the input string to Pig Latin. If you encounter problems during the deployment of your Web Part now, it will be much easier to debug if there is no custom code being executed. Once you successfully manage to deploy the Web Part, you can then concentrate on developing and debugging the business rules and other logic.

Before you deploy your Web Part, you should sign the assembly. The following steps guide you through the process of signing your assembly.

1. Right-click on the project node and select Properties from the context menu.

2. Click the Signing tab.

3. Check the Sign the assembly check box.

4. Select <New...> from the "Choose a strong name key file" drop-down list.

5. Enter **PigLatin** in the Key file name text box.

6. Uncheck the Protect my key file with a password check box.

7. Click OK.

8. Save your changes and build the project.

Now that your assembly is signed, you need to add a `SafeControl` entry to your web application's `web.config` file. Before you are able to add the `SafeControl` entry to your `web.config`, you need to extract the public key token from your compiled assembly using the following steps.

Extract Public Key Token

The following steps guide you though the process of extracting the public key token from your signed assembly using the .NET Framework Strong Name Utility command-line tool. Take note of the public key token; you will need it in the next step.

1. Open a Visual Studio 2005 Command Prompt window by clicking on Start ➪ Programs ➪ Microsoft Visual Studio 2005 ➪ Visual Studio Tools ➪ Visual Studio 2005 Command Prompt.

2. Type **sn -T <assembly>** where <assembly> is the complete path to the Web Part's assembly within your project. If this path contains spaces, place it within double quotation marks. The command window should look similar to Figure 4-24.

Add Safe Control Entry

The following steps walk you through the process of adding a `SafeControl` entry to the `web.config` file of your web application. Without this entry your Web Part will not run.

1. Navigate to the physical folder that represents the web application that you plan on deploying the Web Part to. If the default settings were used, the path should be something like this:

```
C:\Inetpub\wwwroot\wss\VirtualDirectories\Development80
```

The name of the folder in the directory (`C:\Inetpub\wwwroot\wss\VirtualDirectories`*) that contains the web application is determined by the name you gave the web application as well as the port number used during its creation.*

2. Open the `web.config` file.

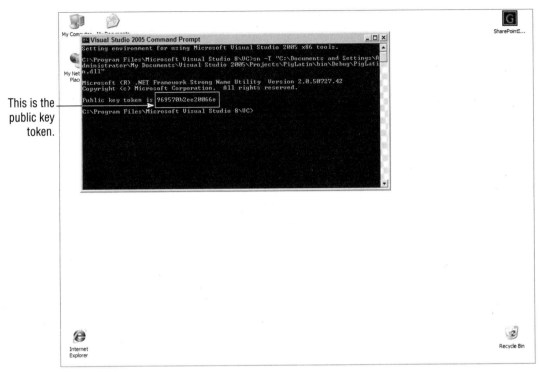

This is the public key token.

Figure 4-24

Take a moment to locate the SafeControls element. Notice that there are several SafeControl elements already defined in your web.config file. Also notice that the entries each contain the complete signature of the assembly that they represent, including the version and the public key token. Because you signed your assembly with a private key in prior steps, you will need the public key you extracted in the previous set of steps.

3. Make a copy of one of the SafeControl entries in the web.config file. Update the Assembly attribute of the copy to the fully qualified name of your Web Part's assembly and the Namespace attribute to the Web Part's namespace. Your SafeControl entry should resemble the following snippet. Make sure that the public key token in your entry matches the public key token you extracted in the previous set of steps.

```
<SafeControl
  Assembly="PigLatin, Version=1.0.0.0, Culture=neutral,
PublicKeyToken=969570b2ee20066e"
  Namespace="PigLatin"
  TypeName="*"
  Safe="True"
  AllowRemoteDesigner="True" />
```

Deploy the Assembly

You now need to place the assembly into the appropriate location, namely the bin folder of the web application that you plan on deploying the Web Part to. Do this by using a post-build event in your project.

1. Right-click on the project node and select Properties from the context menu.

2. Click the Build Events tab.

3. Enter the following command in the "Post-build event command line" text box to copy the `PigLatin.dll` file to the correct location:

```
xcopy PigLatin.dll "C:\Inetpub\wwwroot\wss\VirtualDirectories\
Development80\bin\" /y
```

The trailing slash in the above path will ensure that the bin folder is created if it does not exist. Be sure to update the path to be the correct folder for your web application.

4. Save your changes and build the project.

Create Web Part Definition File

In order to import your Web Part onto a page, you need to create a `.webpart` file. This file, once uploaded, is stored in the content database and tells SharePoint the information it needs to find the Web Part code. It can also be used to set default values for any of your Web Part's properties. Alternatives to this approach are discussed later.

1. Add an XML file to your project, and name it **PigLatinWebPart.webpart**.

2. Add the following code to the `PigLatinWebPart.webpart` file and save the file. Make sure that the public key token in your file matches the public key token extracted in previous steps. Also notice that you are able to set default values for many of the built-in properties as well as any of the public properties defined in your `WebPart` class. You are setting default values for both the `Title` and the `Description` properties below.

```xml
<webParts>
  <webPart xmlns="http://schemas.microsoft.com/WebPart/v3">
    <metaData>
      <type name="PigLatin.PigLatinWebPart, PigLatin, Version=1.0.0.0,
Culture=neutral, PublicKeyToken=969570b2ee20066e" />
      <importErrorMessage>Cannot import this Web Part.</importErrorMessage>
    </metaData>
    <data>
      <properties>
        <property name="Title" type="string">Pig Latin Converter</property>
        <property name="Description" type="string">This Web Part will convert an
input string to its Pig Latin equivalent.</property>
      </properties>
    </data>
  </webPart>
</webParts>
```

Deploy Web Part Definition File

You now need to place the .webpart file into the appropriate location, namely the wpcatalog folder of the web application to which you will deploy the Web Part. Do this by using a post-build event .

1. Right-click on the project node, and select Properties from the context menu.
2. Click the Build Events tab.
3. Enter the following command in the "Post-build event command line" text box to copy the PigLatinWebPart.webpart file to the correct location.

```
xcopy ..\..\PigLatinWebPart.webpart "C:\Inetpub\wwwroot\wss\VirtualDirectories\
Development80\wpcatalog\" /y
```

The trailing slash in the above path will ensure that the wpcatalog folder is created if it does not exist. Be sure to update the path to be the correct folder for you web application.

4. Save your changes and build the project.

Add the Web Part to a Page

The final step in your deployment involves informing SharePoint of the Web Part's existence. There are a few ways to accomplish this task. Keep in mind that if you had deployed this Web Part via a WSS v3 Solution, all of this work would have been done for you. The ways in which you could inform Share-Point of the Web Part are:

❑ Since we copied the .webpart file to the wpcatalog folder, it will automatically appear in the Web Part gallery when we attempt to add a new Web Part via the links at the top of your Web Part zones when editing a page.

❑ Had you not copied the .webpart file to the wpcatalog folder, you could manually import the .webpart file to any page within your site.

❑ Had you not copied the .webpart file to the wpcatalog folder, you could have browsed to the Web Part gallery and added it by clicking on New when viewing the Web Part gallery's Web Parts. SharePoint is smart enough to find your Web Part and display it as an option to add to the gallery. This is possible because of the public access modifier decorating the Web Part class within the assembly (which is in the bin folder).

1. Browse to the WSS v3 site and click on Edit Page under Site Actions.
2. Click in Add a Web Part in one of the two default Web Part zones.
3. Select the Pig Latin Converter Web Part, and click **Add**. Your Web Part should be rendered on the page. Click Exit Edit Mode under the Site Action link.

You can now see your Web Part in its full glory (see Figure 4-25), including your text box and button. You can also click on the button and see that it does indeed post back as you would expect. Remember that you have not added any code to the button click event handler, so nothing is really happening yet. It is up to you to implement the code to convert the input string to Pig Latin. You should know where to find the requirements!

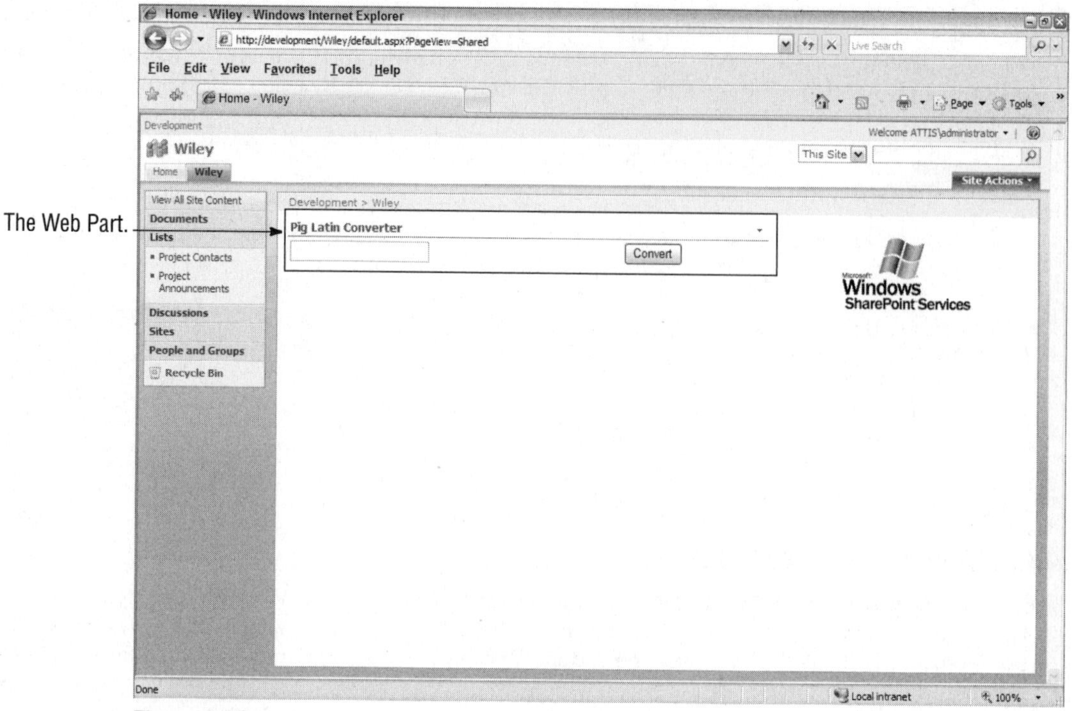

Figure 4-25

Testing and Debugging a Web Part

Any developer, novice or experienced, will of course understand the need to test and debug their code. There are a handful of ways to do this. Because there is no design-time experience for developing Web Parts, and you cannot "run" a Web Part in the traditional sense of running a project, as you can with a web application or a WinForms application, you need to "Attach to Process" to debug your Web Part. The process in this case is the IIS worker process in which the Web Part is running. Regardless of the process used to debug the Web Part, these steps assume that the assembly is in the bin folder of the web application hosting the Web Part, which incidentally is also a best practice. If you plan on deploying the Web Part assembly to the GAC, additional steps need to be performed to get the Visual Studio debugger to successfully debug your assembly. Working under the assumption that you have a Web Part created and have set a breakpoint somewhere in the code that you would like to pause execution on, the steps to debug in this way are as follows. Keep in mind that if your Web Part does not contain any references to WSS v3 objects, it may be easier to debug the Web Part by debugging the web site in which it is hosted.

1.   Open up a Visual Studio 2005 project containing the Web Part you wish to debug.

2.   Select Attach to Process from the Debug menu in Visual Studio 2005.

3. Select the appropriate `w3wp.exe` process in the Attach to Process window. If you see more than one `w3wp.exe` process, simply attach to all of them by holding down the Ctrl key and clicking on all of them one by one, or if you know the correct process, select it.

4. Click the Attach button.

5. Click Attach in the Attach Security Warning dialog box that appears for each process that you are attaching to.

6. Ensure that a break point exists somewhere in your code.

7. Browse to a page containing your Web Part.

8. Perform an action that will enable you to reach the breakpoint. Execution will stop, and you should be able to debug your code as you would any other application.

9. To stop debugging, click the Stop button in the Debug toolbar, press Shift+F5, or select Stop Debugging from the Debug menu.

Although you do not have the luxury of the design-time experience, you do still have all of the rich debugging features that Visual Studio 2005 has to offer available.

Additional Web Part Features

We have only scraped the surface in discussing what Web Parts can do. There are other development options available, but this section briefly discusses only two of those options. Two of the additional available options are:

❑ Connected Web Parts

❑ Custom verbs

Connected Web Parts

Connected Web Parts allow you to have two Web Parts that can exchange information with one another at runtime. A connection between two Web Parts requires that one Web Part be a provider and that the other Web Part be a consumer. The provider Web Part provides some data to the consumer. Think of any type of master-detail scenario as an example. One such example could be a provider Web Part listing some invoices and the details associated with all of the items on each invoice, such as address and total. The provider Web Part would provide the invoice number to the consumer Web Part. The consumer Web Part might list all of the items on the selected invoice. Selecting an invoice in the provider Web Part would automatically display the items on the invoice in the consumer Web Part. More information on the steps required to implement connected Web Parts can be located at http://msdn2 .microsoft.com/en-us/library/ms469765.aspx.

Custom Verbs

Custom verbs allow you to add items to the menu supplied within each Web Part (see Figure 4-26). By default, you see menu items for Minimize, Close, Delete, Modify Shared Web Part, Connections, and Export. You can add items to this menu quite easily by simply overriding the Verbs property of the `WebPart` class.

Web Part
Verbs menu.

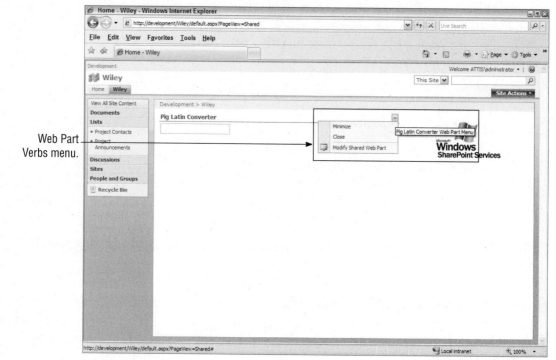

Figure 4-26

Summary

This chapter touched on many of the extensibility points that Windows SharePoint Services v3 (WSS v3) offers. It discussed the structure and content of Site Definitions and how powerful they are when used to provision sites within WSS v3, as well as custom field types and how they can be leveraged to add additional data input and validation options to a WSS v3 list. You reviewed two of the newest additions to the WSS v3 development family: the Feature and Solution Frameworks, and learned about the multitude of elements available when building Features as well as how they are scoped and deployed. Next you explored Solutions, now the preferred way to handle the deployment of many of the SharePoint components, including all of the ones just mentioned. A brief overview of Web Parts glanced over their infrastructure as well as design and security. Finally, you created a sample of each of these components. From the knowledge gained in this chapter, you should now be empowered and motivated to create solutions to the business problems you face using any number of the extensibility points that WSS v3 Framework provides.

Programming Windows SharePoint Services

By Matt Ranlett

Windows SharePoint Services is a lot more than just a set of fancy web pages where you can store your documents and lists. WSS is even more than a host for custom applications and Web Parts. WSS itself is actually a rich platform for application development, complete with a rich object model (OM) and web services layer. This platform allows developers to interact with SharePoint itself — the sites, the lists, and more. By leveraging the SharePoint platform, a developer has the power to create management applications, programmatically interact with lists and document libraries, react to system and user events both before and after they happen, and more. Furthermore, because this platform is exposed to developers both as an object model and as a web services layer, developers have the option of creating windows forms applications, web applications, Web Part applications, system services, and even console applications that can be executed locally on the server or remotely halfway around the world.

Within this chapter, you will learn about the Windows SharePoint Services API. This API includes two major interfaces, an object model you can incorporate directly into your code and a set of web services, which allow you to invoke SharePoint functionality from anywhere on the network. This chapter also covers an introduction to the greatly enhanced event-handling model and a guide to choosing between the object model and web services.

Object Model

The beginnings of any object model exploration should start with a basic understanding of what you're working with. Windows SharePoint Services delivers to developers an object model comprising 30 public namespaces in 10 assemblies. Taken from the Windows SharePoint Services SDK (at http://msdn2.microsoft.com/en-us/library/ms453225.aspx), the following table contains a subset of this list of public namespaces, which assembly files they're each contained in, and a short description of what each namespace offers to developers. For the full list, please refer back to the WSS SDK documentation.

Name	Assembly	Description
Microsoft.SharePoint	Microsoft.SharePoint (in Microsoft.SharePoint.dll)	Provides types and members for working with a top-level site and its subsites or lists
Microsoft.SharePoint .Administration	Microsoft.SharePoint (in Microsoft.SharePoint.dll)	Provides administrative types and members for managing a Microsoft Windows SharePoint Services deployment
Microsoft.SharePoint .Deployment	Microsoft.SharePoint (in Microsoft.SharePoint.dll)	Provides types and members for importing and exporting content between Windows SharePoint Services web sites
Microsoft.SharePoint .Meetings	Microsoft.SharePoint (in Microsoft.SharePoint.dll)	Provides types and members that can be used to customize Meeting Workspace sites
Microsoft.SharePoint .MobileControls	Microsoft.SharePoint (in Microsoft.SharePoint.dll)	Provides server controls for rendering the mobile forms and view pages used in SharePoint lists
Microsoft.SharePoint .Navigation	Microsoft.SharePoint (in Microsoft.SharePoint.dll)	Provides types and members for customizing the navigation structures and site maps of SharePoint web sites
Microsoft.SharePoint .Workflow	Microsoft.SharePoint (in Microsoft.SharePoint.dll)	Provides types and members for associating, initiating, and managing workflow templates and instances

Thirty namespaces sounds like a daunting learning curve, but an understanding of what you're trying to accomplish can help you target which namespace(s) you'll need in your code. Another feature of the SharePoint object model that helps you write code is that the WSS OM is extremely hierarchical — you can navigate from higher-level objects such as the SPSite object all the way down to the SPListItem object and back.

The WSS SDK illustrates this navigation (http://msdn2.microsoft.com/en-us/library/ms473633.aspx) with Figure 5-1 and a description of classes and properties.

Site Architecture and Object Model Overview

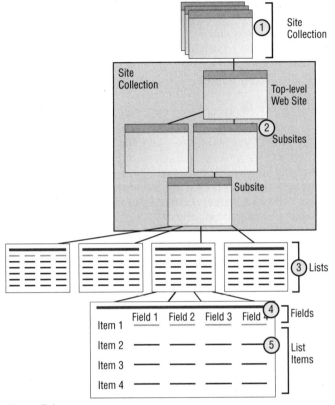

Figure 5-1

- ❑ Each SPSite object represents a site collection and has members that can be used to manage the site collection. The AllWebs property provides access to the SPWebCollection object that represents the collection of all web sites within the site collection, including the top-level site. The Microsoft.SharePoint.SPSite.OpenWeb method of the SPSite class returns a specific web site.

- ❑ Each site collection includes any number of SPWeb objects, and each object has members that can be used to manage a site, including its template and theme, as well as to access files and folders on the site. The Webs property returns an SPWebCollection object that represents all the subsites of a specified site, and the Lists property returns an SPListCollection object that represents all the lists in the site.

- ❑ Each SPList object has members that are used to manage the list or access items in the list. The GetItems method can be used to perform queries that return specific items. The Fields property returns an SPFieldCollection object that represents all the fields, or columns, in the list, and the Items property returns an SPListItemCollection object that represents all the items, or rows, in the list.

❑   Each `SPField` object has members that contain settings for the field.

❑   Each `SPListItem` object represents a single row in the list.

The extremely comprehensive object model is very powerful and bears some investigation into each of the namespaces offered. There isn't space to do that in this chapter, but you will take a look at the largest and most commonly used namespace, `Microsoft.SharePoint`.

Microsoft.SharePoint

The `Microsoft.SharePoint` namespace is by far the most commonly used. Contained in the `Microsoft.SharePoint.dll`, this namespace exposes more than 220 public classes, 9 interfaces, 8 public structures, and over 70 different enumerations. This is the namespace you will turn to in order to find objects like the `SPWeb`, the class that represents a single SharePoint web site, and the `SPList`, the class that represents a single list in a SharePoint web site. In fact, for practically all of the user interface concepts in SharePoint such as sites, features, lists, templates, users, roles, and alerts, you'll find the class corresponding to that concept in the `Microsoft.SharePoint` namespace.

Here is some sample code demonstrating possible uses for this namespace. You'll write a Windows Forms application that creates a new SharePoint site, creates a list in that site, adds a column to the list, and finally adds an item or two to that list.

For the purpose of this and all code demos presented in this chapter, the Visual Studio development environment and the SharePoint server environment are one and the same. While the code can be written in either Visual Basic or in C#, I've called my application `OMExample1` and I've written it in C#. My server's top-level site is `http://localhost`.

1.   Open Visual Studio 2005, and create a new Windows Application project.

2.   Once you have a new application project, add a reference to the `Microsoft.SharePoint.dll` so that you can use the namespaces it provides.

3.   As in the example in Figure 5-2, right-click on the References folder and select Add Reference to get the Add Reference dialog.

4.   Pick the Windows SharePoint Services component, and click OK. Now you can begin actually manipulating the form's elements and editing the code.

Rename the form from `Form1` to `SPMaintForm`. Then place the controls from the following table onto the form and arrange them so that your form looks somewhat like the form in Figure 5-3.

Control Type	Control Name	Description
Textbox	NewSiteNameTextBox	Entry field for users to type in the site's name
Label	NewSiteDirectionsLabel	Directions to the user about the new site name text box

Control Type	Control Name	Description
LinkLabel	NewSiteLinkLabel	Hyperlink to the newly created site
Button	CreateNewSiteButton	Click to create a new site with the user-supplied name and URL.
GroupBox	NewSiteNameGroupBox	Contains all controls dealing with the creation of a new SharePoint web
Textbox	ListNameTextBox	Entry field for users to type in the new list's name
Label	ListNameLabel	Directions for users
GroupBox	NewListGroupBox	Contains all controls involved in the creation of a new list with a custom field type
TextBox	ColumnNameTextBox	Entry field for users to type in the name for the new list field
Label	ColumnNameLabel	Directions for users
Label	ColumnTypeLabel	Directions for user
Radio Button	SingleLineRadioButton	Check for a single-line (Text) column type.
Radio Button	MultiLineRadioButton	Check for a multiple-line (Note) column type.
Radio Button	NumberRadioButton	Check for a numeric (Number) column type.
GroupBox	ColumnPropertiesGroupBox	Contains all controls dealing with the creation of a custom column type in the new list
Button	CreateNewListButton	Click to create a new list with the given name and add a named column of the specified type to the new list.
Textbox	NewItemTitleTextBox	Entry field for users to input the title of the new item
Textbox	NewItemCustomDataTextBox	Entry field for users to input the custom data of their choosing

Continued

Control Type	Control Name	Description
Label	NewItemTitleLabel	Directions for users
Label	CustomColumnDataLabel	Directions for users
Button	AddItemButton	Click to add a new item to your new list in your new site.
GroupBox	NewListItemGroupBox	Contains all controls involved in the creation of a new list item

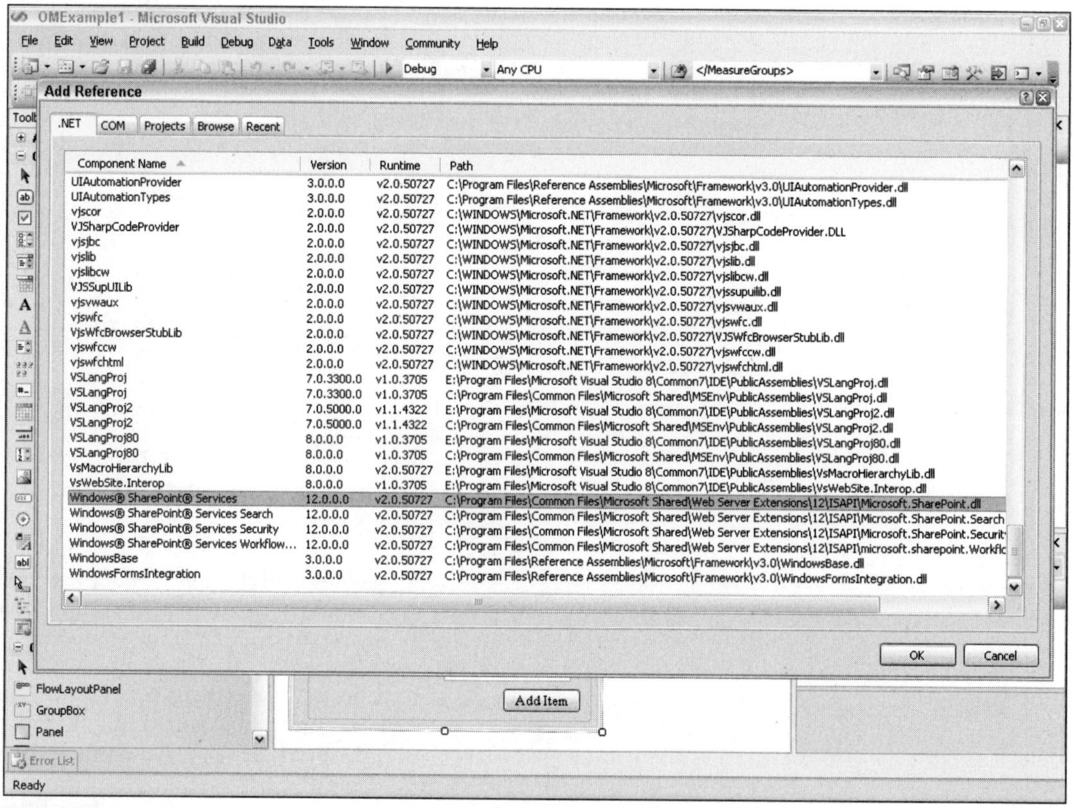

Figure 5-2

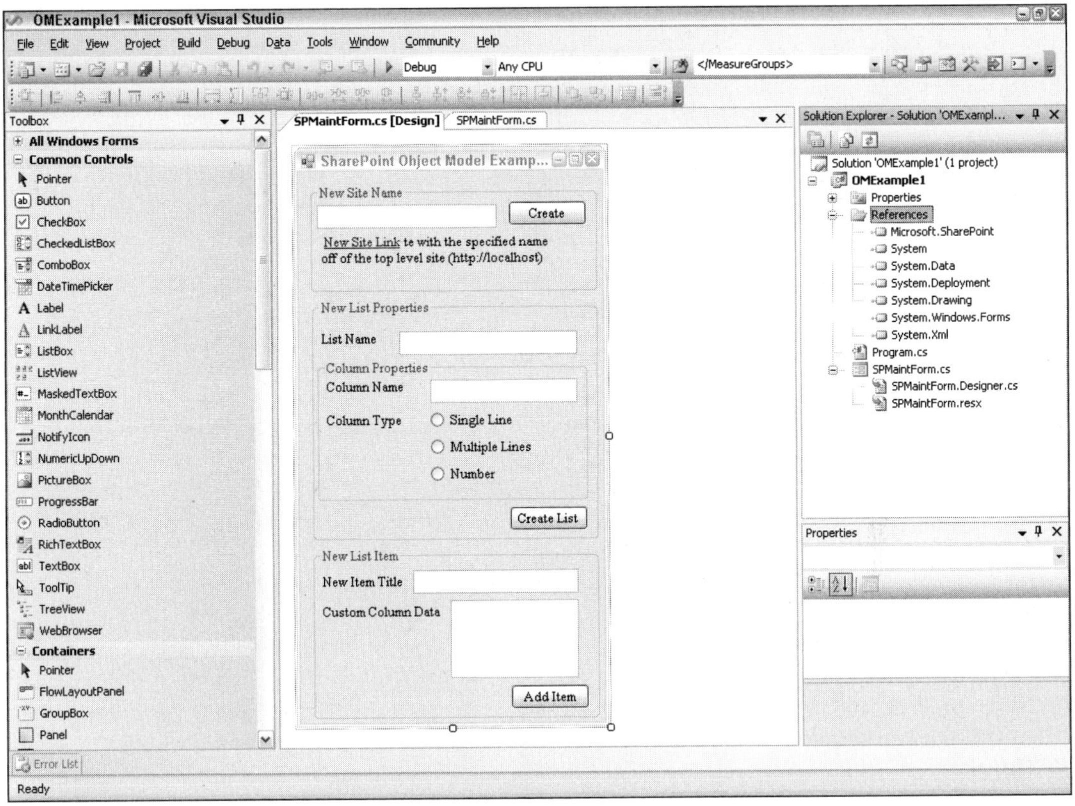

Figure 5-3

Now look at the salient portions of the code in Listing 5-1. The entire solution is provided on the companion web site, at www.wrox.com.

Listing 5-1

```
private void CreateNewSiteButton_Click(object sender, EventArgs e)
{
    ...
    {
        // Get a reference to the top-level site.
        SPSite TopLevelSite = new SPSite("http://localhost");
        SPWeb SharePointWebInstance = TopLevelSite.OpenWeb();
        // Grab our current site's template for use below.
        string CurrentSiteTemplate = SharePointWebInstance.WebTemplate;
```

```
                         // SharePoint is fond of throwing exceptions so be sure to do this
in a Try..Catch.
                    try
                    {
                        ...
                        // Add a new item to the top level site's Webs collection.
                        SharePointWebInstance.Webs.Add(NewSiteNameTextBox.Text,
                                                       NewSiteNameTextBox.Text,
                                                       "New website added with the
OMExample1 test application",

(UInt32)System.Globalization.CultureInfo.CurrentCulture.LCID,
                                                       CurrentSiteTemplate,
                                                       false,
                                                       false);

                        ...
                    }
                    catch (Exception ex)
                    {
                        ...
                    }
                    finally
                    {
                        // Free up your resources!
                        TopLevelSite.Close();
                        SharePointWebInstance.Dispose();
                    }
```

SPSite

This CreateNewSiteButton click event handler contains the bulk of your code for creating a new site. First, you have to establish a reference to the site under which you plan to add a new site. Using the SPSite class and the URL to your top-level site, you get an object that represents the entire site collection. Given your site collection object, you can open a specific web via the OpenWeb() method. You could have identified a site under your top-level site had you passed in a GUID or a site-relative URL, but by not passing in any parameters you elected to open the top-level site at http://localhost. Other interesting methods of the SPSite class include DoesUserHavePermissions(), GetRecycleBinItems(), RecalculateStorageSpaceUsed(), and of course, Delete() and Close().

SPWeb

Once you have opened your top-level web, you discover which template was used so you can use the same template for a consistent look and feel in your new site. Each SPWeb object contains a Webs collection that represents all of its subsites. Adding to this collection adds a new subsite. Notice that you pass a localization ID (frequently hard-coded to 1033 in the WSS SDK examples). This localization ID represents the locale folders under the 12 Hive (typically found at C:\Program Files\Common Files\Microsoft Shared\web server extensions\12). Where you pass in the site template of the current site, you could specify any of the templates in the SiteTemplates directory (..\12\TEMPLATE\SiteTemplates) by name, such as "SPSNEWS" or "PUBLISHING". If you create custom site templates, this is where you can specify your own template's name to dynamically create new sites of your own design. Other interesting methods of the SPWeb class include DoesUserHavePermissions(), GetSubwebsForCurrentUser(), SearchListItems(), and ApplyTheme().

Once you're done adding to your site collection, you need to close any open references to the SPSite and SPWeb classes. However, if you get these references as a shared resource, you should let the platform itself manage the resource to avoid access violation errors. That is to say, if you didn't declare and instantiate the SPWeb object, as would happen if you called SPControl.GetContextWeb, then you cannot call the Dispose method. There is more information about correctly disposing of SharePoint objects in the "Best Practices" section of this chapter.

You've added a new site, but your demo application doesn't stop there. It goes on to create a new custom list in the newly created site and adds a new field to the list. Take a look at this process in Listing 5-2.

Listing 5-2

```
private void CreateNewListButton_Click(object sender, EventArgs e)
{
    ...
    // g\Get a reference to your newly created site.
    SPSite TopLevelSite = new SPSite("http://localhost");
    SPWeb NewSPWebInstance = TopLevelSite.OpenWeb(NewSiteURL);
    // Using the web's Lists property, get a reference to the collection of
lists in the site.
    SPListCollection SiteLists = NewSPWebInstance.Lists;
    try
    {
        // Add a new SPList to the Lists collection.
        NewListID = SiteLists.Add(ListNameTextBox.Text.Trim(),
                            "New list added dynamically via the
OMExample1 sample application",
                                SPListTemplateType.GenericList);
        try
        {
            // Get a reference to our new list.
            SPList NewSPListInstance =
NewSPWebInstance.Lists.GetList(NewListID,
                                                    false);
            // Get the fields collection from our new list so we can add to it.
            SPFieldCollection Fields = NewSPListInstance.Fields;

            // Pick which type of field to create, default to single line text.
            SPFieldType UserChosenFieldType = SPFieldType.Text;
            if (SingleLineRadioButton.Checked)
            {
                UserChosenFieldType = SPFieldType.Text;
            }
            else if (MultiLineRadioButton.Checked)
            {
                UserChosenFieldType = SPFieldType.Note;
            }
            else if (NumberRadioButton.Checked)
            {
                UserChosenFieldType = SPFieldType.Number;
```

```
        }
        ...
        try
        {
            // Add a new field of the chosen type to the fields collection.
            string NewSPFieldInstance = Fields.Add(ColumnNameTextBox.Text,
                                            UserChosenFieldType,
                                            true);
        }
        catch (Exception ex)
        {
            MessageBox.Show("Error encountered attempting to add a new
field" +
                        Environment.NewLine +
                        ex.Message);
        }
    }
    catch (Exception ex)
    {
        MessageBox.Show("Error encountered attempting to identify the new
list" +
                        Environment.NewLine +
                        ex.Message);
    }
}
catch (Exception ex)
{
    MessageBox.Show("Error encountered attempting to create a new list" +
                    Environment.NewLine +
                    ex.Message);
}
finally
{
    TopLevelSite.Close();
    NewSPWebInstance.Dispose();
}
...
}
```

SPListCollection

This function starts out by going back to the top-level site to try to find your current web. Notice this time that when you call the OpenWeb() function, you are passing in a string which is the relative URL from the top-level site. This enables you to open the site you just created. The SPWeb NewSPWebInstance object has a property called Lists, which holds a collection of all the lists contained in this site. Adding a new SPList object to this collection adds a new list to the site. Likewise, removing a list from a collection would remove it from a site. Another method of finding a specific list is to start with the SPContext's AllWebs[] property and passing in the desired site name as an index to retrieve the specific SPWeb object. Once you have the specific SPWeb, use the SPWeb.Lists[] property to retrieve a handle to the desired list. Note that the SPContext object refers to the current HTTP request to a SharePoint site and is best used in web applications.

```
SPList currentList = SPContext.Current.List;
SPWeb currentSite = SPContext.Current.Web;
SPSite currentSiteCollection = SPContext.Current.Site;
SPWebApplication currentWebApplication = SPContext.Current.Site.WebApplication;
```

Given the SPWeb object, the SPListCollection.Add() method creates a new list and accepts the name, description, and list type as arguments and returns the GUID of the newly created list. This is extremely helpful because to do any further operations on the list itself, you'll need this GUID.

SPList

Given the GUID returned by the SPListCollection.Add() method, you can instantiate a reference to your newly created list in the form of a SPList object and manipulate it's properties. For the purposes of this example, you're going to add a custom column based on user input. Other interesting methods on the SPList object include DoesUserHavePermissions(), IsContentTypeAllowed(), and WriteRssFeed().

SPFieldCollection

Every SPList object has a Fields property, which contains a collection of SPField objects associated with a particular list. The code in Listing 5-2 retrieves this collection for use because, like all of the other SharePoint collection properties you've worked with so far, adding to the collection adds a new field.

SPFieldType

Before you add a new field to the SPFieldCollection, check the user input portions of your application to see which SPFieldType the user selected. Using the SPFieldType enumeration, you are able to set a field to one of thirty-two options, including the Text, Note, and Number you're using here. Other options include CrossProjectLinks for Meeting Workspaces and Users to represent SharePoint users.

Now that you've created a new web and put a new list with a custom field into that list, do the work of adding an item to that list. Listing 5-3 illustrates just that task.

Listing 5-3

```
private void AddItemButton_Click(object sender, EventArgs e)
{
    ...
    // Get a reference to our newly created site.
    SPSite TopLevelSite = new SPSite("http://localhost");
    SPWeb NewSPWebInstance = TopLevelSite.OpenWeb(NewSiteURL);
    // Using the web's Lists property, get a reference to the collection of
lists in the site.
    SPListCollection SiteLists = NewSPWebInstance.Lists;
    try
    {
        // Find our list.
        SPList TargetList = SiteLists.GetList(NewListID,
                                              false);
        // Get the ListItems collection from the web.
        SPListItemCollection ListItems = TargetList.Items;
        try
```

```
                    {
                        // Add a new ListItem.
                        SPListItem NewItem = ListItems.Add();
                        // Populate the title field.
                        NewItem["Title"] = NewItemTitleTextBox.Text;
                        // Check the type of the custom field.
                        double NumberField = 0;
                        if (NumberField.GetType() !=
NewItem.Fields[NewFieldName].FieldValueType)
                        {
                            // If we're a text type of field, assign the text value of
the text box.
                            NewItem[NewFieldName] = NewItemCustomDataTextBox.Text;
                        }
                        else
                        {
                            // If our field is a number, we must convert the typed
value to a double.
                            Double.TryParse(NewItemCustomDataTextBox.Text, out
NumberField);
                            NewItem[NewFieldName] = NumberField;
                        }
                        // Persist changes to the SharePoint content database.
                        NewItem.Update();
                    }
                    catch (Exception ex)
                    {
                        MessageBox.Show("Error encountered attempting to add a new item
to the list" +
                                        Environment.NewLine +
                                        ex.Message);
                    }
                }
                catch (Exception ex)
                {
                    MessageBox.Show("Error encountered attempting to identify the new
list" +
                                    Environment.NewLine +
                                    ex.Message);
                }
                finally
                {
                    TopLevelSite.Close();
                    NewSPWebInstance.Dispose();
                }
                ...
            }
```

SPListItems

Again, in Listing 5-3, you start with the now familiar process of obtaining a reference to your web. You drill down through the SPWeb to the list. The SPList object predictably exposes an Items collection, which contains all of the SPListItem objects associated with this particular list. However, adding a new item to a list is not as simple as calling SPList.Items.Add(). Well, actually it is that simple, but after you've added the SPListItem, you need to populate the fields and call the SPListItem.Update() method. As you see in the code above, the SPListItem is returned by the SPList.Items.Add() function. Given this reference to the list item, you can populate the fields using an indexer to specify which field is being updated. Thanks to your user input selection of text or number, you have to handle attempts to add numbers to your custom field. It is worth noting here that SPFieldType.Number maps to a System.Double. For a full list of these mappings between SharePoint SPFieldTypes and .NET types, refer to the following table, which can also be found in the Windows SharePoint SDK. Once both fields have been set to your desired values, you call the SPListItem.Update() method to save the changes to the SharePoint content database. Following that, you dispose of any open references that need to be freed.

Name	Format
Attachments	System.Boolean
Boolean	System.Boolean
Calculated	N/A
Choice	System.String
Computed	N/A
Counter	System.Int32
CrossProjectLink	System.Boolean
Currency	System.Double
DateTime	System.DateTime
GridChoice	System.String
Guid	System.Guid
Integer	System.Int32
Lookup	System.String
MaxItems	System.Int32
ModStat	System.Int32
MultiChoice	System.String
Note	System.String
Number	System.Double
Recurrence	System.Boolean

Continued

Name	Format
Text	System.String
Threading	System.String
URL	System.String, System.String
User	System.String
Note	System.String

With the code complete, you can run the application.

After filling in all of the required user input fields and pressing all the buttons in the right order, you should get a new SharePoint web under your top-level site.

1. Click on the hyperlink on the OMExample1 form to go to the new web's home page. Your screen should look something like Figure 5-4.

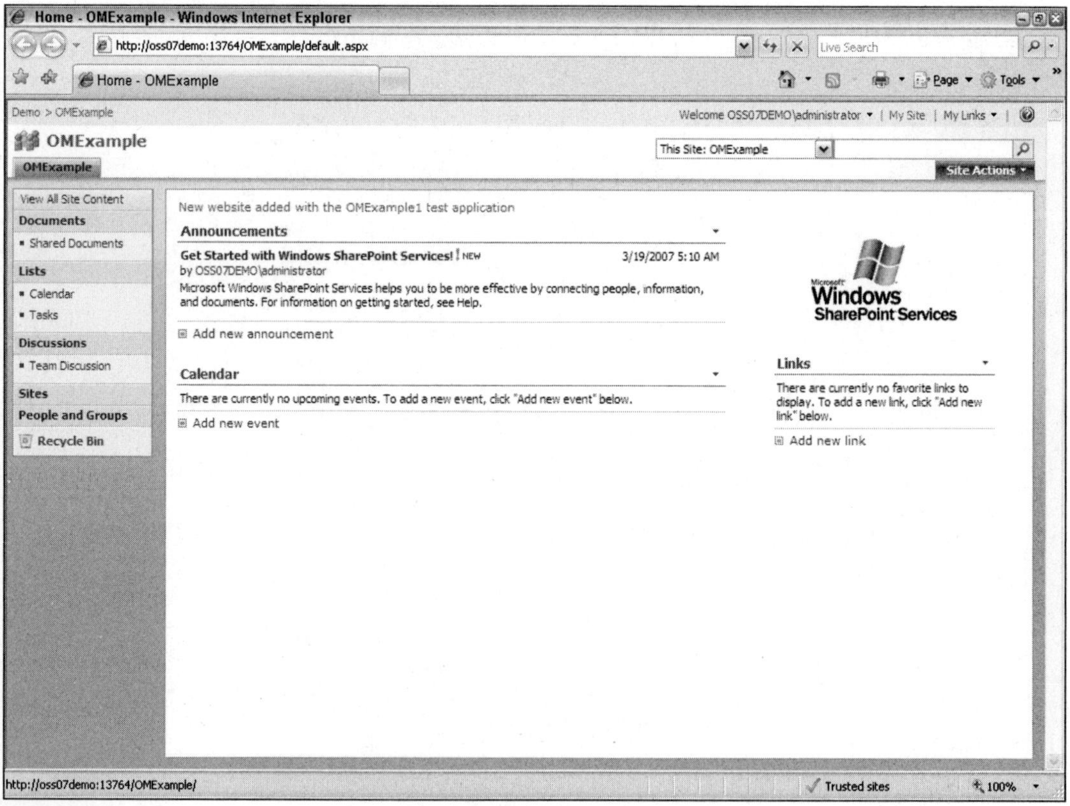

Figure 5-4

2. Click on the Lists link in the Quick Launch bar to verify that the new list has been created, as shown in Figure 5-5

3. Open the new list to verify that the data has, in fact, been added, as shown in Figure 5-6.

4. Open the item to validate that the data looks right and that the custom field is of the type you expect. In my sample run I chose to use a MultiLine field type, shown in Figure 5-7.

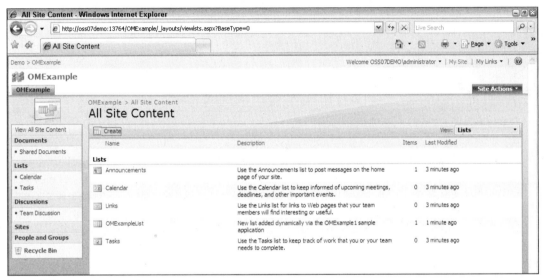

Figure 5-5

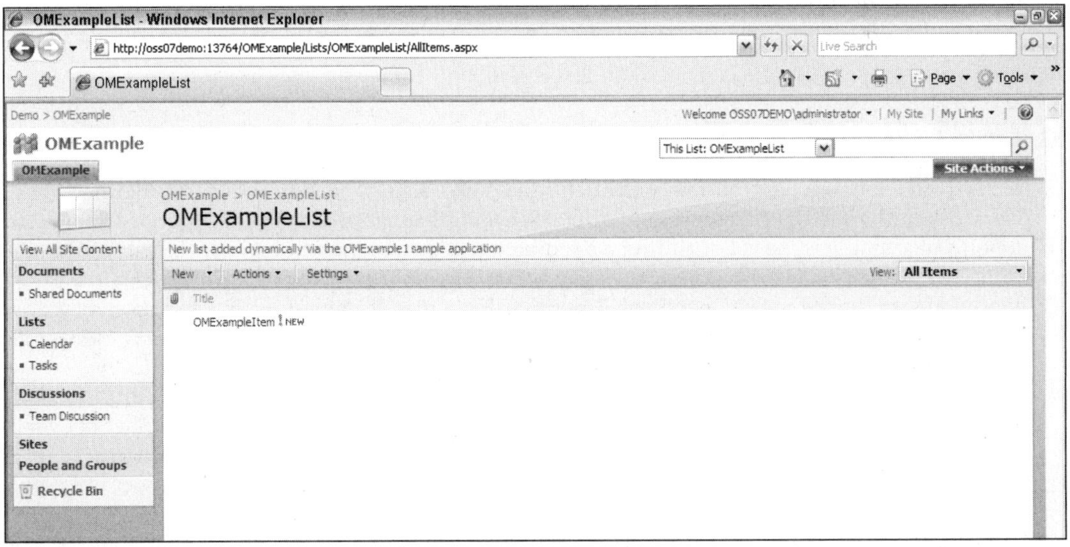

Figure 5-6

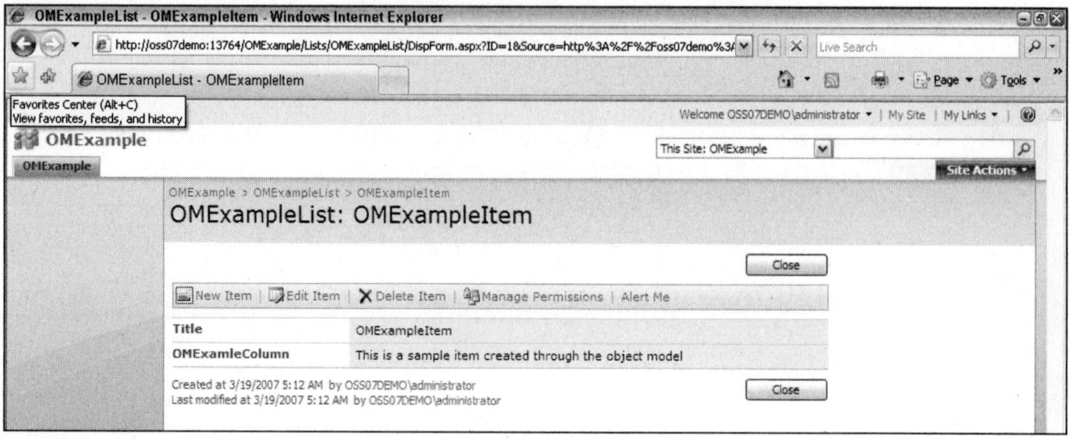

Figure 5-7

This fairly trivial example only scratches the surface of the enormous programming power offered by the `Microsoft.SharePoint` namespace. You've looked at only 6 of the 220 public classes, 2 of the 70 different enumerations, and none of the public interfaces or structures. Learn more about the `Microsoft.SharePoint` namespace in the Windows SharePoint Services SDK: `http://msdn2.microsoft.com/en-us/library/microsoft.sharepoint.aspx`.

Microsoft.SharePoint.Workflow

One of the most exciting new namespaces in SharePoint v3 is the Workflow namespace. Workflow is a new .NET 3.0 technology designed to support long running transactions with multiple points of interaction. While Windows SharePoint Services comes with a few built-in workflows, you have the ability to create your own workflows using the `Microsoft.SharePoint.Workflow` namespace. This topic is so deeply intensive that we've devoted an entire chapter to it later in the book, Chapter 15.

Event Handling

WSS v2 offered developers the ability to catch certain user actions in code and react programmatically. These user actions triggered a set of asynchronous events that happened after the user had completed the action. An example is the act of adding a document to a document library. A developer could catch the `DocumentAdded` event and perform some action. Unfortunately for v2 developers, all of the event handlers were "after-the-fact" handlers. You can't stop a user from performing an action with an event handler. Another limitation of v2 event handlers is that you can only catch events on document and forms libraries.

Fortunately for you, all of this has changed. Now, WSS v3 has a vastly increased number of events developers can take advantage of. These events include "before-the-fact" or synchronous events as well as "after-the-fact" or asynchronous events as illustrated in Figure 5-8. As a developer interested in catching SharePoint events, you are no longer limited to only document libraries and forms libraries. Now you have the ability to catch events on practically every list type that SharePoint offers, as well as at the site level, list, or library level, and at the individual file level. Combine the increase in available functionality of event handlers with Workflow and you'll really have a flexible system.

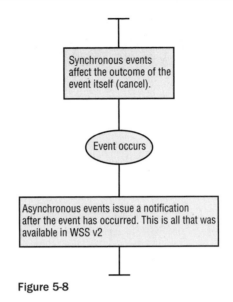

Figure 5-8

Receiving SharePoint Events

To catch SharePoint events at an item level, your classes must inherit from the SPItemEventReceiver base class. From this inheritance, your class will be able to take advantage of the methods shown in the following table.

Public Methods	
Name	**Description**
ContextEvent	Item level event reaction to a SPContext class method call
ItemAdded	Asynchronous after event that occurs after a new item has been added to its containing object
ItemAdding	Synchronous before event that occurs when a new item is added to its containing object
ItemAttachmentAdded	Asynchronous after event that occurs after a user adds an attachment to an item
ItemAttachmentAdding	Synchronous before event that occurs when a user adds an attachment to an item
ItemAttachmentDeleted	Asynchronous after event that occurs when after a user removes an attachment from an item
ItemAttachmentDeleting	Synchronous before event that occurs when a user removes an attachment from an item

Continued

Name	Description
ItemCheckedIn	Asynchronous after event that occurs after an item is checked in
ItemCheckedOut	Asynchronous after event that occurs after an item is checked out
ItemCheckingIn	Synchronous before event that occurs as a file is being checked in
ItemCheckingOut	Synchronous before event that occurs after an item is checked out
ItemDeleted	Asynchronous after event that occurs after an existing item is completely deleted
ItemDeleting	Synchronous before event that occurs before an existing item is completely deleted
ItemFileConverted	Asynchronous after event that occurs after a file has been transformed by the SPFile.Convert method
ItemFileMoved	Occurs after a file is moved
ItemFileMoving	Occurs when a file is being moved
ItemUncheckedOut	Synchronous before event that occurs when an item is being unchecked-out
ItemUncheckingOut	Synchronous before event that occurs when an item is being unchecked-out
ItemUpdated	Asynchronous after event that occurs after an existing item is changed, for example, when the user changes data in one or more fields
ItemUpdating	Synchronous before event that occurs when an existing item is changed, for example, when the user changes data in one or more fields

Protected Methods

Name	Description
DisableEventFiring	Prevents events from being raised (inherited from SPEventReceiverBase)
EnableEventFiring	Enables events to be raised (inherited from SPEventReceiverBase)

You can also catch events at the List (SPListEventReceiver), Web (SPWebEventReceiver), Email (SPEmailEventReceiver), and Feature (SPFeatureReceiver) levels.

Write Code to Cancel an Item Deletion

Let's look at a sample event handler to help understand the core concepts behind handling events. Since your previous levels of functionality left you completely unable to prevent an action on a non-document-library list, in this example you'll stop someone from deleting an announcement. While you will be working with the AnnouncementsList type, the following table is a list of available list template types:

List Template Type	Template ID
Custom List	100
Document Library	101
Survey	102
Links List	103
Announcements List	104
Contacts List	105
Events List	106
Tasks List	107
Discussion Board	108
Picture Library	109

To find these list IDs and the IDs of additional list template types, navigate to the Features directory under the \12\TEMPLATE folder on your SharePoint server. Find the folder for the list you are looking for in the Features directory and open the List Templates folder under that. If you were looking for the AnnouncementsList type, you'd navigate to C:\Program Files\Common Files\Microsoft Shared\ web server extensions\12\TEMPLATE\FEATURES\AnnouncementsList\ListTemplates. Open the XML file in here to find the code represented by Listing 5-4. Pick out the Template ID Type value (Type = 104).

Listing 5-4

```
Announcements.xml
<?xml version="1.0" encoding="utf-8"?>
<Elements xmlns="http://schemas.microsoft.com/sharepoint/">
    <ListTemplate
        Name="announce"
        Type="104"
        BaseType="0"
        OnQuickLaunch="TRUE"
        SecurityBits="11"
        Sequence="320"
        DisplayName="$Resources:core,announceList;"
```

```
            Description="$Resources:core,announceList_Desc;"
            Image="/_layouts/images/itann.gif"/>
    </Elements>
```

To create and use your sample event handler, you'll need to do two things. First, you'll need to create the code that will run whenever you catch your desired event. Then you'll need to create a Feature to activate your event handler. Features are described in more depth in Chapter 4, so you won't be focusing on this portion of the task in great detail.

Open Visual Studio and start a new C# Class Library project called `EventHandlerExample1`. Since event handlers are part of the object model, the first thing you'll need to do is to add a reference to the `Microsoft.SharePoint` namespace.

1. Right-click on the References folder and select Add. In the Add Reference dialog, .NET tab, scroll to the bottom and select the `Microsoft.SharePoint` namespace.

2. Next, you'll want to rename `Class1.cs` to `CancelAnnouncementDeleteHandler.cs`.

You're now ready to begin writing your code.

The `CancelAnnouncementDeleteHandler` class needs to inherit from the `SPItemEventReceiver` class to function, so next to the class name put: `SPItemEventReceiver`. This will give you access to the methods listed in the previous table. You are trying to prevent an item from being deleted, so you will be overriding the `ItemDeleting` method, as shown in Figure 5-9.

In the `ItemDeleting` method, you'll cancel the deletion before it happens. Your code should look like Listing 5-5.

Listing 5-5

```
using System;
using System.Collections.Generic;
using System.Text;
using Microsoft.SharePoint;

namespace EventHandlerExample1
{
    class CancelAnnouncementDeleteHandler: SPItemEventReceiver
    {
        public override void ItemDeleting(SPItemEventProperties properties)
        {
            string HandledMessage = ("Announcements can not be deleted from this
list");
            properties.ErrorMessage = HandledMessage;
            properties.Cancel = true;
        }
    }
}
```

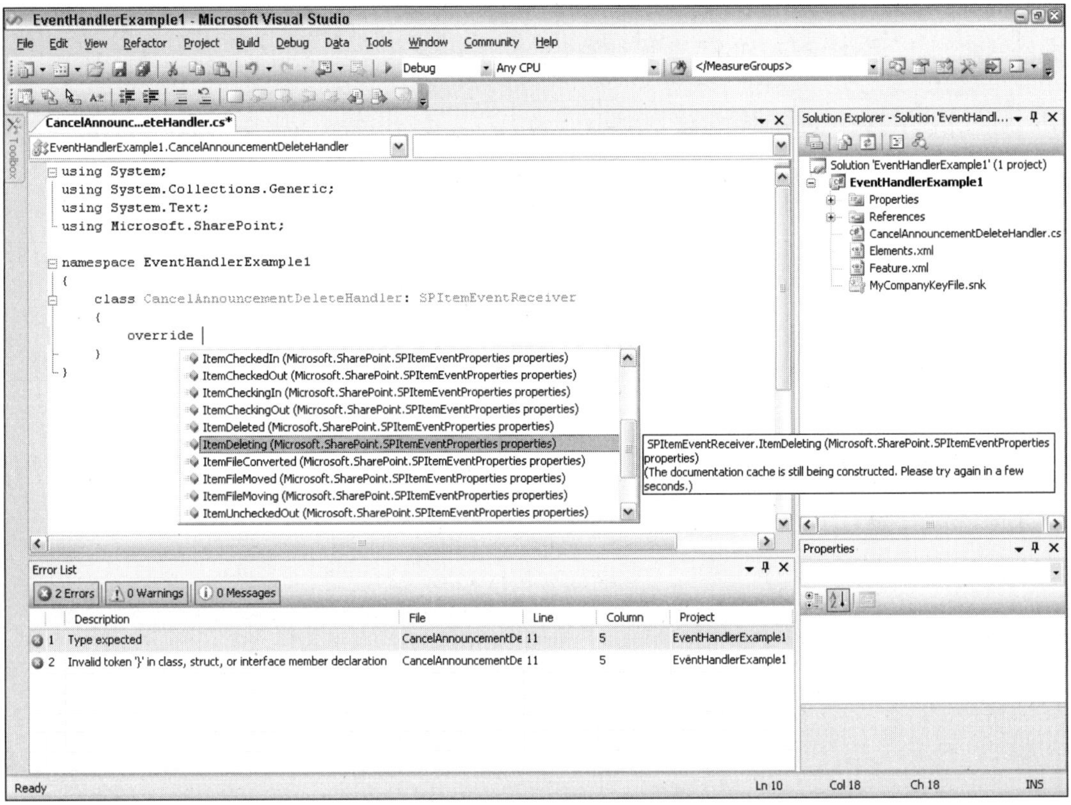

Figure 5-9

The next step in getting your event handler to work is to compile your DLL and deploy it to the GAC. Deploying an assembly to the GAC requires a strongly named assembly, so in the Project Properties dialog, click the Signing tab and check the box to sign the assembly, as in Figure 5-10. Be sure to create a new key file if you haven't already. Build the project and deploy it to the GAC by entering the following command into the SDK command prompt, as in Figure 5-11.

```
gacutil /i "C:\Documents and Settings\Administrator\My Documents\Visual Studio 2005\
Projects\EventHandlerExample1\bin\Debug\EventHandlerExample1.dll"
```

Verify successful deployment by finding your file in the C:\Windows\assembly folder. Normally, this GAC deployment would be automated with post-build steps or batch files, but it is presented in manual detail here as a learning exercise.

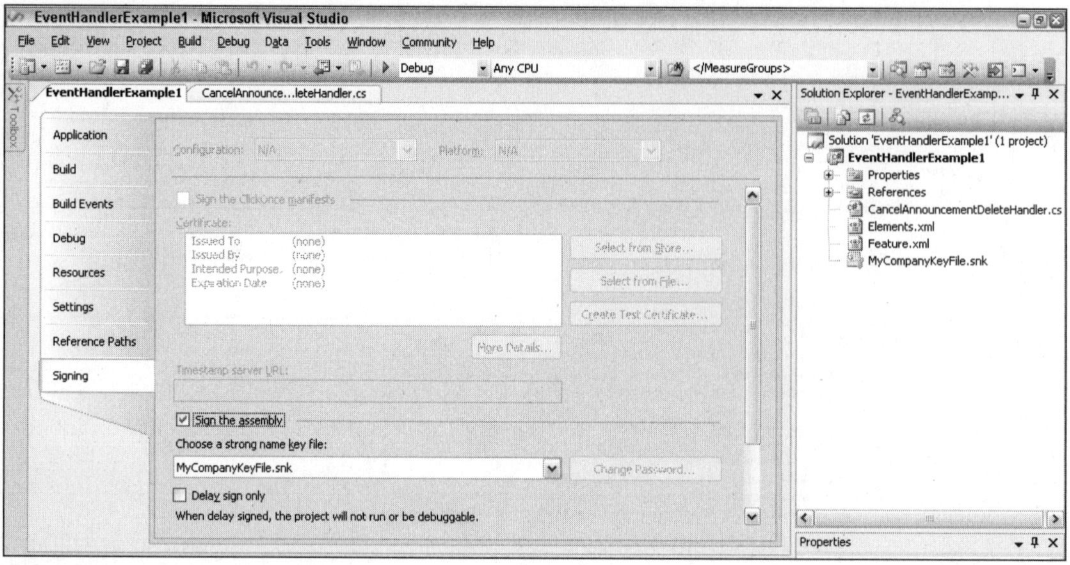

Figure 5-10

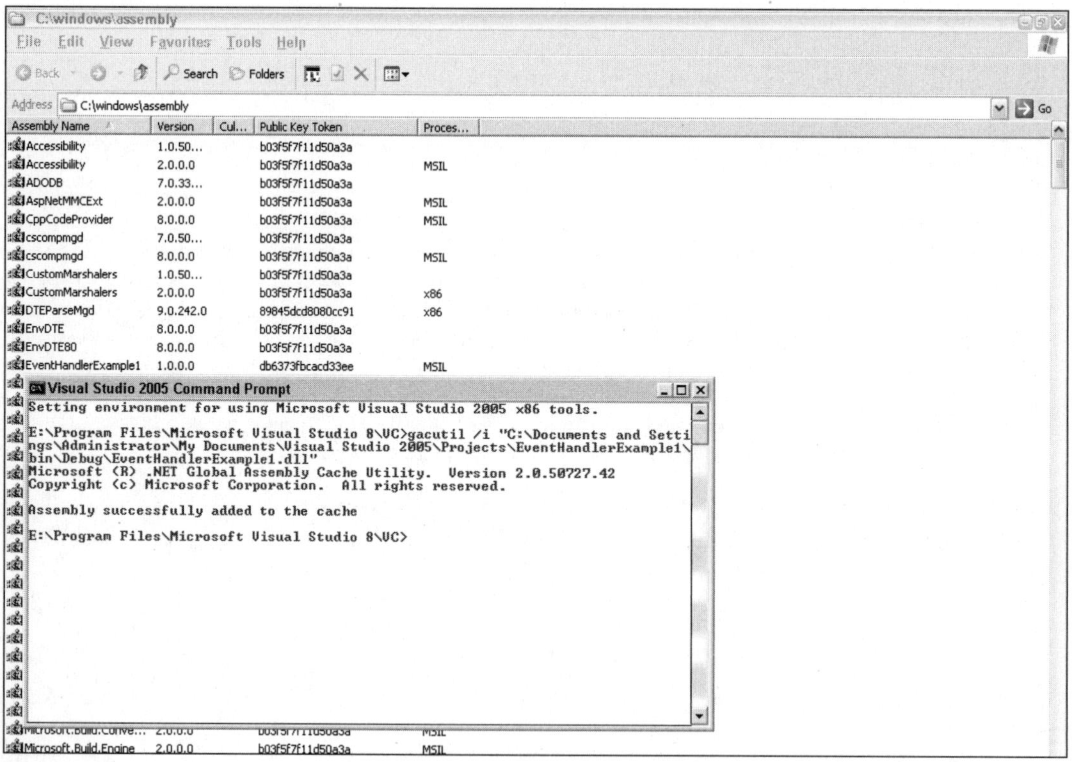

Figure 5-11

Create a Feature to Enable the Event Handler

The next task is to create and deploy a Feature that activates your event handler.

1. Back in Visual Studio, add two new XML files to the project. Call the first XML file, `Feature.xml`, and the second file `Elements.xml`.

2. Next, navigate to an existing feature in the `C:\Program Files\Common Files\Microsoft Shared\web server extensions\12\TEMPLATE\FEATURES` folder. You need to create a new folder for your event handler. Create a new folder with the same name as your event handler, as in Figure 5-12.

3. While you're in the FEATURES directory, here's an example of using one of the Microsoft provided Features for your own `Feature.xml` and `Elements.xml`. Navigate into the AnnouncementsList folder and open `Feature.xml`. Copy the contents of the Announcements `Feature.xml` file into your own `Feature.xml` file in Visual Studio. Now navigate down into the `AnnouncementsList\ListTemplate` folder and copy the contents of `Announcements.xml` into your `Elements.xml` file in Visual Studio. Now it's time to update your `Feature.xml` and `Elements.xml` files to match your event handler project.

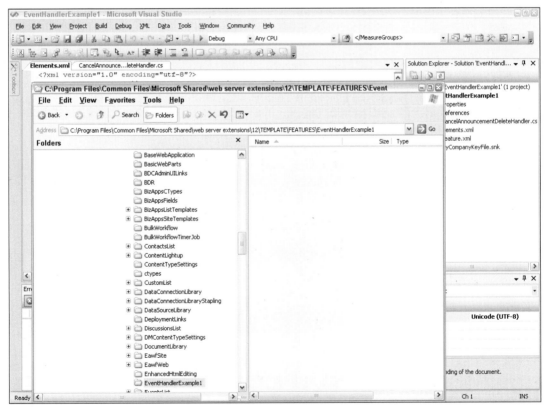

Figure 5-12

4. Start with `Feature.xml`. You'll need a unique `Feature Id` value, so generate a new GUID with the Create GUID tool on the Visual Studio Tools menu. Next you want to give your Feature a title and description to match its purpose. Finally, set the scope of the Feature to `Web`. Remove any additional elements such as `Version` and `Hidden`. When you're finished, your `Feature.xml` file should look like Listing 5-6:

Listing 5-6

```
<?xml version="1.0" encoding="utf-8"?>
<Feature Id="85DA483B-C3D4-4b5c-8F3A-89331E996305"
    Title="EventHandlerExample1"
    Description="An event handler which will cancel the deletion of an
announcements list item and insert a new item announcing that a delete attempt was
made"
    Scope="Web"
    xmlns="http://schemas.microsoft.com/sharepoint/">
        <ElementManifests>
                <ElementManifest Location="Elements.xml"/>
        </ElementManifests>
</Feature>
```

5. With `Elements.xml`, you need to create a `Receivers` node in your XML. In `Elements.xml`, the `Receivers` node has the following elements and attributes. The `ListTemplateID` indicates which template type this event handler targets (see the table in the "Write Code to Cancel an Item Deletion" section); in this case, the Announcements List type is 104. The name of the receiver is the name of the project. The type of receiver is the function you've overridden in your DLL. The `SequenceNumber` is a unique number that identifies this Feature. Microsoft has reserved a significant number of these sequence numbers, but any above 20,000 should be available. The Assembly name is your DLL name, version number, culture, and `PublicKeyToken`.

6. To get the `PublicKeyToken` value, find your DLL in the GAC (`C:\Windows\Assembly`), right-click on it and select Properties. Copy the public key from the properties dialog as illustrated in Figure 5-13. Finally, the class element contains the `Namespace.classname` of your event handler class.

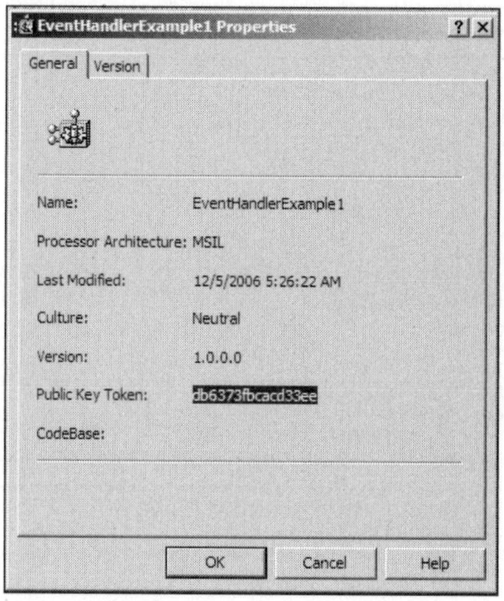

Figure 5-13

The `Elements.xml` file should look like Listing 5-7.

Listing 5-7

```xml
<?xml version="1.0" encoding="utf-8"?>
<Elements xmlns="http://schemas.microsoft.com/sharepoint/">
        <Receivers ListTemplateId="104">
                <Receiver>
                        <Name>EventHandlerExample1</Name>
                        <Type>ItemDeleting</Type>
                        <SequenceNumber>20000</SequenceNumber>
                        <Assembly>
                                EventHandlerExample1, Version=1.0.0.0,
                                culture=neutral, PublicKeyToken=db6373fbcacd33ee
                        </Assembly>

<Class>EventHandlerExample1.CancelAnnouncementDeleteHandler</Class>
                        <Data></Data>
                        <Filter></Filter>
                </Receiver>
        </Receivers>
</Elements>
```

7. Now, it's time to save `Feature.xml` and `Elements.xml` and copy them from your project folder to the Features folder you created above.

8. The next steps are to install and activate the Feature with the `stsadm.exe` tool and to attempt to delete an announcement. To use `stsadm`, open a command prompt window and navigate to the bin directory under the 12 folder. First, you need to install the Feature in the site collection. Use the following command:

```
C:\Program Files\Common Files\Microsoft Shared\Web server
extensions\12\BIN\stsadm.exe -o installfeature -filename
EventHandlerExample1\Feature.xml
```

   The parameters to `stsadm` to install a new feature are `-o installfeature` to indicate which action you're performing and `-filename` (*Feature Folder Name*\Feature.xml) to indicate which feature you're installing.

9. Once you've installed the Feature, the final step is to activate this Feature. This task can be done from inside the SharePoint UI, but for your purposes `stsadm.exe` works just as well (since you're already in the command dialog, you'll just activate the Feature from here). Use the following command:

```
C:\Program Files\Common Files\Microsoft Shared\Web server
extensions\12\BIN\stsadm.exe -o activatefeature -filename
EventHandlerExample1\Feature.xml -URL http://localhost
```

   The parameters to `stsadm` to activate a new feature are `-o activatefeature` to indicate which action you're performing, `-filename` (*Feature Folder Name*\Feature.xml) to indicate which feature you're installing, and `-URL` *url* to indicate which Web you're activating for.

   You should have a command window that looks like the one in Figure 5-14.

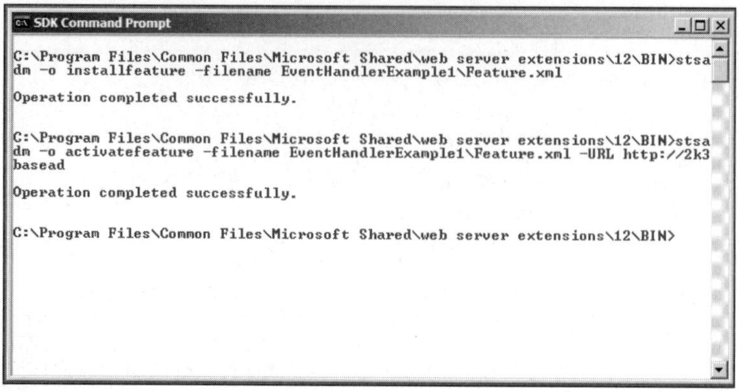

Figure 5-14

Now go to your site and create an Announcements list and put a few items in it. I've done so with my Sample Announcements list. Select an item and try to delete it. You should get an error message that reads "Announcements can not be deleted from this list" (see Figures 5-15 and 5-16).

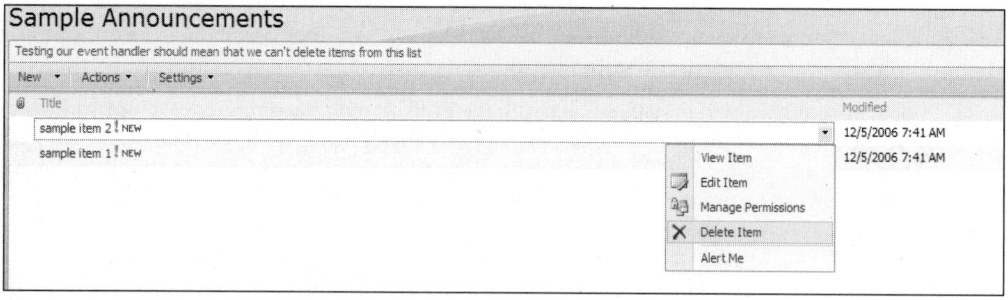

Figure 5-15

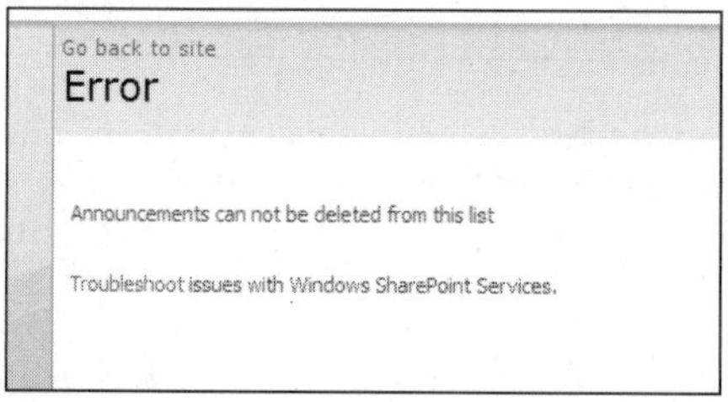

Figure 5-16

Web Services

This chapter provides a tiny glimpse of the power in the SharePoint object model that you as a developer can take advantage of. Augmenting the powerful object model is a services layer that allows developers to call into the SharePoint object model from anywhere.

Best Practices Coding Techniques

As you've seen so far in this chapter, writing code for the SharePoint object model requires the instantiation of lots of objects such as SPWeb, SPSite, and more. Many of these objects implement the IDisposable interface and should be disposed of after they've been used to prevent these objects from remaining in memory.

Scott Harris and Mike Ammerlaan from Microsoft have written an excellent article outlining these best practices recommendations titled "Best Practices: Using Disposable Windows SharePoint Services Objects" (http://msdn2.microsoft.com/en-us/library/aa973248.aspx#sharepointobjmodel__otherobjectsthatrequire-disposal). Any developer interested in writing code targeting the SharePoint platform should read this article. Scott and Mike illustrate many great practices, and they warn you about the times that you shouldn't automatically dispose of every disposable object.

Whereas the object model is organized into namespaces, the web services are grouped logically into 20 different web services. The following table identifies the web services and the methods they expose:

Web Service	Description and Location	Methods
Admin Web Service	Provides methods to manage site collections.	CreateSite
	http://<AdminSite>/_vti_adm/Admin.asmx	DeleteSite
		GetLanguages
		RefreshConfigCache
Alerts	Provides methods for working with alerts on lists and document libraries.	DeleteAlerts
	http://<Site>/_vti_bin/Alerts.asmx	GetAlerts
Authentication	Provides methods to authenticate users to SharePoint.	Login
	http://<Site>/_vti_bin/Authentication.asmx	Mode
Copy	Provides methods for copying files to and from Share-Point sites.	CopyIntoItems
	http://<Site>/_vti_bin/Authentication.asmx	CopyIntoItemsLocal
		GetItem

Continued

Web Service	Description and Location	Methods
Document Workspace	Provides methods for managing Document Workspace sites and the data they contain.	CanCreateDwsUrl
	`http://<Site>/_vti_bin/Dws.asmx`	CreateDws
		CreateFolder
		DeleteDws
		DeleteFolder
		FindDwsDoc
		GetDwsData
		GetDwsMetaData
		RemoveDwsUser
		RenameDws
		UpdateDwsData
Forms	Provides methods for returning forms that are used in the user interface when working with the contents of a list.	GetForm
	`http://<Site>/_vti_bin/Forms.asmx`	GetFormCollection
Imaging	Provides methods that enable you to create and manage picture libraries.	CheckSubwebAndList
	`http://<Site>/_vti_bin/Imaging.asmx`	CreateNewFolder
		Delete
		Download
		Edit
		GetItemsByIds
		GetItemsXMLData
		GetListItems
		ListPictureLibrary
		Rename

Web Service	Description and Location	Methods
Imaging (*continued*)		Upload
List Data Retrieval	The adapter service used to perform queries against sites and lists in WSS. http://<*Site*>/_vti_bin/DspSts.asmx	Query
Lists	Provides methods for working with lists and list data. http://<*Site*>/_vti_bin/Lists.asmx	AddAttachment
		AddDiscussionBoardItem
		AddList
		AddListFromFeature
		ApplyContentTypeToList
		CheckInFile
		CheckOutFile
		CreateContentType
		DeleteAttachment
		DeleteContentType
		DeleteContentTypeXmlDocument
		DeleteList
		GetAttachmentCollection
		GetList
		GetListAndView
		GetListCollection
		GetListContentType
		GetListContentTypes
		GetListItemChanges

Continued

Web Service	Description and Location	Methods
Lists (*continued*)		GetListItemChangesSinceToken
		GetListItems
		GetVersionCollection
		UndoCheckOut
		UpdateContentType
		UpdateContentTypesXmlDocument
		UpdateContentTypeXmlDocument
		UpdateList
		UpdateListItems
Meetings	Enables you to create and manage Meeting Workspace sites. http://<*Site*>/_vti_bin/ Meetings.asmx	AddMeeting AddMeetingFromICal CreateWorkspace DeleteWorkspace GetMeetingsInformation GetMeetingWorkspaces RemoveMeeting RestoreMeeting SetAttendeeResponse SetWorkspaceTitle UpdateMeeting UpdateMeetingFromICal
People	Provides methods for working with WSS Principals. http://<*Site*>/_vti_bin/ People.asmx	ResolvePrincipals SearchPrincipals

Web Service	Description and Location	Methods

Permissions	Provides methods for working with the permissions for a site or list.
	
	`http://<Site>/_vti_bin/`
	`Permissions.asmx`
		`AddPermission`
		
		`AddPermissionCollection`
		
		`GetPermissionCollection`
		
		`RemovePermission`
		
		`RemovePermissionCollection`
		
		`UpdatePermission`

Site Data	Provides methods that return metadata or list data from sites or lists in Microsoft Windows SharePoint Services.
	
	`http://<Site>/_vti_bin/SiteData`
	`.asmx`
		`EnumerateFolder`
		
		`GetAttachments`
		
		`GetChanges`
		
		`GetContent`
		
		`GetList`
		
		`GetListCollection`
		
		`GetListItems`
		
		`GetSite`
		
		`GetSiteAndWeb`
		
		`GetSiteUrl`
		
		`GetURLSegments`
		
		`GetWeb`

Sites	Provides a method for returning information about the collection of site templates on the virtual server.
	
	`http://<Site>/_vti_bin/Sites`
	`.asmx`
		`ExportWeb`
		
		`GetSiteTemplates`

Continued

Web Service	Description and Location	Methods
Sites (*continued*)		GetUpdatedFormDigest
		ImportWeb
Search	The QueryService class is the entry point for calling the Search in Microsoft Windows SharePoint Services Query web service.	Query
	http://<*Site*>/_vti_bin/ spsearch.asmx	QueryEx
		Registration
		Status
Users and Groups	Provides methods for working with users, roles, and groups.	AddGroup
	http://<*Site*>/_vti_bin/ usergroup.asmx	AddGroupToRole
		AddRole
		AddRoleDef
		AddUserCollectionToGroup
		AddUserCollectionToRole
		AddUserToGroup
		AddUserToRole
		GetAllUserCollectionFromWeb
		GetGroupCollection
		GetGroupCollectionFromRole
		GetGroupCollectionFromSite
		GetGroupCollectionFromUser
		GetGroupCollectionFromWeb
		GetGroupInfo
		GetRoleCollection

Web Service	Description and Location	Methods
Users and Groups (*continued*)		GetRoleCollectionFromGroup
		GetRoleCollectionFromUser
		GetRoleCollectionFromWeb
		GetRoleInfo
		GetRolesAndPermissionsForCurrentUser
		GetRolesAndPermissionsForSite
		GetUserCollection
		GetUserCollectionFromGroup
		GetUserCollectionFromRole
		GetUserCollectionFromSite
		GetUserCollectionFromWeb
		GetUserInfo
		GetUserLoginFromEmail
		RemoveGroup
		RemoveGroupFromRole
		RemoveRole
		RemoveUserCollectionFromGroup
		RemoveUserCollectionFromRole
		RemoveUserCollectionFromSite
		RemoveUserFromGroup
		RemoveUserFromRole
		RemoveUserFromSite
		RemoveUserFromWeb
		UpdateGroupInfo

Continued

Web Service	Description and Location	Methods
Users and Groups (*continued*)		UpdateRoleDefInfo
		UpdateRoleInfo
		UpdateUserInfo
Versions	Provides methods for working with file versions. http://<*Site*>/_vti_bin/ Versions.asmx	DeleteAllVersions
		DeleteVersion
		GetVersions
		RestoreVersion
Views	Provides methods for working with views of lists. http://<*Site*>/_vti_bin/Views.asmx	AddView
		DeleteView
		GetView
		GetViewCollection
		GetViewHtml
		UpdateView
		UpdateViewHtml
		UpdateViewHtml2
Web Part Pages	Provides methods for working with Web Parts. http://<*Site*>/_vti_bin/ WebPartPages.asmx	AddWebPart
		AddWebPartToZone
		AssociateWorkflowMarkup
		ConvertWebPartFormat
		DeleteWebPart
		ExecuteProxyUpdates
		FetchLegalWorkflowActions

Web Service	Description and Location	Methods
Users and Groups (*continued*)		GetAssemblyMetaData
		GetBindingResourceData
		GetCustomControlList
		GetDataFromDataSourceControl
		GetFormCapabilityFromDataSourceControl
		GetSafeAssemblyInfo
		GetWebPart
		GetWebPart2
		GetWebPartCrossPageCompatibility
		GetWebPartPage
		GetWebPartPageConnectionInfo
		GetWebPartPageDocument
		GetWebPartProperties
		GetWebPartProperties2
		GetXmlDataFromDataSource
		RemoveWorkflowAssociation
		RenderWebPartForEdit
		SaveWebPart
		SaveWebPart2
		ValidateWorkflowMarkupAndCreateSupportObjects
Webs	Provides methods for working with sites and subsites.	CreateContentType
	http://<*Site*>/ _vti_bin/Webs.asmx	CustomizeCss

Continued

Web Service	Description and Location	Methods
Webs (*continued*)		DeleteContentType
		GetActivatedFeatures
		GetAllSubWebCollection
		GetColumns
		GetContentType
		GetContentTypes
		GetCustomizedPageStatus
		GetListTemplates
		GetWeb
		GetWebCollection
		RemoveContentTypeXmlDocument
		RevertAllFileContentStreams
		RevertCss
		RevertFileContentStream
		UpdateColumns
		UpdateContentType
		UpdateContentTypeXmlDocument
		WebUrlFromPageUrl

Let's look at an example of web services in action. Consider the following scenario: You are a developer at an organization that deals with a considerable number of external clients from a variety of companies. Your organization has decided that it wants to expose a series of SharePoint extranet portals so your company's information workers can collaborate with these external clients. You've created several SharePoint groups for your users, corresponding to their company names and their department names. Your job as the SharePoint developer is to create a mechanism to automatically add these individuals to the correct SharePoint security groups.

1. Open Visual Studio 2005, and create a new C# Class Library project called Sharepoint .Wrappers. You're creating a class library (DLL) because this lets you remain flexible in terms of how to use your code. You have the option to integrate with Windows applications or a web application.

2. Once you have a new class library project started, your first task is to identify which web service you want to use. Right-click the Web References folder and select Add Web Reference. Since you're developing on a machine with WSS installed on it, in the Web References dialog, select the option to list the web services on this machine.

3. From the list of web services that comes back, pick the UserGroup web service, name the web reference SharePoint.UserGroup and click OK (see Figure 5-17). Visual Studio will automatically generate a proxy class to use in the rest of your code.

4. Under the new Web References folder in the Solution Explorer, select the Sharepoint .Usergroup reference. In the Properties window, change the URL Behavior from Dynamic to Static. This will create an app.config that points to your SharePoint site (see Figure 5-18).

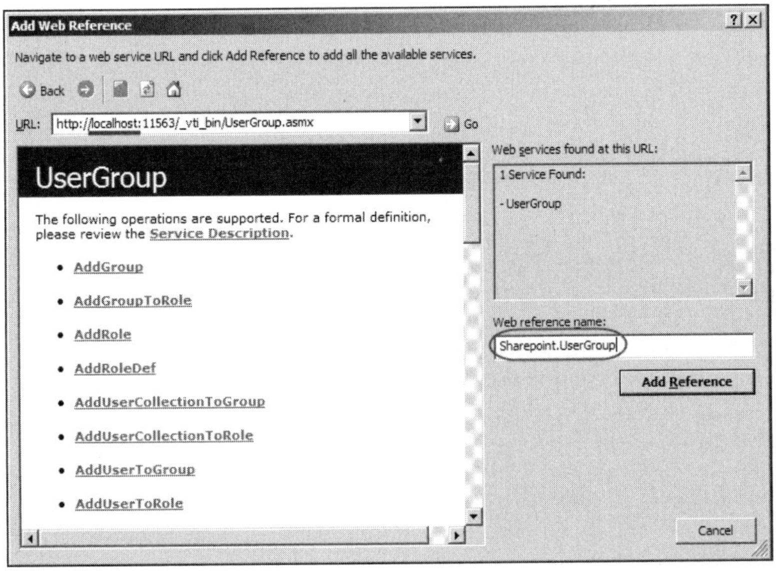

Figure 5-17

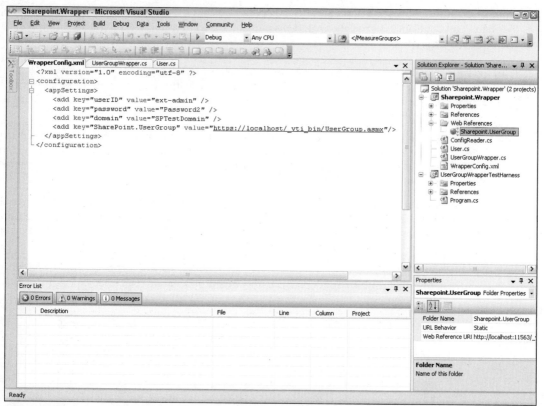

Figure 5-18

Since you're not sure what kind of application you'll be integrating with and DLLs don't get to read their own `app.config` files, you'll create your own configuration file and your own config reader class. Start by adding a new XML file to the project called `WrapperConfig.xml`. Copy the contents of the `app.config` into the XML file and change it to match the sample in Listing 5-8.

Listing 5-8

```xml
<?xml version="1.0" encoding="utf-8" ?>
<configuration>
        <appSettings>
                <add key="userID" value="sampleUser" />
                <add key="password" value="Password2" />
                <add key="domain" value="SPServerDomain" />
                <add key="SharePoint.UserGroup"
value="http://localhost/_vti_bin/UserGroup.asmx"/>
        </appSettings>
</configuration>
```

This custom configuration file contains the URL for your SharePoint site and the user name and password of a user who has access to the web services. This config file can be read by the following class, shown in Listing 5-9.

Listing 5-9

```
/// <summary>
/// Summary description for Config_XmlDocument.
/// </summary>
public class Config
{
        private XmlTextReader _XmlDocument = null;
        private string _uid = string.Empty;
        private string _pwd = string.Empty;
        private string _domain = string.Empty;
        private string _WebServiceURI = string.Empty;

        public string UserID { get {return _uid;}}
        public string Password { get {return _pwd;}}
        public string Domain { get {return _domain;}}
        public string WebServiceURI{ get {return _WebServiceURI;}}


    //private Config myConfig = null;

    public Config()
        {
                // Put the DLL and config in a well-known location.
        string DLLPath = @"c:\Program
Files\ProSharePoint07\Sharepoint.Wrapper\WrapperConfig.xml";
                _XmlDocument = new XmlTextReader(DLLPath);
        // Read our config file.
                GetCredentialsFromConfig();
        }

        private void GetCredentialsFromConfig()
    {
        // Read through the XML file to the end.            while
(_XmlDocument.Read())
        {
            // If we're looking at an element.
            if (XmlNodeType.Element == _XmlDocument.NodeType)
            {
                // If our element is a name-value pair.
                if (2 == _XmlDocument.AttributeCount)
                {
                    // Get the key and value.
                    string keyName =
_XmlDocument.GetAttribute("key").ToString();
                    string keyValue =
_XmlDocument.GetAttribute("value").ToString();
```

```
                        switch (keyName)
                        {
                            case "userID":
                            {
                                _uid = keyValue;
                                break;
                            }
                            case "password":
                            {
                                _pwd = keyValue;
                                break;
                            }
                            case "domain":
                            {
                                _domain = keyValue;
                                break;
                            }
                            case "SharePoint.UserGroup":
                            {
                                _WebServiceURI = keyValue;
                                break;
                            }
                        } // End switch.
                    } // End if key pair.
                } // End if element.
            } // End while.
        } // End GetCredentialsFromConfig.
    } // End class.
```

You'll also want to create some mechanism for storing and easily passing around information about the users you're adding and removing from SharePoint. Create a structure that looks like this:

```
public struct User
{
    public string groupNames;
    public string userName;
    public string userLoginName;
    public string userEmail;
    public string userNotes;
}
```

Now let's take a look at some code back in your main `Sharepoint.Wrapper` class. First, include the Web Reference proxy class in the using statements at the top:

```
using Sharepoint.Wrapper.Sharepoint.UserGroup;
```

Next, you'll need to establish a connection to SharePoint. This means that you'll need to pass the credentials of a user who has access to the web services. Fortunately, you've identified just such a user in your config file. Create a method called `DefineCredentials` that connects us to the SharePoint UserGroup web service. This has been done for you in Listing 5-10.

Listing 5-10

```
        /// <summary>
        /// Use the ConfigReader class to read our XML defined uid, pwd, and domain
name for our
        /// WS user.          /// </summary>
        private void DefineCredentials(UserGroup instance)
        {
            Config _Config = new Config();
            string userid = _Config.UserID;
            string pass = _Config.Password;
            string domain = _Config.Domain;
            instance.Credentials = new System.Net.NetworkCredential(userid, pass,
domain);
        }
```

The UserGroup proxy class, instantiated here as the object instance, has a .Credentials property. Here is where you can store your NetworkCredential. This simple mechanism, passing in the user name, password, and domain, eliminates the requirement to have the executing application be executed by administrative users. Most online examples of the Credentials property use the DefaultCredentials, but that copies the current user's credentials and that might not be sufficient.

Now that you've got access to the web services, call one. In the scenario outlined above, you need to be able to add users to multiple groups so I've implemented the User structure's groupNames string as a pipe ('|') delimited string. This enables the calling application to call the AddUserToGroups function and pass all the groups in at once. Of course, SharePoint won't be expecting that, so you'll implement some custom business logic to break apart that string, as shown in Listing 5-11.

Listing 5-11

```
        /// <summary>
        /// Add an AD user defined by the login name (DOMAIN\username) to a
preexisting SharePoint group.
        /// </summary>
        /// <param name="newUser"></param>
        /// <returns>0 = success, -1 = failure (look in the eventlog for an
exception detail</returns>
        public int AddUserToGroups(User newUser)
        {
            try
            {
                // Get a reference to our SharePoint site (the site URL is defined
in the
                // web reference's path. Be sure this is correct).
                UserGroup instance = new UserGroup();
                DefineCredentials(instance);

                // Break apart the comma delimited  groupNames field.
                char[] stringSeparators = new char[] { '|' };
                string[] _SPGroupNames =
newUser.groupNames.Split(stringSeparators);
```

```
                    // For each entry in our array of group names, add the user to the
        specified group.
                    foreach (string _GroupName in _SPGroupNames)
                    {
                        try
                        {
                            // Invoke the web service via this proxy call.
                            instance.AddUserToGroup(_GroupName,
                                newUser.userName,
                                newUser.userLoginName,
                                newUser.userEmail,
                                newUser.userNotes);
                        }
                        catch (Exception ex)
                        {
                            ErrorLog(ex, newUser);
                            return FAILURE_RESULT;
                        }
                    }
                    return SUCCESS_RESULT;
                }
                catch (Exception ex)
                {
                    ErrorLog(ex, newUser);
                    return FAILURE_RESULT;
                }
            }
```

You've just implemented `AddUserToGroups()`, so now all that's missing is the inverse function, `RemoveUserFromGroups()`. This code is pretty similar, but notice that the Remove web service itself requires fewer parameters (see Listing 5-12).

Listing 5-12

```
            /// <summary>
            /// Remove an AD user defined by the login name (DOMAIN\username) from a
        preexisting SharePoint group.
            /// </summary>
            /// <param name="newUser"></param>
            /// <returns>0 = success, -1 = failure (look in the eventlog for an
        exception detail</returns>
            public int RemoveUserFromGroups(User newUser)
            {
                try
                {
                    // Get a reference to our SharePoint site (the site URL is defined
        in the
                    // web reference's path. Be sure this is correct).
                    UserGroup instance = new UserGroup();
                    DefineCredentials(instance);

                    // Break apart the comma delimited groupNames field.
                    char[] stringSeparators = new char[] { '|' };
```

```
                string[] _SPGroupNames = newUser.groupNames
.Split(stringSeparators);

                // For each entry in our array of group names, remove the user from
the specified group.
                foreach (string _GroupName in _SPGroupNames)
                {
                    try
                    {
                        // Invoke the web service via this proxy call.
                        instance.RemoveUserFromGroup(_GroupName,
                            newUser.userLoginName);
                    }
                    catch (Exception ex)
                    {
                        ErrorLog(ex, newUser);
                        return FAILURE_RESULT;
                    }
                }
                return SUCCESS_RESULT;
        }
        catch (Exception ex)
        {
            ErrorLog(ex, newUser);
            return FAILURE_RESULT;
        }
    }
}
```

This class library will now add and remove users from multiple groups with a single call. Let's build a test harness to try this out. Add a new Console Application project to your solution by clicking File ➪ New ➪ Project in Visual Studio. Select a new C# Windows Console Application, and name it UserGroupWrapperTestHarness. Add a reference to the Sharepoint.Wrappers.DLL you've just built by right-clicking on the UserGroupWrapperTestHarness project's References folder and selecting Add Reference. In the Add Reference dialog, select the Projects tab and pick the Sharepoint.Wrappers namespace from the list, as in Figure 5-19.

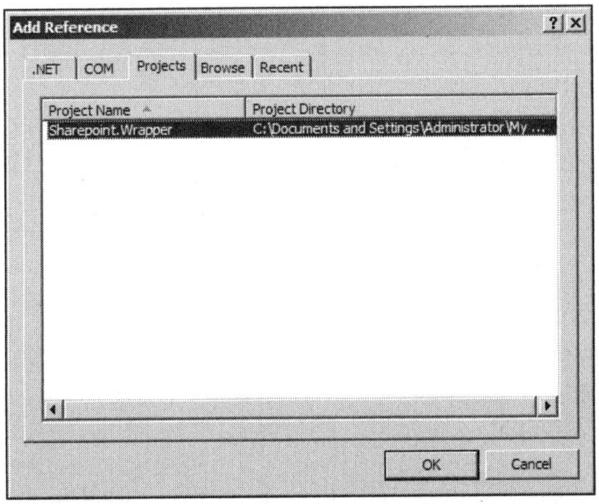

Figure 5-19

Now that the project is ready, rename `Class1.cs` to `TestHarness.cs` and put the test code (see Listing 5-13) inside.

Listing 5-13

```
using System;
using System.Text;
using Sharepoint.Wrappers;

namespace UserGroupWrapperTestHarness
{
    class TestHarness
    {
        static void Main(string[] args)
        {
            int wsRequestResult = UserGroupWrapper.SUCCESS_RESULT;
            User testUser = new Sharepoint.Wrappers.User();

            testUser = ResetTestUser(testUser);

            UserGroupWrapper AddRemover = new
Sharepoint.Wrappers.UserGroupWrapper();

            // Assumptions:  1) The domain is SPTestDomain.
            //               2) User mranlett is a valid Active Directory user.
            //               3) SharePoint groups called "Cool Group" and "Lame
Group" have
            //                  already been created.
            Console.WriteLine("Press 1 to add mranlett to the MattTest Group.");
            Console.WriteLine("Press 2 to remove mranlett from the MattTest
Group.");
            Console.WriteLine("Press 3 to add mranlett to a nonexistant group.");
            Console.WriteLine("Press 4 to remove mranlett from a nonexistant
group.");
            Console.WriteLine("Press 5 to add a nonexistant user to the MattTest
Group.");
            Console.WriteLine("Press 6 to remove a nonexistant user from the
MattTest Group.");
            Console.WriteLine("Press 7 to call Add with the wrong LoginName.");
            Console.WriteLine("Press 8 to call Remove with the wrong LoginName.");
            Console.WriteLine("Press 9 to call Add with the wrong e-mail
address.");
            Console.WriteLine("");
            Console.WriteLine("Press 0 to run the all the test cases at once.");
            Console.WriteLine("Then press ENTER. Any other input is not supported
");
            Console.WriteLine("and may break the test harness.");
            Console.WriteLine("");
            Console.WriteLine("We expect pressing 3, 4, 7, and 8 to generate
eventlog errors");
            Console.WriteLine("the other test pass with no errors.");

            int userInput = Console.Read();
```

```
            switch (userInput)
            {
                case 48: // 48 is hex for 0
                    {
                        // Add a valid user to a valid group.
                        Console.WriteLine("testing the ability to add a valid user
to a valid group");
                        wsRequestResult = AddRemover.AddUserToGroups(testUser);
                        if (UserGroupWrapper.SUCCESS_RESULT == wsRequestResult)
                        {
                            Console.WriteLine("");
                            Console.WriteLine("valid user successfully added to a
valid group");
                        }
                        else
                        {
                            Console.WriteLine("");
                            Console.WriteLine("** error attempting to add a valid
user to a valid group. \n This is unexpected and needs to be researched");
                        }

                        // Remove a valid user from a valid group.
                        Console.WriteLine("testing the ability to remove a valid
user from a valid group");
                        wsRequestResult =
AddRemover.RemoveUserFromGroups(testUser);
                        if (UserGroupWrapper.SUCCESS_RESULT == wsRequestResult)
                        {
                            Console.WriteLine("");
                            Console.WriteLine("valid user successfully removed from
a valid group");
                        }
                        else
                        {
                            Console.WriteLine("");
                            Console.WriteLine("** error attempting to add a valid
user to a valid group. \n This is unexpected and needs to be researched");
                        }

                        // Add a valid user to an invalid group.
                        Console.WriteLine("testing the ability to add a valid user
to an invalid group");
                        testUser.groupNames = testUser.groupNames + "|BoogaBooga";
                        wsRequestResult = AddRemover.AddUserToGroups(testUser);
                        if (UserGroupWrapper.SUCCESS_RESULT == wsRequestResult)
                        {
                            Console.WriteLine("");
                            Console.WriteLine("** added a valid user to an invalid
group successfully. \n This is unexpected and needs to be researched");
                        }
                        else
                        {
                            Console.WriteLine("");
                            Console.WriteLine("error attempting to add a valid user
to an invalid group. This is expected");
                        }
```

```
                         // Remove a valid user from an invalid group.
                         testUser = ResetTestUser(testUser);
                         testUser.groupNames = "MattTest||IT Department||Home
Owners||BoogaBooga";
                         wsRequestResult = AddRemover
.RemoveUserFromGroups(testUser);
                         if (UserGroupWrapper.SUCCESS_RESULT == wsRequestResult)
                         {
                             Console.WriteLine("");
                             Console.WriteLine("** removed a valid user from an
invalid group successfully. \n This is unexpected and needs to be researched");
                         }
                         else
                         {
                             Console.WriteLine("");

                             Console.WriteLine("error attempting to removed a valid
user from an invalid group. \n This is expected");
                         }


                         // Add an invalid user (valid LoginName, invalid userName)
to a valid group.
                         testUser = ResetTestUser(testUser);
                         testUser.userName = "ClownNose";
                         wsRequestResult = AddRemover.AddUserToGroups(testUser);
                         if (UserGroupWrapper.SUCCESS_RESULT == wsRequestResult)
                         {
                             Console.WriteLine("");
                             Console.WriteLine("invalid user name with valid user
login successfully added to a valid group.\n The user name property is not a
validated field.");
                         }
                         else
                         {
                             Console.WriteLine("");
                             Console.WriteLine("** error attempting to add an
invalid user name with valid user login to a valid group. \n This is unexpected and
needs to be researched");
                         }


                         // Remove an invalid user (valid LoginName, invalid
userName) from a valid group.
                         testUser = ResetTestUser(testUser);
                         testUser.userName = "mranlet";
                         wsRequestResult =
AddRemover.RemoveUserFromGroups(testUser);
                         if (UserGroupWrapper.SUCCESS_RESULT == wsRequestResult)
                         {
                             Console.WriteLine("");
                             Console.WriteLine("invalid user name with valid user
login successfully removed from a valid group.\n The user name property is not a
validated field.");
                         }
                         else
```

```
                {
                    Console.WriteLine("");
                    Console.WriteLine("** error attempting to remove an
invalid user name with valid user login from a valid group. \n This is unexpected
and needs to be researched");
                }

                // Add an invalid user (invalid LoginName) to a valid
group.
                testUser = ResetTestUser(testUser);
                testUser.userLoginName = @"FakeDomain\BadUID";
                wsRequestResult = AddRemover.AddUserToGroups(testUser);
                if (UserGroupWrapper.SUCCESS_RESULT == wsRequestResult)
                {
                    Console.WriteLine("");
                    Console.WriteLine("** invalid user login successfully
added to a valid group. \n This is unexpected and needs to be researched");
                }
                else
                {
                    Console.WriteLine("");
                    Console.WriteLine("error attempting to add an invalid
user login to a valid group");
                }

                // Remove an invalid user (invalid LoginName) from a valid
group.
                testUser = ResetTestUser(testUser);
                testUser.userLoginName = @"FakeDomain\BadUID";
                wsRequestResult =
AddRemover.RemoveUserFromGroups(testUser);
                if (UserGroupWrapper.SUCCESS_RESULT == wsRequestResult)
                {
                    Console.WriteLine("");
                    Console.WriteLine("** invalid user login successfully
removed from a valid group. \n This is unexpected and needs to be researched");
                }
                else
                {
                    Console.WriteLine("");
                    Console.WriteLine("error attempting to remove an
invalid user login from a valid group");
                }

                // Add an invalid user (invalid e-mail address) to a valid
group.
                testUser = ResetTestUser(testUser);
                testUser.userEmail = "notmyemail@wrongdomain.com";
                wsRequestResult = AddRemover.AddUserToGroups(testUser);
                if (UserGroupWrapper.SUCCESS_RESULT == wsRequestResult)
                {
                    Console.WriteLine("");
                    Console.WriteLine("invalid user e-mail successfully
added to a valid group. \n e-mail is not a validated field.");
```

```
                }
                else
                {
                        Console.WriteLine("");
                        Console.WriteLine("** error attempting to add an
invalid user e-mail successfully added to a valid group. \n This is unexpected and
needs to be researched");
                }

                // Add a user to a group they're already in.
                testUser = ResetTestUser(testUser);
                wsRequestResult = AddRemover.AddUserToGroups(testUser);
                wsRequestResult = AddRemover.AddUserToGroups(testUser);
                if (UserGroupWrapper.SUCCESS_RESULT == wsRequestResult)
                {
                        Console.WriteLine("");
                        Console.WriteLine("valid user successfully added to a
valid group twice. \n No problems readding a valid user.");
                }
                else
                {
                        Console.WriteLine("");
                        Console.WriteLine("** error attempting to add a valid
user to a valid group twice. \n This is unexpected and needs to be researched");
                }

                // Remove a user from a group they're not in.
                testUser = ResetTestUser(testUser);
                wsRequestResult =
AddRemover.RemoveUserFromGroups(testUser);
                wsRequestResult =
AddRemover.RemoveUserFromGroups(testUser);
                if (UserGroupWrapper.SUCCESS_RESULT == wsRequestResult)
                {
                        Console.WriteLine("");
                        Console.WriteLine("valid user successfully removed from
a valid group twice. \n No problem removing non-existant users.");
                }
                else
                {
                        Console.WriteLine("");
                        Console.WriteLine("** error attempting to add a valid
user to a valid group. \n This is unexpected and needs to be researched");
                }
                Console.Read();
                break;
            }
        case 49: // 49 is hex for 1
            {
                // Press 1 to add mranlett to the MattTest Group.
                AddRemover.AddUserToGroups(testUser);
                break;
            }
        case 50: // 50 is hex for 2
```

```
            {
                // Press 2 to remove mranlett from the MattTest Group..
                AddRemover.RemoveUserFromGroups(testUser);
                break;
            }
        case 51: // 51 is hex for 3
            {
                // Press 3 to add mranlett to a nonexistant group.
                testUser.groupNames = testUser.groupNames + "|BoogaBooga";
                AddRemover.AddUserToGroups(testUser);
                break;
            }
        case 52: // 52 is hex for 4
            {
                // Press 4 to remove mranlett from a nonexistant group.
                testUser.groupNames = testUser.groupNames + "|BoogaBooga";
                AddRemover.RemoveUserFromGroups(testUser);
                break;
            }
        case 53: // 53 is hex for 5
            {
                // Press 5 to add a nonexistant user to the MattTest Group.
                testUser.userName = "ClownNose";
                AddRemover.AddUserToGroups(testUser);
                break;
            }
        case 54: // 54 is hex for 6
            {
                // Press 6 to remove a nonexistant user from the MattTest
Group.
                testUser.userName = "mranlet";
                AddRemover.RemoveUserFromGroups(testUser);
                break;
            }
        case 55: // 55 is hex for 7
            {
                // Press 7 to call Add with the wrong LoginName.
                testUser.userLoginName = @"FakeDomain\BadUID";
                AddRemover.AddUserToGroups(testUser);
                break;
            }
        case 56: // 56 is hex for 8
            {
                // Press 8 to call Remove with the wrong LoginName.
                testUser.userLoginName = @"FakeDomain\BadUID";
                AddRemover.RemoveUserFromGroups(testUser);
                break;
            }
        case 57: // 57 is hex for 9
            {
                // Press 9 to call Add with the wrong e-mail address.
                testUser.userEmail = "notmyemail@wrongdomain.com";
                AddRemover.AddUserToGroups(testUser);
                break;
            }
```

```
                }
            }
            Console.WriteLine("");
            Console.WriteLine("");
            Console.WriteLine("End of test cases. Press Enter 2 times to exit");
            Console.Read();
            Console.Read();
            Console.Read();
            Console.Read();

        }

        private static User ResetTestUser(User testUser)
        {
            testUser.groupNames = "Cool Group|Lame Group";
            testUser.userName = "mranlett";
            testUser.userLoginName = @"SPTestDomain\mattr";
            testUser.userEmail = "mranlett@devcow.com";
            testUser.userNotes = "This is a ficticious user added by the web
service";

            return testUser;
        }
    }
}
```

Running this test code will print out your successful and unsuccessful progress. Notice that you have several places where you expect to receive errors. SharePoint relies on Active Directory (in this example) to authenticate users, so your user must already have been created. This example does not actually create new groups, so the groups must preexist. These test cases help illustrate the power and limitations of two simple web services calls.

Deciding between the Object Model and Web Services

Now that you are beginning to appreciate the power and flexibility of the object model and web services, your next decision is to decide between them. Fortunately, there is an easy rule of thumb for deciding between the SharePoint object model and the SharePoint Web Services — where is your code going to be executed? If you're building code that is executed on the SharePoint server, whether in a server application, a service, or a Web Part, use the object model. Directly hooking into the object model is faster and more efficient than using web services. However, web services grant you the flexibility to take your code away from the server. If your requirements include remote applications, even if your servers and workstations are on the same domain, you have to use web services.

Summary

Windows SharePoint Services 2007 provides the foundation for all of the Office Server 2007 products, including the Microsoft Office SharePoint Server. Part of this foundation is a rich object model, web services façade, and an eventing subsystem that is publicly available for developers. The object model, available to code running locally on the SharePoint server, contains 30 namespaces with thousands of classes. These all work together to provide the developer with nearly every bit of functionality available through the user interface. SharePoint's web services have progressed quite a lot since the 2003 version of WSS. Gone are the ugly CAML statements of the previous version, replaced by 20 fully functional ASP.Net 2.0-based web services. Combine these powerful APIs with the newly enhanced SharePoint event system to create richly functional and extremely responsive applications.

This chapter began an examination of the SharePoint object model by looking at the highly comprehensive `Microsoft.SharePoint` namespace. Using this namespace, sample code was presented that creates a new SharePoint site, a new list in that site, and new list items in that list. Event handling, a subset of the functionality presented by the object model, was explored next with a sample Feature that prevents the deletion of items from a SharePoint Announcements list. The final API explored in this chapter was the web services layer. The sample application presented here used the Users and Groups web service to automatically place new users into SharePoint security groups. The chapter concluded with a brief overview of the decision points between writing object model code and web services code.

A Sample Collaboration Solution

By Jeff Julian

Creating software for SharePoint that links individuals together to complete tasks makes up the majority of work for a SharePoint developer. The SharePoint system is created for collaboration and designed to allow others to add functionality for more collaboration.

This chapter shows you how to build a new collaboration solution using the extensibility features of SharePoint, and walks you through a sample project using the key extension models of SharePoint. Although the user or administrator can handle many scenarios by employing the customization features available through the browser interface, more complex situations require the services of a developer, who will use tools such as SharePoint Designer and Visual Studio.

The Project

A problem has been identified by the human resources staff of XYZ, Inc. The staff is looking for a new solution to the age-old problem of controlling the hiring process within the company. The organization needs a new way to track jobs, managers, and potential applicants across the entire organization.

Currently, XYZ uses different documents and email to create different jobs in the organization. When a hiring manager has a new position open, they create a Word document that has the job name, description, pay scale, hiring date, and experience level. This document is emailed to the HR director where they assign a member of the HR staff to the job. The HR staff member then starts looking for different applicants and creates a list of resumes to send back to the hiring manager. At this point, the hiring manager looks through the list of applicants and starts scheduling interviews with the qualified applicants.

After the interview has taken place, the different interviewers fill out a form that rates the applicant based on fitness for the criteria in the interview process. These documents are collected by the hiring manager, and eventually a candidate is offered a job.

This process works well for the organization but is very difficult to audit when reviewing the hiring results for the company. The jobs also start slipping through the cracks when the HR director is either out of the office or busy.

Expecting significant company growth in the near future, the HR director has requested a computerized solution that will centralize the hiring process and make it more visible to the various stakeholders. The company has recently upgraded its intranet to Microsoft Office SharePoint Server 2007 and would like to use this as the application interface. The staff has been trained on how to use the different types of sites and has Microsoft Office 2007 installed on their desktops.

Designing a Solution

The following solutions will be used to solve the HR hiring problem, using Microsoft Office SharePoint Server 2007. Note that the tools are also available in Windows SharePoint Services 3.0.

1. A dedicated site for the hiring process.

2. A list of departments participating in the application.

3. A list of jobs opening with job details and hiring managers.

4. A list of applicants for each job and a place to attach resumes.

5. An RSS feed for the jobs and applicants, which allows only the HR director to subscribe.

6. An email to be delivered to the hiring manager when a new applicant is entered into the system.

Due to time constraints on the development team, this is the only functionality that will be created for this phase. Later phases will add the functionality for the interview process, but this portion of work will solve the majority of the problems the HR department is facing.

This application uses common SharePoint development approaches to solve this problem. Refer to Windows SharePoint Services 3.0 SDK and Microsoft Office SharePoint Server 2007 SDK to help answer any questions about the object model discussed.

Creating Dedicated Site

This project requires a dedicated site for the HR department and hiring managers to visit and use the application. For this example, create a site called Hiring Management and link it off of the main SharePoint portal for the corporation's intranet. Select the template `Blank Site` and URL name `hiringmanagement` for the new site. Review Figure 6.1 to confirm the settings used in creating the site. Use Chapters 3 and 4 to review the steps on creating a site if needed.

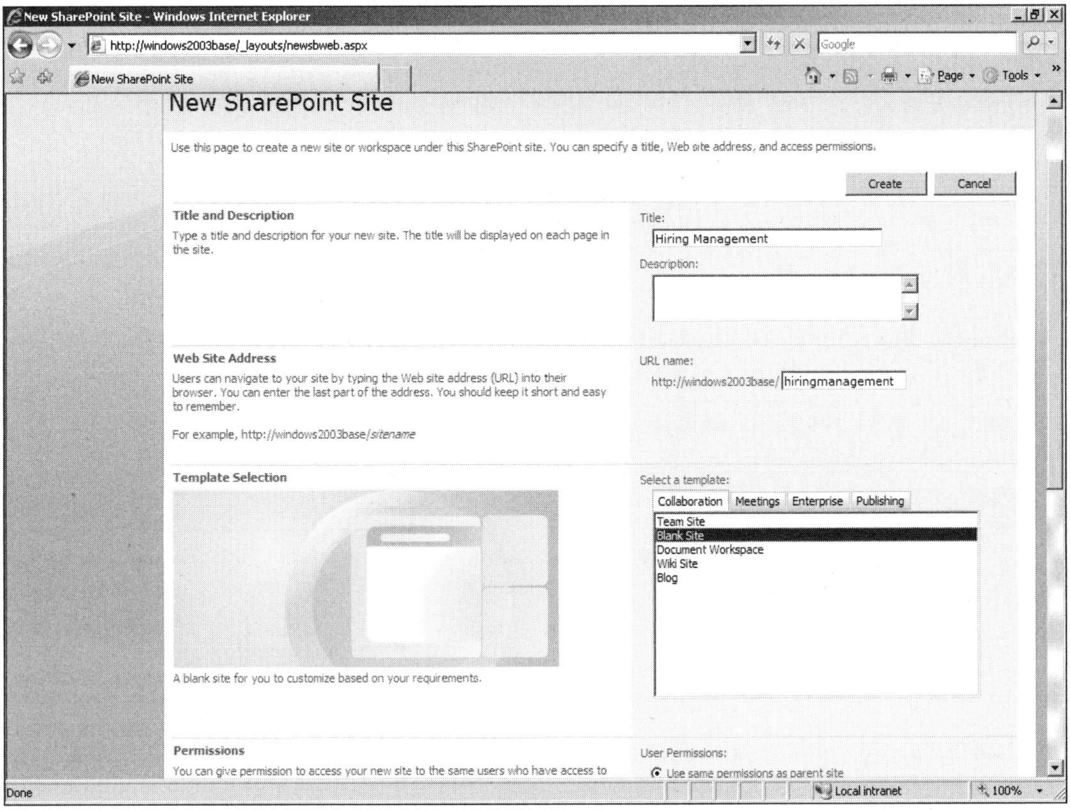

Figure 6.1

The navigation of the blank site is not suited for this application. By default, Documents, Lists, Discussions, Sites, and People and Groups are added as link categories. Since the application is tailored to a specific need, modify the Navigation list in Site Settings to use the categories in the following table. From the default site page, click the Site Actions button and click the Site Settings link. From there, click the Quick Launch link in the Look and Feel section. On this page, add the new headers and remove the unwanted categories.

Category	Description
Staff	Container for all staff related lists
Jobs	Container for job and applicant lists
People and Groups	Original container

The next step is to edit the home page for the site. Since the blank template was chosen, this just requires you to remove the Site Image Web Part. Once this is removed, you can move on to the next step.

Create a Department List

Creating a list of the different departments that participate in the new hiring application gives you the flexibility to add jobs by department. The list also contains the criteria that the hiring manager needs for the department when applicants are entered.

This chapter assumes that you are familiar with creating a list. Using the site management tools, create a list named Departments. The list needs to be a Custom List; use the table below to build the required fields. After the list is created, move the Quick Launch link to the Staff category using the Navigation tools for the site.

To add columns to a custom list, click the List Setting link in the Settings menu on the list. From the Customize Departments screen, click the Create column link in the Columns section.

Note that you should change the name of the Title column to `Department Name`.

Name	Type	Description	Required
Department Name (rename Title)	Single line of text	Name of the department that is participating in the hiring application	Yes
Hiring Manager	Person or Group (People Only)	The hiring manager of the department	Yes

Using the Active Directory or local user management features of the SharePoint installation, add three users, Bob IT, Tom HR, and Alan Sales. These will be used to fill in sample data for this application for a demo and confirmation of functionality.

To confirm that the functionality is correct, add the sample data in the following table, using the new item link of the list:

Department Name	Hiring Manager
Information Technology	Bob IT
Sales	Alan Sales
Human Resources	Tom HR

Once the data is entered, confirm that the data is displayed in the view and move on to the next step.

Create a Jobs List

After the Department list is finished, create a new list for storing the jobs associated with this application. This list is used by the hiring manager to control the open positions in his or her department and by the human resources staff to associate applicants.

Using the site management tools, create a custom list named Jobs. Move this list to the Jobs category, using the Quick Launch navigation tool inside Site Settings.

Using the administration settings for the list, create the columns listed in the following table:

Name	Type	Description	Required
Title (default)	Single line of text	Name of the position	Yes
Department	Lookup (Departments list, Department Name column)	The department the job belongs to	Yes
Internal Description	Multiple lines of text (Rich Text)	The description viewed by employees for this position	No
External Description	Multiple lines of text (Plain Text)	The description used by HR to broadcast the position's availability	Yes
Active	Yes/No	Job active status	N/A
Salary Range	Single line of text	Description of expected salary range	No

Enter the following sample data into the Jobs list using the New Item link.

Information Technology Department Position

- ❑ Title = Software Developer
- ❑ Department = Information Technology
- ❑ Internal Description = Empty
- ❑ External Description = XYZ, Inc. is currently looking for experienced .NET developers to work on their point-of-sale application. Previous experience with C#, SQL Server, and XML is required.
- ❑ Active = Yes
- ❑ Salary Range = $60-70k

Sales Department Position

- ❑ Title = Sales Team Member
- ❑ Department = Sales

❑   Internal Description = Empty

❑   External Description = XYZ, Inc. is currently looking for energetic applicants for promoting their point-of-sale application. This position requires applicants with 2 years of sales experience and individuals who can rebound from rejection.

❑   Active = Yes

❑   Salary Range = $35-45k

Once the data is entered, confirm that the data is displayed in the view and move on to the next step.

Create the Applicant List

The applicant list holds information about applicants who have submitted their resumes for a particular position. If the applicant is approved after human resources' initial screening, HR will create a record in the Applicant list and attach the resume for the hiring manager to review.

In a later step, you revisit this list and associate an event receiver to email hiring managers when a new applicant is added.

Using the site management tools, create a custom list named `Applicant`. Move this list to the Jobs category, using the Quick Launch navigation tool inside Site Settings.

Using the administration settings for the list, create the columns listed below.

Name	Type	Description	Required
Applicant Name (rename Title column)	Single line of text	Name of the applicant	Yes
Job	Lookup (Jobs list, Title column)	The particular position being applied for	Yes
Applied Date	Date and Time (Date Only)	The date the applicant applied for the position	Yes
Email Address	Single line of text	Applicant's email address	Yes
Phone Number	Single line of text	Applicant's phone number	Yes
Notes	Multiple lines of text (Rich Text)	Internal notes from the HR staff to inform the hiring manager of the initial review process	No

The list will use the `Attach File` functionality of the New Item page to post the resumes to the list.

To test the list functionality, enter the following example data. Figure 6-2 shows the example entered into the New Item page.

❑   Applicant Name = John Smith

❑   Job = Software Developer

❑   Applied Date = <Today's Date>

❑   Email Address = <Working Email Address>

❑   Phone Number = (###) ###-####

❑   Notes = This applicant seems extremely qualified for the position based on initial analysis. Next steps will be to review the attached resume and call him.

❑   Attach File = Any PDF available of a reasonable size or example resume.

At this point, the application is functional but lacks some of the extra features added in Windows SharePoint Services 3.0 that help users be more productive by saving them time when applicants and jobs are created.

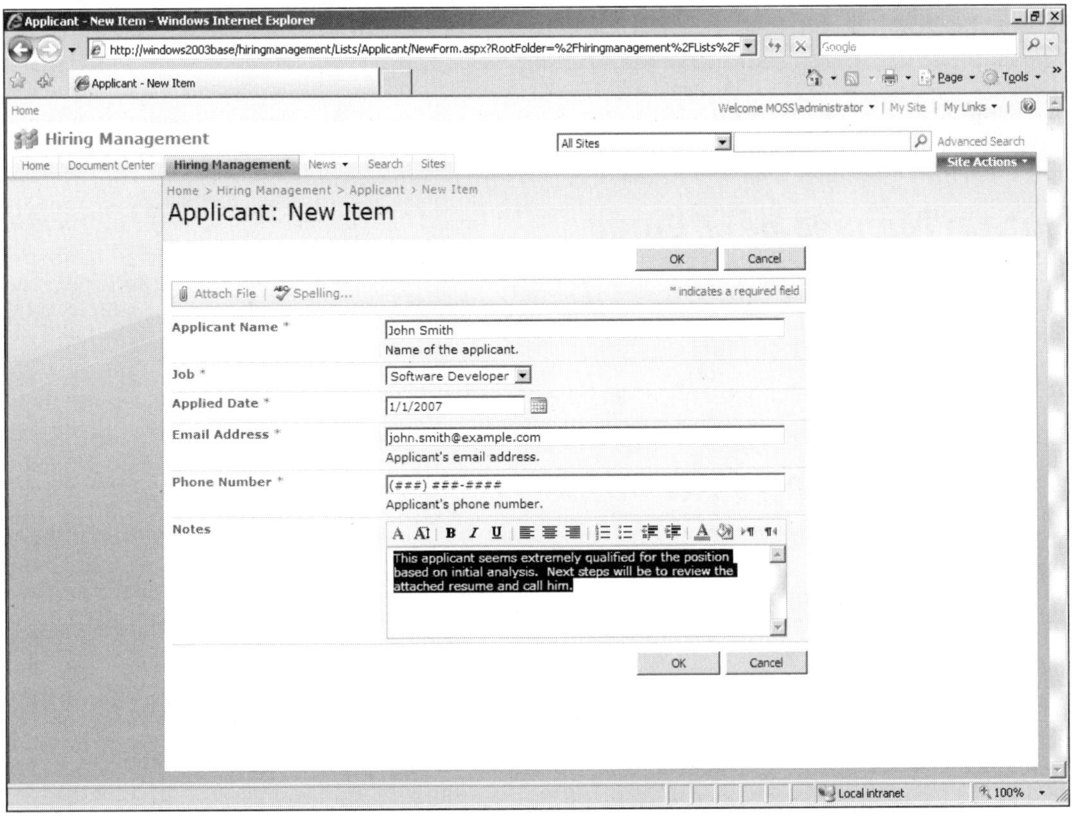

Figure 6-2

Create RSS Feeds

RSS, Really Simple Syndication, is an XML dialect used by subscribers so that they are alerted when content changes. Later chapters in this book cover RSS in more detail. RSS feeds are enabled by default for all lists created in SharePoint, but this application only requires it on some lists.

In the application, different team members will use Outlook 2007 to subscribe as the consumers of these RSS feeds. Unlike email, RSS uses a subscription model to retrieve content instead of a push. This means that Outlook will reload each feed it has in the feed store and look for changes from the previous version. When a new change is found, Outlook will notify the user with an unread mail flag.

The users of this application will subscribe to the RSS feeds generated from the lists based on the need of their role. Review the following table and make the appropriate changes to the application site:

List Name	Enabled	Consumer
Departments	No	Disabled
Jobs	Yes	HR Staff
Applicants	Yes	HR Staff, Department Heads

To turn RSS on or off, use the RSS Settings link in the List Settings. After the page loads, select Yes or No in the List RSS section. Review Figure 6-3 to see the configuration screen.

Set Up Management Email

The department managers would like to receive an email when a new applicant is entered into the system. This email needs to show all the fields of the Applicant List as well as an attachment of the applicant's resume.

SharePoint list alerts would be a good candidate, but since the team wants the emails in a specific format, SharePoint event receivers will be used instead.

SharePoint Event Receivers

SharePoint generates events to notify custom code modules about significant changes, such as the addition or deletion of a list item. The SharePoint object model includes several base classes for building custom event receivers, also called *event handlers*. After choosing the appropriate base class and adding the custom code, you must sign and build the event receiver module and deploy it to the Global Assembly Cache (GAC) on the SharePoint server. After successful deployment, you can associate the event receiver with a site or list.

An event receiver can also be associated with a feature in SharePoint. These features should be created if the action needs to be placed on more than one list or site. Via the Site Settings, the administrator of the site can then toggle the feature on or off based on the current need.

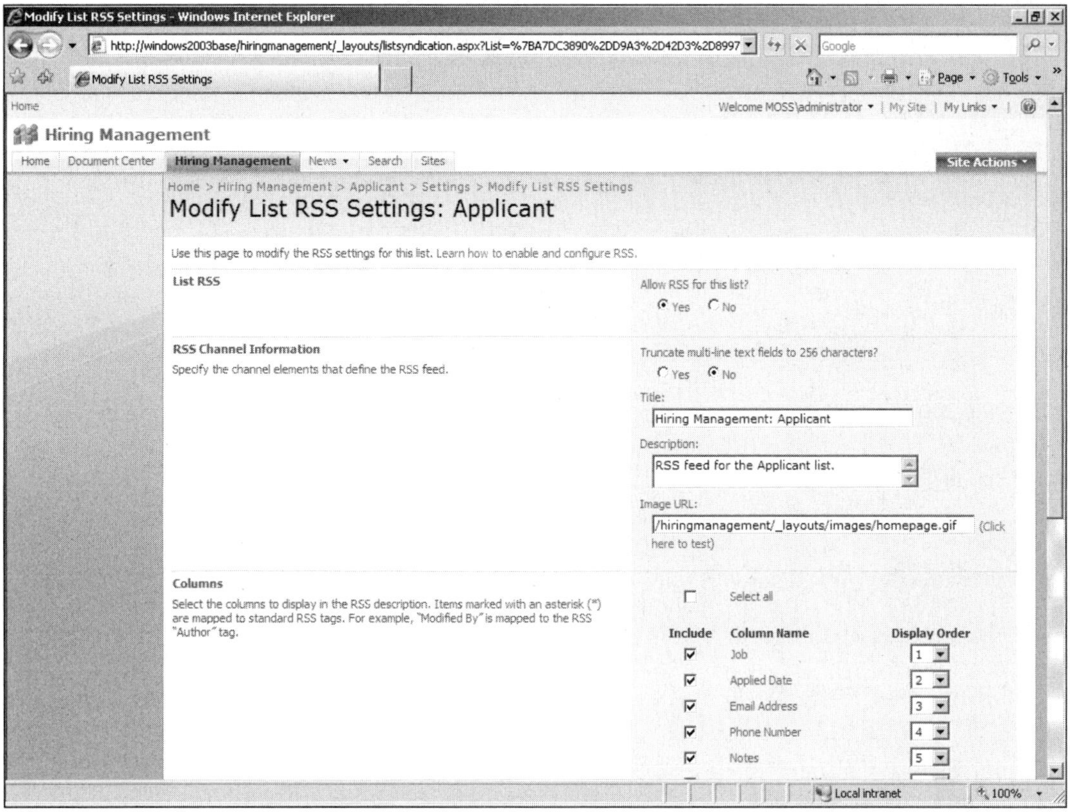

Figure 6-3

The following table lists some event receiver base classes found in the `Microsoft.SharePoint` namespace.

Base Receiver	Events
SPWebEventReceiver	SiteDeleted
SiteDeleting	
WebDeleted	
WebDeleting	
WebMoved	
WebMoving	

Continued

Base Receiver	Events
SPListEventReceiver	FieldAdded
FieldAdding	
FieldDeleted	
FieldDeleting	
FieldUpdated	
FieldUpdating	
SPItemEventReceiver	ItemAdded
ItemAdding	
ItemAttachmentAdded	
ItemAttachmentAdding	
ItemAttachmentDeleted	
ItemAttachmentDeleting	
ItemCheckedIn	
ItemCheckedOut	
ItemCheckingIn	
ItemCheckingOut	
ItemDeleted	
ItemDeleting	
ItemFileConverted	
ItemFileMoved	
ItemFileMoving	
ItemUncheckedOut	
ItemUncheckingOut	
ItemUpdated	
ItemUpdating	

Xyz.HumanResources Class Project

For this application, create a class library project inside Visual Studio to hold the event receiver that will be attached to the Applicant list. The receiver will send an email to the hiring manager when a new applicant is added to one of the manager's openings.

Since the default class file associated with project type is not needed, remove it. Then, associate the `Microsoft.SharePoint.dll` with the project through the Add New References functionality of the project. To find this assembly, use the .NET tab in the reference window and scroll to the appropriate entry.

To associate this project with the SharePoint installation, the compiled library must be added to the Global Assembly Cache. The steps to do this can be found later in this chapter. However, to prepare the assembly for the GAC, this project must be signed. If the project is recompiled after deploying to the GAC and registering to SharePoint for modifications, reset IIS on the SharePoint server to replace the assembly in the ASP.NET cache.

Signing a project is very easy to do and can be achieved by following these steps:

1. In Solution Explorer, right-click on the project name and click Properties.
2. On the left side of the Properties screen, click the Signing tab.
3. Check the `Sign the assembly` box.
4. From the drop-down list below the check box, select the new option.
5. Fill in a name for the key in the `Key file name` text box.
6. Associate a password with the key, and confirm it in the second box.
7. Click the OK button.
8. Close the Properties screen.

Compile the project and check for any errors. If no errors are found, move on to the next step.

Creating an Event Receiver

Next, create a class named `ApplicantEventReceiver`. The class needs to inherit from `SPItemEventReceiver` as it will attach to the `ItemAdded` event of the Applicants list. Due to the amount of objects this project uses in the `Microsoft.SharePoint` namespace, declare the namespace with the C# using statement.

Using the IntelliSense inside Visual Studio 2005, type **override** and select the `ItemAdded` method from the list. Visual Studio will then stub out the method, and it will resemble the following:

```
public override void ItemAdded(SPItemEventProperties properties)
{

}
```

When you attach this event receiver to a list, SharePoint calls the `ItemAdded` method whenever a user adds a new item to that list. The event handler then receives the new item as a property collection. This parameter will be very significant for our event receiver.

The next step is to create a method for loading the `SmtpClient` in `System.Net.Mail` named `LoadSmtpInformation`. This method does not require any parameters and will return the `SmtpClient` object created inside of it. Notice that mail is not handled in .NET 2.0 as it was in .NET 1.x. Developers should review the documentation with .NET 2.0 to become more familiar with this namespace if it is new to them.

After creating the method, add the code to identify the SMTP server information for passing mail through. Due to security issues, adding credentials for the SMTP server may be required. Once completed the method should resemble the following:

```
private SmtpClient LoadSmtpInformation()
{
    SmtpClient client = new SmtpClient();

    client.Host = "server address";
    client.Port = 25;
    client.Credentials = new NetworkCredential("username", "password");

    return client;
}
```

To continue, create the `BuildEmailBody` method, which constructs the message that will be sent to the hiring manager. This method receives the event property list and returns an HTML string.

The method should be similar to the following method, but does not need to be exact:

```
private string BuildEmailBody(SPListItem item)
{
    StringBuilder body = new StringBuilder();

    body.Append("This email has been automatically sent from the Hiring Management
system. <br /><br />");
    body.Append("<table border=\"0\" cellpadding=\"2\" cellspacing=\"0\">");
    body.Append("<colgroup><col width=\"150\" align=\"right\" /><col width=\"350\"
/></colgroup>");
    body.AppendFormat("\r\n<tr><td>Applicant Name:<td><td>{0}<td></tr>",
item["Applicant Name"]);

    SPFieldLookupValue jobValue =
(SPFieldLookupValue)item.Fields["Job"].GetFieldValue((string)item["Job"]);
    body.AppendFormat("\r\n<tr><td>Job:<td><td>{0}<td></tr>",
jobValue.LookupValue);

    body.AppendFormat("\r\n<tr><td>Applied Date:<td><td>{0}<td></tr>",
item["Applied Date"]);
    body.AppendFormat("\r\n<tr><td>Email Address:<td><td>{0}<td></tr>", item["Email
Address"]);
    body.AppendFormat("\r\n<tr><td>Phone Number:<td><td>{0}<td></tr>", item["Phone
Number"]);
    body.AppendFormat("\r\n<tr><td>Notes:<td><td>{0}<td></tr>", item["Notes"]);
    body.Append("</table>");

    return body.ToString();
}
```

Notice that this method uses the item to pull out the different fields added by the end user. The syntax `item["fieldname"]` will return the object equivalent of the field used. Since most of these fields are strings, you can append them to the `StringBuilder` without any formatting concerns.

However, the `Job` field is a lookup on the Jobs list to provide a link back to the job and, beyond that, to the department and hiring manager.

There are two approaches to pulling the display value for this field. If you insert the property item directly like the other fields, SharePoint will return a string with the ID and value, separated by a semicolon and number sign. An example is `"1;#Software Developer"` for the first job created. A better approach, shown above, casts the `Job` property to its true type, which is `SPFieldLookupValue`. Then you call its `LookupValue` method to obtain the default text, which is the job name.

The next step is to create the `LoadHiringManagersEmail` method to fetch the hiring manager's email address. This method uses the lookup techniques described above to find the appropriate email address. You need to navigate through the Job list and Department list to find the `Hiring Manager` information, as shown in the following code sample:

```
private string LoadHiringManagersEmail(SPListItem item)
{
    SPList jobList = item.ParentList.ParentWeb.Lists["Jobs"];
    SPFieldLookupValue jobValue =
(SPFieldLookupValue)item.Fields["Job"].GetFieldValue((string)item["Job"]);
    SPItem jobItem = jobList.Items[jobValue.LookupId];

    SPList departmentList = jobList.ParentWeb.Lists["Departments"];
    SPFieldLookupValue departmentValue =
(SPFieldLookupValue)jobItem.Fields["Department"].GetFieldValue((string)jobItem["Dep
artment"]);
    SPItem departmentItem = departmentList.Items[departmentValue.LookupId];

    SPFieldUserValue hiringManager =
(SPFieldUserValue)departmentItem.Fields["Hiring
Manager"].GetFieldValue((string)departmentItem["Hiring Manager"]);

    return hiringManager.User.Email;
}
```

Notice that this example navigates through the list and uses a new value object to pull the user information named `SPFieldUserValue`. *This object is utilized by fields that use the SharePoint list item type for user lookup. The property* `User` *includes a property named* `Email` *as well as many other key fields for identifying the user.*

Now pull the previous two methods together by creating a `BuildMailMessage` method that will call them and build the `MailMessage` for sending through the `SmtpClient`. This method will accept the list passed through the `ItemAdded` event and return a `MailMessage` object. This message object will also need to include the attachments of the applicant list as email attachments. This can be achieved by using the `Attachments` list inside the list item object. Once finalized, the method should be close to the following:

```
private MailMessage BuildMailMessage(SPListItem item)
{
    MailMessage message = new MailMessage();
```

```
        SPList list = item.ParentList;

        message.From = new MailAddress("humanresources@xyz.local");
        message.To.Add(new MailAddress(LoadHiringManagersEmail(item)));

        message.IsBodyHtml = true;
        message.Body = BuildEmailBody(item);
        message.Subject = "Hiring Management - Applicant Created";

        for (int attachmentIndex = 0; attachmentIndex < item.Attachments.Count;
attachmentIndex++)
        {
            string url = item.Attachments.UrlPrefix +
item.Attachments[attachmentIndex];
            SPFile file = list.ParentWeb.GetFile(url);

            message.Attachments.Add(new Attachment(file.OpenBinaryStream(),
file.Name));
        }

        return message;
    }
```

The final logic needed for this event receiver is to call the SMTP object builder and call the last method you created. To do this, add the following lines of code to the `ItemAdded` method created in the first step of this class:

```
SPListItem item = properties.ListItem;
SmtpClient client = LoadSmtpInformation();

client.Send(BuildMailMessage(item));
```

Now, compile the code and repeat until no errors are found. The next steps will be to deploy the assembly to the SharePoint server and attach the event receiver to the applicant list.

The final code for the event receiver should be close to the following:

```
using System;
using System.Collections.Generic;
using System.Text;
using System.Net.Mail;

using Microsoft.SharePoint;

namespace Xyz.HumanResources
{
    public class ApplicantEventReceiver : SPItemEventReceiver
    {
        public override void ItemAdded(SPItemEventProperties properties)
        {
            SPListItem item = properties.ListItem;
            SmtpClient client = LoadSmtpInformation();
```

```
            client.Send(BuildMailMessage(item));
        }

        private SmtpClient LoadSmtpInformation()
        {
            SmtpClient client = new SmtpClient();

            client.Host = "mail.geekswithblogs.com";
            client.Port = 25;
            client.Credentials = new
System.Net.NetworkCredential("jjulian@geekswithblogs.com", "erjiiu");

            return client;
        }

        private string BuildEmailBody(SPListItem item)
        {
            StringBuilder body = new StringBuilder();

            body.Append("This email has been automatically sent from the Hiring
Management system. <br /><br />");
            body.Append("<table border=\"0\" cellpadding=\"2\"
cellspacing=\"0\">");
            body.Append("<colgroup><col width=\"150\" align=\"right\" /><col
width=\"350\" /></colgroup>");
            body.AppendFormat("\r\n<tr><td>Applicant Name:<td><td>{0}<td></tr>",
item["Applicant Name"]);

            SPFieldLookupValue jobValue =
(SPFieldLookupValue)item.Fields["Job"].GetFieldValue((string)item["Job"]);
            body.AppendFormat("\r\n<tr><td>Job:<td><td>{0}<td></tr>",
jobValue.LookupValue);

            body.AppendFormat("\r\n<tr><td>Applied Date:<td><td>{0}<td></tr>",
item["Applied Date"]);
            body.AppendFormat("\r\n<tr><td>Email Address:<td><td>{0}<td></tr>",
item["Email Address"]);
            body.AppendFormat("\r\n<tr><td>Phone Number:<td><td>{0}<td></tr>",
item["Phone Number"]);
            body.AppendFormat("\r\n<tr><td>Notes:<td><td>{0}<td></tr>",
item["Notes"]);
            body.Append("</table>");

            return body.ToString();
        }

        private MailMessage BuildMailMessage(SPListItem item)
        {
            MailMessage message = new MailMessage();
            SPList list = item.ParentList;

            message.From = new MailAddress("humanresources@xyz.local");
            message.To.Add(new MailAddress(LoadHiringManagersEmail(item)));
```

```
                message.IsBodyHtml = true;
                message.Body = BuildEmailBody(item);
                message.Subject = "Hiring Management - Applicant Created";

                for (int attachmentIndex = 0; attachmentIndex < item.Attachments.Count;
attachmentIndex++)
                {
                     string url = item.Attachments.UrlPrefix +
item.Attachments[attachmentIndex];
                     SPFile file = list.ParentWeb.GetFile(url);

                     message.Attachments.Add(new Attachment(file.OpenBinaryStream(),
file.Name));
                }

                return message;
        }

        private string LoadHiringManagersEmail(SPListItem item)
        {
            SPList jobList = item.ParentList.ParentWeb.Lists["Jobs"];
            SPFieldLookupValue jobValue =
(SPFieldLookupValue)item.Fields["Job"].GetFieldValue((string)item["Job"]);
            SPItem jobItem = jobList.Items[jobValue.LookupId];

            SPList departmentList = jobList.ParentWeb.Lists["Departments"];
            SPFieldLookupValue departmentValue =
(SPFieldLookupValue)jobItem.Fields["Department"].GetFieldValue((string)jobItem["Dep
artment"]);
            SPItem departmentItem = departmentList.Items[departmentValue.LookupId];

            SPFieldUserValue hiringManager =
(SPFieldUserValue)departmentItem.Fields["Hiring
Manager"].GetFieldValue((string)departmentItem["Hiring Manager"]);

            return hiringManager.User.Email;
        }
    }
}
```

Deploying an Event Receiver

You could deploy this event handler by wrapping it within a SharePoint feature package, which would make is available for reuse in other lists. This would be an excellent approach if you had built a general-purpose event handler to produce email messages based on a parameterized template. As you gain SharePoint development skills, you might want to tackle that challenge.

However, the version implemented above is very specific to this hiring process example, so you want to restrict its use to that scenario. To accomplish this type of restricted deployment, you can build a console application that deploys the event handler by invoking the SharePoint object model. This approach has the added advantage of enabling you to update the event handler simply by replacing the assembly in the GAC and recycling IIS.

First, use Visual Studio to create a console application. In the Main method, create a SPSite object to access the hiring management site. Next, create an SPWeb object and assign it to the OpenWeb method on the site object. This object will allow the user to find the applicant list on the SharePoint server.

After opening the web object, load the applicant list using the Lists property. On the list, find the EventReceivers collection and use the Add method to pass the appropriate fields that identify the assembly containing the receiver and the receiver class itself. Some of the values needed to build the type string can be retrieved from the GAC tools provided in the .NET SDK.

Once the receiver is associated with the list, write a completed message to the console and prompt the user for input so that the application does not close before the user can ensure that the application was successful.

This method should look similar to the example here:

```
static void Main(string[] args)
{
    SPSite site = new SPSite("http://server/hiringmanagement/");
    SPWeb web = site.OpenWeb();
    SPList list = web.Lists["Applicant"];

    string assemblyName = "Xyz.HumanResources, Version=1.0.0.0, Culture=neutral,
PublicKeyToken=TOKEN";
    string className = "Xyz.HumanResources.ApplicantEventReceiver";

    list.EventReceivers.Add(SPEventReceiverType.ItemAdded, assemblyName,
className);

    Console.WriteLine(" - Registered - ");
    Console.Read();
}
```

To confirm that the receiver was registered correctly, add an applicant to one of the jobs created early and check the email of the hiring manager that the job was associated with. Make sure that the test includes sample resume attachments, to review the complete functionality.

Project Review

At this point, the project should be completely functional based on the requirements and can be placed into a testing environment to ensure that no bugs are lingering and then reviewed by the IT and HR departments for approval.

After final testing, deploy this site to the production SharePoint server for the organization and remove all sample data.

Summary

The sample application described in this chapter is just one of the many different applications that can be created using the existing functionality of SharePoint. These applications will help SharePoint gain popularity in the organization by extending the rich collaboration already offered with organization specific needs, making teams more productive.

This chapter showed a simple, but quite powerful, use of the SharePoint object model and Visual Studio development environment in a real-world scenario. The most complicated aspect of SharePoint programming is learning how to navigate through the object model to find the information you need for your purposes. The best way to climb that learning curve is by building applications like the one shown here.

7

RSS, Blogs, and Wikis

By Jeff Julian

RSS, blogs, and Wikis were added inside Windows SharePoint Services 3.0 to let teams collaborate beyond what was once available. This chapter explains what these technologies are, common uses of them, and how to use them with Windows SharePoint Services 3.0.

Each section defines what these technologies are and exposes the extension points open to developers to add more functionality than what is in the box.

RSS

RSS (Really Simple Syndication) is an XML document specification used as a generic approach to exposing data to other tools for reading. Many sites now use RSS to deliver content such as search results, weblogs, and news.

Due to the simplicity and usefulness of RSS, it is one of the largest implementations of XML worldwide. People consume the feeds to keep up to date with a wide range of content via subscriptions so that they don't need to remember to visit the sites of interest. Without RSS, web users are required to visit web sites over and over throughout the day or hour to keep them informed of the most current data. This process can lead to a lot of repetitive reading as well as missing timely information. RSS resolves these issues. When paired with an aggregator, and the surfing is done, you can read new items as they arrive automatically.

This approach is somewhat similar to receiving email but uses a very different delivery technique. Unlike email, an RSS feed is hosted by the information provider, instead of delivered to the subscriber. Email typically uses a protocol called Simple Mail Transfer Protocol (SMTP) to communicate with the recipient through an email server. An RSS feed is generated directly by a web site and uses the Hypertext Transfer Protocol (HTTP) as its delivery protocol.

Overview of RSS

RSS is a simple XML format that defines a channel containing items that carry the actual information being delivered to the RSS consumer. These items use various XML elements to describe the title, content, and other metadata useful to whatever tools the consumer employs to process the RSS feed. The most common consumer of RSS is a tool known as an aggregator.

Aggregators consume several RSS feeds via subscriptions and pull the data from each feed on a regular interval, typically 60 minutes. Once the aggregator parses the XML, it will highlight the changes found from the previous pull. With tooling like this, users can easily see what is different from the last time they checked. Later, this chapter demonstrates how to use Outlook 2007 to subscribe to RSS feeds from SharePoint. Listing 7-1 is an example of an RSS feed based on a SharePoint list and the items of that list.

Listing 7-1: A sample RSS feed generated by a document repository

```xml
<?xml version="1.0" encoding="UTF-8"?>
<rss version="2.0">
  <channel>
    <title>Document Center: Announcements</title>
    <link>http://w2k3base/Docs/Lists/Announcements/AllItems.aspx</link>
    <description>RSS feed for the Announcements list.</description>
    <lastBuildDate>Sun, 15 Oct 2006 16:00:42 GMT</lastBuildDate>
    <generator>Windows SharePoint Services V3 RSS Generator</generator>
    <ttl>60</ttl>
    <image>
      <title>Document Center: Announcements</title>
      <url>/Docs/_layouts/images/homepage.gif</url>
      <link>http://w2k3base/Docs/Lists/Announcements/AllItems.aspx</link>
    </image>
    <item>
      <title>Welcome to the managed document repository site.</title>
      <link>http://w2k3base/Docs/Lists/Announcements/DispForm.aspx?ID=1</link>
      <description><![CDATA[<div><b>Body:</b> <div
        class=ExternalClassDA26385B52A04A558486A1CC03599E76>
        Welcome to your new managed document repository site. Use this
        site to centrally manage documents in your enterprise.</div></div>]]>
      </description>
      <author>W2K3BASE\administrator</author>
      <pubDate>Mon, 02 Oct 2006 16:36:35 GMT</pubDate>
      <guid isPermaLink="true">
        http://w2k3base/Docs/Lists/Announcements/DispForm.aspx?ID=1
      </guid>
    </item>
  </channel>
</rss>
```

Structure of an RSS Document

RSS documents have a top-level element, known as the document element, to define the document. This document element is named `rss` and has an attribute named `version` that indicates which version of the RSS specification is being used.

Inside the document element, the element named `channel` is used to hold the RSS items, but it can also contain other elements such as `title`, `description`, and `link` to describe the document in more detail (see the following table).

Name	Description
`title`	The title of the SharePoint page
`link`	The URL of the corresponding page
`description`	Basic text that describes the RSS feed
`lastBuildDate`	Date the feed was generated
`generator`	Describes the RSS generation tool used to build the feed
`ttl`	How long this feed will be cached in minutes from the last time it was built

The `item` elements hold the data for each piece of information shared within the RSS feed. As in the channel element, each item can contain `title`, `link`, and `description` elements to describe the item. In addition, an item can include several other descriptive elements, as shown in the following table. The `author` element indicates who created the item, and in SharePoint this will be a user account name. The `pubDate` element specifies the creation date of the item. The `guid` element is a unique identifier for the item. RSS readers typically use this key to find the correct item in the local cache even if its title or description has changed. If the `guid` value is a URL the attribute `isPermalink` will be `true` to indicate that the `guid` is actually a link to the item. Often this link will point to an expanded version of the article if the item contains only a summary.

Since RSS can be implemented differently depending on the source, review the official specification for the RSS 2.0 at `http://blogs.law.harvard.edu/tech/rss`.

Name	Description
`title`	The title of the item represented
`link`	The URL of the item
`description`	Information about the item
`author`	The account of the item's creator
`pubDate`	Date the item was published
`guid`	The unique identifier of this item. Hyperlinks are used in SharePoint, since they are always unique.

News Aggregators

RSS is a fairly simple XML dialect. To harness its real power, you need a tool that can read RSS documents and present the items in a useful way. In addition, the tool must have the ability to check one or more RSS feeds on a regular interval and update the display accordingly. This type of tool is often called a news aggregator.

The typical news aggregator has a similar interface to a mail reader and allows users to easily add their RSS feeds for subscription. In Office 2007, Outlook has news aggregation features, providing the typical office worker with an aggregator without additional downloading. Many news aggregators are available as free downloads or as packaged software, and several of these are written as .NET applications, such as RSS Bandit and NewsGator.

Other forms of news aggregators take the form of a browser. These aggregators display the content of a feed using HTML rendering and allow you to view the content of a feed without the need to understand XML. These tools are typically web applications and can be used from any computer that has an Internet connection. In Microsoft's Internet Explorer 7, the ability to subscribe to RSS feeds is built into the core functionality and plays a major part in compelling users to upgrade. The following table lists examples of news aggregators:

Name	URL
Internet Explorer 7	http://www.microsoft.com/windows/ie
Microsoft Office Outlook 2007	http://office.microsoft.com
RSS Bandit	http://www.rssbandit.org
NewsGator	http://www.newsgator.com
Bloglines	http://www.bloglines.com
Live.com	http://www.live.com
SharpReader	http://www.sharpreader.net
Pluck	http://www.pluck.com
FeedReader	http://www.feedreader.com

Thanks to the simple mechanics of a news aggregator, it is fairly easy for a developer to create their own. First, the tool must have a data store for retaining the different feeds of a user's subscription. They can use a database, XML file, or other proprietary form of storage. Next, the aggregator must have the ability to retrieve the feeds from the web. This process is typically multi-threaded to allow for multiple feeds to be pulled at the same time. Finally, the aggregator needs the ability to remember what items the user has read and to show the items that have not been reviewed.

Using RSS in Office Outlook 2007 and Internet Explorer

Internet Explorer 7 and Outlook 2007 now have built-in support for aggregating RSS feeds. Since both applications use the same RSS data store, you will see the same items regardless of whether you are running Outlook or Internet Explorer.

The ability of Outlook 2007 to include RSS feeds in its classic email view is a boon for those of us who "live in Outlook." In a SharePoint environment, you can use this feature to keep abreast of changes in your collaborative sites as you deal with your normal email tasks. Figure 7-1 shows the Outlook 2007 view of an RSS feed from a SharePoint document library.

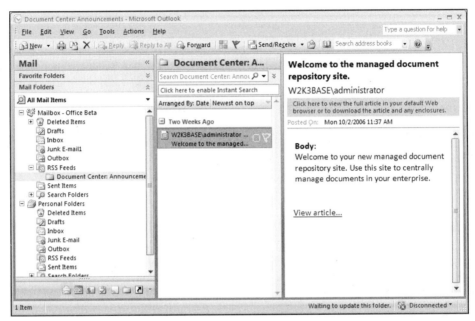

Figure 7-1

Uses of RSS within SharePoint

The addition of RSS to SharePoint couldn't come at a better time. Now that RSS is a proven medium for syndication and with Microsoft releasing tools to view and subscribe to the feeds, SharePoint needs the ability to publish RSS. Since lists are used to store the data in SharePoint, this is the perfect place to expose them to users of the content. The `channel` element of RSS represents the list in the feed and each piece of content inside the list defines the `item` elements.

For developers, RSS is a great data source they can use inside their applications where this type of data is needed. These applications can be client-based or web applications as long as they have the ability to call out and load the content over HTTP. Using simple XML parsing, developers can load the feeds they need and display the data in their user interfaces. In SharePoint, every list has the ability to host an RSS feed. By default, the RSS feed is turned on and can be managed through the list's Action menu as shown in Figure 7-2.

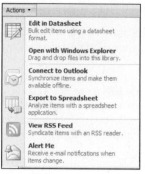

Figure 7-2

Here are the steps for accessing an RSS feed for a document library. You will learn about RSS feeds for blogs later in this chapter.

1.   Click on a document library link from the Quick Launch bar on a SharePoint site.

2.   At the top of the library, click the Action link.

3.   From the list (see Figure 7-2), select View RSS Feed.

To subscribe, copy the URL and import it into your aggregator.

Configuring RSS Settings

In your SharePoint site, the content of some list might be too sensitive for allowing RSS access. Other lists might be updated so frequently that you need to include up to the maximum items. These are features you can manipulate via administration for every list or library that offers RSS. In the following steps, you will walk through how to configure the RSS feeds for a Task list that is part of the Team Site template for SharePoint:

1.   Click the link for Task under Lists from the Quick Launch bar.

2.   Click the Settings link at the top of the list.

3.   Under the Communications section, click the RSS settings link. This screen will resemble Figure 7-3.

4.   To modify whether the list offers RSS, click the Yes or No radio button under Allow RSS for this list? in the List RSS section.

5.   To set a maximum length for the content description, click the Yes or No radio button under Truncate multi-line text fields to 256 characters? in the RSS Channel Information section.

6.   To change the title of the RSS feed, edit the text box labeled Title in the RSS Channel Information section.

7. To change the description of the RSS feed, modify the description text box in the RSS Channel Information section.

8. RSS feeds can use an image to better identify the feed in aggregators. To change the default image, enter the image URL in the text box labeled Image Url in the RSS Channel Information section. To test the image for correctness, click the Click here to test link next to the Image Url text box.

9. From the list of columns available for this list, select the columns you would like to display as part of the RSS feed in the Columns section. These columns will show up as different elements of the `item` field or embedded in the `description` field.

10. To alter the number of items in the feed, change the value of the Maximum items to include text box in the Item Limit section.

11. To add or subtract the amount of days an item will appear in the feed, change the value of the Maximum days to include text box in the Item Limit section.

12. Click the OK button to publish the changes.

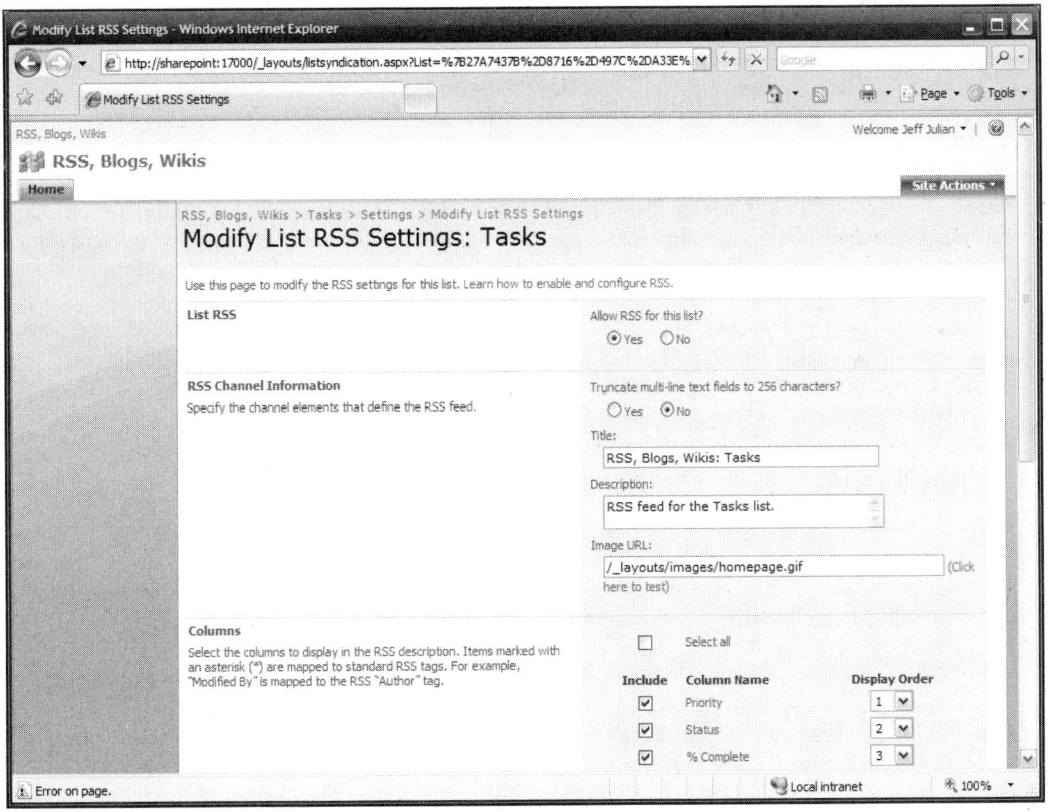

Figure 7-3

Blogs

Weblogs, also known as blogs, are a very useful way to deliver content to an interested audience on a regular basis. Unlike the early days of the web, blogs have easy-to-use tools for publishing new content. Paired with RSS, the readers of a blog can easily get the latest post from your site using the aggregation tools discussed earlier in this chapter.

Blogs were created in the late 1990s and with the advent of XML, RSS shortly followed. Together blogs and RSS started gaining popularity and each year, more and more people started using them. Even though the stereotypical blog user is a teenager, many blogs and blog communities have formed in the Microsoft technology field and have become a popular way of getting up-to-date information about upcoming technologies and ways of using current ones. Microsoft sites like MSDN and TechNet give readers the ability to get to know more about what Microsoft is doing straight from the employee's mouths.

Overview of Blogs

Blogs are very simple by nature. The typical blog has a main page for delivering content in reverse chronological order. Blogs also allow the author to categorize the content so that readers can pick and choose what is most relevant to them. To add to a blog, owners log in to a secure portion of their site and using a simple HTML creation tool, publish new content easily. Other techniques, such as using third-party tools located on the owner's machine to publish content via well-known weblog APIs to the blog server, are gaining popularity. Microsoft Office Word 2007 can be used as one of these tools.

Blogs are not just for letting people know about your vacation. They are also a good medium for technical information such as coding techniques, new tools you found to make development easier, and information about current projects. These different categories require a blogging tool to have different security layers for divulging information due to the sensitive nature of some of it. With the typical blogging tools available, this security layer is absent; so proprietary information is typically kept outside of a blog.

In Windows SharePoint Services 3.0, weblog tools have been added to allow users to use this technique of posting information to other users paired with a security layer to give only authenticated users the information they are allowed to see. Since blog content lives in SharePoint, new RSS features are available so that users can subscribe to the blog using their aggregators to get the latest data as it changes.

Using SharePoint, companies can use this technique to easily publish data about projects, teams, the business, and executives to their employees using tools they already have in their environment. Information that was once scattered over an intranet using different techniques can now be placed in a central repository, and with enterprise search, users can now easily find the content they have access to.

Blogs and teams go hand in hand in Windows SharePoint Services 3.0. When a team uses SharePoint to collaborate, there is a need to publish small amounts of data along with larger documents. Before, members could use documents or announcements to publish this form of data, but it was never easy to create the content or let others on the team know where the content was. The blog feature in SharePoint adds another avenue to publish content, allowing only individuals who have access to the data to review it.

Teams are not the only members of a company that can benefit from the use of blogs. Many companies are now getting executives involved as well. Laying out corporate strategies, energizing employees, announcing mergers and acquisitions are all different pieces of information that could be published in an executive blog while still giving the executive the assurance that this information will be kept secure.

Creating a Blog Site with WSS 3.0

These are the steps to create a blog site using Windows SharePoint Services 3.0:

1. Click on the Site Action button in the top-right corner of the parent site where the blog resides.

2. From the drop-down list, click the Create Site link (see Figure 7-4).

3. Fill out the New SharePoint Site page.

   ❑ Follow the steps to add a site to SharePoint.

   ❑ Select the template Blog in the list on the Collaboration tab (see Figure 7-5).

   ❑ Click the Create button when you are finished.

Once you have created your blog, you need to customize it to fit your team. This includes adding the appropriate categories, setting blog permissions, changing the theme, and adding other links to important blogs. Figure 7-6 shows us a sample of a new blog site created in this way.

Figure 7-4

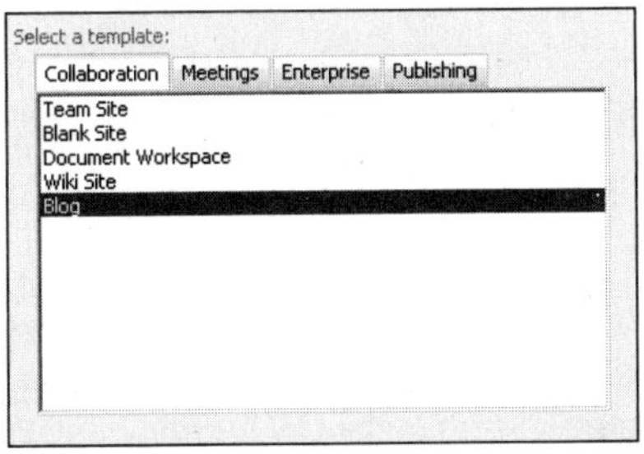

Figure 7-5

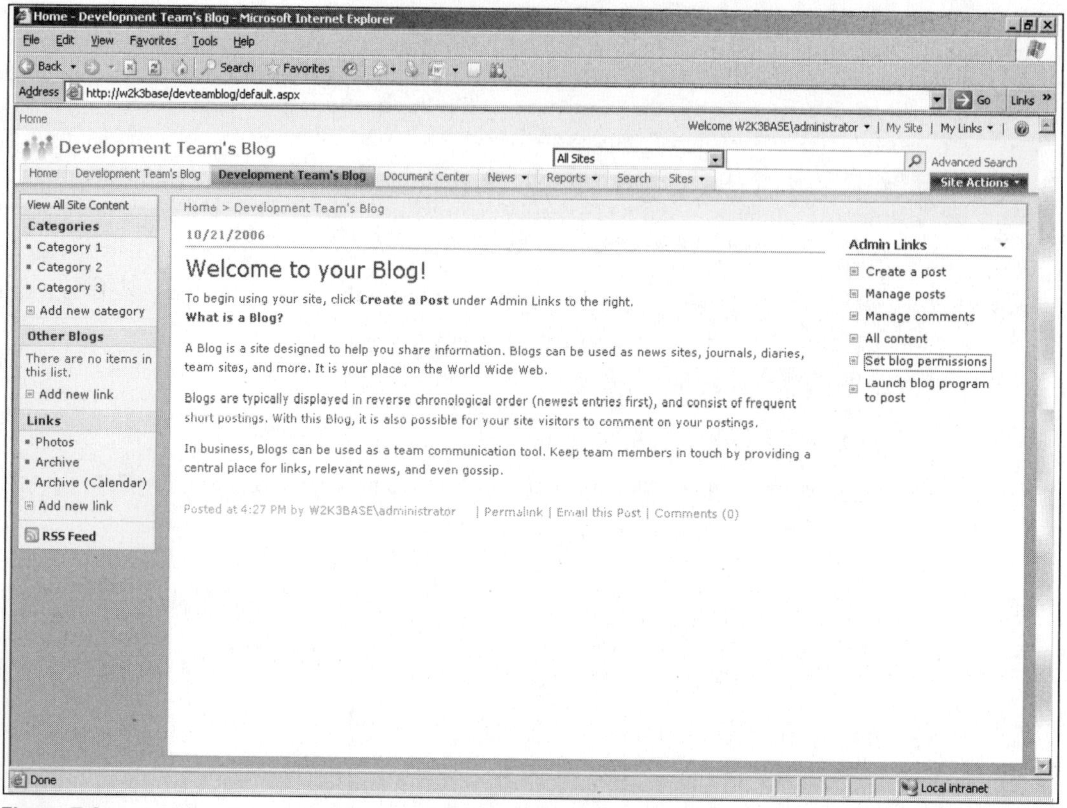

Figure 7-6

Customizing a Blog and Adding Categories

You will typically customize a new blog site to better fit your needs. The look and feel of your blog should fit the characteristics of the team or person it represents. Changing the theme of your blog is quite simple, and the following steps will walk you through the process:

1. Click on the Site Actions button and select Site Settings.

2. Under Look and Feel, click the Site theme link.

3. In the list of themes, select the one you like, using the preview window to decide.

4. Click the Apply button.

Now that you have a new look for your blog, set up the categories to help organize the articles. Categories are held in a SharePoint list and to change this list, click on the Categories header on the left side of the blog. After the list view has loaded, click the New button above the view. Insert the title of the category in the text box on the New Item page and press the OK button. Now you can assign blog posts to that category if the topic of the post relates to the category.

To edit a category, load the category list view and click on the Edit icon on the right side of the list. After the edit page loads, change the title of the category and click the OK button. If you would just like to delete the category at this time, click the Delete Item link above the title text box.

Setting Blog Permissions

Because of its rich feature set, a SharePoint blog site offers many ways to filter content based on security settings. You can set permissions on who can post, read posts, write comments, add to lists, and upload content to its libraries associated with the blog. The following steps walk you through setting permissions on the blog you just created.

Since some data within an internal-use blog may be sensitive, SharePoint allows you to set permissions that regulate which users are allowed to read or manipulate the blog, as described in the following steps:

1. Under the Admin Links, use one of the following options:

    ❏ For post, click Manage posts.

    ❏ For comment, click Manage comments.

    ❏ For categories, click All content, and under Lists, click Categories.

2. Inside the Settings menu, click List Settings.

3. In the Permissions and Management section, click Permissions for this list.

4. Inside the New menu, click Add Users.

    If the New menu is not available, the list's permissions are inherited from the parent site. Under the Actions menu, click Edit Permissions. You will then be alerted that you are about to create unique permissions for the list and asked if you want to continue. Click the OK button. Return to step 4 after this.

5. Inside the Add Users section, find or type the groups or users you want to add permissions for in the Users/Groups field.

6. In the Give Permissions section, select the options for your users or groups.

7. Click the OK button.

The technique to setting the edit access to the blog involves five steps:

1. Under the Admin Links, use one of the following options:

    ❏ For post, click Manage posts.

    ❏ For comment, click Manage comments.

    ❏ For categories, click All content, and under Lists, click Categories.

2. Inside the Settings menu, click List Settings.

3. Under General Settings, click Advanced settings.

4. Inside the Item-level permissions section, use the appropriate option for Edit access.

    Note to set read access, select the specific option for Read access.

5. Click the OK button.

Creating and Managing Blog Posts

Once you have all the permissions set , you are ready to start publishing. SharePoint includes fairly simple tools for writing articles, but you can also produce content via Microsoft Office Word 2007 or any other tool that can produce HTML streams. Let's walk through the steps creating a new blog post using SharePoint:

1.   From the homepage of the blog, click Create a post under Admin Links.

2.   Create a title for the post and place it in the Title box.

3.   With the rich content editor, create the content for the post inside the Body section.

4.   Select a category from the category list that best represents this post.

5.   If an alternative publish date is required, select it using the date tools in the Published section.

6.   Click the publish button or Save as Draft if the content is not finished.

Congratulations, you are now a blogger. Now you might want to modify your new post. One mistake many bloggers commonly make is editing their post without identifying their updates.

This mistake mainly affects RSS subscribers because RSS feeds are modified once a new post is available. If something changes, the post will then be marked for review again in their aggregator if they have already read through the post. Without an update technique, the reader will have to review the entire message and find what has changed. To get around this, bloggers use an Update header at the bottom of the post and add their new changes using a red font.

The following steps use that technique to modify the post:

1.   From the homepage of our blog, click Manage posts under Admin Links.

2.   From the drop-down list within the title of the post we just created, click Edit item.

3.   Move to the bottom of the post and create a new line.

4.   With the font color tool, change the color to red.

5.   Enter [Update: I am modifying this post] on the new line.

6.   Click the Publish button at the top or bottom of the page.

Configuring Content Approval for Blogs

Most blogging tools offer content approval. Because of a new form of spam known as Comment Spam, blog comments are a new medium for spammers to get their content out. These spam comments are not typically designed to drive a blogger to their site, but to use the blogger's search engine optimization to help boost their sites up in a search engine's ranking algorithms. If a blog is not public, this will not need to be a concern of yours.

Comments are not the only place you can enforce approval. In a group blog, team members will be allowed to create content, but it must be reviewed by the lead. For an executive blog, an assistant might be required to review a post for grammatical errors before it is published. Due to all these requirements, content approval is made available for posts, comments, and categories. If articles published to this blog need approval, execute these steps:

1. Under the Admin Links, use one of the following options:

   ❑ For post, click Manage posts.

   ❑ For comment, click Manage comments.

   ❑ For categories, click All content, and under Lists, click Categories.

2. Within the Settings list, select List Settings.

3. Inside the General Settings section, click Versioning settings.

4. Within Content Approval, select Yes to turn on content approval.

5. Click the OK button.

Now that you have turned on content approval, it's time to walk through the steps to approve or reject an item:

1. Under the Admin Links, use one of the following options:

   ❑ For post, click Manage posts.

   ❑ For comment, click Manage comments.

   ❑ For categories, click All content, and under Lists, click Categories.

2. Click on an item in the list using the Title column.

3. Click Approve/reject Item from the bar at the top of the page.

4. Inside Approval Status, select Approved, Rejected, or Pending.

5. If a comment is required to why this option was selected, enter it in the Comment box.

6. Click the OK button.

Changing Skins of SharePoint Blogs

Personalization is important to many bloggers. Since this is a place to display information about themselves and their work, it needs to look the way they prefer. With SharePoint, it is very easy to change the theme of your site, but this section walks through the steps for those who are not familiar with the process:

1. From the home page of the blog, click the Site Actions button.

2. Click the Site Settings link from the list.

3. Under the Look and Feel section, click the Site Theme link.

4. From the list of options, click one and preview.

5. After your final selection, click the Apply button.

Changing RSS Settings for a Blog

Although you can view a blog site by pointing your browser at it, as we discussed earlier, RSS is one of the most powerful features of today's blogging world. RSS aggregators work in the background of the user's machine to ensure that the user is alerted to the arrival of useful articles in a timely way. However, in a SharePoint environment, the use of a blog may be slightly different from that of the typical public blog. Because of this, you will learn the process of toggling RSS feeds on and off for a SharePoint blog. Figure 7-7 demonstrates the RSS settings for a site.

1. Navigate to the default page for the SharePoint blog.
2. Click the Site Actions link in the top-right corner.
3. Click the Site Settings link in the menu.
4. Under the Site Administration section, click the RSS link.
5. Check or uncheck the checkbox labeled Allow RSS feeds in this site.

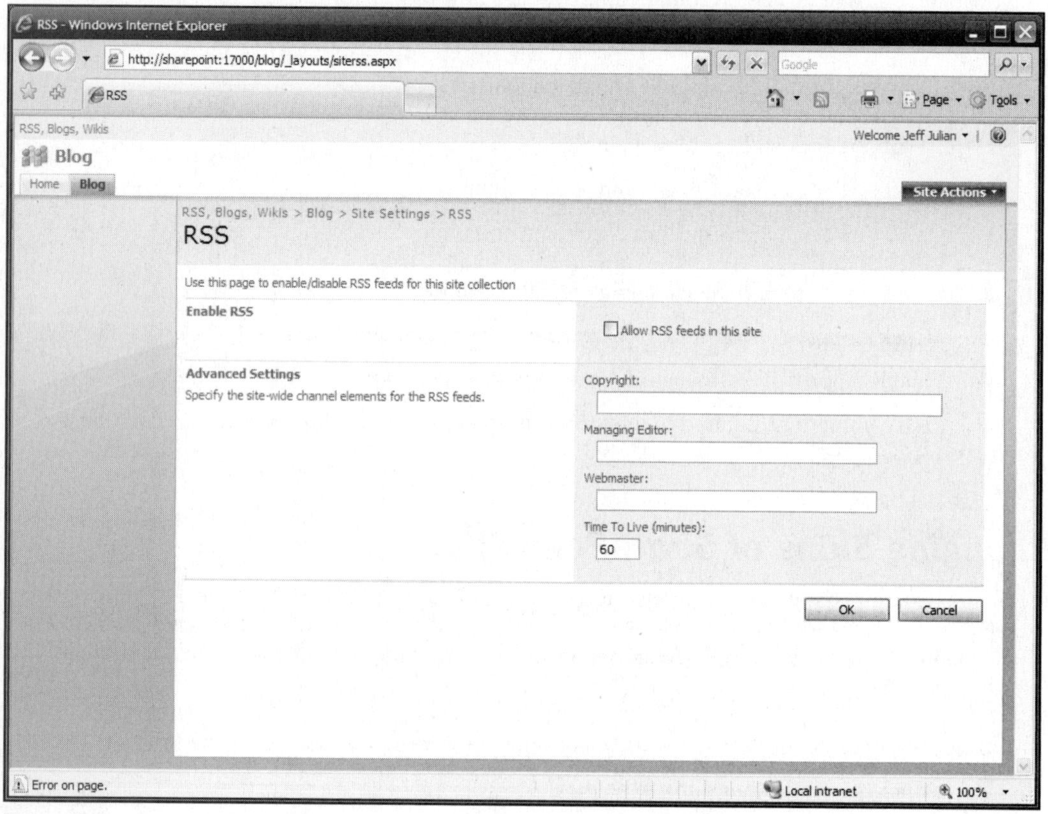

Figure 7-7

6. At this point, you may enter the copyright, managing editor, webmaster, and time to live for the feed in the appropriate fields.

7. Click the OK button to publish your changes.

If you disabled the RSS feed, when you visit the default page for the blog you will notice that the RSS icon and subscription link are missing from the Quick Launch bar.

Wikis

A Wiki is a type of web site that allows visitors to easily change the content of existing pages and add new pages on the fly. Once you visit a Wiki page, if you have permissions, editing the content is a button click away. If you want to create a new page, edit the page and use a simple markup language known as WikiText to add a link to the page you want to create. Return to the main page and once you click the link, the page is created and ready for content.

Wikis were formed in the 1990s by Ward Cunningham, who was looking for an easy way to create content and have it be maintained by a public. Ward initially launched WikiWikiWeb as the first Wiki, and adoption of the technology started booming. Wikis have joined the mainstream with sites like Wikipedia, a huge searchable repository of information on every topic imaginable that allows visitors to modify encyclopedia entries as events happen.

This growing popularity prompted the addition of Wikis to Windows SharePoint Services 3.0. Teams can use this approach to keep documentation, internal development standards, meeting notes, and any other content that can be shared and modified with ease. Using the security model of SharePoint sites, allowing member access is quite simple. The following section covers how to start a Wiki using SharePoint as well as securing your Wiki. SharePoint does not require the user to know Hypertext Markup Language (HTML), allowing for more users to build pages without any background in web design. Figure 7-8 demonstrates what a Wiki in SharePoint looks like after creation.

Implementing Wikis

Windows SharePoint Services 3.0 allows you to add a Wiki to an existing site with a Wiki Page Library, or create a completely separate site for a Wiki using a Wiki Site template. The next section discusses both procedures.

Creating a Wiki Page Library

1. Navigate to the default page of the site where you want to add the Wiki Page Library.

2. Click the View All Site Content link at the top of the Quick Launch bar.

3. Click the Create link at the top of the page.

4. In the Libraries section, click the Wiki Page Library link.

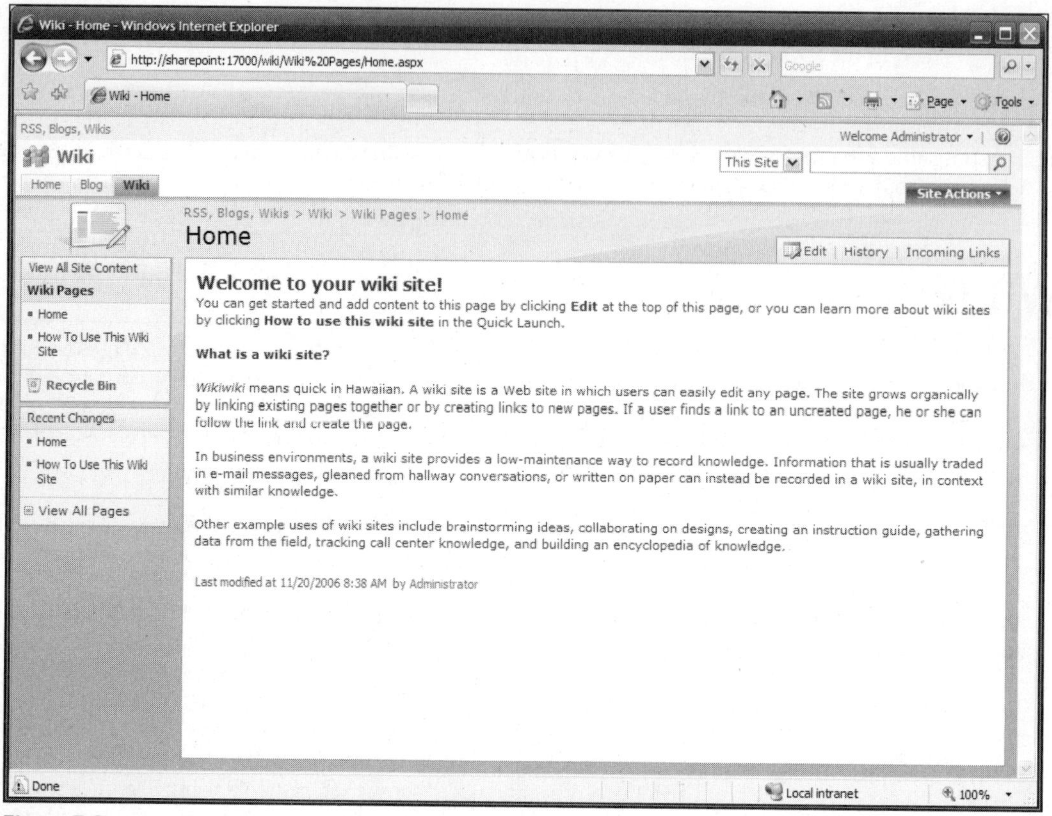

Figure 7-8

5. In the Name and Description section, fill in the name and description in the appropriate text boxes for this Wiki library.

6. Choose if you want this Wiki to show on the Quick Launch bar under the Navigation section.

7. Click the OK button to publish your changes. (See Figure 7-9.)

Creating a Wiki Site

Now it's time to create a Wiki site of your own.

1. Navigate to the parent site's default page that the Wiki Site will reside under.

2. Click the Site Actions button in the top-right corner.

3. Click the Site Settings link from the list.

4. Under the Site Administration section, click the Sites and Workspaces link.

5. Add the title and description of the Wiki in the appropriate fields under the Title and Description section.

6. In the Web Site Address box, fill in the value for the ending URL for the Wiki.

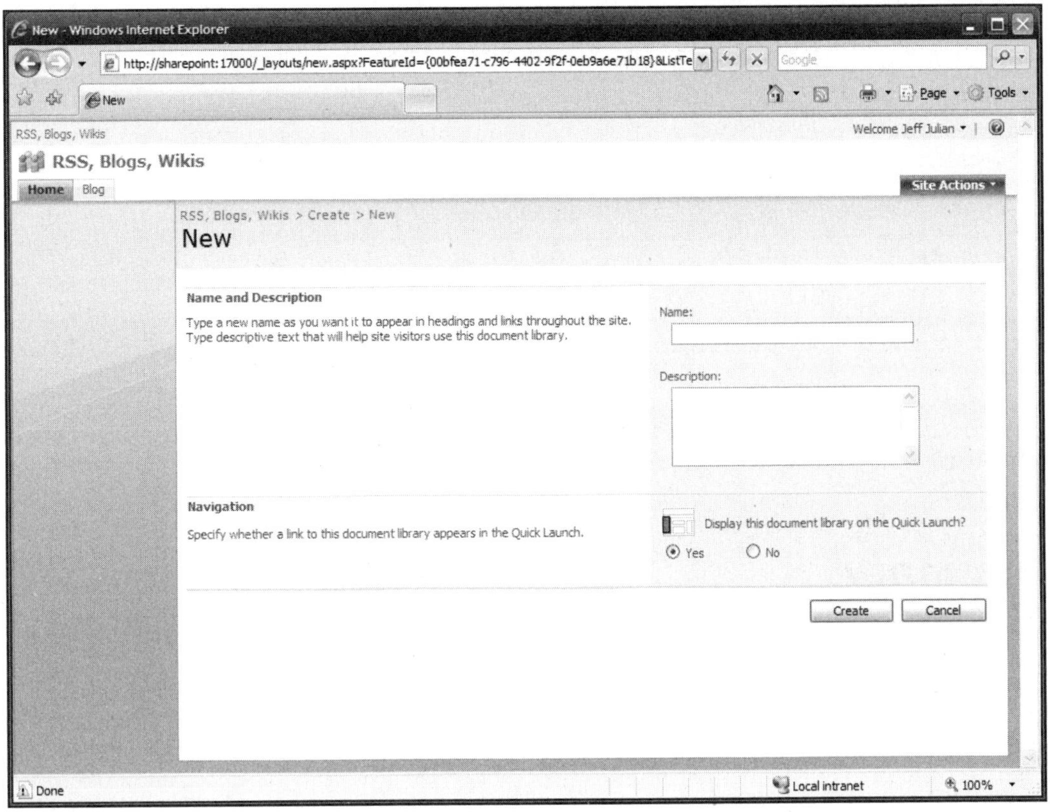

Figure 7-9

7.   Select the Wiki Site template inside the Collaboration tab under the Template Selection section.

8.   Select the appropriate permissions under the Permissions section.

9.   Determine if you want the site to show up in the Quick Launch bar and at the top of the link bar on the parent site under the Navigation section.

10. Click the OK button to publish the changes.

Using Wiki Tools in SharePoint 2007

The power of a Wiki tool is the ease of content creation. In Windows SharePoint Services 3.0, the Wiki tools satisfy this by making it very easy to change content and add new pages. The Rich Test Editor that is part of SharePoint removes the need for the typical WikiText syntax for basic formatting of content. Figure 7-10 shows what options are available to format content in SharePoint.

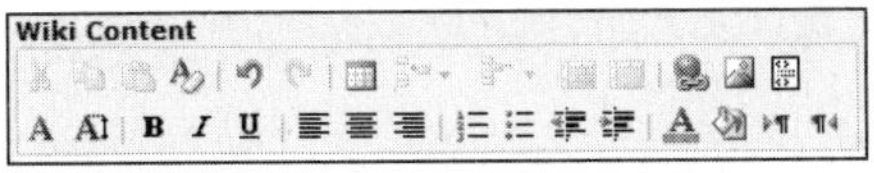

Figure 7-10

One of the features all Wikis need that a Rich Text Editor cannot fulfill is the ability to create links within the code that drive the creation of other Wiki pages. To create these links, place [[and]] around the words you would like the page name to be. If the page name should be different than the text displayed, after [[enter the page name, then place a pipe character, |, and enter the text you would like to have displayed on the page, followed by]]. The following table offers some examples:

Name	Description
Basic link	[[PageName]]
Link with alternative text	[[PageName|Page Text In Content]]

After saving your changes, click on the link, and if the page does not exist, you're asked to create the content of this page. It is good practice to stub in data about these pages when you generate links for them to ensure that read-only content viewers can click the links.

Summary

At this point, you should have a basic understanding of RSS, blogs, and Wikis, and are hopefully ready to get started working with them. With these enhancements to Windows SharePoint Services 3.0, hopefully the outcome is that you can build SharePoint sites that allow your team to collaborate in new ways. RSS gives you a new way, other than email, to alert interested readers about what has changed in SharePoint, and with Outlook 2007 and Internet Explorer 7, this format can easily be placed into your toolbox. Blogging gives you the avenue to publish small amounts of content and give others the opportunity to comment on it. Wikis allow teams to easily create content pages and build on them over time without prior knowledge of HTML.

Building Personalized Solutions

By Brendon Schwartz

A *portal* is a single point of entry for a family of web sites. Often these sites have complex relation-ships, such as multiple tree structures or a complicated grid or network topology. The portal takes care of common tasks such as user login, authentication, authorization, and personalization. In addition, the portal typically provides common user interface artifacts such as master pages and themes, giving the underlying sites a common appearance that can be easily personalized to suit each user's tastes. Finally, most portals offer artifacts such as "breadcrumb" controls that simplify navigation into the underlying sites.

ASP.NET 2.0 contains most of the building blocks you need to construct a portal, and several starter kits are available to help do that, such as DotNetNuke. SharePoint 2007 (that is, WSS 3.0 and MOSS 2007) uses these ASP.NET features, so you can build portals that greatly simplify access to complex SharePoint site topologies.

This chapter introduces you to the key concepts of building a SharePoint portal site:

- ❏ Using built-in features such as profiles, colleagues, and audiences
- ❏ Creating custom applications by developing with the Profiles API
- ❏ Managing membership by designing your own custom people picker
- ❏ Working with audiences programmatically

Building Rich Portal Solutions on SharePoint

Portals were originally created by providers of large public Internet services, such as Yahoo and MSN, that manage thousands of content-rich sites under a common umbrella. However, as corporate intranets and extranets have become more complex, portals have become popular aspects of company infrastructure. They provide employees and business partners with easy access to information such as company news, contact lists, documents, and reports. In addition, portals serve as entry points to back-end business services such as purchasing, manufacturing, and accounting. Human resources departments are deploying portals that provide convenient access to public documents such as the employee handbook as well as private access to an employee's own records. Furthermore, many HR portals include self-help features for tasks such as updating information related to health insurance and retirement plans.

As the needs of these applications have grown, the applications running these sites have grown. They have become easier to customize and have started to use more powerful user data. The portals used by many companies take the form of many different applications today as follows:

- ❏ Standard sets of web pages
- ❏ Content Management Servers (CMS systems)
- ❏ User portal-based applications
- ❏ Internal portals for company use
- ❏ External portals for business-to-business use

Although it is difficult to be everything to everyone, Windows SharePoint Services provides a framework that Office SharePoint Server builds upon to build these types of portal systems. One of the most important features needed for a portal are the user profiles. Each user has a set of profile data that can be used to display information to other users or determine which content the user should see. The profile data can be managed easily from a central location and can be shared across multiple web applications. This data can be imported from other sources or used from a central source.

SharePoint also includes the My Site feature that enables each user to create a personal site with public and private views. This enables users to save, manage, and share information much more conveniently than older file-sharing techniques allowed. This chapter looks at how to manage My Site with the user interface as well as through the object model.

To make the sites dynamic, SharePoint uses audiences to determine the correct content to display to the right users. In addition to audiences, you can use specific Web Parts to show data about yourself and other Colleagues. This allows you to set up a group of users that match a certain profile to be shown the data they need immediately.

Membership and User Profiles

User profiles are a collection of information that can be imported from a database or manually entered. The data in a user profile can then also be further customized by the user. Profiles store personal information about the users in your company or organization. All of the user profiles are stored in Profile

Services, which is part of the Shared Service Provider for the site collection. User profiles can be helpful when you need to determine some type of personal information about another user. Also, user profiles help by pointing out the connections, or relationships, that a user has with other users. For example, a manager would be able to see other managers in the organization, and use them as a resource when help is needed.

You can use user profiles through the user interface or through the APIs provided by the object model. There are many ways that user profiles can be helpful to an organization. For example, if a department is trying to use an unfamiliar program, they could search all of the user profiles to find someone who lists using that product as one of their skills. If there are only a handful of people in the organization who have experience using that product, the user profiles would provide a way to find them quickly and get the help needed. Figure 8-1 shows an advanced search of user profiles.

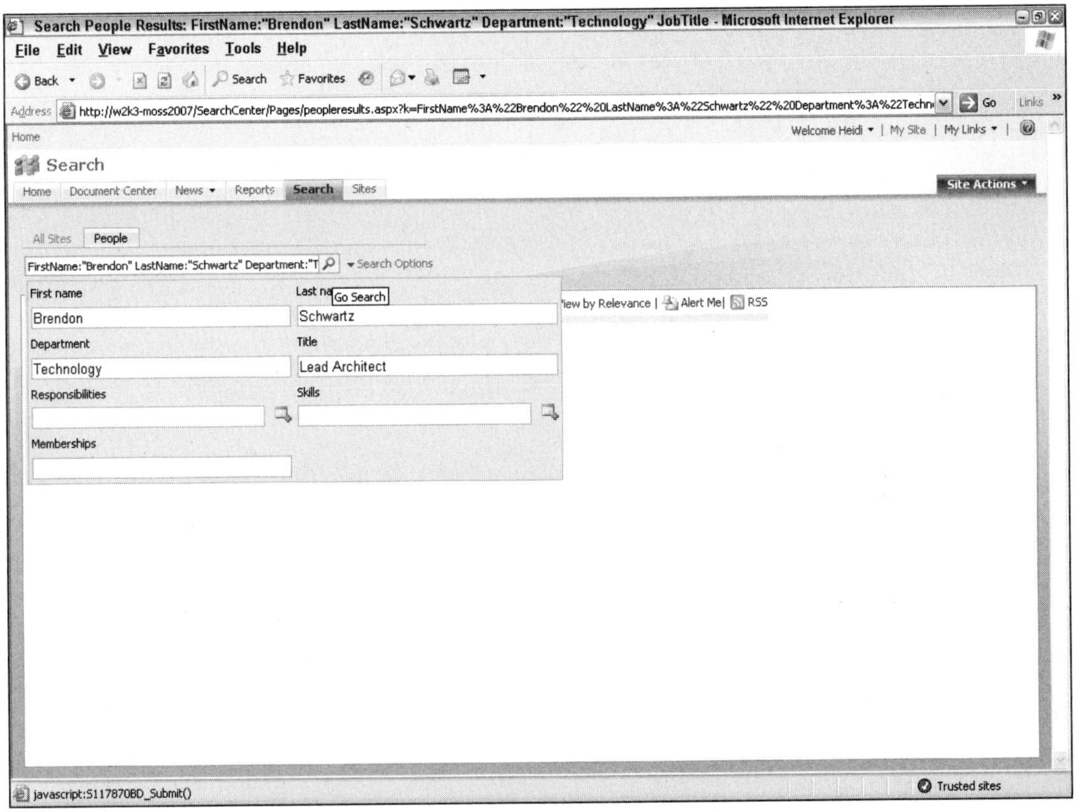

Figure 8-1

Managing a User Profile

To update the user profile, end users will use their My Site page, the administrator will use the Shared Service Provider, and you as the developer can access web services or the object model. When users set up a My Site page, there are five links provided in the Get Started with My Site section to help them personalize their site. The first link allows the user to describe themselves, and it takes the user to a personal profile form. The personal profile is where users can view and modify available user profile fields about themselves. Filling in the information is part of the process of creating memberships and helps other people find them through enterprise search, and also give colleagues some information about each other. This type of information can be very useful in large organizations, where many people don't know what others do or how to find them.

User profile data can be imported from many different connections such as Active Directory or another third-party data store. The administrator can manage the user profiles through the Shared Service Provider User Profiles and Properties screen. From this screen you can add, view, and create new imports for the user profile as well as manage the profile properties of each user. (See Figure 8-2.)

Although the administrator may already have some information set up to be displayed, each user should fill out all of the optional information to create a more robust site and user profile system. It is helpful for users to provide as much information as possible in their profiles, to increase the effectiveness of searches within your organization.

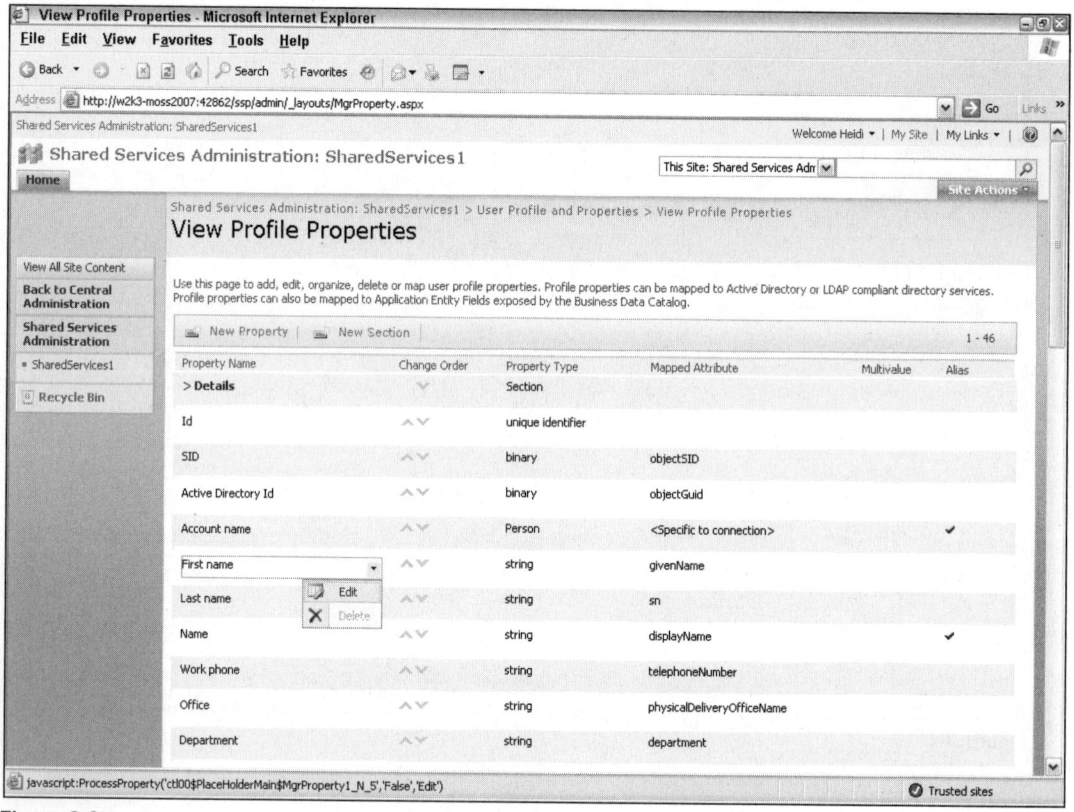

Figure 8-2

Setting Up Connections

To pull user profile information into SharePoint's user profile system, SharePoint sets up a connection to a data store that provides user information. This can include Active Directory, a Lightweight Directory Access Protocol (LDAP) server, or Business Data Catalog. There are two connection types used to bring the profile data into SharePoint.

❑   Master Connection

❑   Sub Connection

A master connection is used as the primary source of the profile data. The master connection is set up to use either Active Directory or LDAP. Sub connections are used to provide supplemental information to the user profile system of SharePoint. The Business Data Catalog can be used as a supplemental store.

User Profile API

The SharePoint Administration Site enables administrators to create and update user profiles as well as manage them from a central location. There are many times when more functionality is required, and custom code can be used to easily extend the user profiles. The primary namespace that was used in SharePoint 2003 for profiles was `Microsoft.SharePoint.Portal.UserProfiles`. This namespace has now been replaced by the `Microsoft.Office.Server.UserProfiles` namespace.

Each SharePoint web application uses a Shared Service Provider to manage the user profile data store. Because web applications can use the same Shared Service Provider, more than one SharePoint web application can use the same set of users stored in the User Profile section.

If you want to import a set of users from another application, SharePoint provides you with a few options. You can use the Business Data Catalog or the built-in APIs from the SharePoint object model, or even the user profile web services. If you are importing users on a regular basis and want to keep two systems synchronized, then the Business Data Catalog is probably the right solution. But if you are creating Web Parts or simple management tools, then the API or web services will provide you with the ability to create those.

To set up users in your SharePoint web application, you can either use the user interface that is provided or you can programmatically create users in custom code. You will look at how to create the users in code shortly. The two major classes that are used are:

❑   `UserProfile` class

❑   `UserProfileManager` class

Let's take a look at the classes that are used and how to work with the User Profile API in code.

Managing Users in the User Profile

UserProfileManager is the main object for accessing the user profile data stored on the web application's shared service. This class can be used to create users, delete users, and provide information about the profile service.

> When working with the object model classes make sure to add a reference to the Windows SharePoint Services DLL as well as the required Microsoft Office SharePoint Server components' DLLs. If you don't have a reference to System.Web.dll, then you will need to add that also.

Creating a UserProfileManager is straightforward and can be done with the new syntax for SharePoint 2007. The following simple console application creates a UserProfileManager that is connected to the ServerContext of a SharePoint site. Then it displays the number of user profiles in the console window.

To create your own console application that displays the number of users in a site follow these steps:

1. Open Visual Studio, and create a new console application called UserProfileManagerApp.

2. Make sure to add the SharePoint references:

```
using Microsoft.SharePoint;
using Microsoft.Office.Server;
using Microsoft.Office.Server.UserProfiles;
```

3. Then in the main function, add the following code:

```
using System;
using Microsoft.SharePoint;
using Microsoft.Office.Server;
using Microsoft.Office.Server.UserProfiles;
namespace UserProfileManagerApp
{
    class Program
    {
        static void Main(string[] args)
        {
            try
            {
                using (SPSite spSite = new SPSite(@"http://localhost"))
                {
                    ServerContext siteContext = ServerContext.GetContext(spSite);
                    UserProfileManager pmManager =
                            new UserProfileManager(siteContext);
                    Console.WriteLine("Number of users: " + pmManager.Count);
                }
            }
            catch (Exception exp)
            {
```

```
                    Console.WriteLine(exp.Message);
            }
        }
    }
}
```

In addition to the `Count` property, the `UserProfileManager` class contains methods to manage user profile data, including the following:

Name	Description
CreateUserProfile	Creates a user profile with the provided values. If the profile already exists, an exception is thrown.
GetUserProfile	Returns a reference to the user profile specified.
RemoveUserProfile	Removes user profiles. The method has multiple overrides to provide options when deleting users.
UserExists	Returns a value indicating whether the user for a specified account name has a profile.

Creating New User Profiles

Creating a new user in the user profile system only requires that the user name match an existing user in the current SharePoint site.

A good policy when creating user profiles is to check to make sure that the profile does not exist already. Although the profile system doesn't let you add a new profile if one already exists, it is much better practice to use the built-in methods for checking for the user, than to try to manage the exceptions that occur when trying to add the user a second time. In some cases, there are no built-in methods for performing a check and you must use the `try/catch` method. This is true when looking for a specific list in the object model.

The following code adds a new profile after checking to make sure that the user doesn't already have one:

1. Using the console application above, add the new code to check if a user exists before you create a new user and profile:

```
using System;
using Microsoft.SharePoint;
using Microsoft.Office.Server;
using Microsoft.Office.Server.UserProfiles;
namespace UserProfileManagerApp
{
    class Program
    {
```

```
            static void Main(string[] args)
            {
                try
                {
                    using (SPSite spSite = new SPSite(@"http://localhost"))
                    {
                        ServerContext siteContext = ServerContext.GetContext(spSite);
                        UserProfileManager pmManager =
                                new UserProfileManager(siteContext);
                        Console.WriteLine("Number of users: " + pmManager.Count);
                        string strUserName = "wrox\\brendon";
                        UserProfile newUser = null;
                        if (!pmManager.UserExists(strUserName))
                        {
                            newUser = pmManager.CreateUserProfile(strUserName);
                        }
                    }
                }
                catch (Exception exp)
                {
                    Console.WriteLine(exp.Message);
                }
            }
        }
    }
```

Deleting User Profiles

The code for deleting profiles is very similar to the code for adding them, except that the method RemoveUserProfile is used. This method accepts either the user's name or the GUID that is the unique key for the user.

The following code removes the profile that was created in the preceding example. This process does not delete the user from the main connection such as Active Directory. Deleting the user from Active Directory will still have to be done from outside SharePoint.

Remember that you are also checking to see if the user profile exists before you can delete it. If the user profile does not exist, then you do not have to take any action.

```
using System;
using Microsoft.SharePoint;
using Microsoft.Office.Server;
using Microsoft.Office.Server.UserProfiles;
namespace DeleteUser
{
    class Program
    {
        static void Main(string[] args)
        {
            try
            {
                using (SPSite spSite = new SPSite(@"http://localhost"))
```

```
        {
            ServerContext siteContext = ServerContext.GetContext(spSite);
            UserProfileManager pmManager =
                        new UserProfileManager(siteContext);
            Console.WriteLine("Number of users: " + pmManager.Count);
            string strUserName = "wrox\\brendon";
            if (pmManager.UserExists(strUserName))
            {
                pmManager.RemoveUserProfile(strUserName);
            }
        }
    }
    catch (Exception exp)
    {
        Console.WriteLine(exp.Message);
    }
    Console.ReadLine();

        }
    }
}
```

Working with User Profiles

At the core of the user profile objects is the `UserProfile` class, which represents a single instance of a user profile. Once you have an object of this type, you can read and change the profile properties, assuming that the code is running with appropriate privileges.

To retrieve a profile, you just provide the user's name or GUID, as shown here:

1. Open Visual Studio and create a new console application called `RetrieveUser`.

2. Make sure to add the SharePoint references:

```
using System.Collections.Generic;
using Microsoft.SharePoint;
using Microsoft.Office.Server;
using Microsoft.Office.Server.UserProfiles;
```

3. Now get a reference to the correct SharePoint site and `UserProfileManager` associated with that site:

```
using System;
using System.Collections.Generic;
using Microsoft.SharePoint;
using Microsoft.Office.Server;
using Microsoft.Office.Server.UserProfiles;

namespace RetrieveUser
{
    class Program
    {
        static void Main(string[] args)
        {
```

```
                try
                {
                    using (SPSite spSite = new SPSite(@"http://localhost"))
                    {
                        ServerContext siteContext = ServerContext.GetContext(spSite);
                        UserProfileManager pmManager =
                                new UserProfileManager(siteContext);
                    }
                }
                catch (Exception exp)
                {
                    Console.WriteLine(exp.Message);
                }
            }
        }
    }
```

4. Check if the user exists, and get the user profile if the user is available:

```
using System;
using System.Collections.Generic;
using Microsoft.SharePoint;
using Microsoft.Office.Server;
using Microsoft.Office.Server.UserProfiles;

namespace RetrieveUser
{
    class Program
    {
        static void Main(string[] args)
        {
            try
            {
                using (SPSite spSite = new SPSite(@"http://localhost"))
                {
                    ServerContext siteContext =
ServerContext.GetContext(spSite);
                    UserProfileManager pmManager =
                            new UserProfileManager(siteContext);
                    string strUserName = "devcow\\brendon";
                    UserProfile userProfile = null; [Author: Why is this variable
called "newUser" when it actually holds the profile for an existing user? In fact,
why isn't it called something like "userProfile" since that's what it is?i have
updated the variable,thanks,brendon]
                    if (pmManager.UserExists(strUserName))
                    {
                        userProfile = pmManager.GetUserProfile(strUserName);
                    }
                }
            }
            catch (Exception exp)
            {
```

```
                    Console.WriteLine(exp.Message);
                }
            }
        }
    }
```

The UserProfile class contains many useful properties that can be leveraged when programming with the User Profile services of SharePoint 2007. The following table describes two properties used to identify the user profile and to return information about a given user profile.

Name	Description
ID	The unique GUID value of the current user profile. This value can be used when working with the UserProfile in the UserProfileManager.
Item	Contains a property value for the current user profile.

The UserProfileManager contains the list of user profile properties that are stored in the user profile data store. These properties are stored in the Shared Service Provider of the web site related to the UserProfileManager. To determine which properties are needed in the user profile store, use the UserProfileManager class. It is important to remember the difference between the name and the DisplayName when dealing with properties in SharePoint. The *name* is the value used when getting and setting the values, and the *DisplayName* is what is shown on the user interface. Sometimes these can be the same, but they are usually different. The IsRequired field shows which properties need to have values entered when the profile is updated in the user interface.

The following code sample demonstrates some of the default property values of the UserProfileManager. The code loops through all of the properties that have been created for the user profiles in the Shared Service. This will display the Name, Display Name, Description, and if the field is required in the console application you just created above.

```
//Get the properties of the Property Manager
foreach (Property property in pmManager.Properties)
{
    Console.WriteLine("Name: " + property.Name);
    Console.WriteLine("DisplayName: " + property.DisplayName);
    Console.WriteLine("Description: " + property.Description);
    Console.WriteLine("Required: " + property.IsRequired);
}
```

Setting User Profile Value Properties

User profile value properties can be entered and edited through the administrative screen, the user's My Site, or through code. The site administrator is also able to add properties to a user profile. These properties provide metadata that describes the user such as email, manager, and skills. You can have as many properties on a user to provide information about that user as needed. These properties can be set through an import from another system such as Active Directory or the Business Data Catalog.

> Only the properties that have been created for the user have values, and the rest of the properties will not contain any value. It is good to check to make sure that the property exists for the user before trying to use the value.

The collection returned from the UserProfile class is a set of Name/Value pairs. Name is simply set as a string value that can be shown to the user, but Value is now a collection called UserProfileValueCollection. Value is a collection in SharePoint 2007 because the properties now have the ability to contain multivalues, which is something you will look at shortly. For now, just return the values as the value field.

The following code shows how you can loop through each value and display the results to the command window:

Using the RetrieveUser console application above, add the following lines to the main method:

```
foreach (KeyValuePair<string,UserProfileValueCollection> NameValues in userProfile)
{
    // Displays all of the name value pairs
    Console.WriteLine(NameValues.Key + ": " + NameValues.Value);
}
```

Now that you have seen what the values are for the properties of your user, you can add the correct values for the fields that are missing but required. You can also update the properties that are already set in the user profile.

Setting Single Value Properties

The standard type of property contained in the UserProfile class is a single value property. This property contains a Name/Value pair that has the information entered about the user.

To update the properties through the SharePoint object model follow these steps:

1. Create a console application called UserProfileProperties.

2. Add the references to SharePoint:

```
using System;
using System.Collections.Generic;
using Microsoft.SharePoint;
using Microsoft.Office.Server;
using Microsoft.Office.Server.UserProfiles;
```

3. Connect to the user profile store and then retrieve a user from the data store. Once you have the user, you can use the indexer method to get the property that is expected. Add the following code to the main method to perform these actions:

```
try
{
```

```
            using (SPSite spSite = new SPSite(@"http://localhost"))
            {
                ServerContext siteContext = ServerContext.GetContext(spSite);
                UserProfileManager pmManager =
                        new UserProfileManager(siteContext);
                string strUserName = "devcow\\brendon";
                UserProfile userProfile = null;
                if (pmManager.UserExists(strUserName))
                {
                    userProfile = pmManager.GetUserProfile(strUserName);
                }
            }
        }
        catch (Exception exp)
        {
            Console.WriteLine(exp.Message);
        }
```

4. Update a value such as Department. To persist the values back to the user profile system, you must call the `Commit()` method on the `UserProfile` that has new changes. This allows you to make many changes in memory and then commit all of the changes at once.

```
using System;
using System.Collections.Generic;
using Microsoft.SharePoint;
using Microsoft.Office.Server;
using Microsoft.Office.Server.UserProfiles;

namespace UserProfileProperties
{
    class Program
    {
        static void Main(string[] args)
        {
            try
            {
                using (SPSite spSite = new SPSite(@"http://localhost"))
                {
                    ServerContext siteContext = ServerContext.GetContext(spSite);
                    UserProfileManager pmManager =
                            new UserProfileManager(siteContext);
                    string strUserName = "devcow\\brendon";
                    UserProfile userProfile = null;
                    if (pmManager.UserExists(strUserName))
                    {
                        userProfile = pmManager.GetUserProfile(strUserName);
                        userProfile["Department"].Value = "Information Technology";
                        userProfile.Commit();
                    }
                }
            }
            catch (Exception exp)
            {
```

```
                    Console.WriteLine(exp.Message);
                }
            }
        }
    }
```

Setting the value requires knowing the string name of the field. SharePoint helps provide a base set of values used in the user profile system. These values are in a class called `PropertyConstants`. The `PropertyConstants` class only contains a set of constants that return the correct string value that is used for the name of the user profile property it refers to.

For example the value of `PropertyConstants.WorkPhone` is `WorkPhone`, whereas the value for `UserGuid` is `UserProfile_GUID`.

As you can see, some of the values are the same, but some can be different. The `PropertyConstants` class will help you retrieve and set all of the common properties in the user profile.

Look at how the following code uses the `PropertyConstants`, as well as a string, to set the value of each property.

5. Update another property, this time using the `PropertyConstants` class:

```
userProfile = pmManager.GetUserProfile(strUserName);
userProfile [PropertyConstants.WorkPhone].Value = "555-555-5555";
userProfile.Commit();
```

Multivalue Properties

A big improvement in SharePoint 2007 is the use of properties called multivalue properties. Sometimes you want the ability to store more than one value for a given field. This can come in very handy for multiple value properties such as sales area if you cover more than one area. Microsoft has some standard fields that are already set up for multivalue use such as Responsibilities, Skills, Past Projects, Interests, and Schools.

To determine whether the property is a multivalued property, the property `IsMultiValued` is provided. This value is a read-only property and can only be set by creating the user profile property as a multi-value property.

As you saw earlier, the multiple values have to be returned as a collection, and these values are returned as an `ArrayList` object. However, if you just display the properties value, the first element of the collection is the value that is displayed.

To add multiple values to the property, just call the `Add` method on the returned `ArrayList` property collection of the user:

```
Property skillProperty =
            pmManager.Properties.GetPropertyByName(PropertyConstants.Skills);
if (skillProperty.IsMultivalued)
{
    if (pmManager.UserExists(strUserName))
    {
        newUser = pmManager.GetUserProfile(strUserName);
```

```
        newUser[PropertyConstants.Skills].Add("ASP.NET");
        newUser[PropertyConstants.Skills].Add("SQL Server");
        newUser.Commit();
    }
}
```

Each value in the user interface will be separated by a single character. The default character that is used is the comma. Some values might contain a comma, so SharePoint 2007 allows you to modify the separator character of a multivalue property. Use the MultiValueSeparator enumeration to select a different value for the property's Separator value. There are four values to choose from in the MultiValueSeparator class. The most common separator values are provided for you, as well as an Unknown value.

❏   Comma

❏   Semicolon

❏   Newline

❏   Unknown

When using the multivalue properties, you will need to pick which type of separator you will use. If the property type is a multivalue, set the separator:

```
property.Separator = MultiValueSeparator.Semicolon;
```

Providing Properties in Choice Lists

In addition to having the ability to add multiple values to a property, you can also allow your users to select from a list of possible values known as a choice list. There are three different values that can be set for the ChoiceList property as follows:

❏   **None** — The property is not currently using a choice list.

❏   **Closed** — The choices have been added to the property and the users cannot edit the choices

❏   **Open** — Users and administrators can add new choices to the list.

User Profile Relationships

Some of the most common methods return information about the user or provide the application with more information about a user, such as relationships to other profiles. The UserProfile class is full of information about the user — such as lists of Managers and Peers — and provides the ability to create the user's personal site. The user will have access to this site by using the My Site link in the user interface of SharePoint.

The following table lists the UserProfile methods:

Name	Description
Colleagues	Returns a ColleagueManager to work with the current colleagues

Continued

Name	Description
GetCommonManager	Gets the user profile of the common managers of the current user
GetDirectReports	Returns a list of UserProfiles that contains the users that report to the current user
GetManager	Gets the current user's immediate manager
GetManagers	Returns a list of all the managers that the current user reports to
GetPeers	Gets a list of user profiles of all users that are the current user's peers
Memberships	Returns a list of the current user's memberships
RefreshManagers	Updates the list of managers the user has as associations

Adding the SharePoint People Picker to the Web Site

The people pickers in SharePoint make it easy to work with any of the users from the data source locations. To work with the control in the user interface, add the PeopleEditor control, as shown in the following code, to a Web Part or web page, and then you will have full control over how the people picker control is displayed and interacts with the user. You will be able to set properties of the PeoplePicker to modify how it is displayed. This is the same control that is used in a list or profile. The following code adds the PeoplePicker to a Web Part, but it could just as easily be added to a web page.

1. Start off by creating a new Web Part called PeoplePickerWebPart.

2. Add the required references:

```
using System;
using System.Runtime.InteropServices;
using System.Web.UI;
using System.Web.UI.WebControls.WebParts;
using System.Xml.Serialization;

using Microsoft.SharePoint;
using Microsoft.SharePoint.WebControls;
using Microsoft.SharePoint.WebPartPages;
using System.Web.UI.WebControls;
```

3. In the CreateChildControls method create a new instance of the PeopleEditor control:

```
PeopleEditor PeoplePickerControl = new PeopleEditor();
this.Controls.Add(PeoplePickerControl);
base.CreateChildControls();
```

4. Update some of the properties of the control, such as allowing the control so that they are empty, allowing the end user to type in information, and changing the look and feel by changing the button names:

```
using System;
using System.Runtime.InteropServices;
using System.Web.UI;
using System.Web.UI.WebControls.WebParts;
using System.Xml.Serialization;

using Microsoft.SharePoint;
using Microsoft.SharePoint.WebControls;
using Microsoft.SharePoint.WebPartPages;
using System.Web.UI.WebControls;

namespace PeoplePickerWebPart
{
    public class AgentPicker : System.Web.UI.WebControls.WebParts.WebPart
    {
        protected override void CreateChildControls()
        {
            try
            {
                PeopleEditor PeoplePickerControl = new PeopleEditor();
                PeoplePickerControl.AllowEmpty = true;
                PeoplePickerControl.AllowTypeIn = true;
                PeoplePickerControl.BrowseButtonImageName = "browse";
                PeoplePickerControl.BrowseButtonToolTip = "Pick an Agent";
                PeoplePickerControl.CheckButtonImageName = "Validate user";
                PeoplePickerControl.ErrorMessage = "No Agent Found";

                this.Controls.Add(PeoplePickerControl);
                base.CreateChildControls();
            }
            catch (Exception ex)
            {
                Literal _ErrorMessageLiteral = new Literal();
                _ErrorMessageLiteral.Text = "Custom Error: " + ex.Message;

                this.Controls.Clear();
                this.Controls.Add(_ErrorMessageLiteral);
            }
        }
    }
}
```

Developing Using the User Profile Change Log

When working with changes to used profiles, the UserProfileChangeQuery class provides the ability to filter based on the following types:

❏   Add

❏   Anniversary

- ❑ Colleague
- ❑ Delete
- ❑ DistributionListMembership
- ❑ MultiValueProperty
- ❑ PersonalizationSite
- ❑ QuickLink
- ❑ SingleValueProperty
- ❑ SiteMembership
- ❑ Update
- ❑ UpdateMetadata
- ❑ UserProfile
- ❑ Weblog

To filter, set one of these values to true once you have created an instance of the class. Multiple filter values can be set to true. The anniversary value will return all profile values that have dates in them. SharePoint considers each date field an anniversary and will create an anniversary event when the date reaches the machine date.

Each change type has a class that is associated with it that contains specific information for that type of change.

The UserProfile class contains methods to get changes about the user or the user's colleagues.

Name	Description
CurrentChangeToken	Represents a timestamp of the last time the current user was modified
GetChanges	Returns a collection of the changes that have happened to the current user
GetColleagueChanges	Returns a collection of changes that have happened to all of the colleagues associated with the current user

To get the change information, you must get the user profile and call the method GetChanges as follows:

1. Create a new console application named ProfileChanges.

2. Add the required SharePoint references:

```
using System;
using System.Collections.Generic;
using Microsoft.SharePoint;
using Microsoft.Office.Server;
using Microsoft.Office.Server.UserProfiles;
```

3. Get a reference to the Site and User Profile Manager.

```
try
{
    using (SPSite spSite = new SPSite(@"http://localhost"))
    {
        ServerContext siteContext = ServerContext.GetContext(spSite);
        UserProfileManager pmManager = new UserProfileManager(siteContext);
    }
}
catch (Exception exp)
{
    Console.WriteLine(exp.Message);
}
```

4. Determine and set the range for the number of days you want to look at in changes, then set the change token that will be used with that amount of time. This example uses the last 30 days.

```
// Display the changes that have occurred in the last month
DateTime dtNumberDays = DateTime.UtcNow.Subtract(TimeSpan.FromDays(30));
// Create a change token to compare the number of days
UserProfileChangeToken upChangeToken = new
        UserProfileChangeToken(dtNumberDays);
```

5. Now create a query object to determine which changes will be returned. For this example, set the Anniversary and Colleague changes to true, and set the ChangeTokenStart value from the change token created above.

```
// Create a query object to determine which changes are displayed
UserProfileChangeQuery QueryAnniversayAndColleagues = new
            UserProfileChangeQuery(false,true);
QueryAnniversayAndColleagues.ChangeTokenStart = upChangeToken;
QueryAnniversayAndColleagues.Anniversary = true;
QueryAnniversayAndColleagues.Colleague = true;
```

6. Now perform the standard steps to get a user profile, and this time call the method GetChanges with the query object you just created.

```
string strUserName = "heididev\\brendon";
if (pmManager.UserExists(strUserName))
{
    UserProfile spMyUser = pmManager.GetUserProfile(strUserName);

    UserProfileChangeCollection MyUserProfileChanges =
            spMyUser.GetChanges(QueryAnniversayAndColleagues);
}
```

7. Loop through each change in the returned collection of user profile changes, determine what type of change it is, and display information about that type of change:

```
try
{
    using (SPSite spSite = new SPSite(@"http://localhost"))
```

```
        {
            ServerContext siteContext = ServerContext.GetContext(spSite);
            UserProfileManager pmManager = new UserProfileManager(siteContext);

            // Gets some subset of changes from a user profile.

            // Display the changes that have occurred in the last month
            DateTime dtNumberDays = DateTime.UtcNow.Subtract(TimeSpan.FromDays(30));
            // Create a change token to compare the number of days
            UserProfileChangeToken upChangeToken = new
                        UserProfileChangeToken(dtNumberDays);

            // Create a query object to determine which changes are displayed
            UserProfileChangeQuery QueryAnniversayAndColleagues = new
                        UserProfileChangeQuery(false,true);
            QueryAnniversayAndColleagues.ChangeTokenStart = upChangeToken;
            QueryAnniversayAndColleagues.Anniversary = true;
            QueryAnniversayAndColleagues.Colleague = true;

            string strUserName = "heididev\\brendon";
            if (pmManager.UserExists(strUserName))
            {
                UserProfile spMyUser = pmManager.GetUserProfile(strUserName);

                UserProfileChangeCollection MyUserProfileChanges =
                        spMyUser.GetChanges(QueryAnniversayAndColleagues);

                foreach (UserProfileChange MyUserChange in MyUserProfileChanges)
                {
                    Console.WriteLine(MyUserChange.EventTime.ToString());
                    if (MyUserChange is UserProfileAnniversaryChange)
                    {
                        UserProfileAnniversaryChange AnniversryEvent =
                                (UserProfileAnniversaryChange)MyUserChange;
                        Console.WriteLine(AnniversryEvent.Anniversary);
                        Console.WriteLine(AnniversryEvent.ProfileProperty);
                    }
                    else if (MyUserChange is UserProfileColleagueChange)
                    {
                        UserProfileColleagueChange ColleagueEvent =
                                (UserProfileColleagueChange)MyUserChange;
                    }
                }
            }
        }
    }
}
catch (Exception exp)
{
    Console.WriteLine(exp.Message);
}
```

Building My Sites

My Sites are personalized sites that can be set up in SharePoint for and by each user individually. Each site can be provisioned on an as-needed basis to save disk space. It's similar to having self-serving Windows SharePoint Services sites, each set up for a different user. Although it is similar, SharePoint has added some features of My Site that make it useful for individual portals. Every site is different, based on the personalized settings that each user sets up for their own site. My Sites are central locations where users can store and manage information and documents that are specific to the user, such as Excel workbooks used to maintain sales for that person's region. Types of information that can be stored and managed on a user's My Site include: documents, tasks, calendars, links, and contacts. It is also a good way for other users in your organization to look up information about a user, including his responsibilities, skills, interests, and even current projects that he is working on.

My Sites have three basic pages that can be used for different purposes throughout the site:

- ❑ Public Profile Page
- ❑ Personal Site Page
- ❑ Personalization Page

Basic templates are provided for each type of page to give users a place to start. Also, each My Site page has a bar of links at the top of the page that can be used for easy navigation between these three different types of sites.

The Public Profile Page

The first page is the public profile page, called My Profile, which can be viewed by anyone in the organization. The administrator gets to decide how the page will look, but the users can add as much or as little information as they want. Privacy groups can be set up to let users decide who can view some of the information on their public site. Items such as skills, interests, distribution list memberships, a list of all colleagues, and other information can be set to only be seen by certain groups, such as a user's manager or workgroup members. This places some of the control of sensitive data in the user's hands and gives each user the ability to show only the information about themselves that they feel comfortable sharing.

The Personal Site Page

The second page that can be used is a personal site, and it is called My Home. Naturally, users access this site by clicking on My Home on the top link bar of My Site. The users are their own administrators for their personal site, and they are provided with a home page that only they can view. Since this page can only be viewed by the user, he or she is able to choose the look and layout of the site. Also, as administrators, users can create and manage as many pages as they want to for their site. With the exception of the private home page, personal site pages are set up to be shared with other selected people in the organization. Personal sites allow many users to work together on projects and store documents that can be shared by setting up list, document library, and workspace pages in their personal site.

The Personalization Page

The third page that is used is the personalization site, which is managed by the site administrator. It has the look and feel of the main site, except that changes have been made to identify it as another My Site page. There are also navigation sections at the top, and then four Web Part zones below. The zones, made up of the top, middle left, middle right, and bottom can be personalized. The content in each of them can be moved, deleted, or have new items added. However, these personalization sites can only be provided and changed by administrators or by content providers. The personalization site stores information that is personalized for each user, and allows special targeting to the user. Different groups in the organization can use this information to create sites that are personalized for each user, depending on their needs. This is discussed in more detail later in this chapter under "SharePoint Audiences."

This type of page is very useful for presenting content that is personal to each user, and could not be posted publicly. For example, a manager could set up a personalization site that keeps track of annual reviews. When a user clicks on the site, all of her previous reviews can be seen, but she would only be able to view her own reviews. All of the personalization sites for each person are linked together to create a collection of sites, and there is a personalized navigation bar that gives the user easy access to their information.

Creating Your First My Site

To create your first My Site page, follow these steps:

1. On the top right of the main screen, click My Site to create your My Site as the logged-in user. The very first time that a logged-in user clicks on the My Site link, SharePoint will create the site. You have to wait a few seconds while SharePoint sets up your personal site for the first time and creates the default document libraries and lists.

2. The first prompt that appears asks if you would like to have a quick link icon added to your personal site. This quick link icon will appear on the left of the Open and Save As dialog boxes inside of your windows applications. If you click Yes, then your personal site will be the first to appear in the drop-down list of locations when you create Meeting and Document Workspace sites. This also sets your My Site page to the default personal site. After SharePoint has set up your My Site, it is up to you to personalize it. Figure 8-3 shows the setup page you access to begin creating your own My Site page.

> When personalizing My Site, information from the user profile will be displayed in the Public profile page when set to a visible Privacy setting. This allows for personalization based on the preferences of the user.

3. You can also keep a list of all of your favorite web sites so that you can access them from any computer where you have access to the network and are able to open My Site. At the top right of all pages on My Site, there is a link to the My Links page (this page can also be accessed by clicking on Links under My Profile on the Quick Launch). The My Links page lets you manage all of your links, as well as allowing access to sites where you are a member.

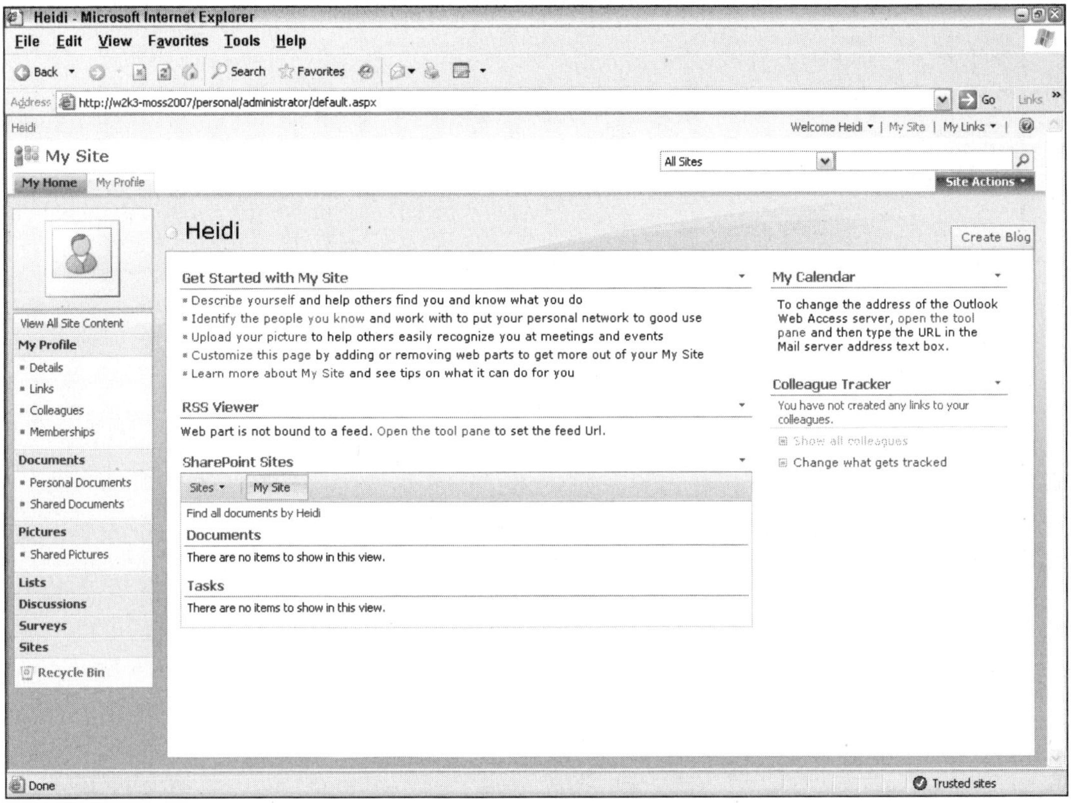

Figure 8-3

4. Once the profile has been imported or created a logged-in user can navigate to their My Site. Click on the link to "describe yourself," and there each available profile can be filled in with details such as a brief personal description, a photo, and the skills and responsibilities that you possess. As you can see in Figure 8-4, some properties can be edited and some cannot. These properties can also be modified using the object model.

5. Depending on how many user profile properties are configured on the site, there could be a lot of information that can be filled in, to give other people an inside look into each user. These profile properties can be modified or extended through the Shared Service Provider. This type of information sharing can also create an integrated organization, where people can see information about other users and relationships they have to others users with a customized set of data for each user. In fact SharePoint will monitor this data and make connections to other users such as colleagues.

To the right of the fields is a drop-down box to select who the field will be shown to. Each field can be set to its own different value — such as Only Me, My Manager, My Workgroup, My Colleagues, and Everyone. This way, when logged in, you can fill something out but choose to only show it to certain groups. There are also a few fields that are set to Everyone and cannot be changed. When all changes have been made, click Save and Close at the top of the page.

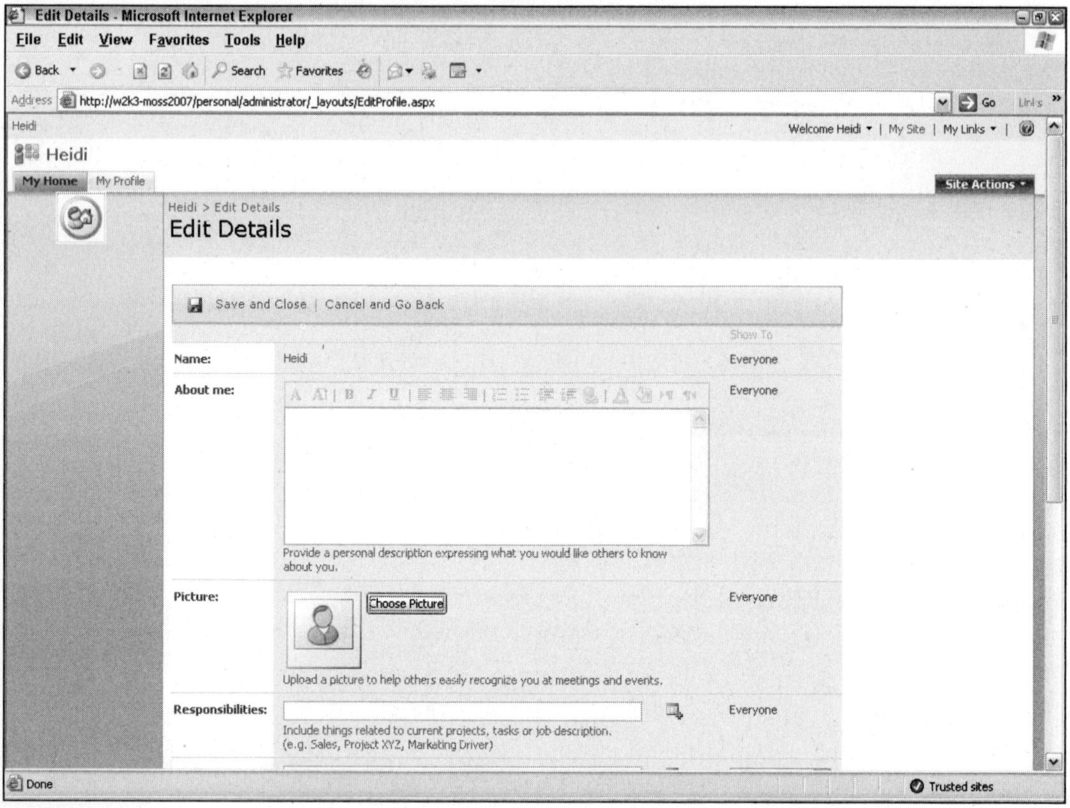

Figure 8-4

These security settings for visibility are known as the policy settings. In the Shared Service Provider, each field can be set to a default privacy setting as well as have a value set indicating if the policy is Required, Optional, or Disabled. In addition to this setting, the site administrator can determine if the user can change the default privacy setting or not.

Identifying People You Know

The second link, Identify the people you know, lets the logged-in user identify people they know and work with. This creates a membership in SharePoint known as Colleagues. This helps you organize and manage your relationships to other users in the site. When users click Identify the people you know or the Colleagues link under the My Profile in My Site, a page where you can add colleagues and organize them into groups will be displayed. The users that are added will appear in the Colleague Tracker Web Part as well as any changes that a user has performed. Because the Colleagues are part of the `PrivacyPolicy` items, you have the option to set the visibility of the colleagues added to a profile.

Uploading Your Picture

To visually help identify a user, each profile has an associated picture. Clicking the Upload your picture link allows end users to modify their profile by displaying the Edit Details page used for the rest of the profile details. The profile property `Picture` allows end users to add a picture of themselves. This property is set to a field type of image and can be viewed by everyone. Fields can be of different types and can even be custom fields created through code.

Using a picture can be useful in large and small organizations, so that people can identify other people. In a large organization that may have many branches in different geographic locations, it could help someone put a face with a name of someone they talk to on the phone. In a small organization, it could help out new employees that have to meet a lot of new people all at once. If you add a picture to your profile, it will be shown on the upper-left corner of your My Site, and the file will also be listed in the Documents section.

> Each My Site is just a site that is created for each user. All information and data is stored in a list on each site, so make sure to monitor the size of the My Site collection

Customizing Your My Site Page

Just like any site page, the My Site portal page can be customized with the user interface and Web Parts. Click the Customize this page link, and the page is shown in Edit Mode. The screen is split into zones, and My Site can be arranged in any way that is best for the user. The Get Started editing links can be taken away or moved to the bottom of the screen after setup, when they won't be used as much anymore. If you frequently use the My Calendar feature, it can be moved to the very top, so that it is the first thing you see on My Site. If there is a feature that is never used, for example if there are no RSS feeds set up, then that feature can be deleted from the page. Later on, if the user wants to add an RSS feed, they can add the Web Part back in by coming to this page and clicking on one of the Add a Web Part links in whatever zone they want it to show up in.

Using Help For End Users

SharePoint makes it easy to find out more information about the topic you are working with, and My Site is no different.

Click the Learn more about My Site link, which offers helpful tips. You can direct the end users to this location so that they can spend some time reviewing the information, as it can help them better understand My Site and how to use it. It will also introduce them to new uses for My Site, which will make it a more powerful tool for you and the organization.

Maintaining a Secure My Site

Privacy policies are built into SharePoint to protect the user from displaying information to users who should not be able to the view the data. When selecting data, there are many options that can be used as listed in the following Privacy enumerations. The end user can modify these settings on the profile page, while you as the developer will programmatically update these settings via the `Profile` property.

- ❑ **Public** — Everyone
- ❑ **Contacts** — Colleagues
- ❑ **Organization** — Workgroup members
- ❑ **Manager** — Manager

❑   **Private** — Only the user

❑   **NotSet** — Provides a default privacy setting

These restrictions apply to most of the My Site functionality.

The `UserProfileManager` class uses the method `GetPrivacyPolicy` to return the `PrivacyPolicyManager` for the current user. This manager will allow you to update these profile properties through code. To see how the `PrivacyPolicyManger` works, take a look at the following example:

1.   Start by creating a console application named `PrivacyPolicyApp`.

2.   Add the required SharePoint references:

```
using System;
using System.Collections.Generic;
using Microsoft.SharePoint;
using Microsoft.Office.Server;
using Microsoft.Office.Server.UserProfiles;
```

3.   Get the site and `UserProfileManager` references:

```
try
{
    using (SPSite spSite = new SPSite(@"http://localhost"))
    {
        ServerContext siteContext = ServerContext.GetContext(spSite);
        UserProfileManager pmManager = new UserProfileManager(siteContext);
    }
}
catch (Exception exp)
{
    Console.WriteLine(exp.Message);
}
```

4.   Return the `PrivacyPolicyManager`, and loop through each `PolicyItem` in the site displaying relevant information about each item:

```
try
{
    using (SPSite spSite = new SPSite(@"http://localhost"))
    {
        ServerContext siteContext = ServerContext.GetContext(spSite);
        UserProfileManager pmManager = new UserProfileManager(siteContext);
        string strUserName = "wrox\\brendon";

        PrivacyPolicyManager ppmPolicyManager = pmManager.GetPrivacyPolicy();

        foreach(PrivacyPolicyItem tempItem in ppmPolicyManager.GetAllItems())
        {
            Console.WriteLine(tempItem.DisplayName);
            Console.WriteLine(tempItem.DefaultPrivacy);
            Console.WriteLine(tempItem.PrivacyPolicy);
            Console.WriteLine(tempItem.Group);
        }
```

```
    }
}
catch (Exception exp)
{
    Console.WriteLine(exp.Message);
}
```

The following code looks at the actual properties of a user and sets some of the privacy profile settings:

1. Start by creating a console application named `UserPrivacyPolicyApp`.

2. Add the required SharePoint references:

```
using System;
using System.Collections.Generic;
using Microsoft.SharePoint;
using Microsoft.Office.Server;
using Microsoft.Office.Server.UserProfiles;
```

3. Get the site and `UserProfileManager` references:

```
try
{
    using (SPSite spSite = new SPSite(@"http://localhost"))
    {
        ServerContext siteContext = ServerContext.GetContext(spSite);
        UserProfileManager pmManager = new UserProfileManager(siteContext);
    }
}
catch (Exception exp)
{
    Console.WriteLine(exp.Message);
}
```

4. Get the reference to the user set in code and get the collection of properties:

```
string strUserName = "heididev\\brendon";

if (pmManager.UserExists(strUserName))
{
    UserProfile spUser = pmManager.GetUserProfile(strUserName);
    PropertyCollection pcCollection = pmManager.Properties;
}
```

5. From the properties collection get a property named `MLSNumber`. You will want to add this property from the Shared Service Provider if it does not exist.

```
Property property = pcCollection.GetPropertyByName("MLSNumber");
```

6. Set the privacy setting for the field to only be seen by you, the Manager:

```
property.DefaultPrivacy = Privacy.Manager;
```

7. Set the field to be a mandatory field that must be entered:

```
property.PrivacyPolicy = PrivacyPolicy.Mandatory;
```

8. Remember to always call the `Commit` function to save your changes in SharePoint:

```
try
{
    using (SPSite spSite = new SPSite(@"http://localhost"))
    {
        ServerContext siteContext = ServerContext.GetContext(spSite);
        UserProfileManager pmManager = new UserProfileManager(siteContext);
        string strUserName = "heididev\\brendon";

        if (pmManager.UserExists(strUserName))
        {
            UserProfile spUser = pmManager.GetUserProfile(strUserName);
            PropertyCollection pcCollection = pmManager.Properties;
            Property property = pcCollection.GetPropertyByName("MLSNumber");
            property.DefaultPrivacy = Privacy.Manager;
            property.PrivacyPolicy = PrivacyPolicy.Mandatory;
            property.Commit();
        }
    }
}
catch (Exception exp)
{
    Console.WriteLine(exp.Message);
}
```

Programmatically Using My Site

My Site is full of information about a user, and most of the relevant information is available through the SharePoint object model. Common actions that you can perform are to get My Site links as well as the user's My Site location. The next section looks at how to programmatically get this information.

Creating A My Site for Users

Some users in your system may need to have a My Site set up for them before they click on the My Site link themselves. This could happen when you are setting up users who store documents securely on their My Site page but mainly save those documents through rich client tools like Microsoft Office 2007 or a third-party application that can communicate with SharePoint 2007. When creating a My Site for a user, SharePoint provides a method called CreatePersonalSite, which is part of the UserProfile class. Most of the methods and properties used for creating My Site functionality are based on a single user created from the UserProfile class. This is due to the fact that the information is created from the user's profile and relationships.

To create the site, start by getting a reference to a new user or an already existing user, then call the CreatePersonalSite() method to create the My Site. These two steps are shown in the following code, where you perform the basic steps to get the profile manager and then make a call to the CreatePersonalSite() for the provided user.

```
try
{
    using (SPSite spSite = new SPSite(@"http://localhost"))
    {
        ServerContext siteContext = ServerContext.GetContext(spSite);
        UserProfileManager pmManager = new UserProfileManager(siteContext);
        string strUserName = "wrox\\brendon";
        if (pmManager.UserExists(strUserName))
        {
            UserProfile spUser = pmManager.GetUserProfile(strUserName);
            Console.WriteLine("This may take a few minutes...");
            spUser.CreatePersonalSite();
        }
    }
}
catch (Exception exp)
{
    Console.WriteLine(exp.Message);
}
```

Creating a new site can take up to a few minutes, depending on how fast the server is and how much load the server is under at the moment. Make sure that you let the user know that his My Site is being provisioned and that it could take a few minutes.

Remember that if the My Site has already been created, it will not overwrite the My Site that is available. Instead, an exception will be thrown stating that the user already has a personal site created, and it will show the personal site's address.

Getting My Site Personal Information

In addition to providing methods for working with the My Site, the UserProfile class can also return information about the user's personalized data that makes up the My Site. In fact, with the object model that the Microsoft SharePoint team provides, you could create your own My Site or even add to the existing one.

The My Site that is provisioned is just a regular SharePoint site and can be modified with the SharePoint object model once you get a reference to the current site.

The following table shows some of the common personalized information provided in the UserProfile class that helps you view or update data:

Name	Description
PersonalizationLinks	Returns the set of links used for the Personalization links bar.
PersonalSite	Returns an object of type SPSite that represents the My Site of the current user.
PersonalUrl	Gets the URL for the My Site of the user that can be modified when logged in as the current user.

Continued

Name	Description
`PublicUrl`	Gets the URL of the current users My Site that can be viewed by any user. The sections marked as being viewable in the public profile are available.
`QuickLinks`	Gets the `QuickLinkManager` object for this user profile.

The `PersonalSite` property can be used to prevent the users My Site from being created twice. This property uses the user profile information to determine whether the My Site has been created already. The following code demonstrates how you might check to see if the user already has a My Site:

```
try
{
    using (SPSite spSite = new SPSite(@"http://localhost"))
    {
        ServerContext siteContext = ServerContext.GetContext(spSite);
        UserProfileManager pmManager = new UserProfileManager(siteContext);
        string strUserName = "wrox\\brendon";
        if (pmManager.UserExists(strUserName))
        {
            UserProfile spUser = pmManager.GetUserProfile(strUserName);
            if (spUser.PersonalSite == null)
            {
                Console.WriteLine("This may take a few minutes...");
                spUser.CreatePersonalSite();
            }
            else
            {
                SPSite personalSite = spUser.PersonalSite;
                Console.WriteLine("personalSite.Url: " + personalSite.Url);
            }
        }
    }
}
catch (Exception exp)
{
    Console.WriteLine(exp.Message);
}
```

To view the locations of the My Site for a user, locate or type the name of the user that you need the information for, and then display either the `PersonalUrl` or the `PublicUrl`. The personal URL displays the location of the site that the user can log in to and edit. If the site is not associated with the currently logged-in user, the page will redirect the user to the View All Content page, but if it is the personal My Site of the logged-in user, My Site will appear and can be edited by the user.

When the user has a My Site already created, the `PersonalUrl` and the URL of the `SPSite` returned in the `PersonalSite` will be the same. If the user has not already set up a My Site, the personal and public URLs that are returned are also the same. This is due to the fact that the personal URL is updated when the My Site is actually created.

Sometimes, you will want to provide a link to the My Site of a user for other users to view. In that case, use the `PublicUrl` of the user's My Site to display the URL that any user can see. This page can show information that has been correctly set up in the privacy policies and will display information according to which user you are logged in as. The following code displays the URL information of the current user to the console application. The URLs that are displayed are the `PersonalUrl` and `PublicUrl` of the current user.

```
try
{
    using (SPSite spSite = new SPSite(@"http://localhost"))
    {
        ServerContext siteContext = ServerContext.GetContext(spSite);
        UserProfileManager pmManager = new UserProfileManager(siteContext);
        string strUserName = "wrox\\brendon";
        if (pmManager.UserExists(strUserName))
        {
            UserProfile spUser = pmManager.GetUserProfile(strUserName);
            Console.WriteLine("spUser.PersonalUrl");
            Console.WriteLine(spUser.PersonalUrl);
            Console.WriteLine("spUser.PublicUrl");
            Console.WriteLine(spUser.PublicUrl);
        }
    }
}
catch (Exception exp)
{
    Console.WriteLine(exp.Message);
}
```

In addition to retrieving the URL properties and SharePoint site of the My Site, you can also work with the user's links. You can use either the `QuickLinks` or the `PersonalizationLinks` from the user's profile. If you select `GetItems()` without providing a privacy policy enumeration, then the default will be `Privacy.Private`. You may want to add a link to every user's profile or just display the user's link on another Web Part. The following code shows how to get a user's links and display them in the console window:

```
try
{
    using (SPSite spSite = new SPSite(@"http://localhost"))
    {
        ServerContext siteContext = ServerContext.GetContext(spSite);
        UserProfileManager pmManager = new UserProfileManager(siteContext);
        string strUserName = "heididev\\sam";
        if (pmManager.UserExists(strUserName))
        {
            UserProfile spMyUser = pmManager.GetUserProfile(strUserName);
            QuickLinkManager linkManager = spMyUser.QuickLinks;
            foreach (QuickLink link in linkManager.GetItems())
            {
                Console.WriteLine(link.Title + " : " + link.Url);
            }
        }
    }
}
```

```
        }
        catch (Exception exp)
        {
            Console.WriteLine(exp.Message);
        }
```

Colleagues

You can use Colleagues to gather information about related contacts in SharePoint. Colleagues are other users in the system that are your managers, peers, or direct reports. These users are automatically added as colleagues by SharePoint 2007. You might have colleagues that are part of your organization that do not fit into one of these categories. This could be a person in another department, who is not part of your reporting structure. You can add these users as colleagues who will appear in the My Site page. Figure 8-5 shows the Colleagues page. Here you can add, and manage colleagues and view the relationships among colleagues.

Once the colleagues have been added, you can display them with the Colleague Tracker Web Part, which is loaded with Microsoft Office SharePoint Server 2007. By default, each user's My Site page contains a Colleague Tracker Web Part to easily view the colleagues each user has. Colleagues can also be used to narrow the searches that are performed on the site.

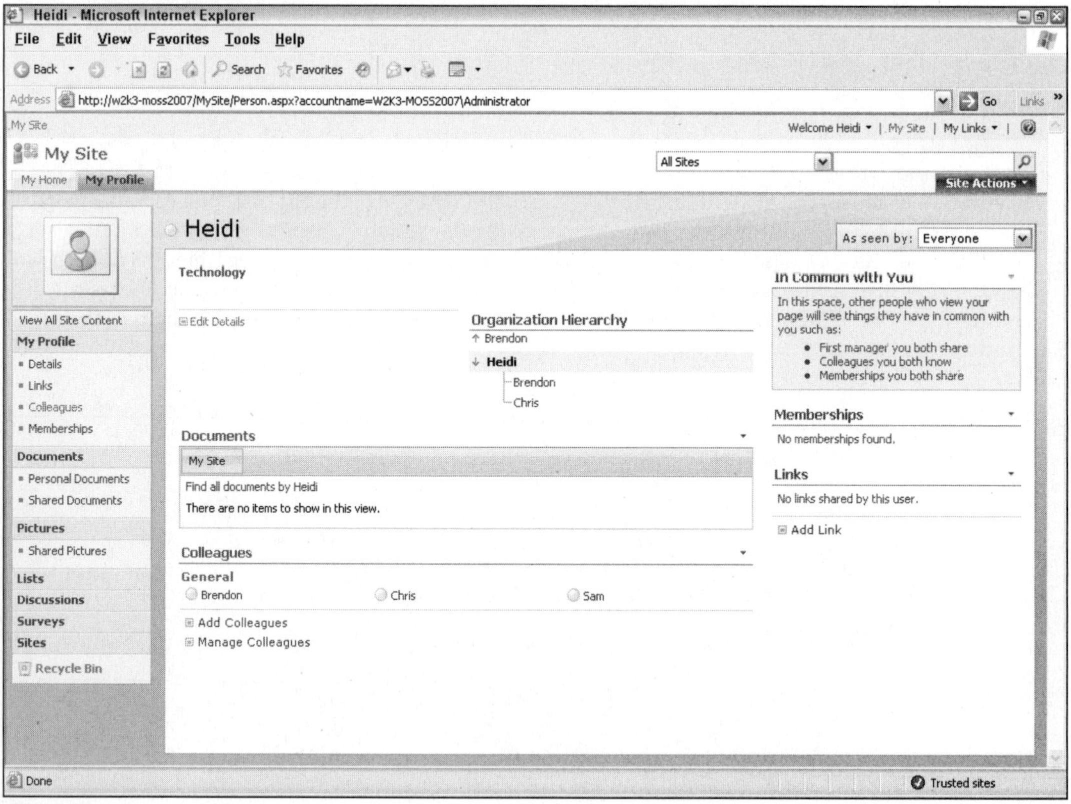

Figure 8-5

The UserProfile class contains a property named Colleagues that returns the colleague's manager for the current user, who can be used to work with the colleagues of the user. Once you have a reference to the ColleagueManager you can add, remove, or list the colleagues of the user. There are even built-in methods to list the common colleagues as well as colleagues of colleagues. The following table lists the ColleagueManager methods for managing a user's colleagues:

Name	Description
Create	Creates a Colleague object with the specified type and privacy level
DeleteAll	Removes all of the colleagues associated with the user
GetColleaguesOfColleagues	Gets the set of colleague's colleagues
GetCommonColleagues	Gets the colleagues that the user and the colleague have in common or share
GetItems	Returns the set of all colleagues based on the privacy settings
IsColleague	Determines whether the specified user is a colleague of this colleague

To add a new colleague, use the built-in method, IsColleague, to check whether the user is already a colleague. If the user is not a colleague, then make a call to the Create method, as follows:

1. Start by creating a console application named ColleagueManagerApp.

2. Add the required SharePoint references:

```
using System;
using System.Collections.Generic;
using Microsoft.SharePoint;
using Microsoft.Office.Server;
using Microsoft.Office.Server.UserProfiles;
```

3. Get a reference to the ColleagueManager from the UserProfile object:

```
spMyUser = pmManager.GetUserProfile(strUserName);
ColleagueManager cmColleagues = spMyUser.Colleagues;
```

4. Display the number of colleagues that have a privacy setting of Public:

```
int NumColleages = cmColleagues.GetItems(Privacy.Public).GetLength(0);
Console.WriteLine(NumColleages);
```

5. Check to see if the provided user is a colleague of the first user. If the user is not a colleague, add the user as a colleague:

```
string strNewColleague = "heididev\\sam";
UserProfile spMyColleague = pmManager.GetUserProfile(strNewColleague);
```

```
if (!cmColleagues.IsColleague(spMyColleague.ID))
{
        cmColleagues.Create(spMyColleague,
                            ColleagueGroupType.Peer,
                            "Peers",
                            false,
                            Privacy.Public);
}
```

6.   Loop through each colleague and display them to the console window:

```
try
{
    using (SPSite spSite = new SPSite(@"http://localhost"))
    {
        ServerContext siteContext = ServerContext.GetContext(spSite);
        UserProfileManager pmManager = new UserProfileManager(siteContext);
        string strUserName = "heididev\\brendon";
        if (pmManager.UserExists(strUserName))
        {
            UserProfile spMyUser = pmManager.GetUserProfile(strUserName);
            ColleagueManager cmColleagues = spMyUser.Colleagues;

            int NumColleages = cmColleagues.GetItems(Privacy.Public).GetLength(0);
            Console.WriteLine(NumColleages);

            string strNewColleague = "heididev\\sam";
            UserProfile spMyColleague = pmManager.GetUserProfile(strNewColleague);
            if (!cmColleagues.IsColleague(spMyColleague.ID))
            {
                cmColleagues.Create(spMyColleague,
                                    ColleagueGroupType.Peer,
                                    "Peers",
                                    false,
                                    Privacy.Public);
            }

            foreach (Colleague tempColleague in cmColleagues.GetItems(Privacy.Public))
            {
                Console.WriteLine(tempColleague.Title);
                Console.WriteLine(tempColleague.GroupType);
                Console.WriteLine(tempColleague.IsAssistant);
                Console.WriteLine(tempColleague.IsInWorkGroup);
            }
        }
    }
}
catch (Exception exp)
{
    Console.WriteLine(exp.Message);
}
```

By using the `ColleagueManager` class, you can remove all of the colleagues of a single user. However, if you want to delete just one colleague, you need to get a reference to that colleague and then call the `Delete` method from the `Colleague` class.

Membership

Similarly to colleagues, memberships provide relationships between the user and content. Content can be related to the user through automatic association or you can use the object model. Standard functionality includes such things as determining memberships, providing the ability to create new memberships, and displaying information about current memberships.

There are two types of membership:

- ❑ Distribution List (DL) memberships
- ❑ Microsoft Windows SharePoint Services 3.0 site memberships

The difference between the two types of memberships is that one is created from the Active Directory directory service and the other is created from SharePoint sites.

Again, just like the colleagues, the memberships that a user has are displayed on the My Site. When another user views the common page, also known as the Profile page, the common memberships with that user will also be shown.

There are two sets of classes to use when programming with the membership relationships that allow you to work with the membership groups and the memberships themselves. The classes are:

- ❑ `MembershipGroup`
- ❑ `Membership`

Both of these classes have a manager class that is associated with them to manage the collections of these items. The manager class allows you to add, display or change the membership objects that they contain.

Working with Membership Groups

You will use the membership groups to add users as a member of a distribution list or to a SharePoint site membership. The membership groups use a number of public properties to describe the membership group itself. The following table lists some useful properties of the class:

Name	Description
CreateMemberGroup	Allows developers to create members groups from the object model
Count	Returns the number of member groups that are associated with the user
GetMemberGroupBySourceAndSourceReference	Returns a specific `MemberGroup` based on the source and name of the source reference

The following code uses the `UserProfile` class to get the membership groups that the user has and then display the number of memberships the user has. In addition to showing the values of the `Membership` class, the `MembershipGroupManager` is used to get the list of groups:

```
try
{
    using (SPSite spSite = new SPSite(@"http://localhost"))
    {
        ServerContext siteContext = ServerContext.GetContext(spSite);
        UserProfileManager pmManager = new UserProfileManager(siteContext);
        string strUserName = "wrox\\brendon";
        if (pmManager.UserExists(strUserName))
        {
            UserProfile spMyUser = pmManager.GetUserProfile(strUserName);
            MemberGroupManager mgmMemberGroups = pmManager.GetMemberGroups();

            int NumMemberships = mgmMemberGroups.Count;
            Console.WriteLine("Number of Memberships: " + NumMemberships);
        }
    }
}
catch (Exception exp)
{
    Console.WriteLine(exp.Message);
}
```

If the installation of SharePoint is new, no membership groups may have been created yet. To add a new group, use the `MemberGroupManager` and create a new group with the `Create` method. Now that you have a `MemberGroup`, you can display the group with the properties of the `MemberGroup` class, which are discussed in the following table:

Name	Description
Count	Returns the number of members associated the member group
Description	A description of the text describing the member group
DisplayName	Name used when the member group is displayed in the user interface
Source	The GUID of the source member group
SourceReference	The value that makes the member group unique in the source
Url	The location of the membership group's URL

When creating new groups, the `sourceReference` string must be different for each `MembershipGroup` you add, or they must have a different source location. An error will be displayed if you try to add the same source more than once. You can however have the same `sourceReference` name if it's from different source. A source must be a valid GUID that can be user created, or it can be one of the predefined types. The following sources are part of the `PrivacyPolicyIDConstants` enumeration class:

- ❑ MembershipsFromDistributionLists
- ❑ MembershipsFromSharePointSites
- ❑ MyColleaguesOnMySite
- ❑ MyColleaguesRecommendations
- ❑ MyPersonalizationLinksOnMySite

1. Start by creating a console application named `MembershipManagerApp`.

2. Add the required SharePoint references:

```
using System;
using System.Collections.Generic;
using Microsoft.SharePoint;
using Microsoft.Office.Server;
using Microsoft.Office.Server.UserProfiles;
```

3. Get the site and `UserProfileManger` reference.

4. Get the list of `MemberGroups` for the user; if there are zero groups create a new one. Make this new list a `DistributionList`.

```
if (mgmMemberGroups.Count == 0)
{
        // Create new member group
        MemberGroup newGroup = mgmMemberGroups.CreateMemberGroup(
                    PrivacyPolicyIdConstants.MembershipsFromDistributionLists,
                    "Wrox SP Reviewers List",
                    "Wrox Review",
                    "Reviewers list",
                    "http://localhost",
                    "Wrox");
}
```

5. Display the number of groups that are in the list:

```
        int NumMemberships = mgmMemberGroups.Count;
        Console.WriteLine("Number of Memberships: " + NumMemberships);
```

6. Loop through each member group and display it to the console window:

```
try
{
    using (SPSite spSite = new SPSite(@"http://localhost"))
    {
        ServerContext siteContext = ServerContext.GetContext(spSite);
        UserProfileManager pmManager = new UserProfileManager(siteContext);
```

```
            string strUserName = "wrox\\brendon";
            if (pmManager.UserExists(strUserName))
            {
                UserProfile spMyUser = pmManager.GetUserProfile(strUserName);
                MemberGroupManager mgmMemberGroups = pmManager.GetMemberGroups();

                if (mgmMemberGroups.Count == 0)
                {
                    // Create new member group
                    MemberGroup newGroup = mgmMemberGroups.CreateMemberGroup(
                            PrivacyPolicyIdConstants.MembershipsFromDistributionLists,
                            "Wrox SP Reviewers List",
                            "Wrox Review",
                            "Reviewers list",
                            "http://localhost",
                            "Wrox");
                }

                int NumMemberships = mgmMemberGroups.Count;
                Console.WriteLine("Number of Memberships: " + NumMemberships);

                foreach (MemberGroup tempMemberGroup in mgmMemberGroups)
                {
                    Console.WriteLine(tempMemberGroup.DisplayName);
                    Console.WriteLine(tempMemberGroup.Description);
                    Console.WriteLine(tempMemberGroup.MailNickName);
                    Console.WriteLine(tempMemberGroup.Source);
                    Console.WriteLine(tempMemberGroup.SourceReference);
                }
            }
        }
    }
    catch (Exception exp)
    {
        Console.WriteLine(exp.Message);
    }
```

Now that you have membership groups, you can create a membership relation to one of the users in your SharePoint system. Use the GetMemberGroupBySourceAndSourceReference() method of the MemberGroupManager class to get a reference to the MemberGroup. Make sure to use the correct source and sourceReference to return the right group. If you create your own source, make sure to store it in a permanent location such as a database to be able to retrieve it for use with the Get statements. You can also iterate through each of the items until you find the right one. Once you have the reference to the user and the membership groups, call the Create method of the MembershipManager class.

The membership item has the same privacy policy as other items in the My Site. When you set the membership relationship, be sure to provide the right level of privacy. This also applies to the GetItems method of the membership manager, which is used to retrieve the Membership objects. The default privacy policy is Private, so make sure to specify a different level if required. The following code shows how to get the membership groups of a user and then check for a specific group:

1. Start by creating a console application named MembershipManagerApp.

2. Add the required SharePoint references:

```
using System;
using System.Collections.Generic;
using Microsoft.SharePoint;
using Microsoft.Office.Server;
using Microsoft.Office.Server.UserProfiles;
```

3. Get the site and `UserProfileManger` reference.

4. Return the `DistributionLists` with a reference of Wrox for the current user.

```
MemberGroup mgMemberGroup =
        mgmMemberGroups.GetMemberGroupBySourceAndSourceReference(
                PrivacyPolicyIdConstants.MembershipsFromDistributionLists,
                "Wrox");
```

5. Check to see if the user already has a membership; if the user doesn't, create a new membership to the group:

```
MembershipManager mmMemberships = spMyUser.Memberships;

//Create a new membership with the current user
if (mmMemberships[mgMemberGroup] == null)
{
        mmMemberships.Create(mgMemberGroup,
                           MembershipGroupType.UserSpecified,
                           "Wrox Reviewers",
                           Privacy.Public);
}
```

6. Display all the memberships the user has to the console window:

```
try
{
    using (SPSite spSite = new SPSite(@"http://localhost"))
    {
        ServerContext siteContext = ServerContext.GetContext(spSite);
        UserProfileManager pmManager = new UserProfileManager(siteContext);
        string strUserName = "wrox\\brendon";
        if (pmManager.UserExists(strUserName))
        {
            UserProfile spMyUser = pmManager.GetUserProfile(strUserName);
            MemberGroupManager mgmMemberGroups = pmManager.GetMemberGroups();

            MemberGroup mgMemberGroup =
                    mgmMemberGroups.GetMemberGroupBySourceAndSourceReference(
                            PrivacyPolicyIdConstants.MembershipsFromDistributionLists,
                            "Wrox");

            MembershipManager mmMemberships = spMyUser.Memberships;

            //Create a new membership with the current user
```

```
                    if (mmMemberships[mgMemberGroup] == null)
                    {
                      mmMemberships.Create(mgMemberGroup,
                                           MembershipGroupType.UserSpecified,
                                           "Wrox Reviewers",
                                           Privacy.Public);
                    }

                    foreach (Membership tempMembership in mmMemberships.GetItems(Privacy.Public))
                    {
                        Console.WriteLine(tempMembership.GroupType);
                        Console.WriteLine(tempMembership.Title);
                        Console.WriteLine(tempMembership.Url);
                        Console.WriteLine(tempMembership.MembershipGroup.MailNickName);
                    }
                }
            }
        }
        catch (Exception exp)
        {
            Console.WriteLine(exp.Message);
        }
```

SharePoint Audiences

SharePoint allows content providers to customize information by using audience targeting through a rules based system. An audience is a collection of users that someone wants to target. Audiences can be groups of people from the Windows security groups, or they can be groups that include people based on rules you set up. They are able to do this by using personalization sites to target users based on information in their user profiles. For example, an audience can be created that includes all members of the accounting department. Once that audience is created, it can then be used to target members of that audience in order to provide custom content to them. Pages and listings can be targeted to an audience to enhance the user experience and provide meaningful custom content. Figure 8-6 shows the list of audiences as they would appear in the Shared Service Provider.

In SharePoint 2007 you can perform audience targeting on a rules-based audience, Windows SharePoint Services groups, and memberships.

Creating an Audience

Audiences can only be created and managed by the administrator from the Shared Services Administration page or by using the object model. To create an audience, follow these steps:

1. Inside the Shared Service Provider page click Audiences, and the Manage Audiences page comes up, which will allow you to manage and compile the audiences you have created.

2. To view one of the existing audiences, click the View Audiences link.

3. To create a new audience, click Create audience, and you are able to define the settings for the audience you would like to create. The first thing needed is a unique name that will easily identify the audience. A description can also be added, along with the owner of the audience. The last option is to include either users who meet all of the rules of the audience, or just any of the rules.

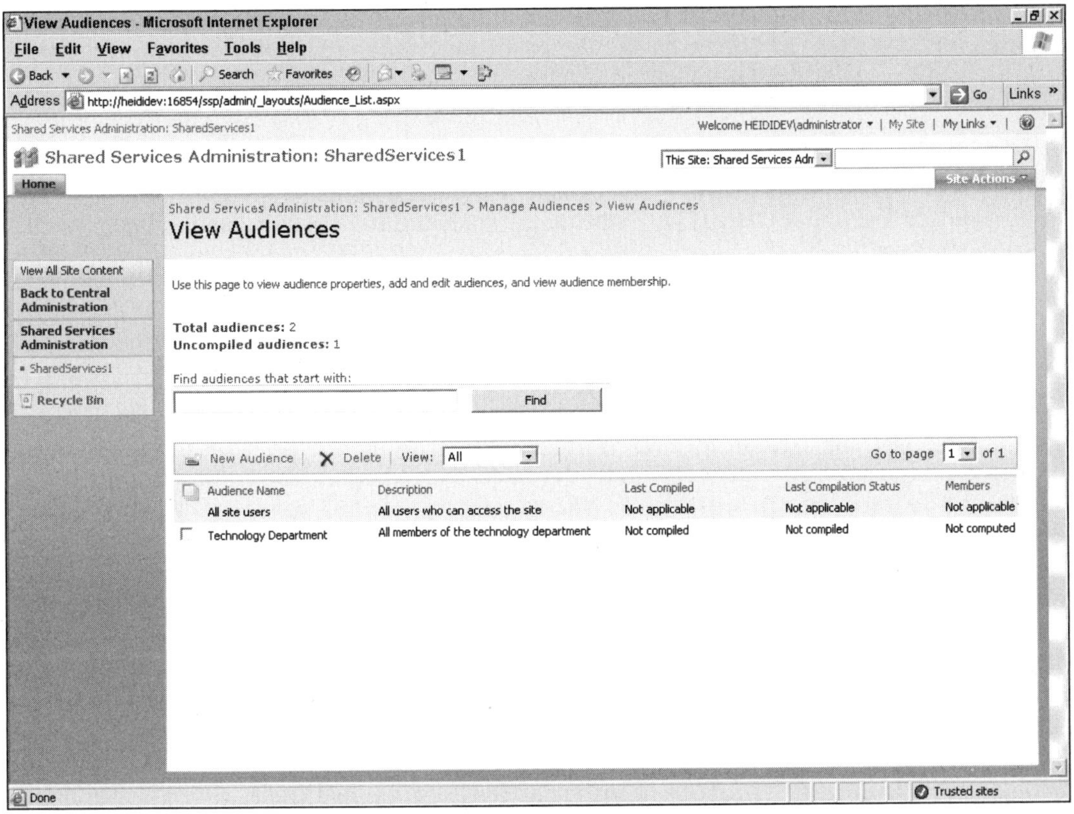

Figure 8-6

Creating Audience Rules

Once an audience is created, you must define the rules that users must meet to be included in the audience. The rules you are able to define use simple queries that will either include or exclude users from the audience. When using the user interface to create rules governing who to include in your audience, you are limited to only six elements in your rules. If a rule has more than six elements that are used, then it must be created by using the object model.

When entering rules using the user interface, each rule asks you to define an operand, an operator, and a value. The operand is the user or the property that you are looking to include in the audience. This is either a user or a property. Select User when you want to add a rule that is based on distribution list membership, a reporting structure, or a security group. When User is chosen as the operand, the only available options for the operator are Reports Under and Member Of. The value must then be a user of the organization. Alternatively, choose a profile property when you want to choose one of the properties that are listed on the drop-down menu.

The operator is what determines how the operand is evaluated, and ultimately whether a user is included in the audience or not. The list of operators that are available to choose from will change, depending on the operand that was chosen. The value is the single value that you want to compare the operand to, using the rule of the chosen operator. The following example should help clarify the different parts used when defining a rule. If the operand is "First name", the operator is "Contains", and the value is "tom", then every user whose first name contains the letters "tom" will be included in the audience. However, it's important to note that this will include anyone by the name of Tom or Tommy, but not anyone with the name of Thomas.

Once you have added a rule, the View Audience Properties page is shown. There, the audience properties and rules are displayed for review. From this page, there are links to edit the audience properties, view the membership, and compile the audience. Also, under the Audience Rules section, the rules can be clicked on to edit them.

Audience Targeting

In the past, SharePoint Portal Server 2003 allowed audience targeting to be done based on a fairly small set of rules. However, Office SharePoint Server 2007 allows you to target an audience based on a lot more information, including groups, distribution list (DL) memberships, and rules-based audiences. Instead of making you target the entire list, SharePoint Server 2007 also lets you target content just by using a list item, making it much more efficient. This type of audience targeting is made possible by using filters on user profiles and by using personalized Web Parts to display content. There are no default Web Parts set up on a page, but each site utilizes different filter Web Parts that help determine which Web Parts on the page should be shown to the user who is visiting the site. It is also interesting to know that SharePoint Server 2007 can automatically find all of the sites that are targeted to a particular user.

Targeting Content

Once you have created an audience, you can then start targeting content for that audience. As an example, using your My Site page, on the Quick Launch, select the page you would like to use for audience targeting.

1. Click on the list or document library you would like to use, and the list of items will be displayed.

2. From there, click on the Settings tab, and choose List Settings or Document Settings to pull up all of the settings for that page.

3. Under General Settings, click on Audience targeting settings.

4. Check the Enable audience targeting check box, which will enable audience targeting for the chosen list or document library.

When audience targeting is enabled, a column is added to the list or document library. The data in this new column will be used by Web Parts to filter the list or library contents based on the user information provided. This enables the content in that Web Part to be customized to the specific user or audience. SharePoint Server 2007 gives you the ability to target items or links in a list to an audience by using Web Parts that are able to recognize membership in that audience. When this is done, only members of that particular audience are able to see the targeted items in that Web Part.

A great example of how this could be used is a human resources department at a large company. The department could use a News Web Part on their home page that would use audience targeting to deliver news items that are relevant to certain users based on audience targeting. For example, if a company wanted to distribute sensitive information that only applied to executive-level managers or higher, they could use audience targeting to accomplish this. By using this method, the new information would only be shown to users it applied to, and important messages could be delivered to executives in an efficient manner without going to lower-ranking employees.

After audience targeting has been enabled, the Settings page for the list or library you changed will show the newly created column. Under the list of all columns, there is a new one listed, the Target Audiences column. The column heading is Audience Targeting, but it is not required. If you click on the column, you will be taken to the Edit page. On this page, you can change the column name, add a description, and change whether or not information is required for this column. However, you are also given the option to allow a global audience, allow distribution lists, and allow SharePoint Groups. All of these options are initially checked but can be changed if you prefer to not allow them. There is also a button that will allow you to delete this column if it is no longer needed. If it is deleted, the next time you go back to the Audience Targeting, the Enable audience targeting check box will not be checked, and therefore audience targeting will not be enabled unless you enable it again.

1. After audience targeting has been enabled, go back to the List page and add a new list item by clicking New and then the item type.

2. On the New Item page, there is now a field to fill in for Target Audiences. You can now choose from the audiences that have been created to target this list item to.

3. Click on the browse icon to pull up a list of available audiences that have been created. Distribution lists and security groups can also be used in this field, but only after they have been imported. One option that can be chosen is All site users, which will allow everyone to see this list. If you are working with a document library where audience targeting has been enabled, audience targeting can be set when you edit or upload a document in the same way as discussed here.

Displaying Targeted Content

Once the audience targeting has been set up on the content, the web site must be changed to display it.

1. Log on to SharePoint using one of the accounts that can modify the Shared View.

2. Click on the link to edit the page, and the page will then be displayed with the Web Part zones.

3. Choose one of the zones, and click to add a Web Part.

4. Click on the check box in the Default group next to the Content Query Web Part to add a Content Query Web Part to the page. This will enable you to show the targeted content from your site to users when they pull up the web page.

5. When the Web Part has been added, stay in edit mode for the page, and click on the edit link on the Content Query Web Part. Choose to Modify Shared Web Part.

6. The Web Part settings page will show up on the right side of the page, where the Content Query Web Part can be modified.

7. Click on the plus sign next to the word Query to expand the Query topic section.

8. Change the List Type to match your audience targeting page, whether it's a specific list (like a tasks list or a links list) or a document library.

9. Next, check the apply audience filtering box under Audience Targeting.

10. Once these changes have been made, click on OK. Now, the list or document library that you selected will only show up for the users that have been targeted in the chosen audience.

Working with the Audiences API

When working with the Audiences API, SharePoint 2007 has introduced a new namespace implemented in `Microsoft.Office.Server.Audience`. The SharePoint team has left the previous SharePoint 2003 version to maintain backward compatibility, but you should work with the new namespace when creating new applications.

> **Code and namespaces that are marked as deprecated or obsolete may not function as expected in new versions of SharePoint. Make sure to test your code to make sure that everything still works as it did in SharePoint 2003.**

The major use of audiences is to ensure that content is delivered to the right people. Although it may seem like this can be used to secure locations and documents, audience targeting is not used as a security mechanism in SharePoint 2007.

To pull the right information about users, audiences must be compiled based on the rules provided. When the rule is being compiled, SharePoint will use information from Active Directory as well as SharePoint itself and store the compiled data result into the database. When external data changes, SharePoint will not recompile the data automatically, and the audience must be recompiled once again.

As with the other objects you have seen, the audience API has a manager that is used as the top-level object when working with the site. The `AudienceManager` class uses the server context to retrieve the correct `AudienceManager` data. Take a look at the following code and notice that the syntax is very similar to the `UserProfile` store. One reason that this may look similar is because the audience system is part of the user profile system. The difference is just that the data is stored in a separate database table.

```
using System;
using System.Collections.Generic;
using System.Text;
using Microsoft.SharePoint;
using Microsoft.Office.Server;
using Microsoft.Office.Server.Audience;

namespace Audiences
{
    class Program
    {
        static void Main(string[] args)
        {
            try
            {
                using (SPSite spSite = new SPSite(@"http://localhost"))
                {
                    ServerContext siteContext = ServerContext.GetContext(spSite);
                    AudienceManager amManager = new AudienceManager(siteContext);

                    if (!amManager.Audiences.CompileInProgress)
                    {
```

```
                       Console.WriteLine(amManager.Audiences.Count);
                   }
               }
           }
           catch (Exception exception)
           {
               Console.WriteLine(exception.ToString());
           }
       }
   }
}
```

Adding New Audiences

When working with either a simple audience rule or a complex audience rule, you can create the audience with the `AudienceCollection` object that is returned from the Audience Manager.

The `Audience` class has a number of useful properties that can be displayed and objects that can be updated. These would be objects such as `Audience Name`, AudienceRules, and `AudienceDescription`. You will use these properties and objects in code shortly.

To create a simple audience, use the site elements server context to retrieve the `AudienceManager` class and the `AudienceCollection`. It is always a good idea to check if the audience already exists on the current site. If you try to add an audience twice, an exception will be thrown that notifies you that the duplicated name is already available for the current site.

1. Start by creating a console application named `AudienceApp`.

2. Add the required SharePoint references:

```
using System;
using System.Collections.Generic;
using System.Text;
using Microsoft.SharePoint;
using Microsoft.Office.Server;
using Microsoft.Office.Server.Audience;
```

3. Get the site and `AudienceManager` reference:

```
try
{
    using (SPSite spSite = new SPSite(@"http://localhost"))
    {
        ServerContext siteContext = ServerContext.GetContext(spSite);
        AudienceManager amManager = new AudienceManager(siteContext);
    }
}
catch (Exception exception)
{
    Console.WriteLine(exception.Message);
}
```

4. Get a collection of all of the Audiences in the site:

```
AudienceCollection acCollection = amManager.Audiences;
```

5. Check if an audience named Marketing Department already exists, and if it doesn't, create the audience:

```
string strName = "Marketing Department";
string strDescription = "All members of the marketing department";

if (!acCollection.AudienceExist(strName))
{
    acCollection.Create(strName, strDescription);
}
```

6. Loop through each of the audiences and display the `AudienceName`, `AudienceSite`, and `MembershipCount`:

```
try
{
    using (SPSite spSite = new SPSite(@"http://localhost"))
    {
        ServerContext siteContext = ServerContext.GetContext(spSite);
        AudienceManager amManager = new AudienceManager(siteContext);

        AudienceCollection acCollection = amManager.Audiences;
        string strName = "Marketing Department";
        string strDescription = "All members of the marketing department";

        if (!acCollection.AudienceExist(strName))
        {
            acCollection.Create(strName, strDescription);
        }

        foreach (Audience tempAudience in acCollection)
        {
            Console.WriteLine(tempAudience.AudienceName);
            Console.WriteLine(tempAudience.AudienceSite);
            Console.WriteLine(tempAudience.MemberShipCount);
        }
    }
}
catch (Exception exception)
{
    Console.WriteLine(exception.Message);
}
```

Adding Rules to Your Audience

Rules help to determine who the targeted information will be displayed to. The rules are string-based values that are evaluated by an operator. Each rule contains a left operand value used for the `AudienceRule` class, an operator value provided when creating a new rule, and a value for comparing the operand. The standard operators AND/OR can be used when creating your rules. In addition to the AND/OR operators, you can use parentheses to create more complex rules. However, you are allowed a maximum of three levels of parentheses nesting.

Supported Audience Rules include the following:

- ❏   =
- ❏   >
- ❏   >=
- ❏   <
- ❏   <=
- ❏   Contains
- ❏   Reports Under
- ❏   <>
- ❏   Not contains
- ❏   AND
- ❏   OR
- ❏   (
- ❏   )
- ❏   Member of

When creating an audience, it is a good idea to check if the audience already has rules associated with the audience. If there are rules associated with the audience, you should create a new AND rule that will include both the old rules and the new rules you are adding.

Make sure to call the Commit method on the audience once you have added all of the rules to make the new rules take effect on the server.

1. Start by creating a console application named AudienceApp.

2. Add the required SharePoint references:

```
using System;
using System.Collections.Generic;
using System.Text;
using Microsoft.SharePoint;
using Microsoft.Office.Server;
using Microsoft.Office.Server.Audience;
```

3. Get the site and AudienceManager reference.

4. Get a collection of all of the audiences in the site:

```
AudienceCollection acCollection = amManager.Audiences;
```

5. Check to see if the audience already exists. If so, retrieve the audience from SharePoint, and if it doesn't, create the new one:

```
Audience.string strName = "Technology Department";
string strDescription = "All members of the technology department";
Audience TechAudience = null;
if (acCollection.AudienceExist(strName))
{
    TechAudience = acCollection[strName];
}
else
{
    TechAudience = acCollection.Create(strName, strDescription);
}
```

6. Get the rules that are associated with the audience. If the audience already has rules associated with it, then create a new rule component that will AND the old rules and the new rules together. Otherwise, just create a new empty `ArrayList`.

```
ArrayList techRules = TechAudience.AudienceRules;
if (techRules == null)
{
    techRules = new ArrayList();
}
else
{
    techRules.Add(new AudienceRuleComponent(null, "AND", null));
}
```

7. Finally, add two new rules to the audience that will limit the people in the audience. These rules are also combined by the AND operator. You can use any of the operators seen in the list above, depending on the type of comparison you wish to apply.

```
try
{
    using (SPSite spSite = new SPSite(@"http://localhost"))
    {
        ServerContext siteContext = ServerContext.GetContext(spSite);
        AudienceManager amManager = new AudienceManager(siteContext);

        AudienceCollection acCollection = amManager.Audiences;

        string strName = "Technology Department";
        string strDescription = "All members of the technology department";
        Audience TechAudience = null;
        if (acCollection.AudienceExist(strName))
        {
            TechAudience = acCollection[strName];
        }
        else
        {
            TechAudience = acCollection.Create(strName, strDescription);
```

```
        }

        ArrayList techRules = TechAudience.AudienceRules;
        if (techRules == null)
        {
            techRules = new ArrayList();
        }
        else
        {
            techRules.Add(new AudienceRuleComponent(null, "AND", null));
        }

        AudienceRuleComponent arRule1 = new AudienceRuleComponent("FirstName",
    "Contains", "H");
        techRules.Add(arRule1) ;

        AudienceRuleComponent arRule2 = new AudienceRuleComponent(null, "AND", null);
        techRules.Add(arRule2);

        AudienceRuleComponent arRule3 = new AudienceRuleComponent("BrokerID", "=",
    "090101");
        techRules.Add(arRule3);

        TechAudience.AudienceRules = techRules;
        TechAudience.Commit();
    }
}
catch (Exception exception)
{
    Console.WriteLine(exception.Message);
}
```

Removing Audiences

You may need to manage the audiences by removing one of the existing audiences created from the Shared Service Provider Central Administration page or from your code. SharePoint makes it easy to remove the audience by using the GUID of the audience or the name of the audience.

In contrast to adding an audience, you should now make sure that the audience does exist, to prevent an exception from being thrown. The following code removes an audience called Technology Department:

```
try
{
    using (SPSite spSite = new SPSite(@"http://localhost"))
    {
        ServerContext siteContext = ServerContext.GetContext(spSite);
        AudienceManager amManager = new AudienceManager(siteContext);

        string strName = "Technology Department";

        if (amManager.Audiences.AudienceExist(strName))
        {
            amManager.Audiences.Remove(strName);
        }
```

```
        }
    }
    catch (Exception exception)
    {
        Console.WriteLine(exception.Message);
    }
```

Working with Audience Memberships

Most companies want to know which users are in each audience, so SharePoint has provided a way to get the memberships associated with an audience. Use the `Audience` class, and call the method `GetMembership` to return a list of memberships as shown in the following code:

```
try
{
    using (SPSite spSite = new SPSite(@"http://localhost"))
    {
        ServerContext siteContext = ServerContext.GetContext(spSite);
        AudienceManager amManager = new AudienceManager(siteContext);

        string strName = "Technology Department";
        Audience TechAudience = amManager.Audiences[strName];

        ArrayList TechAudienceMembers = TechAudience.GetMembership();

        foreach (UserInfo TechUser in TechAudienceMembers)
        {
            Console.WriteLine(TechUser.PreferredName);
            Console.WriteLine(TechUser.NTName);
            Console.WriteLine(TechUser.Email);
        }
    }
}
catch (Exception exception)
{
    Console.WriteLine(exception.Message);
}
```

Summary

There are many aspects to creating a personalized solution with SharePoint. You have covered many different areas from user profiles to audiences. You have looked at how to make sites more personalized by using the features of My Site. These tasks could be done with the user interface, but the new object model functionality provides the ability to perform all of these actions with code. In this chapter, you have seen how to:

❑   Manage users and user profile data

❑   Create Web Parts and web pages that use the built-in controls like the people picker

❏   View and query the users' change logs

❏   Create a user's My Site programmatically

❏   Create colleagues and memberships using the object model

❏   Update a site's audience data

❏   Create new rules for audiences in a site

Now that you have seen how to update many aspects of the personalization through code, the next chapter looks at how to perform enterprise searches. This personalization data can help return the correct search results and limit the visibility of what a user can view.

Using Enterprise Search

By John Alexander

An important part of content management support for a portal is the ability to search. Enterprise Search is a term for using technologies to gather and index content across the entire enterprise and make it accessible for use in governing and running the enterprise. To accomplish this, the content is "crawled" or retrieved by the search engine before the content is analyzed for indexing.

Search capability has been greatly enhanced in Microsoft Office SharePoint Server 2007. With Enterprise Search, you are now able to crawl several different content sources, configure enhanced relevancy information, and set search scopes, all from a consistent search environment between Microsoft Office SharePoint Server and Windows SharePoint Services 3.0.

In this chapter, you will:

- ❏ Explore the Enterprise Search architecture
- ❏ Discover the Query object model
- ❏ Work with the Search web service

Introduction to Enterprise Search

The Microsoft Office SharePoint Server (MOSS) Enterprise Search functionality allows you to search and crawl very diverse content sources, both internally and externally. This shared service also returns those results within a specific security context. Enhanced and expanded, the results can be filtered and made relevant to the people who need the information and are supposed to have it. This compelling set of features can be customized quite heavily through the extensive object model exposed by MOSS 2007 Enterprise Search.

A growing number of organizations are using this functionality to enable searches over content that was previously unreachable with earlier search technologies. That content exists in many different systems and folders, and by combining MOSS Enterprise Search with the Business Data Catalog, virtually all content within a given enterprise can now be queried regardless of its source.

Understanding how you want to search is just as important as what you want to search. What metadata should be crawled, the keywords to be used, and the scope of the search itself are all key factors in developing a successful Enterprise Search strategy.

SharePoint Server Enterprise Search Object Model Architecture

The MOSS object model exposes its search features through a `SearchContext` object and several subordinate objects, as listed in the following table.

Name	Description
SearchContext	The `SearchContext` object is the top-level Enterprise Search object and is responsible for returning the server, shared service provider, or site search context.
ContentSource	The `ContentSource` object is responsible for content crawl definition configuration, and scheduling. Each content source may be searched or "crawled" for a search result set based on a given criteria.
LogViewer	The `LogViewer` object is responsible for returning the Crawl Log data, which can be filtered on a set of criteria.
Keywords	The `Keywords` object is responsible for the keyword's definition and management, which enables more flexible search results and is essential for functionality such as link recommendations or "Best Bets."
Propagation	The `Propagation` object is responsible for pushing the context index between the index service and the query service, if they are running on separate servers.
Ranking	The `Ranking` object is responsible for Ranking Engine parameter customization and allows the changing of the ranking context of the search results.

Name	Description
Schema	The Schema object is responsible for managing the metadata property schema. This property schema consists of two types of properties: managed and crawled. The managed property is configured directly by an administrator, whereas the crawled property is discovered during a content crawl.
Scopes	The Scopes object is responsible for defining and working with search scopes. A search scope in Microsoft Office SharePoint Server 2007 has been enhanced beyond a single scope of content from a content source. Now, the scope can be defined as a collection of items that share a common element as part of a search result.

Working with Content Sources

Content sources are essential to your Enterprise Search strategy. They provide the content that is indexed, crawled, and then returned to the user for further action. Microsoft Office SharePoint Server 2007 provides several content source types, which are all derived from the ContentSource.

The following table describes the Enterprise content object model in greater detail.

Name	Description
BusinessDataContentSource	The BusinessDataContentSource enables the crawling of any given Business Data Catalog content sources. This content source has a prerequisite of requiring the corresponding Application to have been registered within the Business Data Catalog.
CustomContentSource	The CustomContentSource is used for building and crawling custom content sources.
ExchangePublicFolderContentSource	The ExchangePublicFolderContentSource enables the crawling of any given Exchange Public Folder content sources.
FileShareContentSource	The FileShareContentSource enables the crawling of any given file share content sources available to Microsoft Office SharePoint Server 2007.
HierarchicalContentSource	The HierarchicalContentSource is the base class for the ExchangePublicFolderContentSource, the FileShareContentSource, and the LotusNotesContentSource.

Continued

Name	Description
LotusNotesContentSource	The LotusNotesContentSource enables the crawling of any given Lotus Notes content sources.
SharePointContentSource	The SharePointContentSource enables the crawling of all Windows SharePoint Services 3.0 content sources. This is the only content source that needs no additional configuration beyond a starting address, as the Search service will crawl the appropriate content automatically.
WebContentSource	The WebContentSource enables the crawling of a given web content source

Combined with the each content source is the ability to schedule the crawl for that content source. This is accomplished through the Schedule object, which is used to configure either the full or an incremental crawl schedule.

Extending Enterprise Search

The object model exposed by Enterprise Search makes it completely customizable. You can extend and customize it as necessary with the ability to crawl virtually any content, index it, and then search it as needed, both directly through Microsoft Office SharePoint Server 2007 and through your own applications.

Working with the Query Object Model

SharePoint Server exposes a powerful object model for querying content from varied sources. With it, you can do both keyword- and SQL-based queries, as you discovered earlier in the chapter. Start with the SearchContext object and move on programmatically from there.

Programmatically Returning the SearchContext

You can understand the extensibility of the Enterprise Search object model by examining this short code example that returns a SearchContext. Once you have that, you can walk through the rest of the object model and customize the search functionality as you see fit.

```
using System;
using System.Collections;
using System.Text;
using Microsoft.Office.Server.Search.Administration;
using Microsoft.SharePoint;
    class Program
    {
        static void Main(string[] args)
        {
            string siteURL = "http://windows2003Base ";
            SearchContext context;
            using(SPSite spSite = new SPSite(siteURL))
```

```
        {
            context = SearchContext.GetContext(spSite);
        }
        Content sspContent = new Content(context);
        ContentSourceCollection sspContentSources = sspContent.ContentSources;
        foreach (ContentSource contentSource in sspContentSources)
        {
            Console.WriteLine("Content Source: " + contentSource.Name )
        }
    }
}
```

Using the Enterprise Search Web Service

In addition to using the Query object model, you can access Microsoft Office SharePoint using the Enterprise Search Query web service.

Working with the Proxy Object

You have two options for working with the Enterprise Search Query web service `Proxy` object:

❑   Use Visual Studio to add a Web Reference and then use the generated proxy in your code.

❑   Use `XSD.exe` to generate the proxy from the web service schema. You will typically choose this option if you wish to have greater control over the structure and functionality of your proxy class.

Web Methods

The following Web Methods are exposed by the Web Service provided by Enterprise Search.

GetPortalSearchInfo

The `GetPortalSearchInfo` Web Method returns search results based upon given search input criteria as an XML string.

GetSearchMetadata

The `GetSearchMetadata` Web Method returns the search metadata in an ADO.NET `DataSet` object. The metadata results `DataSet` contains two Data Tables, one for the properties related to the search service and the other for any scopes related to the search service.

Query

The `Query` Web Method returns search results based on given search input criteria as an XML string.

The `Query` method returns the following properties if none are specified in the Query XML request:

❑   Date

❑   Description

❑   Relevance

❑   Title

QueryEx

The `QueryEx` Web Method returns search results based upon given search input criteria as a `DataSet`.

The `QueryEx` Web Method returns the following properties if none is specified in the Query XML request:

- `Author`
- `CollapsingStatus`
- `ContentClass`
- `Description`
- `HitHighlightedProperties`
- `HitHighlightedSummary`
- `IsDocument`
- `Path`
- `PictureThumbnailURL`
- `Rank`
- `SiteName`
- `Size`
- `Title`
- `WorkId`
- `Write`

Configuring Enterprise Search

Before exploring the search capabilities of Microsoft Office SharePoint Server 2007, first you must configure it. Begin by navigating to SharePoint 3.0 Central Administration and clicking on the link to Shared Services Administration, as illustrated in Figure 9-1.

Now that you have navigated to the Shared Services Administration page, click on the Search Settings link, as illustrated in Figure 9-2.

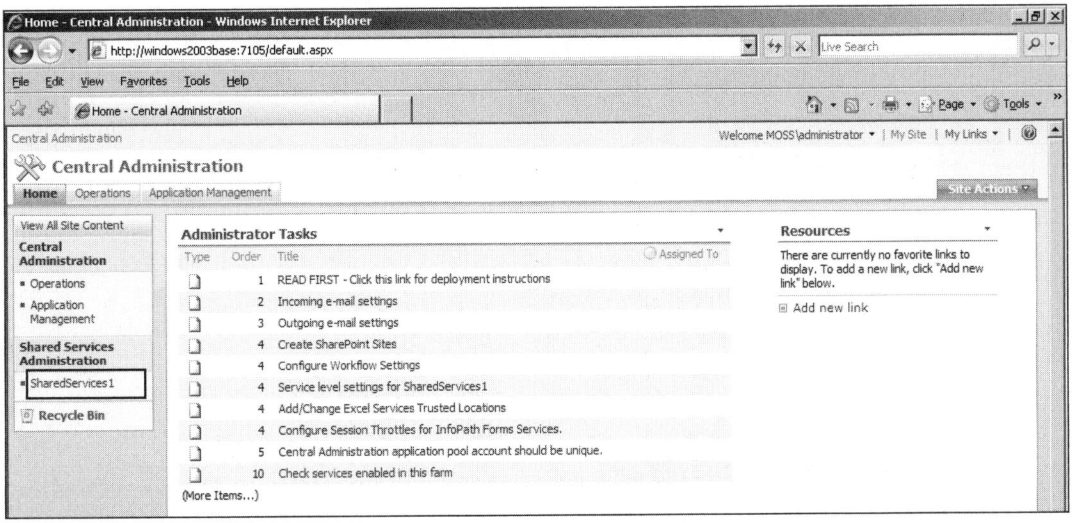

Figure 9-1: Select Shared Services from the Central Administration Page

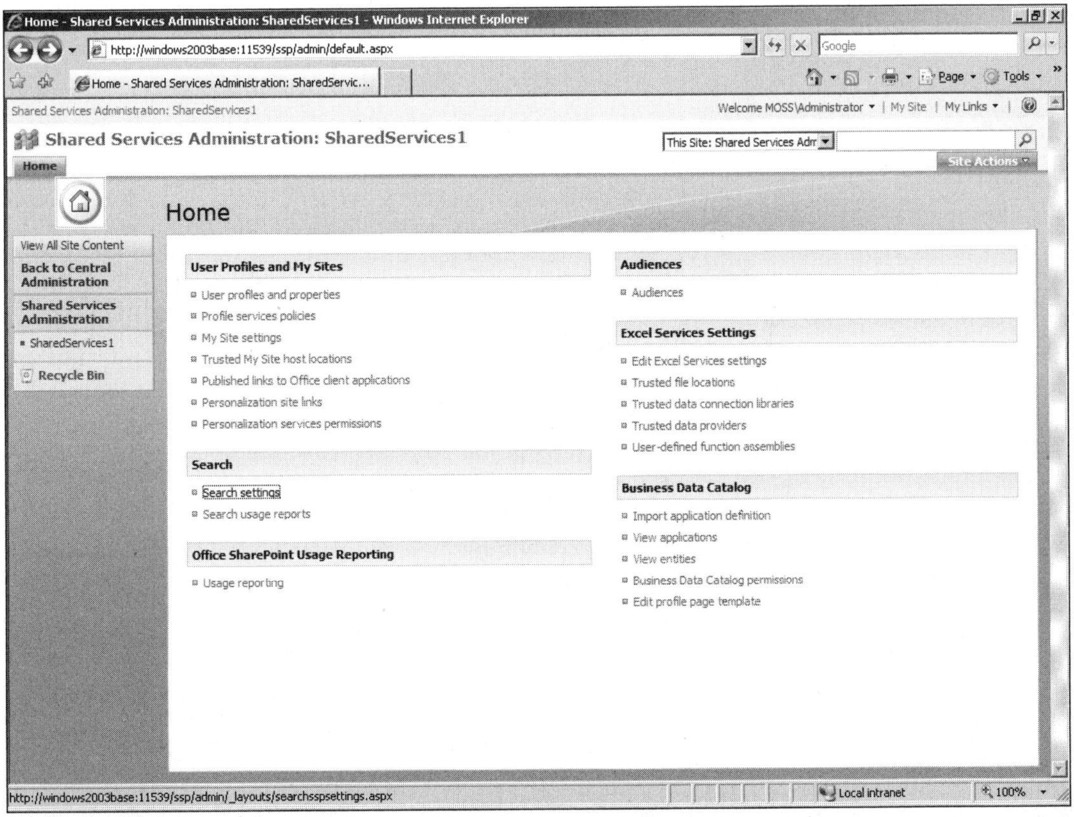

Figure 9-2: Selecting Search Settings from Shared Services Administration Page

There are seven steps involved in configuring Search Settings. They are:

1. Add a content source.

2. Monitor the crawl status.

3. Map the properties.

4. Add a custom tab.

5. Add search pages.

6. Recrawl the content source.

7. Query the content source.

The following sections detail each step for you.

Adding a Content Source

You first need to tell Enterprise Search where it should crawl for content. This is known as the content source.

1. After clicking the Search Settings link, you are presented with several choices. Click on Content Sources and Crawl Schedules to manage existing content sources or to add a new one, as illustrated in Figure 9-3.

2. The next step is to decide what content source you are going to pull from. To assist in that process, you can consider the following questions:

   ❑ Can the content be crawled through an existing ContentSource type? If the answer is yes, you can choose from the list of the currently installed content sources.

   ❑ Have you determined the scope of your content? If the answer is no, you'll want to determine scope before proceeding, as this can greatly impact the amount of time the crawl will take. For example, you'll most likely want to limit your search based on file attributes (a particular location or given file type) or on a rule or set of rules (all sales documents created between April 2006 and June 2006) in order to make the search queries as relevant as possible.

   ❑ Have you determined the properties that you will map to? This is important, as it allows you to link the query and the crawl results.

   Answering these questions beforehand will assist you in accurately planning your content source.

3. In this case, simply point this content source at a web site and then crawl a subset of the content, as illustrated in Figure 9-4.

4. For this example, enter **P2P** into the Name field on the Add Content Source page.

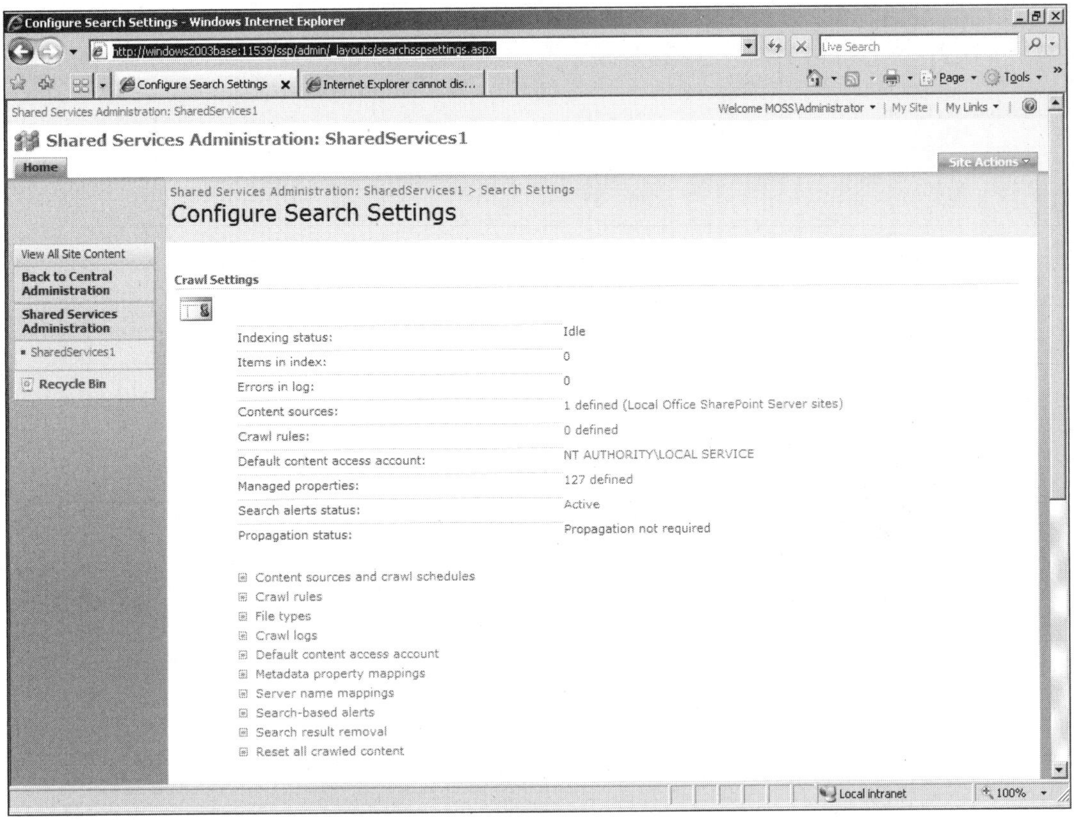

Figure 9-3: Configure Search Settings Page

5. Now, select the type of content to be used. In this example, choose Web Site.

Following that, you need to configure the starting URL of the web site that you want to have crawled by Enterprise Search.

You can add multiple URLs in this pane to be crawled simply by pressing the Return key while inside the pane. Keep in mind when adding multiple web addresses that you are limited to one per line.

Enter **http://www.wrox.com** in the Starting Addresses field.

In addition to entering the general information about the content source, you can also specify the crawling behavior, page depth, and server hop configuration. This information section of the Add Content Source page is available at the bottom portion of the page, as illustrated in Figure 9-5. All of this information gives you significant control over not just what content you crawl but also the level and location of that content.

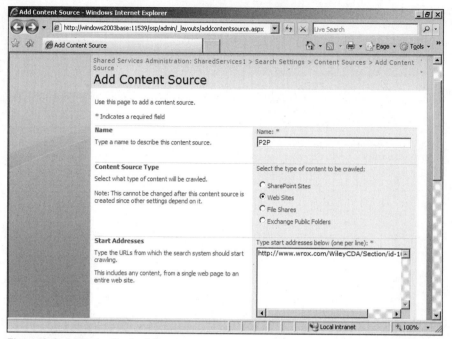

Figure 9-4: Adding a Content Source

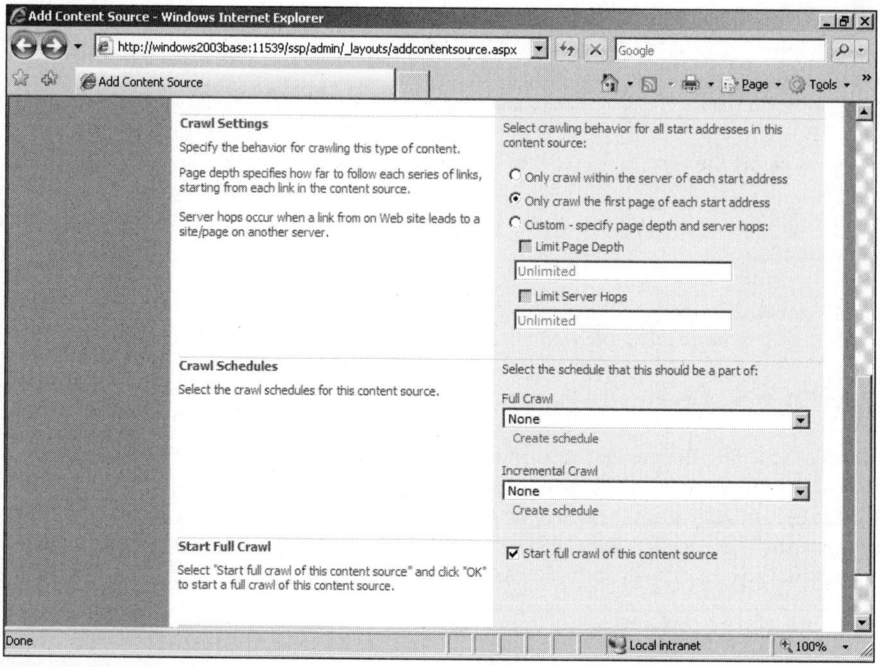

Figure 9-5: Bottom Half of Add Content Source Page

You also can determine at this point whether or not to do a full crawl by selecting the Start full crawl of this content source check box.

When would you want to do an incremental crawl rather than a full crawl? In order to do an incremental crawl, you first must do a full crawl of the content source. Incremental crawls may then be scheduled independently of full crawls and consume much fewer resources than a full crawl. Therefore, you want to schedule an incremental crawl at a time when demand on that particular content source is at a low point.

After entering the content source information, press the OK button located at the bottom of the Add Content Source page.

Monitoring Crawl Status

After clicking the OK button on the Add Content Source, you are redirected to the Manage Content Sources page, as illustrated in Figure 9-6. From this page, you can see the status of the current registered content sources and also access the Crawl Log.

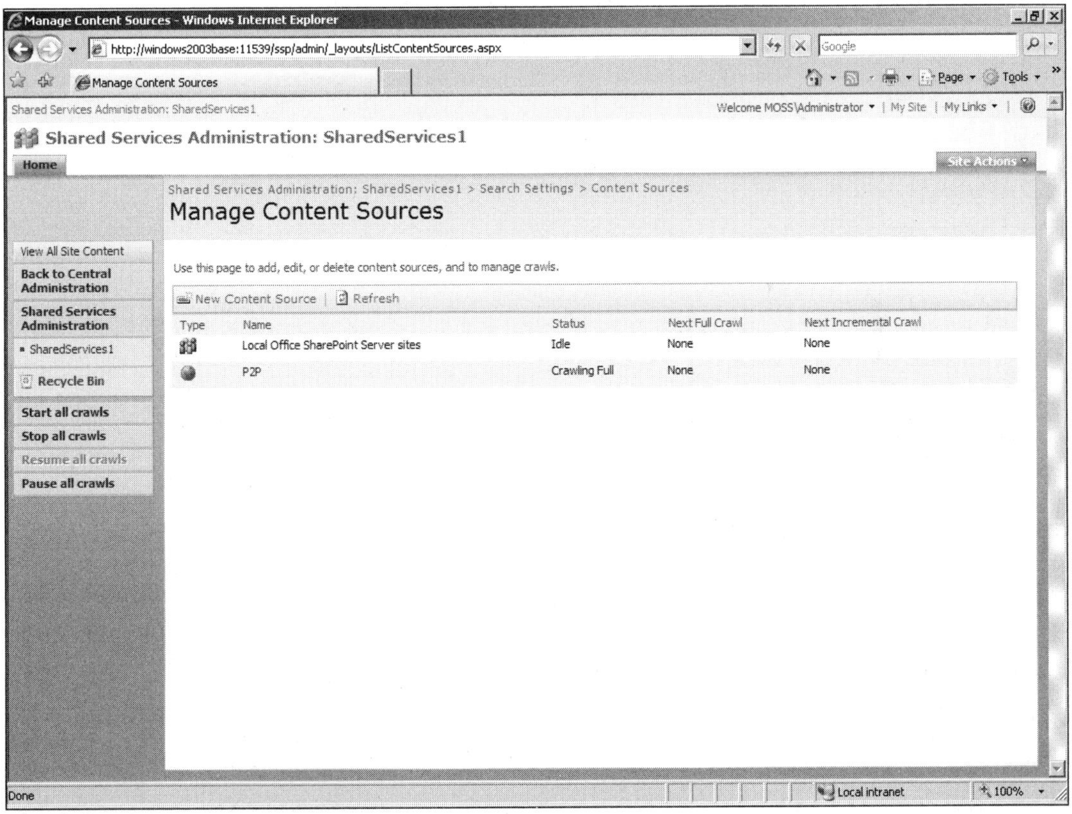

Figure 9-6: Managing Content Sources

Once you've mapped your properties, create a place for the content source results. You don't have to do this, as `SearchCenter` displays the results in the default location, but it will assist in organization, especially if you have multiple content sources.

Mapping Properties

In order to search, you need to know what to search. This is accomplished by mapping crawlable properties for the content source. To do so, execute the following steps:

1. Navigate back to the Search Settings page, as illustrated previously in Figure 9-3, and click on the Metadata Property Mappings link. This is the repository for Administrator configured properties (metadata) and crawler discovered properties (crawled). As you are crawling a web page, you want to map some crawled properties.

2. Click the Crawled Properties button, as illustrated in Figure 9-7. This takes you to the Metadata Property Mappings Crawled Properties View page. This page lists the available content sources and property counts for each.

3. Next, scroll down to find the DESCRIPTION property, and click on it. You will map this crawled property to a managed property in order to support the search query.

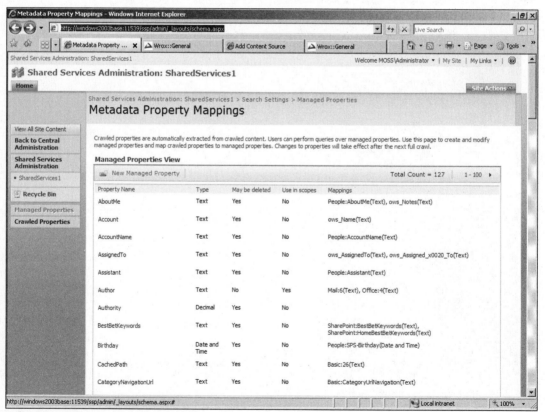

Figure 9-7: Properties Mapping Page

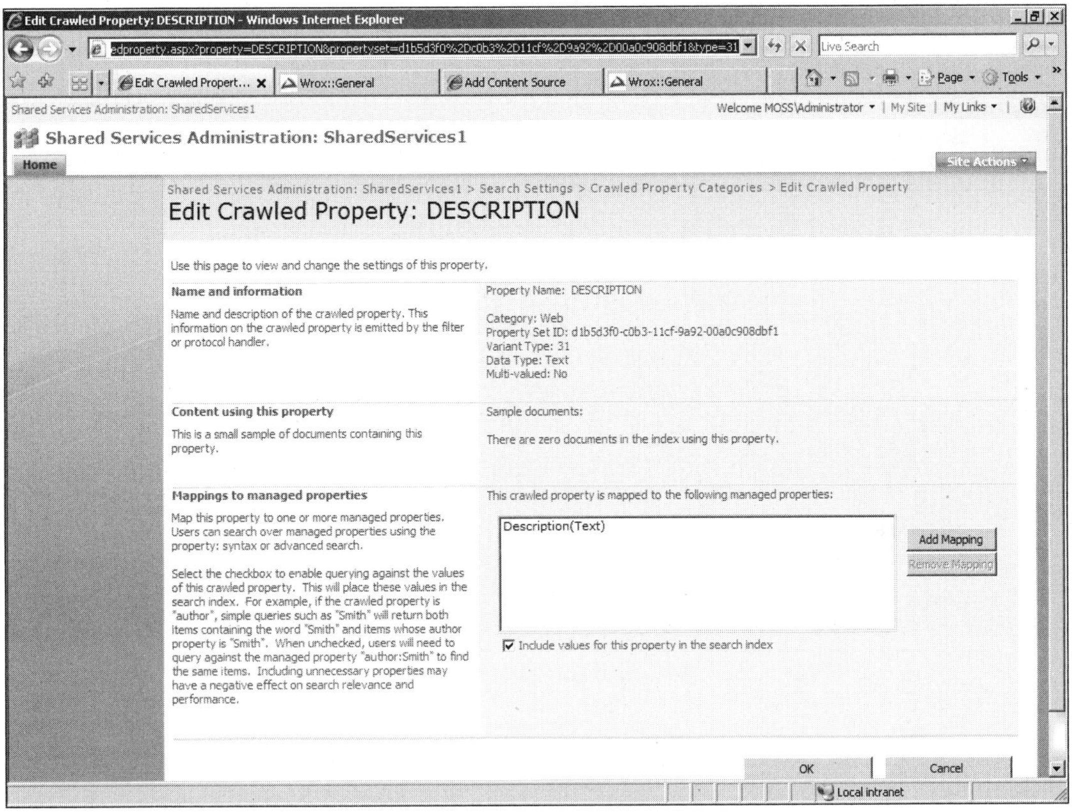

Figure 9-8: Crawled Property Description Page

4. You are then taken to the Edit Crawled Property: DESCRIPTION page, as illustrated in Figure 9-8. Click the Add Mapping button and scroll down to find the `Description` managed property. Click on the property and click OK.

Adding a Custom Tab for Search Results

Once you've mapped your properties, the next thing to do is to create a place for the content source results. You don't have to do this, as `SearchCenter` displays the results in the default location, but it will assist in organization especially if you have multiple content sources.

1. Navigate to `http://<site>/SearchCenter/Pages/default.aspx`.

2. Click Site Actions to access the command menu, as illustrated in Figure 9-9.

3. Click Edit Page on the Site Actions menu.

4. Click Add New Tab to navigate to the page illustrated in Figure 9-10.

5. In the Tab Name field, type **Wrox P2P**.

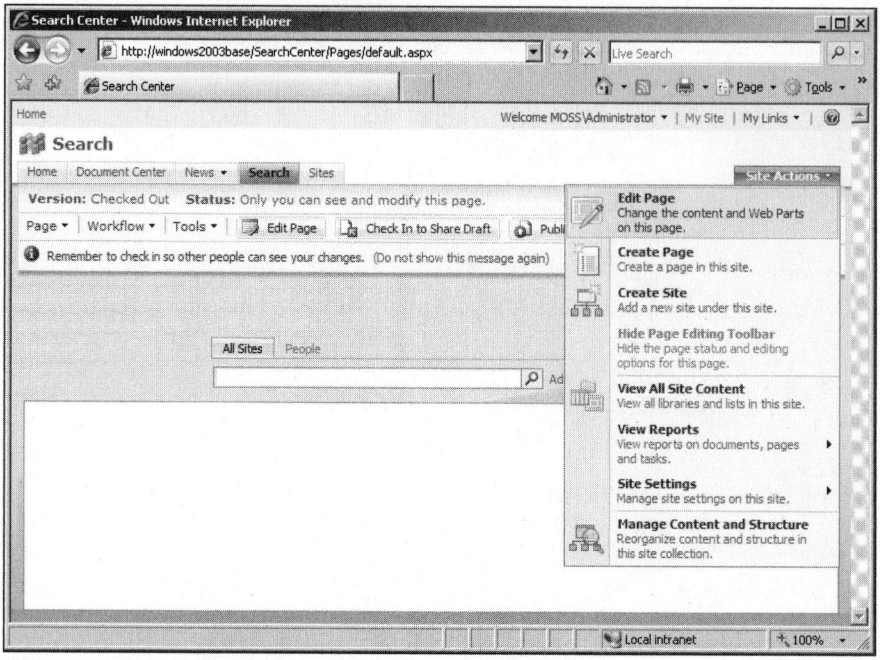

Figure 9-9: Site Actions Menu with Edit Page Highlighted

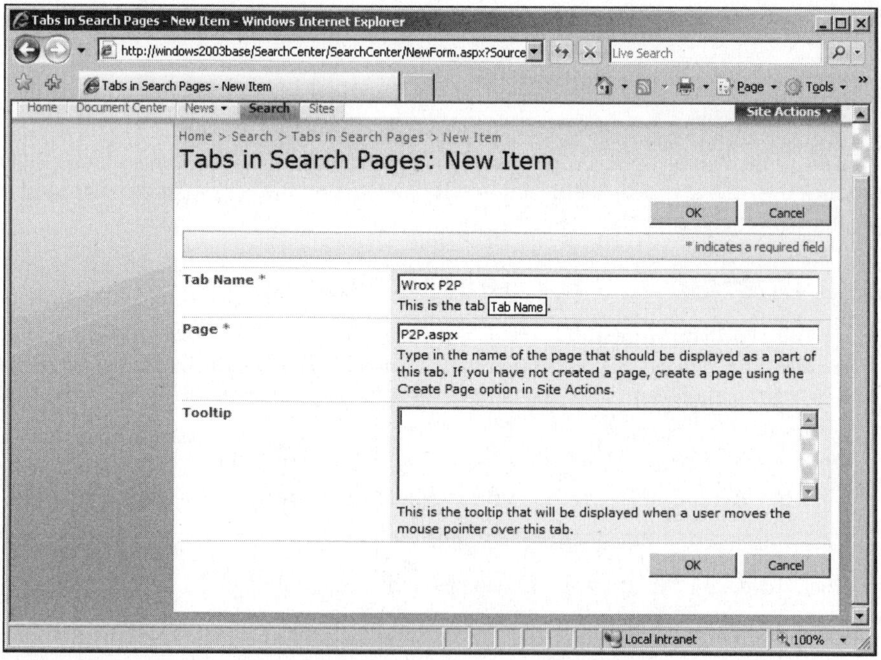

Figure 9-10: Creating a New Tab for the Custom Content Source

6. Next, in the Page field, type **P2P.aspx**.

7. Click the OK button to create the custom tab.

You also need to create a tab for the results as well. Repeat steps 3 through 6 with the following exceptions. For step 4, type **p2p Results.aspx** in the Tab Name field. For step 5, type **p2presults.aspx** in the Page field.

Adding Search Pages to Custom Tabs

In order to be able to view the pages that you added in the fields of the custom search tabs, you need to create them. Navigate back to the Search Center to get started.

1. Click Site Actions to access the command menu again.

2. Click Edit Page on the Site Settings menu.

3. In the URL Name field, type **p2p**.

4. In the Title field, type **P2P** Search.

5. Select (Welcome Page) Search Page in the Page Layout list.

6. Click Create to create the new page referenced in the P2P.

You're getting close to the fruits of your labor. Next, you need to create the page for Search Results. Navigate back to the Search Center to get started.

1. Click Site Actions to access the command menu again.

2. Click Edit Page from the Site Settings menu.

3. In the URL Name field, type **p2presults**.

4. In the Title field, type **P2P Results**.

5. Select (Welcome Page) Search Page in the Page Layout list.

6. Click Create to create the new page referenced in the P2P Results.

Recrawling the Content Source

In order to pick up the changes of your new mapped properties, you need to recrawl the content source.

1. To recrawl, navigate to the Manage Content Sources page.

2. Click on the P2P content source, and click the Open Menu button.

3. Select Start Full Crawl to recrawl the web content source.

Querying the Content Source

Now navigate back to the Search Center and click on the Wrox P2P tab.

Type **ASP.NET** in the Search Box, and click Enter. Your results should be as illustrated in Figure 9-11.

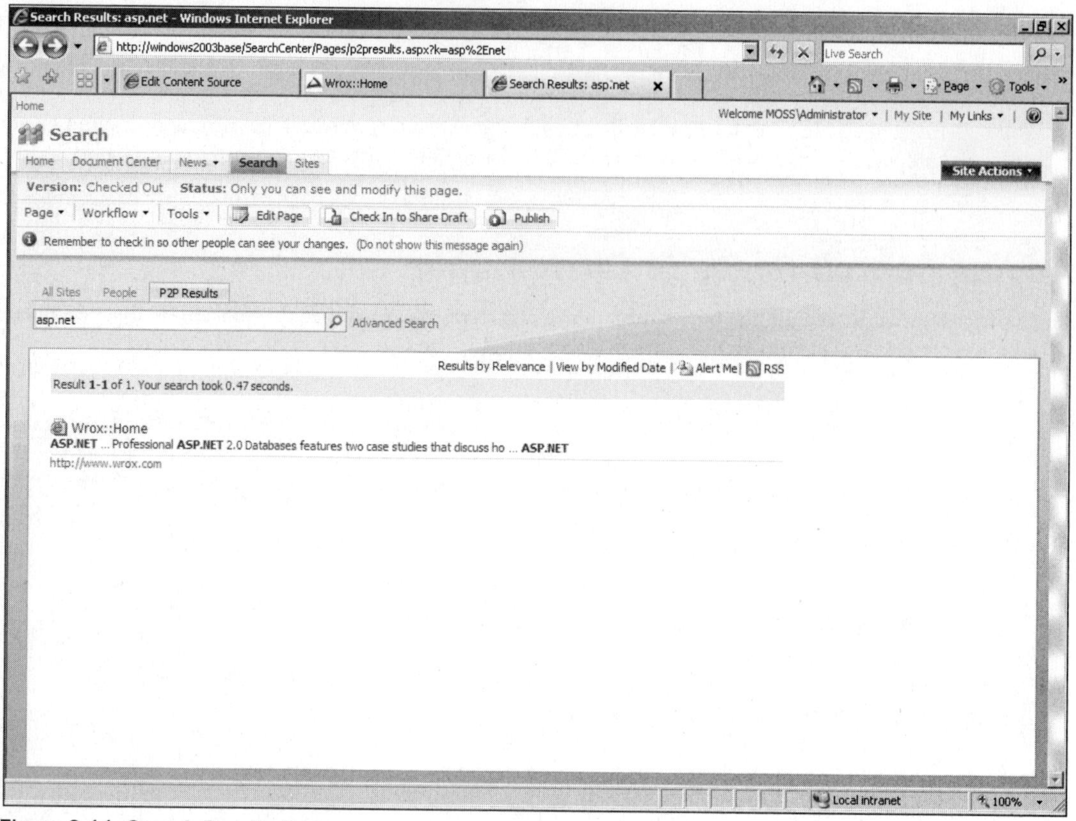

Figure 9-11: Search Results Page

Summary

Search capability, for so long the bane of the SharePoint developer, has been greatly enhanced in Microsoft Office SharePoint Server 2007. You are now able to crawl several different content sources, configure relevancy information and ratios and external business applications using the Business Data Catalog.

In this chapter, you discovered the Enterprise Search object model, learned how to customize the Search UI, and explored the Query object model. By utilizing these extensibility points, you can greatly customize Enterprise Search for your organization. In addition, you also learned to use the Search web service to pull query results back. In the next chapter, you'll discover the power of the Business Data Catalog.

10

Using the Business Data Catalog

By John Alexander

Up until now the options have been limited for effectively searching line-of-business data. Enter the Business Data Catalog (BDC), a shared service that exposes data from enterprise line-of-business applications to Microsoft Windows SharePoint Services 3.0 and Office SharePoint Server 2007. The *Business Data Catalog* is a metadata mapping shared service, enabling line-of-business applications to make data available as Office SharePoint Server 2007 properties.

When you add an application into the BDC, all the exposed application data (types and properties) is made available to all SharePoint Server functionality, either as metadata for other applications and services, Web Parts, or business data lists. This powerful new shared service exposed by Microsoft Office SharePoint Server will be a major element in any integration strategy, as you will see throughout the chapter.

> Note that this chapter focuses on creating applications in the BDC as opposed to consuming them. For a broader discussion of consuming Business Data Catalog applications, please refer to Beginning SharePoint 2007: Building Team Solutions with MOSS 2007 *by Amanda Murphy and Shane Perran, published by Wrox Press.*

In this chapter, you will:

- ❑ Explore the architecture of the Business Data Catalog
- ❑ Learn how to plan best practices for the Business Data Catalog
- ❑ Add an application to the Business Data Catalog
- ❑ Configure an application and expose properties and types through the Business Data Catalog
- ❑ Modify an Application Definition file and add a custom action that is exposed within several Web Parts on the portal

Business Data Catalog Architecture

The BDC has several moving pieces associated with it. Therefore, it's important to examine from a high level the different parts and components that make up the BDC. In order to use the BDC features within SharePoint, such as Business Data Web Parts and Business Data columns in lists, you must first define the metadata.

Major Components of the Business Data Catalog

Following is a short description of the major components that compose the BDC, as illustrated in Figure 10-1.

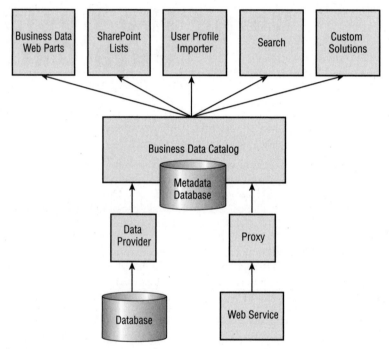

Figure 10-1

Applications

An application is the integration gateway used by the Business Data Catalog. It defines the data entities exposed by a specific line-of-business applicationApplication instance. Once registered, Applications expose the data within instances of business applications that can be surfaced on the portal site through either Web services or databases as LOB data sources and then used through the BDC.

LOB Data Source

LOB Data Source is used to connect an external line-of-business application to the BDC for use within a Microsoft Office SharePoint Server portal site. In Microsoft Office SharePoint Server 2007, the data source can either consist of a database or a web service. When using a database-centric data source, the data provider used is ADO.NET. For a web service, the data provider is accessed through the corresponding web service proxy class.

Surfacing Endpoints

Surfacing endpoints on a portal site consume the information supplied by installed applications in the BDC, such as Web Parts, lists, user profiles, or Search. They can also exist as part of a custom-developed solution using the object model.

Business Data Catalog Communication Service

The BDC is the integration shared service used by Microsoft Office SharePoint Server to connect line-of-business applications with surfacing endpoints. It is one of the shared services provided by Microsoft Office SharePoint Server.

Metadata Database

The Metadata database is the repository used by the Business Data Catalog to store connection and hierarchical information about each of the installed applications. Originally called the "application registry," the corresponding tables are prefixed with AR_ as a holdover from that period. It's important to understand that while the Business Data Catalog stores the application configuration and connection in the database, it connects to the LOB application and exposes the underlying live data from the application as needed.

Hierarchy of the Metadata Model

The heart of communication in the Business Data Catalog is the Metadata Container Model, as illustrated in Figure 10-2. It is the object model that corresponds to the Application Definition file used to register a line-of-business application and is used by the Business Data Catalog to navigate through the hierarchal definition provided upon application registry.

LOBSystem

The LOBSystem is the topmost definition for the line-of-business application. Hierarchically speaking, it is the root from which the rest of the application springs. Everything that defines the application begins with the LOBSystem. The LOBSystem must have a unique name and is either defined as a database or web service type. As it is the heart of the line-of-business application, LOBSystem derives directly from the MetadataObject.

LOBSystemInstances

The LobSystemInstances collection contains system instance-specific objects for each business application.

The LobSystemInstance object represents a specific instance of a line-of-business application that is integrated by the Business Data Catalog. Thus, the LobSystemInstance object is responsible for supplying both connection string parameters and authentication settings' information to the Business Data Catalog. This object requires a unique name because of the instance association.

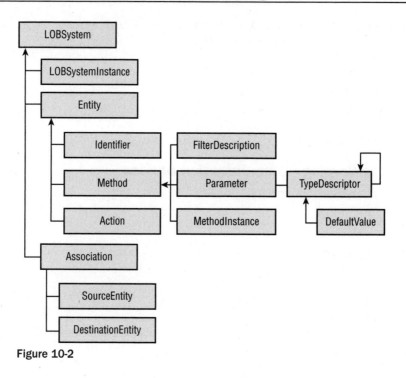

Figure 10-2

Entities

There is an `Entities` collection within each `LobSystemInstance`. The `Entity` element corresponds to each data entity that is a part of the `Application` instance. Each entity can have its own methods, properties, actions, and filters (and other elements defined by you as well). Entities can also be associated with one another, providing relationships that can be used in Web Parts and lists. The following table lists the top-level properties and container elements found within the entity.

Name	Description
Actions	Container element for `Action`
EstimatedInstanceCount	Estimated count of entity instances
Identifiers	Container element for `Identifier`
Methods	Container element for `Method`

Identifiers

Regardless of whether you are using a web service proxy or an ADO.NET data provider, the Entity element has an optional `Identifier`. In most cases, you will want to have an identifier associated with an `Entity`, because without it the `Entity` is little more than a data repository that will be used as a part of another associated `Entity`. However, when you include an `Identifier` with an `Entity`, you can then create custom actions and many other features that you will see firsthand when you substantially modify the `CustomerAddress Entity` later in the chapter.

Parameters

As with any data entity you'd care to manipulate, you'll frequently want to filter or limit the resultset in some form or fashion. The `Parameters` collection within the `Entity` is used just for that purpose (namely, to enable you to parameterize the `Entity` queries).

Methods

Each `Entity` can have one or more `Method` elements. The purpose of a `Method` is to provide an interaction mechanism for the `Entity`. Each method defines a set of input and return parameters, filters, and specific instance information.

MethodInstance

A `Method` is not executable, but a `MethodInstance` is. A `MethodInstance` is used to determine how the `Method` will be used, what will be used as parameters and then what return types (or parts of return types) specifically will be returned. Given this, you can use the same `Method` to satisfy different requirements by adding a new `MethodInstance` element and setting the parameters accordingly.

Finders

`Finder` Methods assist with choosing a specific `MethodInstance` for usage. This `MethodInstance` returns all specific `Entity` instances. For example, the SQL statement associated with a `Finder` method has no WHERE clause:

```
SELECT * FROM Products
```

To be considered a `Finder` method, the method must expose filterable parameters, return `Entity` collections that contain a primary key, and have only a single associated `MethodInstance`.

SpecificFinders

`SpecificFinder` Methods assist you with choosing a specific `MethodInstance` for usage as well. However, this `MethodInstance` returns all specific `Entity` instances for a given criteria. For example, the SQL statement associated with a `SpecificFinder` method has a corresponding WHERE clause:

```
SELECT * FROM Products WHERE ProductID = productNo
```

To be considered a `SpecificFinder` method, the method must expose a parameter that contains a key for a specific `Entity` instance, return corresponding `Entity` fields that include a primary key for that instance, and have only a single associated `MethodInstance`.

FilterDescriptors

`FilterDescriptors` allow for greater control over user input before passing it to the corresponding line-of-business application. Business Data Catalog `FilterDescriptors` are an excellent illustration of the relationship between the Business Data Catalog and the line-of-business application. The BDC provides filter criteria to the line-of-business application's corresponding method. The actual filtering of the requested data takes place in the line-of-business application method that then surfaces the data through the BDC. These objects determine the valid criteria for the MethodInstance.

Filters are implemented through the use of filter patterns to appropriately match the filtering requirements of the line-of-business application. The following table lists the different types of valid filter patterns within an Entity's MethodInstance.

Filter Pattern	Description
Comparison	Enables exact searches based on the comparison criteria defined.
LastIDSeen	Allows for grouping ID enumerators to assist with MethodInstance call performance optimization.
Limit	Enables searches to have a defined limit of returned results.
Password	Used in conjunction with the UserName filter pattern.
SSOTicket	Specifies that the MethodInstance should pass in the related SSOTickets as part of the call.
UserContext	Allows for specifying searches within the given user context. When used, the corresponding domain and user name will be appended to the MethodInstance Method call by the Business Data Catalog.
UserName	Specifies that searches should use a specific SSO (Single Sign-On) User Name as part of a parameter when calling a specific MethodInstance.
UserProfile	Enables the Business Data Catalog to pass back the corresponding user profile property (from the user's UserProfile) as part of the MethodInstance call upon setting the UserProfilePropertyName parameter.
Wildcard	Allows for filtering of "where like value" specified by the wildcard character defined by the LOBSystem Object. Enables criteria searches such as "Starts With."

Associations

Associations define relationships between Entities within a line-of-business application. An association is defined by the SourceEntity instance and DestinationEntity instance contained within. Both the SourceEntity and DestinationEntity must be within the same LOBSystem. In order to facilitate foreign key relationships, an association can have multiple SourceEntities, but many only contain a single DestinationEntity. The MethodInstances for the associations can be in any Entity.

You must define any Entity referenced in an Association before defining the Entity that contains the Association. This is due to the way that the Application Definition file is parsed. As it is parsed top-down, you'll get an error if you reference an Entity before it has been defined.

The XML Application Definition File in Detail

The metadata model is exposed as XML in the Application Definition file. Within Microsoft Office Share-Point Server 2007, both `Model` and `Resource` Application Definition file types are supported. The `Model` Application Definition file, which is the type you will typically use, contains the structure and metadata necessary for application registration. The `Resource` file type is similar in concept to an include file, in that the information they contain will update any corresponding settings in the Metadata repository. In MOSS 2007, `Resource` files can either be of the `LocalizedNames`, `Properties`, or `Permissions` type. Listing 10-1 illustrates the application definition file for selected tables (Product and ProductReview) of the Adventureworks 2005 sample database. Use the object model explanation you read previously in the chapter to assist you in analyzing the structure of this file. Engaging in this exercise will aid in your understanding of how the Application Definition file works.

> ### Do I Really Have to Deal with the XML Directly?
>
> While the object of this chapter is to assist you with a deep understanding of the Business Data Catalog application definition, the answer is no. You can use some of the visual tools that allow you to build and edit the Application Definition File. Some of these are from the BDC team at Microsoft, while others are from ISV or community sources. Use the search term "Business Data Catalog tools" in your favorite search engine for more information.

Listing 10-1: The database application definition file

```xml
<?xml version="1.0" encoding="utf-8" standalone="yes"?>
<LobSystem xmlns:xsi="http://www.w3.org/2001/XMLSchema-instance"
xsi:schemaLocation="http://schemas.microsoft.com/office/2006/03/BusinessDataCatalog
BDCMetadata.xsd" Type="Database" Version="1.0.0.0" Name="AdventureWorksLOBSystem"
xmlns="http://schemas.microsoft.com/office/2006/03/BusinessDataCatalog">
    <Properties>
        <Property Name="WildcardCharacter" Type="System.String">%</Property>
    </Properties>
    <LobSystemInstances>
        <LobSystemInstance Name="AdventureWorksInstance">
            <Properties>
                <Property Name="DatabaseAccessProvider" Type=
"Microsoft.Office.Server.ApplicationRegistry.SystemSpecific.Db.DbAccessProvider">
SqlServer</Property>
                <Property Name="AuthenticationMode"
Type="Microsoft.Office.Server.ApplicationRegistry.SystemSpecific.Db
.DbAuthenticationMode">PassThrough</Property>
                <Property Name="RdbConnection Data Source" Type="System.String">
(local)</Property>
                <Property Name="RdbConnection Initial Catalog" Type=
"System.String">AdventureWorks</Property>
                <Property Name="RdbConnection Integrated Security" Type=
"System.String">SSPI</Property>
```

```xml
                    <Property Name="RdbConnection Pooling" Type="
System.String">false</Property>
                </Properties>
            </LobSystemInstance>
        </LobSystemInstances>
    <Entities>
        <Entity EstimatedInstanceCount="0" Name="Production.Product">
            <Properties>
                <Property Name="DefaultAction" Type="System.String">
View Profile</Property>
            </Properties>
            <Identifiers>
                <Identifier TypeName="System.Int32" Name="ProductID" />
            </Identifiers>
            <Methods>
                <Method Name="GetProduction.Product">
                    <Properties>
                        <Property Name="RdbCommandText" Type="System.String">Select
ProductID,Name,ProductNumber,MakeFlag,FinishedGoodsFlag,Color,SafetyStockLevel,
ReorderPoint,StandardCost,ListPrice,Size,SizeUnitMeasureCode,WeightUnitMeasureCode,
Weight,DaysToManufacture,ProductLine,Class,Style,ProductSubcategoryID,ProductModelID,
SellStartDate,SellEndDate,DiscontinuedDate,rowguid,ModifiedDate From Production
.Product Where (ProductID&gt;=@GeneratedMinProductID) and (ProductID&lt;=
@GeneratedMaxProductID)</Property>
                        <Property Name="RdbCommandType" Type=
"System.Data.CommandType, System.Data, Version=2.0.0.0, Culture=neutral,
PublicKeyToken=b77a5c561934e089">Text</Property>
                    </Properties>
                    <FilterDescriptors>
                        <FilterDescriptor Type="Comparison" Name="ProductID" />
                    </FilterDescriptors>
                    <Parameters>
                        <Parameter Direction="In" Name="@GeneratedMinProductID">
                            <TypeDescriptor TypeName="System.Int32"
IdentifierName="ProductID" AssociatedFilter="ProductID" Name="ProductID">
                                <DefaultValues>
                                    <DefaultValue
MethodInstanceName="Production.ProductFinder" Type="System.Int32">0</DefaultValue>
                                    <DefaultValue MethodInstanceName=
"Production.ProductSpecificFinder" Type="System.Int32">0</DefaultValue>
                                </DefaultValues>
                            </TypeDescriptor>
                        </Parameter>
                        <Parameter Direction="In" Name="@GeneratedMaxProductID">
                            <TypeDescriptor TypeName="System.Int32" IdentifierName=
"ProductID" AssociatedFilter="ProductID" Name="ProductID">
                                <DefaultValues>
                                    <DefaultValue MethodInstanceName=
"Production.ProductFinder" Type="System.Int32">9999999</DefaultValue>
                                    <DefaultValue MethodInstanceName=
"Production.ProductSpecificFinder" Type="System.Int32">9999999</DefaultValue>
                                </DefaultValues>
                            </TypeDescriptor>
                        </Parameter>
```

```
                    <Parameter Direction="Return" Name="Production.Product">
                        <TypeDescriptor TypeName="System.Data.IDataReader,
System.Data, Version=2.0.3600.0, Culture=neutral, PublicKeyToken=b77a5c561934e089"
IsCollection="true" Name="Production.ProductDataReader">
                            <TypeDescriptors>
                                <TypeDescriptor
TypeName="System.Data.IDataRecord, System.Data, Version=2.0.3600.0,
Culture=neutral, PublicKeyToken=b77a5c561934e089"
Name="Production.ProductDataRecord">
                                    <TypeDescriptors>
                                        <TypeDescriptor TypeName=
"System.Int32" IdentifierName="ProductID" Name="ProductID" />
                                        <TypeDescriptor TypeName=
"System.String" Name="Name" />
                                        <TypeDescriptor TypeName=
"System.String" Name="ProductNumber" />
                                        <TypeDescriptor TypeName=
"System.Boolean" Name="MakeFlag" />
                                        <TypeDescriptor TypeName=
"System.Boolean" Name="FinishedGoodsFlag" />
                                        <TypeDescriptor TypeName=
"System.String" Name="Color" />
                                        <TypeDescriptor TypeName=
"System.Int16" Name="SafetyStockLevel" />
                                        <TypeDescriptor TypeName=
"System.Int16" Name="ReorderPoint" />
                                        <TypeDescriptor TypeName=
"System.Decimal" Name="StandardCost" />
                                        <TypeDescriptor TypeName=
"System.Decimal" Name="ListPrice" />
                                        <TypeDescriptor TypeName=
"System.String" Name="Size" />
                                        <TypeDescriptor TypeName=
"System.String" Name="SizeUnitMeasureCode" />
                                        <TypeDescriptor TypeName=
"System.String" Name="WeightUnitMeasureCode" />
                                        <TypeDescriptor TypeName=
"System.Decimal" Name="Weight" />
                                        <TypeDescriptor TypeName=
"System.Int32" Name="DaysToManufacture" />
                                        <TypeDescriptor TypeName=
"System.String" Name="ProductLine" />
                                        <TypeDescriptor TypeName=
"System.String" Name="Class" />
                                        <TypeDescriptor TypeName=
"System.String" Name="Style" />
                                        <TypeDescriptor TypeName=
"System.Int32" Name="ProductSubcategoryID" />
                                        <TypeDescriptor TypeName=
"System.Int32" Name="ProductModelID" />
                                        <TypeDescriptor TypeName=
"System.DateTime" Name="SellStartDate" />
                                        <TypeDescriptor TypeName=
"System.DateTime" Name="SellEndDate" />
```

```
                                                <TypeDescriptor TypeName=
"System.DateTime" Name="DiscontinuedDate" />
                                                <TypeDescriptor TypeName="System.Guid"
Name="rowguid" />
                                                <TypeDescriptor TypeName=
"System.DateTime" Name="ModifiedDate" />
                                        </TypeDescriptors>
                                    </TypeDescriptor>
                                </TypeDescriptors>
                            </TypeDescriptor>
                        </Parameter>
                    </Parameters>
                    <MethodInstances>
                        <MethodInstance Type="Finder" ReturnParameterName=
"Production.Product" ReturnTypeDescriptorName="Production.ProductDataReader"
ReturnTypeDescriptorLevel="0" Name="Production.ProductFinder" />
                        <MethodInstance Type="SpecificFinder" ReturnParameterName=
"Production.Product" ReturnTypeDescriptorName="Production.ProductDataReader"
ReturnTypeDescriptorLevel="0" Name="Production.ProductSpecificFinder" />
                    </MethodInstances>
                </Method>
            </Methods>
            <Actions>
                <Action Position="1" IsOpenedInNewWindow="false" Url="http://
windows2003base:11539/ssp/admin/Content/Production.Product.aspx?ProductID={0}"
ImageUrl="/_layouts/1033/images/viewprof.gif" Name="View Profile">
                    <ActionParameters>
                        <ActionParameter Index="0" Name="ProductID" />
                    </ActionParameters>
                </Action>
            </Actions>
        </Entity>
        <Entity EstimatedInstanceCount="0" Name="Production.ProductReview">
            <Properties>
                <Property Name="DefaultAction" Type="System.String">View Profile<
/Property>
            </Properties>
            <Identifiers>
                <Identifier TypeName="System.Int32" Name="ProductReviewID" />
            </Identifiers>
            <Methods>
                <Method Name="GetProduction.ProductReview">
                    <Properties>
                        <Property Name="RdbCommandText" Type="System.String">
Select ProductReviewID,ProductID,ReviewerName,ReviewDate,EmailAddress,Rating,
Comments,ModifiedDate From Production.ProductReview Where (ProductReviewID&gt;=
@GeneratedMinProductReviewID) and (ProductReviewID&lt;=
@GeneratedMaxProductReviewID)</Property>
                        <Property Name="RdbCommandType" Type=
"System.Data.CommandType, System.Data, Version=2.0.0.0, Culture=neutral,
PublicKeyToken=b77a5c561934e089">Text</Property>
                    </Properties>
                    <FilterDescriptors>
```

```
                        <FilterDescriptor Type="Comparison" Name="ProductReviewID" />
                    </FilterDescriptors>
                    <Parameters>
                        <Parameter Direction="In" Name=
"@GeneratedMinProductReviewID">
                            <TypeDescriptor TypeName="System.Int32" IdentifierName=
"ProductReviewID" AssociatedFilter="ProductReviewID" Name="ProductReviewID">
                                <DefaultValues>
                                    <DefaultValue MethodInstanceName=
"Production.ProductReviewFinder" Type="System.Int32">0</DefaultValue>
                                    <DefaultValue MethodInstanceName=
"Production.ProductReviewSpecificFinder" Type="System.Int32">0</DefaultValue>
                                </DefaultValues>
                            </TypeDescriptor>
                        </Parameter>
                        <Parameter Direction="In" Name=
"@GeneratedMaxProductReviewID">
                            <TypeDescriptor TypeName="System.Int32" IdentifierName=
"ProductReviewID" AssociatedFilter="ProductReviewID" Name="ProductReviewID">
                                <DefaultValues>
                                    <DefaultValue MethodInstanceName=
"Production.ProductReviewFinder" Type="System.Int32">9999999</DefaultValue>
                                    <DefaultValue MethodInstanceName=
"Production.ProductReviewSpecificFinder" Type="System.Int32">9999999</DefaultValue>
                                </DefaultValues>
                            </TypeDescriptor>
                        </Parameter>
                        <Parameter Direction="Return" Name=
"Production.ProductReview">
                            <TypeDescriptor TypeName="System.Data.IDataReader,
System.Data, Version=2.0.3600.0, Culture=neutral, PublicKeyToken=b77a5c561934e089"
IsCollection="true" Name="Production.ProductReviewDataReader">
                                <TypeDescriptors>
                                    <TypeDescriptor TypeName=
"System.Data.IDataRecord, System.Data, Version=2.0.3600.0, Culture=neutral,
PublicKeyToken=b77a5c561934e089" Name="Production.ProductReviewDataRecord">
                                        <TypeDescriptors>
                                            <TypeDescriptor TypeName=
"System.Int32" IdentifierName="ProductReviewID" Name="ProductReviewID" />
                                            <TypeDescriptor TypeName=
"System.Int32" Name="ProductID" />
                                            <TypeDescriptor TypeName=
"System.String" Name="ReviewerName" />
                                            <TypeDescriptor TypeName=
"System.DateTime" Name="ReviewDate" />
                                            <TypeDescriptor TypeName=
"System.String" Name="EmailAddress" />
                                            <TypeDescriptor TypeName=
"System.Int32" Name="Rating" />
                                            <TypeDescriptor TypeName=
"System.String" Name="Comments" />
                                            <TypeDescriptor TypeName=
"System.DateTime" Name="ModifiedDate" />
```

```
                                        </TypeDescriptors>
                                    </TypeDescriptor>
                                </TypeDescriptors>
                            </TypeDescriptor>
                        </Parameter>
                    </Parameters>
                    <MethodInstances>
                        <MethodInstance Type="Finder" ReturnParameterName=
    "Production.ProductReview" ReturnTypeDescriptorName=
    "Production.ProductReviewDataReader" ReturnTypeDescriptorLevel="0" Name=
    "Production.ProductReviewFinder" />
                        <MethodInstance Type="SpecificFinder" ReturnParameterName=
    "Production.ProductReview" ReturnTypeDescriptorName=
    "Production.ProductReviewDataReader" ReturnTypeDescriptorLevel="0" Name=
    "Production.ProductReviewSpecificFinder" />
                    </MethodInstances>
                </Method>
            </Methods>
            <Actions>
                <Action Position="1" IsOpenedInNewWindow="false" Url="http://
    windows2003base:11539/ssp/admin/Content/Production.ProductReview.aspx?ProductReviewID=
    {0}" ImageUrl="/_layouts/1033/images/viewprof.gif" Name="View Profile">
                    <ActionParameters>
                        <ActionParameter Index="0" Name="ProductReviewID" />
                    </ActionParameters>
                </Action>
            </Actions>
        </Entity>
    </Entities>
</LobSystem>
```

So let's explore the file, starting with the outermost element, LobSystem. As previously discussed, the LOBSystem element contains the top-level definition for a line-of-business application.

LOBSystem Element Detailed Breakdown

Everything that defines the application begins with the LOBSystem. The LOBSystem must have a unique name and is either defined as a database or web service type, as illustrated in the following code snippet.

```
<LobSystem xmlns:xsi="http://www.w3.org/2001/XMLSchema-instance" xsi:
schemaLocation="http://schemas.microsoft.com/office/2006/03/BusinessDataCatalog
BDCMetadata.XSD" xmlns="http://schemas.microsoft.com/office/2006/03/
BusinessDataCatalog" Type="Database" Version="1.0.0.0"
Name="AdventureWorksLOBSystem">
```

The following table describes the children of the LobSystem element.

Child	Description
Associations	Container element for related Association collection.
Entities	Container element for related Entity collection.

Child	Description
LobSystemInstances	Container element for related LobSystemInstance collection.
Type	The type of system. Currently either "Database" or "Web Service."
Version	The version of the application definition. The Business Data Catalog prevents you from overwriting a system with the same name and a lower version number.

SystemUtility, ConnectionManager, and EntityInstance are all valid attributes of LobInstance. However, they are included for extensible LobSystem types, which will be supported in a future version of SharePoint Server.

In addition to the child attributes for LOBSystem, you can also use the following properties to assist you with using wildcards.

Properties within LOBSystem

The LOBSystem properties enable you to configure the top-level object container according to the requirements of your external system. As illustrated in the following code snippet, you can accomplish customizations such as specifying the wildcard character to be used in searching.

```
<Properties>
<Property Name="WildcardCharacter" Type="System.String">
%
</Property>
</Properties>
```

The following table describes the properties that the LobSystem object accepts for database systems.

Filter Properties	Description
WildcardCharacter	The system-specific wildcard string. The wildcard filter replaces "*" in the filter value with this string. For example, the SQL Server wildcard string is "%".
WildcardCharacterEscapeFormat	This is the system-specific wildcard string escape sequence in the filter.

LOBSystemInstances Detailed Breakdown

The LOBSystemInstances' properties enable you to do tasks such as determining how you will connect to the application or setting the mode of authentication, as shown in Listing 10-2.

Listing 10-2: LobSystemInstances

```
<LobSystemInstances>
<LobSystemInstance Name="AdventureWorksInstance">
```

```
<Properties>
<Property Name="AuthenticationMode" Type="System.String">
 PassThrough
</Property>
<Property Name="RdbConnection Data Source" Type="System.String">
DN\SQLEXPRESS
</Property>
<Property Name="RdbConnection Initial Catalog" Type="System.String">
AdventureWorks
</Property>
<Property Name="RdbConnection Integrated Security" Type="System.String">
SSPI
</Property>
<Property Name="RdbConnection Pooling" Type="System.String">
False
</Property>
</Properties>
</LobSystemInstance>
</LobSystemInstances>
```

Following are the properties that the LobSystemInstance object accepts for database systems.

Property	Comments
AuthenticationMode	Mode of authentication.
DatabaseAccessProvider	The specific database provider used in accessing the application.
NumberOfConnections	The maximum number of allowed simultaneous system connections. Set the value to -1 if you wish to have an unlimited number of connections.
RdbConnection Data Source	
RdbConnection Integrated Security	
RdbConnection Initial Catalog	
RdbConnection Pooling	Each of these properties deal with connecting to the database. Through these you can specify the data source, the default database, and whether you want to use integrated security or take advantage of connection pooling.
SecondarySsoApplicationId	The SSO enterprise application definition credential store ID for secondary credentials.

Property	Comments
SsoApplicationId	The SSO enterprise application definition that contains credentials used for database connections' information.
SsoProviderImplementation	The ISsoProvider implementation fully qualified type name containing the database account credentials.

Connecting to Databases

In order to import an application definition, such as the one in Code Listing 10-1, navigate to the shared services' Control Panel page. Next, click the Import Application Definition link, as illustrated in Figure 10-3.

Next, browse for the file as illustrated in Figure 10-4. Scroll down to the bottom of the page, and click the Import button. At this point, the XML file will be imported into the Business Data Catalog, ready for you to use in your MOSS 2007 applications.

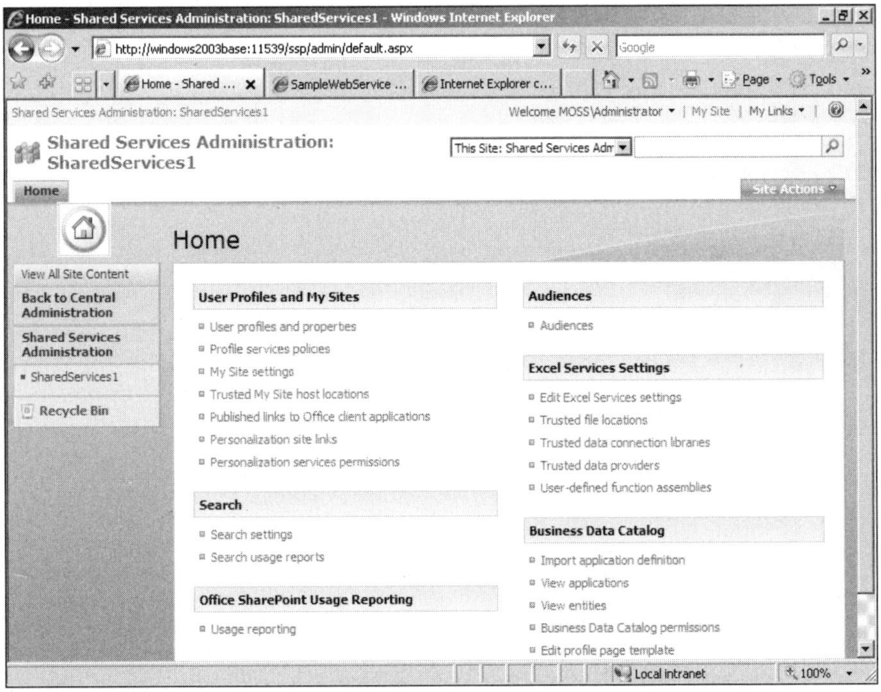

Figure 10-3

The database Application Type *is fairly straightforward to use and is covered in Beginning SharePoint 2007: Building Team Solutions with MOSS 2007 by Amanda Murphy and Shane Perran, published by Wrox Press. As working with the web service application type is a more advanced topic, that is where the bulk of remaining time in this chapter is spent. Keep in mind that working with Web Parts is the same for either application type.*

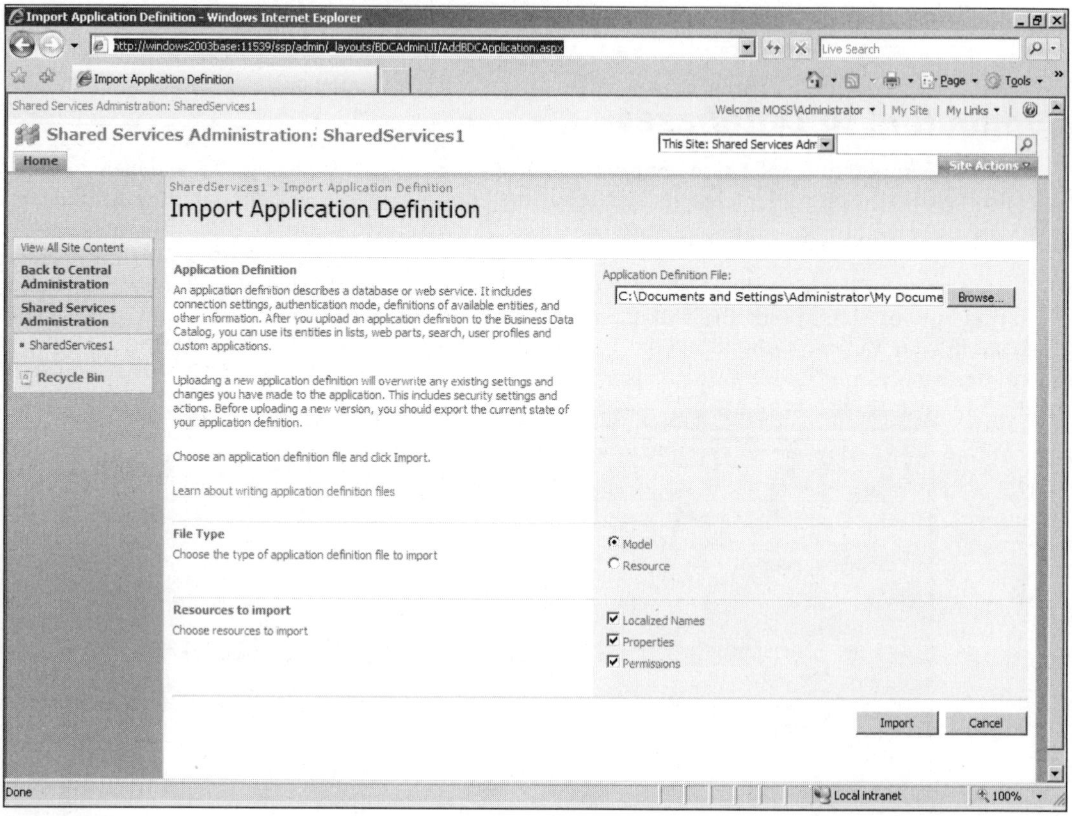

Figure 10-4

Connecting to Web Services

You connect database applications through ADO.NET. All other applications, such as SAP R/3, or Microsoft Dynamics, use web services to connect to the Business Data Catalog. A great place to start is to examine the SampleWebService sample Application Definition file. First, this section explores the web service application definition–specific settings, and then later you modify the file to add a custom action.

Following is a high-level overview of web-service-specific settings for each of the Business Data Catalog elements.

Web Service Specific Properties of the LobSystem Object

For web-service-specific systems, these additional `LobSystem` object properties may be used. As might be expected, these properties deal with the security and communication aspects of a web service Business Data Catalog application, as illustrated in the following table.

Property	Description
WebProxyServerConfiguration	Configuration file location path.
WebServiceProxyNamespace	Designated namespace used for web service proxy class generation.
WebServiceProxyProtocol	Web service protocol.
WebServiceProxyType	Fully qualified type name of a type in place of the autogenerated web service proxy.
WsdlFetchAuthenticationMode	Authentication mode used while fetching the Web Service Discovery Language (WSDL) file.
WsdlFetchSsoApplicationId	Fully qualified type name of the Single Service Offering Provider Interface (`ISsoProvider`) credential store implementation used while fetching the web services discovery document or WSDL file.
WsdlFetchSsoProviderImplementation	Fully qualified type name of the Single Service Offering Provider Interface (`ISsoProvider`) implementation used while fetching the web services discovery document or WSDL file.
WsdlFetchUrl	URL used for web service discovery.

Web Service Specific Properties of the LobSystemInstance Object

For web-service-specific systems, these additional `LobSystemInstance` object properties can be used. As might be expected, these properties deal with the security and communication aspects of a web service Business Data Catalog application instance.

Property	Description
NumberOfConnections	Maximum number of simultaneous connections to allow to the system. If the value is -1, there is no maximum.
SecondarySsoApplicationId	ID of the SSO enterprise application definition that stores credentials used, `Username` filter, and `Password` filter.

Continued

Property	Description
SsoProviderImplementation	Fully qualified type name of the ISsoProvider implementation that stores credentials used to call the web service.
WebServiceAuthenticationMode	Authentication mode used to invoke web service methods.
WebProxyServerConfiguration	Proxy server URL. Requests to fetch WSDL or invoke web service methods are routed through this proxy server.
WebServiceSsoApplicationId	ID of the SSO enterprise application definition that stores credentials used to call the web service.
WebServiceUrlOverride	URL for override.

The power that the Business Data Catalog provides is impressive. In the following web service application definition file, Listing 10-3, all related functionality is exposed. You can expose all of your underlying application data through the set of corresponding Web Methods.

Listing 10-3: The web service application definition file

```
<?xml version="1.0" encoding="utf-8" standalone="yes"?>
<LobSystem xmlns:xsi="http://www.w3.org/2001/XMLSchema-instance"
xsi:schemaLocation="http://schemas.microsoft.com/office/2006/03/BusinessDataCatalog
BDCMetadata.xsd" Type="WebService" Version="1.0.0.0" Name="SampleWebService"
xmlns="http://schemas.microsoft.com/office/2006/03/BusinessDataCatalog">
  <Properties>
    <Property Name="WebServiceProxyNamespace"
Type="System.String">SampleWebServiceProxy</Property>
    <Property Name="WildcardCharacter" Type="System.String">$</Property>
    <Property Name="WsdlFetchUrl"
Type="System.String">http://localhost:8081/SampleWebServices/Service.asmx</Property
>
  </Properties>
  <AccessControlList>
    <AccessControlEntry Principal="MOSS\administrator">
      <Right BdcRight="Edit" />
      <Right BdcRight="Execute" />
      <Right BdcRight="SetPermissions" />
      <Right BdcRight="SelectableInClients" />
    </AccessControlEntry>
    <AccessControlEntry Principal="MOSS\john">
      <Right BdcRight="Edit" />
      <Right BdcRight="Execute" />
      <Right BdcRight="SetPermissions" />
      <Right BdcRight="SelectableInClients" />
    </AccessControlEntry>
  </AccessControlList>
```

```xml
    <LobSystemInstances>
      <LobSystemInstance Name="SampleWebServiceInstance">
        <Properties>
          <Property Name="LobSystemName"
Type="System.String">SampleWebService</Property>
        </Properties>
      </LobSystemInstance>
    </LobSystemInstances>
    <Entities>
      <Entity EstimatedInstanceCount="10000" Name="Customer">
        <Properties>
          <Property Name="Title" Type="System.String">Name</Property>
          <Property Name="DefaultAction" Type="System.String">View Profile</Property>
        </Properties>
        <AccessControlList>
          <AccessControlEntry Principal="MOSS\administrator">
            <Right BdcRight="Edit" />
            <Right BdcRight="Execute" />
            <Right BdcRight="SetPermissions" />
            <Right BdcRight="SelectableInClients" />
          </AccessControlEntry>
          <AccessControlEntry Principal="MOSS\john">
            <Right BdcRight="Edit" />
            <Right BdcRight="Execute" />
            <Right BdcRight="SetPermissions" />
            <Right BdcRight="SelectableInClients" />
          </AccessControlEntry>
        </AccessControlList>
        <Identifiers>
          <Identifier TypeName="System.String" Name="CustomerID" />
        </Identifiers>
        <Methods>
          <Method Name="GetChildCustomersForCustomer">
            <AccessControlList>
              <AccessControlEntry Principal="MOSS\administrator">
                <Right BdcRight="Edit" />
                <Right BdcRight="Execute" />
                <Right BdcRight="SetPermissions" />
                <Right BdcRight="SelectableInClients" />
              </AccessControlEntry>
              <AccessControlEntry Principal="MOSS\john">
                <Right BdcRight="Edit" />
                <Right BdcRight="Execute" />
                <Right BdcRight="SetPermissions" />
                <Right BdcRight="SelectableInClients" />
              </AccessControlEntry>
            </AccessControlList>
            <Parameters>
              <Parameter Direction="In" Name="custid">
                <TypeDescriptor TypeName="System.String" IdentifierName="CustomerID"
Name="custid" />
              </Parameter>
              <Parameter Direction="Return" Name="Customers">
```

```xml
                    <TypeDescriptor TypeName="SampleWebServiceProxy.Customer[],
SampleWebService" IsCollection="true" Name="ArrayOfCustomer">
                      <TypeDescriptors>
                        <TypeDescriptor TypeName="SampleWebServiceProxy.Customer,
SampleWebService" Name="Customer">
                          <TypeDescriptors>
                            <TypeDescriptor TypeName="System.String"
IdentifierName="CustomerID" Name="CustomerID" />
                            <TypeDescriptor TypeName="System.String" Name="Name" />
                            <TypeDescriptor TypeName="System.Int64" Name=
"WorkPhoneNumber" />
                            <TypeDescriptor TypeName="System.Int64" Name="
MobilePhoneNumber" />
                            <TypeDescriptor TypeName="System.String" Name="Industry" />
                            <TypeDescriptor TypeName="System.String" Name="WebSite" />
                          </TypeDescriptors>
                        </TypeDescriptor>
                      </TypeDescriptors>
                    </TypeDescriptor>
                  </Parameter>
                </Parameters>
              </Method>
              <Method Name="GetCustomerIDs">
                <AccessControlList>
                  <AccessControlEntry Principal="MOSS\administrator">
                    <Right BdcRight="Edit" />
                    <Right BdcRight="Execute" />
                    <Right BdcRight="SetPermissions" />
                    <Right BdcRight="SelectableInClients" />
                  </AccessControlEntry>
                  <AccessControlEntry Principal="MOSS\john">
                    <Right BdcRight="Edit" />
                    <Right BdcRight="Execute" />
                    <Right BdcRight="SetPermissions" />
                    <Right BdcRight="SelectableInClients" />
                  </AccessControlEntry>
                </AccessControlList>
                <Parameters>
                  <Parameter Direction="Return" Name="CustomerIDs">
                    <TypeDescriptor TypeName="System.String[]" IsCollection="true" Name=
"ArrayOfString">
                      <TypeDescriptors>
                        <TypeDescriptor TypeName="System.String" IdentifierName=
"CustomerID" Name="CustomerID" />
                      </TypeDescriptors>
                    </TypeDescriptor>
                  </Parameter>
                </Parameters>
                <MethodInstances>
                  <MethodInstance Type="IdEnumerator" ReturnParameterName="CustomerIDs"
ReturnTypeDescriptorName="ArrayOfString" ReturnTypeDescriptorLevel="0" Name=
"GetCustomerIDsInstance">
                    <AccessControlList>
                      <AccessControlEntry Principal="MOSS\administrator">
```

```xml
                    <Right BdcRight="Edit" />
                    <Right BdcRight="Execute" />
                    <Right BdcRight="SetPermissions" />
                    <Right BdcRight="SelectableInClients" />
                  </AccessControlEntry>
                  <AccessControlEntry Principal="MOSS\john">
                    <Right BdcRight="Edit" />
                    <Right BdcRight="Execute" />
                    <Right BdcRight="SetPermissions" />
                    <Right BdcRight="SelectableInClients" />
                  </AccessControlEntry>
                </AccessControlList>
              </MethodInstance>
            </MethodInstances>
          </Method>
          <Method Name="GetCustomers">
            <AccessControlList>
              <AccessControlEntry Principal="MOSS\administrator">
                <Right BdcRight="Edit" />
                <Right BdcRight="Execute" />
                <Right BdcRight="SetPermissions" />
                <Right BdcRight="SelectableInClients" />
              </AccessControlEntry>
              <AccessControlEntry Principal="MOSS\john">
                <Right BdcRight="Edit" />
                <Right BdcRight="Execute" />
                <Right BdcRight="SetPermissions" />
                <Right BdcRight="SelectableInClients" />
              </AccessControlEntry>
            </AccessControlList>
            <FilterDescriptors>
              <FilterDescriptor Type="Wildcard" Name="Name" />
              <FilterDescriptor Type="Limit" Name="Limit" />
            </FilterDescriptors>
            <Parameters>
              <Parameter Direction="In" Name="name">
                <TypeDescriptor TypeName="System.String" AssociatedFilter="Name"
Name="name" />
              </Parameter>
              <Parameter Direction="In" Name="limit">
                <TypeDescriptor TypeName="System.Int32" AssociatedFilter="Limit"
Name="limit" />
              </Parameter>
              <Parameter Direction="Return" Name="Customers">
                <TypeDescriptor TypeName="SampleWebServiceProxy.Customer[],
SampleWebService" IsCollection="true" Name="ArrayOfCustomer">
                    <TypeDescriptors>
                      <TypeDescriptor TypeName="SampleWebServiceProxy.Customer,
SampleWebService" Name="Customer">
                        <TypeDescriptors>
                          <TypeDescriptor TypeName="System.String"
IdentifierName="CustomerID" Name="CustomerID" />
                          <TypeDescriptor TypeName="System.String" Name="Name" />
                          <TypeDescriptor TypeName="System.Int64" Name=
```

```
  "WorkPhoneNumber" />
                        <TypeDescriptor TypeName="System.Int64" Name=
  "MobilePhoneNumber" />
                        <TypeDescriptor TypeName="System.String" Name="Industry" />
                        <TypeDescriptor TypeName="System.String" Name="WebSite" />
                      </TypeDescriptors>
                    </TypeDescriptor>
                  </TypeDescriptors>
                </TypeDescriptor>
              </Parameter>
            </Parameters>
            <MethodInstances>
              <MethodInstance Type="Finder" ReturnParameterName="Customers"
  ReturnTypeDescriptorName="ArrayOfCustomer" ReturnTypeDescriptorLevel="0" Name=
  "FindCustomerInstances">
                  <AccessControlList>
                    <AccessControlEntry Principal="MOSS\administrator">
                      <Right BdcRight="Edit" />
                      <Right BdcRight="Execute" />
                      <Right BdcRight="SetPermissions" />
                      <Right BdcRight="SelectableInClients" />
                    </AccessControlEntry>
                    <AccessControlEntry Principal="MOSS\john">
                      <Right BdcRight="Edit" />
                      <Right BdcRight="Execute" />
                      <Right BdcRight="SetPermissions" />
                      <Right BdcRight="SelectableInClients" />
                    </AccessControlEntry>
                  </AccessControlList>
                </MethodInstance>
              </MethodInstances>
            </Method>
            <Method Name="GetCustomerByID">
              <AccessControlList>
                <AccessControlEntry Principal="MOSS\administrator">
                  <Right BdcRight="Edit" />
                  <Right BdcRight="Execute" />
                  <Right BdcRight="SetPermissions" />
                  <Right BdcRight="SelectableInClients" />
                </AccessControlEntry>
                <AccessControlEntry Principal="MOSS\john">
                  <Right BdcRight="Edit" />
                  <Right BdcRight="Execute" />
                  <Right BdcRight="SetPermissions" />
                  <Right BdcRight="SelectableInClients" />
                </AccessControlEntry>
              </AccessControlList>
              <Parameters>
                <Parameter Direction="In" Name="id">
                  <TypeDescriptor TypeName="System.String" IdentifierName="CustomerID"
  Name="id" />
                </Parameter>
                <Parameter Direction="Return" Name="Customer">
```

```xml
            <TypeDescriptor TypeName="SampleWebServiceProxy.Customer,
SampleWebService" Name="Customer">
                <TypeDescriptors>
                    <TypeDescriptor TypeName="System.String"
IdentifierName="CustomerID" Name="CustomerID" />
                    <TypeDescriptor TypeName="System.String" Name="Name" />
                    <TypeDescriptor TypeName="System.Int64" Name="WorkPhoneNumber" />
                    <TypeDescriptor TypeName="System.Int64" Name="MobilePhoneNumber" />
                    <TypeDescriptor TypeName="System.String" Name="Industry" />
                    <TypeDescriptor TypeName="System.String" Name="WebSite" />
                    <TypeDescriptor
TypeName="SampleWebServiceProxy.CustomerAddress[], SampleWebService" IsCollection=
"true" Name="CustomerAddresses">
                        <TypeDescriptors>
                            <TypeDescriptor TypeName=
"SampleWebServiceProxy.CustomerAddress, SampleWebService" Name="CustomerAddress">
                                <TypeDescriptors>
                                    <TypeDescriptor TypeName="System.String" Name=
"BlockNumber" />
                                    <TypeDescriptor TypeName="System.String" Name="Street" />
                                    <TypeDescriptor TypeName="System.String" Name="City" />
                                    <TypeDescriptor TypeName="System.String" Name=
"StateProvince" />
                                    <TypeDescriptor TypeName="System.String" Name=
"CountryRegion" />
                                    <TypeDescriptor TypeName="System.String" Name=
"PostalCode" />
                                </TypeDescriptors>
                            </TypeDescriptor>
                        </TypeDescriptors>
                    </TypeDescriptor>
                </TypeDescriptors>
            </TypeDescriptor>
        </Parameter>
    </Parameters>
    <MethodInstances>
        <MethodInstance Type="SpecificFinder" ReturnParameterName="Customer"
ReturnTypeDescriptorName="Customer" ReturnTypeDescriptorLevel="0" Name=
"FindCustomerInstance">
            <AccessControlList>
              <AccessControlEntry Principal="MOSS\administrator">
                <Right BdcRight="Edit" />
                <Right BdcRight="Execute" />
                <Right BdcRight="SetPermissions" />
                <Right BdcRight="SelectableInClients" />
              </AccessControlEntry>
              <AccessControlEntry Principal="MOSS\john">
                <Right BdcRight="Edit" />
                <Right BdcRight="Execute" />
                <Right BdcRight="SetPermissions" />
                <Right BdcRight="SelectableInClients" />
              </AccessControlEntry>
            </AccessControlList>
        </MethodInstance>
```

```xml
            </MethodInstances>
          </Method>
        </Methods>
        <Actions>
          <Action Position="1" IsOpenedInNewWindow="false"
Url="http://windows2003base:11539/ssp/admin/Content/Customer.aspx?CustomerID={0}"
ImageUrl="/_layouts/1033/images/viewprof.gif" Name="View Profile">
            <ActionParameters>
              <ActionParameter Index="0" Name="CustomerID" />
            </ActionParameters>
          </Action>
        </Actions>
      </Entity>
      <Entity EstimatedInstanceCount="10000" Name="Region">
        <Properties>
          <Property Name="Title" Type="System.String">Name</Property>
          <Property Name="DefaultAction" Type="System.String">View Profile</Property>
        </Properties>
        <AccessControlList>
          <AccessControlEntry Principal="MOSS\administrator">
            <Right BdcRight="Edit" />
            <Right BdcRight="Execute" />
            <Right BdcRight="SetPermissions" />
            <Right BdcRight="SelectableInClients" />
          </AccessControlEntry>
          <AccessControlEntry Principal="MOSS\john">
            <Right BdcRight="Edit" />
            <Right BdcRight="Execute" />
            <Right BdcRight="SetPermissions" />
            <Right BdcRight="SelectableInClients" />
          </AccessControlEntry>
        </AccessControlList>
        <Identifiers>
          <Identifier TypeName="System.String" Name="RegionID" />
        </Identifiers>
        <Methods>
          <Method Name="GetRegions">
            <AccessControlList>
              <AccessControlEntry Principal="MOSS\administrator">
                <Right BdcRight="Edit" />
                <Right BdcRight="Execute" />
                <Right BdcRight="SetPermissions" />
                <Right BdcRight="SelectableInClients" />
              </AccessControlEntry>
              <AccessControlEntry Principal="MOSS\john">
                <Right BdcRight="Edit" />
                <Right BdcRight="Execute" />
                <Right BdcRight="SetPermissions" />
                <Right BdcRight="SelectableInClients" />
              </AccessControlEntry>
            </AccessControlList>
            <FilterDescriptors>
              <FilterDescriptor Type="Wildcard" Name="Name" />
            </FilterDescriptors>
```

```
            <Parameters>
              <Parameter Direction="In" Name="name">
                <TypeDescriptor TypeName="System.String" AssociatedFilter="Name"
Name="name" />
              </Parameter>
              <Parameter Direction="Return" Name="Regions">
                <TypeDescriptor TypeName="SampleWebServiceProxy.Region[],
SampleWebService" IsCollection="true" Name="ArrayOfRegion">
                  <TypeDescriptors>
                    <TypeDescriptor TypeName="SampleWebServiceProxy.Region,
SampleWebService" Name="Region">
                      <TypeDescriptors>
                        <TypeDescriptor TypeName="System.String"
IdentifierName="RegionID" Name="RegionID" />
                        <TypeDescriptor TypeName="System.String" Name="Name" />
                        <TypeDescriptor TypeName="System.String" Name="Group" />
                        <TypeDescriptor TypeName="System.Decimal"
Name="SalesLastYear" />
                        <TypeDescriptor TypeName="System.Decimal" Name="SalesYTD" />
                      </TypeDescriptors>
                    </TypeDescriptor>
                  </TypeDescriptors>
                </TypeDescriptor>
              </Parameter>
            </Parameters>
            <MethodInstances>
              <MethodInstance Type="Finder" ReturnParameterName="Regions"
ReturnTypeDescriptorName="ArrayOfRegion" ReturnTypeDescriptorLevel="0"
Name="FindRegionInstances">
                <AccessControlList>
                  <AccessControlEntry Principal="MOSS\administrator">
                    <Right BdcRight="Edit" />
                    <Right BdcRight="Execute" />
                    <Right BdcRight="SetPermissions" />
                    <Right BdcRight="SelectableInClients" />
                  </AccessControlEntry>
                  <AccessControlEntry Principal="MOSS\john">
                    <Right BdcRight="Edit" />
                    <Right BdcRight="Execute" />
                    <Right BdcRight="SetPermissions" />
                    <Right BdcRight="SelectableInClients" />
                  </AccessControlEntry>
                </AccessControlList>
              </MethodInstance>
            </MethodInstances>
          </Method>
          <Method Name="GetRegionByID">
            <AccessControlList>
              <AccessControlEntry Principal="MOSS\administrator">
                <Right BdcRight="Edit" />
                <Right BdcRight="Execute" />
                <Right BdcRight="SetPermissions" />
                <Right BdcRight="SelectableInClients" />
              </AccessControlEntry>
```

```
                  <AccessControlEntry Principal="MOSS\john">
                    <Right BdcRight="Edit" />
                    <Right BdcRight="Execute" />
                    <Right BdcRight="SetPermissions" />
                    <Right BdcRight="SelectableInClients" />
                  </AccessControlEntry>
                </AccessControlList>
                <Parameters>
                  <Parameter Direction="In" Name="id">
                    <TypeDescriptor TypeName="System.String" IdentifierName="RegionID"
Name="id" />
                  </Parameter>
                  <Parameter Direction="Return" Name="Region">
                    <TypeDescriptor TypeName="SampleWebServiceProxy.Region,
SampleWebService" Name="Region">
                      <TypeDescriptors>
                        <TypeDescriptor TypeName="System.String"
IdentifierName="RegionID" Name="RegionID" />
                        <TypeDescriptor TypeName="System.String" Name="Name" />
                        <TypeDescriptor TypeName="System.String" Name="Group" />
                        <TypeDescriptor TypeName="System.Decimal" Name="SalesLastYear" />
                        <TypeDescriptor TypeName="System.Decimal" Name="SalesYTD" />
                      </TypeDescriptors>
                    </TypeDescriptor>
                  </Parameter>
                </Parameters>
                <MethodInstances>
                  <MethodInstance Type="SpecificFinder" ReturnParameterName="Region"
ReturnTypeDescriptorName="Region" ReturnTypeDescriptorLevel="0" Name=
"FindRegionInstance">
                    <AccessControlList>
                      <AccessControlEntry Principal="MOSS\administrator">
                        <Right BdcRight="Edit" />
                        <Right BdcRight="Execute" />
                        <Right BdcRight="SetPermissions" />
                        <Right BdcRight="SelectableInClients" />
                      </AccessControlEntry>
                      <AccessControlEntry Principal="MOSS\john">
                        <Right BdcRight="Edit" />
                        <Right BdcRight="Execute" />
                        <Right BdcRight="SetPermissions" />
                        <Right BdcRight="SelectableInClients" />
                      </AccessControlEntry>
                    </AccessControlList>
                  </MethodInstance>
                </MethodInstances>
              </Method>
            </Methods>
            <Actions>
              <Action Position="1" IsOpenedInNewWindow="false"
Url="http://windows2003base:11539/ssp/admin/Content/Region.aspx?RegionID={0}"
ImageUrl="/_layouts/1033/images/viewprof.gif" Name="View Profile">
                <ActionParameters>
                  <ActionParameter Index="0" Name="RegionID" />
```

```
          </ActionParameters>
        </Action>
      </Actions>
    </Entity>
    <Entity EstimatedInstanceCount="10000" Name="Address">
      <Properties>
        <Property Name="Title" Type="System.String">AddressID</Property>
        <Property Name="DefaultAction" Type="System.String">View Profile</Property>
      </Properties>
      <AccessControlList>
        <AccessControlEntry Principal="MOSS\administrator">
          <Right BdcRight="Edit" />
          <Right BdcRight="Execute" />
          <Right BdcRight="SetPermissions" />
          <Right BdcRight="SelectableInClients" />
        </AccessControlEntry>
        <AccessControlEntry Principal="MOSS\john">
          <Right BdcRight="Edit" />
          <Right BdcRight="Execute" />
          <Right BdcRight="SetPermissions" />
          <Right BdcRight="SelectableInClients" />
        </AccessControlEntry>
      </AccessControlList>
      <Identifiers>
        <Identifier TypeName="System.String" Name="AddressID" />
      </Identifiers>
      <Methods>
        <Method Name="GetAddresses">
          <AccessControlList>
            <AccessControlEntry Principal="MOSS\administrator">
              <Right BdcRight="Edit" />
              <Right BdcRight="Execute" />
              <Right BdcRight="SetPermissions" />
              <Right BdcRight="SelectableInClients" />
            </AccessControlEntry>
            <AccessControlEntry Principal="MOSS\john">
              <Right BdcRight="Edit" />
              <Right BdcRight="Execute" />
              <Right BdcRight="SetPermissions" />
              <Right BdcRight="SelectableInClients" />
            </AccessControlEntry>
          </AccessControlList>
          <FilterDescriptors>
            <FilterDescriptor Type="Wildcard" Name="CustomerID" />
          </FilterDescriptors>
          <Parameters>
            <Parameter Direction="In" Name="name">
              <TypeDescriptor TypeName="System.String"
AssociatedFilter="CustomerID" Name="name" />
            </Parameter>
            <Parameter Direction="Return" Name="Addresses">
              <TypeDescriptor TypeName="SampleWebServiceProxy.CustomerAddress[],
SampleWebService" IsCollection="true" Name="CustomerAddresses">
                <TypeDescriptors>
```

```
                    <TypeDescriptor TypeName="SampleWebServiceProxy.CustomerAddress,
        SampleWebService" Name="CustomerAddress">
                        <TypeDescriptors>
                          <TypeDescriptor TypeName="System.String" Name="CustomerID" />
                          <TypeDescriptor TypeName="System.String"
        IdentifierName="AddressID" Name="AddressID" />
                          <TypeDescriptor TypeName="System.String" Name="BlockNumber" />
                          <TypeDescriptor TypeName="System.String" Name="Street" />
                          <TypeDescriptor TypeName="System.String" Name="City" />
                          <TypeDescriptor TypeName="System.String" Name="StateProvince" />
                          <TypeDescriptor TypeName="System.String" Name="CountryRegion" />
                          <TypeDescriptor TypeName="System.String" Name="PostalCode" />
                        </TypeDescriptors>
                      </TypeDescriptor>
                    </TypeDescriptors>
                  </TypeDescriptor>
                </Parameter>
              </Parameters>
              <MethodInstances>
                <MethodInstance Type="Finder" ReturnParameterName="Addresses"
        ReturnTypeDescriptorName="CustomerAddresses" ReturnTypeDescriptorLevel="0" Name=
        "GetAddressesInstance">
                  <AccessControlList>
                    <AccessControlEntry Principal="MOSS\administrator">
                      <Right BdcRight="Edit" />
                      <Right BdcRight="Execute" />
                      <Right BdcRight="SetPermissions" />
                      <Right BdcRight="SelectableInClients" />
                    </AccessControlEntry>
                    <AccessControlEntry Principal="MOSS\john">
                      <Right BdcRight="Edit" />
                      <Right BdcRight="Execute" />
                      <Right BdcRight="SetPermissions" />
                      <Right BdcRight="SelectableInClients" />
                    </AccessControlEntry>
                  </AccessControlList>
                </MethodInstance>
              </MethodInstances>
            </Method>
            <Method Name="GetAddressesForCustomer">
              <AccessControlList>
                <AccessControlEntry Principal="MOSS\administrator">
                  <Right BdcRight="Edit" />
                  <Right BdcRight="Execute" />
                  <Right BdcRight="SetPermissions" />
                  <Right BdcRight="SelectableInClients" />
                </AccessControlEntry>
                <AccessControlEntry Principal="MOSS\john">
                  <Right BdcRight="Edit" />
                  <Right BdcRight="Execute" />
                  <Right BdcRight="SetPermissions" />
                  <Right BdcRight="SelectableInClients" />
                </AccessControlEntry>
              </AccessControlList>
              <Parameters>
```

```
            <Parameter Direction="In" Name="custid">
              <TypeDescriptor TypeName="System.String"
IdentifierEntityName="Customer" IdentifierName="CustomerID" Name="custid" />
            </Parameter>
            <Parameter Direction="Return" Name="Addresses">
              <TypeDescriptor TypeName="SampleWebServiceProxy.CustomerAddress[],
SampleWebService" IsCollection="true" Name="CustomerAddresses">
                <TypeDescriptors>
                  <TypeDescriptor TypeName="SampleWebServiceProxy.CustomerAddress,
SampleWebService" Name="CustomerAddress">
                    <TypeDescriptors>
                      <TypeDescriptor TypeName="System.String" Name="CustomerID" />
                      <TypeDescriptor TypeName="System.String" IdentifierName=
"AddressID" Name="AddressID" />
                      <TypeDescriptor TypeName="System.String" Name="BlockNumber" />
                      <TypeDescriptor TypeName="System.String" Name="Street" />
                      <TypeDescriptor TypeName="System.String" Name="City" />
                      <TypeDescriptor TypeName="System.String" Name="StateProvince" />
                      <TypeDescriptor TypeName="System.String" Name="CountryRegion" />
                      <TypeDescriptor TypeName="System.String" Name="PostalCode" />
                    </TypeDescriptors>
                  </TypeDescriptor>
                </TypeDescriptors>
              </TypeDescriptor>
            </Parameter>
          </Parameters>
        </Method>
        <Method Name="GetAddressByID">
          <AccessControlList>
            <AccessControlEntry Principal="MOSS\administrator">
              <Right BdcRight="Edit" />
              <Right BdcRight="Execute" />
              <Right BdcRight="SetPermissions" />
              <Right BdcRight="SelectableInClients" />
            </AccessControlEntry>
            <AccessControlEntry Principal="MOSS\john">
              <Right BdcRight="Edit" />
              <Right BdcRight="Execute" />
              <Right BdcRight="SetPermissions" />
              <Right BdcRight="SelectableInClients" />
            </AccessControlEntry>
          </AccessControlList>
          <Parameters>
            <Parameter Direction="In" Name="id">
              <TypeDescriptor TypeName="System.String" IdentifierName="AddressID"
Name="id" />
            </Parameter>
            <Parameter Direction="Return" Name="Address">
              <TypeDescriptor TypeName="SampleWebServiceProxy.CustomerAddress,
SampleWebService" Name="CustomerAddress">
                <TypeDescriptors>
                  <TypeDescriptor TypeName="System.String" Name="CustomerID" />
                  <TypeDescriptor TypeName="System.String" IdentifierName=
"AddressID" Name="AddressID" />
```

```
                    <TypeDescriptor TypeName="System.String" Name="BlockNumber" />
                    <TypeDescriptor TypeName="System.String" Name="Street" />
                    <TypeDescriptor TypeName="System.String" Name="City" />
                    <TypeDescriptor TypeName="System.String" Name="StateProvince" />
                    <TypeDescriptor TypeName="System.String" Name="CountryRegion" />
                    <TypeDescriptor TypeName="System.String" Name="PostalCode" />
                  </TypeDescriptors>
                </TypeDescriptor>
              </Parameter>
            </Parameters>
            <MethodInstances>
              <MethodInstance Type="SpecificFinder" ReturnParameterName="Address"
ReturnTypeDescriptorName="CustomerAddress" ReturnTypeDescriptorLevel="0" Name=
"FindAddressInstance">
                <AccessControlList>
                  <AccessControlEntry Principal="MOSS\administrator">
                    <Right BdcRight="Edit" />
                    <Right BdcRight="Execute" />
                    <Right BdcRight="SetPermissions" />
                    <Right BdcRight="SelectableInClients" />
                  </AccessControlEntry>
                  <AccessControlEntry Principal="MOSS\john">
                    <Right BdcRight="Edit" />
                    <Right BdcRight="Execute" />
                    <Right BdcRight="SetPermissions" />
                    <Right BdcRight="SelectableInClients" />
                  </AccessControlEntry>
                </AccessControlList>
              </MethodInstance>
            </MethodInstances>
          </Method>
        </Methods>
        <Actions>
          <Action Position="1" IsOpenedInNewWindow="false"
Url="http://windows2003base:11539/ssp/admin/Content/Address.aspx?AddressID={0}"
ImageUrl="/_layouts/1033/images/viewprof.gif" Name="View Profile">
            <ActionParameters>
              <ActionParameter Index="0" Name="AddressID" />
            </ActionParameters>
          </Action>
          <Action Position="1" IsOpenedInNewWindow="true"
Url="http://maps.google.com/maps?f=l&amp;hl=en&amp;q=%20{0}%20{1}%20{2}%20{3}%20{4}
%20&amp;ie=UTF-8&amp;om=1&amp;z=15&amp;iwloc=addr&amp;oe=UTF-8&amp;sa=N&amp;tab=wl"
ImageUrl="" Name="View Location on Map">
            <ActionParameters>
              <ActionParameter Index="0" Name="BlockNumber" />
              <ActionParameter Index="1" Name="Street" />
              <ActionParameter Index="2" Name="City" />
              <ActionParameter Index="3" Name="StateProvince" />
              <ActionParameter Index="4" Name="PostalCode" />
              <ActionParameter Index="5" Name="CountryRegion" />
            </ActionParameters>
          </Action>
        </Actions>
      </Entity>
```

```xml
<Entity EstimatedInstanceCount="10000" Name="Order">
  <Properties>
    <Property Name="Title" Type="System.String">OrderID</Property>
    <Property Name="DefaultAction" Type="System.String">View Profile</Property>
  </Properties>
  <AccessControlList>
    <AccessControlEntry Principal="MOSS\administrator">
      <Right BdcRight="Edit" />
      <Right BdcRight="Execute" />
      <Right BdcRight="SetPermissions" />
      <Right BdcRight="SelectableInClients" />
    </AccessControlEntry>
    <AccessControlEntry Principal="MOSS\john">
      <Right BdcRight="Edit" />
      <Right BdcRight="Execute" />
      <Right BdcRight="SetPermissions" />
      <Right BdcRight="SelectableInClients" />
    </AccessControlEntry>
  </AccessControlList>
  <Identifiers>
    <Identifier TypeName="System.String" Name="OrderID" />
  </Identifiers>
  <Methods>
    <Method Name="GetOrdersForCustomerAndRegion">
      <AccessControlList>
        <AccessControlEntry Principal="MOSS\administrator">
          <Right BdcRight="Edit" />
          <Right BdcRight="Execute" />
          <Right BdcRight="SetPermissions" />
          <Right BdcRight="SelectableInClients" />
        </AccessControlEntry>
        <AccessControlEntry Principal="MOSS\john">
          <Right BdcRight="Edit" />
          <Right BdcRight="Execute" />
          <Right BdcRight="SetPermissions" />
          <Right BdcRight="SelectableInClients" />
        </AccessControlEntry>
      </AccessControlList>
      <FilterDescriptors>
        <FilterDescriptor Type="Comparison" Name="CurrencyCode">
          <Properties>
            <Property Name="Comparator" Type="System.String">Equals</Property>
          </Properties>
        </FilterDescriptor>
      </FilterDescriptors>
      <Parameters>
        <Parameter Direction="In" Name="custid">
          <TypeDescriptor TypeName="System.String" IdentifierEntityName=
"Customer" IdentifierName="CustomerID" Name="custid" />
        </Parameter>
        <Parameter Direction="In" Name="regid">
          <TypeDescriptor TypeName="System.String" IdentifierEntityName=
"Region" IdentifierName="RegionID" Name="regid" />
        </Parameter>
        <Parameter Direction="In" Name="curcode">
```

```xml
                <TypeDescriptor TypeName="System.String" AssociatedFilter=
"CurrencyCode" Name="curcode" />
            </Parameter>
            <Parameter Direction="Return" Name="Orders">
                <TypeDescriptor TypeName="SampleWebServiceProxy.Order[],
SampleWebService" IsCollection="true" Name="ArrayOfOrder">
                    <TypeDescriptors>
                        <TypeDescriptor TypeName="SampleWebServiceProxy.Order,
SampleWebService" Name="Order">
                            <TypeDescriptors>
                                <TypeDescriptor TypeName="System.String" IdentifierName=
"OrderID" Name="OrderID" />
                                <TypeDescriptor TypeName="System.String" Name="CustomerID" />
                                <TypeDescriptor TypeName="System.String" Name="RegionID" />
                                <TypeDescriptor TypeName="System.String" Name="CurrencyCode" />
                                <TypeDescriptor TypeName="System.Decimal" Name="SubTotal" />
                                <TypeDescriptor TypeName="System.String" Name="OrderDate" />
                                <TypeDescriptor TypeName="System.String" Name="ShipDate" />
                            </TypeDescriptors>
                        </TypeDescriptor>
                    </TypeDescriptors>
                </TypeDescriptor>
            </Parameter>
        </Parameters>
    </Method>
    <Method Name="GetOrderByID">
        <AccessControlList>
            <AccessControlEntry Principal="MOSS\administrator">
                <Right BdcRight="Edit" />
                <Right BdcRight="Execute" />
                <Right BdcRight="SetPermissions" />
                <Right BdcRight="SelectableInClients" />
            </AccessControlEntry>
            <AccessControlEntry Principal="MOSS\john">
                <Right BdcRight="Edit" />
                <Right BdcRight="Execute" />
                <Right BdcRight="SetPermissions" />
                <Right BdcRight="SelectableInClients" />
            </AccessControlEntry>
        </AccessControlList>
        <Parameters>
            <Parameter Direction="In" Name="id">
                <TypeDescriptor TypeName="System.String" IdentifierName="OrderID"
Name="id" />
            </Parameter>
            <Parameter Direction="Return" Name="Order">
                <TypeDescriptor TypeName="SampleWebServiceProxy.Order,
SampleWebService" Name="Order">
                    <TypeDescriptors>
                        <TypeDescriptor TypeName="System.String" IdentifierName="OrderID"
Name="OrderID" />
                        <TypeDescriptor TypeName="System.String" Name="CustomerID" />
                        <TypeDescriptor TypeName="System.String" Name="RegionID" />
                        <TypeDescriptor TypeName="System.String" Name="CurrencyCode" />
```

```xml
                    <TypeDescriptor TypeName="System.Decimal" Name="SubTotal" />
                    <TypeDescriptor TypeName="System.String" Name="OrderDate" />
                    <TypeDescriptor TypeName="System.String" Name="ShipDate" />
                  </TypeDescriptors>
                </TypeDescriptor>
              </Parameter>
            </Parameters>
            <MethodInstances>
              <MethodInstance Type="SpecificFinder" ReturnParameterName="Order"
ReturnTypeDescriptorName="Order" ReturnTypeDescriptorLevel="0" Name=
"FindOrderInstance">
                <AccessControlList>
                  <AccessControlEntry Principal="MOSS\administrator">
                    <Right BdcRight="Edit" />
                    <Right BdcRight="Execute" />
                    <Right BdcRight="SetPermissions" />
                    <Right BdcRight="SelectableInClients" />
                  </AccessControlEntry>
                  <AccessControlEntry Principal="MOSS\john">
                    <Right BdcRight="Edit" />
                    <Right BdcRight="Execute" />
                    <Right BdcRight="SetPermissions" />
                    <Right BdcRight="SelectableInClients" />
                  </AccessControlEntry>
                </AccessControlList>
              </MethodInstance>
            </MethodInstances>
          </Method>
          <Method Name="GetOrders">
            <AccessControlList>
              <AccessControlEntry Principal="MOSS\administrator">
                <Right BdcRight="Edit" />
                <Right BdcRight="Execute" />
                <Right BdcRight="SetPermissions" />
                <Right BdcRight="SelectableInClients" />
              </AccessControlEntry>
              <AccessControlEntry Principal="MOSS\john">
                <Right BdcRight="Edit" />
                <Right BdcRight="Execute" />
                <Right BdcRight="SetPermissions" />
                <Right BdcRight="SelectableInClients" />
              </AccessControlEntry>
            </AccessControlList>
            <Parameters>
              <Parameter Direction="Return" Name="Orders">
                <TypeDescriptor TypeName="SampleWebServiceProxy.Order[],
SampleWebService" IsCollection="true" Name="ArrayOfOrder">
                  <TypeDescriptors>
                    <TypeDescriptor TypeName="SampleWebServiceProxy.Order,
SampleWebService" Name="Order">
                      <TypeDescriptors>
                        <TypeDescriptor TypeName="System.String" IdentifierName=
"OrderID" Name="OrderID" />
                        <TypeDescriptor TypeName="System.String" Name="CustomerID" />
```

```xml
                        <TypeDescriptor TypeName="System.String" Name="RegionID" />
                        <TypeDescriptor TypeName="System.String" Name="CurrencyCode" />
                        <TypeDescriptor TypeName="System.Decimal" Name="SubTotal" />
                        <TypeDescriptor TypeName="System.String" Name="OrderDate" />
                        <TypeDescriptor TypeName="System.String" Name="ShipDate" />
                      </TypeDescriptors>
                    </TypeDescriptor>
                  </TypeDescriptors>
                </TypeDescriptor>
              </Parameter>
            </Parameters>
            <MethodInstances>
              <MethodInstance Type="Finder" ReturnParameterName="Orders"
ReturnTypeDescriptorName="ArrayOfOrder" ReturnTypeDescriptorLevel="0" Name=
"FindOrderInstances">
                <AccessControlList>
                  <AccessControlEntry Principal="MOSS\administrator">
                    <Right BdcRight="Edit" />
                    <Right BdcRight="Execute" />
                    <Right BdcRight="SetPermissions" />
                    <Right BdcRight="SelectableInClients" />
                  </AccessControlEntry>
                  <AccessControlEntry Principal="MOSS\john">
                    <Right BdcRight="Edit" />
                    <Right BdcRight="Execute" />
                    <Right BdcRight="SetPermissions" />
                    <Right BdcRight="SelectableInClients" />
                  </AccessControlEntry>
                </AccessControlList>
              </MethodInstance>
            </MethodInstances>
          </Method>
        </Methods>
        <Actions>
          <Action Position="1" IsOpenedInNewWindow="false" Url="http://
windows2003base:11539/ssp/admin/Content/Order.aspx?OrderID={0}" ImageUrl=
"/_layouts/1033/images/viewprof.gif" Name="View Profile">
            <ActionParameters>
              <ActionParameter Index="0" Name="OrderID" />
            </ActionParameters>
          </Action>
        </Actions>
      </Entity>
      <Entity EstimatedInstanceCount="10000" Name="LineItem">
        <Properties>
          <Property Name="Title" Type="System.String">ProductName</Property>
          <Property Name="DefaultAction" Type="System.String">View Profile</Property>
        </Properties>
        <AccessControlList>
          <AccessControlEntry Principal="MOSS\administrator">
            <Right BdcRight="Edit" />
            <Right BdcRight="Execute" />
            <Right BdcRight="SetPermissions" />
            <Right BdcRight="SelectableInClients" />
```

```
      </AccessControlEntry>
      <AccessControlEntry Principal="MOSS\john">
        <Right BdcRight="Edit" />
        <Right BdcRight="Execute" />
        <Right BdcRight="SetPermissions" />
        <Right BdcRight="SelectableInClients" />
      </AccessControlEntry>
    </AccessControlList>
    <Identifiers>
      <Identifier TypeName="System.String" Name="OrderID" />
      <Identifier TypeName="System.String" Name="ProductID" />
    </Identifiers>
    <Methods>
      <Method Name="GetLineItemsForOrder">
        <AccessControlList>
          <AccessControlEntry Principal="MOSS\administrator">
            <Right BdcRight="Edit" />
            <Right BdcRight="Execute" />
            <Right BdcRight="SetPermissions" />
            <Right BdcRight="SelectableInClients" />
          </AccessControlEntry>
          <AccessControlEntry Principal="MOSS\john">
            <Right BdcRight="Edit" />
            <Right BdcRight="Execute" />
            <Right BdcRight="SetPermissions" />
            <Right BdcRight="SelectableInClients" />
          </AccessControlEntry>
        </AccessControlList>
        <Parameters>
          <Parameter Direction="In" Name="ordid">
            <TypeDescriptor TypeName="System.String" IdentifierEntityName="Order"
IdentifierName="OrderID" Name="ordid" />
          </Parameter>
          <Parameter Direction="Return" Name="LineItems">
            <TypeDescriptor TypeName="SampleWebServiceProxy.LineItem[],
SampleWebService" IsCollection="true" Name="ArrayOfLineItem">
              <TypeDescriptors>
                <TypeDescriptor TypeName="SampleWebServiceProxy.LineItem,
SampleWebService" Name="LineItem">
                  <TypeDescriptors>
                    <TypeDescriptor TypeName="System.String" IdentifierName=
"OrderID" Name="OrderID" />
                    <TypeDescriptor TypeName="System.String" IdentifierName=
"ProductID" Name="ProductID" />
                    <TypeDescriptor TypeName="System.String" Name="ProductName" />
                    <TypeDescriptor TypeName="System.Int32" Name="OrderQty" />
                    <TypeDescriptor TypeName="System.Decimal" Name="UnitPrice" />
                    <TypeDescriptor TypeName="System.Decimal" Name="LineTotal" />
                  </TypeDescriptors>
                </TypeDescriptor>
              </TypeDescriptors>
            </TypeDescriptor>
          </Parameter>
        </Parameters>
```

```
                </Method>
                <Method Name="GetLineItemByID">
                  <AccessControlList>
                    <AccessControlEntry Principal="MOSS\administrator">
                      <Right BdcRight="Edit" />
                      <Right BdcRight="Execute" />
                      <Right BdcRight="SetPermissions" />
                      <Right BdcRight="SelectableInClients" />
                    </AccessControlEntry>
                    <AccessControlEntry Principal="MOSS\john">
                      <Right BdcRight="Edit" />
                      <Right BdcRight="Execute" />
                      <Right BdcRight="SetPermissions" />
                      <Right BdcRight="SelectableInClients" />
                    </AccessControlEntry>
                  </AccessControlList>
                  <Parameters>
                    <Parameter Direction="In" Name="ordid">
                      <TypeDescriptor TypeName="System.String" IdentifierName="OrderID"
Name="ordid" />
                    </Parameter>
                    <Parameter Direction="In" Name="prodid">
                      <TypeDescriptor TypeName="System.String" IdentifierName="ProductID"
Name="prodid" />
                    </Parameter>
                    <Parameter Direction="Return" Name="LineItem">
                      <TypeDescriptor TypeName="SampleWebServiceProxy.LineItem,
SampleWebService" Name="LineItem">
                        <TypeDescriptors>
                          <TypeDescriptor TypeName="System.String" IdentifierName="OrderID"
Name="OrderID" />
                          <TypeDescriptor TypeName="System.String" IdentifierName=
"ProductID" Name="ProductID" />
                          <TypeDescriptor TypeName="System.String" Name="ProductName" />
                          <TypeDescriptor TypeName="System.Int32" Name="OrderQty" />
                          <TypeDescriptor TypeName="System.Decimal" Name="UnitPrice" />
                          <TypeDescriptor TypeName="System.Decimal" Name="LineTotal" />
                        </TypeDescriptors>
                      </TypeDescriptor>
                    </Parameter>
                  </Parameters>
                  <MethodInstances>
                    <MethodInstance Type="SpecificFinder" ReturnParameterName="LineItem"
ReturnTypeDescriptorName="LineItem" ReturnTypeDescriptorLevel="0" Name=
"FindLineItemInstance">
                      <AccessControlList>
                        <AccessControlEntry Principal="MOSS\administrator">
                          <Right BdcRight="Edit" />
                          <Right BdcRight="Execute" />
                          <Right BdcRight="SetPermissions" />
                          <Right BdcRight="SelectableInClients" />
                        </AccessControlEntry>
                        <AccessControlEntry Principal="MOSS\john">
                          <Right BdcRight="Edit" />
```

```
              <Right BdcRight="Execute" />
              <Right BdcRight="SetPermissions" />
              <Right BdcRight="SelectableInClients" />
          </AccessControlEntry>
        </AccessControlList>
      </MethodInstance>
    </MethodInstances>
  </Method>
  <Method Name="GetLineItems">
    <AccessControlList>
      <AccessControlEntry Principal="MOSS\administrator">
        <Right BdcRight="Edit" />
        <Right BdcRight="Execute" />
        <Right BdcRight="SetPermissions" />
        <Right BdcRight="SelectableInClients" />
      </AccessControlEntry>
      <AccessControlEntry Principal="MOSS\john">
        <Right BdcRight="Edit" />
        <Right BdcRight="Execute" />
        <Right BdcRight="SetPermissions" />
        <Right BdcRight="SelectableInClients" />
      </AccessControlEntry>
    </AccessControlList>
    <Parameters>
      <Parameter Direction="Return" Name="LineItems">
        <TypeDescriptor TypeName="SampleWebServiceProxy.LineItem[],
SampleWebService" IsCollection="true" Name="ArrayOfLineItem">
          <TypeDescriptors>
            <TypeDescriptor TypeName="SampleWebServiceProxy.LineItem,
SampleWebService" Name="LineItem">
              <TypeDescriptors>
                <TypeDescriptor TypeName="System.String" IdentifierName=
"OrderID" Name="OrderID" />
                <TypeDescriptor TypeName="System.String" IdentifierName=
"ProductID" Name="ProductID" />
                <TypeDescriptor TypeName="System.String" Name="ProductName" />
                <TypeDescriptor TypeName="System.Int32" Name="OrderQty" />
                <TypeDescriptor TypeName="System.Decimal" Name="UnitPrice" />
                <TypeDescriptor TypeName="System.Decimal" Name="LineTotal" />
              </TypeDescriptors>
            </TypeDescriptor>
          </TypeDescriptors>
        </TypeDescriptor>
      </Parameter>
    </Parameters>
    <MethodInstances>
      <MethodInstance Type="Finder" ReturnParameterName="LineItems"
ReturnTypeDescriptorName="ArrayOfLineItem" ReturnTypeDescriptorLevel="0" Name=
"FindLineItemInstances">
        <AccessControlList>
          <AccessControlEntry Principal="MOSS\administrator">
            <Right BdcRight="Edit" />
            <Right BdcRight="Execute" />
            <Right BdcRight="SetPermissions" />
```

```
                        <Right BdcRight="SelectableInClients" />
                    </AccessControlEntry>
                    <AccessControlEntry Principal="MOSS\john">
                        <Right BdcRight="Edit" />
                        <Right BdcRight="Execute" />
                        <Right BdcRight="SetPermissions" />
                        <Right BdcRight="SelectableInClients" />
                    </AccessControlEntry>
                  </AccessControlList>
                </MethodInstance>
              </MethodInstances>
            </Method>
          </Methods>
          <Actions>
            <Action Position="1" IsOpenedInNewWindow="false"
Url="http://windows2003base:11539/ssp/admin/Content/LineItem.aspx?OrderID={0}&amp;P
roductID={1}" ImageUrl="/_layouts/1033/images/viewprof.gif" Name="View Profile">
              <ActionParameters>
                <ActionParameter Index="0" Name="OrderID" />
                <ActionParameter Index="1" Name="ProductID" />
              </ActionParameters>
            </Action>
          </Actions>
        </Entity>
      </Entities>
      <Associations>
        <Association Name="CustomerToChildCustomers"
AssociationMethodEntityName="Customer"
AssociationMethodName="GetChildCustomersForCustomer"
AssociationMethodReturnParameterName="Customers"
AssociationMethodReturnTypeDescriptorName="ArrayOfCustomer"
AssociationMethodReturnTypeDescriptorLevel="0" IsCached="true">
          <AccessControlList>
            <AccessControlEntry Principal="MOSS\administrator">
              <Right BdcRight="Edit" />
              <Right BdcRight="Execute" />
              <Right BdcRight="SetPermissions" />
              <Right BdcRight="SelectableInClients" />
            </AccessControlEntry>
            <AccessControlEntry Principal="MOSS\john">
              <Right BdcRight="Edit" />
              <Right BdcRight="Execute" />
              <Right BdcRight="SetPermissions" />
              <Right BdcRight="SelectableInClients" />
            </AccessControlEntry>
          </AccessControlList>
          <SourceEntity Name="Customer" />
          <DestinationEntity Name="Customer" />
        </Association>
        <Association Name="CustomerAndRegionToOrders"
AssociationMethodEntityName="Order"
AssociationMethodName="GetOrdersForCustomerAndRegion"
AssociationMethodReturnParameterName="Orders"
AssociationMethodReturnTypeDescriptorName="ArrayOfOrder"
AssociationMethodReturnTypeDescriptorLevel="0" IsCached="true">
```

```
        <AccessControlList>
          <AccessControlEntry Principal="MOSS\administrator">
            <Right BdcRight="Edit" />
            <Right BdcRight="Execute" />
            <Right BdcRight="SetPermissions" />
            <Right BdcRight="SelectableInClients" />
          </AccessControlEntry>
          <AccessControlEntry Principal="MOSS\john">
            <Right BdcRight="Edit" />
            <Right BdcRight="Execute" />
            <Right BdcRight="SetPermissions" />
            <Right BdcRight="SelectableInClients" />
          </AccessControlEntry>
        </AccessControlList>
        <SourceEntity Name="Customer" />
        <SourceEntity Name="Region" />
        <DestinationEntity Name="Order" />
      </Association>
      <Association Name="CustomerToAddresses" AssociationMethodEntityName="Address"
AssociationMethodName="GetAddressesForCustomer"
AssociationMethodReturnParameterName="Addresses"
AssociationMethodReturnTypeDescriptorName="CustomerAddresses"
AssociationMethodReturnTypeDescriptorLevel="0" IsCached="true">
        <AccessControlList>
          <AccessControlEntry Principal="MOSS\administrator">
            <Right BdcRight="Edit" />
            <Right BdcRight="Execute" />
            <Right BdcRight="SetPermissions" />
            <Right BdcRight="SelectableInClients" />
          </AccessControlEntry>
          <AccessControlEntry Principal="MOSS\john">
            <Right BdcRight="Edit" />
            <Right BdcRight="Execute" />
            <Right BdcRight="SetPermissions" />
            <Right BdcRight="SelectableInClients" />
          </AccessControlEntry>
        </AccessControlList>
        <SourceEntity Name="Customer" />
        <DestinationEntity Name="Address" />
      </Association>
      <Association Name="OrderToLineItems" AssociationMethodEntityName="LineItem"
AssociationMethodName="GetLineItemsForOrder"
AssociationMethodReturnParameterName="LineItems"
AssociationMethodReturnTypeDescriptorName="ArrayOfLineItem"
AssociationMethodReturnTypeDescriptorLevel="0" IsCached="true">
        <AccessControlList>
          <AccessControlEntry Principal="MOSS\administrator">
            <Right BdcRight="Edit" />
            <Right BdcRight="Execute" />
            <Right BdcRight="SetPermissions" />
            <Right BdcRight="SelectableInClients" />
          </AccessControlEntry>
          <AccessControlEntry Principal="MOSS\john">
            <Right BdcRight="Edit" />
            <Right BdcRight="Execute" />
```

```
                <Right BdcRight="SetPermissions" />
                <Right BdcRight="SelectableInClients" />
            </AccessControlEntry>
        </AccessControlList>
        <SourceEntity Name="Order" />
        <DestinationEntity Name="LineItem" />
      </Association>
    </Associations>
</LobSystem>
```

Adding a Custom Action to an Application Definition File

Now that you have seen the different elements that compose an Application Definition file, this section
will walk you through modifying the SampleWebService sample from MSDN to add a full Address
Entity instead of an Address child within the Customer Entity.

> *The setup instructions for the* SampleWebService *can be found on this book's companion web site.*
> *You'll need to install the* SampleWebService *before attempting to test the changes to the application*
> *definition.*

You start by examining the Address entity in the original file. Note that Address is really nothing more
than a blob of data. It has no way to identify specific instances of the Address entity and no facility. In
order to make this a first class entity, you'll make these changes and more.

```
      <Entity EstimatedInstanceCount="10000" Name="Address">
        <Properties>
          <Property Name="Title" Type="System.String">StateProvince</Property>
        </Properties>
        <Methods>
          <Method Name="GetAddresses">
            <Parameters>
              <Parameter Direction="Return" Name="Addresses">
                <TypeDescriptor TypeName="SampleWebServiceProxy.CustomerAddress[],
SampleWebService" IsCollection="true" Name="CustomerAddresses" >
                  <TypeDescriptors>
                    <TypeDescriptor TypeName="SampleWebServiceProxy.CustomerAddress,
SampleWebService" Name="CustomerAddress" >
                      <Properties>
                        <Property Name="FormatString" Type="System.String">{0}, {1},
{2}, {3} - PostalCode, {4}</Property>
                      </Properties>
                      <TypeDescriptors>
                        <TypeDescriptor TypeName="SampleWebServiceProxy
.CustomerStreet, SampleWebService" Name="Street">
                          <TypeDescriptors>
                            <TypeDescriptor TypeName="System.String"
Name="BlockNumber" />
                            <TypeDescriptor TypeName="System.String" Name="Street" />
                          </TypeDescriptors>
                        </TypeDescriptor>
                        <TypeDescriptor TypeName="System.String" Name="City" />
                        <TypeDescriptor TypeName="System.String" Name="StateProvince" />
```

```
                    <TypeDescriptor TypeName="System.String" Name="CountryRegion" />
                     <TypeDescriptor TypeName="System.String" Name="PostalCode" />
                  </TypeDescriptors>
                </TypeDescriptor>
              </TypeDescriptors>
            </TypeDescriptor>
          </Parameter>
        </Parameters>
        <MethodInstances>
            <MethodInstance Type="Finder" ReturnParameterName="Addresses"
   ReturnTypeDescriptorName="CustomerAddresses" ReturnTypeDescriptorLevel="0"
   Name="GetAddressesInstance" />
          </MethodInstances>
        </Method>
      </Methods>
    </Entity>
```

Modifying an Application Definition File

After examining the web service Application Definition file, you can now modify it to make the
`Customer Address Entity` into a first class member.

1. Before undertaking the modification, you need to replace the information in the `WsdlFetchUrl`
property with your server information.

```
<Property Name="WsdlFetchUrl" Type="System.String">http://localhost:8081/
SampleWebServices/Service.asmx</Property>
  </Properties>
```

2. The first item you need to add to the `Address Entity` is an `Identifier`. Without the
`Identifier` in place, the `Entity` is nothing more than a data instance. If you want to use it
in a meaningful way within the portal site, then this is a crucial first step. So to do this, inside
the `Address Entity`, immediately following the `Properties` element, add the `Identifier`:

```
  </Properties>
  <Identifiers>
  <Identifier TypeName="System.String" Name="AddressID" />
  </Identifiers>
```

This enables the Entity to expose individual instances based on the identifier.

3. Now that an `Identifier` has been added to the `Address Entity`, the next step is to expand
the data choices provided by the `Entity`. This is accomplished by expanding the `Methods`, as
illustrated in the following code sample. The first method is used as the destination.

```
<Method Name="GetAddressesForCustomer">
    <Parameters>
    <Parameter Direction="In" Name="custid">
      <TypeDescriptor TypeName="System.String" IdentifierEntityName="Customer"
    IdentifierName="CustomerID" Name="custid" />
    </Parameter>
    <Parameter Direction="Return" Name="Addresses">
    <TypeDescriptor TypeName="SampleWebServiceProxy.CustomerAddress[],
    SampleWebService" IsCollection="true" Name="CustomerAddresses">
```

```
<TypeDescriptors>
<TypeDescriptor TypeName="SampleWebServiceProxy.CustomerAddress, SampleWebService"
Name="CustomerAddress">
<TypeDescriptors>
  <TypeDescriptor TypeName="System.String" Name="CustomerID" />
  <TypeDescriptor TypeName="System.String" IdentifierName="AddressID"
Name="AddressID" />
  <TypeDescriptor TypeName="System.String" Name="BlockNumber" />
  <TypeDescriptor TypeName="System.String" Name="Street" />
  <TypeDescriptor TypeName="System.String" Name="City" />
  <TypeDescriptor TypeName="System.String" Name="StateProvince" />
  <TypeDescriptor TypeName="System.String" Name="CountryRegion" />
  <TypeDescriptor TypeName="System.String" Name="PostalCode" />
  </TypeDescriptors>
  </TypeDescriptor>
  </TypeDescriptors>
  </TypeDescriptor>
  </Parameter>
  </Parameters>
  </Method>

<Method Name="GetAddressByID">
 <Parameters>
 <Parameter Direction="In" Name="id">
  <TypeDescriptor TypeName="System.String" IdentifierName="AddressID" Name="id" />
  </Parameter>
 <Parameter Direction="Return" Name="Address">
  <TypeDescriptor TypeName="SampleWebServiceProxy.CustomerAddress, SampleWebService"
Name="CustomerAddress">
 <TypeDescriptors>
  <TypeDescriptor TypeName="System.String" Name="CustomerID" />
  <TypeDescriptor TypeName="System.String" IdentifierName="AddressID"
Name="AddressID" />
  <TypeDescriptor TypeName="System.String" Name="BlockNumber" />
  <TypeDescriptor TypeName="System.String" Name="Street" />
  <TypeDescriptor TypeName="System.String" Name="City" />
  <TypeDescriptor TypeName="System.String" Name="StateProvince" />
  <TypeDescriptor TypeName="System.String" Name="CountryRegion" />
  <TypeDescriptor TypeName="System.String" Name="PostalCode" />
  </TypeDescriptors>
  </TypeDescriptor>
  </Parameter>
  </Parameters>
 <MethodInstances>
  <MethodInstance Type="SpecificFinder" ReturnParameterName="Address"
ReturnTypeDescriptorName="CustomerAddress" ReturnTypeDescriptorLevel="0" Name=
"FindAddressInstance" />
  </MethodInstances>
  </Method>
```

Notice that by adding these methods to the Address Entity, a specific instance can be retrieved and an association can be supported. This is important because it enables items to be surfaced through Web Parts and actions to be added for those instances.

4. Even though the `Entity`'s method capabilities have been substanstially enhanced, in order to utlize this, the `Address Entity` needs to be associated with the `Customer Entity`. Once this is done, when a `Customer` is chosen, the corresponding `Addresses` can be displayed. To add an `Association`, add the following shaded code immediately before the `Associations` ending tag.

```
<Association Name="CustomerToAddresses" AssociationMethodEntityName="Address"
AssociationMethodName="GetAddressesForCustomer"
AssociationMethodReturnParameterName="Addresses"
AssociationMethodReturnTypeDescriptorName="CustomerAddresses"
AssociationMethodReturnTypeDescriptorLevel="0" IsCached="true">
  <SourceEntity Name="Customer" />
  <DestinationEntity Name="Address" />
  </Association>
 </Associations>
  </LobSystem>
```

5. As discussed earlier, actions can be added to an `Entity` to perform additional functions. In this case, `CustomerAddresses` can be mapped via URL to display location information for the given customer address. In order to add the action, you need to add the following code immediately following the `Methods` closing tag. Note that you are adding actions to display the location in both Microsoft Live Maps and Google Maps to illustrate the flexibility of `Actions`.

```
   </Methods>
   <Actions>
        <Action Position="1" IsOpenedInNewWindow="true" Url="http://maps.google
.com/maps?f=l&amp;hl=en&amp;q=%20{0}%20{1}%20{2}%20{3}%20{4}%20&amp;ie=UTF-8&amp;om=
1&amp;z=15&amp;iwloc=addr&amp;oe=UTF-8&amp;sa=N&amp;tab=wl" ImageUrl="" Name="View
in Google Maps">
            <ActionParameters>
                <ActionParameter Index="0" Name="BlockNumber" />
                <ActionParameter Index="1" Name="Street" />
                <ActionParameter Index="2" Name="City" />
                <ActionParameter Index="3" Name="StateProvince" />
                <ActionParameter Index="4" Name="PostalCode" />
                <ActionParameter Index="5" Name="CountryRegion" />
            </ActionParameters>
        </Action>
        <Action Position="1" IsOpenedInNewWindow="true" Url="http://maps.live.com/
?q={0}%20{1}%20{2}%20{3}%20{4}%20{5}&amp;mkt=en-US&amp;FORM=BDRE" ImageUrl=""
Name="View In Live Map">
            <ActionParameters>
                <ActionParameter Index="0" Name="BlockNumber" />
                <ActionParameter Index="1" Name="Street" />
                <ActionParameter Index="2" Name="City" />
                <ActionParameter Index="3" Name="StateProvince" />
                <ActionParameter Index="4" Name="PostalCode" />
                <ActionParameter Index="5" Name="CountryRegion" />
            </ActionParameters>
        </Action>   </Actions>
```

6. Now that the `Address Entity` has been modified, you must move the `Address Entity` after the `Customer Entity`.

7. Before testing the modifications, save the file. Next, return to the Application Definition Import page and import your file to register the application within the Business Data Catalog.

8. Now, test that application and view the address location.

Working with Business Data Catalog in Web Parts

There are several Web Parts specifically designed for surfacing Business Data Catalog application data. Currently, there are five Web Parts set apart for this use. The following table lists the five Web Parts and their usage:

Web Part	Description
Business Data Action	Enables the use of an action via a URL for a given Entity.
Business Data Item	Used to display a specific single Entity instance.
Business Data Item Builder	Enables the creation of dynamic Entity instances based on a querystring from a URL and surfaces it through a profile page.
Business Data List	Used to display a list of Entity instances.
Business Data Related List	Allows associated Entity instances to be displayed.

Programming Using the Runtime API

The Microsoft Office SharePoint Server 2007 Runtime object model allows you to navigate through the hierarchical structure of the registered line-of-business application. This example helps pull together many of the concepts in this chapter. It's time to walk through creating a simple application to illustrate navigating the API structure programmatically.

Step 1: Preliminary Set Up

Before you can work with the code, there is a bit of housekeeping to take care of. The following steps will assist in performing a preliminary setup:

1. After launching Microsoft Visual Studio 2005, create a Console Application Project.

2. Add these references by browsing to the following paths:

   ❑ `C:\Program Files\Common Files\Microsoft Shared\Web Server Extensions\12\ISAPI\Microsoft.SharePoint.dll`

   ❑ `C:\Program Files\Common Files\Microsoft Shared\Web Server Extensions\12\ISAPI\microsoft.sharepoint.portal.dll`

   ❑ `C:\Program Files\Common Files\Microsoft Shared\Web Server Extensions\12\ISAPI\Microsoft.Office.Server.dll`

You should now have three references, as illustrated in the rectangle shown in Figure 10-5.

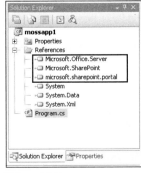

Figure 10-5

3. Add the following references at the top of `Program.cs`:

```
using Microsoft.Office.Server.ApplicationRegistry.MetadataModel;
using Microsoft.Office.Server.ApplicationRegistry.Infrastructure;
```

4. After the class definition, add a constant for the shared service server name:

```
class MOSSInfo
{
    const string _sSPName = "SharedServices1";
```

5. Inside of the Main function, add the following lines. These lines will control the program's execution.

```
static void Main(string[] args)
{
    ConnectToSharedResourceProvider();
    DisplayLOBSystemInformation();
    Console.WriteLine("Press any key to exit...");
    Console.Read();
}
```

Step 2: Connect to the SharedServicesProvider Instance

After the Main function, add the following function. This function is responsible for setting your SharedServices provider instance.

```
static void ConnectToSharedResourceProvider()
{
    SqlSessionProvider.Instance().SetSharedResourceProviderToUse(_sSPName);
}
```

Step 3: Display LOBSystemInstances

After the ConnectToSharedResourceProvider that you just added, add the following function:

```
static void DisplayLOBSystemInformation()
{
```

```
            NamedLobSystemInstanceDictionary sysInstances =
    ApplicationRegistry.GetLobSystemInstances();
            Console.WriteLine("Listing system instances...");
            foreach (String name in sysInstances.Keys)
            {
                Console.WriteLine( "LOBSystemInstance: " + name);
            }
        }
```

When run, this will display the line-of-business application instances, as illustrated in Figure 10-6.

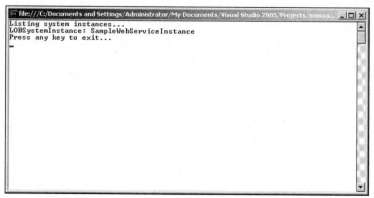

Figure 10-6

Step 4: Display Entities within the Line-of-Business Application

Within the DisplayLOBSystemInformation function, add the following shaded lines to display the Entities contained inside the line-of-business application (LOBSystemInstance):

```
        static void DisplayLOBSystemInformation()
        {

            NamedLobSystemInstanceDictionary sysInstances =
    ApplicationRegistry.GetLobSystemInstances();
            Console.WriteLine("Listing system instances...");
            foreach (String name in sysInstances.Keys)
            {
                Console.WriteLine( "LOBSystemInstance: " + name);

                NamedEntityDictionary entities =
    ApplicationRegistry.GetLobSystemInstanceByName(name).GetEntities();
                foreach (Entity entity in entities.Values)
                {
                    Console.WriteLine(" ");
                    Console.WriteLine("     Entity: " + entity.Name);
                }
            }
        }
```

When run, this will display the `Entities` within the line-of-business application instances as illustrated in Figure 10-7.

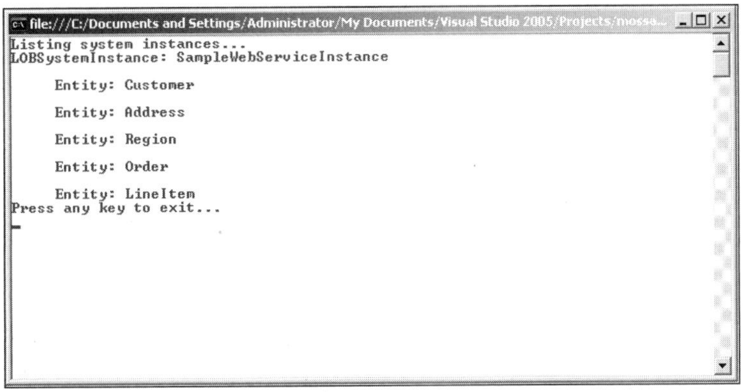

Figure 10-7

Step 5: Display Associations for Entities

Within the `DisplayLOBSystemInformation` function, add the following shaded lines to display `Associations` for the `Entities` contained inside the line-of-business application (`LOBSystemInstance`):

```
static void DisplayLOBSystemInformation()
{
    NamedLobSystemInstanceDictionary sysInstances =
ApplicationRegistry.GetLobSystemInstances();
    Console.WriteLine("Listing system instances...");
    foreach (String name in sysInstances.Keys)
    {
        Console.WriteLine( "LOBSystemInstance: " + name);
        NamedEntityDictionary entities =
ApplicationRegistry.GetLobSystemInstanceByName(name).GetEntities();


        foreach ( Entity entity in entities.Values)
        {
            Console.WriteLine(" ");
            Console.WriteLine("    Entity: " + entity.Name);
            View view = entity.GetFinderView();
            NamedAssociationDictionary sourceAssociations =
entity.GetSourceAssociations();
            NamedAssociationDictionary destinationAssociations =
entity.GetDestinationAssociations();


            foreach (Field field in view.Fields)
            {
                Console.WriteLine("        Field: " +
field.DefaultDisplayName + ", " + field.TypeDescriptor.TypeName);
```

```
                                   }

                          Console.WriteLine(" ");
                          foreach (Association association in
    sourceAssociations.Values)
                          {
                                  Console.WriteLine("           Source Association: " +
      association.Name);
                          }

                          Console.WriteLine(" ");
                          foreach (Association association in
    destinationAssociations.Values)
                          {
                                  Console.WriteLine("           Destination Association: "
      + association.Name);
                          }

                  }

              }
          }
```

When run, this will display the `Associations` for the `Entities` within the line-of-business application instances, as illustrated in Figure 10-8.

Summary

As demonstrated throughout this chapter, the Business Data Catalog is a metadata mapping shared service, enabling line-of-business applications to make data available as Office SharePoint Server 2007 properties and is an effective tool for Enterprise Application Integration strategies. You began your journey with an introduction to Business Data Catalog, starting with an architectural overview. Next, you explored the Metadata object model, which is crucial to manipulating and navigating BDC applications programmatically. After that grounding, you then learned about the XML Application Definition file and dove deeply into it, both from the database and web service type. The applications within the Business Data Catalog expose their data (types and properties), making it available to all SharePoint Server functionality, as metadata for other applications and services, Web Parts, and business data lists. The majority of the time was spent on the web service application definition because it is less straightforward than the database type. You then finished the chapter with a walk through the runtime API, examining several examples to see how to effectively use it.

```
file:///C:/Documents and Settings/Administrator/My Documents/Visual Studio 2005/Projects/mossa...   _ |B| X|
Listing system instances...
LOBSystemInstance: SampleWebServiceInstance

    Entity: Customer
        Field: CustomerID, System.String
        Field: Name, System.String
        Field: WorkPhoneNumber, System.Int64
        Field: MobilePhoneNumber, System.Int64
        Field: Industry, System.String
        Field: WebSite, System.String

        Source Association: CustomerToChildCustomers
        Source Association: CustomerAndRegionToOrders
        Source Association: CustomerToAddresses

        Destination Association: CustomerToChildCustomers

    Entity: Address
        Field: CustomerID, System.String
        Field: AddressID, System.String
        Field: BlockNumber, System.String
        Field: Street, System.String
        Field: City, System.String
        Field: StateProvince, System.String
        Field: CountryRegion, System.String
        Field: PostalCode, System.String

        Destination Association: CustomerToAddresses

    Entity: Region
        Field: RegionID, System.String
        Field: Name, System.String
        Field: Group, System.String
        Field: SalesLastYear, System.Decimal
        Field: SalesYTD, System.Decimal

        Source Association: CustomerAndRegionToOrders

    Entity: Order
        Field: OrderID, System.String
        Field: CustomerID, System.String
        Field: RegionID, System.String
        Field: CurrencyCode, System.String
        Field: SubTotal, System.Decimal
        Field: OrderDate, System.String
        Field: ShipDate, System.String

        Source Association: OrderToLineItems

        Destination Association: CustomerAndRegionToOrders

    Entity: LineItem
        Field: OrderID, System.String
        Field: ProductID, System.String
        Field: ProductName, System.String
        Field: OrderQty, System.Int32
        Field: UnitPrice, System.Decimal
        Field: LineTotal, System.Decimal

        Destination Association: OrderToLineItems
Press any key to exit...
```

Figure 10-8

11

Building Document Management Solutions

By John Holliday

The term "document management" has become a catch-all phrase for anything having to do with documents in an enterprise setting. It is an overly broad term that covers many different aspects of managing documents, from access control to version control to the auditing, review, and approval of content. To understand what document management means in the SharePoint environment, it helps to consider the evolution of document management systems over the last decade or so. It also helps to appreciate the value that SharePoint provides as a development platform for document management solutions.

Early document management systems were focused primarily on keeping track of revisions to documents that involved multiple authors, and operated in a manner similar to source code control systems. Individual authors checked out documents, thereby locking them so that other authors could not overwrite their changes. System administrators could specify who had permission to view or edit documents, and could generate reports of document activity. Other functions included the ability to automatically number each major or minor revision and revert at any time to a specific version of the document, generating the final content from information stored within the database.

The notion of metadata became a key characteristic of legacy document management systems. *Metadata* is information about a document, as opposed to the document content itself. For example, the current version number is an example of metadata, since it is information about the document. Other examples are the title, subject, comments and keywords associated with the document.

Most document management systems store document metadata in a central database. In fact, many of the early document management systems were written as database applications. This worked well at a time when the only business process being modeled was the generic document revision cycle. It starts to break down, however, when you want to model other business processes.

This is where SharePoint emerges as a superior platform for developing document management solutions. SharePoint refines the notion of document metadata to distinguish between system, class, and instance metadata. System-level metadata is maintained internally by SharePoint for all documents. Class-level metadata is stored within the SharePoint database for a given document library or content type and can be customized easily to include domain-specific information. Instance-level metadata is stored within each document instance as a set of document properties, and moves along with the physical document. This is especially important for managing documents in disconnected environments.

Because the term document management is so imprecise, it follows that the idea of what comprises a document management solution might be different depending on the context. One solution might implement a custom document approval process. Another might apply a business rule to determine who has access to a given set of documents. Yet another might apply a set of business rules that capture information about milestones achieved as a document is being edited.

So, what is a document management solution and how do you go about building one in SharePoint? The best way to answer this question is to examine the tools provided by the SharePoint platform in the context of a real scenario.

This chapter develops a solution for managing project proposals. The solution distinguishes between fixed-bid and time-and-material projects and provides metadata for controlling the content of each proposal as it evolves through the revision cycle. The solution will include custom fields for specifying the fixed-bid amount and the estimated hours for time-and-materials projects.

While developing a document management solution, it quickly becomes evident that business rules control not only the type of metadata that can be associated with a document but the range of acceptable values for each field. When a document is first created and at any stage during the revision cycle, the business rules examine the metadata and perform the appropriate actions to ensure that the document state is valid. This collection of business rules is often called a *content management policy* because it summarizes your policies and procedures for a particular type of document.

As you work through the chapter, developing the proposal management solution, you will explore SharePoint content types as a way to capture the essential characteristics of a document in one place. Content types offer tremendous advantages when building document management solutions; they allow you to encapsulate class-level metadata and associate it with code you can run on the server to implement custom business rules. The proposal management solution will include two policies: one to limit the acceptable bid amounts to a certain pre-approved range of values, and another to require a minimum number of estimated hours for time-and-material projects.

Finally, the chapter develops an extensible framework for defining document management policies using XML in conjunction with SharePoint event receivers. You also create custom commands that enable system administrators to use the STSADM command-line tool to administer proposal management policies after the solution is deployed.

Understanding the Document Lifecycle

Effective document management requires an understanding of the document lifecycle and the transformations that can occur as a document moves from one phase to the next. The basic document lifecycle consists of three phases: creation, revision, and publication. Each phase can be broken down into sub-phases that describe the different stages through which a typical document progresses over time (see Figure 11-1).

When a document is created, some information is needed to determine its initial content. You can call this *initiating metadata* for lack of a better term. At the very least, the initiating metadata for a SharePoint document consists of the location of the document template that should be used. Typically, the document template itself takes care of collecting any additional information that might be required to render the document in its initial state. For example, when creating a new proposal in Word, you might popup a dialog to interrogate the user prior to rendering the default document content.

After the document is created, its content is edited through one or more revision cycles. Throughout these iterations, various contributors may check out the document for editing and then check it back in until certain milestones have been achieved. The determination of whether a given milestone has been reached is often subjective, as there can be many different types of milestones, depending on the type of document and the kind of solution being developed. Nevertheless, to the extent you can identify such milestones, you can develop supporting metadata for them.

A typical requirement of a document management solution is to keep track of when changes are made and by whom. SharePoint supports this directly for all lists and list items. Another typical requirement is to enforce a particular numbering scheme for tracking versions, enforce checkout/checkin policies, or customize the way notifications are sent when changes are made.

Publication usually involves moving the finished document into a separate repository or routing it to one or more people for approval or review. As part of the publication process, it might be necessary to clean up the document content or convert it to a special file format for publication. For example, after publishing a document it might be necessary to convert it to PDF to ensure that it can be viewed by users who don't have Microsoft Word on their desktops.

Chapter 12 examines the publication phase and SharePoint's built-in support for automatic document conversion.

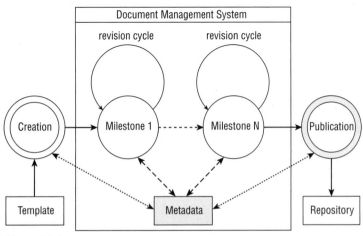

Figure 11-1

Defining Metadata Using Content Types

Metadata is the fuel that drives document management in SharePoint 2007, and the best way to work with document metadata is to define a content type. There are many benefits to using content types; the main one being that content types allow us to specify the custom fields needed to manage a document as it moves through the different stages of its lifecycle.

Solution developers are used to working with classes and objects, and properties and methods, where each class defines the properties and methods for instances of that class. They then create objects to represent instances of each class and invoke methods on those objects to apply business rules that retrieve or modify the state of the properties associated with each instance. Building document management solutions will be much easier if you can map the core elements (document, metadata, repository, etc.) onto familiar abstractions like *class* and *object* that you are used to working with.

SharePoint 2007 content types provide just such an abstraction. The content type acts as a sort of document class, defining the columns and event receivers that comprise each instance. The columns are like properties, and the event receivers are like methods. Take it one step further and say that the `ItemAdding` event receiver acts as a `constructor`, and the `ItemDeleting` event receiver acts as a *destructor* for each document instance.

The first step in defining a new content type is to determine from which of the built-in content types to derive the new content type. In object-oriented terms, you are choosing the base class for the new content type. SharePoint includes a number of default content types, all derived from the System content type, which serves as the root of the content type hierarchy.

Figure 11-2 shows some of the default content types and their identifiers.

SharePoint employs a special numbering scheme for identifying each content type, which it uses as a shortcut for creating new content type instances. Without such a numbering scheme, it might have been prohibitive to enable content type inheritance, since SharePoint would have needed to search through the database trying to resolve content type dependencies. This way, it only needs to examine the identifier, which it reads from right to left. For example, the Picture content type identifier is 0x010102, which SharePoint reads as id 02 (Picture) derived from Document (0x0101) derived from Item (0x01) derived from System (0x).

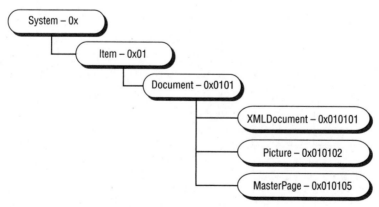

Figure 11-2

For custom content types that you define yourself, the identifier includes a suffix, which is the globally unique identifier (GUID) associated with our type, separated by 00 as a delimiter. For example, the project proposal content type defined later in this chapter has the ID

0x0101004A257CD7888D4E8BAEA35AFCDFDEA58C

Again, reading from right to left, you have 4A257CD7888D4E8BAEA35AFCDFDEA58C derived from Document (0x0101) derived from Item (0x01) derived from System (0x). The 00 serves as a delimiter between the GUID and the rest of the identifier, as shown in Figure 11-3.

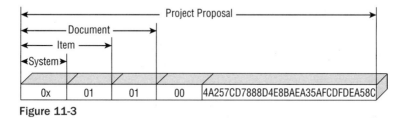

Figure 11-3

Each content type references a set of columns (also called fields), which compose the metadata associated with the type. It is important to note that content types do not declare columns directly. Instead, each content type includes column references that specify the identifiers of columns declared elsewhere within the SharePoint site. Column references are declared in XML using FieldRef elements.

Our project proposal content type is based on the built-in Document content type, which provides the following metadata fields:

❑ **Name** — The name of the file that contains the document content

❑ **Title** — The title of the document (inherited from the Item content type)

Next, you select from the built-in SharePoint fields to capture the common elements of a project proposal:

❑ **Author (Text)** — The author of the proposal

❑ **Start Date (DateTime)** — The date on which the project will start

❑ **End Date (DateTime)** — The date on which the project will end

❑ **Status (Choice)** — The current document status

❑ **Comments (Note)** — Additional comments

❑ **Keywords (Text)** — Keywords

In addition to the built-in columns, you need a few additional columns to complete the type definition.

❑ **ProposalType (Choice)** — The kind of proposal

❑ **EstimatedCost (Currency)** — The total cost of the proposed work

❑ **BidAmount (Currency)** — The proposed amount of the bid

❑ **EstimatedHours (Number)** — The total number of hours

❑ **HourlyRate (Currency)** — The proposed hourly rate

SharePoint provides two methods for declaring content types: using XML or using the Windows SharePoint Services object model. In actual practice, a hybrid approach is often useful. This is because while XML makes it easier to declare fields and other elements at a high level, it also makes it harder to work with the content type from elsewhere in your solution. Once the essential elements have been identified, the object model provides more control over how those elements are used and how they interact with one another. What you need is an easy way to declare the type while preserving your ability to add enhanced functionality through code.

The following sections explore both methods. You will use XML to declare the metadata for your custom project proposal content type and then the object model to control the behavior of each instance. As an alternative to using XML for the content type declaration, you will also explore ways to create content types entirely through code.

Declaring Content Types Using XML

To define a content type using XML, the following steps are required:

1. Create a content type definition file.

2. Create a field definition file that describes any custom fields.

3. Create a feature definition file that references the content type definition.

4. Install the feature into SharePoint.

The Content Type Definition File

Listing 11-1 shows the content type definition XML for the project proposal type. The content type ID is specified and indicates that the project proposal inherits the fields of the built-in Document type. The content type name "Project Proposal" is used to reference our type from code and from the SharePoint user interface.

Listing 11-1: Project proposal content type definition

```
<?xml version="1.0" encoding="utf-8"?>
<Elements xmlns="http://schemas.microsoft.com/sharepoint/">
        <!-- _filecategory="ContentType" _filetype="Schema"
_filename="contenttype.xml" _uniqueid="cff96a1e-6a52-4462-a3d0-d01471b8bfef" -->
        <ContentType ID="0x0101004a257cd7888d4e8baea35afcdfdea58c"
                Name="Project Proposal"
                Group="ProSharePoint2007"
                Description="A Content Type for Managing Project Proposals"
                Version="0">
                <FieldRefs>
                        <FieldRef ID="{246D0907-637C-46b7-9AA0-0BB914DAA832}"
Name="Author"/>
```

```
                              <FieldRef ID="{76A81629-44D4-4ce1-8D4D-6D7EBCD885FC}"
          Name="Subject" />
                              <FieldRef ID="{9DC4BA7E-6C50-4e24-9797-355131089A2E}"
          Name="ProposalType" Required="TRUE"/>
                              <FieldRef ID="{24A18FDA-927A-4232-88AE-F713FFD3FBB4}"
          Name="EstimatedCost"/>
                              <FieldRef ID="{41495470-9EA3-46e0-9A34-0E0C3DE1A445}"
          Name="BidAmount"/>
                              <FieldRef ID="{D46C0900-5617-414c-97E5-E5626DBC1495}"
          Name="EstimatedHours"/>
                              <FieldRef ID="{79368859-EAF8-4361-8A9D-C3CBD9C88697}"
          Name="HourlyRate"/>
                              <FieldRef ID="{64cd368d-2f95-4bfc-a1f9-8d4324ecb007}"
          Name="StartDate" />
                              <FieldRef ID="{8A121252-85A9-443d-8217-A1B57020FADF}"
          Name="EndDate" />
                              <FieldRef ID="{1DAB9B48-2D1A-47b3-878C-8E84F0D211BA}"
          Name="Status" />
                              <FieldRef ID="{52578FC3-1F01-4f4d-B016-94CCBCF428CF}"
           Name="Comments" />
                              <FieldRef ID="{B66E9B50-A28E-469b-B1A0-AF0E45486874}"
          Name="Keywords" />
                        </FieldRefs>
                </ContentType>
        </Elements>
```

Adding fields to a content type requires the use of `FieldRef` elements. This is because content types do not declare fields directly but instead refer to site columns that are defined globally within the current SharePoint execution context.

You will see shortly how site columns are declared, but for now note that each `FieldRef` element specifies the unique identifier of a separate Field element defined elsewhere within the solution. This includes both the built-in site columns that are shipped with Windows SharePoint Services, and any custom fields you define.

This presents a bit of a problem when building content type definition files. You already know the identifiers of the custom fields because you created them yourself. But for the built-in site columns, you first have to locate the appropriate identifiers that are recognized by SharePoint. When creating content types through the user interface, SharePoint looks up the field identifiers automatically. A bit of additional work is required when building a solution that installs custom content types at runtime.

The built-in site columns are declared in the `fieldswss.xml` file, which is located in the `12\TEMPLATE\ FEATURES\fields` folder. To declare a content type based on built-in site columns, you must search through this file to find the field you want, and then copy the GUID from the file into your content type definition XML.

To simplify the process of looking up field identifiers, use a simple XSL style sheet to display the `fieldswss.xml` file as an HTML table. The style sheet shown in Listing 11-2 produces the table shown in Figure 11-4.

Listing 11-2: XSL style sheet to locate built-In field IDs

```xml
<?xml version="1.0" encoding="utf-8"?>
<xsl:stylesheet version="1.0"
        xmlns:xsl="http://www.w3.org/1999/XSL/Transform"
        xmlns:wss="http://schemas.microsoft.com/sharepoint/">
        <xsl:output method="html" version="1.0" encoding="utf-8" indent="yes"/>
        <xsl:template match="wss:Elements">
                <html>
                        <body>
                                <h2>SharePoint v3 Built-In Fields</h2>
                                <table border="0" width="100%"
style="font-size:9pt;">
                                        <tr bgcolor="#9acd32">
                                <th align="left">Group</th>
                                <th align="left" width="100">Field</th>
                                <th align="left">Type</th>
                                <th align="left">Declaration</th>
                        </tr>
                        <xsl:apply-templates>
                            <xsl:sort select="@Group"/>
                            <xsl:sort select="@Name"/>
                        </xsl:apply-templates>
                    </table>
            </body>
        </html>
    </xsl:template>
    <xsl:template match="wss:Field">
        <tr>
            <td width="100"><xsl:value-of select="@Group"/></td>
            <td width="100"><xsl:value-of select="@Name"/></td>
            <td width="100"><xsl:value-of select="@Type"/></td>
            <td>
                &lt;FieldRef ID=&quot;<xsl:value-of select="@ID"/>&quot;
                    Name=&quot;<xsl:value-of select="@Name"/>&quot; /&gt;
            </td>
        </tr>
    </xsl:template>
</xsl:stylesheet>
```

This table comes in handy when writing content type definition XML files. In this example, you include not only the group, field name, and underlying data type but also a text string you can easily copy and paste into the content type definition file.

The Field Definition File

For the five custom fields of the project proposal, you have to create a set of site columns that will be deployed along with the solution. Site columns are defined in XML using CAML Field elements. Each Field element declares the unique identifier, field type, field name, description and other properties.

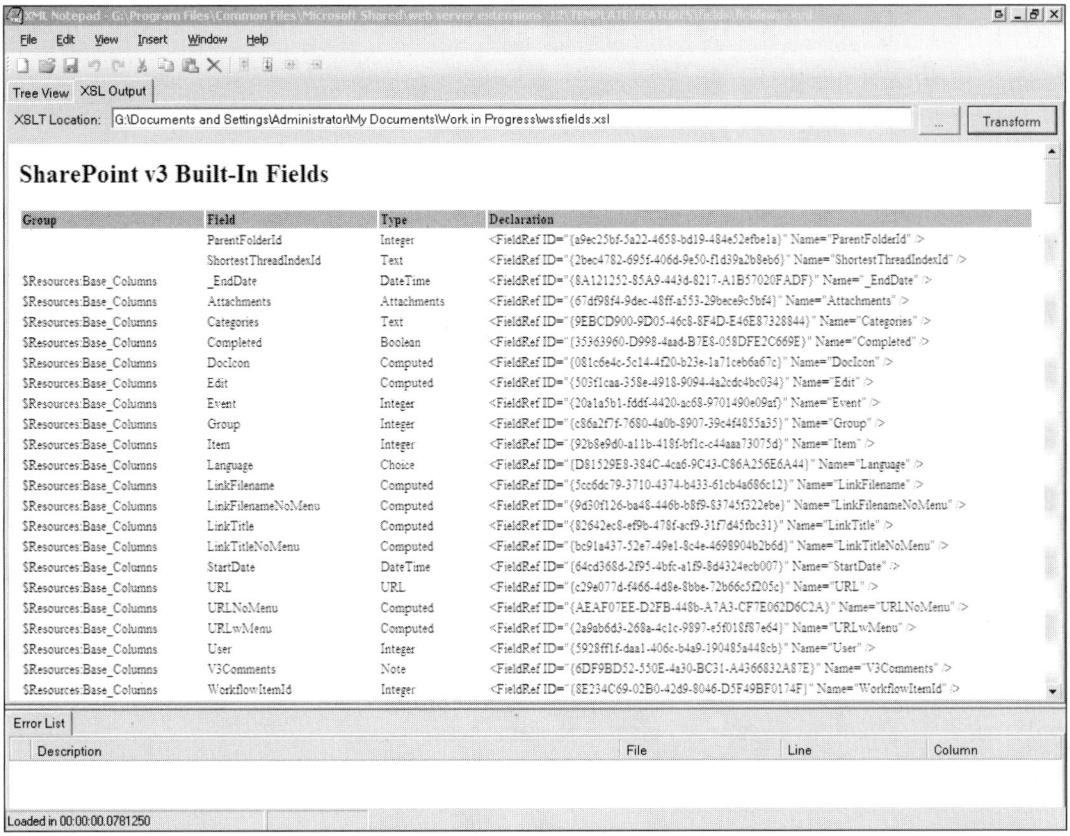

Figure 11-4

Listing 11-3 shows the custom field declarations for the project proposal content type.

Listing 11-3: Project proposal custom field declarations

```
<?xml version="1.0" encoding="utf-8"?>
<Elements xmlns="http://schemas.microsoft.com/sharepoint/">
    <Field
        ID="{9DC4BA7E-6C50-4e24-9797-355131089A2E}"
        Description="Select the proposal type from the available choices."
        Type="Choice"
        Name="ProposalType"
        DisplayName="Proposal Type"
        StaticName="_ProposalType"
        >
        <CHOICES>
          <CHOICE>$Resources:ProposalManager,_Choice_FixedBid</CHOICE>
          <CHOICE>$Resources:ProposalManager,_Choice_TimeAndMaterials</CHOICE>
```

```
                </CHOICES>
        </Field>
        <Field
            ID="{24A18FDA-927A-4232-88AE-F713FFD3FBB4}"
            Description="The estimated cost of performing the work."
            Type="Currency"
            Name="EstimatedCost"
            DisplayName="Estimated Cost"
            StaticName="_EstimatedCost"
            />
        <Field
            ID="{41495470-9EA3-46e0-9A34-0E0C3DE1A445}"
            Description="The total bid amount"
            Type="Currency"
            Name="BidAmount"
            DisplayName="Bid Amount"
            StaticName="_BidAmount"
            />
        <Field
            ID="{D46C0900-5617-414c-97E5-E5626DBC1495}"
            Description="The estimated person-hours for the project."
            Type="Number"
            Name="EstimatedHours"
            DisplayName="Estimated Hours"
            StaticName="_EstimatedHours"
            />
        <Field
            ID="{79368859-EAF8-4361-8A9D-C3CBD9C88697}"
            Description="The negotiated hourly rate."
            Type="Currency"
            Name="HourlyRate"
            DisplayName="Hourly Rate"
            StaticName="_HourlyRate"
            />
</Elements>
```

A Note about Resources

SharePoint uses a special syntax to enable XML definition files to reference strings and other resources at runtime. This powerful new feature enables developers to create more robust solutions with built-in localization support. Resource tags can also be used to keep the code synchronized with the XML definition files, thereby saving time during development.

The $Resources part of the tag indicates that the string should be retrieved from a RESX file stored in the 12\Resources folder. The next part of the tag specifies the name of the RESX file and the resource identifier to retrieve. In this case, the 12\Resources\ ProposalManager.resx file contains a string resource named _Choice_FixedBid that in turn holds the text "Fixed Bid".

The Feature Definition File

The final step is to create a feature definition that references the content type so you can activate the feature within the SharePoint environment. Listing 11-4 shows the feature definition file for the Proposal Management application.

Listing 11-4: Proposal management feature declaration

```
<Feature  Title="ProposalManagerFeature"
    Id="63d38c9c-3ada-4e07-873f-a278443e910c"
    Description=""
    Version="1.0.0.0"
    Scope="Web"
    Hidden="TRUE"
    DefaultResourceFile="core"
    ReceiverAssembly="ProposalManager, Version=1.0.0.0, Culture=neutral,
PublicKeyToken=9f4da00116c38ec5"
    ReceiverClass="ProSharePoint2007.ProposalManagerFeature"
    xmlns="http://schemas.microsoft.com/sharepoint/">
</Feature>
```

Defining Content Types in Code

There are many advantages to using the Windows SharePoint Services 3.0 object model instead of XML to define content types. These advantages include:

❑ No need to refer to the GUIDs of built-in site columns

❑ The ability to create dynamic types that depend on runtime conditions

❑ The ability to build a library of reusable content type components

Automatic Resolution of Built-In Field Identifiers

Setting up field references for content types declared using XML requires that the unique field identifier be known ahead of time. When creating field references in code, you only need to supply the associated field name. SharePoint retrieves the identifier automatically.

For example, the following code segment creates a `Project Proposal` content type based on the built-in `Document` type, and then adds an Author column to the new content type. The Author column is provided by SharePoint as one of the built-in site columns available in the Document Columns group.

```
using (SPSite site = new SPSite("http://localhost")) {
    using (SPWeb web = site.OpenWeb()) {
        SPContentType baseType =  web.AvailableContentTypes["Document"];
        SPContentType proposal = new SPContentType(
            baseType, web.ContentTypes, "Project Proposal");
        web.ContentTypes.Add(proposal);
        proposal.FieldLinks.Add(new SPFieldLink(web.AvailableFields["Author"]));
    }
}
```

Dynamic Content Type Definitions

With XML content type definitions, the fields are declared statically at design time. Once the content type is deployed and provisioned, its fields cannot be changed without rewriting the solution. On the other hand, by using the object model, you can set up the content type differently depending on external conditions. This way you can build smarter solutions that adjust automatically to accommodate changes in the run-time environment.

Building a Library of Reusable Content Type Components

When working with the Windows SharePoint Services 3.0 object model, it is useful to create a set of helper components to simplify solution development. This can greatly reduce the steps needed to build a solution because the low-level details of working with the object model are tucked away inside higher-level abstractions that are easier to declare and use. This is especially important when building document management solutions based on content types because you ultimately want to encapsulate the business rules within the content type itself. Having a library of core components means that you don't have to start from scratch each time you need a new content type.

Listing 11-5 shows a generic `ContentType` class that is used as a wrapper for the underlying `SPContentType` object instance.

Listing 11-5: A generic content type wrapper class

```
using System;
using Microsoft.SharePoint;

namespace ProSharePoint2007
{
    /// <summary>
    /// A utility class for manipulating SharePoint content types.
    /// </summary>
    public class ContentType
    {
        SPContentType m_contentType = null;

        /// <summary>
        /// Default constructor.
        /// </summary>
        public ContentType()
        {
        }

        /// <summary>
        /// Creates a wrapper for an existing content type instance.
        /// </summary>
        /// <param name="contentType"></param>
        public ContentType(SPContentType contentType)
        {
            m_contentType = contentType;
        }

        /// <summary>
        /// Adds a content type to a SharePoint list.
        /// </summary>
        public static void AddToList(SPList list, SPContentType contentType)
```

```csharp
{
    list.ContentTypesEnabled = true;
    list.ContentTypes.Add(contentType);
    list.Update();
}

/// <summary>
/// Removes a content type from a SharePoint list.
/// </summary>
public static void RemoveFromList(SPList list, string contentTypeName)
{
    foreach (SPContentType type in list.ContentTypes) {
        if (type.Name == contentTypeName) {
            list.ContentTypes.Delete(type.Id);
            list.Update();
            break;
        }
    }
}

/// <summary>
/// Loads a preexisting[content type.
/// </summary>
public virtual SPContentType Create(SPWeb web, string typeName)
{
    try {
        m_contentType = web.AvailableContentTypes[typeName];
    } catch {
    }
    return m_contentType;
}

/// <summary>
/// Creates a new content type.
/// </summary>
public virtual SPContentType Create(SPWeb web, string typeName,
                    string baseTypeName,
                    string description)
{
    try {
        SPContentType baseType = (baseTypeName == null
            || baseTypeName.Length == 0) ?
            web.AvailableContentTypes[SPContentTypeId.Empty] :
            web.AvailableContentTypes[baseTypeName];

        m_contentType = new SPContentType(
            baseType, web.ContentTypes, typeName);
        m_contentType.Description = description;
        web.ContentTypes.Add(m_contentType);
    } catch {
    }
    return m_contentType;
}

/// <summary>
/// Conversion operator to access the underlying SPContentType instance.
```

```
        /// </summary>
        public static implicit operator SPContentType(ContentType t){
            return t.m_contentType;
        }


        #region Field Methods

        /// <summary>
        /// Adds a new field having a specified name and type.
        /// </summary>
        public SPField AddField(string fieldDisplayName,
                      SPFieldType fieldType, bool bRequired)
        {
            SPField field = null;
            try {
                // get the parent web
                using (SPWeb web = m_contentType.ParentWeb) {
                    // create the field within the target web
                    string fieldName =
                        web.Fields.Add(fieldDisplayName,
                                  fieldType, bRequired);
                    field = web.Fields[fieldName];
                    // add a field link to the content type
                    m_contentType.FieldLinks.Add(
                        new SPFieldLink(field));
                    m_contentType.Update(false);
                }
            } catch {
            }
            return field;
        }


        /// <summary>
        /// Adds a new field based on an existing field in the parent web.
        /// </summary>
        public SPField AddField(string fieldName)
        {
            using (SPWeb web = m_contentType.ParentWeb) {
                SPField field = web.AvailableFields[fieldName];
                try {
                    if (field != null) {
                        m_contentType.FieldLinks.Add(
                            new SPFieldLink(field));
                        m_contentType.Update(false);
                    }
                } catch {
                }
            }
            return field;
        }
        #endregion
    }
}
```

With this helper class in the component library, it's easy to declare a new project proposal content type. It can either be instantiated from an XML definition associated with a feature or be created entirely in code. Listing 11-6 shows the declaration for the project proposal type derived from the generic content type wrapper class.

Listing 11-6: Using the content type wrapper class

```
using System;
using System.Collections.Generic;
using System.Text;
using Microsoft.SharePoint;

namespace ProSharePoint2007
{
    /// <summary>
    /// A helper class that encapsulates the ProjectProposal content type.
    /// </summary>
    class ProjectProposalType : ContentType
    {
        /// <summary>
        /// Creates the type using the XML content type definition.
        /// </summary>
        public SPContentType Create(SPWeb web)
        {
            return this.Create(web, "Project Proposal");
        }

        /// <summary>
        /// Creates the type using the SharePoint object model.
        /// </summary>
        public override SPContentType Create(SPWeb web, string typeName,
                           string baseTypeName,
                           string description)
        {
            // Call the base method to create the new type.
            SPContentType tProposal = base.Create(web, typeName,
                baseTypeName, description);

            // Create the fields programmatically.
            if (tProposal != null) {
                // built-in fields
                AddField("Author");
                AddField("Subject");
                AddField("StartDate");
                AddField("EndDate");
                AddField("Status");
                AddField("Comments");
                AddField("Keywords");
                // custom fields
                AddField(Strings._Field_ProposalType);
                AddField(Strings._Field_EstimatedCost);
                AddField(Strings._Field_BidAmount);
                AddField(Strings._Field_EstimatedHours);
```

```
            AddField(Strings._Field_HourlyRate);
        }
        return tProposal;
    }
  }
}
```

This code produces the content type definition shown in Figure 11-5.

In order to use the content type in a SharePoint site, you must deploy the type definition and then attach it to a list or document library for which content types have been enabled. Before you can achieve this, you need an additional piece of helper code to set up the document library to hold the proposal documents.

Listing 11-7 shows a `ProposalLibrary` class created for this purpose. When creating the document library, you remove the default `Document` content type so that users cannot create or upload standard documents. Finally, you create a new instance of the `ProjectProposal` content type and add it to the document library using the `AddToList` static method of the `ContentType` helper class.

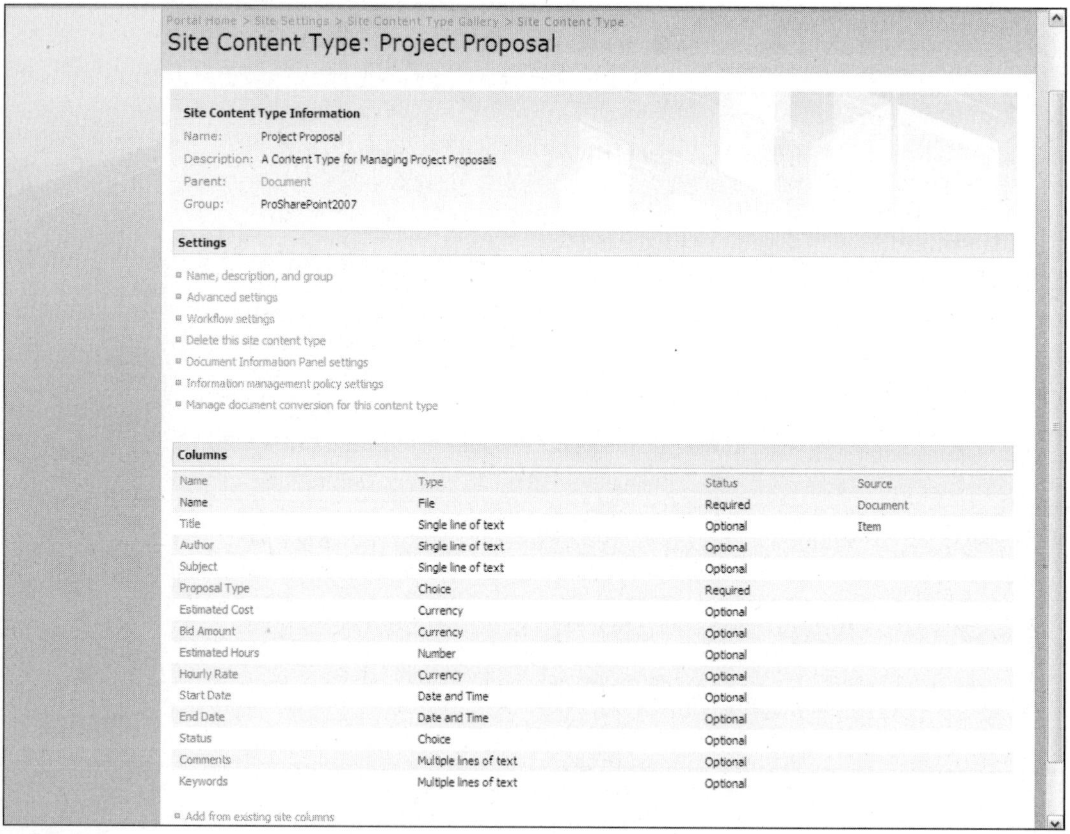

Figure 11-5

Listing 11-7: A custom proposal document library class

```
/// <summary>
/// A class that represents the proposals document library.
/// </summary>
class ProposalDocumentLibrary
{
    SPDocumentLibrary m_docLib = null;
    public ProposalDocumentLibrary(SPWeb web)
    {
        try {
            SPListTemplate template =
                web.ListTemplates["Document Library"];
            System.Guid guid =
                web.Lists.Add(
                    Strings._ProposalLibrary_Title,
                    Strings._ProposalLibrary_Desc,
                    template);
            m_docLib = web.Lists[guid] as SPDocumentLibrary;
        } catch {
        }
        // Initialize the base library properties.
        m_docLib.OnQuickLaunch = true;
        m_docLib.EnableVersioning = true;
        m_docLib.EnableModeration = true;
        m_docLib.EnableMinorVersions = true;

        // Remove the default "Document" content type.
        ContentType.RemoveFromList(m_docLib, "Document");

        // Add the custom proposal content type.
        ContentType.AddToList(m_docLib, new ProjectProposalType().Create(web));
    }
}
```

The easiest way to deploy a new content type is to include it as part of a custom feature. Here, you create a `ProposalManagement` feature to enable all of the proposal management tools on a site. As part of the feature implementation, you create an `SPFeatureReceiver` class for the `FeatureActivated` event that handles the deployment details for your custom content types. Listing 11-8 illustrates this process.

Listing 11-8: Provisioning a content type upon feature activation

```
using System;
using System.Runtime.InteropServices;
using System.Web.UI.WebControls.WebParts;
using Microsoft.SharePoint;
using Microsoft.SharePoint.WebPartPages;
```

```
namespace ProSharePoint2007
{
    [Guid("63d38c9c-3ada-4e07-873f-a278443e910c")]
    partial class ProposalManagerFeature : SPFeatureReceiver
    {
        [SharePointPermission(SecurityAction.LinkDemand, ObjectModel = true)]
        public override void FeatureActivated(
                    SPFeatureReceiverProperties properties)
        {
            if (properties == null) {
                return;
            }

            SPWeb web = properties.Feature.Parent as SPWeb;

            // Create a library to hold the proposals and add a
            // default list view to the left Web Part zone.

            AddListViewWebPart(web,
                new ProposalDocumentLibrary(web),
                "Left", PartChromeType.Default);
        }

        /// <summary>
        /// Creates a ListViewWebPart on the main page.
        /// </summary>
        private void AddListViewWebPart(SPWeb web, SPList list,
                            string zoneId,
                            PartChromeType chromeType)
        {
            // Access the default page of the web.
            SPFile root = web.RootFolder.Files[0];

            // Get the Web Part collection for the page.
            SPLimitedWebPartManager wpm = root.GetLimitedWebPartManager(
            System.Web.UI.WebControls.WebParts.PersonalizationScope.Shared);

            // Add a list view to the bottom of the zone.
            ListViewWebPart part = new ListViewWebPart();
            part.ListName = list.ID.ToString("B").ToUpper();
            part.ChromeType = chromeType;
            wpm.AddWebPart(part, zoneId, 99);
        }
    }
}
```

Now you have a site definition that includes the ProposalManager feature. When a site is created based on this site definition, the FeatureActivated event receiver creates a document library called Project Proposals that is automatically associated with your Project Proposal content type. Figure 11-6 shows the home page of a site created from the site definition.

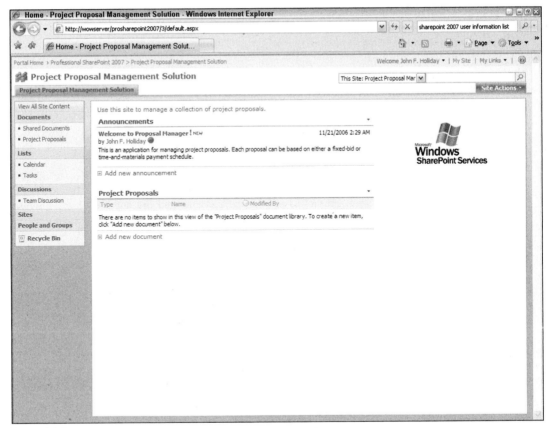

Figure 11-6

Managing Document Creation

In any document management solution, it's important that each new document adhere to organizational standards. This is especially true when metadata is being used to drive business processes. Even with a well-defined set of metadata fields and established guidelines for filling them out, busy knowledge workers often forget to provide this information because they are too focused on the document content. If the metadata is incomplete or inconsistent, then automated business processes that depend on it will fail. This leads to inefficiency and additional costs associated with finding and correcting the missing data.

Windows SharePoint Services 3.0 provides an enhanced callback mechanism that enables solution developers to control the document creation process and take prescriptive action based on the current state of the document. By implementing *event receivers*, you can write custom code that is called during document creation.

Document creation occurs in three stages:

1. The document template is opened in the appropriate editor program. The user edits the content and metadata and then saves the document into the library,

2. SharePoint retrieves the metadata and places it in a property bag, which it passes to the `ItemAdding` event receivers that have been registered for the library.

3. Unless one of the `ItemAdding` receivers cancels the document as noted below, SharePoint uses the properties to construct a new document list item, which is then added to the library. Next it calls the `ItemAdded` event receivers that have been registered for the library.

The `ItemAdding` event is called synchronously, suspending the document creation process until the event receiver returns control to SharePoint. By contrast, the `ItemAdded` event is called asynchronously after the document has been added to the library. Using this architecture, you can implement an `ItemAdding` event receiver to cancel the `Add` operation if the document metadata does not meet your requirements.

The key issues to address are:

1. Have all required metadata fields been supplied with the document?
2. Are the values of the required metadata fields consistent with each other?
3. Is the metadata consistent with our document management policy?

Checking for Required Metadata

First, ensure that all of the required metadata fields have been supplied. For the project proposal, you want to ensure that the user has selected a project type, because the other business rules depend on this value. If it is not supplied, then you reject the document and notify the user.

The usual way to ensure that required metadata fields have been filled out is to set the `Required` attribute to "TRUE" when defining the content type. This works well for simple document types but not in more complex scenarios, where the set of required fields may change depending on an externally defined policy. It may still be necessary to use the `Required` attribute for documents that are created on the client. For instance, Microsoft Word will throw a generic exception instead of displaying a user-friendly error message when the `ItemAdding` event is canceled. Using the `Required` attribute forces the user to enter the item and also enables Word to display a visual cue indicating required fields, as shown in Figure 11-7.

When the `ItemAdding` event receiver is called, SharePoint passes a `SPItemEventProperties` object as a parameter. This object holds the property values for all of the metadata supplied by the user when creating the document. Using this object is a bit tricky because the same type of object is also passed to the other event receiver methods. However, different fields are supplied at different stages of the document lifecycle. The following table shows the relationship between selected fields of the `SPItemEventProperties` object and the Add/Update pairs of event receiver methods.

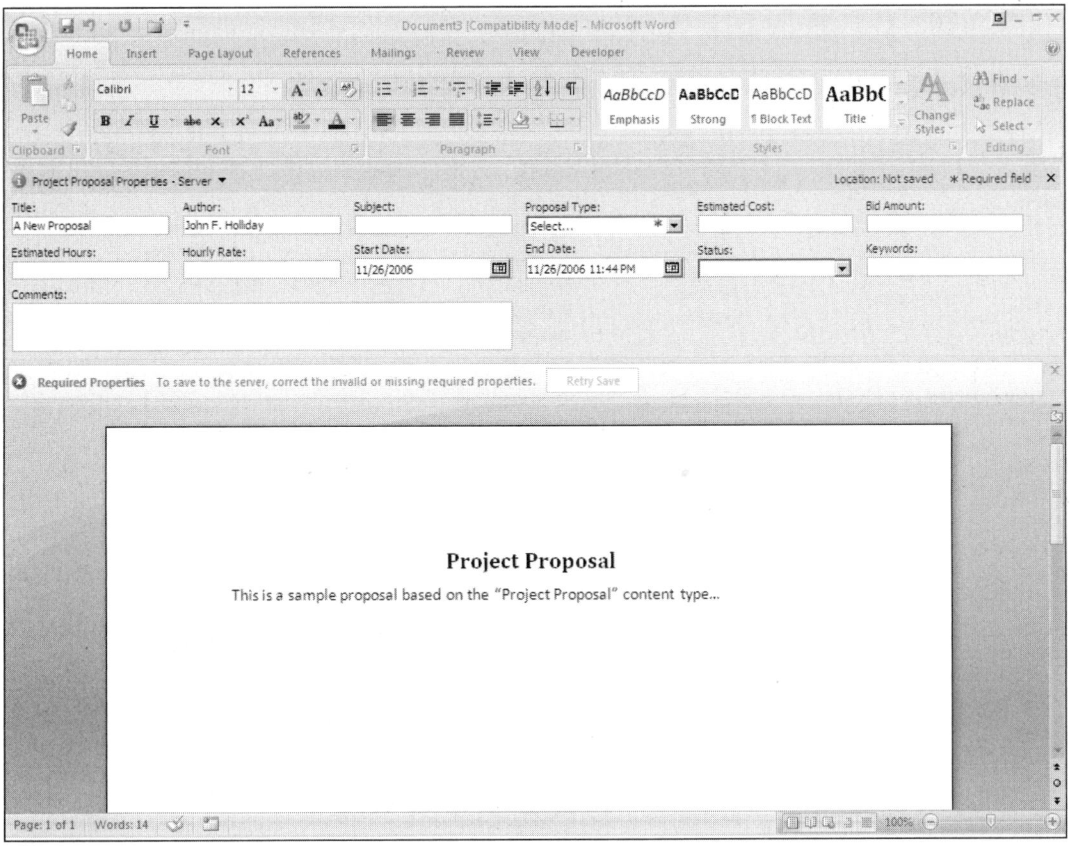

Figure 11-7

Method	Description	Field	Available?	Comments
ItemAdding	Called before an item is added to the list.			
		ListId	Yes	Identifies the list that will contain the new item.
		ListItem	No	The list item has not yet been created.
		Before-Properties	No	Item properties are only available after the item is created.
		After-Properties	Yes	Item properties that will be used to populate the new item.

Continued

Method	Description	Field	Available?	Comments
ItemAdded	Called after an item is added to the list.			
		ListId	Yes	Identifies the containing list.
		ListItem	Yes	Identifies the new list item.
		Before-Properties	No	No item properties existed prior to item creation.
		After-Properties	Yes	Item properties that were used to populate the new item.
ItemUpdating	Called before an item is updated.			
		ListId	Yes	Identifies the containing list.
		ListItem	Yes	Identifies the list item.
		Before-Properties	Yes	Holds a hashtable of item properties before the update.
		After-Properties	Yes	Holds a hashtable of item properties that will be applied when the update is processed.
ItemUpdated	Called after an item is updated.			
		ListId	Yes	Identifies the containing list.
		ListItem	Yes	Identifies the list item.
		Before-Properties	Yes	Holds a hashtable of item properties before the update.
		After-Properties	Yes	Holds a hashtable of item properties after the update.

To make things easier and to simplify the code, you can declare a static class that takes these dependencies into account. Listing 11-9 shows how to implement the ItemAdding event receiver to check for the required metadata using a static wrapper class to process the raw SPItemEventProperties object.

Listing 11-9: ItemAdding event receiver

```
/// <summary>
/// A helper class for testing various conditions on SharePoint list items.
/// </summary>
public class ItemCondition
{
    public static bool HasProposalType(SPItemEventProperties properties)
    {
        object value = properties.AfterProperties["Proposal Type"];
        return value != null && value.ToString() != string.Empty;
    }
}


/// <summary>
/// Synchronous before event that occurs when a new item is added
/// to its containing object.
/// </summary>
/// <param name="properties">
/// A Microsoft.SharePoint.SPItemEventProperties object
/// that represents properties of the event handler.
/// </param>
[SharePointPermission(SecurityAction.LinkDemand, ObjectModel = true)]
public override void ItemAdding(SPItemEventProperties properties)
{
    try {
        ValidateItemProperties(properties);
    } catch (Exception x) {
        properties.ErrorMessage = x.Message;
        properties.Cancel = true;
    }
}


/// <summary>
/// Helper method to determine whether an item meets validation requirements.
/// </summary>
/// <param name="properties"></param>
private void ValidateItemProperties(SPItemEventProperties properties)
{
    if (!ItemCondition.HasProposalType(properties))
        throw new SPItemValidationException(properties, "You must select a proposal
type.");
}
```

Checking Metadata Consistency

In the case of the project proposal, you check for different field values depending on the type of project that was selected. For instance, time-and-material projects require the user to provide an initial estimate of the hours needed to complete the project, while fixed-bid projects require an estimate of the total bid amount. You will use these values later when implementing other business rules, so it is vital that the appropriate values are entered correctly.

When an item is added to a list, SharePoint calls the ItemAdding *event receiver, but it does not call the* ItemUpdating *event receiver. Conversely, when an item is edited, SharePoint calls only the* ItemUpdating *event receiver. Therefore, any consistency checking code should be called from both the* ItemAdding *and the* ItemUpdating *event receivers.*

Postprocessing of Metadata

After a document has been added to the library, it is often useful to perform postcreation tasks such as making entries into a tracking log or notifying users that a new document has been created. In the proposal-tracking system, you want to keep a running record of the progress each proposal makes throughout its lifecycle. You can do this easily by setting up a SharePoint list to record the date and time a given event occurs.

You begin by defining a second content type called a ProposalTrackingRecord and enable it for a custom list called "Proposal History." The ProposalTrackingRecord is derived from the built-in Item content type, and consists of only the title field. Use the title to display the text of the tracking event.

```
<ContentType ID="0x0100a0cada319e714c1fab64c519c065d421"
        Name="Proposal Tracking Record"
        Group="ProSharePoint2007"
        Description="A list item for tracking proposal-specific events."
        Version="0">
        <FieldRefs/>
</ContentType>
```

You can use a ProposalTrackingEvent enumeration to model the different kinds of events you wish to track. In addition to the standard document lifecycle events, you can also capture important proposal-specific milestones such as when a proposal is approved for submission to the client, or when a proposal is accepted by the client.

```
enum ProposalTrackingEvent
{
    Created,
    Modified,
    MajorRevision,
    MinorRevision,
    CheckedOut,
    CheckedIn,
    ApprovedForSubmission,
    AcceptedByClient,
    Published,
    Deleted,
    Archived,
}
```

Finally, in the same way that you created the Proposals document library, you now create the Proposal History custom list and an associated ListView in the right Web Part zone.

```
// Create a custom list to hold the proposal history and
// add a default list view to the right Web Part zone.

AddListViewWebPart(web, new ProposalHistoryList(web),
        "Right", PartChromeType.TitleOnly);
```

To capture postcreation events, implement an `ItemAdded` event receiver for the `ProjectProposal` content type. This event is fired after the metadata has been validated and the new document has been added to the library. When the event receiver is called, you obtain a reference to the Proposal History list and make the appropriate entries using the `AddRecord` helper method:

```
[SharePointPermission(SecurityAction.LinkDemand, ObjectModel = true)]
public override void ItemAdded(SPItemEventProperties properties)
{
    // Add an entry to the proposal history list.
    SPWeb web = properties.ListItem.ParentList.ParentWeb;
    ProposalHistoryList history = ProposalHistoryList.FromWeb(web);
    history.AddRecord(ProposalTrackingEvent.Created,
        properties.AfterProperties);
}
```

Now, whenever a project proposal is added to the proposals library, a new tracking record is created based on the type of event (in this case, `ProposalTrackingEvent.Created`) and the properties stored in the new item. Depending on the event type, you can use these properties to capture a more detailed picture of the context surrounding the event. This analysis could be recorded separately or could cause a custom workflow to be initiated. Figure 11-8 shows the project history list with a tracking record entry.

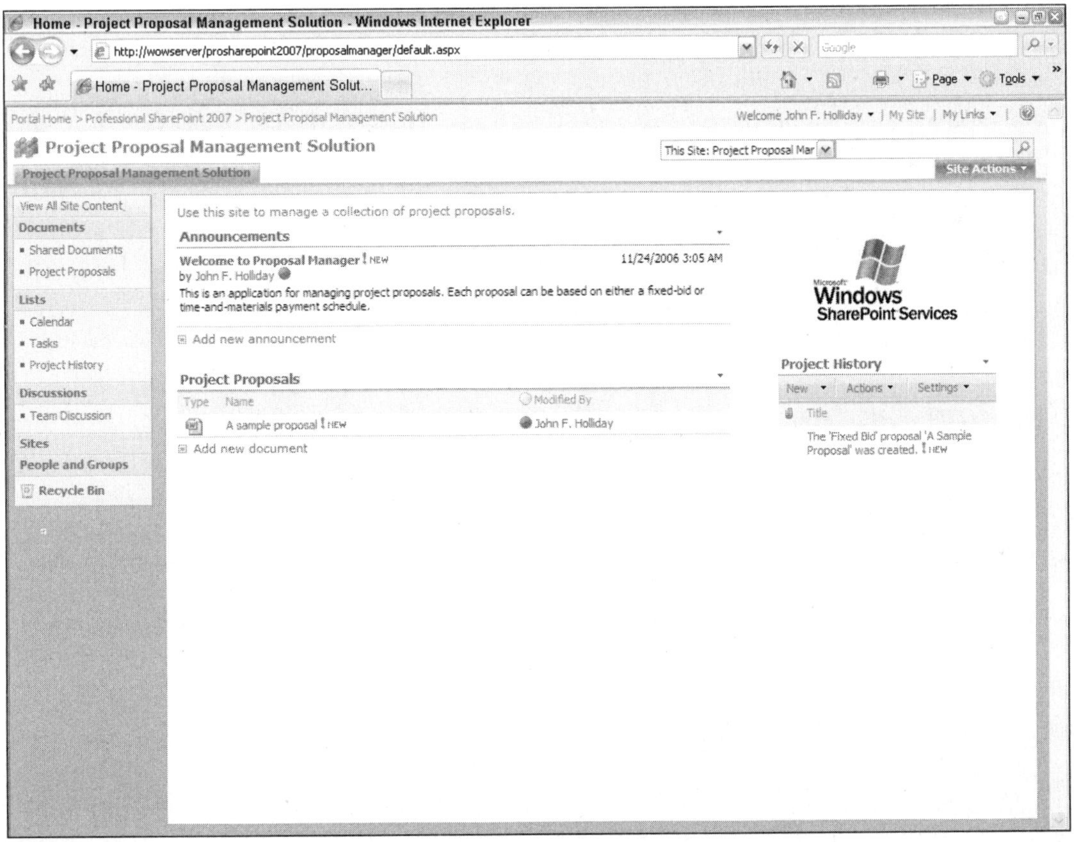

Figure 11-8

Managing the Document Revision Cycle

Referring back to the generic model of the document lifecycle, note that all documents follow the general pattern of creation/revision/publication. Unlike the creation phase, which happens only once, the revision phase occurs repeatedly until the document is ready for publication. During the revision phase, many different types of events can occur, depending on the state of the document metadata and the status of its content.

The SharePoint object model defines eight pairs of events that can occur during the document revision cycle. These are captured by the following elements of the `SPItemEventReceiverType` enumeration. Using these events, you can control all aspects of document revision.

- ❏   `ItemUpdated/Updating`
- ❏   `ItemCheckedIn/CheckingIn`
- ❏   `ItemCheckedOut/CheckingOut`
- ❏   `ItemUncheckedOut/UncheckingOut`
- ❏   `ItemAttachmentAdded/Adding`
- ❏   `ItemAttachmentDeleted/Deleting`
- ❏   `ItemFileMoved/Moving`
- ❏   `ItemDeleted/Deleting`

> *We shall ignore the* `ItemFileConverted` *event and the* `ItemFileMoved/Moving` *event pair because they happen outside the document revision cycle.*

During each stage of the revision cycle, you can use document metadata to analyze the current state of the document in terms of the problem domain and then update the metadata in the appropriate way. This revised metadata can be used to further constrain the behavior of the document or to control the actions of the people involved in editing it.

The following sections explore the construction of both generic and domain-specific tools for analyzing metadata to assist in answering the question "what happens next?" in the context of these events.

Building Custom Tools for Metadata Analysis

Sometimes it is useful to distinguish between metadata maintained by the system and custom metadata you defined within the problem domain. For the former, it's easy to create a library of reusable tools that can be used to quickly analyze system-defined properties. For instance, SharePoint can automatically track major and minor versions of each document in a library and can enforce moderation (approval) and checkout policies. Using the object model components associated with these properties, you can create components that perform useful functions, such as:

- ❏   Determine if the major or minor version number exceeds a certain limit
- ❏   Determine the current approval status of the document

❑   Compute the average length of time a document remains checked out

❑   Count the number of times a given user has checked in or reviewed a document

You can take the same approach for domain-specific metadata such as, in this example, where you might want to define a set of high-level methods for working with project proposals. These general and specific methods can make it much easier to build custom business rules. For example, you might need the following two rules:

❑   Compare the estimated cost of a fixed-bid proposal to a predefined limit.

❑   Compare the estimated man-hours of a time-and-materials proposal to a predefined minimum.

To support these rules, you can create a wrapper class for retrieving the bid amount and estimated hours from a set of project proposal properties. The properties are passed to the SPItemEventReceiver as described earlier. Listing 11-10 shows the ProjectProposal wrapper class that is derived from a generic wrapper for SharePoint list items.

Listing 11-10: A project proposal wrapper class

```
/// <summary>
/// A wrapper class for a project proposal instance.
/// </summary>
class ProjectProposal : SharePointListItem
{
    /// <summary>
    /// Constructs a wrapper for the underlying list item.
    /// </summary>
    public ProjectProposal(SPListItem item):base(item)
    {
    }

    #region Property Value Accessors

    /// <summary>
    /// Retrieves the proposal type as reflected by the item properties.
    /// </summary>
    public static ProposalType GetProposalType(SPItemEventDataCollection
properties)
    {
        ProposalType type = ProposalType.TimeAndMaterials;
        try {
            object value = properties[Strings._Field_ProposalType];
            string choice = value.ToString();
            if (choice.Equals(Strings._Choice_FixedBid))
                type = ProposalType.FixedBid;
        } catch {
        }
        return type;
    }
```

```
/// <summary>
/// Retrieves the proposal bid amount.
/// </summary>
public static decimal GetBidAmount(SPItemEventDataCollection properties)
{
    decimal amount = 0M;
    try {
        object value = properties[Strings._Field_BidAmount];
        amount = Decimal.Parse(value.ToString());
    } catch {
    }
    return amount;
}

/// <summary>
/// Retrieves the estimated person hours for a proposal.
/// </summary>
public static decimal GetEstimatedHours(SPItemEventDataCollection properties)
{
    decimal amount = 0M;
    try {
        object value = properties[Strings._Field_EstimatedHours];
        amount = Decimal.Parse(value.ToString());
    } catch {
    }
    return amount;
}
#endregion
}
```

Ensuring Metadata Consistency between Revisions

Using your library of metadata analysis components, you can easily test for a range of conditions whenever a proposal document is updated. First, you perform the same metadata consistency check as when adding an item, rejecting the update from the ItemUpdating event receiver if a problem exists. Then, you use the project proposal wrapper to test for the two conditions you defined in the business rules.

```
[SharePointPermission(SecurityAction.LinkDemand, ObjectModel = true)]
public override void ItemUpdating(SPItemEventProperties properties)
{
const decimal MinimumBid =5000M;
const decimal MinimumHours = 300M;
try {
    ValidateItemProperties(properties);
    switch (ProjectProposal.GetProposalType(
            properties.AfterProperties)
    {
    case ProposalType.FixedBid: {
        if (ProjectProposal.GetBidAmount(
            properties.AfterProperties) < MinimumBid) {
            throw new ApplicationException(
```

```
                "Bids must be higher than " +
                    MinimumBid.ToString());
        }
        break;
    case ProposalType.TimeAndMaterials: {
        if (ProjectProposal.GetEstimatedHours(
            properties.AfterProperties) < MinimumHours) {
            throw new ApplicationException(
                "Hours must be greater than " +
                    MinimumHours.ToString());
        }
        break;
    }
} catch (Exception x) {
        properties.ErrorMessage = x.Message;
        properties.Cancel = true;
    }
}
```

At this point, you can perform other tests suitable for proposal documents. As more conditions are added, you can easily extend the framework to accommodate them by implementing the appropriate static methods on the `ProjectProposal` class and making the corresponding call from the event receiver.

Managing Checkin and Checkout

SharePoint supports enforced checkout for document libraries and lists. Setting the `ForceCheckout` property to `true` causes SharePoint to require that users check out a document before editing it. However, you may need to place additional constraints on document items. For example, you may need to control which users are allowed to check out a document, or keep track of which users checked out which documents, or calculate the average length of time a given user keeps documents checked out, and so on.

A good example of when this might be necessary is in a document library that is set up to enforce approval via the built-in `_ModerationStatus` field. After the document has been approved, you might wish to prevent users other than the approver from making further changes. You can do this by implementing a `CheckingOut` event receiver, checking the moderation status and then comparing the moderator to the current user. If they do not match and the document has been approved, then you abort the checkout with an appropriate message to the user.

Developing XML-Driven Document Management Solutions

Writing code whenever you want to change the policies associated with a content type can become a tedious operation. It would be better if you could define the more volatile aspects of the policy in an external file and then process that file during execution in order to determine if metadata has been provided consistently and completely. The problem is where should you put the file?

You could certainly put the file in a well-known location, but that would require too much knowledge of the operating environment. What you are really trying to do is separate the policy from your content type implementation so that you can change it more easily.

This section shows how to control the behavior of a class of documents using rules defined in an XML schema associated with a content type. After developing a simple project proposal management schema you create a default policy based on the schema and then attach it to the content type definition. As events are generated by SharePoint during the document revision cycle, you retrieve the policy from the content type and apply the policy.

Developing a Proposal Management Policy Schema

Referring back to the document lifecycle diagram, you can see how policies will affect the overall document revision cycle. Figure 11-9 shows the revision cycle with policies attached. You want to ensure that the total bid amount for fixed-bid proposals is never less than $5000. On the other hand for time-and-materials proposals, you want to reject any revision where the estimated hours are less than 300. And you want to be able to change these values without recoding the solution.

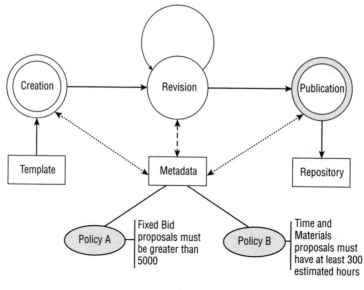

Figure 11-9

You can meet these needs by defining a simple schema to manage project proposals. The schema will distinguish between the two different types of proposals and provide elements for specifying acceptable bid amounts and estimated hours. In addition, you need a way to control what happens when the policy has been violated. This example shows how to display an error message to the user stating the condition and the expected values. Figure 11-10 depicts the proposal management policy schema shown in Listing 11-11.

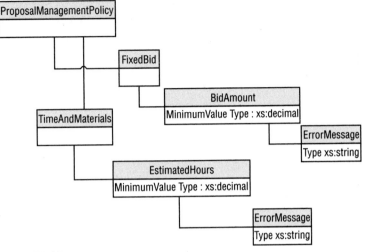

Figure 11-10

Listing 11-11: Proposal management policy schema

```
<xs:element name="ProposalManagementPolicy"
         xmlns:xs="http://www.w3.org/2001/XMLSchema">
<xs:complexType>
    <xs:sequence>
        <xs:element name="FixedBid">
            <xs:complexType>
                <xs:sequence>
                    <xs:element name="BidAmount">
                        <xs:complexType>
                            <xs:sequence>
                                <xs:element
                                    name="ErrorMessage"
                                    type="xs:string" />
                            </xs:sequence>
                            <xs:attribute name="MinimumValue"
                                type="xs:decimal"
                                use="required" />
                        </xs:complexType>
                    </xs:element>
                </xs:sequence>
            </xs:complexType>
        </xs:element>
        <xs:element name="TimeAndMaterials">
            <xs:complexType>
                <xs:sequence>
                    <xs:element name="EstimatedHours">
```

```
<xs:complexType>
    <xs:sequence>
        <xs:element
            name="ErrorMessage"
            type="xs:string" />
    </xs:sequence>
    <xs:attribute name="MinimumValue"
        type="xs:decimal"
        use="required" />
</xs:complexType>
            </xs:element>
        </xs:sequence>
    </xs:complexType>
    </xs:element>
</xs:sequence>
</xs:complexType>
</xs:element>
```

Using this schema definition, you can create a default policy for new project proposals. To make it easier for system administrators who will be editing these files, the example uses a simple value substitution scheme that looks for tokens in the error message text and replaces them with attribute values.

```
<ProposalManagementPolicy
        xmlns="http://schemas.johnholliday.net/proposalmanagementpolicy.xsd">
    <FixedBid>
        <BidAmount MinimumValue="5000">
            <ErrorMessage>The bid amount must be at least $$MinimumValue$$
.</ErrorMessage>
        </BidAmount>
    </FixedBid>
    <TimeAndMaterials>
        <EstimatedHours MinimumValue="300">
            <ErrorMessage>The estimated hours must be at least $$MinimumValue$$
.</ErrorMessage>
        </EstimatedHours>
    </TimeAndMaterials>
</ProposalManagementPolicy>
```

Attaching the Policy to a Content Type

In order for this to work, you need to associate the default policy with the project proposal content type. As it turns out, SharePoint has a built-in facility for doing this.

SharePoint maintains a collection of XML documents for each content type. These documents are accessible through the XmlDocuments Element in the content type definition. There are two ways to associate an XmlDocument with a content type: in the content type definition XML, used to provision the content type, and through the Windows SharePoint Services 3.0 object model. Which method to use depends on when the information is required and whether it will change.

If the information is static or is needed during the provisioning process, then the best option is to include it in the content type definition XML. On the other hand, if the information is dynamic, then the object model is probably the best choice. That way, you can drive other behaviors or control user interactions based on the contents of the associated XML document.

In this example, both conditions are true. You need the information from the default policy during the provisioning process so you can accept or reject new proposals, and you also need the policy information to be dynamic because you want to enable administrative users to modify the policy at any given time.

Adding the default policy to the content type definition XML requires that you insert an XmlDocuments element that contains a child XmlDocument element. You then place the contents of the custom XML document inside the XmlDocument element.

```xml
<?xml version="1.0" encoding="utf-8"?>
<Elements xmlns="http://schemas.microsoft.com/sharepoint/">
<!-- _filecategory="ContentType" _filetype="Schema" _filename="contenttype.xml"
_uniqueid="cff96a1e-6a52-4462-a3d0-d01471b8bfef" -->
<ContentType ID="0x0101004a257cd7888d4e8baea35afcdfdea58c"
    Name="Project Proposal"
    Group="ProSharePoint2007"
    Description="A Content Type for Managing Project Proposals"
    Version="0">
    <FieldRefs>
        <FieldRef ID="{246D0907-637C-46b7-9AA0-0BB914DAA832}" Name="Author"/>
        <FieldRef ID="{76A81629-44D4-4ce1-8D4D-6D7EBCD885FC}" Name="Subject" />
        <FieldRef ID="{9DC4BA7E-6C50-4e24-9797-355131089A2E}" Name="ProposalType"
                            Required="TRUE"/>
        <FieldRef ID="{24A18FDA-927A-4232-88AE-F713FFD3FBB4}" Name="EstimatedCost"/>
        <FieldRef ID="{41495470-9EA3-46e0-9A34-0E0C3DE1A445}" Name="BidAmount"/>
        <FieldRef ID="{D46C0900-5617-414c-97E5-E5626DBC1495}" Name="EstimatedHours"/>
        <FieldRef ID="{79368859-EAF8-4361-8A9D-C3CBD9C88697}" Name="HourlyRate"/>
        <FieldRef ID="{64cd368d-2f95-4bfc-a1f9-8d4324ecb007}" Name="StartDate" />
        <FieldRef ID="{8A121252-85A9-443d-8217-A1B57020FADF}" Name="EndDate" />
        <FieldRef ID="{1DAB9B48-2D1A-47b3-878C-8E84F0D211BA}" Name="Status" />
        <FieldRef ID="{52578FC3-1F01-4f4d-B016-94CCBCF428CF}" Name="Comments" />
        <FieldRef ID="{B66E9B50-A28E-469b-B1A0-AF0E45486874}" Name="Keywords" />
    </FieldRefs>
    <XmlDocuments>
        <XmlDocument NamespaceURI="$Resources:ProposalManager,
ProposalManagementPolicyNamespace">
            <ProposalManagementPolicy>
                <FixedBid>
                    <BidAmount MinimumValue="5000">
                        <ErrorMessage>The bid amount must be at least $$MinimumValue$$
.</ErrorMessage>
                    </BidAmount>
                </FixedBid>
                <TimeAndMaterials>
                    <EstimatedHours MinimumValue="50">
                        <ErrorMessage>The estimated hours must be at least
$$MinimumValue$$.</ErrorMessage>
                    </EstimatedHours>
                </TimeAndMaterials>
            </ProposalManagementPolicy>
        </XmlDocument>
    </XmlDocuments>
</ContentType>
</Elements>
```

SharePoint uses the NamespaceURI attribute to index the collection of XML documents associated with a content type. This means that you must specify a namespace attribute for the XmlDocument element or you will not be able to locate the document when calling the SharePoint object model from your code.

The SharePoint SDK states that you can add any number of XML documents to the XmlDocuments collection, and that any XML document can be used as long as it is valid XML. In practice, I've found that not only must the XML be valid, but it must not cause an exception to be thrown while SharePoint is deserializing the XML fragment. For instance, if namespaces are used, they must resolve properly. Also, it must be an XML fragment and not an XML document. In other words, it must not include an xml directive. If an exception occurs, then SharePoint will silently consume the exception but will not completely load the content type. One side effect of this is that the content type will be created, but without the expected metadata fields. Similarly, if the NamespaceURI attribute is missing, SharePoint will abort the load.

Processing the Policy in Response to Events

The logical place to process policy files is in the synchronous event receiver methods ItemAdding and ItemUpdating, because you can cancel the operation and display an error message to the user. In order for this to work, you need to add a static method to the ProjectProposalType wrapper class.

The ApplyPolicy method extracts the XML document containing our default policy and then uses the XmlSerializer to deserialize it into a C# class. The ProposalManagementPolicy class is shown in Listing 11-12. By passing the SPItemEventProperties parameter along, you can then invoke the appropriate methods on the deserialized class to analyze the properties of the new or modified item in the context of the policy values. You use an extra parameter to specify the context in which the policy is to be applied (add, update, delete, etc.).

```
public static void ApplyPolicy(SPItemEventProperties properties,
                    ProposalManagementPolicy.PolicyContext context)
{
    ProposalManagementPolicy policy = null;
    ProjectProposalType proposalType = new ProjectProposalType();
    using (SPWeb web = properties.OpenWeb())
        {
            if (proposalType.Create(web) != null) {
                string xml = proposalType.GetXmlString(
                    Strings.ProposalManagementPolicyNamespace);
                policy = ProposalManagementPolicy.FromXml(xml);
            } else {
                policy = ProposalManagementPolicy.ReadFrom(
                    Strings.DefaultPolicy);
            }
        }
        if (policy != null) {
            policy.ApplyPolicy(properties.AfterProperties, context);
        }
}
```

Listing 11-12: Proposal management policy class

```
using System;
using System.IO;
using System.Data;
using System.Text;
using System.Diagnostics;
using System.ComponentModel;
using System.Xml;
using System.Xml.Serialization;
using Microsoft.SharePoint;

namespace ProSharePoint2007
{
    [Serializable]
    [XmlType(AnonymousType=true)]
    [XmlRoot(Namespace="", IsNullable=false)]
    public class ProposalManagementPolicy {

        /// <summary>
        /// Specifies the context in which a given policy is being applied.
        /// </summary>
        public enum PolicyContext
        {
            Add,
            Update,
            CheckIn,
            CheckOut,
            Delete
        }

        /// <summary>
        /// Loads a ProposalManagementPolicy object from a file.
        /// </summary>
        public static ProposalManagementPolicy ReadFrom(string fileName)
        {
            XmlSerializer ser = new XmlSerializer(
            typeof(ProposalManagementPolicy), "");
            return (ProposalManagementPolicy)ser.Deserialize(
            new StreamReader(fileName));
        }

        /// <summary>
        /// Loads a ProposalManagementPolicy object from an xml string.
        /// </summary>
        public static ProposalManagementPolicy FromXml(string xml)
        {
            xml = xml.Replace(Strings.XmlDirective_Utf16,
                    Strings.XmlDirective_Utf8).Trim();
```

```
        if (!xml.StartsWith(Strings.XmlDirective_Utf8))
            xml = Strings.XmlDirective_Utf8 + xml;

        XmlSerializer ser = new XmlSerializer(
                    typeof(ProposalManagementPolicy), "");
        return (ProposalManagementPolicy)ser.Deserialize(
                    new StringReader(xml));
    }

    /// <summary>
    /// Loads a ProposalManagementPolicy object from a content type.
    /// </summary>
    /// <param name="contentType">the containing content type instance</param>
    public static ProposalManagementPolicy FromContentType(
                        ContentType contentType)
    {
        string xml = contentType.GetXmlString(
            Strings.ProposalManagementPolicyNamespace);
        XmlSerializer ser = new XmlSerializer(
            typeof(ProposalManagementPolicy), "");
        return (ProposalManagementPolicy)ser.Deserialize(new
StringReader(xml));
    }

    /// <summary>
    /// Applies the policy to a given set of proposal properties.
    /// </summary>
    public void ApplyPolicy(SPItemEventDataCollection properties,
                PolicyContext context)
    {
        // Check the properties to determine if the policy was satisfied.
        switch (ProjectProposal.GetProposalType(properties)) {
            case ProposalType.FixedBid: {
                    ApplyFixedBidPolicy(properties, context);
                    break;
                }
            case ProposalType.TimeAndMaterials: {
                    ApplyTimeAndMaterialsPolicy(properties, context);
                    break;
                }
        }
    }

    /// <summary>
    /// Converts this instance to a text string.
    /// </summary>
    /// <remarks>
    /// Uses the XmlSerializer to produce an XML string representing
    /// the policy.
    /// </remarks>
    public override string ToString()
    {
        // Generate the XML string.
        StringBuilder policy = new StringBuilder();
```

```
        XmlSerializer ser = new XmlSerializer(GetType(), "");
        ser.Serialize(new StringWriter(policy), this);

        // Check for and remove the xml directive.
        string xml = policy.ToString();
        xml = xml.Replace(Strings.XmlDirective_Utf8, "");
        xml = xml.Replace(Strings.XmlDirective_Utf16, "");

        return xml.Trim();
    }

/// <summary>
/// Updates the policy associated with a given content type.
/// </summary>
/// <param name="contentType"></param>
public void UpdatePolicy(ContentType contentType)
{
    // Attach the policy to the content type.
    contentType.AddXmlString(Strings.ProposalManagementPolicyNamespace,
            this.ToString());
}

/// <summary>
/// Applies policies that pertain to fixed bid proposals.
/// </summary>
/// <param name="properties"></param>
void ApplyFixedBidPolicy(SPItemEventDataCollection properties,
            PolicyContext context)
{
    if (ProjectProposal.GetBidAmount(properties)
    < FixedBid.BidAmount.MinimumValue) {
        switch (context) {
            case PolicyContext.Update:
                throw new ProposalManagementPolicyException(
            FixedBid.BidAmount.FormattedErrorMessage);
            }
        }
    }

/// <summary>
/// Applies policies that pertain to time and materials proposals.
/// </summary>
/// <param name="properties"></param>
void ApplyTimeAndMaterialsPolicy(SPItemEventDataCollection properties,
                PolicyContext context)
{
    if (ProjectProposal.GetEstimatedHours(properties)
    < TimeAndMaterials.EstimatedHours.MinimumValue) {
        switch (context) {
            case PolicyContext.Update:
                throw new ProposalManagementPolicyException(
            TimeAndMaterials.EstimatedHours.FormattedErrorMessage);
            }
        }
    }
```

```
        private ProposalManagementPolicyFixedBid fixedBidField;
        private ProposalManagementPolicyTimeAndMaterials timeAndMaterialsField;

        /// <remarks/>
        public ProposalManagementPolicyFixedBid FixedBid {
            get {
                return this.fixedBidField;
            }
            set {
                this.fixedBidField = value;
            }
        }

        /// <remarks/>
        public ProposalManagementPolicyTimeAndMaterials TimeAndMaterials {
            get {
                return this.timeAndMaterialsField;
            }
            set {
                this.timeAndMaterialsField = value;
            }
        }
    }

    #region XML Serialization Support

    /// <remarks/>
    [Serializable]
    [XmlType(AnonymousType=true)]
    public class ProposalManagementPolicyFixedBid {

        private ProposalManagementPolicyFixedBidBidAmount bidAmountField;

        /// <remarks/>
        public ProposalManagementPolicyFixedBidBidAmount BidAmount {
            get {
                return this.bidAmountField;
            }
            set {
                this.bidAmountField = value;
            }
        }
    }

    /// <remarks/>
    [Serializable]
    [XmlType(AnonymousType=true)]
    public class ProposalManagementPolicyFixedBidBidAmount {

        private string errorMessageField;
        private decimal minimumValueField;

        /// <remarks/>
```

```
    public string ErrorMessage {
        get {
            return this.errorMessageField;
        }
        set {
            this.errorMessageField = value;
        }
    }

    /// <summary>
    /// Builds the actual error message by performing field substitutions.
    /// </summary>
    public string FormattedErrorMessage
    {
        get
        {
            return ErrorMessage.Replace(
            "$$MinimumValue$$", MinimumValue.ToString());
        }
    }

    /// <remarks/>
    [XmlAttribute]
    public decimal MinimumValue
    {
        get {
            return this.minimumValueField;
        }
        set {
            this.minimumValueField = value;
        }
    }
}

/// <remarks/>
[Serializable]
[XmlType(AnonymousType=true)]
public class ProposalManagementPolicyTimeAndMaterials {

    private ProposalManagementPolicyTimeAndMaterialsEstimatedHours
        estimatedHoursField;

    /// <remarks/>
    public ProposalManagementPolicyTimeAndMaterialsEstimatedHours
        EstimatedHours {
        get {
            return this.estimatedHoursField;
        }
        set {
            this.estimatedHoursField = value;
        }
    }
}
```

```
/// <remarks/>
[Serializable]
[XmlType(AnonymousType=true)]
public class ProposalManagementPolicyTimeAndMaterialsEstimatedHours {

    private string errorMessageField;
    private decimal minimumValueField;

    /// <remarks/>
    public string ErrorMessage {
        get {
            return this.errorMessageField;
        }
        set {
            this.errorMessageField = value;
        }
    }


    /// <remarks/>
    [XmlAttribute]
    public decimal MinimumValue
    {
        get {
            return this.minimumValueField;
        }
        set {
            this.minimumValueField = value;
        }
    }


    /// <summary>
    /// Builds the actual error message by performing field substitutions.
    /// </summary>
    public string FormattedErrorMessage
    {
        get
        {
            return ErrorMessage.Replace(
            "$$MinimumValue$$", MinimumValue.ToString());
        }
    }
}

public class StringCollection : System.Collections.Generic.List<string> {
}
#endregion
}
```

Now you can modify the `ItemUpdating` event receiver to process the attached policy:

```
[SharePointPermission(SecurityAction.LinkDemand, ObjectModel = true)]
public override void ItemUpdating(SPItemEventProperties properties)
{
    try {
        // Apply the current proposal management policy.
        ProjectProposalType.ApplyPolicy(properties,
            ProposalManagementPolicy.PolicyContext.Update);
    } catch (Exception x) {
        properties.ErrorMessage = x.Message;
        properties.Cancel = true;
    }
}
```

If an exception is thrown during the application of the policy, you set the `ErrorMessage` field and cancel the operation. SharePoint will then display an Error page whenever an attempt is made to update a proposal that does not conform to the established policy, as shown in Figure 11-11.

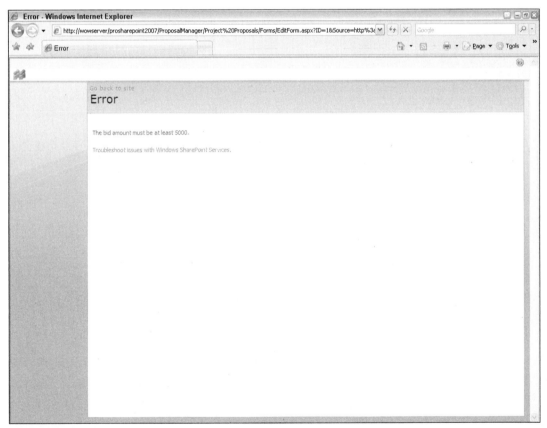

Figure 11-11

Creating Policy Administration Tools

Associating a custom policy file with a content type is powerful, but administrative users will not be able to change the policy unless they can associate a different file with the content type at runtime. Two approaches come to mind. You could provide a custom user interface for entering the acceptable bid amount and estimated hours and then generate an XML file, or you could create a command-line tool.

Working with XML files via command-line utilities is a lot easier than developing a UI, especially if the schema is changing frequently during development. In addition, you might like to enable a machine-driven process or a script to modify the policy rather than require human interaction. Fortunately, the wise and benevolent SharePoint gods made it quite easy to extend the `stsadm` command-line tool with your own custom commands. Listing 11-13 shows a custom `stsadm` extension for setting the proposal management policy that will be applied to new or existing proposals based on your project proposal content type.

Listing 11-13: A custom STSADM command to apply proposal management policy

```
using System;
using System.IO;
using System.Collections.Generic;
using System.Text;
using Microsoft.SharePoint;
using Microsoft.SharePoint.StsAdmin;
using ProSharePoint2007;

namespace ProposalManager.Admin
{
    /// <summary>
    /// Implements a custom STSADM command to display the proposal management
    /// policy specification for a given site.
    /// </summary>
    public class GetProposalPolicy : ISPStsadmCommand
    {
        #region ISPStsadmCommand Members

        string ISPStsadmCommand.GetHelpMessage(string command)
        {
            string msg = "Displays the current Proposal Management policy.";
            return msg + "\n" + "-url <url>\t\tthe url of the site to process";
        }

        int ISPStsadmCommand.Run(string command,
            System.Collections.Specialized.StringDictionary keyValues,
            out string output)
        {
            int result = 1;
            const string ProposalContentTypeName = "Project Proposal";

            try {
            // validate the arguments
            if (keyValues["url"] == null)
                throw new ApplicationException("No url supplied.");
```

```
                      // open the website
                      using (SPSite site = new SPSite(keyValues["url"])){
                          using (SPWeb web = site.OpenWeb()){
                              // load the Project Proposal content type
                              ContentType ctProjectProposal
                                  = new ContentType();
                              if (ctProjectProposal.Create(web,
                                  ProposalContentTypeName) == null) {
                                  throw new ApplicationException(
                                  string.Format(
                                  "Failed to locate Content Type '{0}'",
                                      ProposalContentTypeName));
                              }

                              // load the policy
                              ProposalManagementPolicy policy
                                  = ProposalManagementPolicy.FromContentType(
                                      ctProjectProposal);

                              // convert to text and return result
                              output = policy.ToString();
                              result = 0;
                          }
                      }} catch (Exception x) {
                          output = x.ToString();
                      }

                      return result;
                  }

              #endregion
          }
      }
```

To deploy the command, you simply install the assembly into the Global Assembly Cache and create a command definition file named stsadmcommands.proposalmanager.xml in the 12\CONFIG folder.

```xml
<?xml version="1.0" encoding="utf-8" ?>
<commands>
    <command name="setproposalpolicy"
          class="ProposalManager.Admin.SetProposalPolicy,
              ProposalManager.Admin, Version=1.0.0.0,
              Culture=neutral, PublicKeyToken=3c6b2ee283bb579c"/>
    <command name="getproposalpolicy"
          class="ProposalManager.Admin.GetProposalPolicy,
              ProposalManager.Admin, Version=1.0.0.0,
              Culture=neutral, PublicKeyToken=3c6b2ee283bb579c"/>
</commands>
```

Figure 11-12 shows the new command being executed.

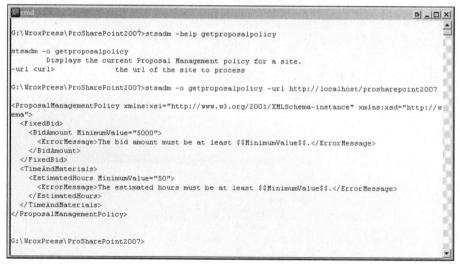

```
G:\WroxPress\ProSharePoint2007>stsadm -help getproposalpolicy

stsadm -o getproposalpolicy
        Displays the current Proposal Management policy for a site.
-url <url>              the url of the site to process

G:\WroxPress\ProSharePoint2007>stsadm -o getproposalpolicy -url http://localhost/prosharepoint2007

<ProposalManagementPolicy xmlns:xsi="http://www.w3.org/2001/XMLSchema-instance" xmlns:xsd="http://w
ema">
  <FixedBid>
    <BidAmount MinimumValue="5000">
      <ErrorMessage>The bid amount must be at least $$MinimumValue$$.</ErrorMessage>
    </BidAmount>
  </FixedBid>
  <TimeAndMaterials>
    <EstimatedHours MinimumValue="50">
      <ErrorMessage>The estimated hours must be at least $$MinimumValue$$.</ErrorMessage>
    </EstimatedHours>
  </TimeAndMaterials>
</ProposalManagementPolicy>


G:\WroxPress\ProSharePoint2007>
```

Figure 11-12

Summary

Managing the document lifecycle depends on metadata. Content types are the way to manage metadata within SharePoint. You can encapsulate document metadata by combining it with custom behaviors implemented in content type event receivers. You then use those custom behaviors to control all aspects of the document creation and revision phases. Constructing reusable libraries of document-specific components can greatly simplify the task of building document management solutions.

You can extend the notion of encapsulation to include high-level document management policies declared using XML. First you create a custom document management policy schema and then use it to create a default set of policies for your content type. Using the Windows SharePoint Services object model, you can attach a default policy to the content type at runtime and then retrieve it, using XML deserialization, to process the policy against individual document items. Finally, you can extend the stsadm command line tool with custom commands specific to your document management solution.

Building Records Management Solutions

By John Holliday

Records management is all about compliance. With the recent increase in legislation surrounding the management of corporate records, companies are faced with the prospect of paying significant fines and other costs associated with keeping accurate records, safeguarding them, and making them available at any time for outside auditors. This dynamic regulatory landscape creates many challenges for managing information effectively. The fundamental question is how to adhere to the new regulatory requirements without interfering with worker productivity. How can companies ensure that compliance, while minimizing the additional costs associated with implementing a given information management policy?

Office SharePoint Server 2007 addresses this requirement in three ways. First, it provides a special site template for creating a records repository with built-in support for storing and managing official documents. Second, it exposes a rich object model designed specifically for records management. Finally, it defines and implements a web service that enables both SharePoint and non-SharePoint applications to interact with records repository sites. This chapter shows you how to work with the records management components to build custom solutions that take advantage of this open architecture.

SharePoint Support for Records Management

There are five core requirements for any records management system:

❑ **Confidentiality** — Confidentiality means access control; you can establish clearly defined policies that govern who has access to official records at any time. It is the responsibility of the records repository to ensure that official records are maintained securely. This means that once a record is stored in the repository, no one can access it except those with the appropriate permissions. It is possible that this group may not include the original author of a given document.

❑ **Information integrity** — Information integrity means that official records must not be altered after they have been placed in the repository. This includes alteration of the document content as well as the document metadata. Information integrity also covers the need to continuously update records to minimize the presence of outdated or inaccurate information.

❑ **High availability** — High availability means that official records must be available at any given time to support outside processes that may have nothing to do with the core business function. This goes beyond network bandwidth and has more to do with the need to decouple the repository from other enterprise information stores so that requests for official records are not tied to other business processes.

❑ **Adherence to policy** — It is important to establish clearly defined policies that govern the way in which records are stored, and to prove that those policies were followed. In fact, in some sense all of the other requirements fall under the general umbrella of information management policy.

*It is interesting to note that the records management tools provided by the Office SharePoint Server system are implemented in the **Microsoft.Office.Policy** assembly.*

❑ **Audit ability** — Audit ability makes it possible to log all changes made to records after they have been stored in the repository. Once an official file is created, the repository must keep track of everything that happens to the document, including information such as the date and time of a change and who made it.

The central feature of a records management system is the records repository. As the primary access point for records entering and exiting the system, the records repository provides the only real point of control over how official records are stored. You need to control both the storage medium and the mechanisms used to move documents into and out of the repository. By controlling access to the repository, you can ensure the confidentiality of records. By controlling the storage medium, you can ensure record integrity and guarantee high availability. By controlling the mechanisms used to move documents into and out of the repository, you can apply business rules to ensure adherence to established policy and maintain clear audit trails.

Office SharePoint Server 2007 provides several layers of support for building records management solutions. These include the ability to:

❑ Set up and configure a records repository according to a custom set of rules

❑ Ensure that records are not altered after being placed in a repository

❑ Set up multiple locations within a repository to organize different types of records

❑ Set up retention policies based on retention schedules

❑ Capture records from external sources

❑ Route records to the correct location within the repository

❑ Manage physical (nonelectronic) records

❏ Specify an action to take when the expiration date is reached

❏ Set up auditing policies to log all activity against a record library

❏ Generate administrative reports of record usage

The SharePoint records management components are implemented in the `Microsoft.Office.Policy` assembly, located in the `12\ISAPI` folder of the SharePoint server. This assembly contains the namespaces shown in the following table:

Namespace	Description
`Microsoft.Office.RecordsManagement` `.RecordsRepository`	Implements components for setting up a records repository and declares the `IRouter` interface. Defines the data structures used for passing information to and from the Official File web service.
`Microsoft.Office.RecordsManagement` `.SearchAndProcess`	Implements a component architecture for finding and processing records within the repository.
`Microsoft.Office.RecordsManagement` `.InformationPolicy`	Implements the Information Management Policy infrastructure and exposes components for creating custom policies, policy features, and resources. Includes components for building custom administrative tools.
`Microsoft.Office.RecordsManagement` `.PolicyFeatures`	Provides additional support for developing custom policies. Implements the default barcode and label components and defines the primary interfaces used for barcode generation and expiration.
`Microsoft.Office.RecordsManagement` `.Holds`	Implements the `Hold`, `HoldsField`, and `HoldStatusField` components. Includes base implementations of UI controls for the hold and hold status fields.
`Microsoft.Office.RecordsManagement` `.Reporting`	Implements the reporting infrastructure, including a default reporting gallery and the custom query control. Includes components for injecting audit information into Excel spreadsheets.

The SharePoint Records Repository

Office SharePoint Server 2007 includes a default implementation of a records repository in the form of the Records Center site template. This template implements the Official File web service and provides all the core functionality needed to build records management solutions. The diagram in Figure 12-1 shows the architecture of a Records Center site.

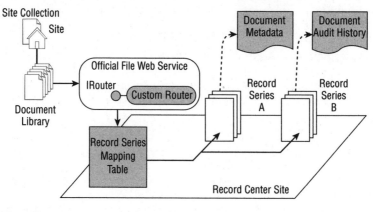

Figure 12-1

A document library is configured to send documents to a central site based on the Records Center site template. Site administrators set this up at the document library level using the user interface. Alternatively, a document library can be configured automatically via the object model or as part of a feature activation. Users can manually select the Send To command from the document library menu to initiate the transfer of documents to the repository. Alternatively, documents can be transferred automatically by a workflow or other process.

SharePoint accesses the Official File web service exposed by the Records Center site to obtain a list of RecordRouting objects. RecordRouting objects specify the locations within the repository that can accept records of a given type. SharePoint maps the name of the content type associated with each document to the name of the routing record to determine which RecordRouting object to use.

SharePoint then submits the file to the repository. The repository loads any custom routers to give them a chance to perform special processing for a given file. Custom routers have the opportunity to examine the document content and metadata and may choose to reject the file, canceling the submission. The submitted file is moved into the appropriate storage location. Matching document metadata is automatically promoted to the document library level within the repository to support auditing and reporting. If a policy has been attached to the document library, then the policy is applied.

Using the Official File Web Service

The Official File web service provides a standardized means of managing a records repository and has been designed to support records management architectures that may use mechanisms other than those provided by the SharePoint platform. By implementing the Official File web service contract, any system can participate in the Office SharePoint Server records management scheme.

Figure 12-2 shows the methods and structure of the Official File web service as defined by the Office SharePoint Server object model.

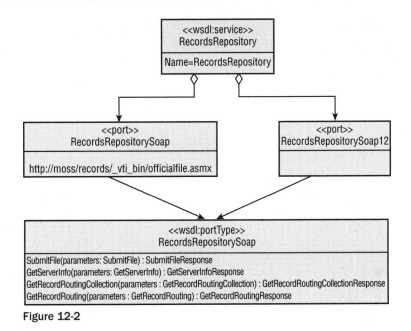

Figure 12-2

The Official File web service can be used to implement a simple Windows Forms application that lets the user select local files and then save them to a Records Center site. The first step is to create a Records Center site to use for testing.

Setting Up the Records Center Site

To create a Records Center site, use the built-in Records Center site template installed by the Publishing feature. From the Site Actions menu of the top-level site, select Create Site and then select Records Center from the Enterprise tab in the Template Selection section of the New SharePoint Site page.

> *The Office SharePoint Server Publishing feature must be activated in order for the Records Center site template to be shown. For details about activating this feature, see Chapter 13.*

After creating the Records Center site, add a document library to receive the submitted files. For this example, create a new document library named "Legal Agreements," accepting the default settings. Next, add a record routing type to the site by clicking the Configure Record Routing link on the home page to open the Record Routing custom list. Alternatively, you could select New ⇨ New Item from the toolbar of the Record Routing list Web Part.

Figure 12-3 shows the item detail for the Contract record routing type. Note that the Contract record routing type refers to the Legal Agreements document library and specifies an additional alias for documents of type `Agreement`.

Figure 12-4 shows the home page of the resulting Records Center site.

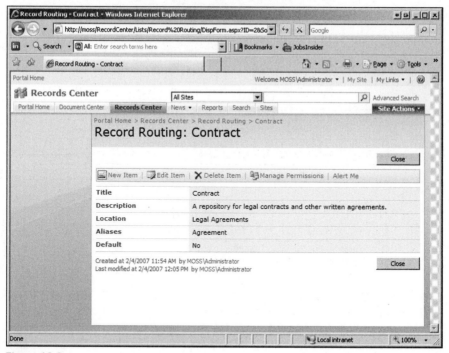

Figure 12-3

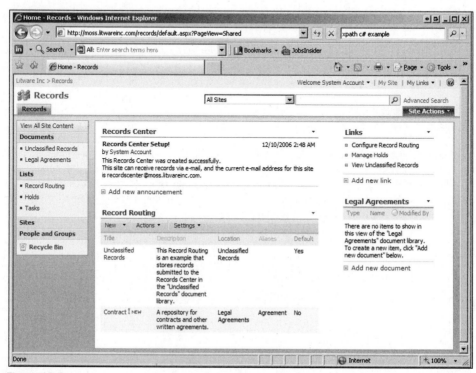

Figure 12-4

Creating the Client Application

The `OfficialFileWebServiceClient` is a Windows Forms application that allows the user to specify a record routing type, a target repository, and a list of local files. Figure 12-5 shows the application user interface.

The user enters the repository URL and then presses the Connect button, which calls the web service to retrieve the list of routing record types available in the repository. The first step is to connect to the web service and then call the `GetRecordRoutingCollection` method to retrieve the record series names.

Connecting to the web service requires a Web Reference for the OfficialFile web service, which is exposed by all top-level sites in a SharePoint Server deployment at the following URL:

```
http://<server>/<portal>/_vti_bin/OfficialFile.asmx
```

Add the Web Reference by navigating to the appropriate portal in the URL field, as illustrated in Figure 12-6.

Adding the Web Reference creates a proxy class for communicating with the web service. In this example, the generated namespace is `OfficialFileService` and the proxy class is named `RecordsRepository` as defined by the web service.

Although the top-level site exposes the web service definition, the actual URL will be set dynamically at runtime. The top-level site is used only to generate the proxy class. This allows the user to work with different repositories. To enable this feature, the URL Behavior *property of the generated proxy class must be set to* Dynamic.

When the user presses the Connect button, a connection to the web service is established using the URL provided in the Repository URL text box and the credentials of the current user.

Next, you need to get the web service proxy and point it at the designated URL, as shown here:

```
OfficialFileService.RecordsRepository m_repository;
m_repository = new OfficialFileService.RecordsRepository();
m_repository.Credentials = System.Net.CredentialCache.DefaultCredentials;
m_repository.Url = repositoryUrl.Text;
```

Figure 12-5

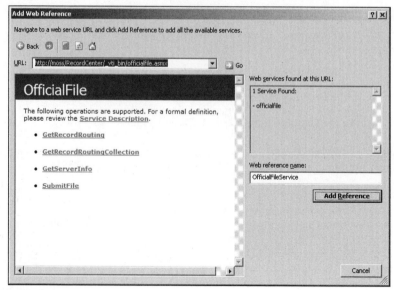

Figure 12-6

To simplify the implementation of the client application, object data sources are used to bind data retrieved from the web service with the controls displayed in the user interface. The drop-down list of routing types is bound to a RoutingTypeList containing RoutingType objects, and the data grid is bound to an OfficialFileCollection containing OfficialFile objects. The RoutingType class is a simple wrapper for the routing type name. The OfficialFile class encapsulates the file path and the ability to submit the file to a records repository. The following code shows the RoutingTypeList and RoutingType utility classes.

```
class RoutingTypeList : List<RoutingType>
{
    public RoutingTypeList() { }
}

class RoutingType
{
    private string m_name;

    public string Name
    {
        get { return m_name; }
        set { m_name = value; }
    }

    public RoutingType(string name)
    {
        m_name = name;
    }
}
```

The `GetRecordRoutingCollection` method returns an XML string containing the available record routing types. For a SharePoint Records Center site, this is the list of items in the Record Routing list. Figure 12-7 shows the return value for the sample Records Center site.

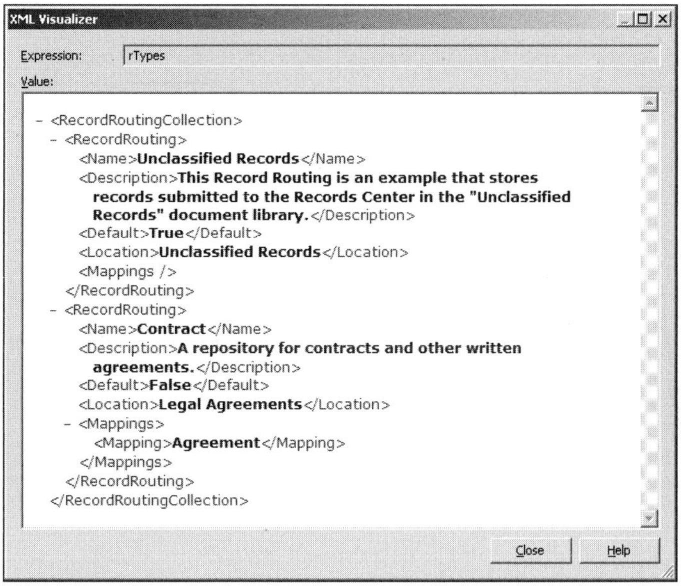

Figure 12-7

If the connection is valid, the other controls are enabled and the drop-down list is populated with the available record routing types. This can be done easily using a simple XPath expression and an `XPathNodeIterator`, adding a new `RoutingType` wrapper object to the data source for each node as shown below.

```
string rTypes = m_repository.GetRecordRoutingCollection();
string expr = "/RecordRoutingCollection/RecordRouting/Name";

XPathDocument doc = new XPathDocument(new StringReader(rTypes));
XPathNavigator nav = doc.CreateNavigator();
XPathNodeIterator iter = nav.Select(expr);

this.routingTypeListBindingSource.Clear();
while (iter.MoveNext())
{
this.routingTypeListBindingSource.Add(
    new RoutingType(iter.Current.Value));
}
```

The data grid is bound to an `OfficialFileCollection` containing `OfficialFile` objects. The `OfficialFile` class encapsulates the file path as well as the ability to submit an official file to a repository. When the user presses the Submit button, the selected files are processed, and the return value from the web service call is displayed in the grid automatically using the `Result` property of the `OfficialFile` class. Listing 12-1 shows the code in the `mainform.cs` file, which delegates the file submit logic to the `OfficialFile` class. Listing 12-2 shows the relevant code from `officialfile.cs`.

Listing 12-1

```
/// <summary>
/// Retrieves the list of files and submits them to the records repository.
/// </summary>
private void DoSubmitFiles()
{
    // Ensure there are files to work on.
    if (this.officialFileCollectionBindingSource.List.Count == 0)
    {
        MessageBox.Show("There are no files in the list.");
        return;
    }
    // Get the selected routing type.
    RoutingType routingType = routingTypeListBindingSource.Current
        as RoutingType;
    if (routingType == null)
    {
        MessageBox.Show("No routing type selected.");
        return;
    }

    // Process each file in the list.
    foreach (OfficialFile officialFile in
        officialFileCollectionBindingSource.List)
    {
        officialFile.Submit(m_repository, routingType);
    }

    // Refresh the UI.
    this.Refresh();
}
```

Listing 12-2

```
class OfficialFile
{
    private string m_result = "Not submitted";

    /// <summary>
    /// A text string representing the result of submitting the file.
    /// </summary>
    public string Result
    {
        get { return m_result; }
        set { m_result = value; }
    }

    private string m_fileName;
```

```csharp
/// <summary>
/// The base file name.
/// </summary>
public string FileName
{
    get { return m_fileName; }
    set { m_fileName = value; }
}

private string m_filePath;

/// <summary>
/// The fully qualified file path.
/// </summary>
public string FilePath
{
    get { return m_filePath; }
    set { m_filePath = value; }
}

/// <summary>
/// Public constructor.
/// </summary>
public OfficialFile(string filePath)
{
    this.FilePath = filePath;
    this.FileName = Path.GetFileName(filePath);
}

/// <summary>
/// Submits the file using the specified routing type.
/// </summary>
public string Submit(OfficialFileService.RecordsRepository repository,
                     RoutingType routingType)
{
    try
    {
        // Retrieve the file data.
        byte[] data = File.ReadAllBytes(this.FilePath);

        // Create a property array.
        OfficialFileService.RecordsRepositoryProperty[] props
            = new OfficialFileService.RecordsRepositoryProperty[1];

        // Specify some property data.
        props[0] = new OfficialFileWebServiceClient.OfficialFileService
                        .RecordsRepositoryProperty();
        props[0].Name = "OriginalPath";
        props[0].Type = "String";
        props[0].Value = this.FilePath;

        // Parse the xml result.
        string result = repository.SubmitFile( data, props,
            routingType.Name, this.FilePath,
            WindowsIdentity.GetCurrent().Name);
```

```
XPathNavigator nav =
    new XPathDocument(
        new StringReader(
            string.Format("<OFS>{0}</OFS>",result)
            )).CreateNavigator();

    XPathNodeIterator iter = nav.Select("/OFS/ResultCode");
    this.Result = iter.MoveNext() ?
        iter.Current.Value : string.Empty;
}
catch (Exception x)
{
    this.Result = x.Message;
}
return this.Result;
    }
}
```

Using the SharePoint Object Model

To illustrate how closely linked the object model is to the web services implementation, the SharePoint object model can be used to submit documents to a Records Center site. Figure 12-8 shows the objects used.

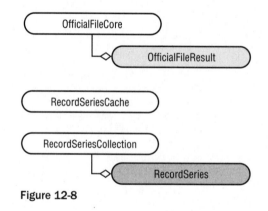

Figure 12-8

The OfficialFileCore class implements a static SubmitFile method, which in turn calls the web service associated with a given SharePoint web site. If the code will be executed on the SharePoint server, you can call this method directly to submit the specified file to the repository instead of calling the web service.

The example in Listing 12-3 (EnumRoutingTypes.cs) implements a custom STSADM command that enables SharePoint server administrators to enumerate the available routing types for a given records repository site.

Listing 12-3

```
using System;
using System.Collections.Generic;
using System.Text;
using Microsoft.SharePoint;
```

```
using Microsoft.SharePoint.StsAdmin;
using Microsoft.Office.RecordsManagement.RecordsRepository;

namespace OfficialFileSTSADMCommand
{
    /// <summary>
    /// Implements a custom STSADM command to enumerate the
    /// record routing types in a records repository.
    /// </summary>
    class EnumRoutingTypes : ISPStsadmCommand
    {
        #region ISPStsadmCommand Members

        string ISPStsadmCommand.GetHelpMessage(string command)
        {
            string msg = "Enumerates the available routing types ";
            msg += "in a records repository site.";
            msg += "\n-url\t<url>\t\tthe url of the Records Center site";
            return msg;
        }

        int ISPStsadmCommand.Run(string command,
            System.Collections.Specialized.StringDictionary keyValues,
            out string output)
        {
            int result = 1;
            string sRepositoryUrl = string.Empty;
            try
            {
                // validate the arguments
                if (null == (sRepositoryUrl = keyValues["url"])
                        || sRepositoryUrl.Length == 0)
                    throw new ApplicationException("No url specified.");

                // open the website
                using (SPSite site = new SPSite(keyValues["url"]))
                {
                    using (SPWeb web = site.OpenWeb())
                    {
                        // Enumerate the routing types using
                        // the RecordSeriesCollection wrapper.
                        RecordSeriesCollection routingTypes =
                            new RecordSeriesCollection(web);

                        if (null == routingTypes || routingTypes.Count == 0)
                        {
                            output = "No routing types were found.";
                        }
                        else
                        {
                            output = string.Format(
                            "Found {0} routing types:", routingTypes.Count);
                            for (int i=0; i < routingTypes.Count; i++)
                            {
                                RecordSeries routingType = routingTypes[i];
                                output += string.Format("\n{0}\n\t{1}\n",
```

```
                                    routingType.Name,
                                    routingType.Description);
                        }
                    }
                }
            }
        }
        catch (Exception x)
        {
            output = x.ToString();
        }
        return result;
    }

    #endregion
    }
}
```

Building a Custom Records Repository

What's interesting about this architecture is that it is not necessary to use a SharePoint site to implement a record repository that SharePoint document libraries can use. Simply by implementing the OfficialFile web service, any repository can be substituted. The steps to accomplish this are straightforward as illustrated in the following example, which implements an image repository for storing image files of various types.

Each image file is stored into a subfolder of the repository root folder, which is created dynamically on the local file system. The subfolder name is the image type as specified by the file extension. Within that folder, the file is stored into a secondary subfolder named according to the current month, day and year. So, for example, the file MyFile.GIF would be stored in C:\ImageRepository\GIF\20070215 if sent to the repository on February 15, 2007.

Creating the Web Service Project

Create a new web service project in Visual Studio 2005 by selecting File ⇨ New ⇨ Web Site. From the New Web Site dialog box, choose the ASP.NET Web Service template and select File System from the Location drop-down. Although it is unnecessary for the service to work, you can rename the Service.cs and Service.asmx files to something more descriptive, like OfficialFileService.cs and OfficialFileService.asmx, respectively.

If you rename these files, be sure to update the CodeBehind *and* Class *attributes in the* .asmx *file with the correct names.*

Edit the code behind file (in this case, OfficialFileService.cs) and modify the WebService attribute so that the namespace matches that of the SharePoint OfficialFile web service. This step is important, because it enables SharePoint to talk to the web service. Without this namespace directive, SharePoint will not recognize the web service as a valid implementation of the OfficialFile web service. The modified declaration should look like the following:

```
[
WebService( Name="ImageRepository",
Namespace = "http://schemas.microsoft.com/sharepoint/soap/recordsrepository/",
Description="An implementation of the OfficialFile Web Service to store image
```

```
files.")
]
[WebServiceBinding(ConformsTo = WsiProfiles.BasicProfile1_1)]
public class OfficialFileService : System.Web.Services.WebService {…}
```

Implementing the OfficialFile Web Service Methods

The OfficialFile web service consists of four methods: GetServerInfo, GetRecordRouting, GetRecordRoutingCollection, and SubmitFile. The return values are either a string describing an error condition or an XML string representing a data value or a result code. The data values are typically short strings, so for most implementations you can use simple string formatting to construct them.

To simplify the handling of known result codes, an enumeration can be used along with an associated wrapper class that implicitly converts the enumeration data type to a string. Listing 12-4 shows a portion of the code in officialfileservice.cs that handles the conversion of result codes.

Listing 12-4

```
/// <summary>
/// The expected result codes for the web service.
/// </summary>
enum ResultCodeType
{
    Success,
    MoreInformation,
    InvalidConfiguration,
    InvalidArgument,
    InvalidUser,
    NotFound,
    FileRejected,
    UnknownError
}

/// <summary>
/// Helper class for returning result codes.
/// </summary>
private class ResultCode
{
    string m_value = null;
    ResultCodeType m_code=ResultCodeType.UnknownError;
    const string fmtResultCode = @"<ResultCode>{0}</ResultCode>";

    public ResultCode(ResultCodeType code)
    {
        m_code = code;
    }

    public ResultCode(string value)
    {
        m_value = value;
    }

    public override string  ToString()
    {
        return string.Format(fmtResultCode,
```

```
                m_value == null ? m_code.ToString() : m_value);
        }

        public static implicit operator string(ResultCode code)
        {
            return code.ToString();
        }
    }
}
```

GetServerInfo

The `GetServerInfo` method returns information on an implementation of the OfficialFile web service. The return value is an XML string matching the following schema:

```
<ServerInfo>
  <ServerType>serverType</ServerType>
  <ServerVersion>serverVersion</ServerVersion>
</ServerInfo>
```

For the image repository, the following code will suffice:

```
/// <summary>
/// Retrieves the server information.
/// </summary>
[WebMethod]
public string GetServerInfo()
{
    try
    {
        StringBuilder sb = new StringBuilder("<ServerInfo>");
        sb.AppendFormat("<ServerType>{0}</ServerType>", "ImageRepository");
        sb.AppendFormat("<ServerVersion>{0}</ServerVersion>",
            Assembly.GetExecutingAssembly().GetName().Version.ToString());
        sb.Append("</ServerInfo>");
        return sb.ToString();
    }
    catch
    {
    }
    // failed for some reason
    return new ResultCode(ResultCodeType.UnknownError);
}
```

GetRecordRouting

The `GetRecordRouting` method gets the properties of a specified record routing type. For this sample image repository implementation, a list of recognized image types is hard-coded using an enumeration. The recognized image types are declared as follows:

```
/// <summary>
/// The recognized image types.
/// </summary>
enum ImageType
{
```

```
    [Description("GIF Image File")]
    GIF,
    [Description("JPEG Image File")]
    JPG,
    [Description("TIFF Image File")]
    TIF,
    [Description("Portable Network Graphics File")]
    PNG
}
```

A useful technique for dealing with enumerations leverages the DescriptionAttribute (declared in System.ComponentModel) along with a wrapper class for retrieving any description that is attached to an enumeration element. For example:

```
/// <summary>
/// Utility class for extracting descriptions from enumerators.
/// </summary>
/// <remarks>Uses reflection to extract the DescriptionAttribute
/// from an enumerator. Returns the enumerator type name
/// if no DescriptionAttribute is found.
/// </remarks>
public class EnumDescription
{
    private string m_str = "";
    ///<summary>Constructor from an enum element.</summary>
    public EnumDescription(Enum value)
    {
        DescriptionAttribute attrib =
            Attribute.GetCustomAttribute(
                value.GetType().GetField(value.ToString()),
                typeof(DescriptionAttribute))
                    as DescriptionAttribute;
        m_str = (attrib == null) ?
            value.ToString() : attrib.Description;
    }
    // support for implicit string conversion
    public static implicit operator string(EnumDescription s)
    {
        return s.m_str;
    }
    // support for explicit string conversion
    public override string ToString()
    {
        return m_str;
    }
}
```

The GetRecordRouting method can be implemented as follows:

```
/// <summary>
/// Returns the routing information for a given record type.
/// </summary>
[WebMethod]
public string GetRecordRouting(string recordRouting) {
const string fmtRoutingType = @"<RecordRouting><Name>{0}</Name>" +
```

```
@"<Description>{1}</Description><Mappings/></RecordRouting>";
    try
    {
        ImageType t = (ImageType)Enum.Parse(
            typeof(ImageType), recordRouting);
        return String.Format(fmtRoutingType, t.ToString(),
            new EnumDescription(t));
    }
    catch
    {
    }
    return new ResultCode(ResultCodeType.InvalidConfiguration);
}
```

GetRecordRoutingCollection

The `GetRecordRoutingCollection` method retrieves the properties of all routing types of the repository. It is essentially a concatenation of the results from the `GetRecordRouting` method for each recognized routing type. Therefore, it can be implemented by iterating over the enumeration of routing types as follows:

```
/// <summary>
/// Returns the collection of recognized routing types.
/// </summary>
[WebMethod]
public string GetRecordRoutingCollection()
{
    StringBuilder sb = new StringBuilder("<RecordRoutingCollection>");
    try
    {
        foreach (ImageType t in Enum.GetValues(typeof(ImageType)))
        {
            sb.Append(GetRecordRouting(t.ToString()));
        }
        sb.Append("</RecordRoutingCollection>");
        return sb.ToString();
    }
    catch
    {
    }
    return new ResultCode(ResultCodeType.InvalidConfiguration);
}
```

SubmitFile

The `SubmitFile` method is the workhorse of the OfficialFile web service. It is responsible for validating the file, applying any policies and finally storing the file into the appropriate location within the repository.

The `ImageRepository` implementation presented here uses a simple hard-coded policy with the following characteristics:

❑   Image files are stored according to file type.

- ❑ The routing record type supplied by the caller is ignored.

- ❑ The source URL is used to determine the file extension.

- ❑ Only recognized file extensions are accepted.

To ensure that the web service works properly when called from a SharePoint site, the result codes should map to the expected result codes as described in the SharePoint SDK. The following table lists the `SubmitFile` result codes expected by the Office SharePoint Server implementation:

Result Code	Description
Success	The file was submitted successfully.
MoreInformation	Required column metadata was not supplied. Additional information can be appended using a `<ResultUrl>...</ResultUrl>` tag to specify the URL of a form the user can use to enter the missing metadata fields.
InvalidConfiguration	The web service is not configured properly. This covers the case where the repository is offline or cannot be reached.
InvalidArgument	One or more arguments were unexpected or were improperly formatted.
InvalidUser	The specified user credentials could not be authenticated or the user does not have the necessary permissions to save the file.
NotFound	The specified user credentials could not be found, or the record routing type was not recognized.
FileRejected	The file was rejected because of a policy violation or for other reasons, such as the file is too large or could not be saved to the specified location.
UnknownError	Some other error occurred during processing.

Unlike the other methods, the `SubmitFile` method accepts an array of `RecordsRepositoryProperty` objects as a parameter. This object is used by callers to specify additional metadata for use by the service when storing the file. Although this property array is ignored by the Image Repository web service, the `RecordsRepositoryProperty` class must still be declared so that SharePoint sites can invoke the method properly.

```
[Serializable]
public struct RecordsRepositoryProperty
{
    public string Name;
    public string Other;
    public string Type;
    public string Value;
}
```

Listing 12-5 (`officialfileservice.cs`) shows the complete `SubmitFile` method implementation.

Listing 12-5

```
/// <summary>
/// Implements the submit method by storing the file into a subfolder
/// of the root (as specified in the web.config file) having the
/// same name as the routing type.
/// </summary>
/// <remarks>
/// This implementation ignores the specified record routing and
/// instead uses the file extension as the routing type. Only
/// recognized file extensions are accepted.
/// </remarks>
[WebMethod]
public string SubmitFile(byte[] fileToSubmit,
    RecordsRepositoryProperty[] properties, string recordRouting,
    string sourceUrl, string userName)
{
    try
    {
        try
        {
            // validate the source URL against the known image types
            // to ensure that the submitted file extension matches
            // a recognized file type
            string ext = Path.GetExtension(sourceUrl).ToUpper()
                            .Substring(1);  // skip the leading dot
            ImageType imageType = (ImageType)
                Enum.Parse(typeof(ImageType), ext);

            // modify the record routing type to match
            // the supplied file extension, ignoring the supplied
            // routing type
            recordRouting = ext;
        }
        catch
        {
            // reject unrecognized file extensions
            return new ResultCode(ResultCodeType.InvalidArgument);
        }

        // get the storage root path from the configuration file
        string path = ConfigurationManager.AppSettings["RepositoryRoot"];
        if (null == path || path.Length == 0) path = @"C:\ImageRepository";

        // open the root folder
        DirectoryInfo storageRoot = Directory.CreateDirectory(path);
        // create a subfolder having the routing type name
        DirectoryInfo routingTypeFolder
            = storageRoot.CreateSubdirectory(recordRouting);
```

```
        // create another subfolder having today's date
        string subpath = DateTime.Today.ToString("yyyyMMdd");
        DirectoryInfo submitFolder
          = routingTypeFolder.CreateSubdirectory(subpath);

        // create a new file having the specified name
        string filePath = Path.Combine(
           submitFolder.FullName, Path.GetFileName(sourceUrl));

        using (FileStream fs = File.Create(filePath))
        {
            // write the bits into the file
            fs.Write(fileToSubmit, 0, fileToSubmit.Length);
        }

        // return the success code
        return new ResultCode(ResultCodeType.Success);
    } catch
    {
    }
    // failed for some reason
    return new ResultCode(ResultCodeType.UnknownError);
}
```

Preparing for Testing from SharePoint

Testing the custom records repository from SharePoint requires a few additional steps to enable SharePoint to locate the repository and communicate with the web service. You need to configure a fixed port number and reconfigure SharePoint to use the custom repository.

Configuring a Fixed Port Number

The default settings for new web site projects in Visual Studio 2005 cause the ASP.NET Development server to generate a port dynamically each time the solution is run. These settings must be changed in order to configure SharePoint to use the service.

Right-click the project name in the Visual Studio Solution Explorer, and open the properties panel. Change the value of the Use dynamic ports property to false. Set the value of the port number property to any value you wish. You may need to rebuild the project before the property becomes editable.

Reconfiguring SharePoint to Use the Custom Repository

Open the SharePoint Central Administration web site and click the Records Center link from the External Service Connections section of the Application Management page. On the Configure Connection to Records Center page, check the Connect to a Records Center radio button and enter the URL of the custom web service, as shown in Figure 12-9.

During development testing, enter the fixed port number used by the ASP.NET Development server. You can obtain this URL by right-clicking on the ASP.NET Development Server task bar icon and then selecting the Show Details command, as shown in Figure 12-10.

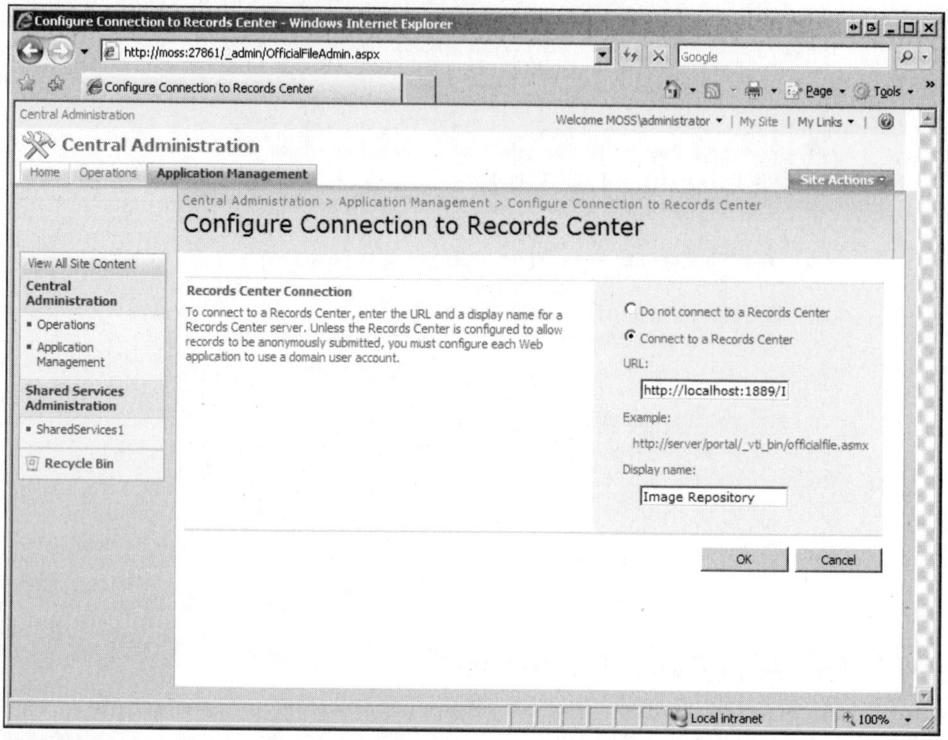

Figure 12-9

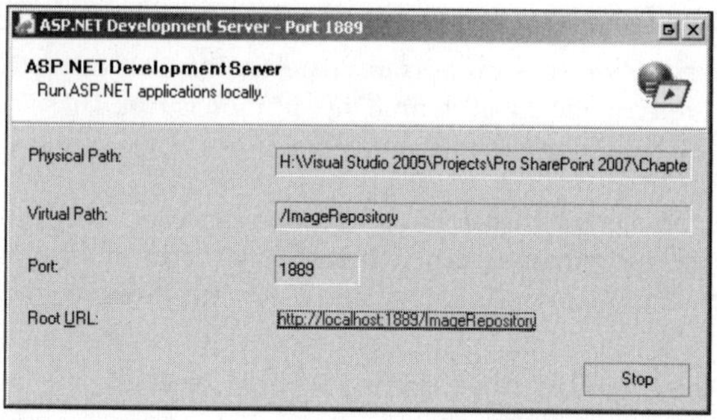

Figure 12-10

After the SharePoint server has been configured, you can send files to the custom repository from any SharePoint document library or picture library, as illustrated in Figures 12-11 and 12-12. Figure 12-11 shows the image repository as an option on the Send To menu. Figure 12-12 shows the resulting image stored in the custom repository.

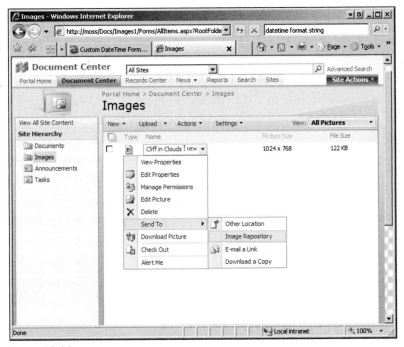

Figure 12-11

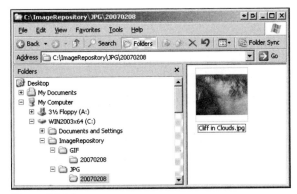

Figure 12-12

Creating a Custom Router

Office SharePoint Server 2007 employs an extensible routing framework to process files that are submitted to a Records Center site. This routing framework is very flexible and supports any number of custom routers, which implement the IRouter interface defined in the SharePoint API. The only limitation of this framework is that only one router can be defined for any given routing type.

The diagram in Figure 12-13 depicts the relationship between a router and the record series.

You create a custom router by implementing the IRouter interface, which declares a single method named OnSubmitFile. If the router has been associated with a record series type, this method is called whenever a file is submitted to a Records Center site, enabling the router to process the file contents and its metadata.

The OnSubmitFile method is called before the standard processing of the file occurs. Depending on the return value, the router can control or override the standard processing sequence. There are two success codes and one error code. Returning a RouterResult value of RejectFile indicates that the record repository should return an error value to the calling application. The values SuccessContinueProcessing and SuccessCancelFurtherProcessing are used to return a success value and then continue or discontinue processing of the document, respectively. Canceling further processing in this context means that the document is not stored into the repository, but the calling application still receives a success code. This means that the router can effectively filter the records going into the repository without notifying the client. De-duplication is one scenario in which this feature can be useful.

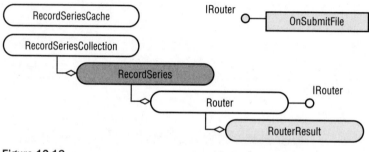

Figure 12-13

Implementing the IRouter Interface

The code shown in Listing 12-6 (EventLogRouter.cs) implements a custom router that appends an entry to the application event log for each document received in the repository.

Listing 12-6

```csharp
using System;
using System.IO;
using System.Diagnostics;
using System.Collections.Generic;
using System.Text;
using Microsoft.Office.RecordsManagement.RecordsRepository;

namespace ProSharePoint2007
{
    /// <summary>
    /// A custom router that writes an entry to the application
    /// event log for each file submitted to the record repository.
    /// </summary>
```

```
public class EventLogRouter : IRouter
{
    RouterResult IRouter.OnSubmitFile(
        string recordSeries,
        string sourceUrl,
        string userName,
        ref byte[] fileToSubmit,
        ref RecordsRepositoryProperty[] properties,
        ref Microsoft.SharePoint.SPList destination,
        ref string resultDetails)
    {
        RouterResult result = RouterResult.SuccessContinueProcessing;

        // Setup the event source and log using the record series name.
        string source = "EventLogRouter";
        if (!EventLog.SourceExists(source))
            EventLog.CreateEventSource(source, "Records Center");

        // Set up the log entry.
        string fileName = Path.GetFileName(sourceUrl);
        string listName = (null==destination) ?
            "unknown" : destination.Title;

        EventLog.WriteEntry(source, "File '"
            + filename + "' was saved by user '"
            + username + "' to list '"
            + listName + "'",
            EventLogEntryType.Information);

        return result;
    }
}
```

Adding the Custom Router to a Records Center Site

Custom routers are deployed using the SharePoint object model. After building the custom router assembly and copying it to the Global Assembly Cache, some additional installation code is required to make the router available to routing types declared within a Records Center site. This code is typically executed during feature activation but can also be executed from a console application or other code that runs directly on the SharePoint server.

Each Records Center site has an associated `RecordSeriesCollection`. This object maintains the list of routing types that the records repository understands. The `RecordSeriesCollection` object also maintains the list of custom routers that are available for use by individual routing types. The first step in making a custom router available is to add the router name, assembly, and class to the `RecordSeriesCollection` associated with a given Records Center site.

Listing 12-7 (`eventlogrouter.cs`) shows the code for a console application that adds or removes the `EventLogRouter` to or from the list of custom routers, which are available for use by routing types associated with a given Records Center site. The user supplies the site URL and a string indicating whether the router should be registered or unregistered.

Listing 12-7

```
using System;
using System.Collections.Generic;
using System.Text;
using Microsoft.Office.RecordsManagement.RecordsRepository;
using Microsoft.SharePoint;

namespace EventLogRouterSetup
{
    /// <summary>
    /// Installs the custom event log router to a Records Center site.
    /// </summary>
    class Program
    {
        const string ROUTER_NAME = "Event Log Router";
        const string ROUTER_CLASS = "ProSharePoint2007.EventLogRouter";
        const string ROUTER_ASSEMBLY =
            "ProSharePoint2007.Chapter12.EventLogRouter"
            + ", Version=1.0.0.0, Culture=neutral"
            + ", PublicKeyToken=0b97b340d4a71524";

        static void Main(string[] args)
        {
            if (args.Length < 2)
            {
                Console.WriteLine(
                    "usage: EventLogRouterSetup "
                    + "[ register | unregister ] <url>"
                );
                return;
            }

            string command = args[0].ToUpper();
            string url = args[1];

            using (SPSite site = new SPSite(url))
            {
                using (SPWeb web = site.OpenWeb())
                {
                    try
                    {
                        RecordSeriesCollection coll
                            = new RecordSeriesCollection(web);
                        switch (command)
                        {
                            case "REGISTER":
                                coll.AddRouter(ROUTER_NAME,
                                    ROUTER_ASSEMBLY, ROUTER_CLASS);
                                break;
                            case "UNREGISTER":
                                coll.RemoveRouter(ROUTER_NAME);
                                break;
                            default:
                                Console.WriteLine("Unrecognized command");
```

```
                              break;
                    }
               }
               catch (Exception x)
               {
                    Console.WriteLine(x.Message);
               }
          }
     }
}
```

Activating the Custom Router for a Routing Type

After the router has been added to a Records Center site, it is available for use by routing types declared within that site. Adding the router to the site does not automatically activate it. Activating the router requires one additional step by the site administrator, which is performed through the SharePoint user interface.

When one or more custom routers have been added to a Records Center site, the Record Routing edit form is extended to include a drop-down list of router names, as shown in Figure 12-14.

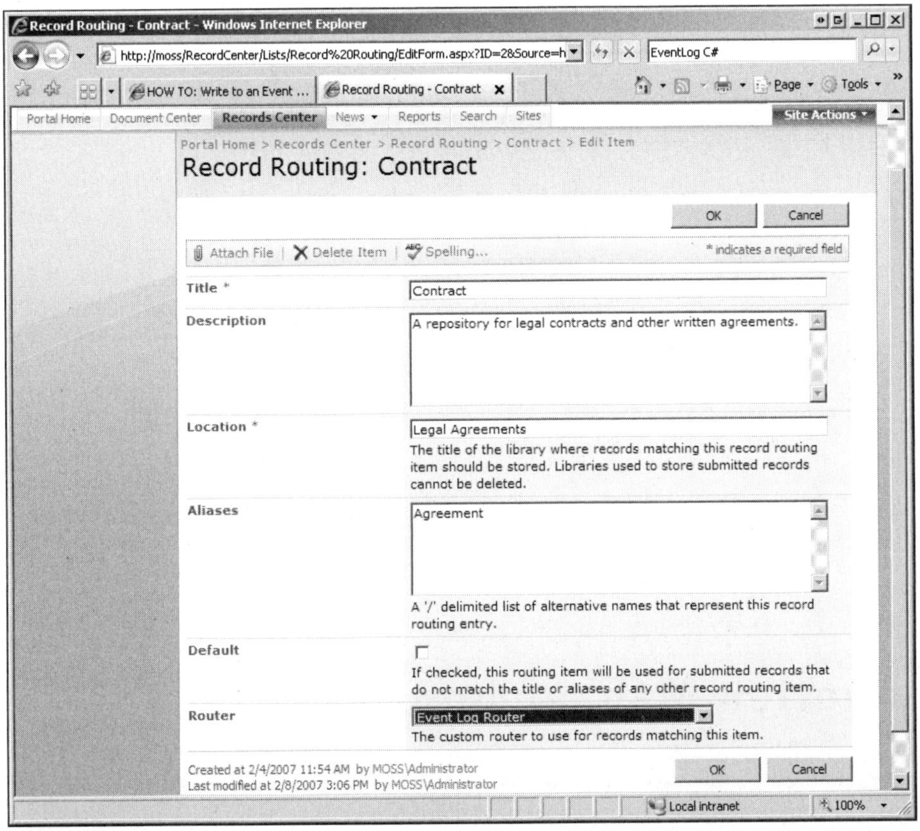

Figure 12-14

Selecting an item from this list activates the custom router for that routing type. Only one router can be chosen for a given routing type. Having done so, any record of that type that is received will now be processed by the custom router. Figure 12-15 shows an entry made to the event log by the custom router when a contract is processed. Figure 12-16 shows the `message detail`.

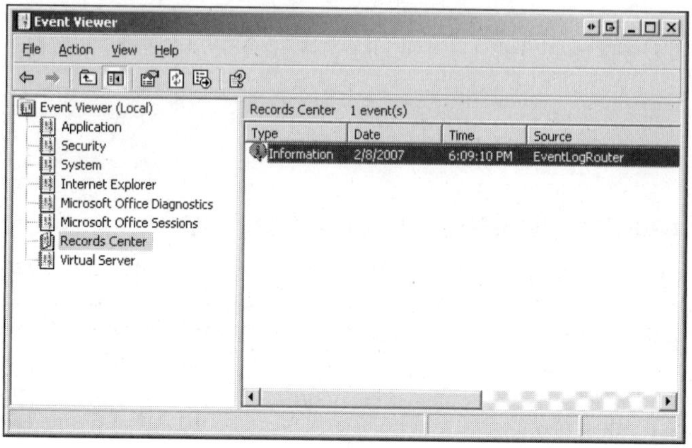

Figure 12-15

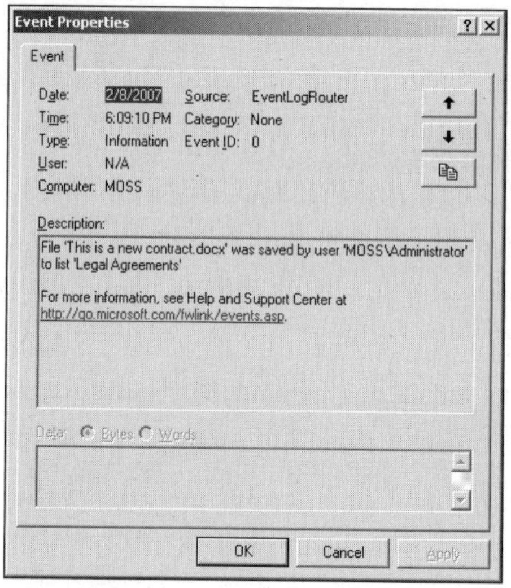

Figure 12-16

Information Management Policy

Office SharePoint Server 2007 makes it possible to establish explicit rules for governing information management through the use of Information Management Policy Features. By implementing a Policy Feature, you can control what happens to selected information as it moves through the enterprise. This is particularly important for records management solutions, where regulatory compliance is driving the solution development effort.

Figure 12-17 shows the Information Management Policy architecture within the Office SharePoint Server 2007 system.

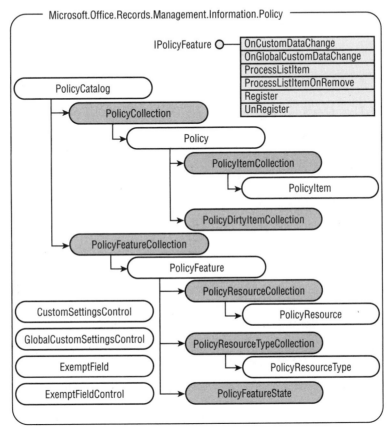

Figure 12-17

You create a policy by implementing one or more policy features and then adding them to the global policy catalog for the SharePoint Server Farm. Each feature can be associated with one or more policy resources, which it consumes in response to events it receives through the IPolicyFeature interface.

Creating a Custom Policy Feature

It is important to understand that Policy Features are attached to content types and are called to act on list items which are instances of the associated content types. Thus, the lifecycle for a Policy Feature includes the following steps:

1.   The Policy Feature assembly is registered in the global policy catalog.

2. The Policy Feature is registered for a given content type. The feature can register custom event receivers for the list or perform other housekeeping chores.

3. As items are added to the list, the `ProcessListItem` method is invoked. This method precedes any event receiver methods which may be associated with the list.

4. Any event receivers associated with the list are called.

5. As items are removed from the list, the `ProcessListItemOnRemove` method is invoked. This method comes after any event receiver methods that may be associated with the list.

6. The Policy Feature is unregistered for the content type.

7. The Policy Feature assembly is removed from the global policy catalog.

Registering a Policy Feature in the Global Policy Catalog

The code shown in Listing 12-8 (`TaskAssignmentPolicyReceiver.cs`) registers a policy feature that prevents the creation of unassigned task items.

Listing 12-8

```
using System;
using System.Collections.Generic;
using System.Text;
using Microsoft.SharePoint;
using Microsoft.Office.RecordsManagement.InformationPolicy;

namespace ProSharePoint2007
{
    public class TaskAssignmentPolicyReceiver : SPFeatureReceiver
    {
        public override void FeatureActivated(
            SPFeatureReceiverProperties properties)
        {
            string sManifest =
            @"<p:PolicyFeature id = ""TaskAssignment""
                xmlns:p=""urn:schemas-microsoft-com:office:server:policy"">
            <p:Name>Task Assignment Policy</p:Name>
            <p:Description>Prevents the creation of unassigned
                task items.</p:Description>
            <p:Publisher>John Holliday</p:Publisher>
            <p:AssemblyName>ProSharePoint2007.Chapter12.TaskAssignmentPolicy,
                Version=1.0.0.0, Culture=Neutral,
                PublicKeyToken=0b97b340d4a71524</p:AssemblyName>
            <p:ClassName>ProSharePoint2007.TaskAssignmentPolicy</p:ClassName>
            </p:PolicyFeature>";
            try
            {
                PolicyFeatureCollection.Add(sManifest);
            }
            catch
            {
            }
        }
    }
```

```
        public override void  FeatureDeactivating(
            SPFeatureReceiverProperties properties)
        {
            PolicyFeatureCollection.Delete("TaskAssignment");
        }
        public override void  FeatureInstalled(SPFeatureReceiverProperties
properties){}
        public override void  FeatureUninstalling(SPFeatureReceiverProperties
properties){}
    }
}
```

Processing List Items

Listing 12-9 (`TaskPolicyFeature.cs`) shows the `IPolicyFeature` implementation.

Listing 12-9

```csharp
using System;
using System.Collections.Generic;
using System.Text;
using Microsoft.SharePoint;
using Microsoft.Office.RecordsManagement.InformationPolicy;

namespace TaskPolicyFeature
{
    /// <summary>
    /// This class prevents the creation of unassigned task items.
    /// </summary>
    public class TaskAssignmentPolicy : IPolicyFeature
    {
        // not used - updates feature state when the
        // custom data information is changed
        void IPolicyFeature.OnCustomDataChange(
            PolicyItem policyItem, SPContentType ct)
        {
        }

        // not used - updates feature state when
        // central administration settings are changed
        void IPolicyFeature.OnGlobalCustomDataChange(PolicyFeature feature)
        {
        }

        // called when list items are added
        bool IPolicyFeature.ProcessListItem(
            SPSite site, PolicyItem policyItem, SPListItem listItem)
        {
            // Checks for task items.
            if (listItem != null && listItem.ContentType.Name == "Task")
            {
                if (listItem["Assigned To"] == null)
                    return false;
```

```
        }
        return true;
    }

    // not used - called for list items that are no longer
    // subject to the policy
    bool IPolicyFeature.ProcessListItemOnRemove(
        SPSite site, SPListItem listItem)
    {
        return true;
    }

    // not used - called when the policy is added to a content type
    void IPolicyFeature.Register(SPContentType ct)
    {
        // register event receivers
        // add or remove fields from the content type
    }

    // not used - called when the policy is removed from a content type
    void IPolicyFeature.UnRegister(SPContentType ct)
    {
        // unregister event receivers
    }
    }
}
```

Summary

Records management is driven by regulatory compliance and the need to ensure the confidentiality, integrity, high availability, adherence to policy, and audit ability of information stored in official records. The central feature of any records management system is the records repository. The Office SharePoint Server 2007 records management features include a default implementation of a records repository in the form of the Records Center site template. This template provides all of the core functionality needed to build records management solutions through the OfficialFile web service and underlying object model.

Office SharePoint Server 2007 uses the OfficialFile web service to maintain a list of RecordRouting objects, which specify the locations within a repository that can accept records of a given type. By implementing the Official File web service contract, any system can participate in the Office SharePoint Server 2007 records management scheme.

Office SharePoint Server 2007 employs an extensible routing framework to process files that are submitted to a Records Center site. Once a router has been associated with a RecordRouting object, its SubmitFile method is called whenever a file is submitted to the site, enabling the router to process the file contents and its metadata. Custom routers are deployed using the SharePoint object model.

Office SharePoint Server 2007 also makes it possible to establish explicit rules for governing information management through the use of Information Management Policy Features. By implementing a Policy Feature, you can control what happens to selected information as it moves through the enterprise.

13

Building Web Content Management Solutions

By John Holliday

Web content management (WCM) encompasses a range of activities having to do with publishing information for consumption through a web interface. Its primary goal is to enable content contributors to collaborate and publish information from a variety of sources in a controlled and consistent manner.

Often, the skills required to maintain branding and consistency do not match the skills needed to produce up-to-date content. The challenge is to empower knowledge workers to keep content up to date without requiring them to understand HTML or user interface design, which is more suited to graphic designers and web developers. At the same time, there is also a need to empower web development teams to manipulate site structure and manage evolving design requirements without having to work directly with content providers.

Web content management solves this problem. Using a WCM system, knowledge workers can edit and publish web pages without having to work directly with web designers, because their submissions are controlled, formatted, and routed automatically by the system. Web designers are free to set up page layouts and styles independently of content authors and vice versa. WCM also provides enhanced collaboration support, allowing content to be moderated and approved before it is made available for public consumption.

Microsoft Office SharePoint Server (MOSS) 2007 includes a robust set of features that provide a complete WCM system built from standard SharePoint components. The following sections describe these features and demonstrate tools and techniques for leveraging them to create custom content-authoring and -publishing applications.

WCM in Office SharePoint Server 2007

The MOSS web content management components are implemented as part of the Microsoft SharePoint publishing framework, which is implemented as a set of Windows SharePoint Services 3.0 features. In other words, the publishing framework is implemented in the same way as any other "feature," which is really a testament to the breadth and effectiveness of the Windows SharePoint Services 3.0 architecture. The following table describes the major components of the Office SharePoint Server 2007 publishing framework:

Features Folder	Description
12\TEMPLATES\FEATURES\ Publishing	Provides the core publishing framework that enables publishing in a web.
	Adds custom actions to the user interface for managing item scheduling from a document library, and for setting up content type conversions.
12\TEMPLATES\FEATURES\ PublishingLayouts	Defines the default layouts that are available for publishing pages.
12\TEMPLATES\FEATURES\ PublishingPrerequisites	Installs a custom event receiver to handle publishing feature activation and deactivation for a site collection.
12\TEMPLATES\FEATURES\ PublishingResources	Installs Web Parts, images, stylesheets and other resources that are used by various components of the publishing framework.
12\TEMPLATES\FEATURES\ PublishingSite	Sets up feature activation dependencies for a publishing site to ensure that the necessary components are in place for a given publishing site.
12\TEMPLATES\FEATURES\ PublishingStapling	Establishes dependencies between publishing features and site templates.
12\TEMPLATES\FEATURES\ PublishingWeb	Defines activation dependencies between publishing features.

The SharePoint Publishing Object Model

The Office SharePoint Server 2007 publishing features work in conjunction with a robust object model that consists of eight public namespaces which are implemented in the `Microsoft.SharePoint .Publishing dll`. The following sections describe each of these namespaces and the components they provide.

Microsoft.SharePoint.Publishing

This namespace contains core components and utility classes that are used by the other publishing components. This includes the page layout framework and foundation classes for pages that use the enhanced caching mechanisms designed especially for web page publishing. This namespace also declares interfaces used to expose document converter settings to end users and to manage Web Part properties between variations.

Variations are a way to publish multiple versions (variations) of a web site from a single set of pages. See the "Using Variations" section for additional details.

Microsoft.SharePoint.Publishing.Administration

These classes are used for content deployment and for migrating content from Microsoft Content Management Server (CMS) 2002 to SharePoint Server 2007.

Microsoft.SharePoint.Publishing.Administration.WebServices

Implements the ContentDeploymentRemoteImport web service that supports remotely executing content deployment jobs.

Microsoft.SharePoint.Publishing.Fields

This namespace defines the base hierarchy for fields, field values, and core field behavior, including HTML and image fields, summary links, schedules, and content type identifiers.

Microsoft.SharePoint.Publishing.Navigation

This namespace provides support for navigating publishing sites. This includes the hierarchical views and specialized site map nodes that take advantage of the enhanced caching support provided by the publishing layer.

Microsoft.SharePoint.Publishing.WebControls

This namespace implements classes that define the appearance and behavior of publishing web controls. It includes a rich set of base controls for handling typical publishing operations such as editing HTML content, browsing for URL assets in a site collection, displaying error messages to end users, and specifying content queries. It also includes extensive support for content validation, scheduling, and setting up variations.

Microsoft.SharePoint.Publishing.WebControls.EditingMenuActions

This namespace implements the custom actions that define the behaviors available through the SharePoint Editing menu. This includes the common actions such as add, remove, check in, and check out, as well as workflow- and publishing-specific functions such as spell checking, workflow approval, and checking for broken links.

Microsoft.SharePoint.Publishing.WebServices

This namespace implements the SharePoint PublishingService and the SharepointPublishingToolboxService components. The PublishingService component provides a SOAP interface for the Publishing web service, which exposes members that can be used to remotely create and manipulate page layouts. The SharepointPublishingToolboxService is used by SharePoint Designer 2007 to retrieve toolbox information for a given page layout.

The SharePoint Publishing Architecture

Web content management boils down to three key activities; *content authoring*, which may involve a revision cycle that requires approval of content prior to publication; *page design and layout*, which may also involve a separate revision/approval cycle; and *page rendering*, which presents the merged content and layout either immediately or on a predefined schedule. Figure 13-1 illustrates the major components of the SharePoint publishing architecture.

Each of these activities carries with it a different set of requirements.

Content authors need a way to contribute material and to collaborate while developing it, preferably using familiar authoring tools and without consuming precious IT resources. Consider an intranet portal that includes information from many different departments, each contributing a different type of information. Some of the content may come from Microsoft Word documents; some from Microsoft Excel spreadsheets; and still other content may come from text files, Microsoft Project plans, presentations, PDF files, and other file formats. The WCM system needs to provide a way for authors to pull content from a variety of sources, while still preserving the distinction between raw content and its presentation.

Web designers create master pages to define the overall look and feel of the site, and then use page layouts to specify where the approved content will be injected into the final rendered page.

> *The master pages used by the SharePoint publishing framework are the same as ASP.NET 2.0 master pages, and the page layout files are the same as ASP.NET 2.0 content pages. The page layout files hold additional markup that is merged with the designated master page to produce the HTML that is rendered in the browser.*

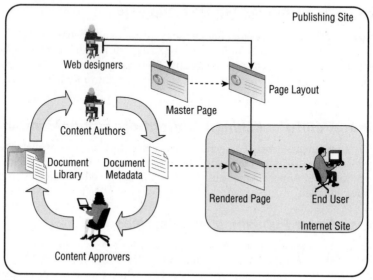

Figure 13-1

With these master pages and page layout files in place, administrators can then change the underlying master page at any time, and content authors can select the page layout they want that is most appropriate for the kind of content being developed. The actual content comes from the metadata associated with a given document library item.

The MOSS 2007 system ships with a set of predefined page layouts for publishing news articles. Each layout is tied to the same underlying content type (Article), but provides different ways to present the article content.

How Page Rendering Works

End users consume content through pages, which are rendered according to rules attached to controls embedded within each page. Each control pulls content from a data source such as a SharePoint list item, and then displays or hides that content based on the current state of the data, the configuration of the site, the permissions of the current user, or other rules that have been specified by the content authors. Figure 13-2 illustrates the Office SharePoint 2007 page rendering architecture.

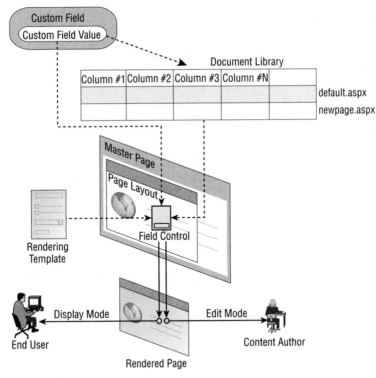

Figure 13-2

477

Everything is tied together using Windows SharePoint Services 3.0 content types and field controls which are aware of the content type to which they are bound. All of the pages involved in the rendering process, including the master page, the page layout, and the content pages, are instances of a content type defined by the publishing framework. Each content type declares the necessary fields (columns) that the publishing framework then uses to store configuration information (in the case of master pages and page layouts), and content metadata (in the case of content pages). The following diagram (see Figure 13-3) illustrates the relationships between the content types declared by the publishing framework.

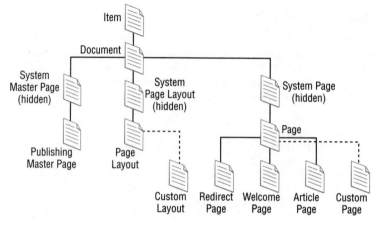

Figure 13-3

The hidden *System Master Page* content type inherits the name and title from its parent types, *Document* and *Item*. It also declares some additional information for the description, primary contact, and the preview image to display in the master page gallery. The derived *Publishing Master Page* does not add any columns, but is provided so that administrators or developers can add additional columns.

The *System Page Layout* content type is similar to the *System Master Page*, but adds a field to hold the identifier of the content type that will provide the rendering column data, as well as a field to keep track of variations. Again, the derived *Page Layout* is provided to enable additional columns to be added.

Finally, the *System Page* content type adds support for scheduled publishing by defining fields to hold the scheduling start and end dates. It includes fields for specifying the primary contact person in charge of the page, the rollup image, and target audiences for the published content. The derived *Page* content type rounds out the set of foundation content types.

To build a custom WCM solution, you can start with the default Page Layout, or you can derive a custom Page Layout if you need to manage a common set of data across multiple pages. You typically then create one or more custom page content types that hold the publishing content supplied by content authors.

Working with Master Pages

Master pages typically contain navigation elements, logos, a search box, a login control, editing controls, CSS references, and other server controls. The easiest way to create a new master page is to open an existing master page using SharePoint Designer 2007 and then save it to the file system. Once you've made the desired customizations, you can then upload it to the master page gallery of a top-level site, or you can package it into a Windows SharePoint Services 3.0 feature for deployment to multiple sites.

If you want to create a master page from scratch, it is still a good idea to start with a copy of an existing master page. This is because there are specific ContentPlaceholder controls that must be present in the master page markup, or SharePoint will throw an exception when the page is displayed. These controls can be placed in a hidden panel to prevent them from rendering HTML content, as shown in the highlighted part of the following code:

```
<%@ Master language="C#" %>
<!DOCTYPE html PUBLIC "-//W3C//DTD HTML 4.01 Transitional//EN"
"http://www.w3.org/TR/html4/loose.dtd">
<%@ Import Namespace="Microsoft.SharePoint" %>
<%@ Register Tagprefix="SPSWC" Namespace="Microsoft.SharePoint.Portal.WebControls"
Assembly="Microsoft.SharePoint.Portal, Version=12.0.0.0, Culture=neutral,
PublicKeyToken=71e9bce111e9429c" %>
<%@ Register Tagprefix="SharePoint" Namespace="Microsoft.SharePoint.WebControls"
Assembly="Microsoft.SharePoint, Version=12.0.0.0, Culture=neutral,
PublicKeyToken=71e9bce111e9429c" %>
<%@ Register Tagprefix="WebPartPages" Namespace="Microsoft.SharePoint.WebPartPages"
Assembly="Microsoft.SharePoint, Version=12.0.0.0, Culture=neutral,
PublicKeyToken=71e9bce111e9429c" %>
<%@ Register Tagprefix="PublishingWebControls"
Namespace="Microsoft.SharePoint.Publishing.WebControls"
Assembly="Microsoft.SharePoint.Publishing, Version=12.0.0.0, Culture=neutral,
PublicKeyToken=71e9bce111e9429c" %>
<%@ Register Tagprefix="PublishingNavigation"
Namespace="Microsoft.SharePoint.Publishing.Navigation"
Assembly="Microsoft.SharePoint.Publishing, Version=12.0.0.0, Culture=neutral,
PublicKeyToken=71e9bce111e9429c" %>
<%@ Register TagPrefix="wssuc" TagName="Welcome"
src="~/_controltemplates/Welcome.ascx" %>
<%@ Register TagPrefix="wssuc" TagName="DesignModeConsole"
src="~/_controltemplates/DesignModeConsole.ascx" %>
<%@ Register TagPrefix="PublishingVariations" TagName="VariationsLabelMenu"
src="~/_controltemplates/VariationsLabelMenu.ascx" %>
<%@ Register Tagprefix="PublishingConsole" TagName="Console"
src="~/_controltemplates/PublishingConsole.ascx" %>
<%@ Register TagPrefix="PublishingSiteAction" TagName="SiteActionMenu"
src="~/_controltemplates/PublishingActionMenu.ascx" %>
<html>
  <WebPartPages:SPWebPartManager runat="server"/>
  <SharePoint:RobotsMetaTag runat="server"/>
  <head runat="server">
    <asp:ContentPlaceHolder runat="server" id="head">
      <title>
        <asp:ContentPlaceHolder id="PlaceHolderPageTitle" runat="server" />
      </title>
    </asp:ContentPlaceHolder>
    <Sharepoint:CssLink runat="server"/>
    <asp:ContentPlaceHolder
id="PlaceHolderAdditionalPageHead" runat="server" />
  </head>
  <body onload="BLOCKED SCRIPT_spBodyOnLoadWrapper();">
```

```
            <form runat="server" onsubmit="return _spFormOnSubmitWrapper();">
              <wssuc:Welcome id="explitLogout" runat="server"/>
              <PublishingSiteAction:SiteActionMenu runat="server"/>
              <PublishingWebControls:AuthoringContainer
      id="authoringcontrols" runat="server">
                  <PublishingConsole:Console runat="server" />
              </PublishingWebControls:AuthoringContainer>
              <asp:ContentPlaceHolder id="PlaceHolderMain" runat="server" />
                  <asp:Panel visible="false" runat="server">
      <asp:ContentPlaceHolder id="PlaceHolderSearchArea" runat="server"/>
      <asp:ContentPlaceHolder id="PlaceHolderTitleBreadcrumb" runat="server"/>
      <asp:ContentPlaceHolder id="PlaceHolderPageTitleInTitleArea"  runat="server"/>
      <asp:ContentPlaceHolder id="PlaceHolderLeftNavBar" runat="server"/>
      <asp:ContentPlaceHolder ID="PlaceHolderPageImage" runat="server"/>
      <asp:ContentPlaceHolder ID="PlaceHolderBodyLeftBorder" runat="server"/>
      <asp:ContentPlaceHolder ID="PlaceHolderNavSpacer" runat="server"/>
      <asp:ContentPlaceHolder ID="PlaceHolderTitleLeftBorder" runat="server"/>
      <asp:ContentPlaceHolder ID="PlaceHolderTitleAreaSeparator" runat="server"/>
      <asp:ContentPlaceHolder ID="PlaceHolderMiniConsole" runat="server"/>
      <asp:ContentPlaceHolder id="PlaceHolderCalendarNavigator" runat ="server" />
      <asp:ContentPlaceHolder id="PlaceHolderLeftActions" runat ="server"/>
      <asp:ContentPlaceHolder id="PlaceHolderPageDescription" runat ="server"/>
      <asp:ContentPlaceHolder id="PlaceHolderBodyAreaClass" runat ="server"/>
      <asp:ContentPlaceHolder id="PlaceHolderTitleAreaClass" runat ="server"/>
      </asp:Panel>
          </form>
        </body>
      </html>
```

Using the Edit Mode Panel Control

The `EditModePanel` control provides a useful mechanism for displaying custom controls that are visible only during page editing. Simply placing a control within the `EditModePanel` control accomplishes the desired result, and it works with any control you want to use. This is nice, because there are many situations in which you want to provide additional information for the author without having to write a lot of code to set up a special authoring environment. In essence, this control allows you to create that environment automatically. The following example pulls in a special stylesheet for use only when the page is in edit mode:

```
<PublishingWebControls:editmodepanel runat="server" id="editmodestyles">
<!— Styles for edit mode only —>
        <SharePointWebControls:CssRegistration
name="<% $SPUrl:~sitecollection/Style Library/~language/Core
Styles/zz2_editMode.css %>" runat="server"/>
</PublishingWebControls:editmodepanel>
```

There can be multiple instances of the `EditModePanel` control on the layout page; so it is easy to configure the page for different editing scenarios. You can also place Web Part zones within the edit mode panel, to allow authors (and only authors) to select additional Web Parts they may need while researching their content. Because they are placed within the `EditModePanel` control, the Web Part zones do not appear on the final rendered page.

Using the AuthoringContainer Control

You can also use the `AuthoringContainer` control on a master page to hold controls that should only be displayed to content authors. However, this control works slightly differently from the `EditModePanel` control. The `AuthoringContainer` control is shown in both edit and view modes, but only for content authors, and not on the final published page. The following code fragment shows the `AuthoringContainer` control with an embedded welcome control that is shown only to authors:

```
<PublishingWebControls:AuthoringContainer id="logincontrols" runat="server">
<div class="login">
<asp:ContentPlaceHolder id="PlaceHolderLogin" runat="server">
<SharePointWebControls:Welcome id="welcome" runat="server"
EnableViewState="false"></SharePointWebControls:Welcome>
    </asp:ContentPlaceHolder>
</div>
</PublishingWebControls:AuthoringContainer>
```

Recall that the page-rendering scheme involves three distinct display modes — *Edit Mode*, when the page is checked out for editing by an author; *Author Review Mode*, when the page is not checked out for editing, but is being reviewed by an author; and *View Mode*, when the page is rendered for final publication. When the page is in Author Review Mode, it might be useful to provide additional information that is intended only for authors. For example, a stock ticker Web Part might be useful for authors who are working on a financial document. Another use might be to display status information related to the document itself.

Working with Page Layouts

By far, the easiest way to create a page layout is to use SharePoint Designer 2007. Whether you ultimately plan to deploy the layout directly to a site or via a solution deployment package, the first step is just to define the layout. SharePoint Designer makes this very easy when you are working directly with a SharePoint site. It becomes a bit more strenuous when you want to work with page layouts in Visual Studio.

Start with an existing page layout by opening a site in SharePoint Designer, and then navigate to the master page gallery, which is located under _catalogs/masterpage. In the gallery, click the Type column to sort the list, and then select the desired layout from the .aspx types. To start with a minimal layout, select the `PageLayoutTemplate.aspx` file. This file uses only two content placeholders, one for the title and another for the main content. For a more typical layout, choose `DefaultLayout.aspx` or one of the Article layouts. Figure 13-4 shows the `ArticleRight` layout opened in SharePoint Designer 2007.

Depending on the layout you choose, SharePoint Designer will populate the SharePoint Controls section of the toolbox with controls that can be used on the chosen page. This collection of controls is determined in part by the content type associated with the layout. Referring back to Figure 13-4, notice the toolbox for the `ArticleRight` layout. Since the `ArticleRight` page layout is associated with the Article Page content type, which is derived from the System Page content type, SharePoint Designer references these content types to retrieve the list of controls that can be used on the page. The Page Fields subsection contains field controls that can be used with the columns specified by the inherited System Page content type. The Content Fields subsection contains controls for fields defined in the Article Page content type itself.

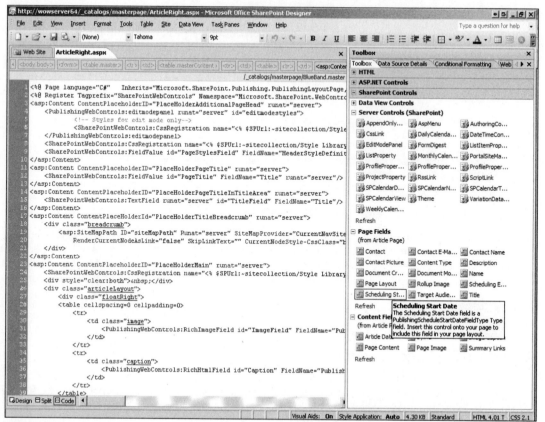

Figure 13-4

Here is where the problem arises for developing page layouts in Visual Studio. The toolbox only works for existing page layouts that reside in a running SharePoint site. This is because SharePoint Designer populates the toolbox by communicating with the SharePoint site in real time. This makes sense because the association between the page layout and the content type is stored as metadata in the pages document library on the site. As soon as you save the layout to a separate file, the link between it and the site is broken, and SharePoint Designer can no longer populate the toolbox.

To work around this problem, take the following steps:

1. Create a SharePoint site to use as a temporary workspace, using one of the publishing templates.

2. Open the site in SharePoint Designer 2007, and then create a new page layout from the File ➪ New menu. Select the SharePoint Content tab, and then click the SharePoint Publishing item in the list on the left side, as shown in Figure 13-5. Select Page Layout from the middle list, and then choose Page Layout Content Types from the Content Type Group drop-down.

3. Select the content type you want to associate with the new page layout, and then specify a name and title, and click OK. SharePoint Designer creates the new page layout and populates the toolbox accordingly.

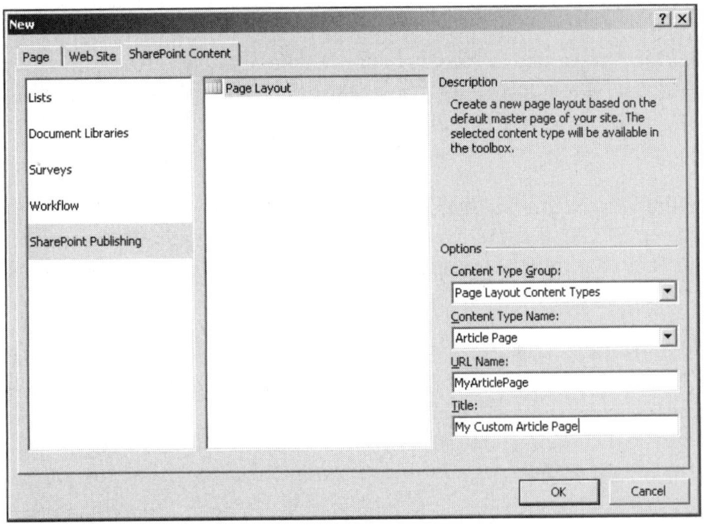

Figure 13-5

Now you can work from within SharePoint Designer to drag and drop controls onto the new page layout. When you are finished designing the page, you can then save it to disk and add it to your Visual Studio solution or to a SharePoint solution package for deployment.

Customizing the Authoring Experience

MOSS 2007 supports two methods for authoring web content. Using the web-based approach, content authors edit content directly in a web browser via server controls included in the SharePoint Publishing object model. Using the smart-client approach, content authors create a document in an application such as Microsoft Word, and then convert the document into HTML using the MOSS 2007 document conversion framework.

There are trade-offs for each method. Authoring content in the browser allows the author to see the content in the context of the page in which it will be rendered, and has the added advantage of incorporating document management features provided by the SharePoint platform. On the other hand, authoring content in a smart-client application is easier for authors already familiar with the application, and for adding preexisting content or developing lengthy reports and complex documents.

The following sections describe each method in detail, and show how to customize and extend the authoring experience.

Web-Based Authoring

The web-based authoring environment consists of two distinct sets of user interface elements. The Page Editing Toolbar enables authors to perform page-level operations, and the HTML Editor Toolbar provides a rich interface for entering HTML content. Both can be customized to create a constrained authoring environment or to ensure the availability of specific resources for authors to use.

The Page Editing Toolbar

The Page Editing toolbar presents a panel of controls that display information to content authors about a publishing page. The toolbar appears at the top of the page and consists of three areas: the Page Status bar, the Page Editing menu, and a group of Quick Access buttons. Figure 13-6 shows the default Page Editing toolbar displayed on the welcome page of a publishing portal site.

In this diagram, the *Version* and *Status* items reflect the current state of the page. The *Page, Workflow,* and *Tools* items are menus that contain a standard set of default commands that apply to all pages regardless of status. To the right of these, the *Edit Page* and *Publish* items are Quick Access buttons that depend on the current page status.

The menu commands displayed on the Page Editing toolbar are declared in a pair of external XML files. The default menu commands are declared in the EditingMenu.XML file, located in the 12\ TEMPLATE\LAYOUTS\EditingMenu folder. While it is possible to edit this file directly, doing so is ill-advised because it contains items that work in conjunction with the publishing framework. Inadvertently modifying or deleting a required command could break the page edit framework. Instead, you can create a separate file to declare custom menu commands, which are loaded into the control after the default menu items are processed.

Figure 13-6

Customizing the Page Editing Menu and Quick Access Button Panel

The EditingMenu.xml file contains a *customfile* element that points to the file containing custom menu commands. By default, this file is named CustomEditingMenu.xml and is located in the Editing Menu folder of the master page gallery associated with the site collection. At runtime, the Page Editing toolbar code searches for the custom definition file and processes the `ConsoleNode` elements it contains to complete the initialization process. For the Quick Access Button Panel, the `QuickAccess.xml` file is used, which refers to `CustomQuickAccess.xml` by default. The `QuickAccess.xml` file and the `EditingMenu.xml` file are structured in the same way.

Each file contains a collection of `ConsoleNode` elements that describe each menu item. These nodes are processed in order from top to bottom. The processing order is important, because it allows you to override the default menu items without editing the primary configuration file, thereby avoiding the risk of breaking the default implementation. To override a default menu item, simply use the same identifier as the item you want to replace.

The following listing shows a portion of the default `EditingMenu.xml` file. At the top is the `customfile` element that references the custom configuration file that should be loaded after the control is initialized. This element is followed by a `references` element containing assembly references, and a `structure` element containing `ConsoleNode` elements. Each `ConsoleNode` element describes an individual menu item.

The `reference` element operates in a similar fashion as the ASP.NET page directive used to register tag prefixes for referencing external user controls. In this case, as highlighted below, the "cms" prefix is declared as a short-hand reference to the `Microsoft.SharePoint.Publishing.WebControls.EditingMenuActions` namespace. This prefix is then used in the `ConsoleNode` elements to specify the `ConsoleAction` classes that are called when the menu command is executed.

```xml
<?xml version="1.0" encoding="utf-8" ?>
<Console>
    <customfile FileName="CustomEditingMenu" />
    <references>
        <reference TagPrefix="cms"
assembly="Microsoft.SharePoint.Publishing,    Version=12.0.0.0, Culture=neutral,
 PublicKeyToken=71e9bce111e9429c"
namespace="Microsoft.SharePoint.Publishing.WebControls.EditingMenuActions"/>
    </references>
    <structure >
        <ConsoleNode Sequence="100"
            NavigateUrl="javascript:" AccessKey="G"
            DisplayText="cms,console_pagesubmenu"
            ImageUrl="/_layouts/images/saveitem.gif"
            UseResourceFile="true"
            UserRights="EmptyMask"
            ID="saPageSubMenu">
            <ConsoleNode
                Action="cms:SavePublishingPageAction"
                DisplayText="cms,console_savechanges"
                ImageUrl="/_layouts/images/saveitem.gif"
                UseResourceFile="true" ID="saSaveChanges"/>
            <ConsoleNode
                Action="cms:SwitchToPublishedModeAction"
                DisplayText="cms,console_reviewmode"
                ImageUrl="/_layouts/images/saveitem.gif"
                UseResourceFile="true" ID="saReviewMode"/>
            <ConsoleNode
                IsSeparatorImage="True"
                UserRights="EmptyMask" />
```

```
<ConsoleNode
        Action="cms:CheckInWithCommentAction"
        HideStates="IsCheckedOutToCurrentUserFalse"
        ImageUrl="/_layouts/images/checkin.gif"
        UseResourceFile="true" ID="saCheckinWithComment"/>
```

The cms prefix is also used here to reference resource strings. This overloaded usage is unrelated to the *reference* element described above. Resource strings in XML definition files follow the general format `<resource filename>`, `<resource identifier>`, directing the system to load a specific resource string from the named resource file. Unlike other resource files that are located in the `12\Resources` folder, the `cms.resx` file is located in the `App_GlobalResources` folder of the root folder for the web application, for example, `c:\inetpub\wwwroot\wss\VirtualDirectories\80\App_GlobalResources`.

The HTML Editor Toolbar

The HTML Editor field control is used in conjunction with columns of type `Page Content` to provide authors with a rich editor for HTML content. Figure 13-7 shows the default HTML Editor field control on a publishing page.

The HTML Editor toolbar is customizable both globally and locally. Global customizations apply to all instances of the HTML Editor field control, and involve adding custom command buttons that invoke custom JavaScript code. Local customizations apply to each control individually, and involve specifying custom styles that authors can apply to selected content, and also defining constraints that hide certain commands based on a set of required permissions.

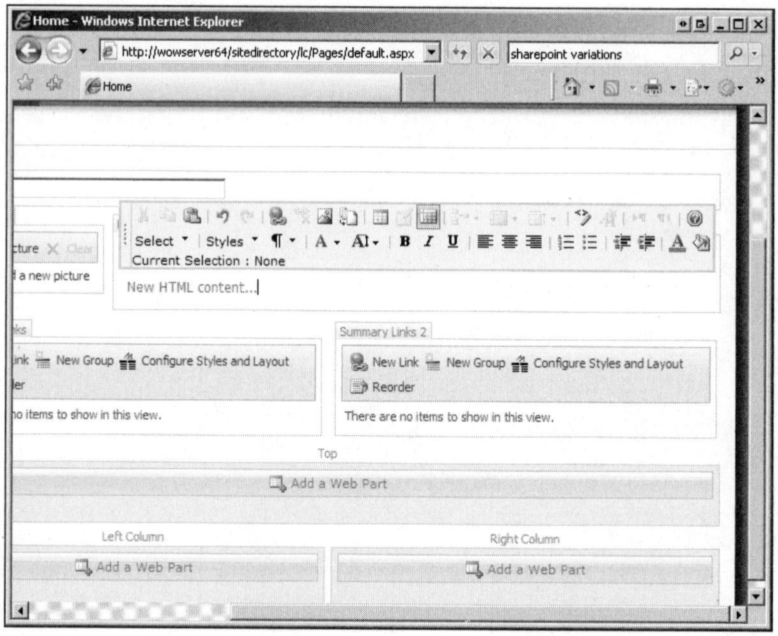

Figure 13-7

Adding Custom Command Buttons

The HTML Editor toolbar buttons are declared in the RTE2ToolbarExtension.xml file, which is located in the Editing Menu folder of the master page gallery associated with the site collection. By default, this file contains only a root node of type RTE2ToolbarExtensions. Custom commands are defined by adding subnodes of type RTE2ToolbarExtraButton nodes, as in the following example:

```
<?xml version="1.0" encoding="utf-8" ?>
<RTE2ToolbarExtensions>
    <RTE2ToolbarExtraButton id="myExtraButton" src="MyExtraButton.js"/>
</RTE2ToolbarExtensions>
```

In this example, the custom button identifier myExtraButton is associated with a JavaScript file, which must be copied to the 12\TEMPLATE\LAYOUTS\1033 folder. This file must contain code that registers the toolbar button and also implements two methods for handling the onClickCallback and onResetStateCallback events. The onClickCallback method is called when the button is clicked, and the onResetStateCallback method is called to reset the button state when any state of the editor is changed.

The following example registers a custom command button that displays an alert message when clicked:

```
// Called when the button is clicked
function onClickMyButton(strBaseElementID, args) {
alert("MyExtraButton was clicked in " + strBaseElementID + ": " + args[1]);
}

// Called when the button is reset
function onResetMyButton(strBaseElementID, args) {
var document = RTE_GetEditorDocument(strBaseElementID);
if (document != null) {
    RTE_RestoreSelection(strBaseElementID);
    return true;
    }
    return false;
}

// Registers the custom button
RTE2_RegisterToolbarButton(

/* button mnemonic */
"MyExtraButton",

/* path to the button icon */
RTE_GetServerRelativeUnlocalizedImageUrl("rte2popup.gif"),

/* text to display next to the icon */
"! Alert",

/* tooltip to display while hovering over the icon */
"Testing toolbar extensibility",

/* method called when the button is clicked */
onClickMyButton,
```

```
/* method called when the button is reset */
onResetMyButton,

/* object passed to the callback methods */
new Array("test","this","button")
);
```

Changing Styles and Branding

A commonly used feature of the HTML Editor is selecting predefined styles to apply to a given content element. For example, to create an unordered list, the author adds a UL element to the page, and then may wish to select a style to be applied to that list. The HTML Editor supports the ability to customize the collection of styles that are presented to the author in the Styles drop-down of the HTML Editor toolbar.

By default, the editor includes a default set of styles. These are loaded into the drop-down by searching through the CSS stylesheets associated with the page for styles with a designated prefix. The default prefix is ms-rteCustom-*XXXX*, where *XXXX* is the name of the CSS class that is displayed in the list. If any CSS classes are found whose names match this prefix, then the default styles are not loaded and the custom styles are loaded instead.

The following example declares a set of custom unordered list styles which are displayed when an unordered list element is selected in the editor:

```
UL.ms-rteCustom-MaroonSmallCaps
{
    color:Maroon;
    font-variant:small-caps;
}
UL.ms-rteCustom-NavySquareBullet
{
    color:Navy;
    list-style-type:square;
}
```

Unlike custom buttons, custom styles are processed locally by each instance of the control, allowing a different set of custom styles to be used for different sections of the page. This is achieved by changing the prefix used to name the CSS classes. The PrefixStyleSheet attribute of the RichHtmlField declaration specifies the prefix to be used.

```
<PublishingWebControls:RichHtmlField id="RegionOne" FieldName="RegionOneContent"
runat="server" PrefixStyleSheet="RegionOne" />

<PublishingWebControls:RichHtmlField id="RegionTwo" FieldName="RegionTwoContent"
runat="server" PrefixStyleSheet="RegionTwo" />
UL.RegionOne-UnorderedList1 { color:Blue; font-size:10pt; }
UL.RegionOne-UnorderedList2 { color:Red; font-size: 8pt; }

UL.RegionTwo-UnorderedList1 { color:Black; font-size:12pt;}
UL.RegionTwo-UnorderedList2 { color:Green; font-size:9pt; border:solid 2px;}
```

Smart-Client Authoring

Smart-client authoring allows content authors to use a client-side application such as Microsoft Word to create content or to import existing content. The term "smart-client authoring" is somewhat of a misnomer because the client-side authoring architecture does not take advantage of any "smart" connection between the client application and the SharePoint environment. Any application that can produce a document of the appropriate type can be used.

Content that is authored on the client is added to a MOSS 2007 publishing site through the use of *document converters*, which are command-line executables invoked by SharePoint on the server to convert a given document from one type to another. Document converters are managed at the server farm level, but individual document converters are scoped to the web application level. In other words, the executable file is installed on the server, but can be enabled or disabled for specific web applications.

The document conversion process is coordinated by two Windows Services. The `DCLoadBalancer` service is responsible for determining where the application should be executed on the server farm. The `DCLauncher` service is responsible for setting up the runtime environment, invoking the converter, and for retrieving and storing the converted document. Document converters are run by the `DCLauncher` service in a very isolated runtime environment to protect the server from potentially dangerous document converters, some of which may have been ported from other environments, and may have been originally designed for other purposes.

Consequently, the `DCLauncher` service creates a locked-down environment within which to run document converters. First, it creates a custom window station and desktop, and logs in as a guest user with a name of the form `HVU_<machinename>`. Then it sets up restricted permissions, basically allowing that guest user access to a single folder. Thus, when a converter runs, it can only read from the document it was given, and can only write to the folder from which it was executed.

Building Custom Document Converters

Implementing a custom document converter requires the following steps:

1. Create an EXE that performs the conversion.
2. Register the converter in the SharePoint environment.
3. Optionally create a custom ASPX page to allow the user to provide converter-specific settings.

The converter EXE file must accept the following parameters:

`-in infile`	The input file containing the document to be converted
`-out outfile.html`	The fully qualified path to the output HTML file
`[ -config config.xml ]`	(optional) path to the configuration settings
`[ -log logfile.log ]`	(option) path to the log file

The following example shows how to implement a simple converter for text files containing a comma-delimited list of values, where the first line contains a list of row headers, and the remaining lines contain column values. The resulting HTML file must contain two sections, an optional <head><style> . . . </style></head> section and a <body> . . . </body> tag. The converter generates a formatted HTML table while ensuring that each row contains the correct number of cells. Extra cells are discarded for any given row.

```csharp
using System;
using System.IO;
using System.ComponentModel;
using System.Collections.Generic;
using System.Text;
using System.Web.UI;

namespace ProSharePoint2007
{
    class SimpleConverter
    {
        enum ArgType { _in, _out, _config, _log, _unknown };

        static void Main(string[] args)
        {
            ArgType m_argType = ArgType._unknown;
            string[] arg = new string[(int)ArgType._unknown];

            foreach (string s in args) {
                if (s[0] == '-' || s[0] == '/')
                    m_argType = (ArgType)Enum.Parse(
typeof(ArgType), s.Replace(s[0].ToString(), "_"));
                else {
                    arg[(int)m_argType] = s;
                    m_argType = ArgType._unknown;
                }
            }
            SimpleConverter.ConvertToHTML(arg[0],arg[1],arg[2],arg[3]);
        }

        /// <summary>
        /// Performs the conversion to HTML
        /// </summary>
        /// <param name="inFile"> comma-delimited strings</param>
        /// <param name="outFile">the HTML output file</param>
        /// <param name="configFile">optional settings file</param>
        /// <param name="logFile">optional log file</param>
        static void ConvertToHTML(string inFile, string outFile,
string configFile, string logFile)
        {
            using (StreamReader reader = new StreamReader(inFile)) {
```

```
                using (HtmlTextWriter writer = new HtmlTextWriter(
new StreamWriter(outFile))) {
                    writer.RenderBeginTag(HtmlTextWriterTag.Html);
                    WriteStyles(reader, writer);
                    WriteBody(reader, writer);
                    writer.RenderEndTag();
                    writer.Close();
                }
            }
        }

        static void WriteStyles(StreamReader reader, HtmlTextWriter writer)
        {
            writer.RenderBeginTag(HtmlTextWriterTag.Head);
            writer.RenderBeginTag(HtmlTextWriterTag.Style);
            writer.WriteLine("TABLE { border-style:solid; border-color:green; }");
            writer.WriteLine("TH { font-weight:bold; font-size:10pt; }");
            writer.WriteLine("TD { font-size:8pt; color:blue; }");
            writer.RenderEndTag();
            writer.RenderEndTag();
        }

        static void WriteBody(StreamReader reader, HtmlTextWriter writer)
        {
            writer.RenderBeginTag(HtmlTextWriterTag.Body);
            writer.RenderBeginTag(HtmlTextWriterTag.Table);
            int i, rows = 0, cols = 0;
            while (!reader.EndOfStream) {
                writer.RenderBeginTag(HtmlTextWriterTag.Tr);
                HtmlTextWriterTag colTag = HtmlTextWriterTag.Td;
                string[] tokens = reader.ReadLine().Split(",".ToCharArray());
                if (rows++ == 0) {
                    cols = tokens.Length;
                    colTag = HtmlTextWriterTag.Th;
                }
                for (i = 0; i < cols; i++) {
                    writer.RenderBeginTag(colTag);
                    if (i < tokens.Length) {
                        writer.Write(tokens[i]);
                    }
                    writer.RenderEndTag();
                }
                writer.RenderEndTag();
            }
            writer.RenderEndTag();
            writer.RenderEndTag();
        }
    }
}
```

Deploying a Custom Converter

Document Converters are deployed at the web application level, using a SharePoint feature definition file and a Document Converter definition file.

Installing and running a document converter on a domain controller (DC) is not supported. This is because all document converters are executed in the context of a restricted local account, which is unavailable on a domain controller.

The following example shows the feature definition XML for the CSV to HTML converter:

```
<Feature xmlns="http://schemas.microsoft.com/sharepoint/"
         Id="{5FD4BBC0-1538-4ead-817A-A637AB66B1FF}"
         Title="Simple Document Converter"
         Description="Converts from CSV to HTML"
         Version="1.0.0.0"
         Scope="WebApplication"
         Hidden="FALSE">
    <ElementManifests>
        <ElementManifest Location="elements.xml"/>
    </ElementManifests>
</Feature>
```

The element manifest contains the converter definition XML:

```
<Elements xmlns="http://schemas.microsoft.com/sharepoint/">
    <DocumentConverter
        Id="{ADE66E1D-2750-44f5-A8BD-435B5BBFDA56}"
        Name="CSV to HTML"
        App="SimpleConverter.exe"
        From="csv"
        To="html"
    />
</Elements>
```

After copying these two files along with the `SimpleConverter.exe` application to a new folder named `12\TEMPLATE\FEATURES\SimpleConverter`, the STSADM command-line utility can be used to install and activate the feature as follows:

```
stsadm -o installfeature -name SimpleConverter
stsadm -o activatefeature -name SimpleConverter -url http://localhost
```

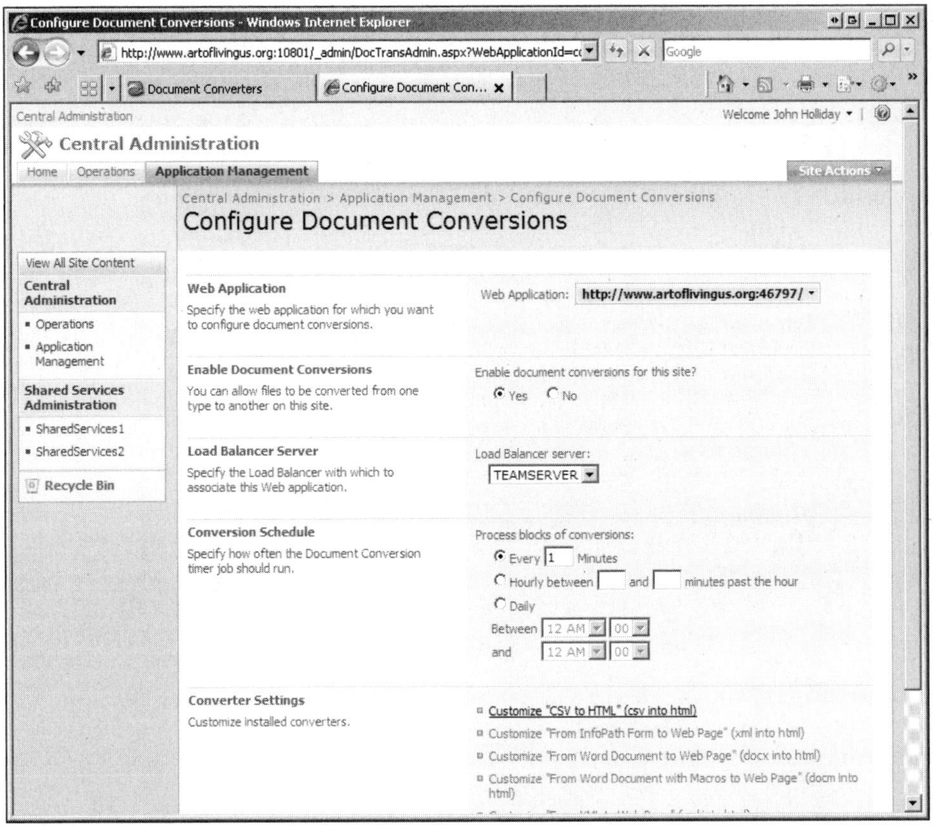

Figure 13-8

Installing and activating the document converter feature makes it available for final configuration from the Central Administration web site for the specified web application. Figure 13-8 shows the *Configure Document Conversions* page after the CSV to HTML converter feature is activated.

Once the document converter is configured, it is available for use by content authors. Typically, an author uploads a document with a given file extension to a document library, and then selects the *Convert Document* menu command. The available document converters for the selected file type are displayed in the drop-down menu, as shown in Figure 13-9.

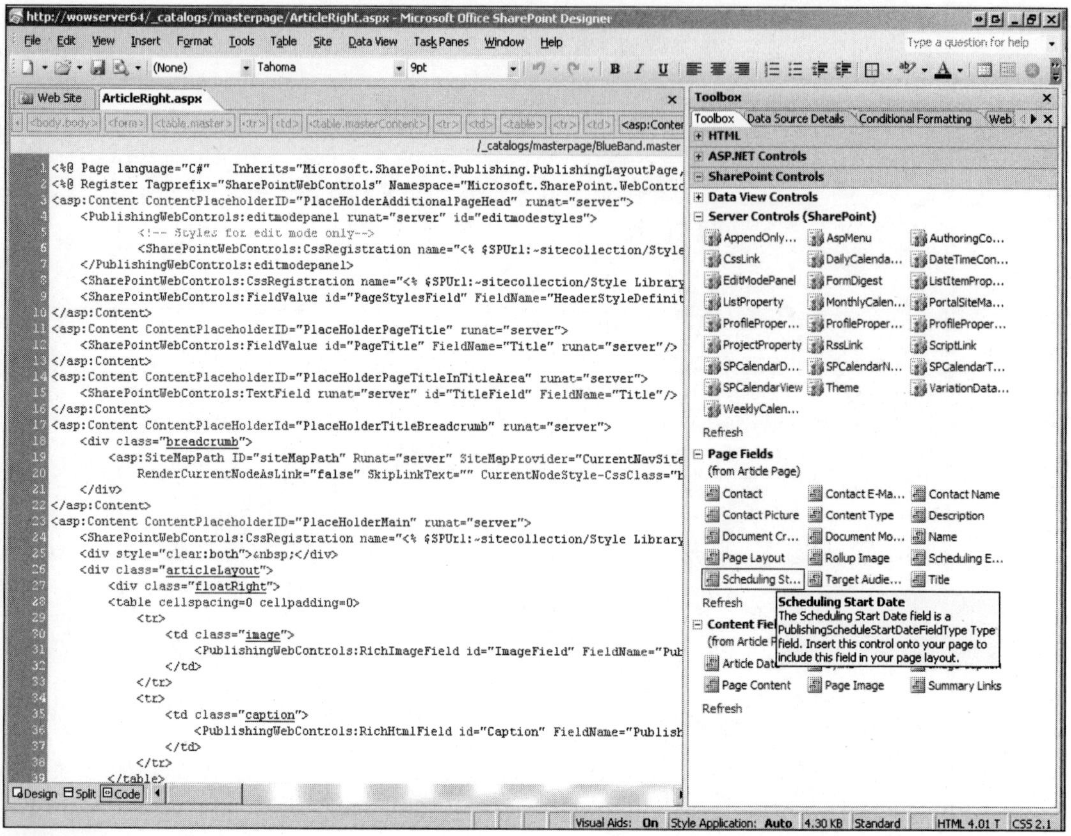

Figure 13-9

Calling Document Converters Programmatically

Under certain conditions, it may be necessary to invoke a document converter programmatically. A common example might be a workflow activity that needs to convert a Microsoft Word document to html. You can invoke a document converter in one of two ways: by calling the `Convert()` method of the `SPFile` object associated with the document, or by adding the document to the `PublishingPages` collection of the publishing web site.

The `PublishingWeb` component is a special component that provides a wrapper around an existing `SPWeb` object that lets you call special methods for working with the Publishing API. The central concept here is that the conversion occurs when the document is added to the `PublishingPages` collection. This may seem counterintuitive outside the context of a user interface, but makes sense when you think about how the publishing system works.

You invoke a document converter by adding a page to the pages collection. The `Add` method takes the GUID of the converter you want to apply and the file to which it should be applied. It is important to understand what happens when using this method. When a page is added to the `PublishingPages` collection, some additional postprocessing occurs after the conversion is finished. This postprocessing step is responsible for extracting the CSS styles from the optional `<style>` section and for extracting the HTML markup from the `<body>` tag of the converted document. This information is then injected into the field controls embedded in the page layout associated with the page.

```
PublishingWeb publishingWeb = PublishingWeb.GetPublishingWeb(web);
PublishingPageCollection pages = publishingWeb.GetPublishingPages();
PublishingPage page = pages.Add("New Page Name",fileToConvert,
    converterId, PageConversionPriority.Immediately);
```

Creating and Using Field Controls

Field controls constitute the "heart" of the MOSS 2007 publishing system. Field controls are aptly named because each control is tightly bound to a field (site column) in the underlying content type associated with a page layout. This tight association can be seen by examining the page layout markup for the standard `WelcomeSplash.aspx` page layout.

```
<table cellpadding="0" cellspacing="6" width="100%" class="splashLinkFrame">
    <tr>
        <td width="50%" valign="top" class="splashLinkArea">
            <PublishingWebControls:SummaryLinkFieldControl
id="SummaryLink1"
FieldName="SummaryLinks"
runat="server"/>
        </td>
    </tr>
</table>
```

The `FieldName` attribute binds the control to the `SummaryLinks` field of the Welcome Page content type (shown in Figure 13-10) with which the `WelcomeSplash.aspx` page layout is associated.

This also means that if the content type is modified, then the field control will no longer work as expected. Modifying content types installed by a feature is generally a bad idea because of other hidden dependencies that may exist between components. To prevent users from removing essential columns from a content type through the UI, you can mark the column as "sealed." This will not, however, prevent the field reference from being removed programmatically.

Field controls essentially define a mapping from one or more columns of the document library item to content which appears somewhere on the page when it is rendered. By placing field controls on the page layout, you are providing a container for authors to enter the metadata, as well as a canvas for displaying that metadata to end users.

Building a Custom Field Control

The many different pieces of the WCM puzzle start to come together when designing custom field controls because you can customize just about anything with a little bit of work. When dealing with so many moving parts, it helps to refer back to the MOSS 2007 object model to gain perspective. For instance, to support different types of rendering, an extra level of indirection is typically added to the implementation of various components. The names are similar in the definition files, but they may refer to different components in the object model. This may not be obvious when looking just at the XML markup.

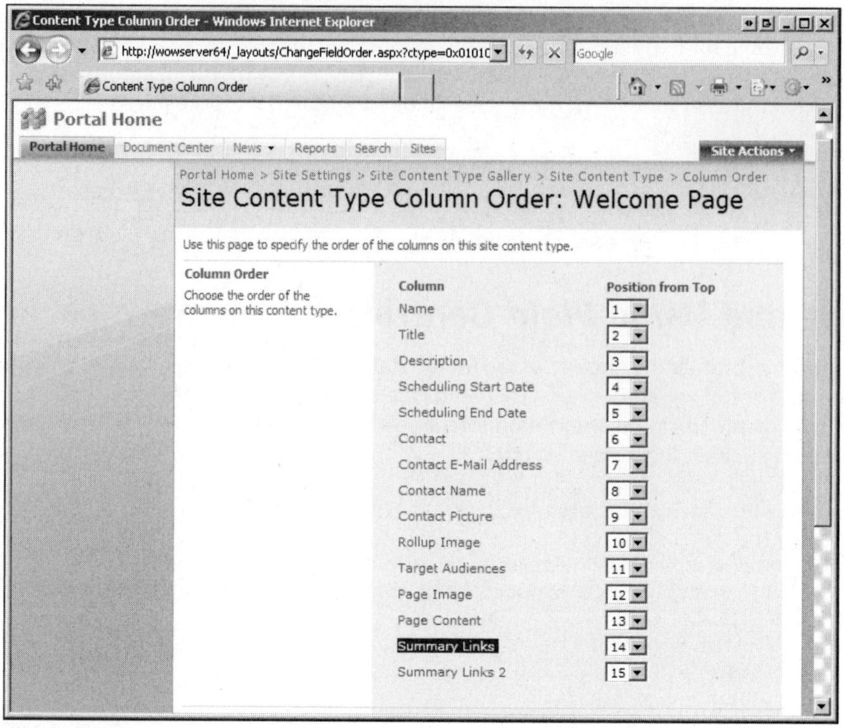

Figure 13-10

It is important to keep in mind that there is an `SPField` object associated with the markup for every field. This object defines both the underlying field data type and the CAML that determines how the field will be rendered in the browser when the user enters or edits the field value. The data for any given field is typically stored in a separate value object, not in the `SPField` object itself. Figure 13-11 shows the core set of publishing fields and their relationships.

It is useful to follow the same pattern when creating custom fields. The following example defines a `MediaField` class, and a corresponding `MediaFieldValue` class that is used to manage metadata about an individual media asset for a portal containing tutorials and other training materials. These classes in turn support the development of a `RichMediaField` field control for displaying rich media content on a publishing page.

```
using System;
using System.Collections.Generic;
using System.Text;
using Microsoft.SharePoint;
using Microsoft.SharePoint.WebControls;

namespace ProSharePoint2007.Chapter13
{
    public class MediaField : SPFieldMultiColumn
    {
        public MediaField(SPFieldCollection fields, string fieldName)
: base(fields, fieldName){}
```

Microsoft.SharePoint

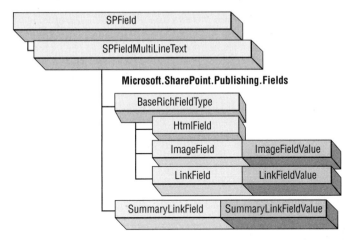

Figure 13-11

```
        public MediaField(SPFieldCollection fields, string typeName,
string displayName) : base(fields, typeName, displayName){}

        public override object GetFieldValue(string value)
        {
            if (String.IsNullOrEmpty(value)) return null;
            return new MediaFieldValue(value);
        }

        public override BaseFieldControl FieldRenderingControl
        {
            get
            {
                return base.FieldRenderingControl;
            }
        }
    }
    public class MediaFieldValue : SPFieldMultiColumnValue
    {
        const int NUM_FIELDS = 2;

        public MediaFieldValue() : base(NUM_FIELDS) { }
        public MediaFieldValue(string value) : base(value) { }
        public MediaFieldValue(string type, string url) : base(NUM_FIELDS)
        {
            this.MediaType = type;
            this.MediaUrl = url;
        }

        public string MediaType
        {
```

```
            get { return this[0]; }
            set { this[0] = value; }
        }

        public string MediaUrl
        {
            get { return this[1]; }
            set { this[1] = value; }
        }
    }
}
```

In this case, the `MediaFieldValue` stores both the media type and its location. Before this field can be used on publishing pages, two additional issues must be addressed:

❑   How to render the field on the new and edit web forms

❑   How to render the field on publishing pages

Rendering Fields in the SharePoint UI

It is important to keep in mind that SharePoint fields are rendered in two entirely different ways. When a list item is created or edited within the SharePoint user interface, its fields are rendered using CAML. When accessed through a publishing page, its fields are rendered using server controls. When building a custom `SPField`-derived object that supports a custom field control, you must support both rendering methods.

```xml
<FieldTypes>
  <FieldType>
    <Field Name="TypeName">Media</Field>
    <Field Name="ParentType">MultiColumn</Field>
    <Field Name="TypeDisplayName">Media File</Field>
    <Field Name="TypeShortDescription">Media File</Field>
    <Field Name="UserCreatable">TRUE</Field>
    <Field Name="ShowInListCreate">TRUE</Field>
    <Field Name="ShowInSurveyCreate">TRUE</Field>
    <Field Name="ShowInDocumentLibraryCreate">TRUE</Field>
    <Field Name="ShowInColumnTemplateCreate">TRUE</Field>
    <Field Name="FieldTypeClass">ProSharePoint2007.Chapter13.MediaField,
ProSharePoint2007.Chapter13.LearningCenter, Version=1.0.0.0, Culture=neutral,
PublicKeyToken=0b97b340d4a71524</Field>
    <PropertySchema>
      <Fields>
        <Field Name="DefaultMediaType" DisplayName="Default Media Type:"
MaxLength="50" DisplaySize="30" Type="Text">
          <Default>SWF</Default>
        </Field>
        <Field Name="DefaultMediaUrl" DisplayName="Default Media Url:"
MaxLength="50" DisplaySize="30" Type="Text">
          <Default></Default>
        </Field>
      </Fields>
    </PropertySchema>
```

```
     <RenderPattern Name="DisplayPattern">
       <Switch>
         <Expr>
           <Column />
         </Expr>
         <Case Value=""/>
         <Default>
           <Column SubColumnNumber="0" HTMLEncode="TRUE"/>
           <HTML><![CDATA[ ]]></HTML>
           <Column SubColumnNumber="1" HTMLEncode="TRUE"/>
         </Default>
       </Switch>
     </RenderPattern>
   </FieldType>
 </FieldTypes>
```

Rendering Fields on Publishing Pages

Once you have determined what kind of field you are working with, you are ready to build the server control that will render the data on publishing pages. This is the control that is referenced from within the page layout file. The key concept here is that the publishing framework needs a way to bind each control to a particular field (column) of the associated list item. This intelligence is implemented in the BaseFieldControl class.

Interestingly, the BaseFieldControl *class and its parent, the* FieldMetadata *class is provided by the core Windows SharePoint Services 3.0 object model and not by the MOSS 2007 publishing framework. The SDK describes the* FieldMetadata *class as an "Abstract class which implements the common functionality for all the Windows SharePoint Services field controls . . . for all fields rendering metadata."*

The BaseFieldControl class encapsulates concepts related to managing the general rendering behavior of a SPField instance. This includes storing and retrieving the list item field value, and formatting the "chrome" that is displayed around the field when it is rendered. Its parent class, the FieldMetadata class, stores a reference to the associated SPField.

The MOSS 2007 publishing framework includes a number of built-in field controls that can handle most publishing scenarios. These controls are designed to work with specific site columns that are also included in the publishing feature set. The following table describes the built-in field controls, their associated site columns and how they are used:

Field Control	Field Type	Description
RichHtmlField	HtmlField	Provides an interactive browser-based environment for editing HTML content
RichImageField	ImageField/ImageFieldValue	Provides a way to direct users to specific locations when browsing for images
RichLinkField	LinkField/LinkFieldValue	Provides a way to direct users to specific locations when browsing for publishing assets

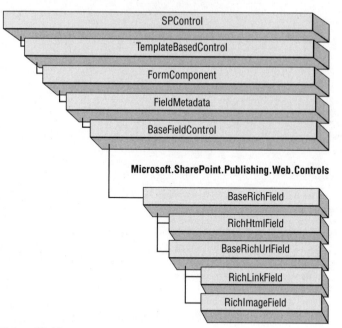

Figure 13-12

Figure 13-12 shows the derivation hierarchy for the default field rendering controls.

The following code fragment shows the rendering template used to display the custom field on publishing pages:

```
<%@ Control Language="C#" Debug="true" %>
<%@ Assembly Name="Microsoft.SharePoint, Version=12.0.0.0, Culture=neutral,
PublicKeyToken=71e9bce111e9429c" %>
<%@ Register TagPrefix="SharePoint" Namespace="Microsoft.SharePoint.WebControls"
Assembly="Microsoft.SharePoint, Version=12.0.0.0, Culture=neutral,
PublicKeyToken=71e9bce111e9429c" %>
<SharePoint:RenderingTemplate ID="MediaFieldRendering" runat="server">
    <Template>
        <table class="ms-form">
            <tr align="left">
                <td>Media Type</td>
                <td>Media Url</td>
            </tr>
            <tr align="left">
                <td>
                    <asp:DropDownList ID="MediaType" runat="server">
                        <asp:ListItem>SWF</asp:ListItem>
                        <asp:ListItem>AVI</asp:ListItem>
                        <asp:ListItem>WMV</asp:ListItem>
```

```
                <asp:ListItem>Camtasia</asp:ListItem>
            </asp:DropDownList>
        </td>
        <td>
            <asp:TextBox ID="MediaUrl" runat="server" />
        </td>
    </tr>
    </table>
</Template>
</SharePoint:RenderingTemplate>
```

Handling View, Edit and Design Mode

`FieldControls` may be displayed in any of several modes. Edit Mode is what the authors see while editing the page. View Mode is what appears when the page is rendered for end users. Design Mode is used to preview what the control will look like in view mode, and is also used to display a design surface for developers using tools like SharePoint Designer 2007.

The preferred approach for developing custom field controls, and the one adopted by Microsoft, is to have separate classes that implement the Edit Mode and View Mode behaviors. The main advantage being that you can delegate the Edit Mode behavior to a separate class that inherits functionality from one of the built-in "selector" classes.

Another approach is to implement the Edit and View Modes in a single class. This has the advantage of placing the entire implementation in one place, but has several disadvantages, the main one being that you are forced to implement everything and cannot easily inherit the base "selector" functionality.

Tips for Writing Field Controls

Field controls may appear on forms pages, so they should be tested in these scenarios as well as in publishing scenarios. For instance, the `edititem.aspx` page is displayed when a user edits the properties of a content type. Custom field controls that have been associated with the content type may be displayed on this page.

Don't use hard-coded styles when developing field controls. Doing so will limit the flexibility of the control and could interfere with custom CSS styles that have been applied to the pages on which they are rendered. This is an important guideline for all display modes, but is particularly important for view mode. If you need to use a special set of CSS styles, then SharePoint provides a mechanism for registering for a specific CSS stylesheet. Using this approach, you are guaranteed that the required style will be loaded at runtime and still allow graphic designers to tweak the styles you have provided.

Minimize database round trips in your field controls. The main point here is that the SharePoint publishing feature takes advantage of certain optimizations to minimize the time needed to render a page. Part of this optimization process involves caching the list item data so that requests for data are handled without having to go back to the database to get it. If you write a field control that makes direct connections to an external database, for example, then you risk a significant performance hit due to the frequency with which published pages are rendered. One way around this is to take advantage of the caching framework provided by ASP.NET 2.0 and the extensions to this framework provided by the SharePoint Publishing API.

Don't forget to implement design-time support for your field controls. This is an important step because your audience includes not only content authors but web designers as well. A good approach is to edit your pages in SharePoint Designer prior to deployment. This will show you exactly what web designers will see when using your controls. The following table describes when to use field controls versus Web Parts:

Need	Field Control	Web Part
Data storage	Field in the page list item	Web part data associated with the page
Location in page	Fixed as a control in the page layout	Fixed as a control in the page layout, but within a Web Part zone
Versioning	Versioned with the page	Versioned with the page, but without historical versions.
Personalization	No	Yes
Standard uses	Used to display content stored within the page	Used to display the result of queries or views of external content.
Example	Rich HTML Field Image Field Summary Links	Content Query Web Part Table of Contents Web Part

Publishing Content on a Schedule

You can control when list items are displayed using scheduled items. A ScheduledItem list item is visible on a published site only between specified start and end dates. Since every published page is a list item, you can effectively control when certain pages appear using this approach.

You create a ScheduledItem list item using the ScheduledItem wrapper class for a given list item. You create the wrapper class instance using a static method of the ScheduledItem class, which is defined in the Microsoft.SharePoint.Publishing namespace. The following example shows how this is done.

```
using Microsoft.SharePoint;
using Microsoft.SharePoint.Publishing;
...
SPListItem item = myList["SelectedItem"];
ScheduledItem scheduledItem = ScheduledItem.GetScheduledItem(item);
scheduledItem.StartDate = DateTime.Parse("1/15/2007");
scheduledItem.EndDate = DateTime.Parse("3/15/2007");
scheduledItem.Schedule();
```

Scheduling an item is equivalent to approving the item for display. You can include an approval comment at the same time the item is scheduled by using the overloaded Schedule (string approvalComment) method. If the specified start date is earlier than the date on which the method is called, then the item is published immediately. You can omit the end date, which publishes the item indefinitely. Otherwise, the item is unpublished on the date specified. When the current date is outside the range of dates specified for a scheduled item, the page is no longer visible.

Using Timer Jobs

You can set up a timer job to publish pages. This approach is useful in many situations. For instance, you can set up a document library that contains job notices and automatically post new job listings on a separate web site as soon as they appear in the list. For this kind of solution, you could use one of the built-in document converters and post the job listing as a Microsoft Word document. You could then set up a timer job that automatically converts the document into an HTML page, which is then published to the site. Both the original document and the converted page are stored in the document library. End users can view the job posting using the styles and presentation defined by the page layout.

Using Variations

Variations are a way to keep web site structure and content synchronized across multiple languages or form factors. You can use variations to publish foreign language versions of a web site or to publish content simultaneously to desktop browsers, mobile phones, or other devices. You can also use variations to implement themes, allowing the user to choose easily between different versions of the same content, applying different master pages and layouts, for example.

The MOSS 2007 variations architecture introduces the concept of a *variation label* to synchronize published content. A variation label is an identifier that describes each version, or variation, of a web site, and its relationship to its source. You can only declare one set of variation labels for a given site collection, and you can only designate one variation label as the source site, with the rest as target sites. As content is published to the source site, the SharePoint publishing framework then propagates the content automatically from the source to the target sites.

Figure 13-13 illustrates the variations architecture.

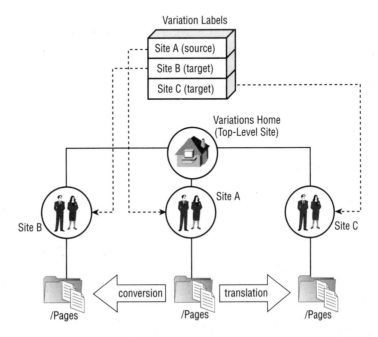

Figure 13-13

Whatever changes are made to the pages of the source site are replicated in the target sites, but the target pages can be associated with different layouts and different master pages. This is done through the property bag associated with a given page layout. When a page layout is associated with a variation label, the label identifier is stored along with the properties of the page layout. This causes special processing to be invoked when content is being propagated from one variation to another.

Since standard SharePoint lists are used to keep track of variations and the relationships between source and target pages, there is an opportunity to develop custom solutions that generate variation reports, or that modify the list programmatically if necessary.

To use the variations framework, you first configure the variations settings (either via the SharePoint user interface or programmatically), and then create the variation labels, electing which Variation is the Source variation. Next, you create the variation hierarchies, and create and approve source pages. As new pages are added to the source site, they must then be translated (manually) and approved before being finally rendered to end users.

Configuring Variations Settings

You configure variations for a site collection from the *Variation Settings* link of the *Site Settings* page. The Variation Home specifies the starting location for variations of the site. This represents the root of variation hierarchy.

You must create variation labels through the SharePoint user interface. The goal is to specify the label name and description, the designated locale, and how its associated site hierarchy should be created when new content is added to the source variation.

To create a variation label, navigate to the Site Settings page of the top-level site, and then select the Variation Labels link. This will display the current list of variation labels. Selecting Create New Label from the drop-down menu displays the page shown in Figure 13-14.

Once the variation labels have been created, and the source variation has been designated, you can create the variation hierarchy. After creating the variation hierarchies, you can only edit the display name and description of the variation labels. The other settings can no longer be modified.

Summary

The MOSS 2007 web content management components are implemented as part of the Microsoft SharePoint publishing framework, which is deployed as a standard set of Windows SharePoint Services 3.0 features. Web designers create master pages to define the overall look and feel of a site, and then use page layouts to specify where the approved content will be injected into the final rendered page. By using master pages and page layout files, web designers can then change the underlying master page at any time, and content authors can select the page layout they want that is most appropriate for the kind of content being developed.

Building a custom WCM solution involves creating one or more custom content types that define the fields associated with the publishing content that will be supplied by content authors, and then associating those content types with one or more page layouts. Page layouts can be created easily using SharePoint Designer 2007, and then deployed using Windows SharePoint Services 3.0 features.

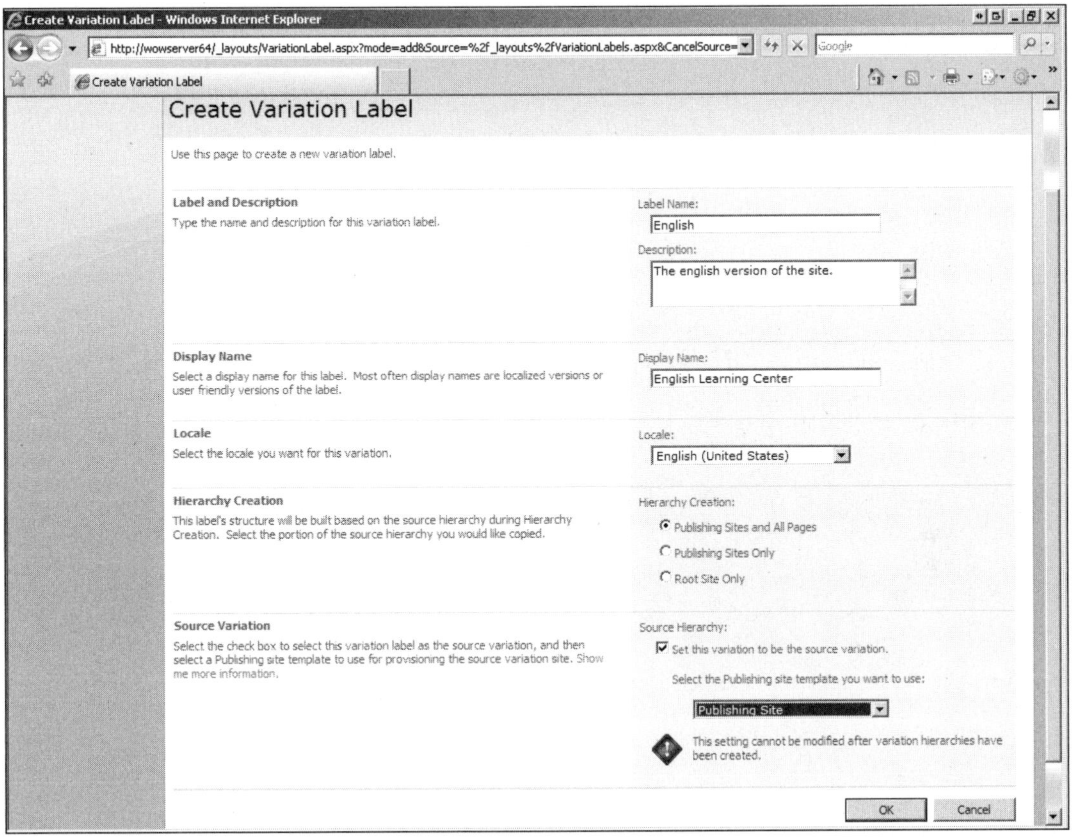

Figure 13-14

MOSS 2007 supports two methods for authoring web content. Using the web-based approach, content authors edit content directly in a web browser via server controls included in the SharePoint Publishing object model. Using the smart-client approach, content authors create a document in an application such as Microsoft Office Word, and then convert the document into an HTML page using the MOSS 2007 document conversion framework. Document converters are deployed at the Web Application level using a SharePoint feature definition file and a document converter definition file.

Field controls constitute the "heart" of the MOSS 2007 publishing system. Field controls are aptly named because each control is tightly bound to a field (site column) in the underlying content type associated with a page layout. Field controls essentially define a mapping from one or more columns of the document library item to content which appears somewhere on the page when it is rendered.

The MOSS 2007 variations architecture introduces the concept of a *variation label* to synchronize published content. As content is published to the source site, the SharePoint publishing framework then propagates the content automatically from the source to the target sites.

14

Electronic Forms in MOSS 2007

By John Holliday

The subject of electronic forms is much broader than SharePoint, but in many ways, getting electronic forms to work in a SharePoint environment brings out many of the core issues involved in realizing their value. In other words, the core value proposition for using electronic forms in the first place is to reduce the effort involved in collecting and manipulating data by capturing and presenting the data in a consistent manner, storing the data in a central location so that it can drive common business processes, and manipulating the data with a common set of business rules. When you think about it, this is why SharePoint and electronic forms fit together so well. It is also why developing an effective electronic forms solution has been so challenging.

InfoPath 2003 was Microsoft's first attempt to capture the essential features required for an effective electronic forms solution. It turned out to be a very difficult problem to solve because data gathering and presentation is such a common requirement that it affects just about every layer of the platform. On the one hand, you want to make it easy for end users to work with the data, so you need a rich user experience whether they are working independently or in a collaborative environment. At the same time, you want to empower developers to build solutions that consume the data efficiently without concern for its origin or final destination. Finally, you want to enable administrators to track and control how the data is used as well as protect critical systems from security risks.

InfoPath 2003 introduced the notion that you could build a rich client application for designing forms based on a reusable description of data, called a schema, and then reuse and manipulate that data outside of the authoring tool. As long as the data conformed to the schema, other tools could work with and modify the data, while ensuring consistency and data integrity. Building on this core concept, SharePoint 2003 offered a central repository called a *form library* that could interpret the schema to surface selected data fields as columns, allowing end users to filter and view form data without having to resort to the original form. The form library concept also enabled end users to create new data by using the form template.

While this was a good start, there were many limitations with the InfoPath 2003 design and implementation. First, although data elements could be promoted to columns in the form library, there was no way to edit those data fields in the library and have that data find its way back into the form. This meant that you could not easily build data-driven solutions that were keyed off of data in the form library because that data was not synchronized with the data in the form.

Another problem with the InfoPath 2003 design was that it was not easy to republish a form without involving the original form designer. For simple, out-of-the-box forms, the problem was masked by the relative ease of publishing forms to a SharePoint site. But as soon as you started to build more sophisticated forms, the problem immediately became apparent, exacerbated in part by the security risks inherent in deploying "smart forms" with built-in intelligence. With InfoPath 2003 and the SharePoint 2003 platform, the only option was to deploy a form template to a form library. But you had to know in advance which library you wanted to publish the template to, and you needed the appropriate permissions to do so. This meant that a site administrator could not easily take the same form and move it to another site. The form developer, or someone familiar with the code within the form would have to be involved in publishing the form to another site, thus creating a potentially serious IT bottleneck.

InfoPath 2007 represents a significant improvement over the previous version by addressing many of these concerns. Some of the solutions are provided by the Windows SharePoint Services 3.0 platform itself.

❑ Form templates can now be attached to content types, giving site administrators the power to redeploy the templates at will without involving IT resources.

❑ Form data fields are now bidirectional, meaning that developers can promote selected fields and have those fields presented as form library columns that end users can edit. The edited field values are then pushed back into the underlying data file and can be used to drive solutions that depend on the data.

❑ Form templates can now be split into separate components, called "template parts," which simplifies the creation of complex forms and makes it easier to reuse your work.

As previously stated, electronic forms are a very large topic that could make up its own book. However, by the time you're finished reading this chapter, you will have a good grasp on how InfoPath forms work and how to employ them in your SharePoint solutions to everyone's benefit. In addition to learning about the typical elements within an InfoPath form, form templates, and data types, you'll learn about InfoPath security and form publishing. Finally, the chapter covers InfoPath Forms Services and how to work with browser-based forms.

The Structure of an InfoPath Form

InfoPath form templates are packaged in ZIP files with an .XSN extension. The ZIP format makes sense for a number of reasons. It is a universally recognized archival format that is supported by most operating systems. It also handles compressed binary formats easily, which enables the form template to include both XML content and precompiled assemblies. Figure 14-1 shows the XSN file for the sample expense report form.

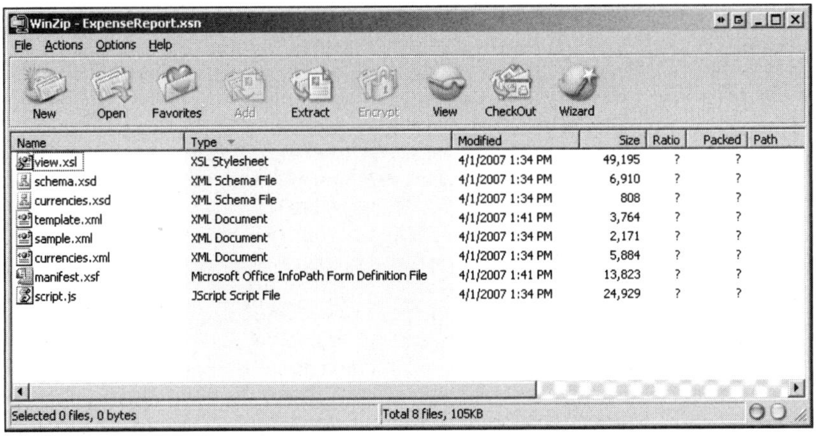

Figure 14-1

The Form Definition File (XSF)

The manifest.xsf file contains XML code that describes all aspects of the form. It includes references to the other files in the archive as well as references to the various schemas used to describe different parts of the form. If you open this file in notepad and scroll through it, you can learn a lot about how InfoPath forms are organized. For instance, you can see many XML elements that describe how the form was last viewed in the InfoPath client application. There are other elements that contain information about the views, the controls used for editing data elements, the menus to display for various parts of the form, and the event handlers to associate with individual controls.

Toward the bottom of the file, there is an xsf:extensions element that warrants some attention. This element is used to bind the form to other platforms, like SharePoint. The following code snippet appears in the manifest for an expense report form that has been published to a SharePoint site.

```
    <xsf:extensions>
        <xsf:extension name="SolutionDefinitionExtensions">
            <xsf2:solutionDefinition runtimeCompatibility="client"
allowClientOnlyCode="no"
xmlns:xsf2="http://schemas.microsoft.com/office/infopath/2006/solutionDefinition/
extensions">
                <xsf2:listPropertiesExtension>
                    <xsf2:fieldsExtension>
                        <xsf2:fieldExtension columnId=
"{b7d7c252-0b51-45a1-9ad2-40f72ea01c85}" readWrite="no" columnName=
"{AE404D63-E85B-4CB9-B0D2-3A39C5411FDB}"></xsf2:fieldExtension>
                        <xsf2:fieldExtension columnId=
"{4cd5d119-c850-4290-a122-7965075ddc69}" readWrite="no" columnName=
"{F97879E7-2A7C-43D6-BF2B-7849DBCAFFD3}"></xsf2:fieldExtension>
                        <xsf2:fieldExtension columnId=
"{da793958-73cb-48ba-8136-bc26e0eaa0db}" readWrite="no" columnName=
"{9FDD772E-194F-4617-8859-1EC2F130564D}"></xsf2:fieldExtension>
```

```
                                    <xsf2:fieldExtension columnId=
"{93506d8c-5341-4357-93ac-93651a045957}" readWrite="no" columnName=
"{A0594F2E-CBE7-4DBD-A0C7-DA800CBAFCEF}"></xsf2:fieldExtension>
                                    <xsf2:fieldExtension columnId=
"{64f1cc9f-5384-46c5-b05a-245b5fefea27}" readWrite="no" columnName=
"{2EBB7411-DD28-4405-96DF-EDB2D9992FB5}"></xsf2:fieldExtension>
                                    <xsf2:fieldExtension columnId=
"{3c459bfc-c753-4ce9-ada1-b46ed76f5d05}" readWrite="no" columnName=
"{B423D728-4EF1-4116-8808-AB0B61E17F5C}"></xsf2:fieldExtension>
                            </xsf2:fieldsExtension>
                        </xsf2:listPropertiesExtension>
                        <xsf2:solutionPropertiesExtension branch="share">
                            <xsf2:contentTypeTemplate site="http://moss/
prosharepoint2007" path="http://moss/prosharepoint2007/Form Templates/
Expense Report.xsn" name="ExpenseReportForm" description="This is a standard
expense report." browserEnable="no"></xsf2:contentTypeTemplate>
                            <xsf2:share formName="ExpenseReport" path="F:\Documents
and Settings\Administrator\My Documents\My Forms\Published\ExpenseReport.xsn"
accessPath="F:\Documents and Settings\Administrator\My Documents\My Forms\
Published\ExpenseReport.xsn"></xsf2:share>
                        </xsf2:solutionPropertiesExtension>
                    </xsf2:solutionDefinition>
                </xsf:extension>
            </xsf:extensions>
```

Notice the `fieldsExtension` section, which includes child elements that signals SharePoint to promote certain form fields to list columns. If this section is included in the form, then the specified fields are promoted. Also notice the `contentTypeTemplate` element within the `solutionPropertiesExtension` section that describes how the form should be bound to a content type. As you work with InfoPath forms in your SharePoint solutions, it is a good idea to poke around inside the generated files once in a while to become familiar with the different parts of the form and how they relate to SharePoint objects.

The Form Schema (XSD)

Every InfoPath form has a schema that describes the data that the form recognizes. When building Share-Point solutions that rely on form data, this is the most important file in the form template. If you are writing managed code that manipulates form data, then you will typically use the XSD.EXE utility along with the schema file to generate C# or VB classes that represent the data elements. You can then call the generated methods to create new data or to work with existing data in a form.

> *The XSD.EXE utility is installed as part of the .NET Framework SDK.*

Listing 14-1 shows the schema for the sample expense report form. It is interesting to note that although this schema was created using InfoPath 2007, the namespace references in the schema refer to InfoPath 2003. This possible oversight does not affect the functionality of the form, since these are merely place-holder URNs that are used only to define the target and default namespaces. It is also interesting to note that the schema is standards compliant with no references to Microsoft schemas other than the two place-holders shown at the top of the file, which are unique to this particular form.

By scanning the form schema, you can quickly see how the data is organized as a hierarchy of complex data types. This maps directly to the tree of elements that InfoPath displays in the Data Source panel.

Each tree node maps to a complex type in the XSD file. For example, the highlighted `addressType` node represents an address block that can be referenced from many places in the schema.

Listing 14-1: Expense report form schema

```
<?xml version="1.0" encoding="UTF-8"?><xs:schema targetNamespace="http://
schemas.microsoft.com/office/infopath/2003/sample/ExpenseReport" xmlns:exp="http://
schemas.microsoft.com/office/infopath/2003/sample/ExpenseReport" xmlns:xs="http://
www.w3.org/2001/XMLSchema" elementFormDefault="qualified" attributeFormDefault=
"unqualified">
        <xs:element name="expenseReport">
            <xs:complexType>
                <xs:sequence>
                    <xs:element name="employee" type="exp:contactType"/>
                    <xs:element name="manager" type="exp:contactType"/>
                    <xs:element name="expenseCode" type="xs:string"/>
                    <xs:element name="startDate" type="xs:date" nillable="true"/>
                    <xs:element name="endDate" type="xs:date" nillable="true"/>
                    <xs:element name="reportDate" type="xs:date" nillable="true"/>
                    <xs:element name="purpose" type="xs:string"/>
                    <xs:element name="notes" type="exp:xhtml" minOccurs="0"/>
                    <xs:element name="currency" type="exp:currencyType"/>
                    <xs:element name="items">
                        <xs:complexType>
                            <xs:sequence>
                                <xs:element name="item" maxOccurs="unbounded">
                                    <xs:complexType>
                                        <xs:sequence>
                                            <xs:element name="date"
type="xs:date" nillable="true"/>
                                            <xs:element name="description"
type="xs:string"/>
                                            <xs:element name="amount"
type="xs:double"/>
                                            <xs:element name="category"
type="xs:string"/>
                                            <xs:element name="currency"
type="xs:string"/>
                                            <xs:element name="rate"
type="xs:double"/>
                                            <xs:element name="totalAmount"
type="xs:double"/>
                                            <xs:any namespace="##other"
processContents="lax" minOccurs="0" maxOccurs="unbounded"/>
                                        </xs:sequence>
                                    </xs:complexType>
                                </xs:element>
                            </xs:sequence>
                        </xs:complexType>
                    </xs:element>
                    <xs:element name="cashAdvance" type="xs:double"/>
                    <xs:element name="total" type="xs:double"/>
                    <xs:element name="subTotal" type="xs:double"/>
```

```
                              <xs:element name="signatures"
type="exp:digitalSignaturesType"/>
                              <xs:any namespace="##other" processContents="lax" minOccurs="0"
maxOccurs="unbounded"/>
                    </xs:sequence>
                    <xs:anyAttribute namespace="http://www.w3.org/XML/1998/
namespace" processContents="lax"/>
              </xs:complexType>
        </xs:element>
        <xs:complexType name="addressType">
              <xs:sequence>
                    <xs:element name="line1" type="xs:string"/>
                    <xs:element name="line2" type="xs:string"/>
                    <xs:element name="line3" type="xs:string"/>
                    <xs:element name="line4" type="xs:string"/>
                    <xs:element name="city" type="xs:string"/>
                    <xs:element name="stateProvince" type="xs:string"/>
                    <xs:element name="postalCode" type="xs:string"/>
                    <xs:element name="country" type="xs:string"/>
                    <xs:any namespace="##other" processContents="lax" minOccurs="0"
maxOccurs="unbounded"/>
              </xs:sequence>
        </xs:complexType>
        <xs:complexType name="companyType">
              <xs:sequence>
                    <xs:element name="name" type="xs:string" minOccurs="0"/>
                    <xs:element name="address" type="exp:addressType" minOccurs="0"/>
                    <xs:element name="identificationNumber" type="xs:string"
minOccurs="0"/>
                    <xs:element name="telephoneNumber" type="xs:string" minOccurs="0"/>
                    <xs:element name="faxNumber" type="xs:string" minOccurs="0"/>
                    <xs:element name="emailAddressPrimary" type="xs:string"
minOccurs="0"/>
                    <xs:element name="webSite" type="xs:anyURI" minOccurs="0"/>
                    <xs:element name="ftpSite" type="xs:anyURI" minOccurs="0"/>
                    <xs:element name="telex" type="xs:string" minOccurs="0"/>
                    <xs:any namespace="##other" processContents="lax" minOccurs="0"
maxOccurs="unbounded"/>
              </xs:sequence>
        </xs:complexType>
        <xs:complexType name="companyWithContactType">
              <xs:complexContent>
                    <xs:extension base="exp:companyType">
                          <xs:sequence>
                                <xs:element name="contact" type="exp:contactType"/>
                                <xs:any namespace="##other" processContents="lax"
minOccurs="0" maxOccurs="unbounded"/>
                          </xs:sequence>
                    </xs:extension>
              </xs:complexContent>
        </xs:complexType>
        <xs:complexType name="contactType">
              <xs:sequence>
                    <xs:element name="name" type="exp:nameType" minOccurs="0"/>
```

```
                    <xs:element name="address" type="exp:addressType" minOccurs="0"/>
                    <xs:element name="identificationNumber" type="xs:string"
minOccurs="0"/>
                    <xs:element name="emailAddressPrimary" type="xs:string"
minOccurs="0"/>
                    <xs:element name="emailAddressSecondary" type="xs:string"
minOccurs="0"/>
                    <xs:element name="telephoneNumberWork" type="xs:string"
minOccurs="0"/>
                    <xs:element name="telephoneNumberHome" type="xs:string"
minOccurs="0"/>
                    <xs:element name="telephoneNumberCell" type="xs:string"
minOccurs="0"/>
                    <xs:element name="telephoneNumberPager" type="xs:string"
minOccurs="0"/>
                    <xs:element name="faxNumber" type="xs:string" minOccurs="0"/>
                    <xs:element name="jobTitle" type="xs:string" minOccurs="0"/>
                    <xs:element name="officeLocation" type="xs:string" minOccurs="0"/>
                    <xs:element name="department" type="xs:string" minOccurs="0"/>
                    <xs:element name="webSite" type="xs:anyURI" minOccurs="0"/>
                    <xs:element name="ftpSite" type="xs:anyURI" minOccurs="0"/>
                    <xs:any namespace="##other" processContents="lax" minOccurs="0"
maxOccurs="unbounded"/>
            </xs:sequence>
        </xs:complexType>
        <xs:complexType name="contactWithCompanyType">
            <xs:complexContent>
                <xs:extension base="exp:contactType">
                    <xs:sequence>
                        <xs:element name="company" type="exp:companyType"/>
                        <xs:any namespace="##other" processContents="lax"
minOccurs="0" maxOccurs="unbounded"/>
                    </xs:sequence>
                </xs:extension>
            </xs:complexContent>
        </xs:complexType>
        <xs:complexType name="digitalSignaturesType">
            <xs:sequence>
                <xs:any namespace="http://www.w3.org/2000/09/xmldsig#"
processContents="lax" minOccurs="0" maxOccurs="unbounded"/>
            </xs:sequence>
        </xs:complexType>
        <xs:complexType name="nameType">
            <xs:sequence>
                <xs:element name="prefix" type="xs:string" minOccurs="0"/>
                <xs:element name="givenName" type="xs:string" minOccurs="0"/>
                <xs:element name="middleName" type="xs:string" minOccurs="0"/>
                <xs:element name="surname" type="xs:string" minOccurs="0"/>
                <xs:element name="suffix" type="xs:string" minOccurs="0"/>
                <xs:element name="singleName" type="xs:string"/>
                <xs:any namespace="##other" processContents="lax" minOccurs="0"
maxOccurs="unbounded"/>
            </xs:sequence>
        </xs:complexType>
```

```
            <xs:complexType name="currencyType">
                <xs:sequence>
                    <xs:element name="name" type="xs:string"/>
                    <xs:element name="symbol" type="xs:string"/>
                    <xs:any namespace="##other" processContents="lax" minOccurs="0"
maxOccurs="unbounded"/>
                </xs:sequence>
            </xs:complexType>
            <xs:complexType name="xhtml" mixed="true">
                <xs:sequence>
                    <xs:any namespace="http://www.w3.org/1999/xhtml"
processContents="lax" minOccurs="0" maxOccurs="unbounded"/>
                </xs:sequence>
            </xs:complexType>
        </xs:schema>
```

The Form Views (XSL)

Views are an important part of a form because they provide a way to present different information, depending on the runtime environment and other factors, including the security profile of the end user. InfoPath form views are defined as XSL stylesheets, which makes them relatively easy to work with. Because they are based on XSL, you can theoretically substitute any XSL code you wish to create your custom views. That said, the default views that are generated by the InfoPath client make heavy use of Microsoft-specific schemas, so in practice, you will not be creating your own views by hand. However, you can and probably will have occasion to edit the XSL files to modify the default behavior.

Most of the conditional formatting rules that you apply to a form end up as XSL code in one or more views. For instance, the following code snippet is taken from the view stylesheet for the report date field of the sample expense report form. The highlighted section shows an example of how XSL is used to format the date if a special formatting function is available.

```
<div>
    <div>
        <font face="Verdana" size="1">Report Date: </font>
    </div>
    <div class="xdDTPicker" title="Report Date" style="WIDTH: 100%; FONT-FAMILY:
Verdana; FONT-SIZE: x-small" noWrap="1" xd:xctname="DTPicker" xd:CtrlId="CTRL97"
tabIndex="-1">
        <span class="xdDTText xdBehavior_FormattingNoBUI" hideFocus="1"
contentEditable="true" tabIndex="0" xd:xctname="DTPicker_DTText"
xd:boundProp="xd:num" xd:datafmt="&quot;date&quot;,&quot;dateFormat:Short
Date;&quot;" xd:innerCtrl="_DTText" xd:binding="exp:reportDate">
            <xsl:attribute name="xd:num">
                <xsl:value-of select="exp:reportDate"/>
            </xsl:attribute>
            <xsl:choose>
                <xsl:when test="function-available('xdFormatting:formatString')">
                    <xsl:value-of select=
```

```
    "xdFormatting:formatString(exp:reportDate,&quot;date&quot;,&quot;dateFormat:Short
Date;&quot;)"/>
            </xsl:when>
            <xsl:otherwise>
                <xsl:value-of select="exp:reportDate"/>
            </xsl:otherwise>
        </xsl:choose>
    </span>
    <button class="xdDTButton" xd:xctname="DTPicker_DTButton"
xd:innerCtrl="_DTButton" tabIndex="-1">
        <img src="res://infopath.exe/calendar.gif"/>
    </button>
    </div>
</div>
```

The Data File (XML)

When you create a new form template or edit the data source, InfoPath generates a sample data file that conforms to the schema and stores it with the form. This is marginally useful during development, because if you want to create sample data, you can simply use the InfoPath client to fill out a form and save the data file, stripping out the InfoPath processing instructions. Also, InfoPath is not consistent about which data fields it populates, leaving many of the fields empty.

Form Templates and Form Data

The InfoPath client reads the information in the form template to display the required views and controls based on the form schema. The user enters data into the controls and then saves the resulting data file either to the local drive or to a centrally accessible form data repository such as a SharePoint form library. The important point to remember here is that the form template is not copied to the form library when the user saves the data file. That only happens when the template is published to the library. *(See the section on form publishing for a more detailed description of the publishing process.)* Since only the form data file is stored into the form library, how does InfoPath know which template to use when the user opens the form?

Well, in the case of SharePoint form libraries, the simple answer is that InfoPath can look at the form library itself to determine which template is associated with the data file and then open the template from there, but form data files can also be stored locally or in a document library or some repository other than SharePoint. In those cases, the information about which template to use is taken from the form data file itself.

Say that you have a form data file on your desktop and you double-click the file to edit the data. InfoPath form data files contain a special processing instruction that tells InfoPath that the data represents an instance of an InfoPath form schema, and where the form template is located. Figure 14-2 shows an example of the processing instruction that is embedded into the form data file.

```
ExpenseReportData.xml - Notepad
File Edit Format View Help
<?xml version="1.0" encoding="UTF-8"?>
<?mso-infoPathSolution solutionVersion="1.0.0.5" productVersion="12.0.0" PIVersion="1.0.0.0"
href="file:///F:\Documents%20and%20Settings\Administrator\My%20Documents\My%20Forms\Published\ExpenseReport.xsn"
name="urn:schemas-microsoft-com:office:infopath:ExpenseReport:-sample-ExpenseReport" ?>
<?mso-application progid="InfoPath.Document" versionProgid="InfoPath.Document.2"?>
<exp:expenseReport xmlns:xhtml="http://www.w3.org/1999/xhtml" xmlns:xsi="http://www.w3.org/2001/XMLSchema-instance"
xmlns:exp="http://schemas.microsoft.com/office/infopath/2003/sample/ExpenseReport"
xmlns:my="http://schemas.microsoft.com/office/infopath/2003/myXSD"
xmlns:xd="http://schemas.microsoft.com/office/infopath/2003" xml:lang="en-us">
        <exp:employee>
            <exp:name>
                <exp:prefix></exp:prefix>
                <exp:givenName></exp:givenName>
                <exp:middleName></exp:middleName>
                <exp:surname></exp:surname>
                <exp:suffix></exp:suffix>
                <exp:singleName>John F. Holliday</exp:singleName>
            </exp:name>
            <exp:address>
                <exp:line1>POB 3998</exp:line1>
                <exp:line2></exp:line2>
                <exp:line3></exp:line3>
                <exp:line4></exp:line4>
                <exp:city>Amelia Island</exp:city>
                <exp:stateProvince>FL</exp:stateProvince>
                <exp:postalCode>32034</exp:postalCode>
                <exp:country>USA</exp:country>
            </exp:address>
            <exp:identificationNumber></exp:identificationNumber>
            <exp:emailAddressPrimary>john@johnholliday.net</exp:emailAddressPrimary>
            <exp:emailAddressSecondary></exp:emailAddressSecondary>
            <exp:telephoneNumberWork></exp:telephoneNumberWork>
            <exp:telephoneNumberHome></exp:telephoneNumberHome>
            <exp:telephoneNumberCell></exp:telephoneNumberCell>
            <exp:telephoneNumberPager></exp:telephoneNumberPager>
            <exp:faxNumber></exp:faxNumber>
            <exp:jobTitle>President</exp:jobTitle>
            <exp:officeLocation></exp:officeLocation>
            <exp:department>Development</exp:department>
            <exp:webSite></exp:webSite>
            <exp:ftpSite></exp:ftpSite>
        </exp:employee>
```

Figure 14-2

This means first and foremost that if the form template is moved from the location referenced in the file, then the data file may not open properly. Although InfoPath can adjust on the fly for most forms by caching the template on the development machine, you will get a warning when opening a template in design mode, as shown in Figure 14-3.

```
Microsoft Office InfoPath                                          x
  ⚠   This form template was published to one location and has been saved or moved to a different location. To ensure
      that forms based on this template work correctly, publish the template again.
                              [  OK  ]
```

Figure 14-3

Working with Data Sources

The data source is the heart of any InfoPath form, and is really the best starting point when designing a form from scratch. Once the data elements are defined, it is easy to place them into views and arrange them on the page. It gets trickier when you need more than one data source in the same form. A form can have one primary data source, also called a data connection, and many secondary data sources that link to external data.

You set up the data sources for a form using the Data Source panel, which is only visible while designing a form.

Consider the common scenario where you want to let the user choose from a list of values in a dropdown list. You could enter the values directly into the control, but that wouldn't allow you to reuse the list in other controls. It is better to set up a secondary data source and then store the list values in a separate XML file that is packaged with the form.

Even though the XML file is stored within the form template file, it is still referred to as an external data source. Later, you can modify the data source or add a new one that retrieves the values dynamically from an external location, such as a SharePoint list, a web service or a SQL database.

When developing forms for SharePoint solutions, it is useful to create a data connection library to make it easier to connect your forms to dynamic data. To create a data connection library, navigate to a SharePoint site that will be accessible from your forms and select Create from the Site Actions menu, and then select `Data Connection Library` from the Libraries section. Figure 14-4 shows the New Data Connection Library page. Once you have created the library, you can begin populating it with data connections.

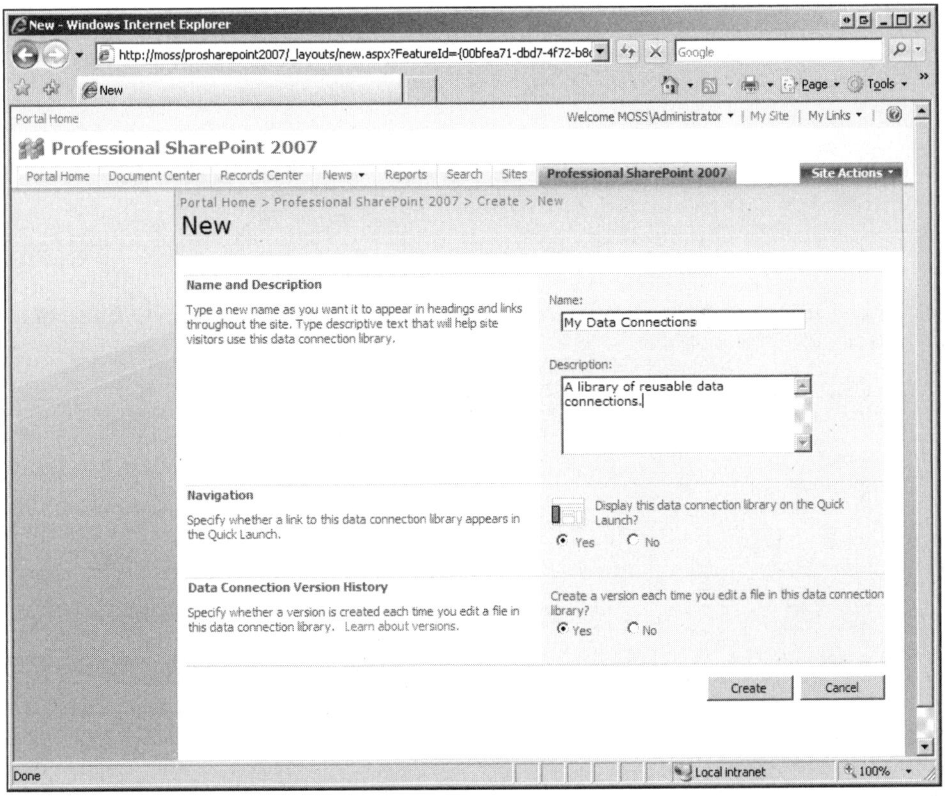

Figure 14-4

Although the Data Connection Library page includes both New and Upload commands, there is really only one command, and that is Upload. In other words, the only way to populate the data connection library is to first create a data connection file locally and then upload it to the library. The easiest way to create a data connection file is to use the Data Connection Wizard in Microsoft Excel 2007. To start the Data Connection Wizard, open Microsoft Excel 2007 and select Data ⇨ From Other Sources ⇨ From the Data Connection Wizard.

Connecting to SharePoint Data

One of the most common scenarios you will encounter when building forms for use in SharePoint solutions is pulling data from a SharePoint site to present users with a dropdown list of items to choose from while completing a form. A typical example is a list of departments in an organization that the user needs to select from. In the following example, you will modify the sample Asset Tracking form to enable a user to choose a department from a SharePoint list instead of typing in the department name.

1. First, create a custom list on a SharePoint site named "Departments" and change the name of the default `Title` field to `Department Name`. You can populate the list with a few department names, as shown in Figure 14-5.

2. Next, open the sample Asset Tracking form in design mode, as shown in Figure 14-6. The Asset Tracking form is one of the sample forms that are included with InfoPath. Notice the text control labeled "Department" associated with the `employeeDepartment` data field.

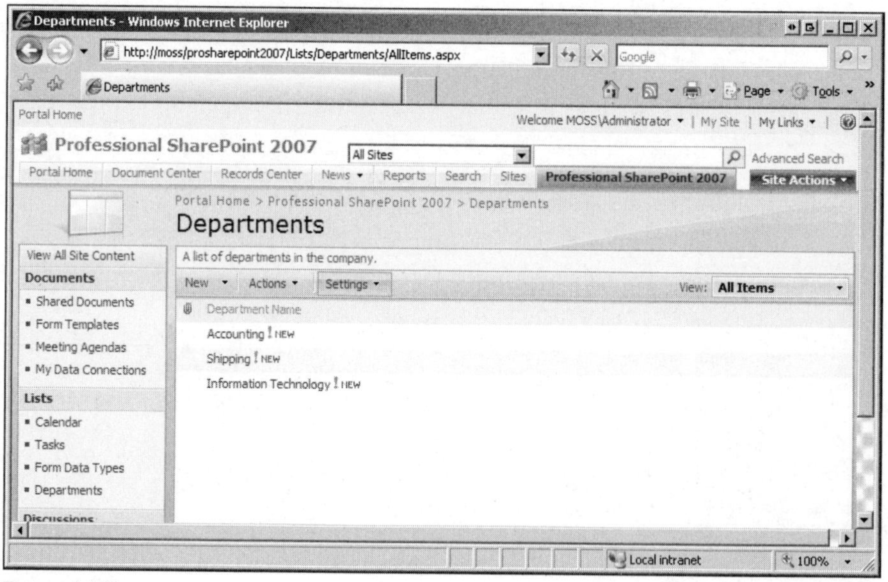

Figure 14-5

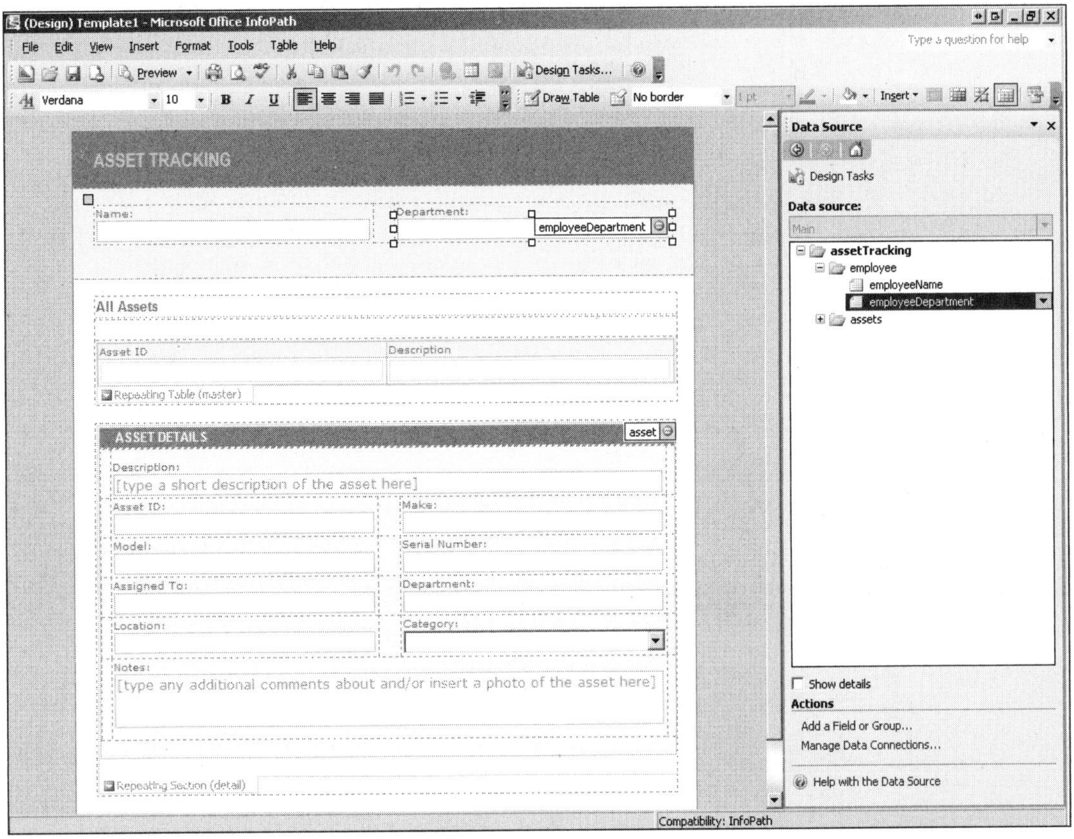

Figure 14-6

3. Select Manage Data Connections... from the Actions section of the Data Source pane and click the Add... button to create a new connection. You will see the Data Connection Wizard.

4. Choose Create a new connection to: and then choose Receive data and click Next.

5. Select SharePoint library or list as the source of the data, and then enter the URL of the Share-Point site containing the custom list. You should now see the Departments list in the dialog, as shown in Figure 14-7.

6. Select the Departments list and click Next to see the fields associated with the list, as shown in Figure 14-8. Place a checkmark next to the fields you want to include in the data connection. For this example, you only need to select the department name and click Next.

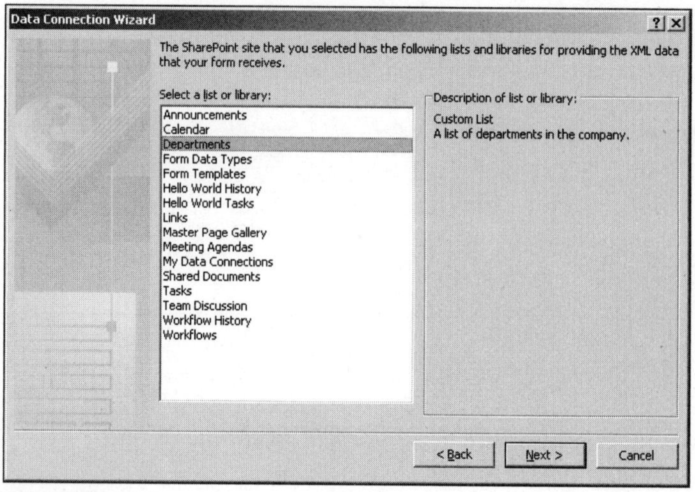

Figure 14-7

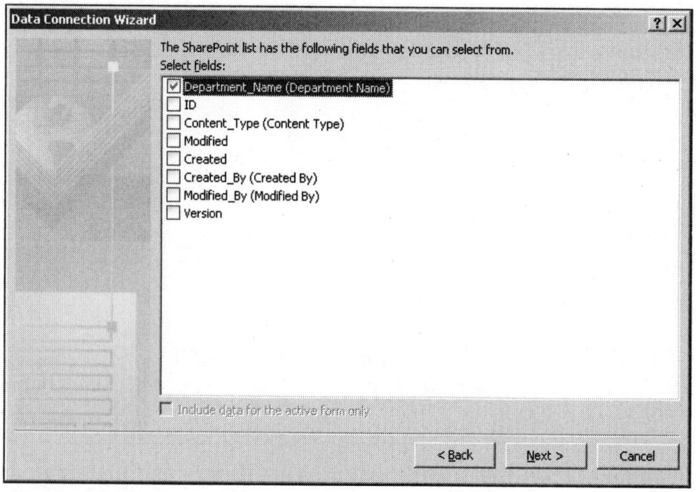

Figure 14-8

7.   The next dialog allows you to place a static copy of the data from the list into the form template for use by disconnected users. For this example, leave the check box deselected and click Next. Click Finish to complete the wizard and then click Close to return to InfoPath.

Now you have a secondary data source named Departments that is connected to a SharePoint list. To see the results in the form, you need to associate the data source with a control. To do that, execute the following steps:

1. Right-click the `TextBox` control, which appears beneath the `"Department:"` label on the form, and select Change To ⇨ Drop-Down List Box from the context menu.

2. Right-click the control again, and choose Properties... from the context menu.

3. In the Drop-Down List Box Properties dialog, select Look up values from an external source, in the List box entries section.

4. Select Departments as the Data Source, and click the button to the right of the Entries text box.

5. Select the `:Department_Name` field, and click OK. To filter out duplicate entries, place a check-mark in the `Show only entries with unique display names` field, as shown in Figure 14-9.

Save and preview the form. Now, when the form starts up, InfoPath attempts to connect to the SharePoint site in order to retrieve the data values for the dropdown list. When this happens, InfoPath issues a warning of a potential security issue as shown in Figure 14-10. Click Yes to skip the dialog. (See the section "Understanding InfoPath Security" for more details about the InfoPath security model.)

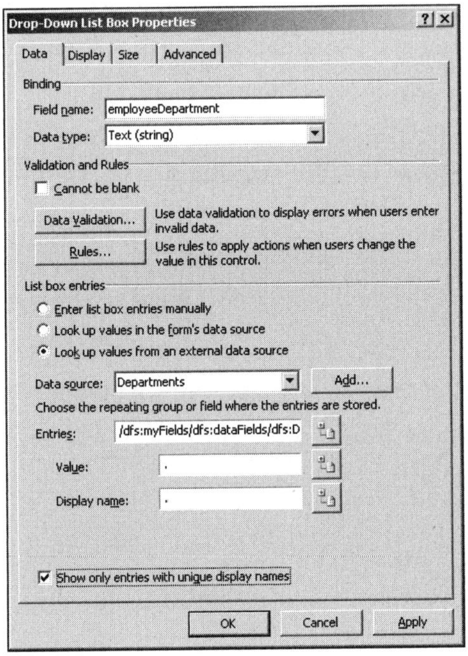

Figure 14-9

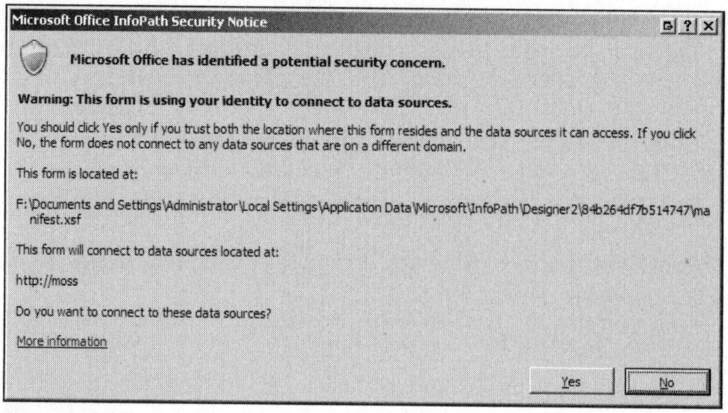

Figure 14-10

When the form opens, the dropdown list is populated with the current values stored in the SharePoint site. Figure 14-11 shows the result. As new departments are added to the list, they will appear in the form the next time it is opened.

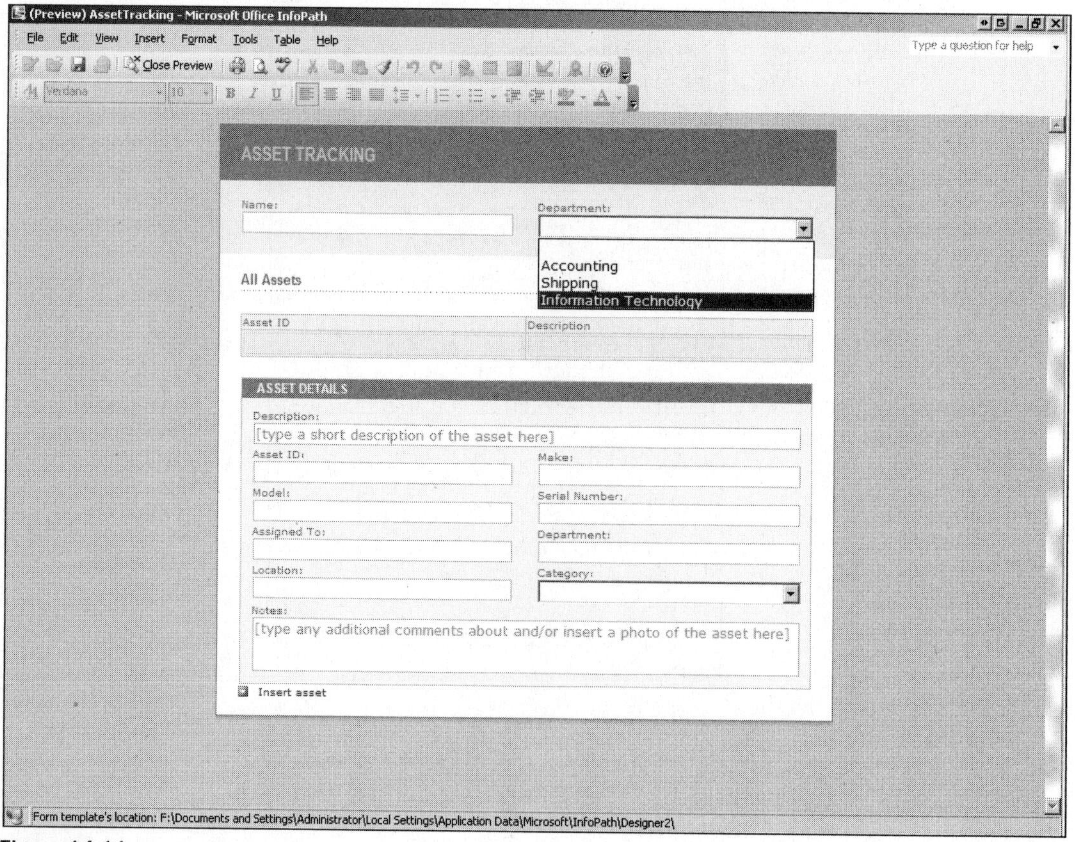

Figure 14-11

Working with Existing Content Types

Often when working with SharePoint forms, you already have a good idea about the structure of the data, especially if it comes from an existing list or content type, but you don't want to link directly to an existing SharePoint list. Instead, you want to use an existing list as a model for the primary data source of the custom form that you are designing. It would be nice to have a way to simply reference an existing content type and then have InfoPath create the primary data source directly. Unfortunately, the current version doesn't let you do this. As a partial work-around, you can create a dummy form and create an external data connection to import the fields from an existing content type.

The steps are:

1. Create a new custom list on a SharePoint site.

2. Select Advanced Settings from the List Settings page, and enable content types for the list.

3. Add the content type you are interested in to the list.

4. Create a dummy InfoPath form. Any kind of form will do, even a blank form.

5. Open the InfoPath Data Connection Wizard by selecting Manage Data Connections... from the Actions section of the Data Source panel.

6. Click Add to create a new external data connection and then click Receive Data in the Create a new connection to: section.

7. Select SharePoint library or list as the source of the data and click Next.

8. Enter the URL of the SharePoint site that contains the list.

9. Select the list that contains the content type, and place a checkmark next to the fields you want to use and click Next.

10. Click Next to skip the part about storing a copy of the data.

11. Enter the name of the content type as the name of the data connection, and click Finish and then Close.

You now have a secondary data source in your form with the same name as the content type. To complete the process, you would then cut and paste the data elements from the secondary schema into the primary data source.

Be Careful When Editing Schema Files

There are still some problems with this approach, however, that are illustrative of the way that InfoPath deals with data sources. First of all, the imported fields are all typed as strings. To correct this, you would have to go back through all of the fields one by one, changing each to the correct data type.

The second problem is that you cannot easily modify the XSD on disk once it has been generated by InfoPath. The prescribed approach is to select Save as Source Files from the File menu and then edit the files you want. InfoPath will recognize that the form was split into source files and will load them back in the next time the file is opened. This works well for certain files, like the XSL files for views. But if you edit the XSD files manually, you may run into problems if you make a mistake. It's easy to break a form this way, and it can be very time-consuming to get it back to a working state.

Understanding InfoPath Security

There are three basic scenarios that a form template must support.

First, you need a way to simply gather data without any special programming or logic. You just want to present a simple dialog to users and let them fill in the fields you have declared in the form schema. Then you want to work with the data they have entered.

In the second scenario, you want to make the form more intelligent and dynamically control what data the user can enter. For example, you might have a list of departments in a SharePoint list, and you want to let the user choose a department name from a dropdown list in the form. For that, you need to put some code in the form to retrieve the list of departments from SharePoint and display them to the user, and so on.

In the third scenario, you need to add more sophisticated logic to the form. For instance, you might need to invoke some supporting code to validate the data, or you may want to include special programming for submitting the form data. These kinds of situations require writing managed code that is attached to the form and is executed on each machine where the form is installed.

Each of these scenarios maps broadly to one of three security modes that InfoPath recognizes. They are, respectively, *restricted mode*, *domain security mode*, and *full trust security mode*.

Restricted Security Mode

Consider the case where you only need to retrieve some data fields from the user. One way to do that might be to copy the XSN file to a central file share or send the XSN file to the user via email.

> *Outlook 2007 has been enhanced to enable users to fill out attached XSN files directly within the email editing environment. This only works for restricted mode templates and only for recipients who also have Outlook 2007 installed.*

Restricted mode basically says that the form does not contain any code and is simply a container for data as described by the form schema. When a form template is published in restricted mode, a special marker is placed in the file.

Restricted mode has its advantages for developing business process automation solutions in SharePoint. Imagine a form that gathers data that is then used to create items and documents in one or more Share-Point document libraries. By coding the form for restricted mode, you could gather the data by sending the form as an email attachment. Outlook 2007 users could then fill out the form directly within Outlook and then forward it to an email-enabled form library to which you've attached a custom event receiver that decodes the form and performs the appropriate steps based on the data in the form.

Domain Security Mode

Domain security mode means that the form cannot connect to any server other than its host. This imposes limitations on how the form is coded. If a form is intended to be run in a browser, then it cannot have any code at all. If it does, then the form validation will fail and the form may not run correctly when deployed. Forms that run in the InfoPath client may contain code and can connect to resources on the same server. This is ideally suited to forms that are deployed to a SharePoint site that need to reference lists in the same domain. These types of forms can reference lists on other domains by using a data connection from a trusted data connection library in a site within the same domain.

Full Trust Security Mode

Fully trusted forms are either digitally signed or have been installed on the machine on which they are run. This includes the SharePoint server, meaning that an administrator has to install a form to the SharePoint server farm before it is fully trusted. It is not enough to simply upload and enable the form. The administrator must have direct access to the server machine so that the form can be properly registered. Once it has been properly registered, a fully trusted form can perform any function the developer can dream up, including accessing data from multiple servers on any domain and calling managed code. Forms that have been uploaded and installed on the server farm can be executed directly within the InfoPath client without being installed on the client machine.

Form Programming

There are three ways you can add intelligence to an InfoPath 2007 form. You can attach conditional rules directly to data elements, you can write script that gets embedded into the form, and you can write managed code that is called from a separate "code behind" assembly. In addition to these choices, there are two ways that you can write managed code. You can install Visual Studio Tools for Applications (VSTA) and launch the development environment from within InfoPath, or you can install Visual Studio Tools for Office (VSTO) and launch InfoPath from within the Visual Studio 2005 IDE. The project structure is the same in both cases, but with VSTO you have more control over the client application. For instance, you cannot write code that modifies the InfoPath 2007 user interface from within a VSTA project. For that, you have to use VSTO.

To start adding code to a form, you must first select the appropriate options in the form itself. Open the form options dialog by choosing Form Options from the Tools menu in InfoPath 2007, and then select the `Programming` category from the list on the left side. In the Programming Language section, you can choose the form template code language from a dropdown list. Selecting JScript or VBScript causes InfoPath to launch the Microsoft Script Editor when you add an event handler to your form. Selecting C# or Visual Basic launches VSTA. If VSTA is not installed, then these options do not appear in the list.

Using Script

If your custom logic does not rely on managed code, you can write it using JScript or VBScript. When you add an event handler to a form that is setup for scripting, you write the code in the Microsoft Script Editor. Figure 14-12 illustrates this with a simple example that overrides the default value of a data field when the form is loaded.

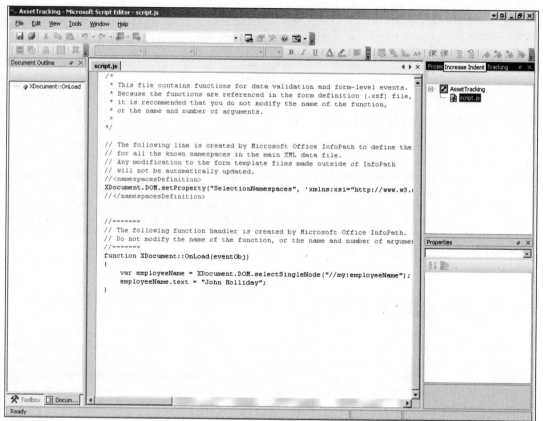

Figure 14-12

Improvements in InfoPath 2007

One thing that has really improved in InfoPath 2007 is the prescriptive guidance that is offered when you are writing script. In InfoPath 2003, you had to continually consult the data source to determine the proper XPath expression to use when accessing the form data model from script. InfoPath 2007 makes it easier by injecting the associated XPath expression into the comment for the event handler. Keep in mind that neither the comment nor the function name is updated if you change the underlying object model, although the link to the generated function remains in place even if the name of the original data element changes.

Using Visual Studio Tools for Applications

Visual Studio Tools for Applications provides a familiar development environment for developing smart forms. If you've developed managed code for InfoPath 2003 forms, you may recall that the solution architecture was somewhat convoluted because of the way Visual Studio communicated with the InfoPath 2003 client. The development picture has improved dramatically with the release of InfoPath 2007 and Visual Studio 2005. First, all of the code is now fully event driven, meaning that there is no special startup code you have to write. Instead, you can simply select the event you want to handle and InfoPath will generate the wrapper code for you, creating a handler on the fly.

Before you can start writing VSTA code, you must install the VSTA IDE on your development machine, as follows:

1. If you haven't done so already, open the Control Panel and select Add/Remove Programs.

2. Find the Microsoft Office InfoPath 2007 in the list, and click Change.

3. Select the VSTA option under .NET Programmability Support to install the IDE.

4. Next, open InfoPath and set up your programming preferences.

5. Select Options from the Tools menu, and then click the Design tab, as shown in Figure 14-13.

6. In the `Programming Defaults` section, select the programming languages you prefer to use when designing forms that run either in InfoPath alone, or in InfoPath and InfoPath Forms Services. Here, you can also set the default location for creating projects.

Once you get all this set up, you can start writing managed code for your forms. To add code for an event, select Tools ➪ Programming from the main menu and then select the event you want to code against. This will open the VSTA IDE and generate the proper declaration for adding your code.

Figure 14-14 shows the VSTA IDE for customizing the Asset Tracking form. Notice that the project contains the appropriate references, and the assembly is signed using a generated public key. While developing your code, you will enjoy the usual benefits of IntelliSense and integrated debugging as well as tight integration with the InfoPath client.

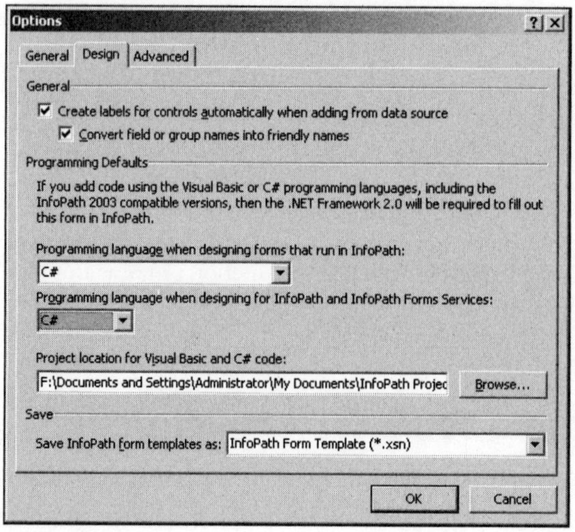

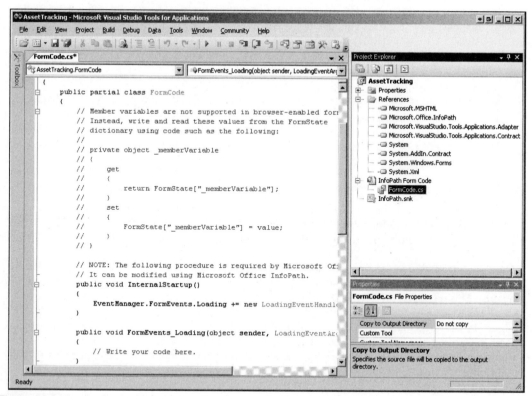

Figure 14-13

Figure 14-14

When you are finished building your code, the generated assembly is added to the form template, as shown in Figure 14-15.

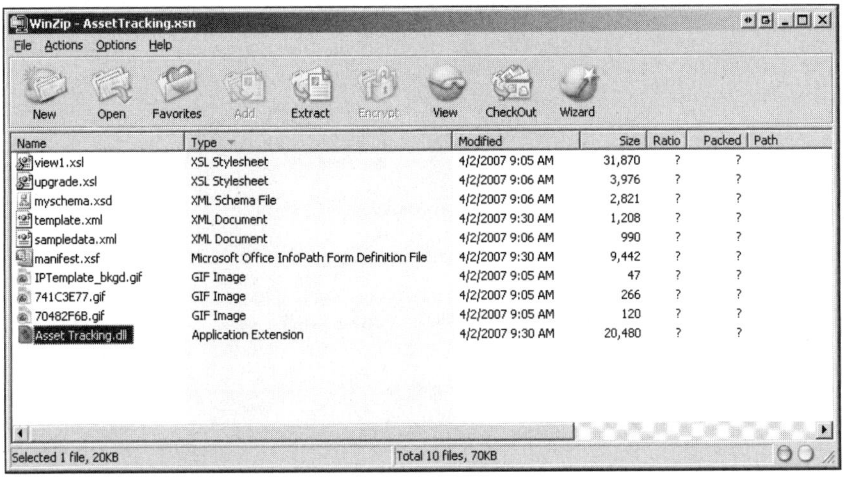

Figure 14-15

Using Visual Studio Tools for Office

Visual Studio Tools for Office provides the most comprehensive development experience available for building smart electronic forms. When you install VSTO, you get a number of project templates for creating solutions at the application level (called "add-ins") and at the document level (generally called "templates"). Use an application- level add-in when you want to customize the authoring experience within the application. Use a document- level template when you want to create a custom document with specialized behavior.

Start by creating a new InfoPath Form Template project. You will find this project template in the Office node of the project type tree in the New Project dialog under your language of choice. Give the project a name and click OK. Figure 14-16 shows the starting layout of a new form template project for customizing the sample Asset Tracking form. The first thing you'll notice is that the InfoPath design surface is hosted within the Visual Studio IDE. This means that you can design your form from within Visual Studio without having to switch back and forth between it and the InfoPath client. You also get the Design Tasks task pane with all the familiar links. Even the logic inspector is hosted within the Visual Studio environment.

Although many of the InfoPath commands are merged into similar locations in the Visual Studio IDE, the form-level event handlers are placed on the Insert menu instead of the Tools menu.

One drawback of the current VSTO implementation is that the property pane is not fully integrated with the InfoPath objects. For example, if you select a data element in the Data Source pane, the Visual Studio Properties pane is not updated to reflect the properties of the selected element. To get to the properties, you have to use the context menu and select the properties... command, which opens a modal dialog for editing the data element.

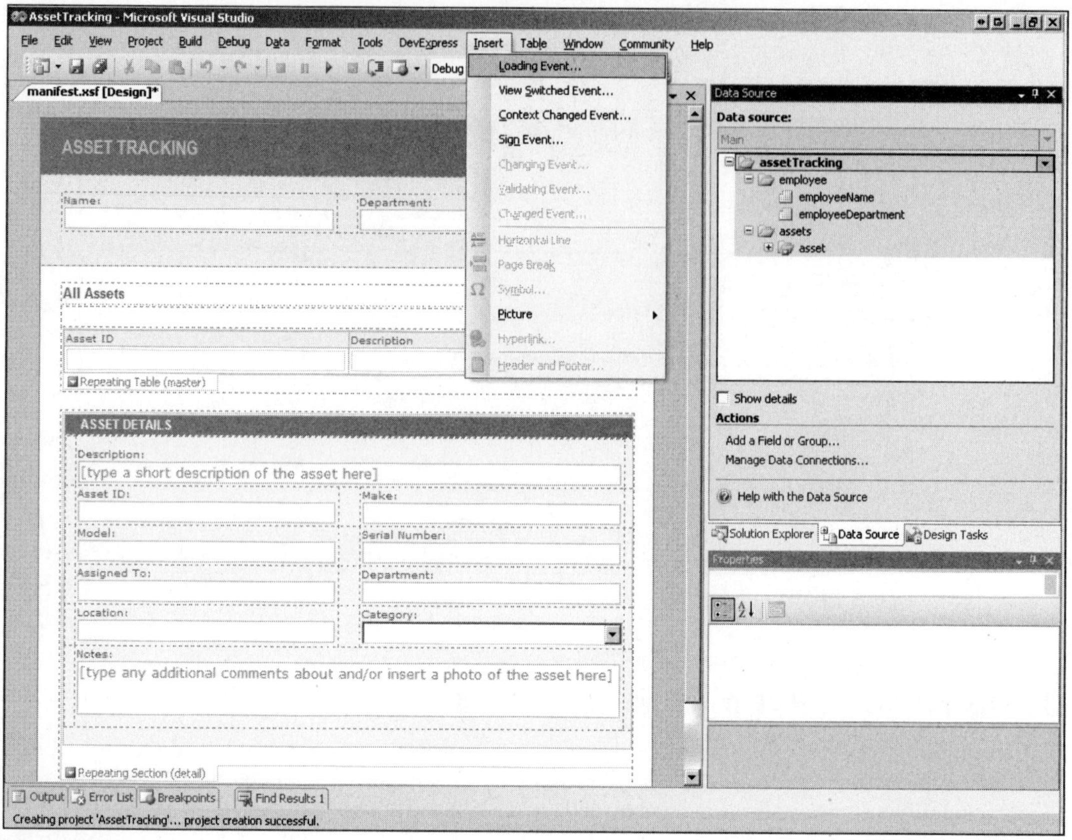

Figure 14-16

The Logic Inspector

When developing code for a form, it is often difficult to keep track of all the places where that code will be invoked within the form. This is mainly because of the fact that custom code can be attached to many form elements, some of which are dependent on other elements. To simplify this process, InfoPath 2007 includes a tool called the *logic inspector* that shows all of the code dependencies for the form in a single dialog. Figure 14-17 shows the logic inspector for the sample Meeting Agenda form, which automatically adjusts the meeting end time whenever the meeting start time is changed.

Using this tool, you can quickly get an overall picture of the code dependencies that exist in a form. This is particularly useful when working with legacy forms that were developed by others. Note that the logic inspector shows all of the logical dependencies that exist for the form, including logic that has been developed in managed code and attached to various elements. Although the managed code is not decompiled, it can be helpful to know which elements depend on which methods.

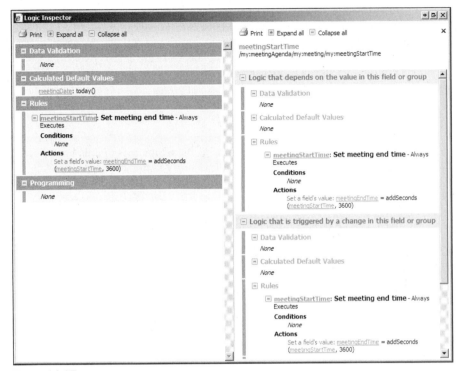

Figure 14-17

Form Deployment and Distribution

There are many ways to deploy and distribute forms, and the method you choose depends on several factors. These include the location from which you want users to access the form and the level of security you want to enforce when the form is filled out. As mentioned earlier, restricted mode forms can be distributed by simply sharing the XSN file, but the usefulness of such forms is limited to simple data gathering. In most cases, you will need to publish your forms. The following sections examine the publishing process in detail.

How Form Publishing Works

InfoPath uses the term *publishing* to refer to the process of preparing a form for distribution and actually placing it into the desired location. Saving a form template and then copying it to another location is not the same as publishing the template. Publishing a template is analogous to compiling a source file for an executable program. You can save the source file as often as you like, but you can't run it until it is compiled. Compiling the file accomplishes several goals. First, it validates the source code so that the programmer can identify and correct logical and syntactical errors. Second, it transforms the source file into a format the target machine can understand.

Form publishing works the same way. InfoPath examines the contents of the form template and validates it, allowing the form developer to correct any problems, and then it transforms the template so that it can run properly in the specified target environment. In the case of a source file, the compiler is only concerned with the runtime execution. In the case of a form template, there are at least two scenarios that have to be covered: the creation and storage of form data when the template is "executed," and the storage and configuration of the form template itself.

Publishing to a SharePoint Site

When a form template is published to a SharePoint site, the template is updated to reflect its new location and the modified template is attached to the form library as the document template for that library. When a new form is created, the form data file contains a reference to the form library. The following example illustrates the steps involved:

1. Open the Meeting Agenda sample form in design mode.

2. Select Publish from the File menu to start the Publishing Wizard.

3. Select To a SharePoint server with or without InfoPath Forms Services, and click Next.

4. Enter the URL of the target site, and select Document Library as the publishing target. You can either create a new library or update an existing one.

5. Select the columns you want to promote, and then click Next. You are presented with a summary page indicating the target library, its location, the server type, and the security level that has been determined by InfoPath based on the form options and other factors such as whether the form contains embedded code. The Meeting Agenda sample is marked as restricted because it does not contain any code, just rules. Restricted mode allows it to run anywhere.

6. Click Publish to complete the wizard and publish the form. You should see a dialog like the one shown in Figure 14-18.

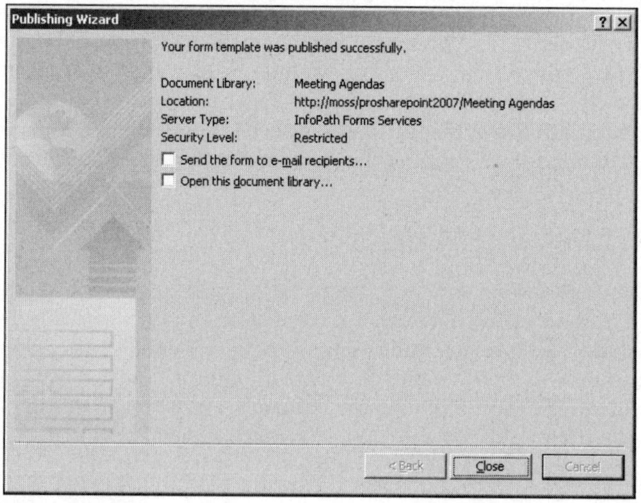

Figure 14-18

Publishing to a Content Type

InfoPath 2007 adds the ability to publish a form to a content type. This is a new feature that eliminates the IT bottleneck associated with publishing a form directly to a form library, as in the previous example. The bottleneck occurs because the publishing step often requires knowledge of how the form works. For example, the person publishing the form has to decide which columns to promote. Typically, this person is the form designer. After the form is up and running, a site administrator may need to deploy the same form to another form library. This means that the form designer must open the form in design mode and repeat the steps required to publish the form to the new location.

Content types eliminate this, allowing site administrators to attach the same form to multiple form libraries without the help of the form designer. They can simply enable the selected content type on the new library by using the SharePoint user interface. The steps for publishing to a content type are similar to those used when publishing to a form library, except that you select Site Content Type in the Publishing Wizard dialog, as shown in Figure 14-19.

Instead of creating or updating a document library, you create or update a content type, as shown in Figure 14-20.

The important part of this process is that the resulting content type will contain a reference to the form template after it is published. It is essential that this reference be accessible to users of the content type. This carries security implications as well, especially for forms that rely on the domain security mode. Recall that domain security mode restricts a form from accessing resources outside its domain. It is important to ensure that the location and file name you choose for such templates is within the same domain as the content type. Typically, this means publishing the form template to a document library on the same site, as shown in Figure 14-21.

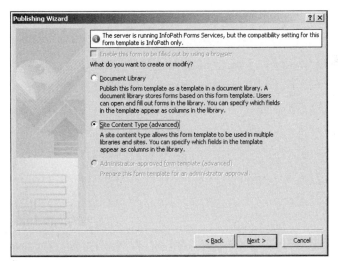

Figure 14-19

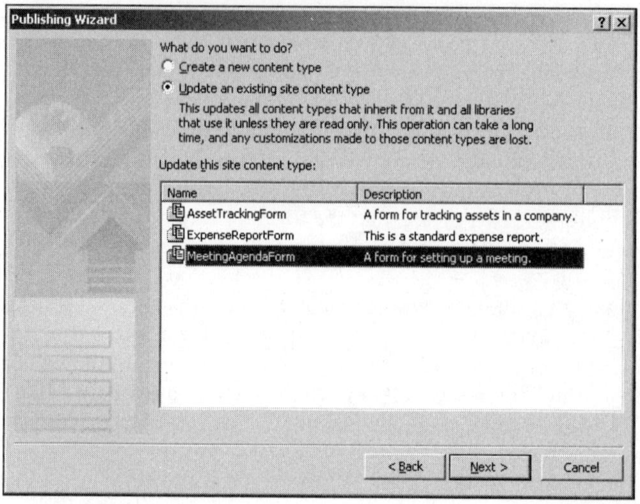

Figure 14-20

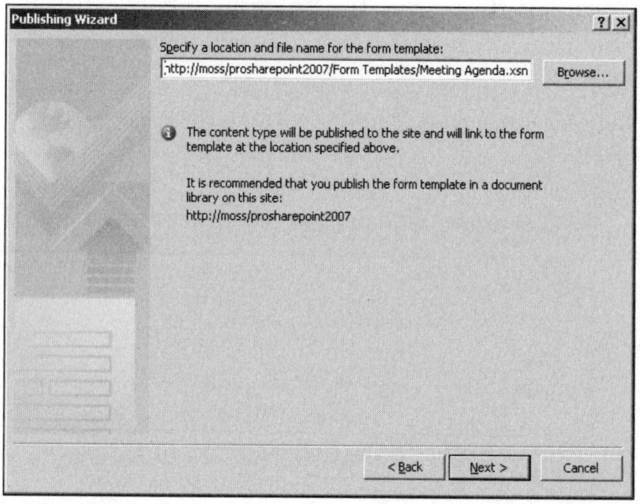

Figure 14-21

Publishing the template and publishing to the content type are two distinct operations. The location and file name you specify in the Publishing Wizard when publishing to a content type is what is written into the content type definition. You have to ensure that the location and file name match the actual location of the form template. If they don't match, then you'll get an error when trying to create form data items from the content type.

When you have completed the Publishing Wizard, you will see a dialog that contains a link to the content type page of the site. From there, you can manage the new content type. Figure 14-22 shows the resulting content type in the SharePoint user interface.

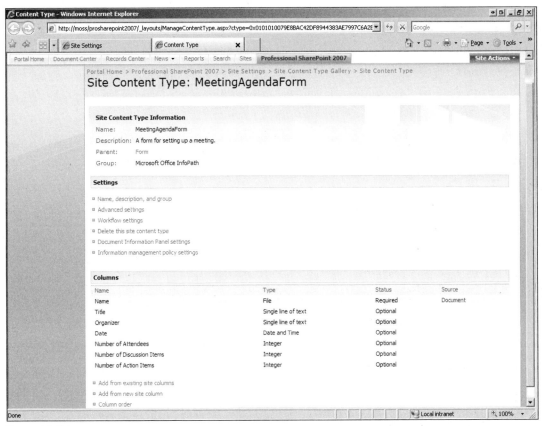

Figure 14-22

Using Browser-Based Forms

One of the most anticipated new features introduced with InfoPath 2007 and MOSS is the ability to gather data using browser-based forms. This capability greatly extends the reach of electronic forms because users are no longer required to have the InfoPath client application installed in order to fill out a form. With InfoPath Forms Services enabled, they can edit many forms directly in their web browser.

Although there are many limitations to the functionality of browser-based forms, they are essential for many critical business solutions. Figure 14-23 shows the sample expense report form open in a web browser.

Although there is a lot of power and value in using browser-based forms, the true intention of this feature is to extend the reach of forms that would otherwise not be available to a significant number of users. It is not intended to replace client-based forms. To get the most benefit from the Forms Services layer, you can create two views within your form — one for the browser and another for the client.

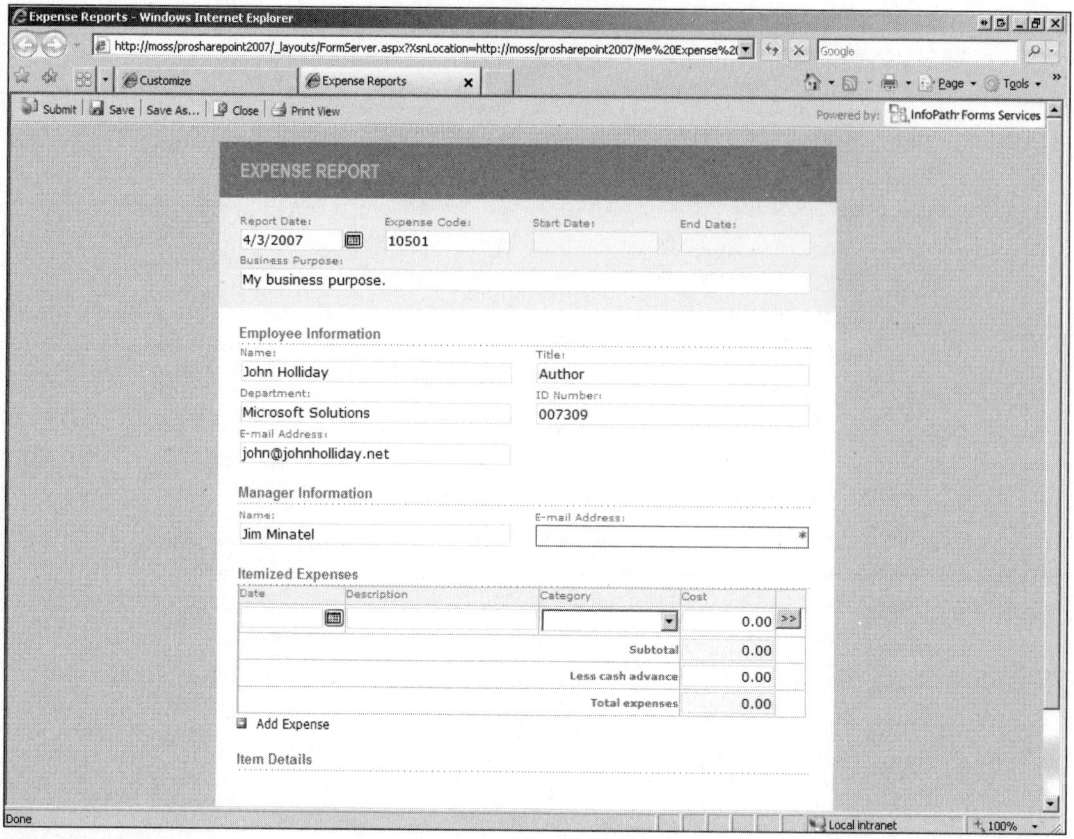

Figure 14-23

With a little planning, you can achieve good results by designing your forms for both environments and then disabling the client-only views when the form is displayed in the browser and vice versa. An example of this approach might be a form that retrieves the information needed to generate a medical patient summary document using Open XML. The form would gather the core data elements for a patient record and then generate the summary document based on the information entered into the form. The browser-based version would only collect basic information using string fields, while the more enhanced client version would use dropdown lists populated directly from SharePoint sites and the like.

This is just one example, but the introduction of browser-based forms generally creates more complexity for the developer. This is partly due to the restrictions that are placed on forms that can be presented in the browser. The first thing to consider when developing browser-based forms is whether your existing forms are compatible with presentation in a browser. InfoPath 2007 provides a lot of help in making this determination by including a fairly sophisticated design checker that searches for and flags compatibility issues that it finds in a given form.

In general, browser-based forms are limited in the following ways:

- ❑ You cannot use JScript or VBScript.
- ❑ You cannot create custom task panes.
- ❑ You cannot use repeating sections in a master/detail relationship.
- ❑ You cannot include placeholder text in controls.
- ❑ You cannot merge forms using custom code.
- ❑ You cannot implement custom save or submit code.
- ❑ You cannot digitally sign the entire form. Only sections can be signed.

Another area of concern is what to surface to the user when a form is presented in the browser. You have a good deal of control over what happens by using the Browser category of the Form Options dialog, as shown in Figure 14-24. However, once you enable a form for display in a browser, many of the other options are affected, as shown in Figure 14-25.

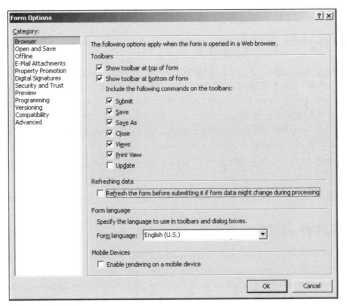

Figure 14-24

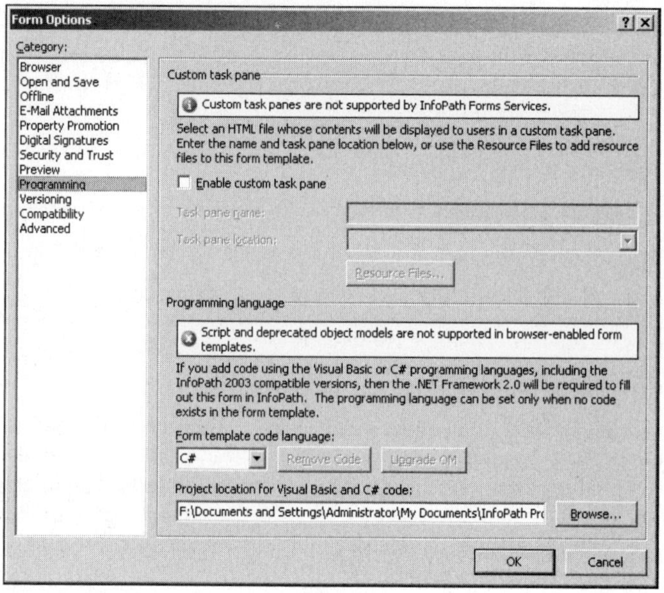

Figure 14-25

Configuring InfoPath Forms Services

InfoPath Forms Services (IFS) is included with MOSS and can also be installed as a separate product. You configure IFS from the Application Management page of the Central Administration web site. The basic configuration options have mostly to do with security and authentication. Many of these options are only necessary because there are so many combinations of features that tend to subvert the security policies that have been put in place by administrators. For example, it is possible for users to upload form templates and then make them browser-enabled. This might go against an organizational policy that requires all forms to be opened on the client. From the IFS administration page, an administrator can enable or disable this feature and choose the desired authentication behavior for all forms deployed to the farm.

Managing Form Templates

Given the ability to gather data via browser-based forms, there is a separate interface that system administrators can use to upload and manage the form templates that are available on the server. Once a form template has been successfully uploaded to the server, it can then be hosted in web pages within a site collection.

The problem with centrally managed form templates is that there may already be instances of the form already in use. This carries implications for what should be done about outstanding data-gathering sessions as well as what to do about future sessions. This problem is exacerbated by the fact that browser-based forms are typically used as part of long-running processes, also known as workflows.

For example, if a workflow starts out using version 1 of a modification form and then that form is upgraded to version 2 while the workflow is hibernating, then problems could arise when the workflow wakes up and the upgraded modification form tries to manipulate the version 1 data. Since there is no way to predict all of the scenarios where this type of conflict can occur, it is left to the administrator to sort it out. This is done from the Upload Form Template page, shown in Figure 14-26.

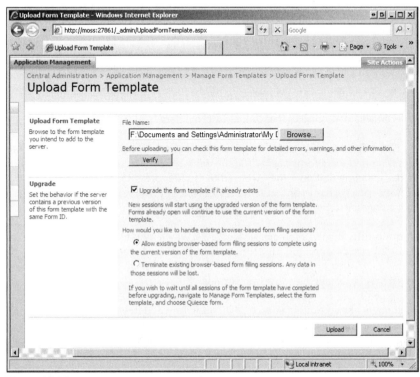

Figure 14-26

Handling Forms Authentication

Consider the case of an InfoPath form that needs to communicate with a remote server to retrieve data for a dropdown list. It does so by supplying user credentials directly to the server, which authenticates the user and returns the result. When that same form is uploaded to IFS, a problem is created because an extra level of indirection is introduced. This is called the *double-hop* or *multi-hop delegation* problem.

This is not an issue when using Kerberos authentication because the user's credentials are embedded inside a Kerberos ticket, which IFS can then use to authenticate the form on the user's behalf. NTLM authentication, on the other hand, requires that the encrypted credentials pass directly between the requesting process and the server. Since the IFS server is not running in a process associated with the form user, the required credentials are not available when the form is loaded, and therefore the form cannot be authenticated in response to the user's request.

Microsoft recommends Single Sign-On (SSO) as the preferred method for dealing with the double-hop problem. SSO is an encrypted database of user credentials that act like a Kerberos ticket without requiring Kerberos authentication protocols. Using SSO, IFS can retrieve the required credentials without risking exposure of those credentials to unauthorized users.

Summary

InfoPath form templates are packaged in ZIP files with an .XSN extension. They contain a manifest that describes all aspects of the form and a schema that describes the data that the form recognizes. When building SharePoint solutions that rely on form data, this is the most important part of the form template. The data source is the heart of any InfoPath form, and is probably the best starting point when designing a form from scratch. A form can have one primary data source, also called a data connection, and many secondary data sources that link to external data.

SharePoint 2003 offered form libraries that could surface selected form data fields as columns, allowing end users to filter and view form data without having to resort to the original form. These columns were unidirectional, meaning that once they were edited in the form library, they could not be written back to the underlying form. Windows SharePoint Services 3.0 form data fields are now bidirectional, allowing for greater consistency in the gathering of form data.

InfoPath form security involves three basic scenarios, which map to the three underlying security models, namely restricted, domain, and full trust modes. Restricted mode forms are used for simple data gathering. Domain forms are limited to data sources within the same domain. Fully trusted forms can run managed code but must first be installed by an administrator.

Form publishing is like compiling source code. InfoPath validates the form and then transforms it as appropriate for the target execution environment. When published to a SharePoint site, a form template is updated to reflect its new location and the modified template is attached to the form library as the document template for that library. When a new form is created, the form data file contains a reference to the form library.

InfoPath 2007 can publish a form to a SharePoint document library and adds the ability to publish a form directly to a content type. Content type publishing eliminates the need for the form designers to be involved in redeploying a form to another form library, thereby relieving the IT bottleneck for site administrators.

InfoPath Forms Services greatly extends the reach of electronic forms because users are no longer required to have the InfoPath client application installed in order to fill out a form. With InfoPath Forms Services enabled, users can edit many forms directly from within their web browser. Browser-based forms have restricted functionality and are not intended to replace client-based forms. Client-based forms may still be required to implement certain types of solutions.

15

Building Workflow Solutions

By Thomas Rizzo and John Holliday

Human-based workflow is increasingly becoming a critical component of enterprise content management systems development. Beyond the need to route content through an organization for review and approval, workflows are growing in complexity, touching a broad range of external systems and driving critical business processes. This chapter examines the various options available for developing SharePoint workflow solutions and will explore in detail the mechanics and the techniques involved. However, before diving into the SharePoint-specific workflow capabilities, it will be helpful to take a closer look at Windows Workflow Foundation, the business process automation platform upon which SharePoint workflow is built.

Workflow Foundation Basics

The Windows Workflow Foundation (WF) is a process automation platform that is integrated into SharePoint as well as many other Microsoft initiatives, including future versions of BizTalk Server and the Microsoft Dynamics product line. WF is the way to build workflow enabled solutions on the Windows platform. It provides a generalized architecture for delivering feature-rich business automation solutions while at the same time preserving the ability to integrate its various components into existing solutions. This includes applications on the server and on the client. It is this flexibility that adds to both its complexity and its power. You can embed custom workflow components into any .NET application, such as a WinForms application, and you can expose the same workflow components as a web service and access them over the Internet. The following sections explore the architectural features that enable this flexibility and highlight those most relevant to SharePoint solution development.

Workflow consists of a runtime engine and a programming model with tools for workflow developers. Windows Workflow Foundation is part of the .NET Framework 3.0 (formally known as

WinFX) that includes the Windows Communication Foundation (WCF, formally known as Indigo) and the Windows Presentation Foundation (WPF, formally known as Avalon). WF provides a common infrastructure that Microsoft as well as third-party vendors will implement.

There are several key concepts that you need to grasp in order to work effectively with WF. These concepts include the different types of workflows you can build with WF, how workflows are structured, the kinds of actions a workflow can perform, and the ways in which a running workflow can communicate with other systems and processes.

There are fundamentally three parts to the WF framework. First, there is the runtime engine, which provides the workflow execution environment, state management, transactions, persistence, and tracking capabilities. Then there is the hosting application, which provides an execution context for the runtime engine along with any application-specific services that may be needed to support the workflows being executed. Finally, there are the activities from which the workflows are built. The WF framework includes a base activity library, which provides out-of-the-box activities as well as the base classes for building your own custom activities.

Figure 15-1 shows the different components of the WF framework.

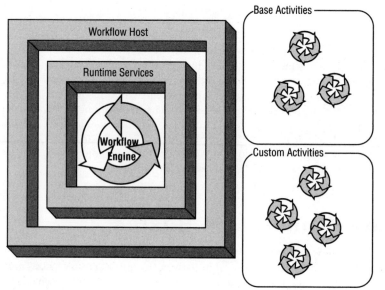

Figure 15-1

Types of Workflows

There are two kinds of workflows: sequential and state machine. This distinction between sequential and state-machine workflows becomes very important from a developer perspective, because when developing real solutions, especially when modeling human-based business processes, it is often necessary to combine both approaches. It is sometimes difficult to choose, and the "right" answer often depends on the complexity of the solution as well as the availability of preexisting workflows and activities.

The fact that workflows are long-running tends to alleviate the pressure to use one approach over the other. As a workflow runs, it may reach a point where additional information is needed and that information is unavailable. This is often the case with human-based business processes, which tend to be event-driven with long gaps between each event. The runtime services component takes care of persisting the workflow state while any additional required information is gathered. Thus, it is possible to use a sequential workflow to model such processes even though the state-machine approach might be easier to implement. Either way, the key take-aways are:

❑   The WF framework is flexible enough to accommodate both modeling styles.

❑   Existing workflow components can be integrated easily into new components to handle changing requirements.

Sequential Workflows

A sequential workflow does what its name implies. It performs one action after another in sequence from start to finish. While it might seem that sequential workflows are rigid and predetermined, you can create conditions in your workflow so that different routes are taken depending on values passed in from outside sources. Those values may come from anywhere, including actions made by end users. These types of workflows can have looping, branching, and other flow of control mechanisms. Workflows that model system behavior are good candidates for sequential workflows. Figure 15-2 shows an example of a sequential workflow in the Visual Studio graphical designer.

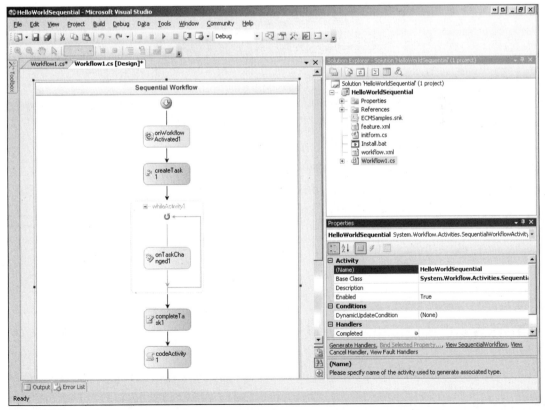

Figure 15-2

State-Machine Workflows

State-machine workflows perform different actions in response to discrete events, which may be generated either from within the workflow or from an external source. Rather than defining a sequential path through the workflow, you define states and state transitions. State-machine workflows are useful when you do not know the sequence of activities that you want to perform or the set of possible combinations of paths through the workflow is too large or complex.

With a state-machine workflow, you have a starting state. You then define state transitions such as moving from state A to state B. The workflow can also skip steps or jump around according to the events that the workflow receives. Transitions in the workflow are triggered by events. These events can be simple (such as the firing of a timer event) or complex (such as detecting the arrival of data from an external data source). Human-based workflows are good candidates for the state-machine approach because of the dynamic and changing nature of those processes.

Figure 15-3 shows a state-machine workflow in the Visual Studio graphical designer.

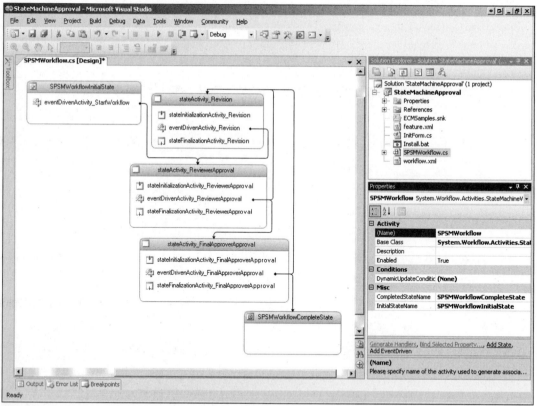

Figure 15-3

Code and No-Code Workflows

There are three basic approaches you can use to build your workflows. These are code, no-code, and code-beside.

Using the code approach, you design your workflow using the Visual Studio 2005 graphical designer. Your workflow design is converted into code using the WF object model, placed in a separate file, and then invoked from the generated `InitializeComponent` method. All of the required code is generated by the designer.

The second approach is to create your workflow using the no-code workflow capabilities. Your workflow is modeled using the eXtensible Application Markup Language (XAML). XAML is a format that allows you to serialize .NET objects as XML and is supported by a number of Microsoft technologies such as the Windows Presentation Framework. When you use XAML with WF, your workflow is saved with a file extension of `.xoml` to differentiate it from other uses of XAML. You then compile the workflow using the workflow command-line compiler (`wfc.exe`) or you can load the `.xoml` file directly into your host application without compiling it. SharePoint Designer 2007 uses no-code workflows in conjunction with declarative rules.

The third approach is a combination of the previous two. You design your workflow using a no-code model to produce an `.xoml` file, and then combine that with a code-based or rules-based implementation. The easiest way to think about this mode is that it is like ASP.NET 2.0, where you have a code-beside file. Besides writing code, you could write a workflow rules file, which is a declarative rules file. When you build workflows against SharePoint with the Visual Studio 2005 workflow designer, this is the default mode that is used.

> *ASP.NET developers use the term "code behind" to refer to code placed in a separate file. ASP.NET 2.0 introduced the new term "code beside" to refer to code placed in separate files that also use partial classes to enable the IDE to regenerate code without affecting the code being written by the developer. The WF designer also generates partial classes using this technique.*

Workflow Activities

The central concept of WF is the notion that a workflow consists of a collection of activities. An activity can be thought of as a discrete unit of behavior. Activities can also contain other activities. You design a workflow by either combining activities in sequence or nesting them one within the other to direct the flow of information over time. Thus, a workflow is itself a type of activity. This ability to compose higher-level activities from simpler ones and to package entire workflows as activities gives WF an almost unlimited range of expressive power.

What Is an Activity?

When thinking about WF activities, it is useful to consider them as you would any other .NET component. In other words, what's under the covers? How are they implemented? What are the pieces that make up an activity and enable it to participate in a workflow? Essentially, there are seven facets to any workflow activity, and the WF framework provides a default implementation for all seven. Since every activity you write will ultimately be derived from one of the base activity classes declared in the `System.Workflow` `.ComponentModel` assembly, your activities will automatically inherit the default implementations. You can, of course, override the defaults.

The following table describes the different parts of a workflow activity:

Component	Description
Designer	A class that implements a visual designer for controlling the appearance of the activity within the graphical designer
Code Generator	A class that is responsible for generating the code needed to implement the activity based on its property settings
Validator	A class that handles property validation to ensure that business rules are honored and the internal state of the activity is consistent with its use
Toolbox Item	A way to represent the activity in the toolbox associated with the graphical designer
Executor	A class that is responsible for providing a method for executing the activity at runtime
Serializer	A class that is responsible for serializing and deserializing the state of the activity
Deployer	A class that is responsible for deploying the activity into the runtime environment

Designer

You declare a designer using the `Designer` attribute as in the following example. You then create a separate class to implement the designer, overriding the default implementation where appropriate. Listing 15-1 declares a custom designer to display a distinctive icon for a custom activity so that workflow developers can identify it easily on the design surface.

Listing 15-1

```
using System;
using System.ComponentModel;
using System.ComponentModel.Design;
using System.Drawing;
using System.Drawing.Drawing2D;
using System.Workflow;
using System.Workflow.Activities;
using System.Workflow.ComponentModel;
using System.Workflow.ComponentModel.Design;

namespace ProSharePoint2007
{
    [Designer(typeof(CustomActivityDesigner), typeof(IDesigner))]
    public class CustomActivity : Activity
    {
```

```csharp
        public static readonly DependencyProperty TextProperty
            = DependencyProperty.Register("Text", typeof(string),
                typeof(CustomActivity));

        public string Text
        {
            get { return (string)base.GetValue(TextProperty); }
            set { base.SetValue(TextProperty, value); }
        }

        protected override ActivityExecutionStatus
        Execute(ActivityExecutionContext executionContext)
        {
            Console.WriteLine(Text);
            return ActivityExecutionStatus.Closed;
        }
    }

    public class CustomActivityDesigner : ActivityDesigner
    {
        protected override void Initialize(Activity activity)
        {
            base.Initialize(activity);
            Bitmap bmp = Properties.Resources.CustomActivityIcon;
            bmp.MakeTransparent();
            this.Image = bmp;
        }

        protected override Size OnLayoutSize(ActivityDesignerLayoutEventArgs e)
        {
            base.OnLayoutSize(e);
            return new Size(96, 96);
        }

        protected override Rectangle ImageRectangle
        {
            get
            {
                const int width = 48;
                Rectangle rc = new Rectangle();
                rc.X = this.Bounds.Left + ((this.Bounds.Width - width) / 2);
                rc.Y = this.Bounds.Top + 4;
                rc.Size = new Size(width,width);
                return rc;
            }
        }

        protected override Rectangle TextRectangle
        {
            get
            {
                Size size = this.Image.Size;
                Rectangle imageRect = this.ImageRectangle;
                return new Rectangle(this.Bounds.Left + 2, imageRect.Bottom,
```

```
                        this.Bounds.Width-4, this.Bounds.Height -
                            imageRect.Height - 1);
                    }
                }
            }
        }
```

Code Generator

You can use a custom code generator to handle special situations that require dynamic code injection. There are many situations where this capability might come in handy, such as generating web service proxies on the fly, but it is probably not very useful for SharePoint workflows.

The way this works is as follows. You create a new class derived from either ActivityCodeGenerator or CompositeActivityCodeGenerator. These base classes are declared in the System.Workflow .ComponentModel.Compiler namespace. In your custom generator class, you override the GenerateCode method. This method is called during workflow compilation by the workflow compiler when your activity is compiled. In order to tell the compiler to use your class instead of the default, you need to decorate your activity with the ActivityCodeGenerator attribute as in the following example:

```
using System;
using System.ComponentModel;
using System.ComponentModel.Design;
using System.Drawing;
using System.Drawing.Drawing2D;
using System.Workflow;
using System.Workflow.Activities;
using System.Workflow.ComponentModel;
using System.Workflow.ComponentModel.Compiler;

namespace ProSharePoint2007
{
    [ActivityCodeGenerator(typeof(CustomActivityCodeGenerator))]
    public class CustomActivity : Activity
    {
        public static readonly DependencyProperty TextProperty
            = DependencyProperty.Register("Text", typeof(string),
                typeof(CustomActivity));

        public string Text
        {
            get { return (string)base.GetValue(TextProperty); }
            set { base.SetValue(TextProperty, value); }
        }

        protected override ActivityExecutionStatus
                Execute(ActivityExecutionContext executionContext)
        {
            Console.WriteLine(Text);
            return ActivityExecutionStatus.Closed;
        }
    }
```

```
public class CustomActivityCodeGenerator : ActivityCodeGenerator
{
    public override void GenerateCode(CodeGenerationManager manager,
            object obj)
    {
        // Cast obj to custom activity type.
        CustomActivity customActivity = obj as CustomActivity;

        // Retrieve a type provider object.
        ITypeProvider typeProvider =
            (ITypeProvider)manager.GetService(typeof(ITypeProvider));

        // ****************************************************
        // Generate code here using the CodeGenerationManager
        // and the CodeDOM.
        // ****************************************************
    }
}
```

Validator

The WF approach to validation is very powerful and is fully integrated within the design environment in real time. This means that as soon as an activity is dropped onto the design surface, the validation framework kicks in to determine if the current set of properties adheres to the rules and constraints defined by the activity itself.

The designer calls the validator object associated with an activity whenever a change is made to any of its properties. For every property that fails validation, the designer displays a smart tag that allows the workflow developer to see immediately that there is a problem. This approach is known as "correct-by-construction" and provides continuous validation, but does not interfere with the design process. As soon as the problem is corrected, the smart tag disappears.

To apply custom validation logic to an activity, you must derive a class from ActivityValidator and override the Validate method. You then use the ActivityValidator attribute to associate the class with your activity.

Toolbox Item

Every activity is associated with a toolbox item that is displayed in the toolbox of the designer. The toolbox item provides both an iconic and textual representation of the activity. In addition to providing a convenient visual representation for the activity, the toolbox item can also initialize the state of an activity when it is dragged onto the design surface. This is the primary reason for implementing a custom toolbox item.

The ActivityToolboxItem class is defined in the System.Workflow.ComponentModel.Design namespace. You define a custom toolbox item by implementing a class that derives from ActivityToolboxItem and then marking up your custom activity to reference your class using the ToolboxItem attribute, as in the following example:

```
using System;
using System.ComponentModel;
```

```
using System.ComponentModel.Design;
using System.Collections;
using System.Drawing;
using System.Workflow.ComponentModel.Compiler;
using System.Workflow.ComponentModel.Serialization;
using System.Workflow.ComponentModel;
using System.Workflow.ComponentModel.Design;
using System.Workflow.Runtime;
using System.Workflow.Activities;
using System.Workflow.Activities.Rules;

namespace ProSharePoint2007.CustomActivities
{
    [ToolboxItem(typeof(TaskReminderToolboxItem))]
    [ToolboxBitmap(typeof(TaskReminderActivity),"TaskReminder.bmp")]
    public partial class TaskReminderActivity: SequenceActivity
    {
        public TaskReminderActivity()
        {
            InitializeComponent();
        }
    }
}
```

Note that to use a custom bitmap, you need two attributes. This is because the base
ActivityToolboxItem class exposes a static method, which the WF designer uses to retrieve
the bitmap from the class associated with the item. That method searches for a ToolboxBitmap
attribute on the class. If none is found, it uses the default image.

In your derived ActivityToolboxItem class, you must mark the class as serializable. This is critical
for the toolbox to be able to load and unload the item and its properties. You can then override the
CreateComponentsCore method to initialize the activity with default properties, or to create additional
subactivities, and the like.

```
using System;
using System.Drawing;
using System.Collections.Generic;
using System.Text;
using System.Workflow.ComponentModel.Design;
using System.Runtime.Serialization;
using System.ComponentModel;
using System.ComponentModel.Design;

namespace ProSharePoint2007.CustomActivities
{
    [Serializable]
    internal sealed class TaskReminderToolboxItem : ActivityToolboxItem
    {
        protected override IComponent[]
```

```
                CreateComponentsCore(IDesignerHost host)
    {
        TaskReminderActivity reminder = new TaskReminderActivity();
        reminder.Description = "Sends reminders to the task assignee.";
        return new IComponent[] { reminder };
    }
  }
}
```

Executor

By definition, an activity represents an action to be performed. It is up to the WF framework to construct the proper context within which to execute the activity and to pass along any required information that enables the activity to run. It is the activity itself that provides the implementation of its core set of actions. This is done by overriding the Execute method, which is declared as follows:

```
protected override ActivityExecutionStatus
    Execute(ActivityExecutionContext context) {...}
```

Whenever a call is made to a method in an activity, a new execution context object is created and configured for that activity. The WF framework uses the `ActivityExecutionContext` object in this way to manage the execution of each activity and to control what the activity is allowed to do. This is particularly important for activities that execute other activities, such as replicator activities, while loops, and the like.

Serializer

In order for workflows to continue running over long periods of time (months or even years), it is necessary to pause their execution and save their state to persistent storage so they can be restarted later. The process of saving a workflow is often called "dehydration," and returning it to the running state is called "hydration" — terms which are reminiscent of the freeze-dried foods often used by campers. In any case, the ability to save and restore a running workflow is one of the key features of the WF framework. Since workflow activities may come from a variety of different vendors and developers, a standardized serialization model is necessary to enable them to work together in the context of a running workflow. It is also the case that different types of activities may require different types of serialization, so it is up to each activity to provide the most appropriate implementation. The base activity classes provide a default serialization framework with which you can interact to control the visibility of properties declared within your activities. This is done using the `DesignerSerializationVisibility` attribute. For more information, see the Windows Workflow Foundation Programming Guide.

Types of Activities

For the sake of completeness, this section describes some of the built-in activities for WF. Not all WF activities are relevant in a SharePoint environment. SharePoint supports a subset of the activities that you will see in the designer. The following table shows the activities that the WF designer supports.

The word Activity has been removed from each name for readability.

Name	Description
CallExternalMethod	This activity invokes a local method on a local service. You need to set the InterfaceType and MethodName properties to let WF know which method to call. This activity works with the HandleExternalEvent activity.
CancellationHandler	This activity contains cleanup code for a composite activity if one part of the activity is canceled before its children are done executing. A good example of this is when one branch of a parallel activity is canceled while the other is executing.
Code	This activity allows you to write code. You should use this activity infrequently and instead encapsulate your custom code into custom activities for reusability.
Compensate	This activity handles failures. With workflows, after you commit a transaction, there may be times when you need to roll back that transaction. However, if the transaction is already committed, you can't roll it back but instead need to run a compensating action to reverse it. This is where you would use this activity.
CompensationHandler	This activity will contain the activities that your workflow will perform if your workflow fails. This activity works with the Compensate activity. The Compensate activity triggers the CompensationHandler activity associated with it.
CompensatableSequence	This activity is a compensatable version of the Sequence activity. It implements the ICompensatableActivity interface.
CompensatableTransactionScope	This is the compensatable version of the TransactionScope activity.
ConditionedActivityGroup	This activity contains child activities that you can use a combination of rules and code to control. Your children activities are evaluated and executed based on your conditions or code. For example, you can place a WhenCondition or UntilCondition on your activities, and these activities or the set of activities will execute until the condition is met.
Delay	If you wanted to wait for a particular time, you would use this activity. You specify the duration for the delay. You use this activity most commonly in a Listen activity to set a timeout or run a scheduled job.

Name	Description
DelayForActivity	Suspends the workflow for a specified length of time.
DelayUntilActivity	Suspends the workflow until a specified date.
EventDriven	This activity contains children activities and is triggered when an event comes in that this activity is expecting. The first child activity in this activity must implement the IEventActivity interface.
EventHandlers	The EventHandlers activity allows you to connect events with activities.
EventHandlingScope	This activity allows you to run the main child activity concurrently with eventhandlers' activities. For example, you may want to run a sequence of activities while listening for a cancellation or a timeout window.
FaultHandler	This activity handles a fault of the type you specify. It is similar to a catch statement in code. You specify the type of fault using the FaultType property. You can have multiple fault handlers to handle different types of faults.
FaultHandlers	This is a composite activity that you can't drop from the toolbox but is added by the designer when you right-click an activity and select View Fault Handlers.
HandleExternalEvent	This activity waits for an external event to occur. Since this activity blocks the execution of the workflow, you will want to use it in a Listen activity so that you can place a Delay activity to perform a timeout.
IfElse	This activity is similar to the If Else statement in programming languages. You specify the conditions, and the workflow runtime evaluates which branch to go down. This activity works with the IfElseBranch activity.
IfElseBranch	This activity contains the activities for the branches in an IfElse activity. You set the conditions on these activities to determine when they should be executed.
InvokeWebService	This activity invokes a web service.
InvokeWorkflow	This activity invokes another workflow. You cannot directly retrieve the output of that workflow but could work through the host application to retrieve the output.

Continued

Name	Description
Listen	This activity contains multiple branches of event-driven activities. You can use the `Delay` activity in a `Listen` activity to simulate a timeout. This activity cannot be used in state-machine workflows.
Parallel	This activity contains two or more sequence activities that execute at the same time. This is not multithreaded parallel processing, since only a single thread can execute inside of a workflow. This activity allows the branches to execute independently.
Policy	This activity is a rules engine that allows you to specify business logic separate form your workflow. The WF designer includes a Rule Set Editor. By default, forward chaining will be used, which means that if a later rule changes a value that a previous rule depended on, the previous rule will be reevaluated.
Replicator	This activity allows you to create multiple instances of an activity. This is useful if you do not know how many times an activity or sequence of activities need to run. With SharePoint for workflows that can have an arbitrary number of approvers.
Sequence	This activity is a composite activity that allows you to run multiple activities in order.
SetState	This activity is what allows you to transition between your states in a state-machine workflow.
State	This activity represents a state in your state-machine workflow.
StateInitalization	This activity contains children activities that are performed when your state is transitioned to. You can only have one initialization activity per state.
StateFinalization	This activity contains children activities that are performed when your state is transitioned out of. There can only be one finalization activity per state.
Suspend	This activity suspends your workflow. This may be useful when your workflow hits an error that it cannot resolve and may require intervention from outside sources such as a human being.

Name	Description
SynchronizationScope	This activity is similar to thread semantics in programming languages that allow you to serialize access to critical pieces of code. The WF runtime will attempt to get a lock on the shared resource and will wait if the lock cannot be obtained.
Terminate	This activity will immediately terminate the workflow. There is no way back from this activity so it should be used if you know there is no way to recover from a fault or the condition that is causing you to terminate the workflow.
Throw	This activity is similar to the Throw statements in programming languages. By using this activity, you are making the thrown exception an explicit piece of your workflow model.
TransactionScope	You wrap transactions with this activity. By scoping the activities you place in this activity in a transaction, you can roll back if there is a failure anywhere in the sequence of activities. You can control the isolation and timeout through the TransactionOptions property. You cannot nest transaction scopes.
WebServiceFault	This activity allows you to raise a SOAP exception.
WebServiceInput	This activity allows you to receive data from a web service.
WebServiceOutput	This activity is used to respond to a web service request.
While	This activity is similar to While loop in programming languages. You set the condition and the loop will keep iterating until that condition is met.

Dependency Properties

When working with the WF framework, especially when working with the graphical designer, it becomes apparent that indirection plays a key role in enabling the power and flexibility of the platform. A big part of this is due to the use of dependency properties. Dependency properties are not unique to the WF framework. They are used extensively in the Windows Presentation Framework (WPF) and are an integral part of the .NET framework, though maybe not heavily used by most SharePoint developers.

Each dependency property is registered at runtime via a call to the static DependencyProperty .Register() method and is wrapped with property accessor methods to make it easy to work with from other code within the activity. The power of indirection comes into play at runtime. You can think of a dependency property as a value-resolution engine that defers the actual resolution until runtime. The way that the resolution happens "depends" on whatever else may be connected to it.

Dependency properties are used to set up a property value deferral system in WF. In a nutshell, dependency properties allow you to establish a loose coupling between objects at runtime. They enable the WF framework to do things like update property values without your having to retrieve them explicitly. For instance, once you declare a dependency property and bind it to a variable inside your activity, WF can wire the dependency property for a given scenario to other objects without having to generate code specific to that scenario. A good example might be a conditional expression editor in the graphical designer. Using dependency properties, such an editor would enable the workflow designer to enter an expression to calculate a condition based on properties declared within an activity, but the editor could defer the actual binding until runtime.

Dependency properties also enable the property owner to be notified when changes are made to a property and have those changes propagated through the system. When you think about it, this is important for workflow activities, which may have many objects that depend on values that come from a variety of different sources at runtime.

Workflow Security

It is important to remember that all workflows run as System Account in WSS and as the App Pool Identity on the server computer and domain. This means that a workflow has SharePoint administrator privileges and whatever computer or domain privileges have been assigned to the App Pool Identity. This carries implications for both the development and deployment of workflows. For example, it might be possible for a user to circumvent SharePoint permissions by using a workflow to perform an action that would otherwise not be allowed. It is up to the workflow developer to build code that protects against this possibility. One way to do that is to impersonate the current user from within a workflow activity, thereby reducing the permissions available to the workflow to those available to the user.

Workflow in MOSS

With a basic grounding in WF fundamentals, it is now possible to understand workflow in the context of Windows SharePoint Services. Since MOSS builds on WSS, it gets all of its workflow capabilities through WSS. Therefore, to understand workflow in MOSS, you also need to examine how WSS hosts the WF runtime.

Recall that Windows Workflow Foundation is not itself an application but merely provides a framework for workflow development. In order to execute a workflow, the WF runtime engine must be hosted within an execution environment. The WF runtime then interacts with that environment through a prescribed set of interfaces in order to create the required conditions for performing each workflow activity. It is important, therefore, to keep in mind that WSS hosts the WF runtime differently than most other applications. This fact becomes immediately apparent as soon as you start to peek inside the WSS host implementation.

The WSS Workflow Architecture

The first thing to consider is the high-level design of the WSS workflow hosting environment. Given the nature of the SharePoint environment, two assumptions are immutable. Workflows will be centered around content, and workflows will involve interactions with people. The following two sections explore these design constraints in greater detail.

SharePoint Workflow is Content-Centric

The content-centric nature of SharePoint workflow is readily apparent, but it also affects the design of the WF hosting environment as implemented within WSS. SharePoint workflows are designed to be attached to documents, list items, and content types. SharePoint list items have been extended specifically to support workflow via the `SPListItem.Workflows` data member. This property maintains the collection of workflow instances currently associated with a list item. Similarly, SharePoint content types support workflow via the `WorkflowAssociations` data member. Since content types operate at the class level (list items are instances of a content type), this data member maintains the collection of workflows (not instances) currently associated with the content type.

SharePoint Workflow Is Human-Based

The human-based nature of SharePoint workflow is also evident in the extensive support given to integrating SharePoint tasks into workflows. As you'll see below, there is a rich palette of task-specific activities that enable two-way interaction between tasks and workflow activities. You can easily create and assign SharePoint tasks from within custom activities, and you can suspend workflow execution until a SharePoint task has been completed.

The SharePoint Workflow Lifecycle

SharePoint workflows are governed by a specific sequence of events that is unique to the SharePoint environment. This is driven by the fact that SharePoint workflows are always connected to some kind of content, such as individual documents, list items, or content types. The following diagram shows the different stages of the SharePoint workflow lifecycle.

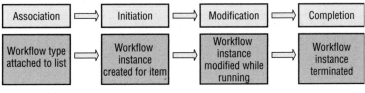

Figure 15-4

Workflow Association

In order for a workflow to run within SharePoint, it must first be associated with a list, either directly or through a content type attached to that list. Once this association has been established, SharePoint uses the association to determine what to do when items are created, modified, or removed from the list. For instance, the association specifies whether the workflow should be started automatically when an item is created, or whether the user should be allowed to start the workflow manually, and so on.

SharePoint maintains a farm-level workflow association table so that WSS can match up the workflow templates with the items the workflow should run on. Workflow templates define the workflow contents using XML that specifies the assemblies and forms associated with the workflow. One such form is the Workflow Association Form, which allows a person with the permission to associate a workflow to set up the default values of workflow properties. For instance, you can use an association form to allow administrators to set up the list of approvers, due dates, or other default parameters.

Workflow Initiation

When a user clicks on an associated workflow to start that workflow, or if the workflow is started automatically when a list item is added or changed, the workflow is said to be *Initiated*. When this happens, an optional Initiation Form is displayed. This form allows users to override any default parameter values that have been set, or add additional parameter values. Often, the Association Form and the Initiation Form are the same, allowing users to modify the same set of parameters that the list administrator has set. After the initiation form is submitted, a new workflow instance is created and attached to the list item. Figure 15- 5 shows the initiation form for the approval workflow.

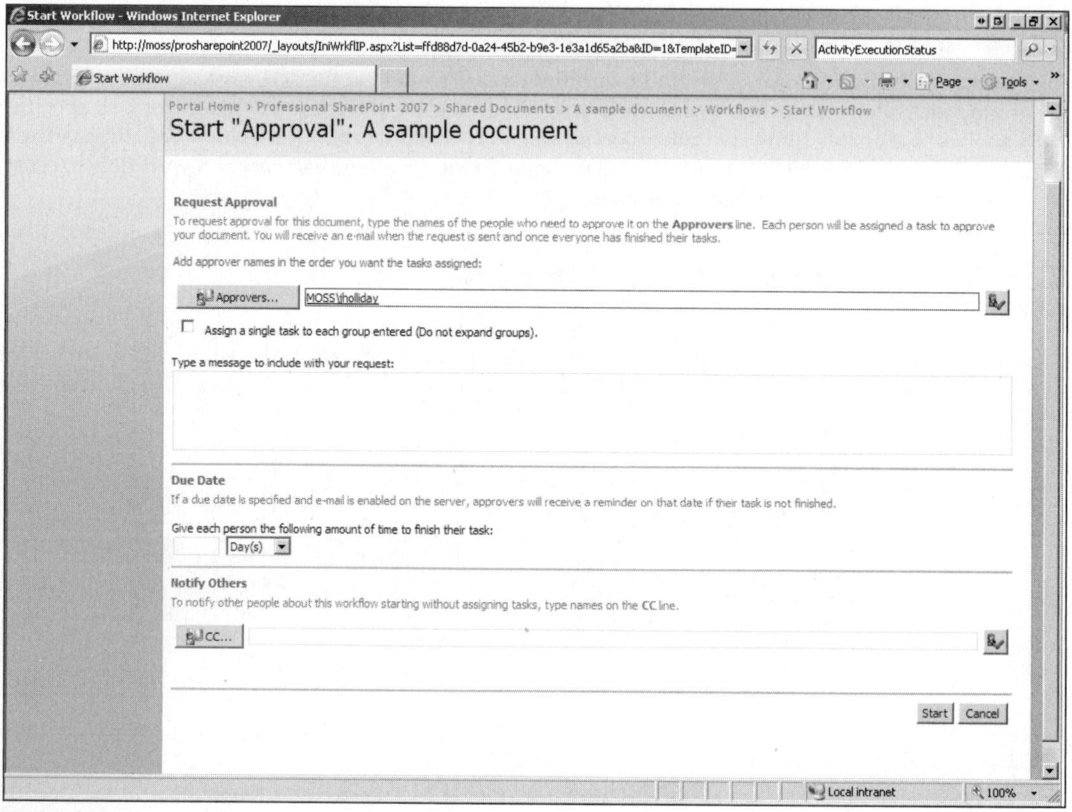

Figure 15-5

There can be multiple workflow instances attached to a single list item, but there can be only one instance of a given workflow type. For example, there cannot be two instances of the approval workflow running on the same item at the same type. But there could be an instance of the approval workflow running at the same time as an instance of the issue-tracking workflow.

Workflow Modification

It may be necessary to modify the workflow after it starts. For instance, with the built-in approval workflow, it might be necessary to add approvers or change the task descriptions and due dates while the workflow is running. To achieve this, SharePoint supports the same workflow modification strategy provided by WF. This involves specifying a Workflow Modification Form to enable users to modify the workflow.

Workflow Status

SharePoint provides built-in support for tracking the progress of a workflow. The workflow history list is a specialized SharePoint list used to record events that occur while the workflow is running. A view of this list is displayed on the workflow status page, allowing the list administrator to review the history of the workflow and understand what has happened as part of the workflow process.

Figure 15-6 shows the workflow status page with a workflow history list.

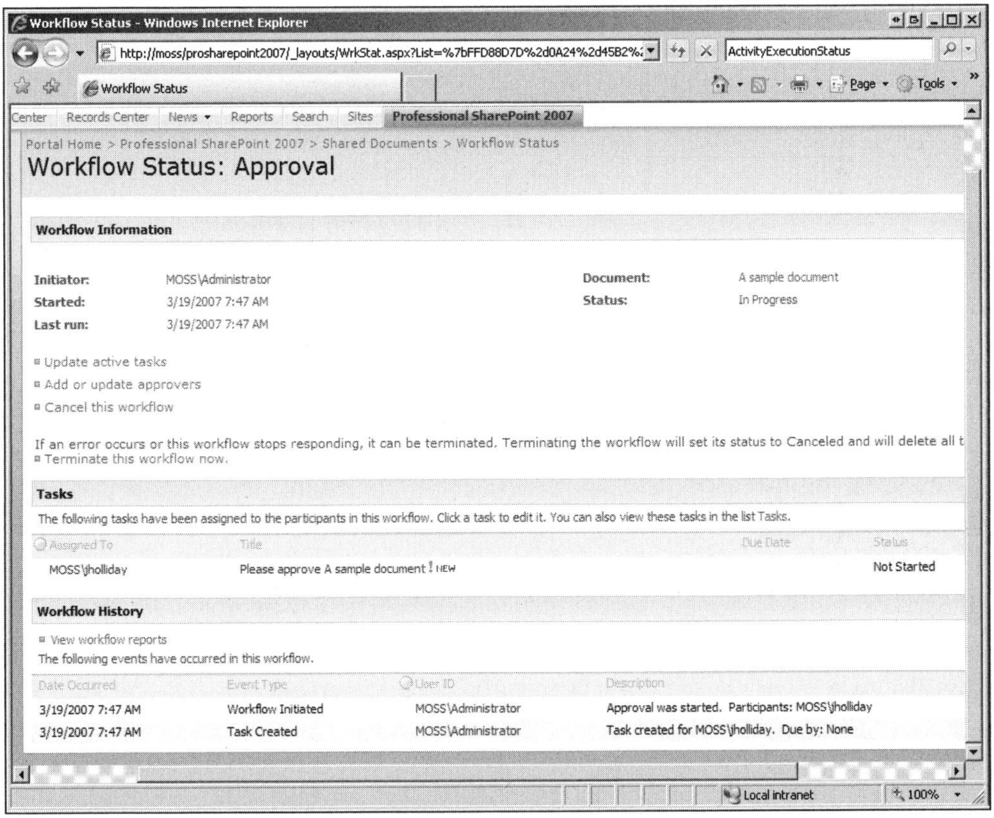

Figure 15-6

The SharePoint Workflow Object Model

The SharePoint workflow layer extends the WF object model by providing support for each stage of the SharePoint workflow lifecycle. This includes objects for starting and managing workflows, the associations between workflows and other SharePoint objects, modifications to running workflows, and coordinating tasks. Figure 15-7 shows the core components and interfaces that make up the SharePoint workflow object model.

Microsoft.Sharepoint.Workflow

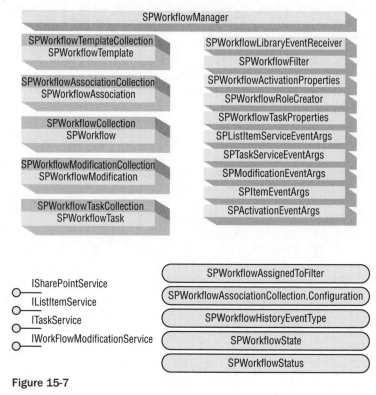

Figure 15-7

Workflow Manager

The SPWorkflowManager class exposes methods you can use to start and control running workflow instances from code. These are the same methods that are called from the SharePoint user interface when a user starts or cancels a workflow manually. You can use this class to perform administrative functions or to generate reports. For example, you can use the GetItemActiveWorkflows method to retrieve a list of all the workflow instances currently running for a given list item.

Workflow Template

The SPWorkflowTemplate class provides a code-based representation of the attributes specified in the workflow.xml file associated with the SharePoint feature used to deploy the workflow. The workflow template provides basic information about the workflow that SharePoint uses to create workflow instances and to manage the workflow lifecycle.

Workflow Association

The SPWorkflowAssociation class is what SharePoint uses to bind a workflow template with a given list or content type. You can use objects of this class to control how the binding is applied when the workflow is run. For example, you can modify the workflow association object to change whether the workflow is started automatically when an item is created, or you can specify which lists are used to create workflow tasks or history list items.

The following code segment uses the SPWorkflowAssociation class to associate a workflow with items in a task list so that the workflow is started automatically when a new task is created:

```
using System;
using System.Globalization;
using System.Collections.Generic;
using System.Text;
using Microsoft.SharePoint;
using Microsoft.SharePoint.Workflow;

namespace ProSharePoint2007.TaskAssociation
{
    class Program
    {
        static void Main(string[] args)
        {
            using (SPSite site =
                new SPSite("http://moss/SiteDirectory/Testing"))
            {
                using (SPWeb web = site.OpenWeb())
                {
                    SPList tasks = web.Lists["Tasks"];
                    SPWorkflowManager wfManager = site.WorkflowManager;
                    SPWorkflowTemplateCollection wfTemplates
                        = wfManager.GetWorkflowTemplatesByCategory(web, null);
                    SPWorkflowTemplate wfTemplate
                        = wfTemplates.GetTemplateByName(
                            "TaskReminder",CultureInfo.CurrentCulture);
                    SPWorkflowAssociation wfAssociation
                        = SPWorkflowAssociation.CreateListAssociation(
                            wfTemplate, wfTemplate.Name, null, null);
                    wfAssociation.AutoStartCreate = true;
                    tasks.AddWorkflowAssociation(wfAssociation);
                }
            }
        }
    }
}
```

Workflow Instance

The SPWorkflow object represents a workflow instance that has been run or is currently running on a list item. You get a SPWorkflow object when you start or resume a workflow from the workflow manager, or when you retrieve the collection of workflows associated with a list item. You can then use the object to retrieve additional information about the workflow instance, such as whether it is completed and the identifiers of objects associated with it.

Workflow Modification

The SPWorkflowModification object is used to apply changes to a running workflow instance. You start by creating the modification object and then call the SPWorkflowManager.ModifyWorkflow method to apply the changes. This is the same object used internally when you create a modification form for a workflow. Because of this, using the SPWorkflowModification object programmatically can be a bit tricky. In particular, the context data specified in the call must match the modification form schema expected by the workflow.

The modification form schema is mapped to the workflow by a GUID that was specified in the associated workflow template. Even if there is no context data available, you still have to supply a well-formed XML string that matches the schema.

Workflow Task

SharePoint uses the native task content type through a derived type called `SPWorkflowTask` and task list support to maintain the tasks that users need to complete. By building on the task type, workflow tasks get the same support as other SharePoint tasks such as the ability to take those tasks offline in Outlook and complete the workflows through the Outlook client.

Outlook assigns the workflow task to the `IPM.Task.Microsoft.Workflow` message class. By using this custom message class, Outlook can perform special activities on the task and display a customized user interface for workflow tasks.

The `SPTask` object exposes a number of additional properties and methods for working with workflows. The following table describes these members.

Property / Method	Description
WorkflowId	Identifies the workflow attached to the item.
AlterTask	Modifies one or more properties in the task item. Modifications can be performed synchronously or asynchronously.
GetExtendedPropertiesAsHashtable	Retrieves the collection of extended properties associated with the task item.
GetWorkflowData	Retrieves the workflow data as a string.

Workflow Roles

One important part of workflows, beyond sequencing the activities that make up your workflow, is the ability to use roles rather than hard-coded names. For example, you may want to create a role called expense approvers so that as approvers change, your workflow does not have to change. Instead, you add or remove people from the role rather than from the workflow.

WF includes a pluggable roles repository that lets you extend the built-in `WorkflowRole` abstract class to implement your own roles repository. Out of the box, WF ships with a role provider for Active Directory through the `ActiveDirectoryRole` class. Active Directory groups provide the role infrastructure. For example, you would create an AD group for expense approvers and then add people to that Active Directory group. WF supports nesting and expansion of groups so that if the Active Directory group contains other groups, WF will expand each group until all users are retrieved for the role.

Beyond supporting Active Directory groups, WF also supports an object model for getting other organizational information about the users in a role. For example, you can use the methods provided by the `System.Workflow.Activities.ActiveDirectoryRole` class to retrieve other roles that relate to the current role.

The SharePoint Workflow Service APIs

To understand how SharePoint workflow really works, you have to take a peek under the covers to see what's going on because the terminology can be confusing. It is doubly confusing when the same terminology refers to different objects, depending on your point of view.

The heart of the SharePoint Workflow architecture centers around four interfaces that provide the methods and events needed to process SharePoint events and manipulate SharePoint objects. These are `ISharePointService`, `IListItemService`, `ITaskService`, and `IWorkflowModificationService`. These services support the SharePoint Workflow Actions and do all of the actual work. In fact, the methods and events of these core services map one-to-one to corresponding activity classes in the `Microsoft.SharePoint.WorkflowActions` namespace. These are the components you use to build your workflows.

Figure 15-8 illustrates the starting portion of a sequential workflow that writes a string to the workflow history list and creates a SharePoint task item. This illustration should give some perspective on how the SharePoint Workflow Service APIs operate in tandem with the workflow activities to accomplish the desired results.

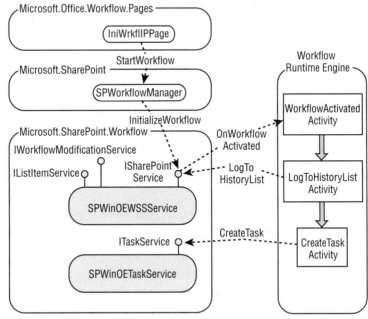

Figure 15-8

The default implementation of the workflow initiation page is a standard web page that hosts the `XMLFormView` control so that it can display and process an InfoPath workflow initiation form. When the user submits the form, the workflow initiation page calls the `SPWorkflowManager` to start the workflow, passing the initial metadata in an XML string. The workflow manager creates a new workflow instance, and then calls into the `ISharePointService` interface of the `SPWinOEWSSService` object to initialize the workflow. That object fires an event that is handled by the `WorkflowActivated` activity, which is always the first activity in a sequential workflow. As the various activities of the workflow are executed, calls are made to the various services to manipulate SharePoint objects and data.

If you want to use this approach for your own custom service, then you must remember to define an interface which is decorated with the `ExternalDataExchange` attribute and has been properly registered with the workflow runtime engine. For more information, see the Windows Workflow Foundation Programming Guide (`http://msdn2.microsoft.com/en-us/library/ms734702.aspx`).

The following tables list the methods and events exposed by the SharePoint Workflow Service APIs.

The ISharePointService Interface

The `ISharePointService` interface specifies the core set of methods and events for managing the workflow at a high level. It also provides catch-all support for performing functions that fall outside the context of a list item, task, or workflow instance. The following tables describe the methods and events that are defined for this interface.

Methods

Method	Description
InitializeWorkflow	This method acts as a placeholder for setting up the correlation token for the workflow instance. It assumes that the workflow identifier will be assigned prior to the call.
LogToHistoryList	Appends an item to the history list associated with a workflow. The history list displays tracking information and acts as a log that the user can review to verify that certain actions were taken and the results of those actions.
SendEmail	Schedules an email message to be sent using the `SPUtility.SendMail` method.
SetState	Changes the currently executing state activity in a state-machine workflow.
UpdateAllTasks	Applies a set of properties to all `SPWorkflowTask` objects in a specified workflow.

Events

Event	Description
OnWorkflowActivated	Called at the beginning of a sequential workflow.
OnWorkflowItemChanged	Called when an item has changed in the list to which the workflow is attached.
OnWorkflowItemDeleted	Called when a list item is deleted from the list to which the workflow is attached.

The ITaskService Interface

The ITaskService interface specifies the methods and events needed to support the manipulation of SharePoint task items, as described in the following table.

Methods

Method	Description
CreateTask	Creates a SharePoint task item.
CreateTaskWithContentType	Creates a SharePoint task item of a given content type. This is used in cases where the list supports multiple content types and you want to create an instance of a specific type.
UpdateTask	Schedules the application of a set of properties to a given task item.
DeleteTask	Schedules the deletion of a task item.
CompleteTask	Marks a task item as complete.
RollbackTask	Rolls back changes made to a task item since the last time changes were committed.

Events

Event	Description
OnTaskCreated	Fires whenever a new task is created
OnTaskDeleted	Fires whenever an existing task is deleted
OnTaskChanged	Fires whenever an existing task is modified

The IListItemService Interface

The following table describes the IListItemService interface, which provides general support for managing non-task-list items.

It is interesting to note that the events declared on this interface are similar to the methods of the SPItemEventReceiver class, except that there are no synchronous events, the ItemAdded event is called ItemCreated, the ItemUpdated event is called ItemChanged, and there is no event for ItemFileConverted.

Methods

Method	Description
CheckInListItem	Checks in a list item with a comment.
CheckOutListItem	Checks out a list item.
CopyListItem	Copies a list item from one list to another.
CreateDocument	Creates a document in a list. You pass in the item properties in a hashtable along with a byte array.
CreateListItem	Creates a new item in a list from properties passed in a hashtable.
DeleteListItem	Removes an item from a list.
InitializeForEvent	This method acts as a placeholder for setting up correlation tokens for the workflow, list, and list item on which the other methods will operate.
UndoCheckOutListItem	Undoes a checkout operation for a list item.
UpdateDocument	Updates a document from properties passed in a hashtable along with new content passed in a byte array.
UpdateListItem	Updates a list item from properties passed in a hashtable.

Events

Event	Description
OnItemAttachmentAdded	Fires after an attachment has been added to an item
OnItemAttachmentDeleted	Fires after an attachment has been deleted from an item
OnItemChanged	Fires after an item has been modified
OnItemCheckedIn	Fires after an item has been checked in

Event	Description
OnItemCheckedOut	Fires after an item has been checked out
OnItemCreated	Fires after an item has been created
OnItemDeleted	Fires after an item has been deleted
OnItemFileMoved	Fires after item's file has been moved
OnItemUncheckedOut	Fires after an item check out has been revoked

The IWorkflowModificationService Interface

This interface supports scenarios in which modifications must be made to a running workflow.

Methods

Method	Description
EnableWorkflowModification	Adds a new SPWorkflowModification object to the workflow depending on whether or not the specified modification already exists within the workflow

Events

Event	Description
OnWorkflowModified	Fires whenever a modification is added to a workflow instance

The MOSS Workflow Implementation

WSS hosts the runtime engine for WF. The WSS host provides a number of key services for WF including persistence, event delivery, timer, history, and reporting and application integration. Some of these services are transparent to you such as the persistence service, while you can program against others using the WSS WF object model.

Activities in MOSS

Activities work differently in SharePoint than in a normal workflow. Typically, when creating a workflow you can write code activities and other kinds of activities and not be concerned about synchronization issues. However, with SharePoint due to optimizations that have been implemented in the SharePoint Workflow Service, it is important to understand the sequence of events that take place when SharePoint-specific workflow activities are interspersed with your own code activities.

The problem is the optimization. When a Windows SharePoint Services 3.0 workflow runs, it may make changes to list items or other data that is ultimately stored within the Windows SharePoint Services 3.0 content database. SharePoint caches all write operations until the next time the workflow reaches a point at which it is waiting for input or is otherwise stalled waiting for some event to occur. At that time SharePoint commits the changes to the content database bypassing the normal write operations that might occur if one were calling the SharePoint object model directly to effect those changes. Instead of calling the object model, SharePoint wraps the write operations into a single SQL transaction and then commits them directly to the content database. This approach, while making SharePoint workflows perform better, has implications for workflow activities that use the object model to manipulate SharePoint data.

It is possible that a code-based activity may commit changes to the SharePoint database ahead of SharePoint activities that execute before the code-based activity is run. This is particularly important for code-based activities that need to check the status of a SharePoint list item. It is also possible that changes made by a code-based activity are subsequently overwritten by cached changes recorded by a prior SharePoint activity. Finally, since all of the uncommitted changes are wrapped in a SQL transaction, unpredictable results can occur when SharePoint attempts to roll back to the previous "commit point" when a failure is encountered. To avoid these kinds of synchronization problems, the recommended approach when building SharePoint workflows is to use the SharePoint Workflow Service API to manipulate SharePoint data.

Core Activities

The activities in this group inherit from the `CallExternalMethodActivity` or `HandleExternalEventActivity` classes, which enable a workflow to communicate with a local service. In this case, the activities correspond to methods and events exposed by the SharePoint Workflow Service APIs. Thus, for each method in the Service API interfaces, there is a corresponding class that serves as a wrapper for the call. This architecture allows service calls to be incorporated easily into the workflow designer.

Declarative, No-Code Activities

The following activities were designed for use in declarative, no-code workflows such as those created in SharePoint Designer 2007 and are not supported by the Visual Studio graphical designer.

Activity	Description
AddArrayToArrayListActivity	Merges two array lists to create a single list that is the sum of the original two.
AddTimeToDateActivity	Adds days, hours, and minutes to a `DateTime` object.
AddToArrayListActivity	Adds a value to an array list.
AddToHashtableActivity	Adds an object and a string key to a hashtable.
ApplyActivation	Applies a set of workflow properties to a workflow instance.
BuildStringActivity	Provides dynamic string formatting by decoding a string expression and performing parameter substitution.

Activity	Description
CheckInItemActivity	Checks in a document to its associated document library.
CheckOutItemActivity	Checks out a document from its associated document library.
ClearArrayListActivity	Removes all items from an array list.
ClearHashtableActivity	Removes all items from a hashtable.
CollectDataTask	Assigns a task to a user, returning the list item ID of the task created when the user submits the task form as complete.
ConvertActivity	Performs basic type conversion on an object.
CopyItemActivity	Copies an item from one list to another.
CreateItemActivity	Creates a new list item or document library item.
CurrentDateActivity	Retrieves the current date.
DeleteItemActivity	Deletes a specified list item or document library item.
EmailActivity	Sends an email message to a specified list of recipients.
FindActivity	Searches for a list item in another list using values taken from the item on which the workflow instance is running.
FindValueActivity	Implements the IDynamicPropertyTypeProvider interface to support dynamic value resolution.
GroupAssignedTask	Assigns a task to a group of users in parallel. Use this activity to assign a task that requires users to enter the information in the task form and then submit the form as completed. All users in the group must submit the form as completed before the activity is considered finished. When a sequence activity is started, the workflow is suspended until the activity is completed.
Helper	Exposes a set of helper methods that enable SharePoint Designer 2007 to map user interface components to high-level commands.
LookupActivity	Looks up data from a list.
MathActivity	Provides a set of fields that can be used to perform simple arithmetic operations.

Continued

Activity	Description
SetFieldActivity	Sets a field in a list item to a specified value.
SetModerationStatusActivity	Sets the content approval status for a list item or a document library item.
SetTimeFieldActivity	Sets the time portion of a DateTime object.
SetVariableActivity	Sets the value of a workflow variable.
TodoItemTask	Assigns a "to do" task to a group of users in parallel.
UndoCheckOutItemActivity	Undoes a document check out operation.
UpdateItemActivity	Updates an item in a list or document library.
UpdateTask	Updates a task list item.
WaitForActivity	Pauses the workflow until the specified list field equals a specified value.

The Built-In Workflows

To show you the basic pieces of how you develop workflows, looking at the out-of-the-box workflows is a great place to start. If you do not have MOSS installed, you will see only the tri-state workflow as part of your WSS deployment. So, you can build workflows on WSS without MOSS, but you don't get the powerful set of built-in workflows that come with MOSS. The following table outlines the capabilities that each of the built-in MOSS workflows provides.

These workflows are not customizable. You cannot take them into Visual Studio to tweak them or modify their flow. This is unfortunate, because if you want to extend the built-in workflows, you have to rewrite them completely. The built-in workflows are complex, so rewriting them is not a simple task. You can, however, embed them into other workflows to incorporate their functionality. For example, you could create a state-machine workflow that calls the built-in approval workflow under certain conditions.

Workflow	Description
Approval	The Approval workflow routes the content for approval. You can set up this workflow as serial or parallel as well as preset the approvers. This could be considered a "workhorse" workflow in the sense that there are many scenarios where it can be used.
Collect Feedback	Routes the content for feedback. When the workflow completes all the feedback is sent to the originator of the workflow.
Collect Signatures	Rather than just sending content for approval, this workflow requires digital signatures on the content. This workflow requires the Office 2007 client and can only be initiated from a client application.

Workflow	Description
Disposition Approval	This workflow works with the records management capabilities of SharePoint. It allows you to manage document expiration and retention.
Group Approval	To support hierarchical approvals, this workflow presents a hierarchical control to select the approvers and stamping rather than signatures for approval.
Translation Management	This workflow is used with the web content management features of SharePoint to support a translation workflow for content to multiple languages.
Issue Tracking	This workflow ships with WSS and is a simple issue-tracking workflow that shows status of active and resolved issues.

Workflow Development

The first step in developing custom workflows is to decide which tools you want to use. Each tool has different capabilities, strengths, and weaknesses. SharePoint Designer 2007 (SPD) presents a declarative workflow design experience and includes a wizard to create workflows that is similar to the Outlook Rules Wizard. Visual Studio 2005, on the other hand, presents a graphical design experience with its integrated workflow designer as well as a low-level code-based design experience with the Visual Studio extensions for WF. Visual Studio gives you more power, but is more complex than SharePoint Designer.

The tool that you decide to use depends on a number of factors. First, you should decide whether you really need to develop a custom workflow at all. The default workflows included with SharePoint resolve a number of business scenarios and are somewhat customizable through various configuration options. If you need something more powerful or customizable, then you should compare the features and capabilities of SharePoint Designer with those of Visual Studio 2005. The following table presents key points of comparison between the two development environments:

Category	SharePoint Designer	Visual Studio
Supported WF Hosts	WSS/MOSS	WSS/MOSS/Others
Development Model	Wizard based	Graphical Designer
Supported Workflows	Sequential Only	Sequential and State Machine
Workflow type	Markup only. The markup file, rules and supporting files are not compiled.	Markup with code-beside compiled into an assembly.

Continued

Category	SharePoint Designer	Visual Studio
Code Beside	No	Yes
Activities	Built-in and use custom activities developed separately.	Built-in; use and develop custom activities.
Forms Technology	Autogenerated, customizable ASP.NET forms	Design forms in any forms technology such as ASP.NET or InfoPath.
Association	Associated automatically with a single list at design time. No other associations are possible.	Can be associated with multiple content types, lists, and document libraries.
Initiation	Initiation forms are supported.	Initiation forms are supported.
Modification	Cannot modify workflow through modification forms.	Modification supported.
Tasks	Supports custom task forms.	Supports custom task forms.
Deployment	Automatically deployed to the associated list.	Must create a separate package and deploy the workflow using SharePoint feature technology.
Debugging	No debugging available.	Debug directly within Visual Studio.

Admittedly, there is a lot to get your head around before you can develop workflows in MOSS. It is a gradual process of becoming familiar with all the moving parts, and then it just starts to click. According to the SharePoint Enterprise Content Management (ECM) team (the ones who developed the SharePoint workflow components), you can make the process easier by taking the time to plan and model the workflow before attempting to implement it. You then create the required forms and activities, implement the workflow, deploy it to the server, and test it.

Plan the Workflow

SharePoint workflows are constrained by two factors: they involve human beings and they are tied to SharePoint content. You can take advantage of these constraints when planning your workflow to stay focused on the requirements and not get distracted by the complexities involved in its design and construction.

What Does It Do?

The first thing to consider is what you want the workflow to do. Remembering that SharePoint workflows are tied to content, an appropriate question might be whether the workflow will manipulate that content. If not, then a declarative approach might suffice or you might be able to develop and debug the workflow outside of the SharePoint environment.

If the workflow needs to manipulate content, then a second question might be what kind of content? If you are developing a custom content type in conjunction with the workflow, then you need to consider how best to incorporate the required metadata. If the metadata that the workflow needs to manipulate is large and complex, then you might consider implementing helper methods in a separate assembly that you can call easily from within the workflow.

Where Does The Data Come From?

Another thing to consider is where the data for the workflow will come from. If coming from the document library or list item to which the workflow instance is attached, then the workflow host created by SharePoint will provide you with the data you need. If, on the other hand, the data comes from another document library or list item, you will need to use the SharePoint object model to retrieve it. This may introduce dependencies and performance constraints you need to consider before getting into the workflow design. The same holds true for data that you retrieve from external data sources. For more information, see the later section about how workflow activities are processed by the SharePoint host.

Where Does The Data Go?

During workflow processing, new data may be created that needs to be stored. If it needs to be written to a SharePoint list item, then you need to consider when and how the data will be committed to the item. This is especially true when developing custom activities that may be reused and incorporated into new workflows, perhaps in novel ways you did not consider when designing the activity. In general, the best way to ensure consistency is to use the interfaces provided by the `Microsoft.SharePoint.Workflow` namespace, namely the `ISharePointService`, `IListItemService`, `ITaskService`, and `IWorkflowModificationService` interfaces.

Who Are the Actors?

It is important to consider who will be performing actions over the life of the workflow. With any workflow, there is at least one actor, namely the workflow itself. SharePoint workflows run as the System Account and therefore have administrator privileges. This means that the workflow can perform actions that other users cannot, including the person who started the workflow. You can take advantage of this when designing workflows that need built-in administrative, logging, or auditing features.

Perhaps no human interaction is necessary at all and the workflow can run to completion on its own. Perhaps you need to take prescriptive action if a user fails to complete a task within a given time limit, or you need to provide a way for list administrators to ignore unresponsive users. Understanding the primary and secondary actors can provide a great deal of clarity when designing workflows, especially when developing workflow models.

Model the Workflow

After planning the workflow, it is very helpful to create a model that captures the overall flow of information. This also helps highlight hidden data dependencies and environmental requirements that would be more difficult to resolve at a later stage in the development process. The model does not have to be complete or even precisely correct. Its main purpose at this stage is to act as a map for the actual workflow design and to pinpoint additional resources which may be required for implementation.

Microsoft Office Visio is a great tool for workflow modeling, because it helps you keep the entire workflow in perspective without getting distracted by low-level design details. For instance, when modeling in Visio, there is no need to decide which activities to use for what purpose or to think about parameter validation, correlation tokens, and the like. By contrast, modeling the same workflow in the Visual Studio graphical designer introduces all these concepts and quickly pulls you away from the high level perspective you want at this stage.

Choose a Visio stencil that best matches the type of workflow you are building. For simple sequential workflows, the basic flowchart stencil should suffice. For more complex sequential workflows where many actors are involved, the cross-functional flowchart stencil works well. Figure 15-9 shows a Visio model of an expense reporting workflow using this approach.

A good rule of thumb is that if you can't capture a sequential workflow in one or two pages, then consider switching to a state machine. The Visio data-flow stencil works well for modeling state-machine workflows. Figure 15-10 shows an example of a state-machine workflow for sending reminders about tasks that are in danger of running behind schedule.

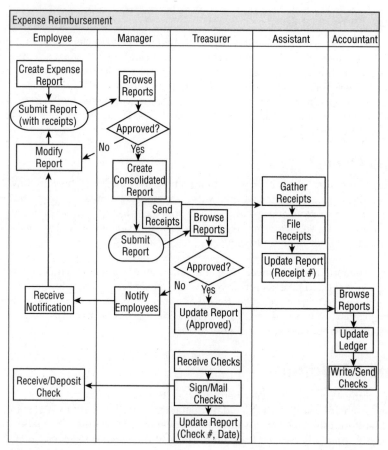

Figure 15-9

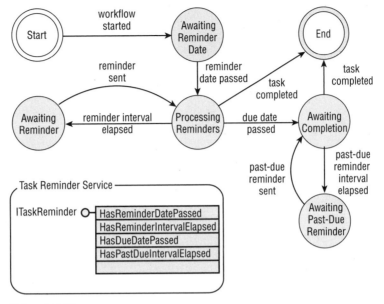

Figure 15-10

Create and Bind Forms

From the model, you should be able to determine what data will be needed at each stage of the workflow. With this information, you can proceed to decide what types of forms will be required and implement prototypes for them. There are four types of forms you can use with a SharePoint workflow: association, initiation, task edit, and workflow modification. You typically create these forms using InfoPath. This is the easiest method for two reasons. First, InfoPath takes care of the low-level details required to publish the form and make it accessible from within your workflow. Second, the default ASPX forms are already implemented and are prewired to store and retrieve data from InfoPath forms, which they host using the `XMLFormView` control. If you decide to replace the default ASPX pages with your own custom forms, then you must implement the required logic yourself. The following sections explain how this is done.

The Association Form

Association forms are used to gather data needed before the workflow starts. This information might include decisions for the workflow administrator, such as who should receive notifications for certain workflow events or where to store workflow tracking information. It is the responsibility of the association form to create an `SPWorkflowAssociation` object that binds the workflow to a given list or content type.

The default association form is implemented in `CstWrkflIP.aspx`, which uses the `XmlFormView` control to host an InfoPath form. If you wish to use simple web controls instead of an InfoPath form, you could use code similar to the following, replacing the code in boldface type with your own custom code that constructs the XML data string:

```
using System;
using System.Web;
```

```
using System.Web.UI;
using System.Web.UI.WebControls;
using Microsoft.SharePoint;
using Microsoft.SharePoint.Workflow;
using Microsoft.SharePoint.WebControls;

namespace ProSharePoint2007
{
    class CustomAssociationPage : Page
    {
        protected Button m_btnSubmit;
        protected TextBox m_editText;
        protected SPWeb m_web;
        protected SPList m_list;
        protected SPList m_taskList;
        protected SPList m_historyList;
        protected string m_taskListName;
        protected string m_historyListName;
        protected SPWorkflowAssociation m_assocTemplate;
        protected SPWorkflowTemplate m_baseTemplate;
        protected string m_workflowName;

        protected override void OnInit(EventArgs e)
        {
            base.OnInit(e);
            m_btnSubmit.Click += new EventHandler(m_btnSubmit_Click);
        }

        protected override void OnLoad(EventArgs e)
        {
            base.OnLoad(e);
            m_web = SPControl.GetContextWeb(this.Context);
            m_taskListName = Request.Params["TaskList"];
            m_historyListName = Request.Params["HistoryList"];
            m_worfklowName = Request.Params["WorkflowName"];
            m_list = m_web.Lists[new Guid(Request.QueryString["List"])];
            m_taskList = m_web.Lists[m_taskListName];
            m_historyList = m_web.Lists[m_historyListName];
            m_baseTemplate = m_web.WorkflowTemplates[
                new Guid(Request.Params["WorkflowDefinition"])];
            m_assocTemplate = null;
        }

        void m_btnSubmit_Click(object sender, EventArgs e)
        {
            DoAssociation(GetFormData());
        }

        protected string GetFormData()
        {
            string xmlData;
            // code to construct an xml string
            // from your web controls
            // for example...
```

```
                xmlData = String.Format(
                    "<MyCustomData>{0}</MyCustomData>",m_editText.Text);
                return xmlData;
            }

            protected void DoAssociation(string xmlFormData)
            {
                if (m_assocTemplate != null)
                {
                    m_assocTemplate.Name = m_workflowName;
                    m_assocTemplate.SetTaskList(m_taskList);
                    m_assocTemplate.SetHistoryList(m_historyList);
                    m_assocTemplate.AssociationData = xmlFormData;
                    m_list.AddWorkflowAssociation(m_assocTemplate);
                }
            }
        }
    }
}
```

The Initiation Form

Initiation forms are used to gather information needed when the workflow starts, such as who shall be assigned a given task or where to place the finished document. Another way to think of the difference between association forms and initiation forms is that association forms apply to the workflow class or type, whereas initiation forms apply to workflow instances. It is the responsibility of the initiation form to actually start the workflow instance.

The default workflow initiation form calls the SPWorkflowManager.StartWorkflow method to create a workflow instance, passing the current list item, the SPWorkflowAssociation object bound to the list and the XML string containing the data entered into the form. When the workflow instance is created, the StartWorkflow method passes the association data and initiation data to the workflow in the SPWorkflowProperties parameter of the OnWorkflowActivated activity.

If you wish to use a web form instead of InfoPath, you could use code similar to the following, replacing the code in boldface type with your own custom code that retrieves the initiation form data from your web controls:

```
using System;
using System.Web;
using System.Web.UI;
using System.Web.UI.WebControls;
using System.Globalization;
using Microsoft.SharePoint;
using Microsoft.SharePoint.Workflow;
using Microsoft.SharePoint.WebControls;
using Microsoft.SharePoint.Utilities;

namespace ProSharePoint2007
{
    class CustomInitiationPage : Page
    {
        protected Button m_btnSubmit;
        protected SPWorkflowAssociation m_assocTemplate;
```

```
protected SPWorkflowTemplate m_baseTemplate;
protected SPWeb m_web;
protected SPList m_list;
protected SPListItem m_listItem;
protected string m_listItemName;
protected string m_listItemUrl;
protected string m_workflowName;

protected override void OnInit(EventArgs e)
{
    base.OnInit(e);
    m_btnSubmit.Click
      += new EventHandler(m_btnSubmit_Click);
}


protected override void OnLoad(EventArgs e)
{
    base.OnLoad(e);
    m_web = SPControl.GetContextWeb(this.Context);
    m_list = m_web.Lists[
      new Guid(Request.QueryString["List"])];
    m_listItem = m_list.GetItemById(
        Convert.ToInt32(Request.Params["ID"],
        CultureInfo.InvariantCulture));
    Guid associationId =
      new Guid(Request.Params["TemplateID"]);
    m_assocTemplate =
      SPWorkflowAssociationCollection
        .GetAssociationForListItemById(
          m_listItem, associationId);
    if (m_assocTemplate == null)
    {
        throw new SPException(
          "Missing Association Template");
    }
    m_baseTemplate = m_assocTemplate.BaseTemplate;
    m_workflowName = m_assocTemplate.Name;
    m_formData = m_assocTemplate.AssociationData;

    if (m_listItem.File != null)
    {
        m_listItemUrl = m_web.Url + "/"
          + m_listItem.File.Url;
    }
    else
    {
        m_listItemUrl = m_web.Url
          + m_listItem.ParentList
            .Forms[PAGETYPE.PAGE_DISPLAYFORM]
            .ServerRelativeUrl + "?ID="
              +
                m_listItem.ID.ToString(
                  CultureInfo.InvariantCulture);
    }
```

```csharp
            if (m_list.BaseType
                != SPBaseType.DocumentLibrary)
            {
                m_listItemName = m_listItem.Title;
            }
            else
            {
                m_listItemName = m_listItem.Name;
                int length = m_listItemName
                                .LastIndexOf('.');
                if (length > 0)
                {
                    m_listItemName
                       = m_listItemName.Substring(0, length);
                }
            }
        }


        /// <summary>
        /// Returns a formatted XML string
        /// containing the form data.
        /// </summary>
        protected string GetInitiationFormData()
        {
            // Pull the data from embedded web controls
            // and format as an XML string.
            return
                "<MyCustomData>Custom Data Goes Here</MyCustomData>";
        }

        void m_btnSubmit_Click(object sender, EventArgs e)
        {
            string urlRedirect = m_list.DefaultViewUrl;
            SPLongOperation operation =
              new SPLongOperation(this);
            try
            {
                operation.Begin();
                try
                {
                    // Start the workflow using
                    // the custom form data.
                    m_web.Site.WorkflowManager
                       .StartWorkflow(
                          m_listItem, m_assocTemplate,
                             GetInitiationFormData());
                }
                catch (UnauthorizedAccessException uex)
                {
                    SPUtility.HandleAccessDenied(uex);
                }
                catch (Exception ex)
                {
                    SPUtility
```

```
                        .TransferToErrorPage(ex.Message);
                }
                operation.End(urlRedirect,
                    SPRedirectFlags.Static,
                    this.Context, null);
            }
            finally
            {
                if (operation != null)
                {
                    operation.Dispose();
                }
            }
        }
    }
}
```

The Task Edit Form

Task edit forms are specialized forms used for interacting with users while the workflow is being processed. It is easy to confuse workflow task edit forms with the standard edit forms used for SharePoint task list items. Task edit forms work with SPWorkflowTask objects, not task list items. SPWorkflowTask is a special derived SPListItem that includes additional fields and methods for working with workflows, such as the workflow identifier and the AlterTask method used to modify task properties.

If you want to use a web form instead of InfoPath, you can use the following code to obtain the underlying task item, and then add your own custom controls to enable the end user to manipulate the task properties. When the user is ready to submit the changes, you can call the AlterTask method as illustrated by the code shown in boldface type.

```
using System;
using System.Collections;
using System.IO;
using System.Web;
using System.Web.UI;
using System.Web.UI.WebControls;
using System.Globalization;
using System.Xml;
using Microsoft.SharePoint;
using Microsoft.SharePoint.Workflow;
using Microsoft.SharePoint.WebControls;
using Microsoft.SharePoint.Utilities;

namespace ProSharePoint2007
{
    class CustomTaskEditPage : Page
    {
        protected Button m_btnSubmit;
        protected SPWeb m_web;
        protected SPList m_list;
        protected SPListItem m_task;
        protected string m_taskName;
        protected string m_workflowName;
        protected string m_formData;
```

```
protected override void OnInit(EventArgs e)
{
    base.OnInit(e);
    m_btnSubmit.Click +=
      new EventHandler(m_btnSubmit_Click);
}

protected override void OnLoad(EventArgs e)
{
    base.OnLoad(e);
    m_web = SPControl.GetContextWeb(this.Context);
    m_list = m_web.Lists[
        new Guid(Request.QueryString["List"])];
    m_task = m_list.GetItemById(
        Convert.ToInt32(Request.Params["ID"],
            CultureInfo.InvariantCulture));
    m_task.CheckPermissions(
        SPBasePermissions.EditListItems);
    Guid workflowInstanceId =

        new Guid((string)m_task[
            SPBuiltInFieldId.WorkflowInstanceID]);
    SPWorkflow workflow =
        new SPWorkflow(m_web, workflowInstanceId);
    SPList parentList = null;
    try
    {
        parentList = workflow.ParentList;
    }
    catch
    {
    }
    if (parentList != null
          && workflow.VisibleParentItem)
    {
        SPWorkflowAssociation parentAssociation
            = workflow.ParentAssociation;
        SPWorkflowTemplate baseTemplate
            = parentAssociation.BaseTemplate;

        m_workflowName = parentAssociation.Name;
        m_taskName = (string)m_task[
            SPBuiltInFieldId.Title];
        m_formData = (string)m_task[
            SPBuiltInFieldId.FormData];
    }
}

static Hashtable XmlToHashtable(string xml)
{
    Hashtable hashtable = new Hashtable();
    XmlTextReader reader = new XmlTextReader(
        new StringReader(xml));
    if (!reader.IsEmptyElement)
    {
        reader.ReadStartElement();
```

```
            while (reader.IsStartElement())
            {
                string text = XmlConvert.DecodeName(
                    reader.LocalName);
                string text2 = reader.ReadInnerXml();
                hashtable[text] = text2;
            }
            if (reader.NodeType != XmlNodeType.None)
            {
                reader.ReadEndElement();
                return hashtable;
            }
            return hashtable;
        }
        return hashtable;
}


void m_btnSubmit_Click(object sender, EventArgs e)
{
    Hashtable formData =
        XmlToHashtable(m_formData);
    using (SPLongOperation operation =
        new SPLongOperation(this))
    {
        string url = null;
        if (!SPUtility.DetermineRedirectUrl(
                m_list.DefaultViewUrl,
            SPRedirectFlags.DoNotEncodeUrl
                | SPRedirectFlags.UseSource,
            this.Context, null, out url))
        {
            url = m_list.DefaultViewUrl;
        }
        try
        {
            operation.Begin();
            if (!SPWorkflowTask.AlterTask(m_task,
                                formData, true))
            {
                SPUtility.TransferToErrorPage(
                    "Rolling back: \n\n{0}",
                    SPResource.GetString(
                        "WorkflowTaskRollbackPageLinkText",
                        new object[0]),
                    url);
            }
            operation.End(url,
                SPRedirectFlags.Static,
                this.Context, null);
        }
        catch
        {
        }
```

```
                    }
                }
            }
        }
    }
```

The Workflow Modification Form

Workflow modification forms are used to modify running workflows. When presented to an end user, this form calls the `SPWorkflowManager.ModifyWorkflow` method, passing its data as an XML string. This string is then passed along to the `OnWorkflowModified` activity in the `ContextData` parameter. Listing 15-2 implements a custom web form that can be used instead of an InfoPath form.

Listing 15-2

```
using System;
using System.Collections;
using System.IO;
using System.Web;
using System.Web.UI;
using System.Web.UI.WebControls;
using System.Globalization;
using System.Xml;
using Microsoft.SharePoint;
using Microsoft.SharePoint.Workflow;
using Microsoft.SharePoint.WebControls;
using Microsoft.SharePoint.Utilities;

namespace ProSharePoint2007
{
    class CustomWorkflowModificationPage : Page
    {
        protected Button m_btnSubmit;
        protected SPWeb m_web;
        protected SPList m_list;
        protected SPListItem m_listItem;
        protected SPWorkflow m_workflow;
        protected SPWorkflowModification m_modification;
        protected Guid m_modificationId;
        protected Guid m_workflowId;
        protected string m_workflowName;
        protected string m_formData;

        protected override void OnInit(EventArgs e)
        {
            base.OnInit(e);
            m_btnSubmit.Click += new EventHandler(m_btnSubmit_Click);
        }

        protected override void OnLoad(EventArgs e)
        {
            base.OnLoad(e);
            m_web = SPControl.GetContextWeb(this.Context);
            m_list = m_web.Lists[new Guid(Request.QueryString["List"])];
```

```
            m_workflowId = new Guid(base.Request.Params["WorkflowInstanceID"]);
            m_modificationId = new Guid(Request.Params["ModificationID"]);
            m_workflow = new SPWorkflow(m_web, m_workflowId);
            SPWorkflowTemplate baseTemplate
                = m_workflow.ParentAssociation.BaseTemplate;
            m_modification = m_workflow.Modifications[ m_modificationId ];
            m_workflowName = m_workflow.ParentAssociation.Name;
            m_listItem = m_workflow.ParentItem;
            string modificationFormat
                = (string)baseTemplate["Modification_Format"];
            if (m_modification == null)
            {
                throw new SPException("Invalid Workflow State");
            }
            m_formData = m_modification.ContextData;
            if (m_workflow.Author != m_workflow.ParentWeb.CurrentUser.ID)
            {
                m_workflow.ParentList.CheckPermissions(
                    SPBasePermissions.EmptyMask
                    | SPBasePermissions.ManageLists);
            }
            if (!string.IsNullOrEmpty(modificationFormat))
            {
                m_formData = string.Format(modificationFormat, m_formData);
            }
        }

    void m_btnSubmit_Click(object sender, EventArgs e)
    {
        using (SPLongOperation operation = new SPLongOperation(this))
        {
            string url = null;
            if (!SPUtility.DetermineRedirectUrl(m_list.DefaultViewUrl,
                SPRedirectFlags.DoNotEncodeUrl | SPRedirectFlags.UseSource,
                this.Context, null, out url))
            {
                url = m_list.DefaultViewUrl;
            }
            try
            {
                operation.Begin();
                m_web.Site.WorkflowManager.ModifyWorkflow(
                    m_workflow, m_modification, m_formData);
                operation.End(url, SPRedirectFlags.Static,
                    this.Context, null);
            }
            catch
            {
            }
        }
    }
}
}
}
```

Identify/Create Activities

Using the model and the forms as a guide, you can begin to identify the workflow activities that satisfy your requirements. Ideally, there will already be a library of suitable activities to choose from. Even if that is the case, you should consider creating your own composite activities and an associated set of service interfaces that encapsulate your solution. Whether you decide to do so or not, this stage in the workflow development process — just prior to implementation — is the ideal time to start thinking about how this workflow can be reused. Packaging existing activities into a reusable set can greatly simplify the development of future workflows that require similar functionality.

Implement the Workflow

After you have identified and/or created the required activities, you are ready to implement the workflow. This can be a quick process or it can take longer, depending on the tool you are using and the development strategy you have chosen. If your development strategy focuses more on reusability, then you will spend more time developing activities than the workflows that use them. In that case, you may elect to add your custom activities to the SharePoint Designer toolbox to enable the creation of workflows using a declarative model. This approach has the advantage of supporting rapid prototyping of your workflows.

Deploy to the Server

Deploying a SharePoint workflow requires the activation of a feature that exposes the workflow and makes it available for association with one or more SharePoint lists. To create a workflow feature, you use the `ElementManifest` element in a `feature.xml` file to reference your `workflow.xml` definition file. You can either configure the file manually or deploy it as part of a SharePoint Solution package.

The steps to deploy a workflow feature manually are:

1. Create a `feature.xml` file and a `workflow.xml` file.
2. Add a reference to the `workflow.xml` file to the element manifest.
3. Add references to the default workflow feature receiver assembly and class.
4. Copy the workflow assembly to the GAC.
5. Create a new FEATURES subfolder under the 12 hive.
6. Copy the `feature.xml` and supporting files to the new folder.

After copying the required files, recycle the SharePoint application pool and activate the feature using STSADM or via the SharePoint UI. At this point, the workflow is available for association with a list.

When you deploy WSS in a farm configuration, the WF runtime is hosted in the WSS process on all front-end machines. Since your workflows are stateful and are persisted to the back-end WSS database, workflows can run on any front-end machine. However, once they are activated, they cannot be distributed across front-end servers but instead must run to completion on the front-end server that initiated the workflow.

The following code shows a feature definition for a simple workflow:

```xml
<?xml version="1.0" encoding="utf-8"?>
<!-- _lcid="1033" _version="12.0.3111" _dal="1" -->
<!-- _LocalBinding -->
<Feature  Id="432CE9D0-5CFB-4765-B8E2-DFDEC25B4DD8"
          Title="Simple Workflow"
          Description="Creates a task and waits for the user to complete it."
          Version="12.0.0.0"
          Scope="Site"
          ReceiverAssembly="Microsoft.Office.Workflow.Feature, Version=12.0.0.0,
Culture=neutral, PublicKeyToken=71e9bce111e9429c"
          ReceiverClass="Microsoft.Office.Workflow.Feature.WorkflowFeatureReceiver"
          xmlns="http://schemas.microsoft.com/sharepoint/">
  <ElementManifests>
    <ElementManifest Location="workflow.xml" />
  </ElementManifests>
  <Properties>
    <Property Key="GloballyAvailable" Value="true" />
    <!-- Value for RegisterForms key indicates the path to the forms relative to
feature file location -->
    <!-- if you don't have forms, use *.xsn -->
    <Property Key="RegisterForms" Value="*.xsn" />
  </Properties>
</Feature>
```

The following code shows the corresponding workflow definition file:

```xml
<?xml version="1.0" encoding="utf-8" ?>
<!-- _lcid="1033" _version="12.0.3015" _dal="1"   -->
<!-- _LocalBinding   -->
<Elements xmlns="http://schemas.microsoft.com/sharepoint/">
  <Workflow
        Name="Simple Workflow"
        Description="Workflow that waits for the user to complete a task."
        Id="37672D19-6909-451e-BDD6-404A9ED2376C"
        CodeBesideClass="ProSharePoint2007.Chapter15.SimpleWorkflow"
        CodeBesideAssembly="ProSharePoint2007.Chapter15., Version=1.0.0.0,
Culture=neutral, PublicKeyToken=ec457ebe7d96977c"
        TaskListContentTypeId="0x01080100C9C9515DE4E24001905074F980F93160"
        AssociationUrl="_layouts/CustomAssociationPage.aspx"
        InstantiationUrl="_layouts/CustomInitiationPage.aspx"
        ModificationUrl="_layouts/CustomModificationPage.aspx">

    <Categories/>
    <!-- Tags to specify InfoPath forms for the workflow; delete tags for forms
that you do not have -->
    <MetaData>
      <StatusPageUrl>_layouts/WrkStat.aspx</StatusPageUrl>
    </MetaData>
  </Workflow>
</Elements>
```

Test and Debug

WSS loads the WF runtime in its own process so debugging a WF workflow is very similar to debugging Web Parts or other applications that are part of the WSS process. Once the debugger is attached to the process, you can set breakpoints in your workflow code.

> It is important to remember while debugging that the SharePoint workflow service APIs do not commit changes to the content database immediately. Instead, they wait until the workflow ends or is suspended waiting for input. Thus, you may not be able to verify those changes from within the debugger until after the workflow runs.

Building Declarative Workflows Using SharePoint Designer 2007

SharePoint Designer (SPD) provides a workflow design experience similar to the Outlook Rules Wizard. You create your linear workflow by specifying conditions and the actions to take based on those conditions. SPD does not use code to create its workflows but instead uses a workflow markup file that includes rules and conditions that WF executes. One thing to realize about SPD is that the target for SPD designed workflows is to allow you to code up business logic for your lists that require you not to write event handlers or other types of code. If you are looking to use SPD to write very complex, intricate workflows, you will find yourself quickly yearning for Visual Studio and the WF designer or you will write custom activities in Visual Studio that you will plug into SharePoint Designer.

The easiest way to understand how to build workflows with SPD is to build a workflow with SPD. There are some concepts you need to wrap your head around when working with SPD workflows before you get started. First, SPD workflows are sequential so modeling complex workflows will be, well, complex. There are probably ways you could build very complex workflows in SPD by using multiple workflows in different lists to mimic state-machine-style workflows, but it's probably easier to just use Visual Studio at that point. Second, debugging is nonexistent in SPD workflows. The closest thing to debugging is writing to the workflow history log. You will find at one point or another, when using the designer, your hands pulling hairs out of your head wondering why your conditions are not being met or your actions being triggered. The rest of this section will step you through the process of building SPD workflows and some of the pitfalls to watch out for.

Creating a Workflow

The following example creates a simple document approval workflow. The workflow will use a number of the built-in activities in SPD. Later, some additional activities written in Visual Studio will be added to further customize the workflow.

To get started, the first thing to do is point SPD at a SharePoint site. In the File menu, under the New menu, there is the Workflow option. There is also an Open Workflow item on the File menu, which makes it easier to go back and open workflows quickly in SPD.

When you create your new workflow, you will need to name the workflow, select the list you want to associate the workflow with, and select the appropriate options. As part of these options, you can have the workflow start manually when a new item is created or when an item is changed. Since SPD workflows are interpreted, SPD has the ability to check the workflow for errors by running the workflow through the compiler. You will also notice that along the bottom of the workflow designer, as shown in Figure 15-11, you can set the initiation variables and general variables for the workflow.

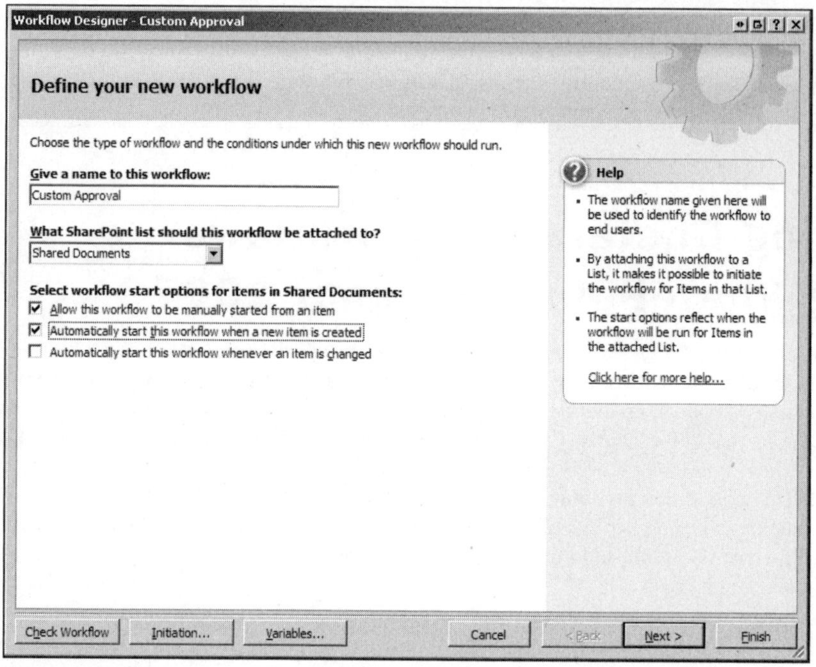

Figure 15-11

SPD stores its workflows in a hidden list called "workflows" under the root of the site. You will find that you cannot open this folder in the browser, since it does not have the standard list files such as `AllItems .aspx` or `EditForm.aspx`. The tasks you create as part of your workflows are always created in the Tasks folder as part of your site's list folders. SPD creates a special content type and task form for your workflow tasks and associates them with the tasks list. If you go to the list settings, you will see your task content types as part of the content types supported by the list. You can view the tasks list through the browser to see the task data.

When you use the logging feature in SPD, SPD places the log entries into the Workflow History list. Some of the columns that you see in this list track the GUID for the parent instance ID, workflow association ID, list ID, dates and times and the description of the event that you either specified or that the workflow infrastructure created. Try previewing this list in the browser from SPD by selecting it and hitting F12 to understand all the columns this list contains.

Workflows can be associated with any list type. The document approval workflow in this example is associated with a document library and started manually. When it is started, the user is prompted to provide a semicolon-delimited list of email addresses for the people who will approve the document. SPD allows you to create initiation variables and will generate an ASP.NET form automatically for you to prompt the user for those variables. Even if you do not need to collect initiation parameters, SPD still generates an ASP.NET form for you to allow users to manually start the workflows you create. The ASP.NET forms that SPD creates are editable in SPD, so you can customize the forms.

The workflow will use a single-line text field to retrieve the email addresses. Any combination of fields could be used, including multiline text fields, numbers, date and time, choice (drop-down or radio button), and yes/no (check box) fields. You can set default values for the different type of initiation parameters. You will see in the ASP.NET page a tag added for a `SPWorkflowDataSource`. This datasource will contain a dataset that contains a row that in turn contains the fields defined in the initiation form. Figure 15-12 shows the user interface for creating the initation form.

As for workflow variables, you can think of these as temporary, workflow-instance-specific variables you can use in your workflows to store dynamic, volatile data. One common usage that you will see for workflow variables is generating dynamic, runtime data in your workflow that you need to stuff into a workflow variable, so you can use it in another step in your workflow.

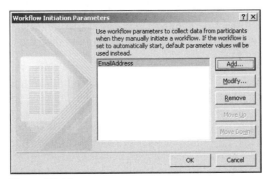

Figure 15-12

Adding Steps, Conditions and Actions

After setting up the list and initiation variables, you can add steps which contain conditions and actions to the workflow. With SPD, you can make an action always occur just by leaving out any conditions in your step but including an action. Since the document approval workflow will always want to take the email addresses, assign to-do items, log to the workflow history, and send email to the approvers, the condition is omitted in this example.

SPD includes a number of predefined conditions which are useful for many scenarios. You can also build your own conditions that allow you to compare any datasource value as part of the condition. You can also use lookups as part of the compared value. For example, you could compare the name of a contact to the name of the approver of the workflow or you could compare the task status to a custom field in your application. Even though SPD allows you to add datasources such as databases, XML files, and other external datasources, the workflow designer itself cannot use or compare to these datasources.

The following table shows the available set of conditions you can use.

Condition Name	Description
Title contains specific keywords	This condition allows you to check to see if the title of the item contains specific keywords.
Modified in a specific date span	You can check to see if the item was modified between two dates. You can either type in a date, use the date value dialog, or specific a lookup. The date value dialog allows you to specify the current date, so you could create a time span from the current date through some future date.
Modified by a specific person	Allows you to specify the modifier to check for. This can be a specific person selected from the address book, a variable, a lookup, or the current user who created the item.
Created in a specific date span	Similar to the modified condition, this condition instead checks the creation date rather than the modified date.
Created by a specific person	Same as the modified by a specific person condition except that this condition checks the creator not the modifier.
Compare "list" field	The "list" part of this condition refers to the current list that you have the workflow associated with. This condition lets you quickly select a field in the current list and compare it to a static value, a lookup or even a regular expression that you specify. An example of a regular expression would be `http://(www\.)?([^\.]+)\.com`, which would match URLs that pointed to `.com` sites.
Compare any data source	This condition allows you compare any two datasources via lookups or static values.
Action Name	Description.
Add time to date	This action allows you to add a certain amount of time such as seconds, minutes, hours, days, months, or years to a value and have the output placed into a workflow variable.
Assign a form to a group	If you need to assign a custom form to a set of users, this action allows you to do that. You will need to use a secondary workflow to set properties on the custom form, since the default property you can set is the description. You can add custom fields as part of the new form. This action does not return an ID for the responses like the Collect data from user action.

Condition Name	Description
Assign a to-do item	This action allows you to set a workflow task for a user or a group, or by using a lookup.
Build dynamic string	When you need to build a string on the fly as part of your workflow, you should use this action. Your dynamic string can use lookups as part of the string. You assign the new string to a variable in your workflow.
Check in item	Allows you to check in an item in a list that has versioning enabled. You can specify a comment as part of the check-in.
Check out item	With this action you can check out an item from a list. You will have to specify a matching value to find the item you want to check out.
Collect data from user	Use this action to pause your workflow while you collect data from the user. You cannot use this with multiple users. SPD will prompt you for fields that you want in your form and who you want to assign the collection to. When the task is assigned to the user, SPD will then output the ID of the task into a variable you specify, so you can use that ID within the workflow.
Copy list item	Copies a list item from one list to another.
Create list item	Allows you to create a new item in the list. SPD will look at the content types associated with the list and pull out the required fields for you to set. You can set optional fields as well with statics or lookup values.
Delete item	Deletes the item.
Discard check out item	Discards the check out of the item.
Do calculation	Performs a calculation on numeric values and then outputs the result to a variable you specify. You can add, subtract, multiply, divide, or mod the values.
Log to history list	Logs the message you specify to the workflow history list. This message can be static or be generated via a lookup. You can also make the value dynamic by using the Build dynamic string action and then placing the output variable of that action in the log.
Pause for duration	Pauses the workflow for the specified number of days, hours, or minutes. You can set the values either statically or via lookup.
Pause until date	Pauses the workflow until the specified date, which could be the current date or a future date and time.

Continued

Condition Name	Description
Send an email	Sends an email. You can dynamically look up the recipients on the to and cc lines. In addition, on the subject line you can type in the subject or look it up. In the email body, you can also type in values or add dynamic lookups.
Set content approval status	Sets the content approval status and allows you to specify comments as part of setting the status.
Set field in current item	Sets the field you specify in the current item. SPD will display the possible values for the field or allow you to type in values, or you can look up values.
Set time portion of date/time field	Allows you to set the time for a date field and output the value into a variable.
Set workflow variable	Sets the value for a workflow variable that you specify either with a static value or lookup.
Stop workflow	Stops the workflow and allows you to log a message. This action is useful if your workflow encounters an error condition that you have predefined.
Update list item	Allows you to update the fields in a list item. You can update multiple fields at once.
Wait for field change in current item	Pauses the workflow until a field changes in the current item. Depending on the type of field you specify, you can perform different comparison operations. Once the field meets the conditions you specify, the workflow continues.

Branching and Parallelism

In SharePoint Designer, you can create IfElse constructs in the designer within a single workflow step. This is useful if you want to test conditions in an if...else construct. Using the else part of the branching is also useful, for example, if you want to log whether the item meets your conditions. You could stop the workflow and write a message to the history log, for instance.

Similarly to the branching within a single step, you can also add parallelism to your workflow by allowing the engine to run actions in parallel rather than serially. This is useful if you want to have a delayed action but do not have the workflow block on the delay. Unfortunately, you cannot interleave serial and parallel activities in a single branch. It's either all serial or all parallel. A good example of using parallel activities is executing a delay or some other type of pause, while you still want to execute other activities such as logging history or changing fields within an item.

A Note about Multithreading

WF does not use multithreading in a single workflow instance. While this may not affect your SPD workflows, you should be aware of this design principle. The reason for this architecture is to simplify your development. You may be wondering how this affects scale or performance. With the types of workflows you are building with SharePoint, namely human-centric workflows, the human delay factor is much larger than the machine delay caused by not having multithreading in WF. The thing to remember is that it is a single thread per workflow instance, so if you have 20 instances of a workflow running, they will execute on multiple threads. It's just that any single instance at any given time will only have a single thread of execution to make sure that you do not have other threads running steps in your workflow.

Putting It All Together

The document approval workflow presents an initiation form to get the reason for the approval from the user. For each approver, it will create a to-do item, log an event, and send an email to that person. The next step is to wait for the approver to approve the task assigned to them and then log an event. Figure 15-13 shows the initiation form for the workflow when a user starts the workflow on an item.

To illustrate the conditions and the actions in the Designer, Figure 15-14 shows the first step in the workflow.

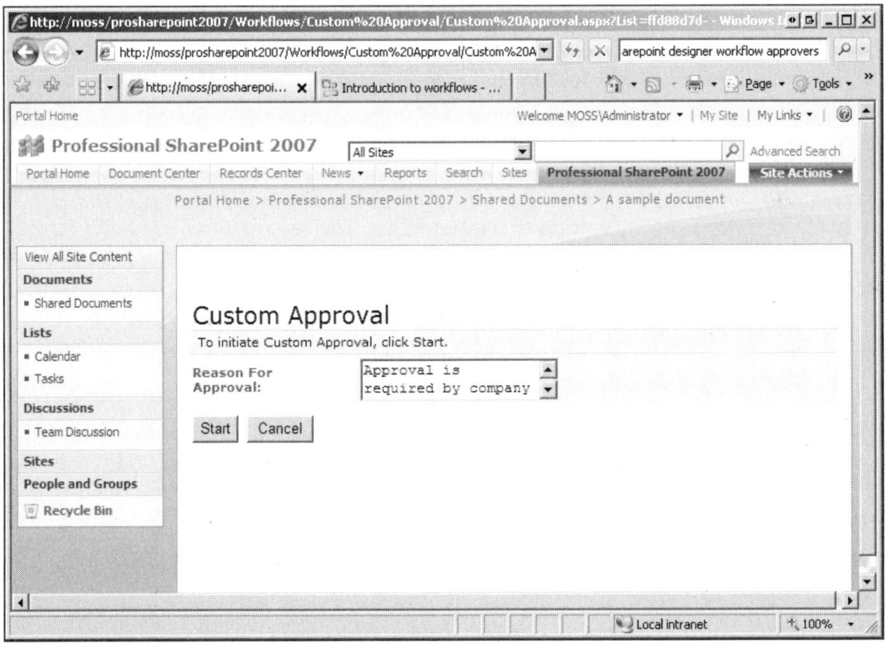

Figure 15-13

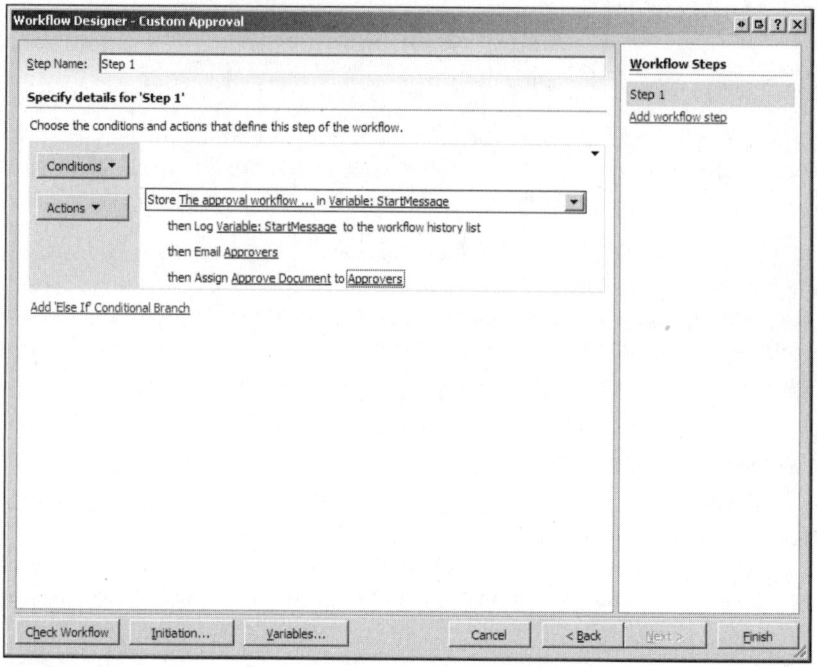

Figure 15-14

To log the name of the approver into the workflow history list, the workflow generates a dynamic string that includes both a static message and the value in the initiation variable collected from the user. This is what the first action does. The second action takes the new dynamic string in the variable and writes it out to the workflow history. Then, the approver is sent an email message containing a link to the document through a workflow lookup. Finally, a to-do item is assigned to the approver to approve the document.

The assign to-do action is at the bottom of the action list. The reason for this is that you will want to be careful in the sequencing of your actions in your workflow. If you had assigned the to-do item anywhere else, the workflow would have assigned the item and then waited for the completion of the item before continuing through the rest of the actions. Parallel actions would not have worked because parallel execution does not guarantee the order in which actions are performed. In this case, the dynamic string needs to be generated before it is written to the workflow history log.

The second step of the workflow looks for the completion status of the to-do item and when it is completed, it logs in the workflow history that the document has been approved and emails the person who created the item that the document has been approved. The way to ensure that the task is complete is to look for the value 1 in the % Complete field. Because this is a number field, the value will range from 0 for not completed to 1 for 100% complete. In order to ensure the correct task item is referenced, a filter is applied that matches the task's workflow item ID to the ID of the item that is being routed. This is critical, since it will make sure that the correct task is associated with the correct item and that the workflow does not get a false positive on the completion if there are multiple workflow tasks running in parallel on multiple items.

Things to Watch Out For

Although it's a powerful tool for workflow development, there are some limitations when building workflows in SharePoint Designer. This section will give you some helpful hints on things to watch out for so that you don't run into these pitfalls when building your own workflows.

Data Types and Data Values

Be careful when comparing data values. Make sure that you know the underlying data type of the items you are comparing and their possible values. For example, the user interface lets you display Number data types as percentages. But the values actually range from 0 to 1. So, if you enter values like 100 or 75, your conditions will not be met.

Circular Workflows

Be careful not to create circular workflows. SPD protects you from creating actions that trigger the same workflow in the same list but may not catch all declarations that result in circular logic. For example, you can't tell a workflow to fire automatically on item change and then have a workflow that changes the saved item in the same list. You would get stuck in an infinite loop as part of the workflow, and SPD will warn you.

SPD will even protect you from circular workflows if you have a workflow in two lists that trigger each other. It does this by using a token. Say that you have a workflow on List A that creates an item in List B. You also have a workflow on List B that creates an item in List A. If these were allowed to run, you would see both lists filling up with items as each in the workflows triggered each other ad infinitum. SPD prevents this by using a token that references each workflow. Even if you manually try to start the workflow on the new item in List A, the item that was created in List B will not trigger the workflow in List B that would have created another item in List A.

Debugging

SPD does not support debugging, so you will have to get used to writing lots of messages to the workflow history log when building your workflows. With the built-in actions, not having debugging is okay. However, when working with complex workflows or with complex conditions, debugging gets very messy. If your workflow starts to get too complex, or you find that debugging is a chore, it's probably time to consider building some custom activities to which you can delegate the complexity. Once you have those activities installed, you can develop more and more complex workflows using the declarative style for which SPD was intended.

Initiation Data

It can be tricky to control the initialization of workflows that start automatically. You can create initiation variables, but be sure to initialize them to default values. Also, if you need to collect and store initiation data from the user, a good way to store it is to use custom fields in the associated list item. The custom fields are available as a hashtable on the list item.

Caching

The final gotcha is workflow timing and caching. Both will affect your workflow in interesting ways and are interrelated.

The SharePoint WF host aggressively caches data and will not make changes to an item until the workflow is completed or dehydrated. SPD addresses the scenario where you create a new item and try to use the new information in that item. However, the scenario you have to watch out for is the one where you modify a field in an item and then try to use the new value later in the same workflow step. You will find that the workflow will end in an error, since it will not be able to find the item yet. This is because the new value has not yet been updated in the content database.

This is especially true for calculated fields because they need to be saved in order to be calculated. The easiest way to resolve this issue is to suspend the workflow for a time interval, which will dehydrate the workflow and save the changes. Then, your workflow will work as you expect.

Building Reusable Workflows Using Visual Studio 2005

Arguably the biggest limitation on using SPD to create workflows is that the workflows you develop cannot be applied to other lists. They are attached directly to the list you are working with. So, if you want the same functionality on another list, you have to create the workflow again on that list, and so on.

Visual Studio provides more control and flexibility when designing workflows, but that power comes as the cost of increased complexity for both development and deployment. In addition, you will have to touch the server installation in order to get your DLL on the server and installed into the Global Assembly Cache (GAC).

There are a couple of prerequisites before you start developing your workflows in Visual Studio. The first is that you want to make sure that you have the Workflow Extensions for Visual Studio 2005 installed on your development machine. This will provide you with the workflow project types and the workflow designer in Visual Studio. Next, depending on whether you are running WSS or MOSS, you will want either the WSS Workflow Developer Starter Kit or the Enterprise Content Management Starter Kit.

The WSS kit includes the Visual Studio templates for building SharePoint workflows and some samples. The ECM kit adds some useful whitepapers, more detailed samples and covers more technologies than just workflows, including records management, encryption, and information rights management. The ECM Starter Kit is included with the Office SharePoint Server SDK.

When building workflows in Visual Studio, you must do so on a server that is running SharePoint because the DLL containing the SharePoint-specific workflow activities is located only on the SharePoint server. You could "remote desktop" into the server to make it easier for your development, but unfortunately you cannot develop workflows on a client machine without SharePoint installed and deploy that workflow to the server.

The first step in developing your workflow is to create a new project. When selecting your project type, select the SharePoint project group and then select either a sequential or a state-machine workflow. Once it is selected and opened, Visual Studio adds a number of capabilities to your workflow project.

First, you will see a `DeploymentFiles` folder that contains the files needed for deploying your workflow into the SharePoint environment. This folder contains a subfolder named `FeatureFiles` that contains the `feature.xml` and `workflow.xml` files to be used for deployment. The `feature.xml` file is a standard SharePoint feature activation file since your workflow will need to be installed and activated on the server. Similarly, the `workflow.xml` file contains the workflow template specification.

Unfortunately, the generated files don't contain any code. Instead, they rely on the developer to insert the appropriate codes using the provided code snippets. The following examples show what they *should* look like after the snippets have been inserted:

feature.xml

```xml
<?xml version="1.0" encoding="utf-8"?>
<!-- _lcid="1033" _version="12.0.3111" _dal="1" -->
<!-- _LocalBinding -->
<Feature   Id="002A7AB6-AC9F-4cc4-BCBD-1FFABDB25846"
           Title="Task Reminder Workflow"
           Description="Sends email reminders to a task assignee."
           Version="12.0.0.0"
           Scope="Site"
           ReceiverAssembly="Microsoft.Office.Workflow.Feature, Version=12.0.0.0,
Culture=neutral, PublicKeyToken=71e9bce111e9429c"
           ReceiverClass="Microsoft.Office.Workflow.Feature.WorkflowFeatureReceiver"
           xmlns="http://schemas.microsoft.com/sharepoint/">
    <ElementManifests>
        <ElementManifest Location="workflow.xml" />
        <ElementFile Location="TaskReminderForm.xsn"/>
    </ElementManifests>
    <Properties>
        <Property Key="GloballyAvailable" Value="true" />
        <Property Key="RegisterForms" Value="*.xsn" />
    </Properties>
</Feature>
```

workflow.xml

```xml
<?xml version="1.0" encoding="utf-8" ?>
<!-- _lcid="1033" _version="12.0.3015" _dal="1"    -->
<!-- _LocalBinding    -->
<Elements xmlns="http://schemas.microsoft.com/sharepoint/">
    <Workflow
        Name="Task Reminder Workflow"
        Description="Sends reminders to a task assignee."
        Id="E37B16BB-B105-4229-B68D-EB17D3F19BAF"
        CodeBesideClass="ProSharePoint2007.TaskReminder.TaskReminder"
        CodeBesideAssembly="ProSharePoint2007.TaskReminder, Version=1.0.0.0,
Culture=neutral, PublicKeyToken=0b97b340d4a71524"
        TaskListContentTypeId="0x01080100C9C9515DE4E24001905074F980F93160"
        AssociationUrl="_layouts/CstWrkflIP.aspx"
        InstantiationUrl="_layouts/IniWrkflIP.aspx"
        ModificationUrl="_layouts/ModWrkflIP.aspx"
        StatusUrl="_layouts/WrkStat.aspx">

        <Categories/>
        <MetaData>
            <Association_FormURN>associationFormURN</Association_FormURN>
```

```
        <Instantiation_FormURN>instantiationFormURN</Instantiation_FormURN>
        <Task0_FormURN>taskFormURN</Task0_FormURN>

        <Modification_GUID_FormURN>modificationURN</Modification_GUID_FormURN>
        <Modification_GUID_Name>Name of Modification</Modification_GUID_Name>

        <AssociateOnActivation>false</AssociateOnActivation>
      </MetaData>
    </Workflow>
</Elements>
```

wsp_structure.ddf

```
;
;*************
; This ddf specifies the structure of the .wsp solution cab file. To customize this:
; 1. Replace "MyFeature" with the name of your own feature.
; 2. Add IP forms for the workflow at the bottom.
;*************
;
.OPTION EXPLICIT        ; Generate errors
.Set CabinetNameTemplate=TaskReminder.wsp
.set DiskDirectoryTemplate=CDROM ; All cabinets go in a single directory
.Set CompressionType=MSZIP;** All files are compressed in cabinet files
.Set UniqueFiles="ON"
.Set Cabinet=on
.Set DiskDirectory1=Package
"..\..\DeploymentFiles\ProductionDeployment\manifest.xml"  manifest.xml
"..\..\DeploymentFiles\FeatureFiles\feature.xml"        TaskReminder\feature.xml
"..\..\DeploymentFiles\FeatureFiles\workflow.xml"       TaskReminder\workflow.xml
"ProSharePoint2007.TaskReminder.dll"        ProSharePoint2007.TaskReminder.dll
;
;*** add IP forms
;"..\..\DeploymentFiles\FeatureFiles\InitiationForm.xsn"
TaskReminder\InitiationForm.xsn
;*** <the end>
```

The project template also creates a second subfolder named *ProductionDeployment*. This folder contains stubs for the solution manifest.xml and a diamond-directive file (.ddf) you can use with the makecab.exe utility to build a SharePoint solution file (.wsp) for deploying your workflow. Again, unfortunately, the generated files have to be modified by hand to change the generated name "MyFeature" to the actual name you choose for the workflow feature. You will also have to modify the wsp_structure.ddf file to include any custom forms you may have added to the project.

> **Be sure to add your custom forms to the** FeatureFiles **folder so that the generated** .ddf **file can locate them.**

The PostBuildActions.bat file contains scripted commands that perform the required deployment steps, such as calling stsadm to install and activate your feature.

The ECM Starter Kit

To understand how this all works, it is instructive to examine the sample projects in the Enterprise Content Management Starter Kit. The ECM Starter Kit is a free download from the Microsoft web site, and is an essential resource for anyone intending to develop SharePoint workflows. Although it deals with much more than workflow, the workflow samples it includes provide a great deal of insight into how best to leverage the WF framework in MOSS. At the time of this writing, it contains about a dozen sample projects, including the `HelloWorldSequential` project, which illustrates the basic structure of a code-based workflow.

The following section examines the `HelloWorldSequential` sample project in detail to better illustrate some of the hidden features of the SharePoint workflow architecture and to show you how to pull everything together when building your own custom workflow solutions.

HelloWorldSequential

The first workflow to examine is the `HelloWorldSequential` workflow. This is a simple workflow that can be associated with a document library to create a "Review This Document" task for a given user. The workflow task includes a link to the document to be reviewed and the workflow uses custom InfoPath forms to capture the user to whom the task will be assigned and to provide instructions for that user to follow as well as a space to record user feedback when the task is performed. The workflow waits for the user to complete the task before continuing. It then marks the task as completed and terminates.

Figure 15-15 illustrates the overall flow.

The different stages of the workflow are described in the next sections.

OnWorkflowActivated

This activity is called at the beginning of every SharePoint sequential workflow. The first order of business is to store the workflow correlation token. This is the identifier that will be used by other activities to refer to the currently running workflow. This activity is derived from `HandleExternalEventActivity` to handle the corresponding event fired by the SharePoint Workflow Service implementation of the `IWorkflowService` interface when the workflow is activated.

```
public Guid workflowId = default(System.Guid);
public Microsoft.SharePoint.Workflow.SPWorkflowActivationProperties
workflowProperties
                = new
Microsoft.SharePoint.Workflow.SPWorkflowActivationProperties();
private void onWorkflowActivated(object sender, ExternalDataEventArgs e)
{
    workflowId = workflowProperties.WorkflowId; //initialize the id

    XmlSerializer serializer = new XmlSerializer(typeof(InitForm));
    XmlTextReader reader = new XmlTextReader(
        new System.IO.StringReader(workflowProperties.InitiationData));
    InitForm initform = (InitForm)serializer.Deserialize(reader);

    assignee = initform.assignee;
    instructions = initform.instructions;
    comments = initform.comments;
}
```

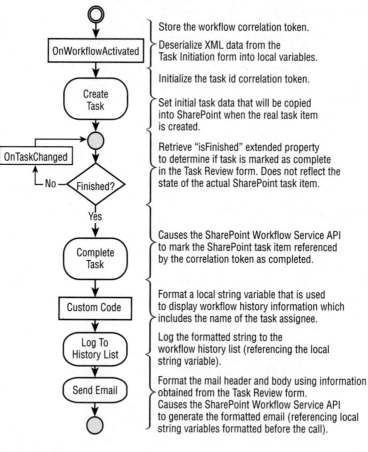

Figure 15-15

The highlighted sections of the above code show the recommended approach for dealing with initiation form data. Using the XSD.exe command-line tool, you can deserialize the form data into a set of .NET classes, which you can then assign to local variables for use in your code. The initiation form data is passed to the workflow in the SPWorkflowActivationProperties object. After deserializing this data to an InitForm instance, the assignee, instructions, and comments variables are initialized accordingly.

CreateTask

This activity acts as a wrapper for the ITaskService.CreateTask method. As is the case with all ExternalDataExchange methods, the MethodInvoking property points to a method you write that is called just prior to the actual method call, giving you the opportunity to set up the properties the external method will use. In the case of ITaskService.CreateTask, you can initialize the properties it will use to create the task, as in the following code from the ECM starter kit:

```
public Guid taskID = default(System.Guid);
public Microsoft.SharePoint.Workflow.SPWorkflowTaskProperties taskProps
    = new Microsoft.SharePoint.Workflow.SPWorkflowTaskProperties();
```

```
private void createTask(object sender, EventArgs e)
{
    taskID = Guid.NewGuid();
    taskProps.Title = "Review this document";
    taskProps.AssignedTo = assignee;
    taskProps.Description = instructions;
    taskProps.ExtendedProperties["comments"] = comments;
    taskProps.ExtendedProperties["instructions"] = instructions;
}
```

There are a couple of important points to note about this code. First, the taskID and taskProps member variables were injected by the designer automatically when the CreateTask activity was added to the workflow. Figure 15-16 shows the property pane for the CreateTask activity in the designer.

The real question at this point is: How do you know that you have to initialize the taskID property with a new GUID? Well, there's good news and there's bad news. The bad news is that it's not obvious. You have to do some digging. Of course, you don't have to do this twice. Once you know how a particular activity works, you don't have to learn it again. But why should you have to in the first place? This is where the documentation could have really helped a lot. But instead of relying on the documentation, it would be better if there were something about the TaskId member that said "initialize me." That's the good news: There is.

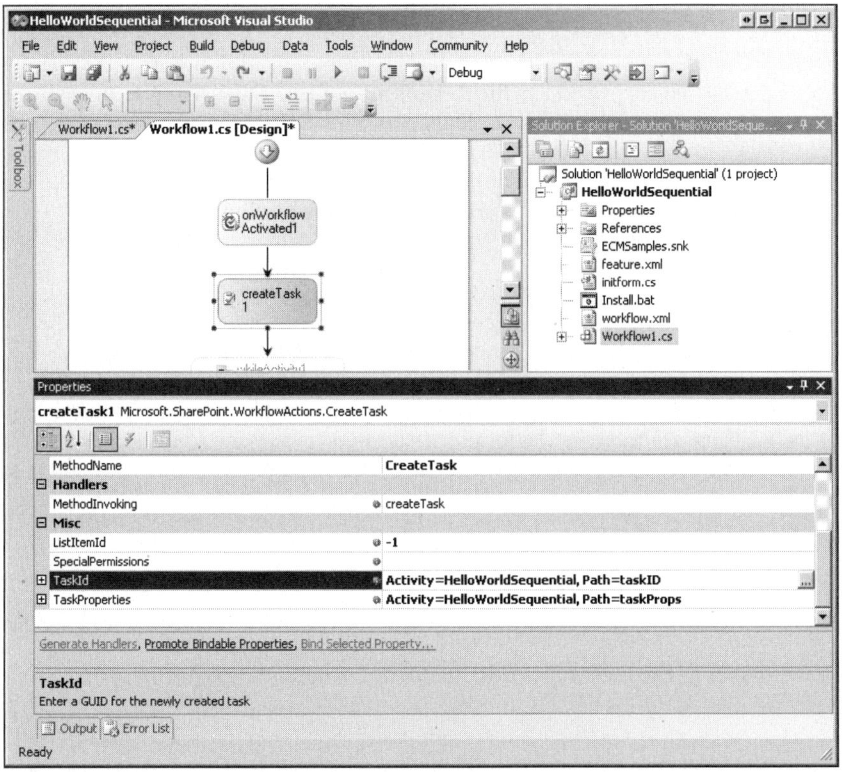

Figure 15-16

If you look at the declaration of the ITaskService interface, it specifies a CorrelationParameter having the name "taskId", as shown below.

```
[ ExternalDataExchange, CorrelationParameter("taskId") ]
public interface ITaskService {...}
```

This says to the WF runtime that whenever it encounters a parameter by that name in any method declared within the interface, treat it as a correlation parameter. Then if you look at the declaration of the CreateTask method, you'll see that it is marked with the CorrelationInitializer attribute, as shown below.

```
[ CorrelationInitializer ]
int CreateTask ( Guid taskId,
    SPWorkflowTaskProperties properties,
    HybridDictionary specialPermissions );
```

This says to the WF runtime that this method initializes the correlation value. With a little experimentation, you can figure out that if the taskId passed to the method is the default GUID, it generates the GUID on its own. But then you would have to wait for a separate event to determine the actual GUID associated with the new task. If you assign the new GUID yourself, you can use the value immediately to perform other work because the CreateTask method will use the GUID you pass in.

Similarly, the taskProps member variable was injected by the designer. This is an instance of the SPWorkflowTaskProperties class and is used to pass data to and from real SharePoint task items. The ITaskService.CreateTask method copies the properties into the new task item. It contains a set of member variables that correspond to the default columns of a task list item, such as the AssignedTo, DueDate, and PercentComplete columns. It also contains a hashtable of extended properties, which is used to map values to custom columns that may be defined for custom task list item types. If an extended property does not map to a custom column, it is stored as a hidden property associated with the item. Hidden properties can be used within the workflow to apply custom business logic.

OnTaskChanged

The OnTaskChanged activity is derived from HandleExternalEventActivity and is called whenever a task is changed. To understand how this activity works, once again you have to refer to the ITaskService interface for clues. If you've worked with the Windows SharePoint Services 3.0 object model, then you become familiar with event receivers. The basic paradigm is that when an event receiver is called, there are before and after properties that correspond to the state of the list item before and after the event, respectively. If you look at the declaration for ITaskService.OnTaskChanged, you'll see that there is a single parameter of type SPTaskServiceEventArgs. This class declares the following four members:

❑ afterProperties

❑ beforeProperties

❑ executor

❑ taskId

The beforeProperties and afterProperties members are instances of SPWorkflowTaskProperties, and as you might expect, they are filled with the state of the task item before and after the OnTaskChanged event, repectively. When the event is fired, the WF runtime calls the method specified by the Invoked property of the OnTaskChanged activity — in this case, the following onTaskChanged method from the ECM starter kit:

```
bool isFinished = false; //user defined variable to store the results of the
isFinished check box on the task form
private void onTaskChanged(object sender, ExternalDataEventArgs e)
{
    isFinished = bool.Parse(afterProps.ExtendedProperties["isFinished"].ToString());
}
```

What's interesting about this code is that the extended properties are used to determine whether the user has checked the isFinished check box on the custom InfoPath edit form. It does not, however, indicate the status of the underlying SharePoint task item.

CompleteTask

When the user indicates that the task is finished by checking the isFinished check box, the workflow then updates the underlying SharePoint task item using the CompleteTask activity. This activity implements the ITaskService.CompleteTask method, which schedules the task to be marked as complete the next time the workflow actions are committed to the content database.

Custom Code Activity

This activity prepares the string that will be used to update the history list in a subsequent activity. This could have been done dynamically by binding a property to the LogToHistoryList activity, but doing it this way is easier since the assignee name is already known. The code in this part simply formats the string that will be written to the log.

Log to History List

This activity updates the history list that is associated with the workflow. You can specify an event type, a description, an outcome, and a duration for the event. In this case, the event type WorkflowCompleted is specified along with the previously formatted description string.

Send Email

The final step in the workflow generates an email via the ISharePointService API. The following MethodInvoking method is called just prior to the actual invocation of the ISharePointService.SendMail method, which this activity acts as a wrapper for:

```
public String completeMailBody = default(System.String);
public System.Collections.Specialized.StringDictionary completeMailHeader = new
System.Collections.Specialized.StringDictionary();
private void sendCompletedMail(object sender, EventArgs e)
{
    completeMailHeader.Add("To", workflowProperties.OriginatorEmail);
    completeMailHeader.Add("Subject", "Task assigned to " + assignee + " is
complete.");
    completeMailBody = "Workflow summary: <br><br>" +
        "Reviewer feedback: " + afterProps.ExtendedProperties["feedback"].ToString();
}
```

The `completeMailBody` and `completeMailHeader` members are bound to the `Body` and `Headers` properties of the `SendMail` activity, as shown in Figure 15-17.

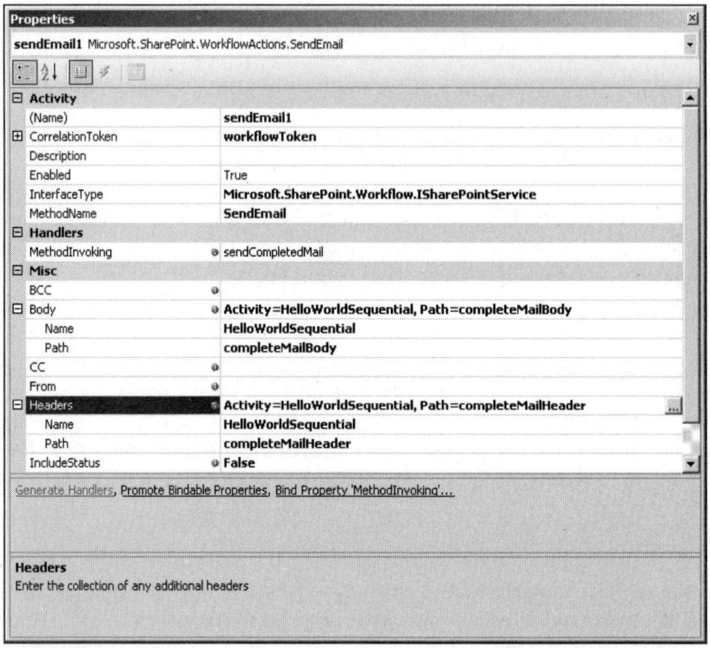

Figure 15-17

Understanding Correlation Tokens

Correlation tokens are so fundamentally important to the SharePoint workflow that it is essential to understand how they work and how to use them correctly. If used improperly, they can produce unexpected results that are difficult to diagnose. This section examines correlation tokens from three perspectives. What are correlation tokens and why are they necessary? How are correlation tokens declared when building custom service interfaces? How are correlation tokens used when building workflows that consume those interfaces?

What Are Correlation Tokens?

Correlation tokens are unique identifiers that enable the WF runtime to establish a mapping between objects declared within a workflow and the environment in which the WF runtime is hosted. They may also reference objects that are maintained by the host. One way to think about correlation tokens is that they are similar to parameter names in a method or function declaration.

When creating a method to add two numbers, you would need to declare two parameters; for example A and B as in the following example:

```
int AddTwoNumbers(int A, int B){...}
```

Similarly, when creating a workflow to transfer data from one list item to another, you need to declare two correlation tokens — one for each list item. Then you can have one activity that retrieves the data from the first item, and another activity later in the workflow that stores the data into the second item. Correlation tokens are, therefore, bound to a particular object and are used by the WF runtime to unambiguously reference that object during the life of the workflow. Correlation tokens are persisted along with the state of each workflow instance so that when the workflow is rehydrated, each token references the same object it did prior to dehydration.

Why Are Correlation Tokens Necessary?

Recall that the WF runtime manages all communication between a workflow and its host environment, in essence acting as a proxy. Correlation tokens are necessary for two reasons. First, they enable software outside the workflow to reference a given workflow instance. For example, when a suspended workflow must be rehydrated to continue processing in response to changes made to a SharePoint task, a correlation token is used to identify the appropriate workflow instance. Second, they enable activities within a given workflow to reference specific objects that may live outside the workflow. For example, when several workflow activities must retrieve or modify data in a SharePoint list item, a correlation token is used to identify the item.

How Are Correlation Tokens Declared?

Since correlation tokens are only required when dealing with external methods and events, it follows that they are tied to the mechanism used to enable a workflow to call an external method or handle an external event. This is accomplished through declarations made in the interfaces used to communicate with those external objects themselves. In other words, since the code that implements the interface is responsible for operating on the object referred to by the correlation token, it is also the responsibility of that same code to declare the need for one or more tokens to identify those objects it wishes to act upon. This architecture comes into play when designing interfaces for use by custom workflow activities.

You can greatly extend the power of custom workflow activities by implementing a companion interface that is marked with the `ExternalDataExchange` attribute. Using this approach can simplify the development of complex workflows by delegating the heavy lifting to external code that can be easily reused.

The `ExternalDataExchange` attribute is defined in the `System.Workflow.Activities` assembly, and is used to mark an interface as a local service, enabling it to be called from the `CallExternalMethod` activity and to fire events to the `HandleExternalEvent` activity. Once you have marked your interface with this attribute, you can use the `CorrelationParameter` attribute to specify the names of parameters you wish to correlate in the methods and events defined by the interface. You can then use the `CorrelationInitializer` attribute to specify a special method that will be called to initialize the correlation value (at the beginning of the workflow), and the `CorrelationAlias` attribute to override the `CorrelationParameter` setting for a specific method or event.

The method you specify as the correlation initializer must be called prior to other methods in the local service interface; otherwise, workflow validation will fail.

The following example shows how these attributes might be used in a companion interface for custom activities that generate email messages to task item assignees as the task due date approaches:

```
[ ExternalDataExchange ]
[ CorrelationParameter("taskId") ]
```

```
public interface ITaskReminderService
{
      [ CorrelationInitializer ]
      void CreateTaskWithReminder(string taskId, string assignee, string text,
TimeSpan daysBeforeDueDate, TimeSpan frequency);

      [ CorrelationAlias("taskId", "e.Id") ]
      event EventHandler<TaskEventArgs> TaskCompleted;
}
```

How Are Correlation Tokens Used?

In general, you will use separate correlation tokens for the workflow itself, each item you need to reference from within the workflow, and each modification. Even if you are referencing only one task from within a workflow, it is vital that you not use the same correlation token for the task that you use for the workflow itself. Doing so may prevent the workflow from being properly rehydrated. For example, when developing composite activities that manage other workflows, you would use a workflow token to reference a given workflow instance in workflow-related activities such as SetState, SendEmail, and UpdateAllTasks. Similarly, when developing workflows that manage tasks, you would use a task token to reference a given task in activities such as CreateTask, UpdateTask, and the like. Modification tokens would be used in the EnableWorkflowModification and OnWorkflowModified activities.

Creating Custom Activities for Use with SharePoint Designer

The Sharepoint Designer toolbox comes with about two dozen or so default workflow activities. You can add your own custom activities to extend that set so that you can create more complex workflows than what is available out of the box. The default activities are defined in a file called WSS.ACTIONS, which resides in the template directory on the SharePoint server. When you open the Workflow Designer for a given site, SharePoint Designer retrieves this file to configure the workflow designer user interface and to format the .xoml file used by SharePoint to implement your workflow.

The XML used in the WSS.ACTIONS file is similar to CAML in many respects. The most significant similarity is the fact that it encapsulates both presentation and functional features of the workflow activities it describes. It is unique, however, in the level of extensibility it supports. Using this file, you can completely customize the SharePoint Designer user interface so that it supports your own private collection of workflow activities. This capability allows you to publish powerful workflow solutions using all the advanced developer features of Visual Studio, while limiting the SharePoint Designer surface area for less technical users.

The following example leverages this capability to extend the workflow designer to support a set of custom-reporting workflow activities tied to a specific SharePoint Site Group. The person designing the workflow can specify the workflow behavior at a high level, for example, selecting which group to be notified of site usage. Under the covers, the custom Usage Reporter activity takes care of the necessary details.

Create and Build the Activity

The first step is to create a custom activity. This example creates a simple activity that writes a message to the event log. The code for this activity is shown in Listing 15-3.

Listing 15-3

```
using System;
using System.ComponentModel;
using System.ComponentModel.Design;
using System.Collections;
using System.Diagnostics;
using System.Drawing;
using System.Workflow.ComponentModel.Compiler;
using System.Workflow.ComponentModel.Serialization;
using System.Workflow.ComponentModel;
using System.Workflow.ComponentModel.Design;
using System.Workflow.Runtime;
using System.Workflow.Activities;
using System.Workflow.Activities.Rules;

namespace ProSharePoint2007
{
    public partial class EventLogger: Activity
    {
        public EventLogger()
        {
            InitializeComponent();
        }

        public static DependencyProperty MessageProperty
            = System.Workflow.ComponentModel.DependencyProperty.Register(
                "Message", typeof(string), typeof(EventLogger));

        [Description(
                "The message text that will appear in the system event log.")]
        [Category("ProSharePoint2007")]
        [Browsable(true)]
        [DesignerSerializationVisibility(
                DesignerSerializationVisibility.Visible)]
        public string Message
        {
            get
            {
                return ((string)(base.GetValue(EventLogger.MessageProperty)));
            }
            set
            {
                base.SetValue(EventLogger.MessageProperty, value);
            }
        }
    }
```

```
            protected override ActivityExecutionStatus
                Execute(ActivityExecutionContext executionContext)
        {
            using (EventLog log = new EventLog("ProSharePoint2007"))
            {
                try
                {
                    log.Source = "EventLogger Activity";
                    log.WriteEntry(this.Message, EventLogEntryType.Information);
                }
                catch
                {
                }
            }
            return ActivityExecutionStatus.Closed;
        }
    }
}
```

The `Message` property will be used to specify the text to be displayed in the event log and the overridden `Execute` method performs the action. In order for the workflow to bind variables to the property for input and output, a `DependencyProperty` object is declared to "promote" the property for use by the workflow.

Deploy and Register the Assembly

The next step is to sign the assembly and deploy it to the Global Assembly Cache. You also have to register the assembly with SharePoint. You do this by editing the `web.config` file for the site you wish to extend. The default location for the `web.config` files is `C:\inetpub\wwwroot\wss\virtualdirectories\`. Beneath that you will find a separate directory for each SharePoint web application. Edit the `web.config` file and search for the following element:

```
<System.Workflow.ComponentModel.WorkflowCompiler>
```

Copy one of the existing elements and modify it to point to your custom activity assembly, as in the following example:

```
<authorizedType Assembly="ProSharePoint2007.Chapter15.EventLoggerActivity,
Version=1.0.0.0, Culture=neutral, PublicKeyToken=0b97b340d4a71524"
    Namespace="ProSharePoint2007" TypeName="*" Authorized="True" />
```

Create an .ACTIONS file

SharePoint Designer 2007 retrieves the descriptions of the actions to be displayed from an XML file. This file describes the public properties exposed by the activity and tells SharePoint Designer how to map those properties into rules that can be displayed to the user. The following code shows the `.ACTIONS` file for the custom `EventLogger` activity:

```
<?xml version="1.0" encoding="utf-8" ?>
<WorkflowInfo>
    <Actions Sequential="then" Parallel="and">
```

```
                <Action Name="Write Message To Event Log"
                ClassName="ProSharePoint2007.EventLogger"
                Assembly="ProSharePoint2007.Chapter15.EventLoggerActivity,
    Version=1.0.0.0, Culture=neutral, PublicKeyToken=0b97b340d4a71524"
                AppliesTo="all" Category="ProSharePoint2007">
                    <RuleDesigner Sentence="Write '%1' to the event log">
                        <FieldBind Field="Message" DesignerType="TextArea"
    Id="1"/>
                    </RuleDesigner>
                    <Parameters>
                        <Paramater Name="Message" Type="System.String, mscorlib"
    Direction="In"/>
                    </Parameters>
                </Action>
            </Actions>
    </WorkflowInfo>
```

The following table summarizes the elements and attributes expected by SharePoint Designer.

Element	Attribute	Description
Actions		Contains a separate Action element for each activity.
Action		Describes a single activity.
	Name	The name that SPD will display in the actions list.
	ClassName	The compiled name of the activity class.
	Assembly	The assembly that contains the activity class. The assembly must reside in the GAC.
	AppliesTo	Specifies the types of lists the activity can be used for. Valid values are list, doclib, or all.
	Category	A text string that SPD will use to organize activites into categories.
RuleDesigner		Contains the field bindings for properties exposed by the activity.
	Sentence	Specifies the format string that SPD will use in the Rules Wizard. You can use numbered format specifiers as placeholders for parameters.
FieldBind		Describes each property of the activity and maps it to a numbered format specifier in the sentence.

Continued

Element	Attribute	Description
	Field	Specifies the corresponding property of the activity. This value must match a parameter entry described below.
	DesignerType	Specifies the type of control to use when the user clicks the link to edit the value.
	Id	Maps the property to the format specifier.
Parameters		Contains the list of parameters.
Parameter		Describes a single parameter.
	Name	Specifies the parameter name used above.
	Type	Indicates the data type of the property.
	Direction	Specifies In to retrieve the property value, or Out to set the property value.

The final step is to copy your custom .ACTIONS file to the following folder:

```
%Program Files%\Common Files\Microsoft Shared\Web Server Extensions\
12\TEMPLATE\1033\Workflow\
```

View the Activity in SharePoint Designer

After copying the .ACTIONS files to the appropriate folder, you should do an IISReset to clear the cache. Now, you can open SharePoint Designer and see the custom activity displayed in the workflow designer, as shown in Figure 15-18.

Summary

Windows Workflow Foundation is the business process automation platform upon which the Share-Point workflow is built and is the way to build workflow-enabled solutions on the Windows platform. Windows Workflow Foundation is not itself an application but merely provides a framework for workflow development.

Windows Workflow Foundation supports both sequential and state-machine workflows. Although state-machine workflows are more natural for modeling human-based workflows, you can also build complex workflows using the sequential model. Whichever approach you choose, workflow activities are the basic building block you will use. Every workflow consists of a collection of activities.

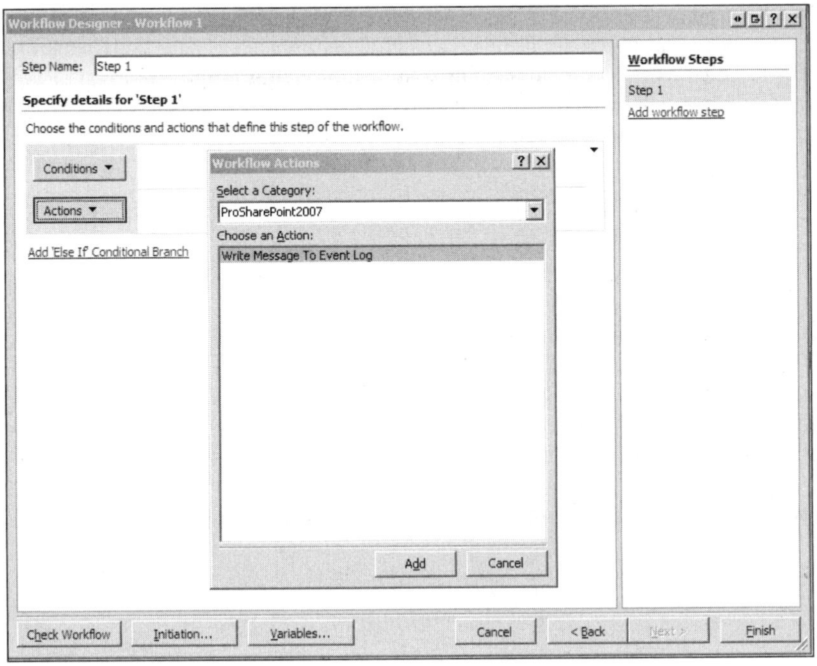

Figure 15-18

A workflow activity is a discrete unit of behavior. Activities can also contain other activities. You design a workflow by either combining activities in sequence or nesting them one within the other to direct the flow of information over time. There are many built-in activities you can use to build workflows, but not all activities are relevant to SharePoint workflows. SharePoint supports a subset of the activities that are available in the Visual Studio graphical designer.

In order to execute a workflow, SharePoint hosts the Workflow Foundation runtime engine. The Workflow Foundation runtime then interacts with MOSS through a prescribed set of interfaces in order to create the required conditions for performing each workflow activity. SharePoint hosts the Workflow Foundation runtime differently than other applications in the way that it caches modifications to SharePoint items until the workflow reaches a point where it needs input or is otherwise suspended.

SharePoint workflows are always tied to content and are designed to be attached to documents, list items, and content types. SharePoint workflows are also optimized for human interaction with a rich palette of task-specific activities that enable two-way communication between tasks and workflow activities. You can easily create and assign SharePoint tasks from within custom activities, and you can suspend work-flow execution until a SharePoint task has been completed.

MOSS ships with a powerful set of built-in workflows that you can use without modification. These include individual and group approval workflows, feedback and signature collection workflows, and translation management and issue tracking workflows.

You can build SharePoint workflows using the Visual Studio 2005 graphical designer or SharePoint Designer 2007, which employs a declarative model based on the eXtensible Application Markup Language (XAML). Deploying a workflow developed in Visual Studio requires the activation of a feature that exposes the workflow and makes it available for association with one or more SharePoint lists. To create a workflow feature, you use the `ElementManifest` element in a `feature.xml` file to reference your `workflow.xml` definition file. You can either configure the file manually or deploy it as part of a SharePoint Solution package. Workflows developed using SharePoint Designer are deployed directly into SharePoint but cannot be reused for other lists.

There are several steps you can take to simplify the development process. These include planning and modeling the workflow before you begin the implementation. When planning a workflow, it is important to give due consideration to the source and disposition of workflow data as well as who the primary actors are and what they will be able to do. Also, there are important security concerns to be aware of when developing workflows for execution in a SharePoint environment, since all workflows run as System Account in WSS and as the App Pool Identity on the server computer and domain. This carries security implications for both the development and deployment of workflows.

The next and final chapter of the book brings everything together in the larger context of business intelligence.

16

Business Intelligence and SharePoint Server 2007

By Matt Ranlett

When someone talks about the newest version of SharePoint Server, the topic of *business intelligence* frequently comes up. What exactly is business intelligence and how can SharePoint 2007 help you get it? This chapter takes the time to explain some core business intelligence concepts and then builds an entire working business intelligence portal using tools as diverse as SQL Server, Microsoft Excel, and Visual Studio.

Business Intelligence Overview

The term "business intelligence" has been bandied about since the 1990s, but there is still a lot of misunderstanding about what business intelligence means. The term was first popularized in 1989 as an umbrella term describing a diverse set of concepts designed to improve business decision making. Business intelligence is the next evolution of data warehousing and reporting. Where the original concept of data warehousing is primarily concerned with the integration of vast amounts of data across multiple business systems, business intelligence technologies help to gather, analyze, and provide access to that integrated store of data in order to make informed strategic business decisions.

Before the advent of the information age in the twentieth century, businesses often struggled to collect high-quality data. Even as data accumulated, businesses lacked the capability to quickly analyze the data and were forced to make strategic decisions based solely on executive intuition. As businesses started automating themselves, more and more high-quality data became available. Database and data-warehousing technologies were invented to store the vast amounts of data. Timeliness of data has been continuously improved as integration and reporting technologies evolved. Current business intelligence specialists practice the art of sifting through the large amounts of data, extracting the pertinent information, and turning it into knowledge upon which actions can be based.

Given this broad definition of business intelligence, the next logical question is why should any organization undergo the effort of building such systems and who are the users of business intelligence? By using business intelligence technologies to track business performance, detect trends, and produce accurate forecasts about the future, businesses hope to turn their wealth of corporate data into a competitive advantage. Where strategic business decisions 100 years ago were largely made by guesswork, business intelligence systems help to eliminate the guesswork by providing much more insight into past performance and more accurate predictions of the future conditions. This high-quality information can actually be targeted at any level of an organization, although most use cases involve upper management.

Key Business Intelligence Concepts

The following business intelligence concepts are common across all technology offerings and are important for the rest of this chapter: OLTP databases, OLAP data warehouses, KPIs, and dashboards.

Business intelligence data is typically gathered by frontline systems that communicate with *online transaction processing* (OLTP) databases. An example of this is a cash register system ringing up customers and recording sales data to a central database. Examples of OLTP databases include Microsoft's SQL Server, Oracle's Oracle 10g, IBM's DB2, and the open-source MySQL database.

The central point of any business intelligence system is its analytical and reporting system. Typically this takes the form of an online analytical processing (OLAP) data warehouse. Data warehouses are the workhorses of any business intelligence system, gathering data from a wide array of data stores (typically OLTP databases), analyzing and optimizing the information, and reporting the results out to users.

Data mining is the process of extracting valid, authentic, and actionable information from large databases. Data mining is used to search large amounts of data to find patterns for the purposes of forecasting. A commonly understood example of data mining is the "customers who bought this item also bought" section on Amazon.com. If you look at a product, Amazon.com's servers will show you other items purchased by customers who purchased the item you are looking at. This kind of pattern matching and trend analysis is being used to increase sales by targeting advertising at specific customers.

Data cubes are logical database constructs where a list of specific data elements is surrounded with descriptive attributes. In reality, these structures are made up of three (or more) dimensional arrays of data, giving the data cube its name. The list of elements is called a fact table, and the descriptive attributes are called dimensions. For example, consider a database table of sales line item details. The raw sales data, numeric data which can be aggregated, would be the facts, the dates, sales person ID, store ID, and geography associated with the raw sales details, which might all be considered dimensions of those facts. Cubes, which enable ad hoc reporting and analysis, are part of the set of data warehouse objects that combine to make OLAP and data mining a powerful tool in the business intelligence toolkit. *Key Performance Indicators*, or KPIs, are metrics that summarize the present state of the business. KPIs are used to measure progress towards an objective. For example, if the objective is to decrease the average duration of support calls from 10 minutes to 6 minutes, the KPI in this scenario would be the average duration of support calls. Identifying the proper metrics to measure is partly an art and partly a science; entire books have been written on this subject.

Dashboards are management tools used to get a snapshot of the business's performance and health. Typically a simple visual collection of graphics based on the metaphor of an instrument panel, dashboards are used to monitor key business indicators and provide a summary of business conditions. Using a dashboard, a business decision maker can quickly ascertain the state and health of the business and make informed tactical and strategic business decisions.

Introducing Microsoft's Business Intelligence Offering

The previous section covered the basic concepts which make up business intelligence implementations. Now that you are able to speak the basic language of business intelligence, it is time to explore Microsoft's offerings in the business intelligence category.

SQL Server 2005

The basis for Microsoft's business intelligence offerings is Microsoft's SQL Server 2005. SQL Server 2005 encapsulates most of the business intelligence functionality we've discussed so far, including an OLTP database, an OLAP database, integration technologies, and reporting technologies. SQL Server 2005 has propelled Microsoft into the forefront of database size and performance capabilities, competing in realms where previously you would only see vendors like Oracle or Teradata. Heavy competition on features and performance, when combined with the single all-inclusive price for all SQL Server technologies make SQL Server perhaps the most widely installed database system in the world.

SQL Server's online analytical processing is served up by the included Analysis Services piece of SQL Server 2005 (SSAS). Analysis Services 2005 is built around a completely new Unified Dimensional Model (UDM), which provides a semantic model that defines business entities, logic, calculations, and metrics. The use of this UDM makes it easier to integrate different sources of data. Users build data cubes out of central fact tables surrounded by dimensions that define the facts. An example of a cube is a fact table of item sales surrounded by dimensions like date/time, geography, clients, and sales promotions

A crucial piece of any business intelligence technology offering is the ability to extract specific data elements from outside data stores, transform it to fit business needs, and load it into the data warehouse. This process of extracting data, transforming it, and loading it is known as ETL (extract, transform, and load). This task is handled by the SQL Server Integration Services (SSIS). SSIS is a complete redesign and rewrite of the original SQL Server technology, Data Transformation Services (DTS). Microsoft SQL Server also provides a native reporting engine which provides the ability to create, manage, secure, and deliver reports in a variety of formats. SQL Server Reporting Services (SSRS) provides solutions for enterprise reporting, ad hoc reporting, web-based reporting, and embedded reporting. New in SSRS 2005 is the Report Builder, an Office-like application that enables end users to build and distribute their own ad hoc reports without requiring support from a corporate IT staff. The SSRS Report Builder tool is a significant addition for SharePoint because it can now participate as a SharePoint document library template just like Word and Excel. Click New in a Report Library, and Report Builder opens to allow your business users to create their own reports.

Other Microsoft Business Intelligence Software Products

While SQL Server is an integral piece of the Microsoft business intelligence offering, it is not the sole BI product offered by Microsoft. Other products in the Microsoft business intelligence offerings include the new Performance Point Server 2007, Microsoft's Business Scorecard Manager 2005, the ubiquitous spreadsheet program Microsoft Office Excel 2007, and of course the focus for this book, Microsoft Office SharePoint Server 2007.

Business Scorecard Manager 2005 is a tool that helps organizations build collections of related KPIs into scorecards. Scorecards enable business decision makers to easily visualize key business data and simplify the measurement of business performance to achieve improved business performance. Scorecards created with BSM 2005 can be displayed on the web or embedded in custom applications. Perhaps no tool is used to analyze business data more frequently than Microsoft Office Excel. The newest version of Microsoft Office Excel 2007 includes new features to improve working with tables and pivot tables, integrate with SQL Server Analysis Services, and, through an all new Excel Services' server-based technology, allow users to securely share and reuse workbooks online.

Performance Point Server 2007 is an integrated performance management application which combines the features of several other products. Included in Performance Point Server are the features to manage company performance such as scorecards, dashboards, reporting, and data analysis. Performance Point Server 2007 works with the familiar Microsoft Office suite and the power of SQL Server. At the time of writing, Performance Point Server 2007 was still in beta.

Microsoft Office SharePoint Server 2007

To understand the evolution of business intelligence features in Microsoft's Office SharePoint Server 2007, one must first understand where SharePoint Portal Server 2003 left off. SharePoint Portal Server 2003, the Office 2003 Web Parts, and Business Scorecard Manager, all provided developers with the ability to build their own dashboard-style applications, which provide upper-level management with the ability to gauge the state of the business at a glance. However, SharePoint Portal Server 2003 did not natively support digital dashboards, leaving the door open for third-party vendors such as ProClarity to build products that integrated with SQL Server and SharePoint to provide solutions.

The team that was building Microsoft Office SharePoint Server 2007 made significant changes based on these lessons learned. Specifically, they enabled SharePoint Server 2007 to easily build such dashboards natively. Business intelligence features now permeate SharePoint Server 2007 and include such elements as the Excel Services, the Business Data Catalog, Business Data SharePoint lists and Web Parts, dashboards, and the Report Center web sites. The rest of this chapter discusses these features in detail.

Building a Business Intelligence Portal

The rest of this chapter builds a single working Business Intelligence Portal based on the Microsoft Adventure Works database. Download the SQL Server 2005 sample database from Microsoft at: `www.microsoft.com/downloads/details.aspx?FamilyID=e719ecf7-9f46-4312-af89-6ad8702e4e6e&DisplayLang=en#filelist`. Install the database by running the AdventureWorksBI `.msi`. Attach the database AdventureWorksDW to your SQL Server. This database has been built by Microsoft specifically to demonstrate Analysis Services' concepts.

The following section of this chapter will focus on building a foundation used throughout the remainder of this chapter. Using Visual Studio, you will create a SQL Server Analysis Services project and create your own simplistic data warehouse and cube.

Building a Cube

The center of Microsoft's business intelligence universe is the SQL Server Analysis Services data cube. Therefore, the first step to taking advantage of the business intelligence features of the Microsoft Office SharePoint Server is to build a cube to work from. Fortunately, this is an extremely easy task thanks to the SQL Server 2005 Analysis Services Cube Wizard. The SSAS Cube Wizard will build a cube for the rest of the examples in this chapter in several easy steps.

Creating an Analysis Services Project

SQL Server 2005 has integrated its design surface into Visual Studio 2005. Therefore, the first step to creating a new cube is to start an Analysis Services project in Visual Studio.

1. To get to this project, open Visual Studio, click Project next to the word Create. Select Business Intelligence from the Project type list on the left, and select Analysis Services Project from the templates list on the right.

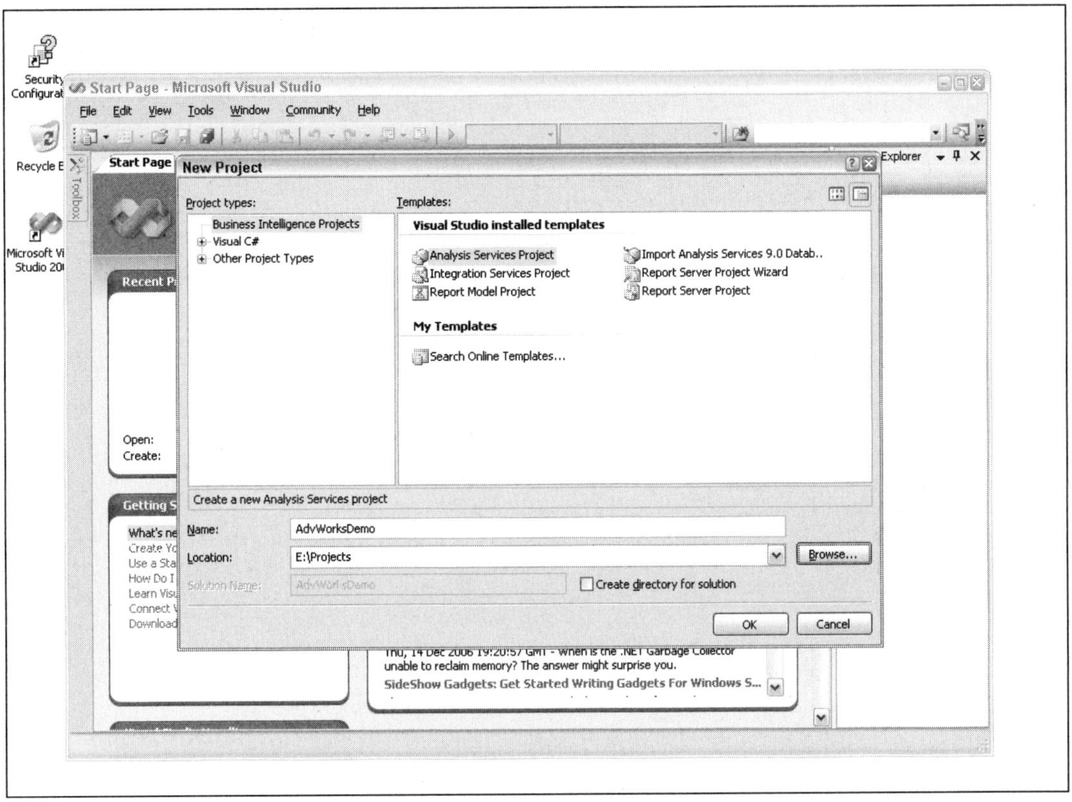

Figure 16-1

2. Name your project **AdvWorksDemo**, and save it in a Projects folder.

3. Deselect the Create directory for solution check box, and your screen should look like Figure 16-1. Click OK.

Create a Data Source

Now, you have the empty shell of an SSAS project. The next step is to connect your project to the database by using the Data Source Wizard.

1. In the Solution Explorer, right-click the Data Sources folder and select New Data Source. This will launch the Data Source Wizard, which will help connect the project to SQL Server.

2. Click next on the Wizard's welcome screen to move on to the Create a new connection screen.

3. Click the new button to create a new data connection. This will bring up the Connection Manager dialog.

4. Identify your SQL Server and the AdventureWorksDW database in the appropriate drop-downs.

5. Test your connection to ensure that your settings are correct, and click OK to return to the main screen, which should now look like Figure 16-2.

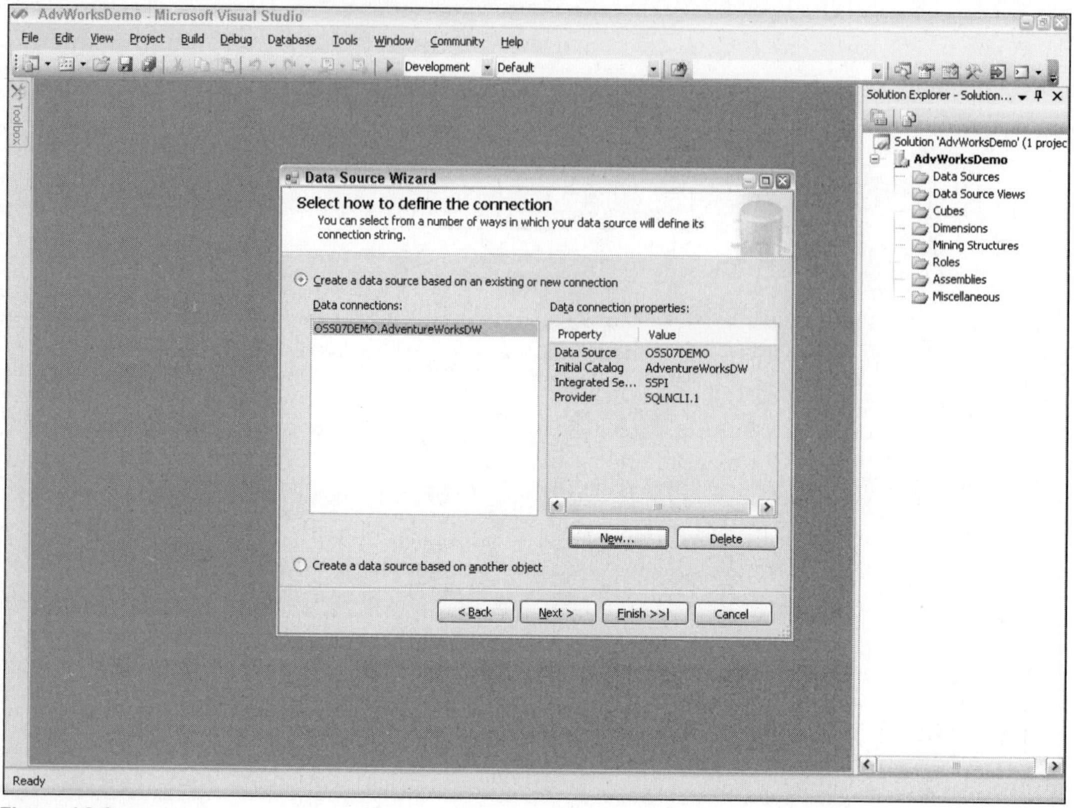

Figure 16-2

6. Click Next to proceed to the Impersonation Information screen. This screen allows you to specify which account to use to connect to SQL Server.

7. For this demo, select Default to use the actual user's Windows identity rather than a service account.

8. Click Next to proceed to the final screen where you can give your connection a name. In Figure 16-3 you can see that I've accepted the default name, AdventureWorksDW.

9. Click Finish to close this dialog and commit your changes.

Create a New Data Source View

Cubes are built on top of logical database views. This layer of abstraction is what enables SSAS cubes to include calculated columns and named queries that do not actually exist in the physical model. The logical view can also be defined as including data from multiple data sources. This enables SSAS to connect to physical data sources such as SQL Server databases or OLE DB databases such as those from Oracle. Creating a new Data Source View is a trivial task thanks to the Data Source View Wizard.

1. The second step in configuring an Analysis Services' project is to identify the data source view. In the Solution Explorer, right-click the Data Source View folder and select New Data Source View.

618

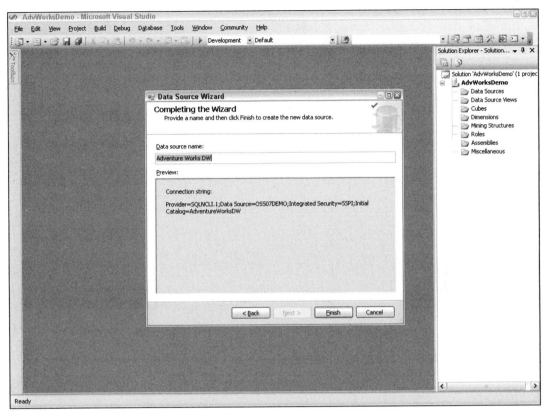

Figure 16-3

2. This will open the Data Source View Wizard. Click Next on the welcome screen to proceed to the Select Data Source screen . This project should only have one data source, so simply click Next.

3. The next screen allows you to select which tables and views you want to include in your data source view. This portion of the process is where you are creating a logical data model of your database. Analysis Services will store metadata about the tables you select such as table and column names and relationships. This logical model of the database is how Analysis Services creates a consistent schema out of different data stores. This is the first step in creating the Unified Dimensional Model upon which Analysis Services is based. In the AdventureWorksDW database, pick the following columns and move them to the Included objects column: DimCurrency, DimCustomer, DimEmployee, DimGeography, DimProduct, DimProductCategory, DimProduct-Subcategory, DimPromotion, DimReseller, DimSalesTerritory, DimTime, FactInternetSales, Fact-ResellerSales, and FactSalesQuota.

4. Click Next to move on to the final screen, where you name your new data source.

5. When you click Finish, you will be presented with a diagram describing the logical model you've just created, as in Figure 16-4. This model is extremely powerful and can even have business logic embedded in it.

6. For example, right-click on the DimCustomer table header and select New Named Calculation.

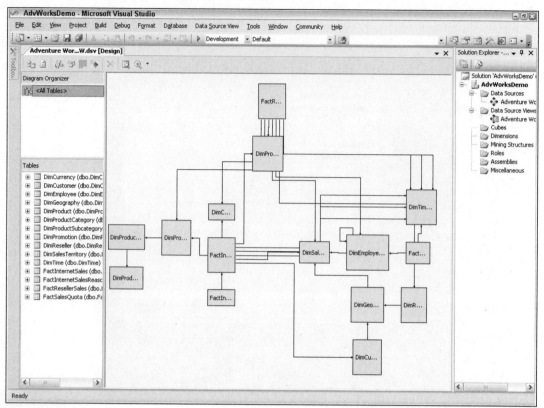

Figure 16-4

7. In the Named Calculation dialog, name the calculation **Full Name**. In the Expression box, type in **FirstName + ' ' + LastName** and click OK. You now have some business logic embedded in your data source view.

8. Validate that you were successful by right-clicking on the table and selecting Explore Data. As in Figure 16-5, this will let you see all of the data in the table, including the new calculated column you just added.

9. The tables in this diagram have names like DimCustomer and FactInternetSales. These names are not very friendly for your future Information Worker users, so rename the table's Friendly Name property to Customer by right-clicking the DimCustomer table and selecting Properties. In the Properties window, change the FriendlyName value from DimCustomer to **Customer**. It is possible to change the friendly table names like this for the rest of the tables in the diagram to provide a consistent friendly feel for future users. In fact, each column in each table also exposes a FriendlyName property. With a little effort, you can truly make your data source view feel very friendly indeed!

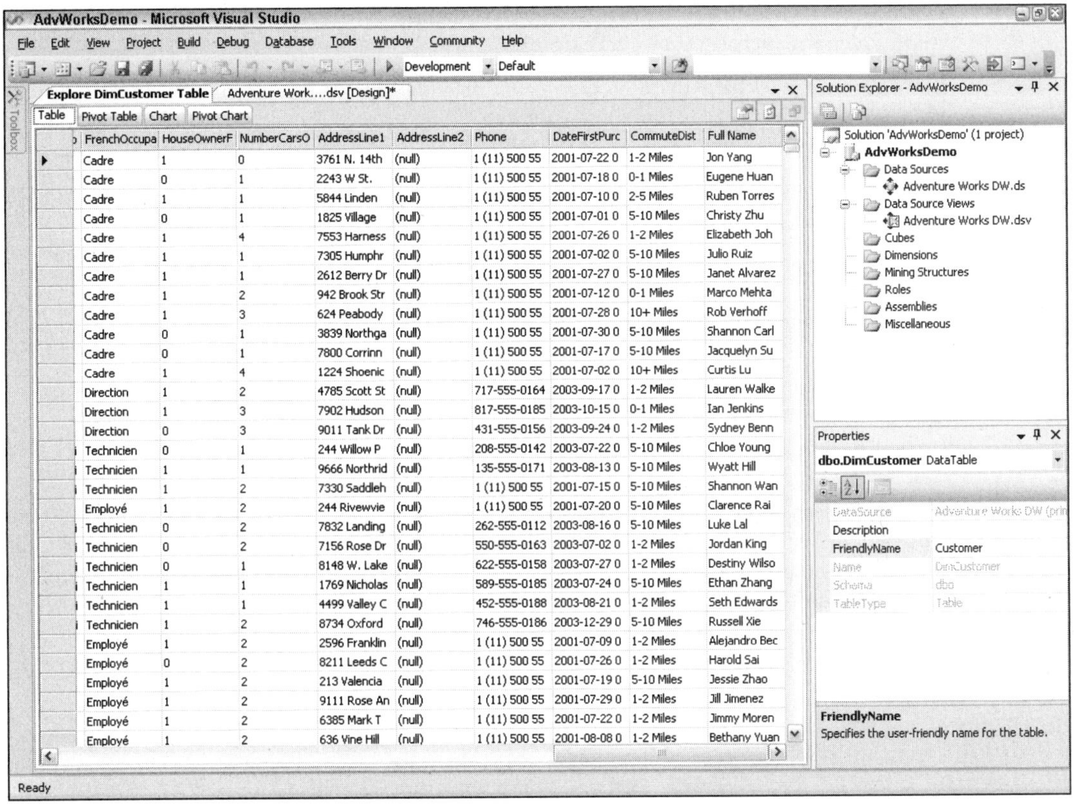

Figure 16-5

Create a New Cube

The next step is to create a cube. The cube, as has been previously stated, is the heart of the solution. The cube you create here is what users in SharePoint and Office will be using.

1. Begin by right-clicking the Cubes folder in the Solution Explorer and selecting New Cube to launch the Cube Wizard.

2. Click Next on the Cube Wizard's welcome screen to get to the Select Build Method screen. Choose to Build the cube using a data source and leave the Auto build box checked.

3. Ensure that the drop-down says to Create attributes and hierarchies, and click Next to select the data source view.

4. As there is only one data source view in this project, click Next to proceed. The wizard will attempt to automatically detect the fact and dimension tables for you, and you can review its progress by clicking Next when it finishes. Microsoft's sample database kindly identifies which tables are fact

tables and which tables are dimension tables by handy prefix, so it will be easy for you to determine which is which.

5. The only thing you have to do on this screen provided the wizard did its job correctly is identify the DimTime table as the Time dimension table. Your screen should now look something like Figure 16-6. In this screenshot, all of the tables have been renamed with FriendlyNames.

6. Because a time dimension table was identified, you must map the time table's columns to the time properties on the Select Time Periods screen using the following values.

   ❑ Map the Year property to the CalendarYear column.

   ❑ Map the Half Year property to the CalendarSemester column.

   ❑ Map the Quarter property to the CalendarQuarter column.

   ❑ Map the Month property to the EnglishMonthName column.

   ❑ Map the Date property to the FullDateAlternateKey column.

7. The next screen is the Select Measures screen. This screen allows you to identify the metrics you care to track with your cube. The Analysis Services Wizard automatically scans the fact tables to identify the columns in the Available measures grid. In this sample, the only column which isn't an actual metric is the Revision number column.

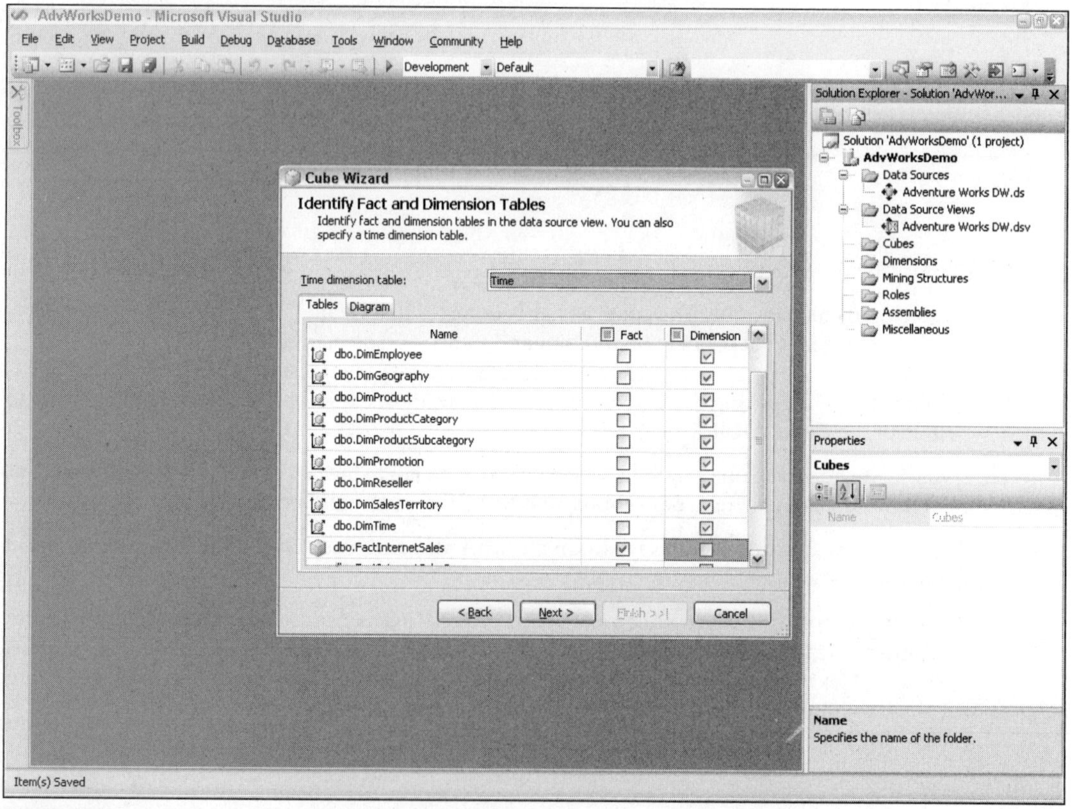

Figure 16-6

8. Click Next to allow the wizard to attempt to automatically detect relationships between the fact and dimension tables. This process will detect and build hierarchies that may or may not be defined in the physical database, such as a relationship between states, regions, and customers. Once all relationships have been detected, click Next again.

9. You will now be at the Review New Dimensions screen. This screen allows you to review the dimension tables which describe the fact tables. The only value that should be changed here is in the Products table; there is a Large Photo attribute, which should be deselected to prevent the database from growing too large with a value that won't be very helpful in this demo.

10. Click Next to proceed to the last screen, where you can assign your cube a name.

11. Click Finish to return to Visual Studio and a color-coded table diagram, as shown in Figure 16-7.

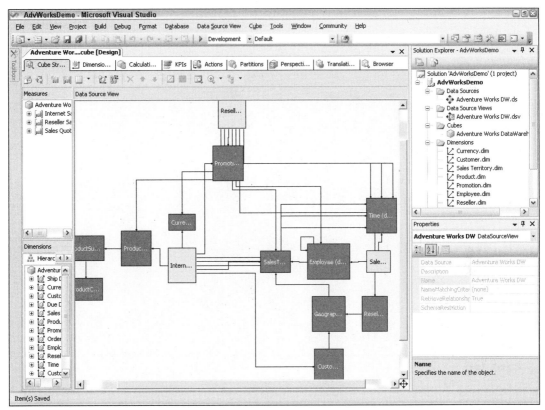

Figure 16-7

Deploying the Cube

All of the work done in the AdvWorksDemo project thus far has not done anything other than create some XML documents. To view these XML documents, right-click on an object such as the Adventure Works DataWarehouse cube object and select View Code. To actually take advantage of the work, you need to deploy these XML documents in SQL Server Analysis Services. SSAS will take the XML definition documents and construct the actual database objects and copy data from the data sources to the

Analysis Services data warehouse objects. To begin the process of deploying your work, right-click on the AdvWorksDemo project in the Solution Explorer and select Deploy. Visual Studio will deploy to Analysis Services, reporting its progress in the bottom-right corner. Once the cube has been deployed, you have the ability to browse the cube and to experience the flexible ad hoc reporting possible right from inside of Visual Studio. Double-Click on the Adventure Works DataWarehouse cube object and select the Browser tab. The main portion of the screen will become a very familiar Office Web Component UI, and you can easily drag fields onto the screen to build a PivotTable in a matter of moments, as in Figure 16-8, where I've decided to examine sales amounts and quantities by geography, by customer, and by quarter.

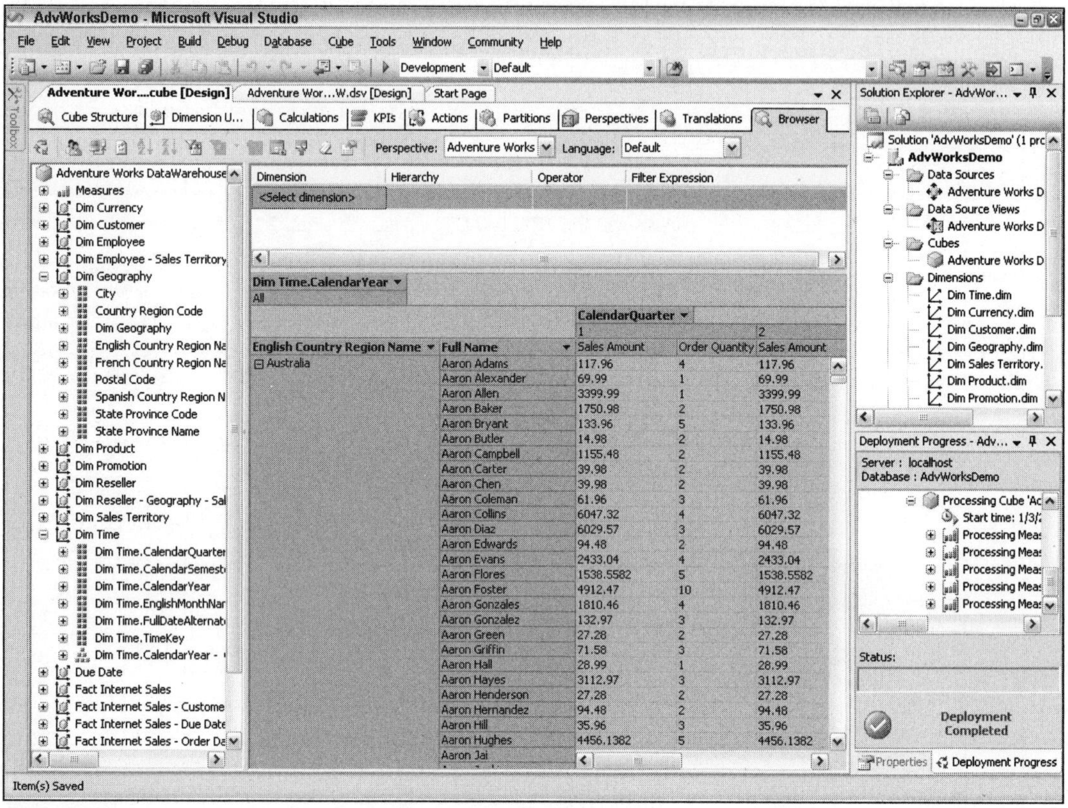

Figure 16-8

Creating Key Performance Indicators in SSAS

You now have the first part of a data warehouse, a cube. Now it is time to add some monitoring capabilities to the cube in the form of some Key Performance Indicators. SSAS is a powerful tool for analysis and incorporating your KPIs directly in the cube is an effective and portable mechanism for identifying the state of the data in the cube.

1. To prepare for the creating KPIs, create a new measure to identify gross profit.

2. Adding the Key Performance Indicators is the next step now that the cube has been defined. Open the Adventure Works DataWarehouse cube object, and click on the KPIs tab.

3. Add a new KPI by clicking on the New KPI button. The blank KPI template will appear. Since AdventureWorks is a (fictional) retail organization, one of the KPIs they care about is whether or not they are making a profit on the merchandise they sell. The first KPI to add is the Gross Profit Margin KPI. Fortunately, Analysis Services ships with a large number of template KPIs, which will help make the creation of KPIs easier.

4. In the Calculation Tools window at the bottom left of the screen, select the Templates tab. Expand the Financial folder and locate the Gross Profit Margin template. Double-click this template to create a new instance of this KPI. Now, you can customize the template to fit the organization's needs. The fields have the following meanings:

   ❑ Name — this is the name of your KPI. The default value of Gross Profit Margin is perfect for this demo.

   ❑ The Associated measure group identifies which fact table to associate the KPI with. Select Fact Internet Sales from the list.

   ❑ The Value Expression identifies how to evaluate the KPI and defaults to gross profit / net sale × 100, which is an adequate expression of the organization's gross profit. The default template text is just a placeholder, so replace the existing text with the following MDX expression. This expression was built by dragging and dropping values from the Calculation Tools' metadata tab:

   SUM([Measures].[Sales Amount]-[Measures].[Tax Amt]- [Measures].[Total Product Cost]) / SUM([Measures].[Sales Amount] - [Measures].[Tax Amt]) × 100

   ❑ The Goal Expression identifies the target value. Remember that KPIs are a measurement of progress towards a *goal*. AdventureWorks would like to earn a 25% profit, so put .25 in the Goal Expression field.

   ❑ The Status indicator drop-down allows you to pick which graphic you want to represent your KPI. Pick the Shapes option.

   ❑ The Status Expression is an MDX expression that evaluates progress towards the goal. Status expressions are represented as a range between –1 (very bad) and +1 (very good). In the provided expression, the KPI will evaluate if the current profit margin minus the goal profit margin is positive. This indicates that AdventureWorks is exceeding its stated goal of a 25% profit margin. If the current gross profit margin calculation minus the goal is a negative number, then AdventureWorks has not met its goal and needs to pay attention to profitability. This is the expression that is provided by the template:

```
IIf
(
    KPIValue( "Gross Profit Margin" ) - KPIGoal( "Gross Profit Margin" )>=0, 1, -1
)
```

   ❑ The trend indicator is a graphic used to identify which direction the company is moving in. Again, refer to the definition of a KPI — *progress* towards a goal. Pick the Status arrow from the list.

❏ The trend expression is an MDX expression that calculates the trend towards achieving the desired goal. This is the provided trend expression:

```
IIf
(
  KPIValue( "Gross Profit Margin" ) >
  ( KPIValue( "Gross Profit Margin" ),
    ParallelPeriod
  (
    [<<Time Dimension Name>>].[<<Time Hierarchy Name>>].[<<Time Year Level Name>>],
    1,
    [<<Time Dimension Name>>].[<<Time Hierarchy Name>>].CurrentMember
  )
  ), 1, -1
)
```

To learn more about Analysis Services, try the sample application included with the AdventureWorksDW database and the tutorial online at http://msdn2.microsoft.com/en-us/library/ms170208.aspx.

Using Excel and Excel Services in Business Intelligence

A majority of organizations keep a large amount of business intelligence logic in Microsoft Excel workbooks. This is because Excel is a tool with a long history and a huge entrenched user base. Information workers are able to manipulate data in a spreadsheet using a variety of the powerful Excel features to quickly and easily create an understanding of what the numbers in that workbook represent. Charts and pivot tables, multiple sheets in a workbook, powerful formulas, and even Visual Basic for Applications, all combine to make Excel a nearly indispensable tool for business today.

Unfortunately, Excel has always been a local or client-side application. The data in multiple Excel workbooks is sometimes difficult to extract, and the business logic embedded in these workbooks is hard to reuse meaningfully across larger organizations. Customers have been asking Microsoft for years to "put Excel on the server" to enable this content and logic reuse. This kind of request has typically been answered by third-party solutions such as SoftArtisan's OfficeWriter (http://officewriter.softartisans.com/officewriter-8.aspx). However, now for the first time since Excel was launched back in 1985 (for the Mac, oddly enough), Excel now has a server component designed to extend and enrich spreadsheet data.

Microsoft Office Excel 2007

Microsoft Office has traditionally been one of the largest sources of revenue for Microsoft, and critical to the ongoing adoption of the Office suite among customers is Microsoft Excel. The 2007 version of Excel comes with some fantastic new features, including but not limited to, the following:

❏ A brand-new user interface starring the new Office Ribbon (designed to help users get faster and better results by bringing to the forefront task-oriented program features).

❏ Enlarged spreadsheet capacity designed to store larger amounts of data.

❏ Improved style choices and conditional formatting help make your tables, charts, and numbers stand out in easy to read and understand ways.

❑ PivotTable and PivotChart wizards use a simple drag and drop interface to radically simplify the previously painful process of creating PivotTables and PivotCharts.

❑ Integration into SQL Server Analysis Services. As in older versions of Excel, you can connect to SQL Server to import external data, but now SSAS data warehouses are one of the available external data sources.

What Is Excel Services?

Excel Services is included with the Enterprise Edition of Microsoft Office SharePoint Server. It is designed to give users the ability to easily and securely share Excel spreadsheets and workbooks. Essentially, Excel Services renders spreadsheets as HTML and JavaScript and delivers the results to the user's browser. No Office clients or viewers are required, and no ActiveX control installation is required either. The user experience is a subset of the full Excel application on the desktop. For instance, the web user can sort and filter data within the browser. If editing is required, a user with the appropriate permissions can open the workbook in Excel and then update the copy on the server.

Excel Services Architecture

Excel Services was designed for scalability and is composed of three distinct components. The Excel Calculation Services component gathers data, performs calculations, and handles user sessions. The Excel Web Access (EWA) Web Part renders a server-based spreadsheet using only DHTML and JavaScript, which enables users to access the spreadsheet from just about any browser and platform. The final piece of Excel Services is the Excel Web Services (EWS) service layer that enables developers to build custom applications that take advantage of Excel workbooks.

Excel Services can be installed in three configurations: the Single Server scenario, the Small Farm scenario, and the Server Farm scenario. In the *Single Server scenario*, most commonly seen in department level servers, all of the required server components are installed on a single server, including SQL Server and SharePoint. In the *Small Farm scenario*, SQL Server is moved to another server while Excel Services and SharePoint share a physical machine. In the *Server Farm scenario*, Excel Services is installed on one or more dedicated servers, apart from SharePoint and SQL Server. In this Server Farm scenario, Excel Calculation Services servers and Web Front End servers (which include Excel Web Access) may be load balanced and increased in number to handle demand as required.

Excel Services Benefits

Okay, so you can put a workbook on the web. How is this better than just storing the workbook in a SharePoint document library or on a network file share? There are several answers to this question. First and foremost is security. As a workbook publisher, you get to decide which portions of the workbook are available online. You could indicate which worksheets or even which tables and charts on a sheet are available. Second, you have the option to save snapshots of data rather than live workbooks. A snapshot only saves data and formatting, not formulas or live data connections. This is useful when you want to protect private business logic and to save data for archival purposes. Third, having the workbook online, combined with the aforementioned security, enables you to have one version of a workbook rather than multiple versions, as frequently happens when Excel workbooks are emailed around and manipulated by multiple individuals. Finally, you have access to the Excel Services API. This enables you to keep your existing business logic in Excel, but to present the data in custom applications.

The following examples walk you through the creation of an Excel workbook, the publication of this workbook to a SharePoint document library, and the consumption of the workbook through both Excel Web Access and the Excel Web Services API.

Build an Excel Workbook

Excel Services is for the "exploration and consumption" of workbooks, but Excel 2007 is still the editor when it comes to creating and modifying workbooks. The following portion will build a simple Excel workbook containing multiple sheets, some live data tied to a database, a pivot table, and some charts. This will show off a few of the newest Excel 2007 features and be the basis for the upcoming Excel Services exploration.

Begin by opening Microsoft Excel. The first thing to do is have a quick peek at some of the great new conditional formatting options, which allow easy visual identification of key data values. This section will start out showcasing some of the neat new features in Excel 2007 and move into some power user content before diving into user defined functions (managed code) and the Excel Web Services API. The power user section below will help you present more compelling spreadsheets online via Excel Services.

Heat Map

A heat map is a quick visual indication of problem areas identified by color-coding the background of the cell a shade from green to red. You can choose the style, but the basic premise is that green numbers (perhaps large numbers) are good, and red numbers (perhaps small numbers) are bad. Using a heat map can help you instantly identify which numbers to pay attention to in a large table of data that might otherwise require deliberate study to find the desired values.

1. In cell A1, type **Random Numbers and a Heat Map**.

2. In cell A2, type **=Rand()** to generate a random number between 0 and 1.

3. Drag the lower-right corner to cell G2 to fill the top row with random numbers.

4. Highlight these numbers, and drag the lower-right corner to row 20 to create a grid of random numbers.

5. Highlight the grid, and on the Home tab of the Ribbon, select Conditional Formatting ⇨ Color Scales.

6. Pick the first entry to create a heat map where the largest numbers are green and the smallest numbers are red.

Data Bars

Similar to heat maps, data bars are background images in a cell. What's nice about data bars is that you can use this bar graph like background to help you visually measure values against each other.

1. In cell I1, type **Random Numbers and Data Bars**.

2. In cell I2, type = **=Rand()** to generate a random number.

3. Drag the lower-right corner down to cell I20 to fill a column with random numbers.

4. Highlight this column, and select Conditional Formatting ⇨ Data Bars.

5. Pick the first entry to create blue data bars that fill the background of the cell with a gradient indicating the largest numbers with proportional fill effects.

6. Rename Sheet1 to **Random Numbers** and click on Sheet2 to enter a clean workbook sheet.

Data from SQL Server

Now it is time to connect to SQL Server and pull in some data. Unfortunately, due to the Excel Services' restrictions, once this data is pulled down from SQL Server, the live connection to the database must be severed or Excel Services won't render the workbook.

1. Click the Data tab.

2. Click the From Other Sources button. Notice the variety of choices, including SQL Server Analysis Services. Pick From SQL Server for this particular exercise.

3. Identify the SQL Server you wish to connect to, and press Next.

4. Select the database you wish to connect to, and select the specific table. For this example, you want to connect to the AdventureWorksDW database and the FactInternetSales table. Click Next.

5. Change the Friendly Name to **InternetSales**, and click Finish.

6. Accept all of the defaults to import the data as a table into the existing worksheet at position A1. Click OK.

7. You now have an Excel table of sales data from the database. Rename this sheet Internet Sales, and click on Sheet3 to enter a clean workbook sheet.

8. Repeat these steps on Sheet3, but this time import the DimProducts table to have a sheet with all the product information. Rename this sheet **Products**.

9. On each of the two new sheets, click the Design tab in the Ribbon, and in the External Table Data section, click the Unlink icon to break the connection between SQL Server and Excel. Failure to do this will cause Excel Services to complain about unsupported features.

Calculated Values

The sales table contains a sales amount and a cost amount column. Add two new columns to calculate profit and profit margin percentage:

1. Insert a new column between the SalesAmount and TaxAmount columns.

2. Rename the column **ProfitAmount**.

3. In the cell, enter the formula =t2-s2 to subtract the TotalProductCost from the SalesAmount. Excel will automatically fill the rest of the column for you.

4. Insert another new column between the new ProfitAmount column and the TaxAmount columns.

5. Rename this column **ProfitMargin**.

6. In the first cell, enter the formula =(ts-s2)/t2 to get the gross profit margin. Excel will automatically fill the rest of the column for you.

When you're finished, your screen should look like Figure 16-9.

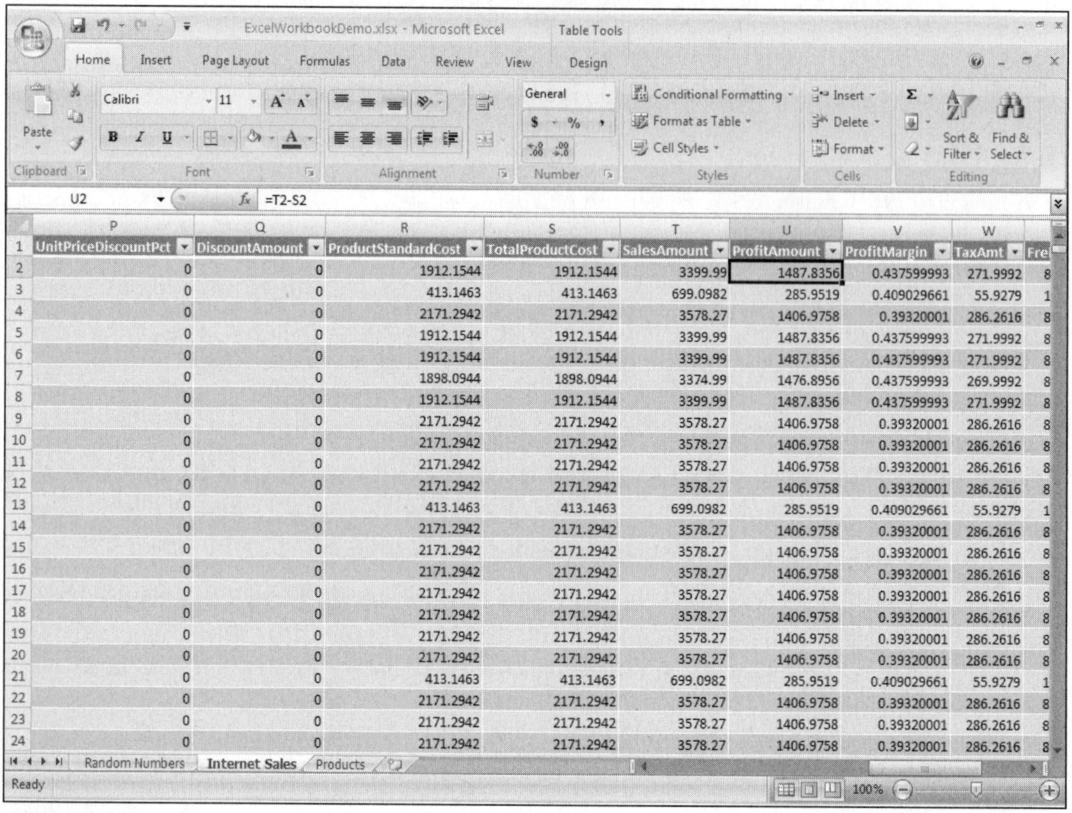

	UnitPriceDiscountPct	DiscountAmount	ProductStandardCost	TotalProductCost	SalesAmount	ProfitAmount	ProfitMargin	TaxAmt	Fre
2	0	0	1912.1544	1912.1544	3399.99	1487.8356	0.437599993	271.9992	8
3	0	0	413.1463	413.1463	699.0982	285.9519	0.409029661	55.9279	1
4	0	0	2171.2942	2171.2942	3578.27	1406.9758	0.39320001	286.2616	8
5	0	0	1912.1544	1912.1544	3399.99	1487.8356	0.437599993	271.9992	8
6	0	0	1912.1544	1912.1544	3399.99	1487.8356	0.437599993	271.9992	8
7	0	0	1898.0944	1898.0944	3374.99	1476.8956	0.437599993	269.9992	8
8	0	0	1912.1544	1912.1544	3399.99	1487.8356	0.437599993	271.9992	8
9	0	0	2171.2942	2171.2942	3578.27	1406.9758	0.39320001	286.2616	8
10	0	0	2171.2942	2171.2942	3578.27	1406.9758	0.39320001	286.2616	8
11	0	0	2171.2942	2171.2942	3578.27	1406.9758	0.39320001	286.2616	8
12	0	0	2171.2942	2171.2942	3578.27	1406.9758	0.39320001	286.2616	8
13	0	0	413.1463	413.1463	699.0982	285.9519	0.409029661	55.9279	1
14	0	0	2171.2942	2171.2942	3578.27	1406.9758	0.39320001	286.2616	8
15	0	0	2171.2942	2171.2942	3578.27	1406.9758	0.39320001	286.2616	8
16	0	0	2171.2942	2171.2942	3578.27	1406.9758	0.39320001	286.2616	8
17	0	0	2171.2942	2171.2942	3578.27	1406.9758	0.39320001	286.2616	8
18	0	0	2171.2942	2171.2942	3578.27	1406.9758	0.39320001	286.2616	8
19	0	0	2171.2942	2171.2942	3578.27	1406.9758	0.39320001	286.2616	8
20	0	0	2171.2942	2171.2942	3578.27	1406.9758	0.39320001	286.2616	8
21	0	0	413.1463	413.1463	699.0982	285.9519	0.409029661	55.9279	1
22	0	0	2171.2942	2171.2942	3578.27	1406.9758	0.39320001	286.2616	8
23	0	0	2171.2942	2171.2942	3578.27	1406.9758	0.39320001	286.2616	8
24	0	0	2171.2942	2171.2942	3578.27	1406.9758	0.39320001	286.2616	8

Figure 16-9

Vlookup Function

You have the sales table and the product table in your workbook, but how do you get data from one sheet into the other? This quick walkthrough will help you put the appropriate product name in the sales table based on the product key.

1. Insert a column between the Product Key and the OrderDateKey.
2. Change the column header name from Column1 to **ProductName**.
3. In cell B2, type the following formula, **=vlookup(A2, Table__._AdventureWorksDW_DimProduct[[ProductKey]:[EnglishProductName]], 6, False)**. This formula identifies the `ProductKey` value as the foreign key, locates it in the named rage in the DimProduct table, and inserts the associated English Product Name (column 6).
4. Excel will automatically fill the column with the correct data as in Figure 16-10.

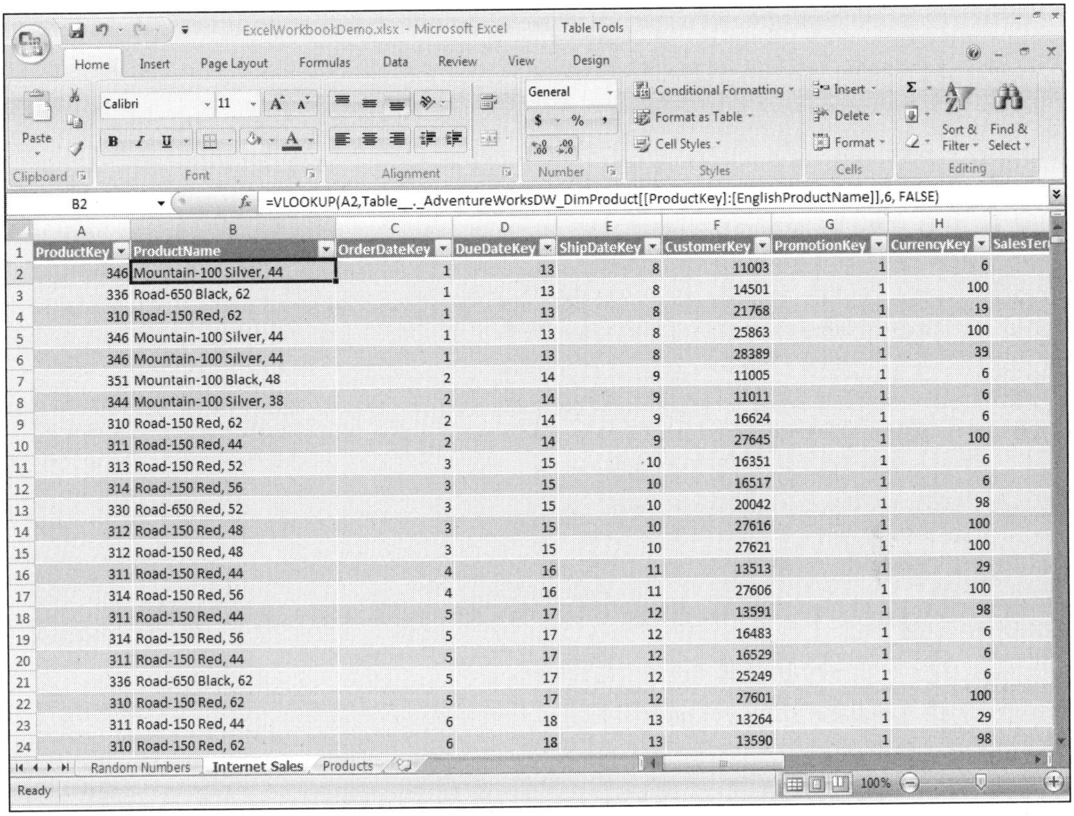

	ProductKey	ProductName	OrderDateKey	DueDateKey	ShipDateKey	CustomerKey	PromotionKey	CurrencyKey	SalesTer
2	346	Mountain-100 Silver, 44	1	13	8	11003	1	6	
3	336	Road-650 Black, 62	1	13	8	14501	1	100	
4	310	Road-150 Red, 62	1	13	8	21768	1	19	
5	346	Mountain-100 Silver, 44	1	13	8	25863	1	100	
6	346	Mountain-100 Silver, 44	1	13	8	28389	1	39	
7	351	Mountain-100 Black, 48	2	14	9	11005	1	6	
8	344	Mountain-100 Silver, 38	2	14	9	11011	1	6	
9	310	Road-150 Red, 62	2	14	9	16624	1	6	
10	311	Road-150 Red, 44	2	14	9	27645	1	100	
11	313	Road-150 Red, 52	3	15	10	16351	1	6	
12	314	Road-150 Red, 56	3	15	10	16517	1	6	
13	330	Road-650 Red, 52	3	15	10	20042	1	98	
14	312	Road-150 Red, 48	3	15	10	27616	1	100	
15	312	Road-150 Red, 48	3	15	10	27621	1	100	
16	311	Road-150 Red, 44	4	16	11	13513	1	29	
17	314	Road-150 Red, 56	4	16	11	27606	1	100	
18	311	Road-150 Red, 44	5	17	12	13591	1	98	
19	314	Road-150 Red, 56	5	17	12	16483	1	6	
20	311	Road-150 Red, 44	5	17	12	16529	1	6	
21	336	Road-650 Black, 62	5	17	12	25249	1	6	
22	310	Road-150 Red, 62	5	17	12	27601	1	100	
23	311	Road-150 Red, 44	6	18	13	13264	1	29	
24	310	Road-150 Red, 62	6	18	13	13590	1	98	

Figure 16-10

PivotTables

PivotTables are an important spreadsheet concept and are frequently used for reporting large amounts of data. The basic premise is that you can take a large table of data and summarize the values based along a different axis. Imagine that you had a large amount of cash register transactions. These would typically be laid out by transaction number and perhaps sorted by time. You could use a pivot table to summarize this data by sales clerk to see which clerk was the busiest.

1. Select the Internet Sales sheet and select the entire Internet Sales table by pressing CTRL+A.
2. Click the Insert tab on the Ribbon and click the PivotTable button.
3. Select PivotTable to bring up the Create PivotTable dialog.
4. Select New Worksheet as the location of the new PivotTable and click OK.
5. You will now be presented with the PivotTable report builder which will help you generate the report.
6. Check the fields TotalProdutCost, SalesAmount, and ProfitAmount to include them as detail fields in the report. Highlight these fields on the report and format them as currency.

7. Drag the ProductName field down to the Report Filter box to enable filtering by product.

8. Check the field ProfitMargin to include it in the report.

9. In the Values box, click the options arrow next to Sum of ProfitMargin, and select the Value Field Settings option.

10. Change the summarize by option from Sum to Average.

11. Select the Average of ProfitMargin on the report, and change the formatting from currency to percentage.

12. Close the Field List task pane, and test your report's filtering capabilities by changing the ProductName value from All to a specific field. Notice that the report values change as different options are selected.

13. Notice that if you double-click on a cell value such as the Sum of SalesAmount, you can drill into the data that makes up this value. In this case, a new sheet will be created which contains the same data as the Internet Sales sheet.

14. Rename the sheet to **PivotReports**.

Adding Charts

Add a chart based on the PivotTable to make the data pop out and easy to understand.

1. On the Insert tab, select to insert a 2-D bar chart.

2. Click the Select Data button on the Design tab to pick the values.

3. Add a series. Call the Series Total Sales Amount ,and pick cell B5 as the value.

4. Add another series, this time called Total Profit Amount. Pick cell B6 as the value.

5. Edit the Horizontal Axis Label so that it says **Totals** instead of "1".

6. Select the Quick Layout button, and pick Layout 5 to automatically create a table under the chart with the report values.

7. Right-click the horizontal axis with the total dollar amounts and select Format Axis. To prevent the axis from appearing too crowded, change the number format to Currency with 0 decimal places. This should make the chart easier to read.

8. Notice that as you change the filter for the PivotTable, the chart values automatically change with it.

Excel Services User Defined Functions

User Defined Functions (UDFs) are developer-created custom functionality that extend the capabilities of Excel. UDFs are created in managed .NET code and are used in workbooks just like the build in Excel formulas, in a cell using the "=MyUDF(A1:B2)" syntax. User Defined Function classes must be marked with the `Microsoft.Office.Excel.Server.Udf.UdfClass` attribute, and UDF methods must be marked with the `Microsoft.Office.Excel.Server.Udf.UdfMethod` attribute or they will be ignored by the Excel Calculation Services. In this demo, you will create a simple UDF that can be used in the workbook sample you created above.

Create a Managed UDF

Text manipulation is not easily accomplished in Excel, but is a snap to handle in C#. This example Managed UDF takes text entered in the spreadsheet and runs it through some C# code to translate the text into Pig Latin.

1. Open Visual Studio.

2. Create a new C# Class Library project. Name your project **ExcelUDFDemo**.

3. Once the project is created, in the Solution Explorer, right-click on the References folder and click Add Reference.

4. Select the Excel Services UDF Framework.

5. In Class1.cs, add this using statement: `using Microsoft.Office.Excel.Server.UDF`.

6. Rename your class from Class1 to **PigLatin**.

7. Decorate your class with the `UdfClass` attribute, as in Figure 16-11.

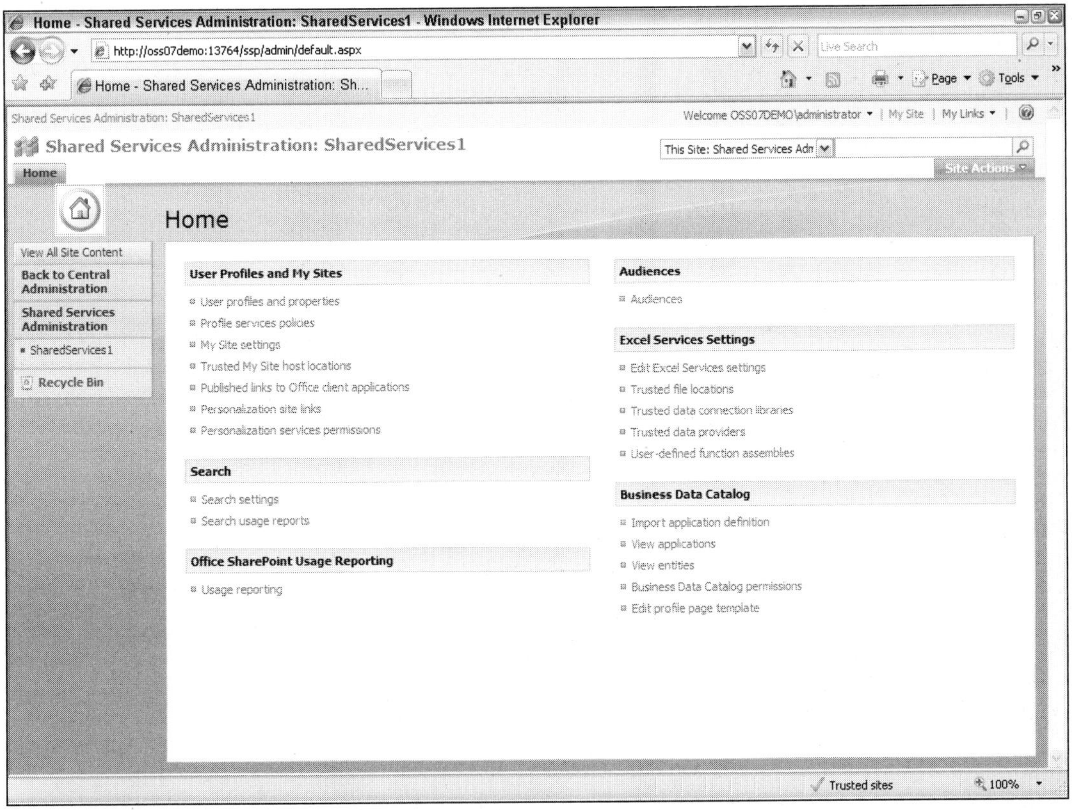

Figure 16-11

8. Create a method to accept a string value and turn it into Pig Latin, as in the following example.

```
[UdfMethod]
     public string MakePigLatin(string ConvertText)
     {
         StringBuilder Response = new StringBuilder();
         String[] Words;
         String TempWord;

         ConvertText = ConvertText.Trim();

         if (ConvertText.Length >= 4)
         {
             Words = ConvertText.Split(' ');

             foreach (String word in Words)
             {
                 if (word.Length != 0)
                 {
                     TempWord = word.Trim();

                     if (TempWord.Length >= 4)
                     {
                         if (!this.IsVowel(TempWord.Substring(0, 1)))
                         {
                             if (!this.IsVowel(TempWord.Substring(1, 1)))
                             {
                                 Response.Append(TempWord.Substring(2,
TempWord.Length - 2) + TempWord.Substring(0, 2) + "ay" + " ");
                             }
                             else
                             {
                                 Response.Append((TempWord.Substring(1,
TempWord.Length - 1) + TempWord.Substring(0, 1) + "ay" + " "));
                             }
                         }
                         else
                         {
                             TempWord = "h" + TempWord;
                             Response.Append(TempWord.Substring(1,
TempWord.Length - 1) + "-" + TempWord.Substring(0, 1) + "ay" + " ");
                         }
                     }
                     else
                     {
                         Response.Append(TempWord + " ");
                     }
                 }
             }

             return Response.ToString(0, Response.Length - 1);
         }
         else
         {
             return ConvertText;
         }
     }
```

```
        }

        private bool IsVowel(String Letter)
        {
            foreach (char vowel in Vowels)
            {
                if (String.Compare(vowel.ToString(), Letter, true) == 0)
                {
                    return true;
                }
            }
            return false;
        }
    }
```

You can find the completed solution along with a Pig Latin Test Harness as `ExcelUDFDemo.zip` *at* `www.wrox.com`.

Deploying the UDF

Your UDF is not functional on your machine and must be deployed to the SharePoint server to work. The following steps walk you through creating a trusted location on your server and deploying the managed assembly:

1. Copy the compiled DLL to the SharePoint server. It is recommended that you create a single location for all UDFs, such as `C:\UDFs`.

2. Launch the SharePoint Central Administrator, and navigate to the Shared Services Administration page.

3. In the Excel Services Settings section, click the Trusted file locations link. Add a trusted file location if one does not already exist.

4. In the trusted file location, identify in the Address box the URL of the SharePoint library where you will be storing your workbooks. On my machine I picked `http://oss07demo:13764/Shared%20Documents`.

5. Set the maximum workbook size up to 30MB or more. Thanks to the large amount of data in the example workbook, you need to increase the size of the searched workbooks or you will get File Not Found errors when you try to view the workbook in your web browser.

6. Under Trust Children, select Children trusted to trust subdirectories.

7. Under the Allow User-Defined Functions section, select User-defined functions allowed.

8. Click OK.

9. Return to the Shared Services Administration page, and click the User-defined function assemblies link under the Excel Services Settings.

10. Add a new User Defined Function.

11. In the Assembly box, type in the following file path: `C:\UDFs\ExcelUDFDemo.dll`.

12. In the Assembly Location selection, choose File Path.

13. Ensure the assembly is enabled (the default selection) and click OK.

14. Restart IIS by clicking Start ➪ Run and typing **iisreset**.

Using the UDF in Excel

Return to the Excel workbook you have been working on. It is time to start using the new User Defined Function you just created.

1. On the Random Numbers sheet, type **=MakePigLatin(A1)** into cell A23. Don't be alarmed when the cell evaluates to #Name? in Excel. User Defined Functions only work when the workbook is displayed by Excel Services.

2. You must name the parameter to your UDF. Highlight cell A1 and click the Formulas tab.

3. Click the Name Manager icon and click Add.

4. Name the selected cell **InputString4PigLatin** and click OK, and you'll be returned to the Name Manager dialog as in Figure 16-12.

5. Close the Name Manager and save the workbook.

Learn more about Excel Services UDFs in the online help documentation here: `http://msdn2 .microsoft.com/en-us/library/ms493934.aspx`.

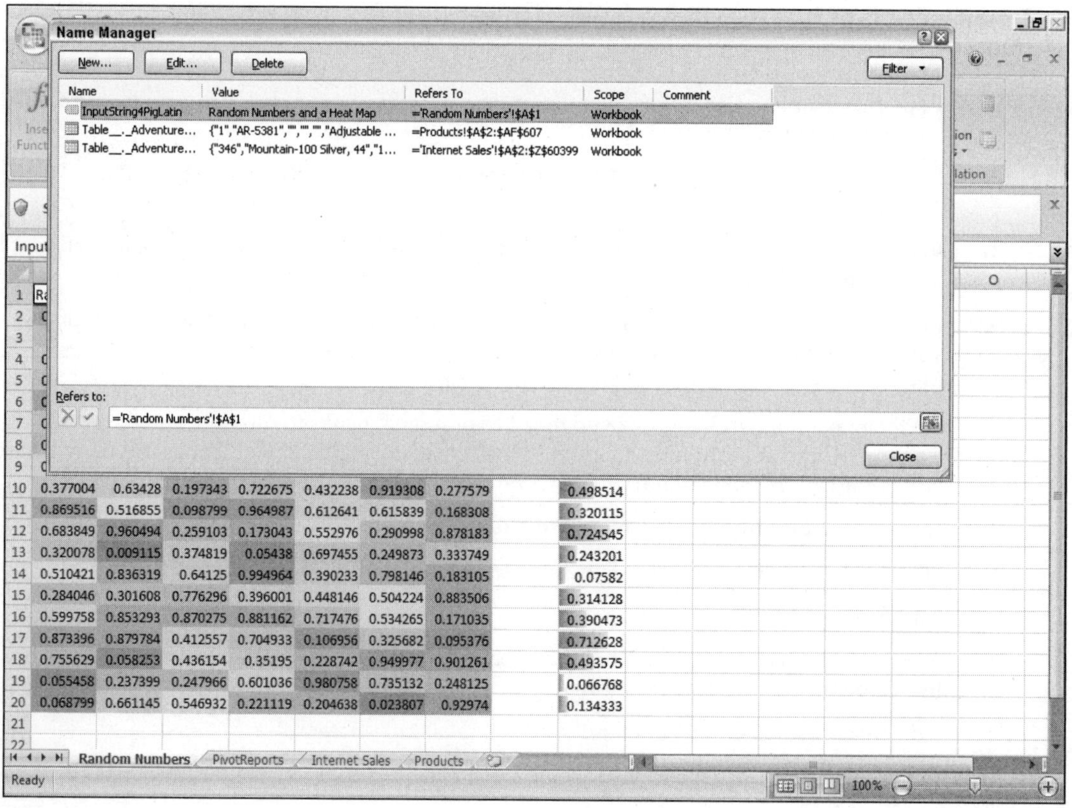

Figure 16-12

Publish with Excel Services

Now you have a workbook. It's time to put that workbook online and examine the features you get with Excel Services. The first step is publishing the workbook.

1. Click the Microsoft Office Button, point to Publish, and click Excel Services.

2. In the File Name box, type in the URL of the document library you identified as a trusted file location for Excel Services, that is, `http://oss07demo:13764/Shared%20Documents/ExcelWorkbookDemo.xlsx`, as in Figure 16-13.

3. Pull down the Save As type drop-down to force Excel to connect to the SharePoint library.

4. Ensure that the Open in Excel Services check box is checked and click Save. The server will process the operation for a while then render the workbook in Internet Explorer as in Figure 16-14. Notice that each of the worksheet tabs and all of the elements on each of those tabs are present. Also notice that the UDF has correctly processed the text in cell A1 into Pig Latin.

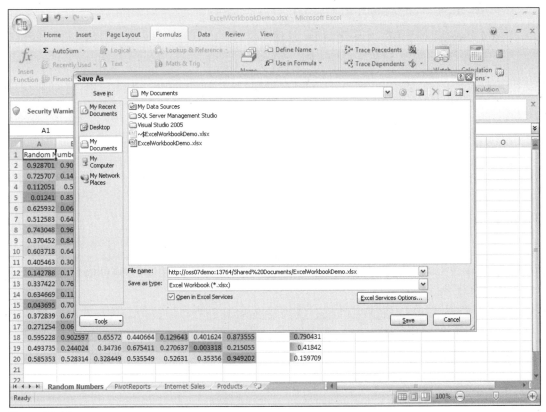

Figure 16-13

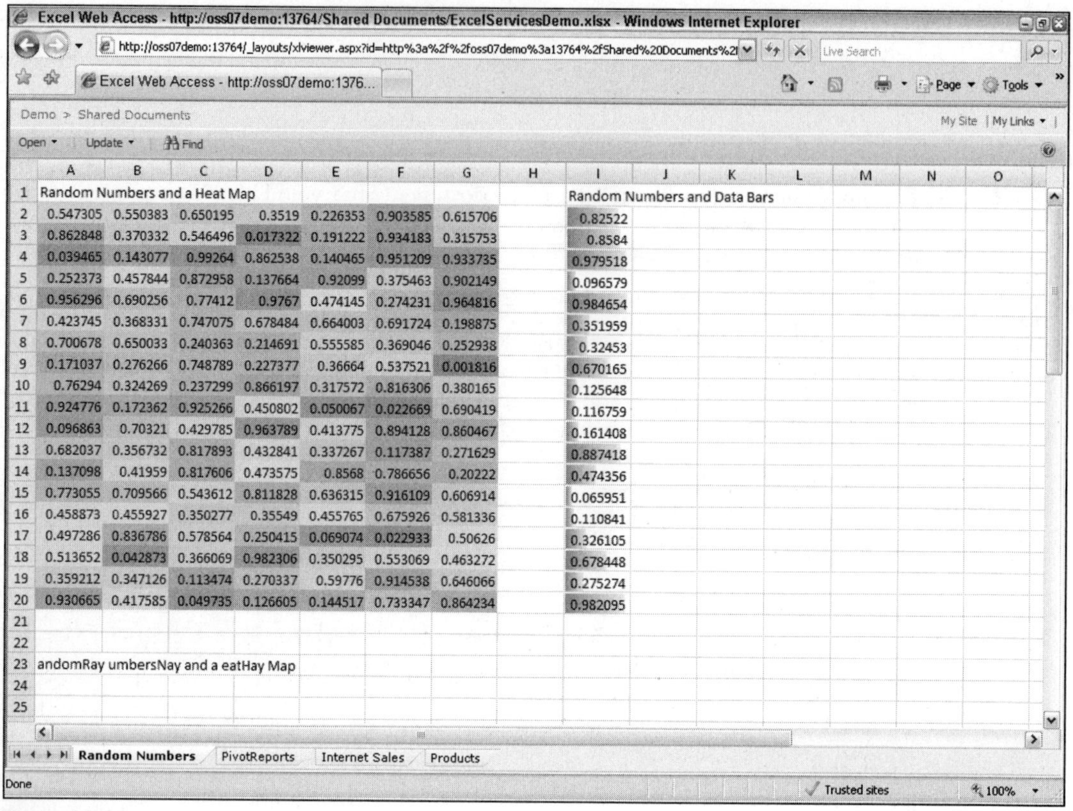

Figure 16-14

Publishing Parts of Workbooks

If security or archival purposes are a concern, you might want to hide portions of the workbook or per-haps only publish a snapshot of the data, which is frozen in time and all external links are removed. The process is almost identical to the steps above, except that now it is time to explore the Excel Services Options dialog.

1. Click the Microsoft Office Button, point to Publish, and click Excel Services.

2. In the Save As dialog that pops up, click the Excel Services Options button .

3. In the Excel Services Options dialog, the Show tab allows you to secure portions of the spread-sheet. Click the drop-down and select Sheets. Remove the InternetSales and Products sheets from the list.

4. Click the Parameters tab. This is where you could specify manually supplied input parameters. This demo doesn't require this, but if you click the Add button you can see that the named parameter, InputString4PigLatin, is an available parameter.

5. In the File Name box, type in the URL of the document library and save the file with a different name, such as `ExcelServicesDemo.xlsx`.

6. Ensure the Open in Excel Services check box is checked and click Save. The server will process the operation for a while then render the workbook in Internet Explorer. Notice that only the selected worksheet tabs and all of the elements on each of those tabs are present.

Programming with the Excel Services API

As you would expect with a SharePoint service, Microsoft's Excel Services exposes an API designed for developers to enable the building of custom applications. There is both an object model accessible on the server and a set of web services accessible from anywhere on the network. In the following example, you will build a tool to open the workbook created above, update certain values to be processed by a formula in an Excel workbook, pull the values back to the custom application, and view the changes on a SharePoint page.

1. Open Visual Studio and create a new C# Windows Application project.

2. Since you'll be working with Excel Web Services, name your application **EWSDemoApp**.

3. In the Solution Explorer, right-click the References folder and select Add Web Reference.

4. In the Add Web Reference dialog, select the services on the local machine and then select the ExcelService at `http://localhost/_vti_bin/ExcelService.asmx`.

5. Name the web reference `SharePoint.ExcelServices`.

6. On the form, place four text boxes and a button according to the following chart. When finished, your form should look something like Figure 16-15.

Name	Type
PigLatinInputTextBox	Textbox
ConnectButton	Button
PigLatinOutputTextBox	Textbox
TotalSalesTextBox	Textbox
TotalCostTextBox	Textbox

7. Add a using statement reference to the EWS proxy class.

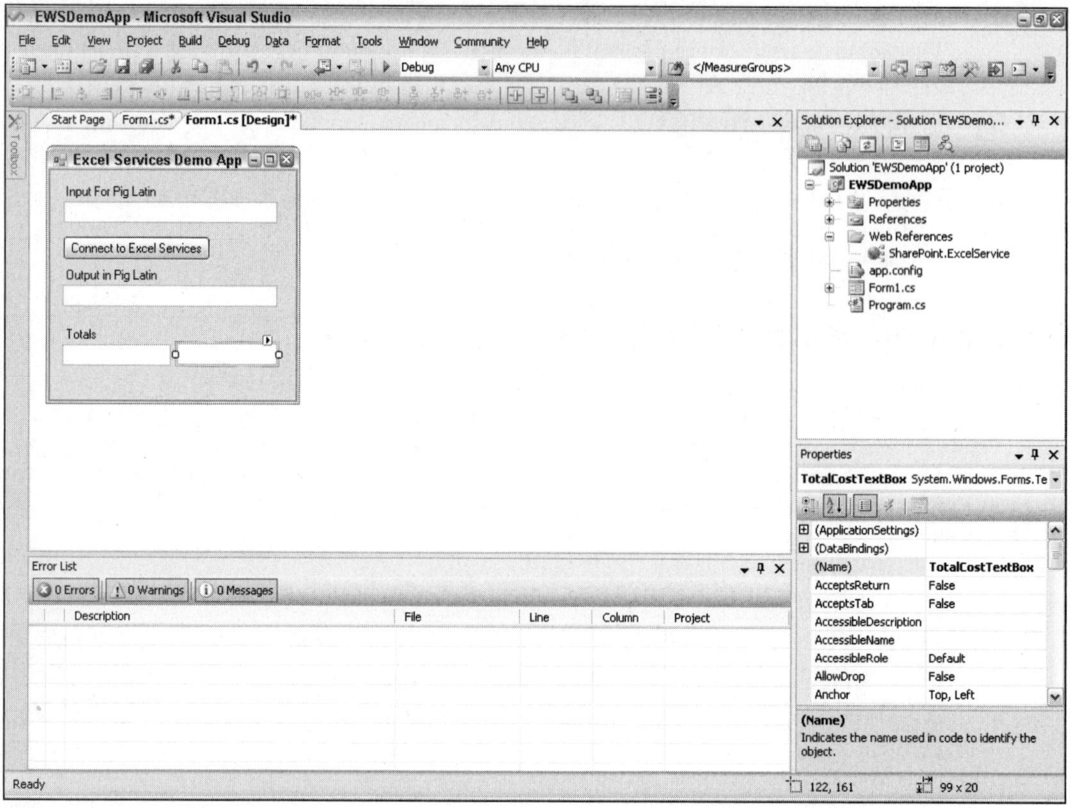

Figure 16-15

8. On the form, click the button to create the button's Click event handler. Add the following code to the `ConnectButton_Click` function:

```
if (PigLatinInputTextBox.Text != String.Empty)
{
    // Create a new instance of the Excel Services web service
    ExcelService es = new ExcelService();
    // Use the default user credentials for web requests
    System.Net.NetworkCredential cred = new System.Net.NetworkCredential
("administrator", "Password1", "oss07demo");
    es.Credentials = cred;

    try
    {
        // Create a status array to capture alerts from SharePoint
        Status[] alertMessages;
        // Open the workbook
        string Session = es.OpenWorkbook("http://oss07demo:13764/
```

```
                Shared%20Documents/ExcelServicesDemo.xlsx",
                                           "en-US",
                                           "en-US",
                                           out alertMessages);
            // Supply the value of the PigLatinInputTextBox to the A1 cell on the
    Random Numbers sheet
            es.SetCellA1(Session, "Random Numbers", "A1", PigLatinInputTextBox.Text);
            // Read the value of cell A23 on the Random Numbers sheet to then
    PigLatinOutputTextBox
            object ResultValue = es.GetCellA1(Session, "Random Numbers", "A23", false,
    out alertMessages);
            PigLatinOutputTextbox.Text = ResultValue.ToString();
            // Read the value of cells A5:B5 on the PivotReport sheet to the
    TotalSalesTextBox and TotalCostTextBox
            object[] RngResultValues = es.GetRangeA1(Session, "PivotReports", "A5:B5",
    true, out alertMessages);
            foreach (object[] RangeValue in RngResultValues)
            {
                TotalCostTextBox.Text = RangeValue[0].ToString();
                TotalSalesTextBox.Text = RangeValue[1].ToString();
            }
            // Close the workbook
            es.CloseWorkbookAsync(Session);
        }
        catch (Exception ex)
        {
            System.Diagnostics.EventLog.WriteEntry("EWS Demo App",
                                        "An error occurred attempting to
    open and manipulate an Excel workbook." + Environment.NewLine
                                        + ex.Message);
        }
    }
}
```

The previous code instantiates an instance of the web service and identifies the credentials that will be used to log in and retrieve workbooks. I've used this method of explicitly identifying the user to demonstrate how you might impersonate a user for the purposes of Excel Web Services. The next step is to identify which workbook you are trying to attach to. For the purpose of this demonstration application, I've connected to the partially published workbook to show that you don't need every sheet available in order to connect with Excel Web Services.

Once you have a connection to the workbook, use the SetCellA1 and GetCellA1 functions to specify which specific cells your are connecting to with Excel A1:B2 syntax. The GetRangeA1 function will return a two-dimensional array matching the area selected from the Excel workbook.

When you have completely coded your application and run it successfully, your screen should look like Figure 16-16.

Learn more about the ExcelService *class in the Microsoft SDK at* http://msdn2.microsoft.com/ en-us/library/microsoft.office.excel.server.webservices.excelservice.aspx.

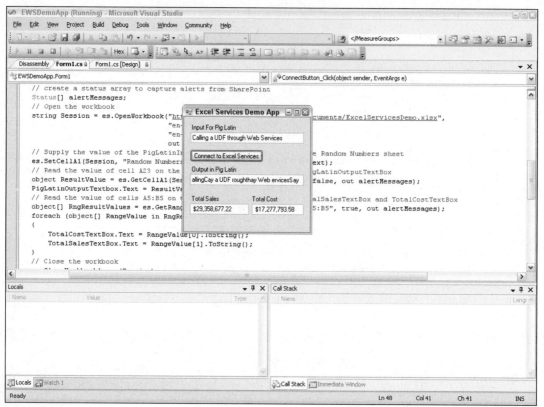

Figure 16-16

Dashboards and Report Center

SharePoint offers multiple mechanisms for displaying business intelligence data. You have already seen Excel spreadsheets integrated in SharePoint pages with the Excel Services rendering engine. Now it is time to examine dashboards and the SharePoint Site Template, Report Center. As with the Excel and Excel Services content, this examination begins with coverage of some power user approaches to business intelligence and then dives into the APIs offered by Office SharePoint Server 2007 Enterprise Edition.

Dashboards

As I previously stated, a dashboard is a visual metaphor of the state and health of the business. A dashboard actually allows multiple applications to work together to display data in one page. A dashboard could be displaying data from SQL Reporting Services, the Business Data Catalog, and Excel Services at the same time. New SharePoint filter Web Parts allow data from multiple sources on a page to be filtered in many different ways. This could allow you to filter a dashboard view comprising SSAS and Excel Services data with a single drop-down.

Office SharePoint Server 2007 ships with a Report Center Site Template, a new Site Template optimized for easy report access and management. The Report Center includes a report library, a data connection library, and a dashboard template. However, any of these Web Parts, such as the dashboard elements and KPIs, can be placed on any page — you are not required to use the Report Center template to access any of SharePoint's business intelligence features.

To begin using the Report Center and the business intelligence Web Parts such as KPI lists, you must first enable the Office SharePoint Server Publishing Infrastructure or you will receive an error message when you attempt to create a new Report Center site. To enable this feature, perform the following steps:

1. Log in as an administrator and click on the Site Actions menu on the top-level site.

2. Click Site Settings.

3. In the Site Collection Administration list, click the Site collection features link.

4. Activate the Office SharePoint Server Publishing Infrastructure feature, as in Figure 16-17.

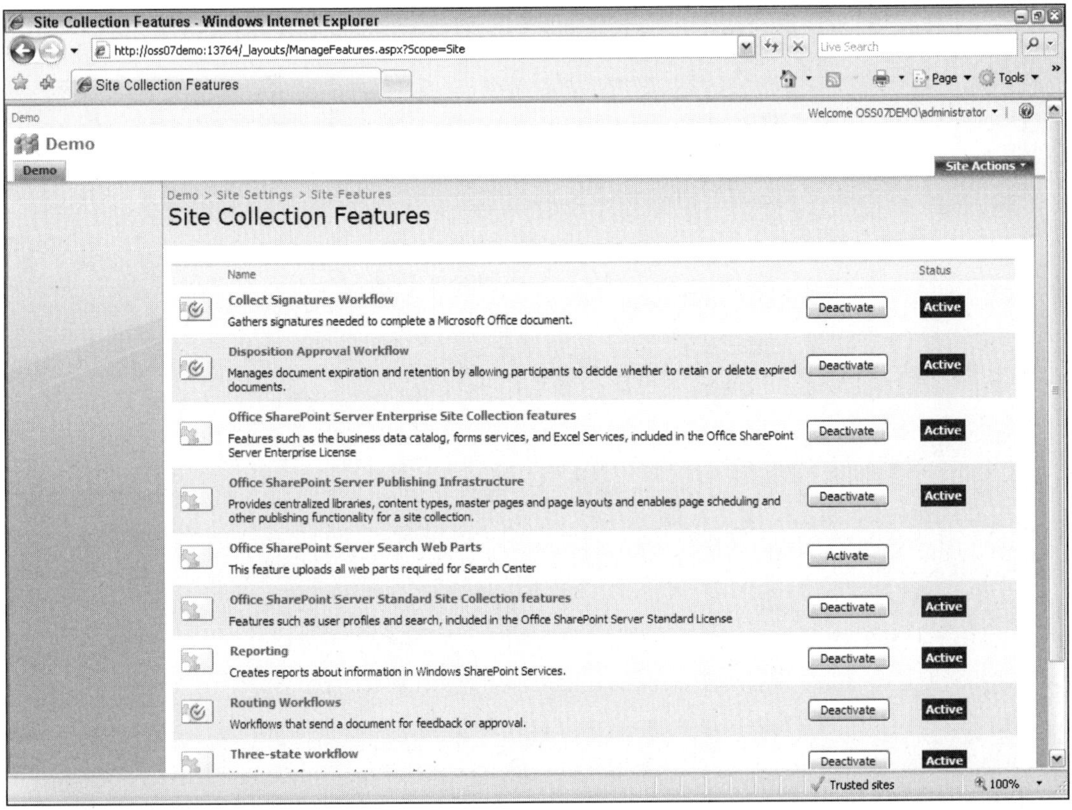

Figure 16-17

Report Center Site Template

To properly explore KPIs and dashboard applications in SharePoint 2007, create a new site with the Report Center template by following these steps:

1. On the top-level site, click the Site Actions menu and select Create to get to the Create options, as seen in Figure 16-18.

2. In the Web Pages list, select Sites and Workspaces to get to the New SharePoint Site page.

3. Fill out the New SharePoint Site page by assigning these values:

   ❑ Title = Dashboard

   ❑ URL name = dashboard

   ❑ Template = Enterprise/Report Center

   ❑ User Permissions = use same permissions as parent site

   ❑ Navigation Inheritance = yes

4. Click create, and your new Report Center site will be generated. Your template site should look like Figure 16-19.

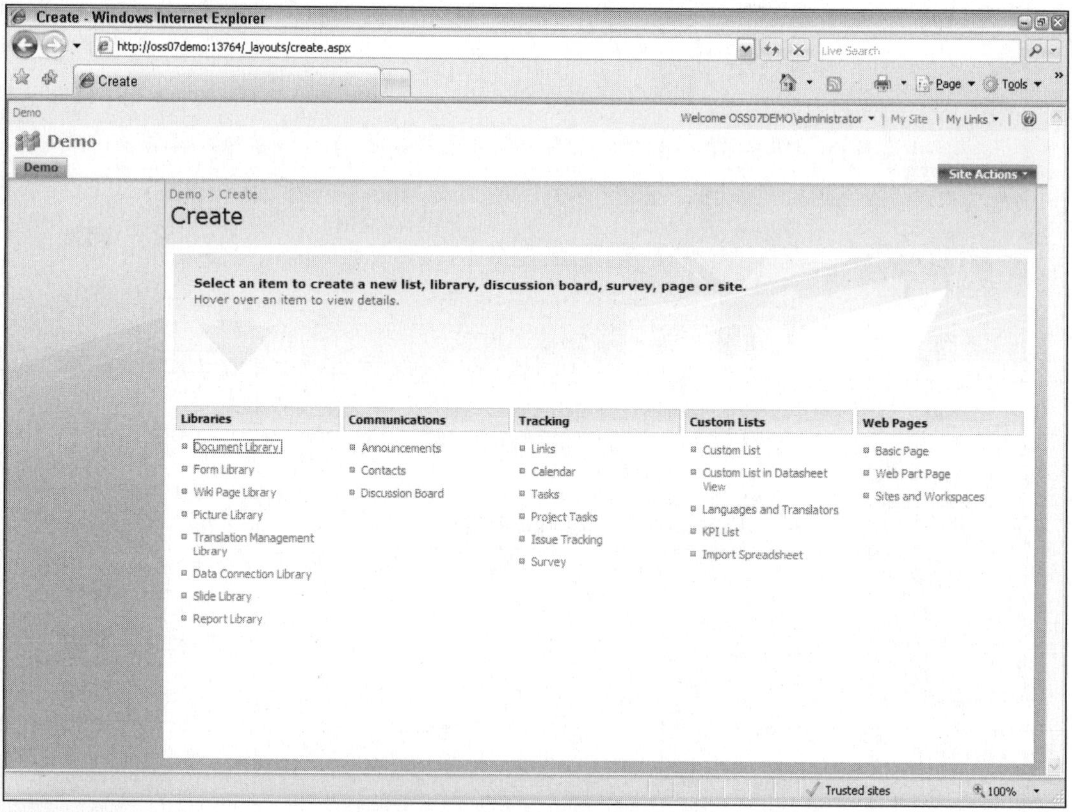

Figure 16-18

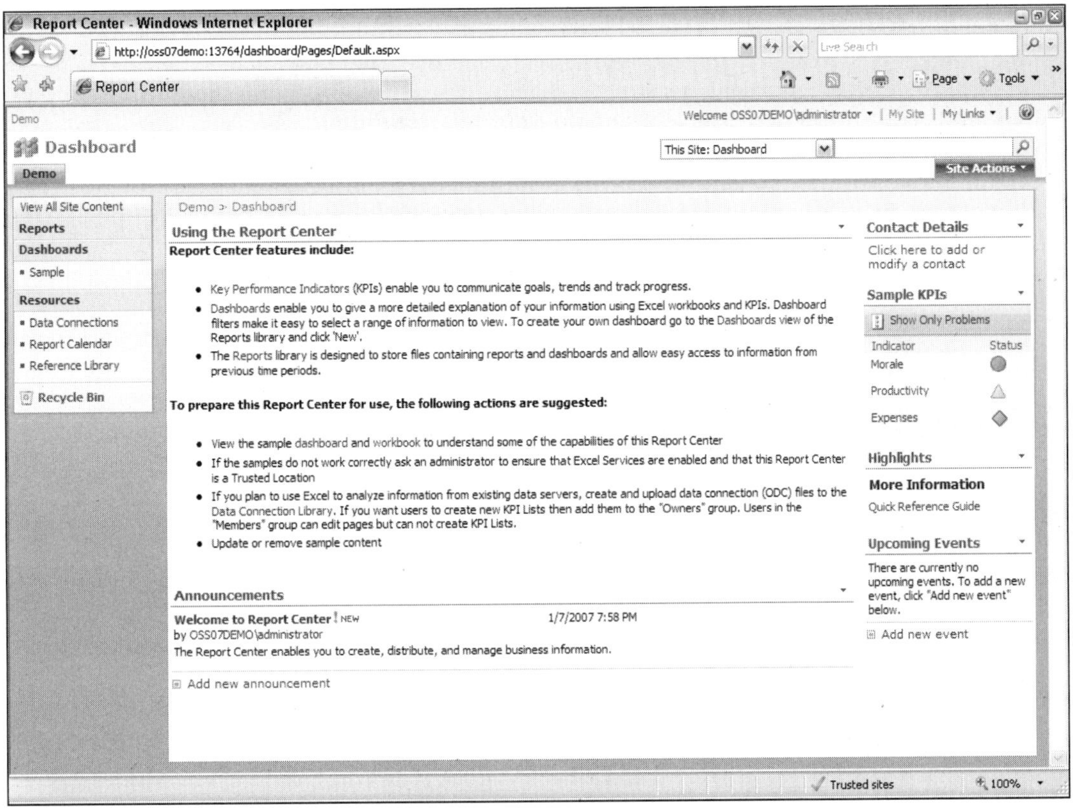

Figure 16-19

KPI And KPI List Web Parts

So far, this chapter has discussed Key Performance Indicators as an excellent mechanism for identifying progress towards a goal. When you want to be focused on a specific numeric target, a simple red/yellow/green indicator is an effective visual indicator for monitoring that progress. Take a look at the variety of different kinds of KPIs you are able to create with SharePoint 2007.

KPI Lists

KPI Lists store individual KPIs for use in Key Performance Indicator Web Parts and KPI Details Web Parts. Create a KPI List by following these steps:

1. In your Report Center site, click Site Actions ➪ Site Settings ➪ :Modify All Site Settings.

2. In the Site Administration group of the Site Settings page, click Site libraries and lists.

3. Click the Create new content link at the top of the Site Libraries and Lists page.

4. In the Custom Lists column, select KPI List.

5. Name the list Demo KPI List and click Create.

Manually Creating a Simple KPI

The easiest way to create a simple KPI is to enter the data manually. This can be extremely useful when the data you wish to represent is not structured or easily accessible programmatically, such as customer feedback in emails. Create a manually updated KPI with these steps:

1. In the Demo KPI List, click New and select Indicator using Manually entered information.

2. Create a manually populated KPI list item by filling out the following values.

- ❑ Name = Happiness with SharePoint 2007
- ❑ Description = Metric to measure overall happiness with SharePoint 2007
- ❑ Comments = Since we're always happy about SharePoint 07, this indicator will always be green!
- ❑ Value = 100
- ❑ Better values are = higher
- ❑ Display green when has met or exceeded goal = 100
- ❑ Display yellow when has met or exceeded warning = 50

3. Click OK to see your new KPI.

KPI Monitoring of SharePoint List Data

If a SharePoint list contains numeric or date-based information, you can use a KPI to distill the list into a single graphical indicator for monitoring purposes. Consider a task list or an issues list. Monitoring the percentage of completed tasks or the number of open issues is simple with some SharePoint list-based KPIs. Create a SharePoint list-based KPI by following these steps:

1. Create a list on the top-level site from which you can draw summarization information. In Figure 16-20, you can see the Demo Issues List I am using in my example.

2. In the Demo KPI List, click New and select the option to create a new indicator using data in the SharePoint list.

3. Fill in the following indicator properties to correctly create the SharePoint list-based KPI, as in Figure 16-21.

- ❑ Name = Issue Resolution Metric
- ❑ Description = Illustrate issue close performance with a KPI
- ❑ List URL = `http://oss07demo:13764/Lists/Demo Issue List.aspx`
- ❑ Value calculation = Percentage of items in the list where:
- ❑ Issue Status is equal to Resolve OR
- ❑ Issue Status is equal to Closed
- ❑ Better values are higher

❏ Display green when has met or exceeded goal 90

❏ Display yellow when has met or exceeded warning 50

4. Click OK to see your new KPI in the KPI List.

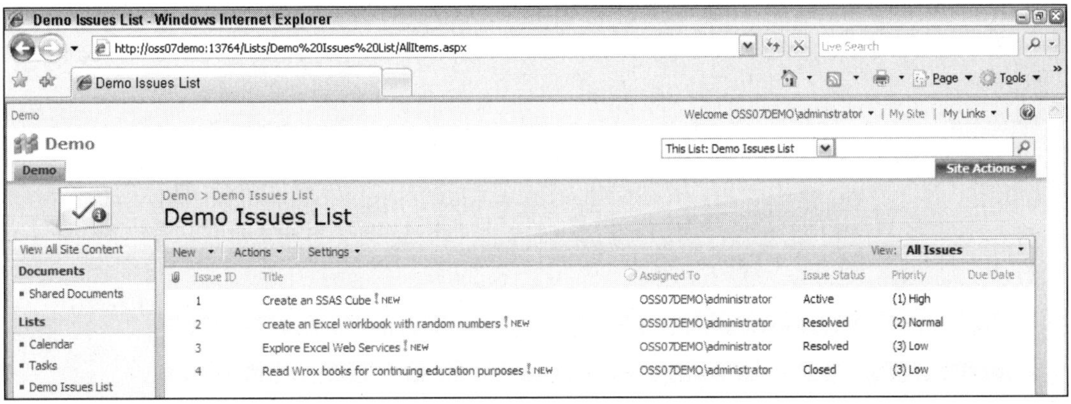

Figure 16-20

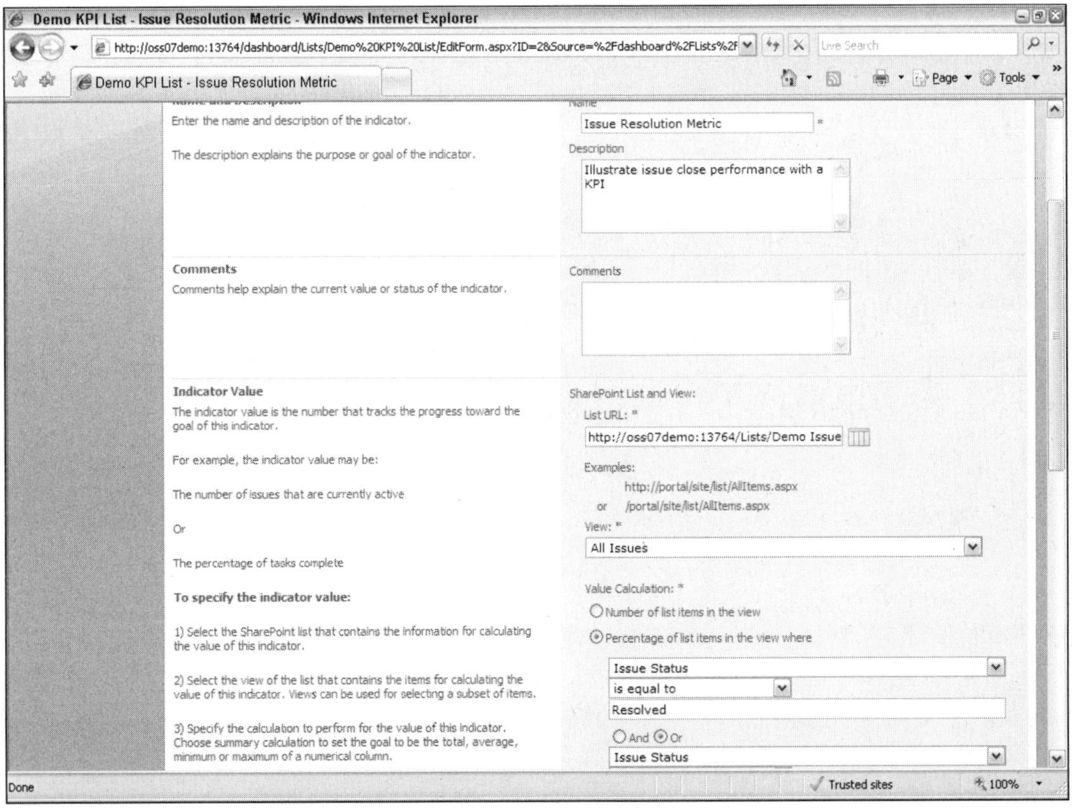

Figure 16-21

Create an Excel Data-Based KPI

Setting up a KPI to monitor the data in an Excel workbook is as simple as using the conditional formatting tools available in Excel 2007. Using Excel Services, as the data in the workbook changes, the KPI can automatically be updated on the web site. Add a new Excel-based KPI by following these steps:

1. In the Demo KPI List, click New and select to create a new indicator using data in Excel workbook.

2. Fill in the following indicator properties to correctly create the Excel workbook based KPI:

- ❑ Name = Sales Totals KPI

- ❑ Description = Base a KPI off values in the PivotTable report

- ❑ Workbook URL = type in the URL or use the workbook picker to find the `ExcelServicesDemo.xlsx` workbook at `/Shared Documents/ ExcelServicesDemo.xlsx`.

- ❑ Cell Address for Indicator Value = Use the select dialog to launch Excel Web Access to pick the value, goal, and warning cells.

3. Click OK to see your new KPI in the KPI List, as in Figure 16-22.

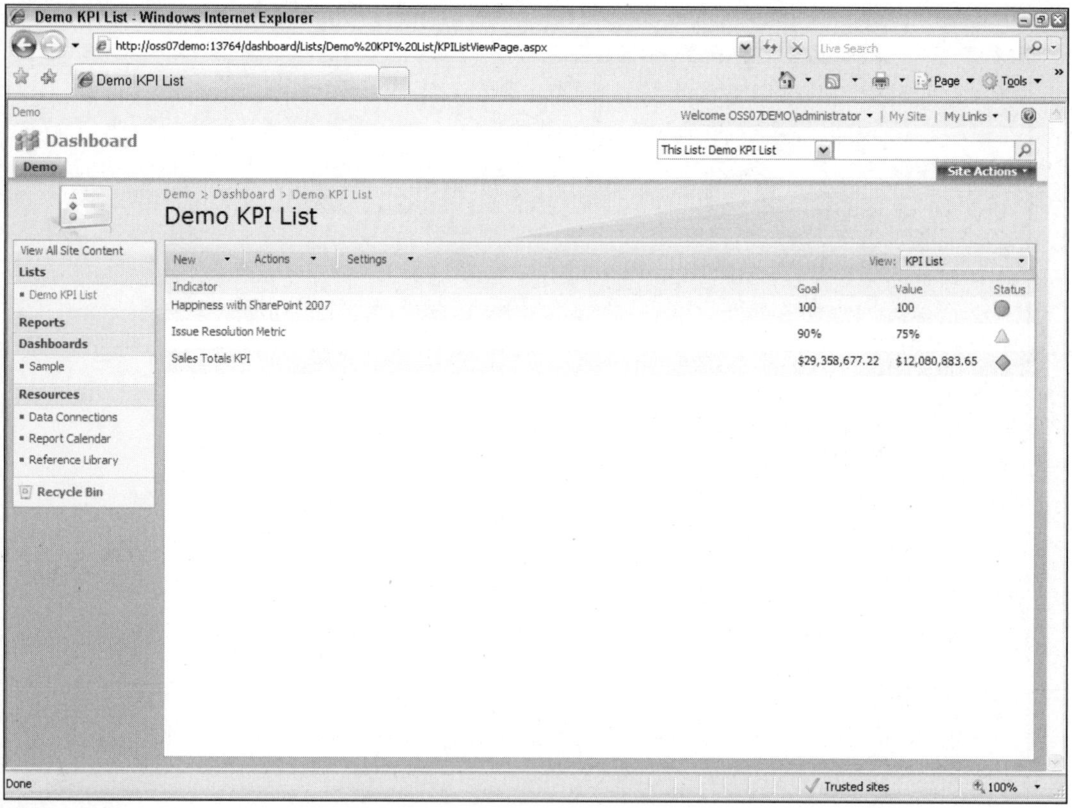

Figure 16-22

Reading and Reporting on SSAS-Based KPIs

When complex KPIs need to be tracked, nothing is better or more appropriate than the full power of SQL Server and the SQL Server Analysis Services. SharePoint 2007 has the ability to consume SSAS KPIs via a live data connection to SQL Server. Create a SSAS KPI by following these directions:

1. Start by adding a data connection to the Report Center's Data Connection Library.

   ❏ On the Report Center site, click Data Connections under Resources on the left navigation bar.

   ❏ Click New.

   ❏ In the Libraries column, click the Data Connection Library Link.

   ❏ Click New Data Connection, and specify a link to an existing cube.

2. Back in the KPI list, create a new indicator using data in SQL Server 2005 Analysis Services with the following values:

   ❏ Data Connection = the path (URL) to the Office Data Connnection (.odc) file

   ❏ Only display KPIs from display folder = chose the folder in SSAS which contains the KPI

   ❏ KPI List = select the KPI you want to show

   ❏ Name = the name which appears in the SharePoint list (be descriptive to help when placing this KPI on a dashboard)

   ❏ Comments = optional

KPI Web Parts

Key Performance Indicator Web Parts display a list of KPIs to help you display your important metrics on your dashboard. KPI Details Web Parts display the details of a single KPI in a more detailed view. Both are in the Dashboard section of the Add Web Parts to Zone dialog. Add them both to your Report Center site by following these steps:

1. In the Report Center site, click the Site Actions button and select Edit Page.

2. In the right zone, click the Add Web Parts button.

3. Scroll down to the Dashboard section, and select both the Key Performance Indicators and KPI Details Web Parts.

4. Click Add and your new Web Parts will appear at the top of the right zone.

5. Now customize the properties of each Web Part to connect to your Demo KPI list.

Programatically Interacting with KPIs

There are several opportunities to interact with KPIs in code that have not been explored in previous code examples. The `Microsoft.SharePoint.Portal` namespace offers dozens of classes such as the following for your use. The inclusion of the classes that make the KPIs themselves give you the opportunity to create your own KPI classes.

Name	Description
`Microsoft.SharePoint.Portal.WebControls .AnalysisServicesKpiNewFormControl`	Create and update individual KPIs with this class.
`Microsoft.SharePoint.Portal.WebControls .KPIConsts`	This base class is used to support classes like the `ExcelCellPicker` and the `IndicatorWebPart`.
`Microsoft.SharePoint.Portal.WebControls .KPIListWebPart`	Control the display of KPIs in the list, including sort order and filtering.
`Microsoft.SharePoint.Portal.WebControls .KpiPostBackEventHandlers`	Catch and potentially override KPI postback events to do things like custom rendering.

SharePoint Filter Web Parts

The simple beauty of a truly functional dashboard is that all of the pieces of the dashboard work in concert to provide a complete understanding of the business. However, what if you're not trying to monitor every bit of data at the same time? What if you'd like the ability to view your sales dashboard by region or by year? Without filter Web Parts, synchronizing the different components could be extremely tedious.

SharePoint 2007's new filter Web Parts help dashboard consumers target the data to the subsets of information they are particularly interested in. This can include filtering by time, location, or other classifications. Filter Web Parts are also providers in the ASP.Net 2.0 Web Part provider-consumer model and can be taken advantage of programmatically in your own Web Parts. To create a consumer Web Part, you have to request the `IFilterValues` interface from the filter provider Web Part. It is important to note that this interface is not restricted to SharePoint and can in fact be implemented in any ASP.NET 2.0 Web Part to allow for connected Web Parts. SharePoint merely leverages the ASP.NET functionality to achieve its goals. The calls to the SharePoint namespaces are to populate parameter values.

This sample code, provided by MSDN (`http://msdn2.microsoft.com/en-us/library/ ms490609.aspx`) illustrates how a filter consumer Web Part will connect to a filter provider Web Part and list the possible filter selections:

```
using System;
using System.Collections.Generic;
using System.ComponentModel;
using System.Text;
using System.Web;
using System.Web.UI;
using System.Web.UI.WebControls;
using aspnetwebparts = System.Web.UI.WebControls.WebParts;
using Microsoft.Office.Server.Utilities;
using wsswebparts = Microsoft.SharePoint.WebPartPages;
using Microsoft.SharePoint.Portal.WebControls;
using System.Collections.ObjectModel;
using Microsoft.SharePoint.Utilities;
using System.Data;
using System.Collections;
```

```
namespace MyWebPartLibrary
{
    public class SimpleFilterConsumerWebPart : aspnetwebparts.WebPart
    {

        List<wsswebparts.IFilterValues> providers = new List<wsswebparts
.IFilterValues>();


        protected override void CreateChildControls()
        {
            base.CreateChildControls();
        }



        [aspnetwebparts.ConnectionConsumer("Simple Consumer", "IFilterValues",
AllowsMultipleConnections = false)]
        public void SetConnectionInterface(wsswebparts.IFilterValues provider)
        {
            this.providers.Add(provider);
            if (provider != null)
            {
                List<wsswebparts.ConsumerParameter> l = new List<wsswebparts
.ConsumerParameter>();
                l.Add(new wsswebparts.ConsumerParameter("Value", wsswebparts
.ConsumerParameterCapabilities.SupportsMultipleValues | wsswebparts
.ConsumerParameterCapabilities.SupportsAllValue));
                provider.SetConsumerParameters(new ReadOnlyCollection<wsswebparts
.ConsumerParameter>(l));
            }
        }

        protected override void RenderContents(HtmlTextWriter output)
        {
            this.EnsureChildControls();
            foreach (wsswebparts.IFilterValues provider in this.providers)
            {
                if (provider != null)
                {
                    string prop = provider.ParameterName;
                    ReadOnlyCollection<String> values = provider.ParameterValues;

                    if (prop != null && values != null)
                    {
                        output.Write("<div>" + SPEncode.HtmlEncode(prop) + ":</div>");
                        foreach (string v in values)
                        {
                            if (v == null)
                            {
                                output.Write("<div>  <i>&quot;
(empty)&quot;/null</i></div>");
                            }
                            else if (v.Length == 0)
                            {
```

```
                                   output.Write("<div>  <i>empty
string</i></div>");
                            }
                            else
                            {
                                output.Write("<div>  " +v + "</div>");
                            }
                        }
                    }
                    else
                    {
                        output.Write("<div>No filter specified (all).</div>");
                    }
                }
                else
                {
                    output.Write("<div>Not connected.</div>");
                }

                output.Write("<hr>");
            }
        }
    }
}
```

Once you have this code compiled, you will put this file into the bin directory or into the GAC to make it available to your site. Add your Web Part to the safe controls and you're ready to go.

The above example shows you at a basic level how to create your own Web Parts, which can be filtered by consume a filter provider Web Part. The next bit of code will show you what it takes to create a custom filter provider. This sample code, also provided by MSDN (http://msdn2 .microsoft.com/en-us/library/ms499375.aspx), describes how to create a filter that implements the ITransformableFilterValues interface to allow a List containing one or more values to be passed to the consumers. Imagine a treeview control or checked list where multiple selections are possible. Again, the interface ITransformableFilterValues is not restricted.

```
using System;
using System.Collections.Generic;
using System.ComponentModel;
using System.Text;
using System.Web;
using System.Web.UI;
using System.Web.UI.WebControls;
using aspnetwebparts = System.Web.UI.WebControls.WebParts;
using Microsoft.Office.Server.Utilities;
using wsswebparts = Microsoft.SharePoint.WebPartPages;
using Microsoft.SharePoint.Portal.WebControls;
using System.Collections.ObjectModel;
using Microsoft.SharePoint.Utilities;
using System.Data;
using System.Collections;
```

```
namespace MyWebPartLibrary
{
    public class RegionFilterWebPart : aspnetwebparts.WebPart, wsswebparts
.ITransformableFilterValues
    {
        CheckBoxList cblRegionList;
        ListItem cbitemRegion;

        public virtual bool AllowMultipleValues
        {
            get
            {
                return true;
            }
        }
        public virtual bool AllowAllValue
        {
            get
            {
                return true;
            }
        }

        public virtual bool AllowEmptyValue
        {
            get
            {
                return false;
            }
        }
        public virtual string ParameterName
        {
            get
            {
                return "Geography";
            }
        }

        public virtual ReadOnlyCollection<string> ParameterValues
        {
            get
            {
                string[] values = this.GetCurrentlySelectedGeographies();
                return values == null ?
                    null :
                    new ReadOnlyCollection<string>(values);
            }
        }


        protected override void CreateChildControls()
        {
```

```
        cblRegionList = new CheckBoxList();
        Controls.Add(cblRegionList);

        cbitemRegion = new ListItem();
        cbitemRegion.Text = "Seattle";
        cblRegionList.Items.Add(cbitemRegion);
        cbitemRegion = null;

        cbitemRegion = new ListItem();
        cbitemRegion.Text = "US";
        cblRegionList.Items.Add(cbitemRegion);
        cbitemRegion = null;

        cbitemRegion = new ListItem();
        cbitemRegion.Text = "World";
        cblRegionList.Items.Add(cbitemRegion);
        cbitemRegion = null;

        cbitemRegion = new ListItem();
        cbitemRegion.Text = "All";
        cblRegionList.Items.Add(cbitemRegion);
        cbitemRegion = null;


        base.CreateChildControls();
    }


    [aspnetwebparts.ConnectionProvider("Region Filter",
"ITransformableFilterValues", AllowsMultipleConnections = true)]
    public wsswebparts.ITransformableFilterValues SetConnectionInterface()
    {
        return this;
    }
    protected override void OnPreRender(EventArgs e)
    {
        base.OnPreRender(e);
    }

    public string[] GetCurrentlySelectedGeographies()
    {
        String[] choices = new String[5];
        bool anythingSelected = false;

        for (int i = 0; i < cblRegionList.Items.Count; i++)
        {
            //get the selected choices
            if (cblRegionList.Items[i].Selected)
            {
                anythingSelected = true;
                if (cblRegionList.Items[i].Text != "All")
                {
                    choices[i] = cblRegionList.Items[i].Text;
                }
                else
```

```
                    {
                        choices = null;
                        return choices;
                    }
                }

            }
            if (!anythingSelected)
                choices = null;

            return choices;
        }

        protected override void RenderContents(HtmlTextWriter output)
        {
            this.EnsureChildControls();
            RenderChildren(output);


        }

    }
}
```

How does consuming this List of filter values differ from the first example? The code in the
OnPreRender function would simply iterate through all of the values in the list to see if it should filter
by that particular value. Here is the code that consumes the multi-select region filter created above:

```
using System;
using System.Collections.Generic;
using System.ComponentModel;
using System.Text;
using System.Web;
using System.Web.UI;
using System.Web.UI.WebControls;
using aspnetwebparts = System.Web.UI.WebControls.WebParts;
using Microsoft.Office.Server.Utilities;
using wsswebparts = Microsoft.SharePoint.WebPartPages;
using Microsoft.SharePoint.Portal.WebControls;
using System.Collections.ObjectModel;
using Microsoft.SharePoint.Utilities;
using System.Data;
using System.Collections;

namespace MyWebPartLibrary
{
    public class DataBoundHeadlinesFilterConsumerWebPart : aspnetwebparts.WebPart
    {

        public class Headline
        {
            private string title;
            private string region;
```

```
        public Headline(string Title, string Region)
        {

            this.title = Title;
            this.region = Region;

        }
        public string Title
        {
            get
            {
                return this.title;
            }
            set
            {
                this.title = value;
            }
        }

        public string Region
        {
            get
            {
                return this.region;
            }
            set
            {
                this.Region = value;
            }
        }



    }

    List<wsswebparts.IFilterValues> providers = new List<wsswebparts
.IFilterValues>();
    List<Headline> headlines;

    DataGrid DataListHeadlines;

    protected override void CreateChildControls()
    {
        DataListHeadlines = new DataGrid();

        headlines = new List<Headline>();

        headlines.Add(new Headline("This week in Redmond", "Redmond"));
        headlines.Add(new Headline("Traffic in Redmond", "Redmond"));
        headlines.Add(new Headline("Sports highlights in Redmond", "Redmond"));
        headlines.Add(new Headline("Bitter cold, wind to follow today's snow",
"Seattle"));
        headlines.Add(new Headline("This week in Seattle", "Seattle"));
        headlines.Add(new Headline("Sports News in US", "US"));
```

```
            headlines.Add(new Headline("This week in the US", "US"));
            headlines.Add(new Headline("This week in the world", "World"));
            headlines.Add(new Headline("Last week sports highlights", "World"));


            DataListHeadlines.ID = "list1";
            Controls.Add(DataListHeadlines);

            base.CreateChildControls();
        }


        [aspnetwebparts.ConnectionConsumer("Headlines Filter", "IFilterValues",
AllowsMultipleConnections = true)]
        public void SetConnectionInterface(wsswebparts.IFilterValues provider)
        {
            if (provider != null)
            {
                this.providers.Add(provider);

                List<wsswebparts.ConsumerParameter> l = new List<wsswebparts
.ConsumerParameter>();
                    l.Add(new wsswebparts.ConsumerParameter("Region",
                        wsswebparts.ConsumerParameterCapabilities
.SupportsMultipleValues | wsswebparts.ConsumerParameterCapabilities
.SupportsAllValue));

                provider.SetConsumerParameters(new ReadOnlyCollection<wsswebparts
.ConsumerParameter>(l));
            }
        }

        protected override void OnPreRender(EventArgs e)
        {
            this.EnsureChildControls();

            // The filtering logic is to perform a union of all of the filters
            // (a logical OR).
            // If we didn't get any filter providers or if any of the filters
            // send the "All" value (i.e. if provider.ParameterValues == null)
            // then we don't need to filter and we can just send back all of
            // the headlines.

            List<Headline> filteredHeadlines = null;

            bool shouldFilter = true;
            if (this.providers.Count == 0)
            {
                shouldFilter = false;
            }
            else if (this.providers.Count > 0)
            {
                foreach( wsswebparts.IFilterValues filter in this.providers)
                {
```

```
                             if (filter.ParameterValues == null)
                             {
                                 // Some filter sent "All" - don't bother with the rest
                                 // of the filtering.
                                 shouldFilter = false;
                                 break;
                             }
                         }
                     }


                 if (!shouldFilter)
                 {
                     // the "filtered" headlines are unfiltered.
                     filteredHeadlines = this.headlines;
                 }
                 else
                 {
                     // Just fill in the headlines that match the filters.

                     filteredHeadlines = new List<Headline>();

                     // Create a lookup from region to a list of headlines which
                     // correspond to that region.
                     Dictionary<string, List<Headline>> regionHeadlineMap = new
Dictionary<string,List<Headline>>();
                     foreach (Headline headline in this.headlines)
                     {
                         List<Headline> headlinesForRegion = null;
                         if (!regionHeadlineMap.TryGetValue(headline.Region, out
headlinesForRegion))
                         {
                             headlinesForRegion = new List<Headline>();
                             regionHeadlineMap.Add(headline.Region, headlinesForRegion);
                         }

                         headlinesForRegion.Add(headline);
                     }

                     foreach (wsswebparts.IFilterValues provider in this.providers)
                     {

                         ReadOnlyCollection<String> values = provider.ParameterValues;
                         if (values != null)
                         {
                             foreach (string v in values)
                             {
                                 if (v == null)
                                 {
                                     // This indicates the "Empty" value, which this
                                     // doesn't apply to headlines, since they all
                                     // have a Region.
```

```
                              }
                              else
                              {
                                  List<Headline> matchedHeadlines;
                                  if (regionHeadlineMap.TryGetValue(v, out
matchedHeadlines))
                                  {
                                      foreach (Headline matchedHeadline in
matchedHeadlines)
                                      {
                                          if (!filteredHeadlines
.Contains(matchedHeadline))
                                          {
                                              filteredHeadlines.Add(matchedHeadline);
                                          }
                                      }
                                  }
                              }
                          }
                      }
                  }
              }

              // Display the filtered headlines.
              DataListHeadlines.DataSource = filteredHeadlines;
              DataListHeadlines.DataBind();

              base.OnPreRender(e);
        }.
    }
}
```

These examples and filter Web Parts in general are explained in more detail in MSDN (http://msdn2.microsoft.com/en-us/library/ms546894.aspx).

Dashboard Applications

With SharePoint 2007, it has never been easier to create a rich dashboard application that can help your business decision makers understand their business in a flash. Building a dashboard is as simple as picking which components to display on the screen.

1.   On the Report Center site, click the Dashboard category on the left navigation bar.

2.   Click New and select Dashboard Page.

3.   Give your new dashboard page a name and URL like **demodash** and click OK.

4.   You now should have a blank dashboard page similar to Figure 16-23.

5.   Now you can pick and choose your KPIs, spreadsheet, and text to populate your dashboard. This is where you need to be familiar with your business to be able to pick the correct data elements to track in order to develop a useful dashboard.

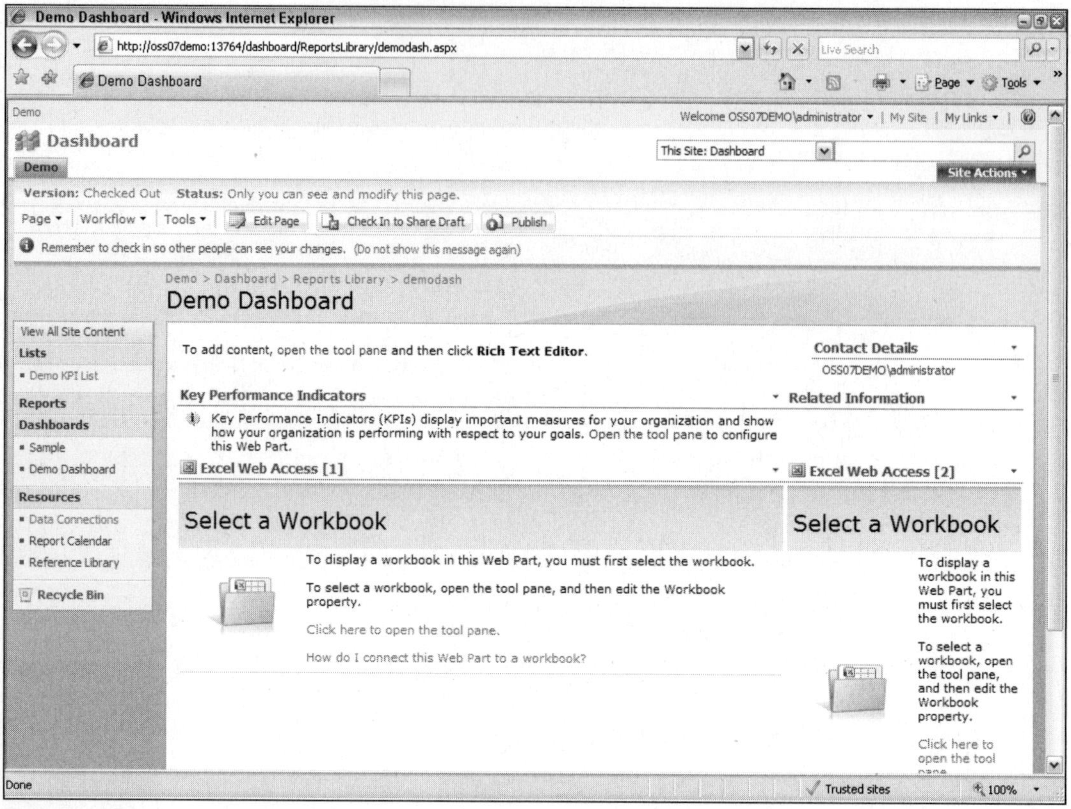

Figure 16-23

Summary

This chapter provided an overview of the significant investment Microsoft has made in business intelligence in the newest version of Microsoft Office Excel 2007 and Microsoft Office SharePoint Server 2007. In this chapter, you have learned about SQL Server Analysis Services and how to tie its business intelligence features into Excel 2007 and SharePoint Server 2007. You've learned about Excel Services, a server component to the Excel 2007 desktop software, which provides a secure mechanism to share and reuse Excel workbooks. Finally, you've learned about the Report Center Site Template, SharePoint dashboards, and KPI Web Parts. These business intelligence features represent a significant part of Microsoft's push to provide businesses insight and better decision-making capabilities through software.

Using the Microsoft Visual Studio 2005 Extension for Windows SharePoint Services 3.0

By Adam Buenz

The Microsoft Visual Studio 2005 Extensions for Windows SharePoint Services 3.0 (VSeWSS) enables SharePoint developers to economically and efficiently build the most customary solutions that target and leverage the SharePoint platform. Typical SharePoint development often consists of repetitive, tedious chores when trying to build the foundation for custom solutions such as Web Parts, Site and List Definitions, content types, and deployable packages for distributing customized content across an enterprise environment. SharePoint as a modular development framework implies that several habitual tasks must be performed when constructing new pieces of functionality, in essence, providing the groundwork to integrate and make use of programmatic assets available in the SharePoint environment. VSeWSS seeks to make the life of a SharePoint developer much more painless, truncate development chores, and provide resourceful methods for deployment of robust SharePoint solutions. In essence, VSeWSS is a way to empower a SharePoint developer with enhanced, integrated development tools that offload some of the overhead that is typically required when building against the SharePoint platform.

As an example, consider the groundwork typically required for building the most common solution SharePoint developers tackle, a minimal custom SharePoint Web Part. Under normal circumstances, to build a simple Web Part, a developer has to start off by modifying a Web Control Library Project to include references to the relevant SharePoint assemblies if leveraging the SharePoint object model; build out the appropriate `using` statements; adjust Web Part class inheritance to target either the `Microsoft.SharePoint.WebPartPages.WebPart` or `System.Web.UI.WebControls.WebParts.WebPart` base class; and if doing something small like writing out a small stream of text, build the appropriate writer method by overriding `RenderWebPart` or `RenderContents`. Following this, for the Web Part to be installed in the GAC, the binary must be signed with a cryptographic key pair, or a security policy may have to be implemented in order to get the appropriate Code Access Security

Rights for deployment in relative bin directories. Once the assembly is built, deployment options have to be considered, since there are various methods to expose and integrate the Web Part into the actual SharePoint environment. Should you auto-create a Web Part description file in the Web Part gallery following the relevant `safecontrol` entries? Or should you create a deployable `.cab` solution with the relevant files? Or should you build a SharePoint Feature to reference and deploy the Web Part? Such tasks are targeted and automated by the VSeWSS, and exploiting them appropriately provides an unparalleled platform for building compelling, extendable SharePoint solutions.

Installation Requirements

The use of VSeWSS requires Windows SharePoint Services 3.0 and Visual Studio 2005 to be installed on the target machine, since most of the assembly references that are going to be used for SharePoint development exist solely on a SharePoint enabled machine. Without WSSv3 and VS2005, the MSI package will not allow the installation to perform.

However, if at some point you want to place the Visual Studio Item and Project templates on another development machine regardless of whether or not WSSv3 is installed, it is feasible to do this after acquiring them from the development machine running SharePoint after successful installation of VSeWSS. This is helpful if you're accustomed to doing development on another machine besides those that are engaged in the preproduction deployment lifecycle in a SharePoint environment. The only caveats to this are that the assembly references that are automatically made when instantiating a new VSeWSS Project or Item template will have to be manually resolved and the embedded SharePoint Solution Generator will not be installed. The latter is a large loss, since it means forgoing several of the runtime debugging options and built-in provisioning features, whose influential aspects will be demonstrated shortly.

Building a Custom Solution Using the VSeWSS

In order to appreciate how VSeWSS can improve the SharePoint development experience by eliminating some of the cyclical activities involved in creating a SharePoint solution, it is best to build a robust example solution employing all of the options that VSeWSS offers. This appendix provides a detailed overview of VSeWSS architecture, showing each element that composes VSeWSS, as well as demonstrating some portions that can be extended to include various enterprise development standards, and explaining how each of the faculties that the extensions provide can be exploited to its maximum potential to construct robust, effective, manageable business solutions (see Figure A-1). The end result, achieved solely by using VSeWSS, is a powerful, easily deployable, manageable corporate policy management site that leverages all of the custom solutions created.

This section starts by building the foundation for a corporate policy management site using a custom Site Definition Project Template, which can provision the new site with appropriate assets needed for global deployment scenarios. Within the site, there will be particular custom files that ought to be included with the rest of the custom content; therefore, the definition of a custom module to be packaged with the Site Definition is provided. Second, a new content type will be generated, since the policy library used for corporate policies will have specific properties (columns), policy templates, listform pages, and event handlers associated with it. Third, there is a demonstration of how to use the List Definition template in order to build a custom document library template to house the relevant documents based on the generated content type, which also plays a pivotal role in the overall site development. Fourth, using the WebPart Project Template to perform one of the most common tasks in SharePoint provides a new way of looking at managing child subsites, since policy document workspaces are frequently used for important pieces of information such as corporate policies. Last, you will see how to propagate the custom development throughout the enterprise easily using the inherent SharePoint solution deployment options, as well as pull the site back down using the stand-alone SharePoint Solution Generator.

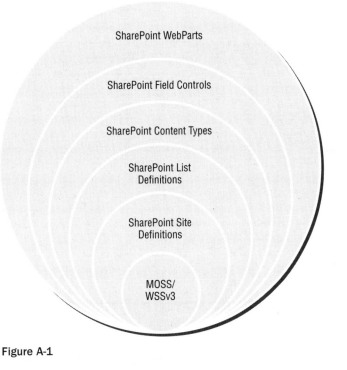

Figure A-1

Architecture of and Extending VSeWSS Item and Project Templates

VSeWSS core functionality is provided as a set of Visual Studio Project and Item Templates for use with C# projects. As I write this, VSeWSS only supports C#, although it would be reasonable to expect VB.NET support in the future. These templates are stored in the appropriate Visual Studio Project and Item template directories:

```
Project Template Directory
C:\Program Files\Microsoft Visual Studio 8\Common7\IDE\ProjectTemplates\
CSharp\SharePoint

Item Template Directory
C:\Program Files\Microsoft Visual Studio 8\Common7\IDE\ItemTemplates\
CSharp\SharePoint
```

The `ProjectTemplates` directory houses all the options that are available when starting with a fresh Visual Studio Project instance; therefore, they are only offered when you are not adding one of the VSeWSS items to a currently existing solution file. Through the project selection screen, you can create a Team Site Definition, Blank Site Definition, List Definition, Web Part, or Empty Project File (See Figure A-2).

Once one of the boilerplate templates is instantiated and a new solution file has been created, the projects that are available in the `ItemTemplates` directory become available within the Solution Explorer. Through the Item Selection screen, you can create a new List Definition, List Definition from content type, content type, field control, Web Part, or module (See Figure A-3).

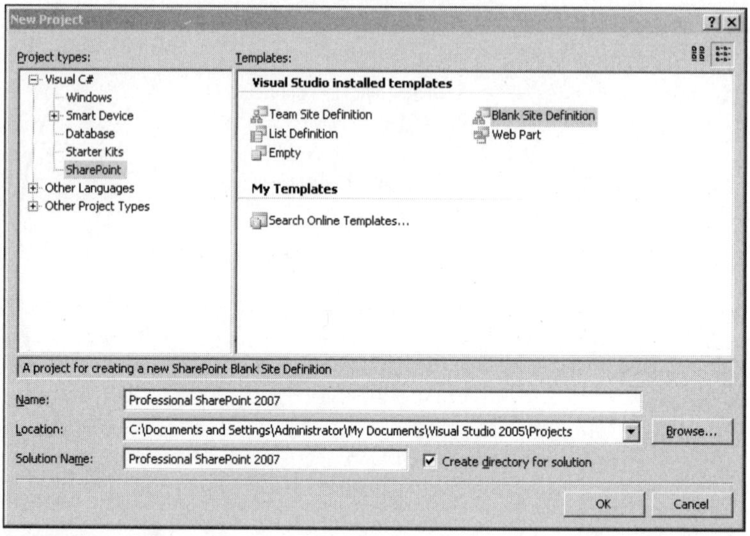

Figure A-2

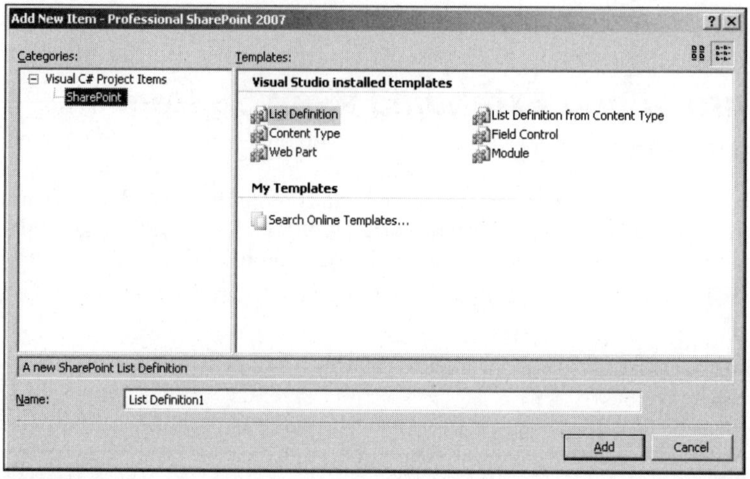

Figure A-3

The Vstemplate Parent Element and Extending the VSeWSS Templates

Each of the VSeWSS Visual Studio project templates is composed of an overlying XML vstemplate project file that defines various attributes about the project, containing a parent VSTemplate node that houses child elements of the project or list instances. Collectively, within the project templates there are two major assets that can be considered universal and one more infrequently used item, which only appears when using the templates that require some user interaction, such as defining base types or provisioning of event receivers. The two common elements are TemplateData and TemplateContent, and the more infrequently used element is WizardData, which is used to harvest extended, user-provided data after the project has been created. Because the template files contain normal XML, it is possible to extend them to include custom attributes in order to promote certain development goals. This activity should be approached with caution, since it is probable that Microsoft will continually add updates to the VSeWSS template packages, which could then negate customizations you make to the bundled files. Therefore, as a best practice it is recommended that you make copies of the relevant template files in a new template in order to construct custom templates that will survive future releases of VSeWSS. That being said, extending the templates to include custom content, code files, and activities is a powerful option that can drastically increase the overall usability of VSeWSS for specific organizations.

Extending TemplateData

TemplateData contains general information about the VSeWSS template that a developer can access from the Visual Studio interface, such as the default name of the template, the project type, the project icon, and whether or not the template will instantiate a new folder. Although a majority of the default settings that are available within the default project template are satisfactory to most SharePoint developers, it is also possible to extend the template to include other options, if desired, simply by modifying the TemplateData section by adjusting the standard elements or adding elements that are not currently built into the parent element. For example, if you're building several Web Parts that are experimental, and therefore are creating and destroying numerous projects, it is useful to set the <PromptForSaveOnCreation> element in the TemplateData element to true. This allows the storage of a SharePoint project in memory, as opposed to storing each created Web Part in the default My Projects folder.

TemplateContent

TemplateContent contains essential material references to obligatory code files, XML files, and cryptographic key pairs, alongside other miscellaneous content that may be mandatory to include if the template is to be useful. Since the TemplateData elements contain references to the files to include in a SharePoint project, they can be modified and extended to include other files in your SharePoint project. This can be extremely useful when development standards within your SharePoint environment need to be maintained, such as enforcing rules necessary for class names to conform to enterprise SharePoint naming conventions or provisioning common sets of helper classes and libraries that are used throughout an organization for conventional activities.

Extending TemplateContent to Include Common Enterprise Classes

Many enterprise environments use defined patterns, such as general exception-handling classes, for all custom development. Doing so provides a uniform pattern for defining an error-catching mechanism, which is easily maintainable, improves overall software standards, and decreases development time. Therefore, if you are using VSeWSS, it is advantageous to initially modify the templates to include some patterns that are considered standards within your corporate environment. As an example, it is feasible to modify the SharePoint WebPart template code file slightly to not only include the relevant codefiles and related project assembly references provided by VSeWSS, but also include references to custom assemblies and include custom code files. Because the Web Part template exists as both a project- and item-level template, it must be modified in both directories.

If a common custom assembly houses the exception-handling classes, simply reference the assembly in the `WebPart.vstemplate` in the `<ItemGroup>` parent element. The exact reference is established in the child element `<Reference Include>`. For example, to add a reference to a general common exception library, add `<Reference Include="ProSharePoint.Practices.Common.Exception.Example" />`. Then, implement a `using` statement in the code for the exception handler by opening the main C# Web Part file (`WebPart1.cs`) in the `ProjectTemplate` and `ItemTemplate` directories and adding `using ProSharePoint.Practices.Common.Exception.Example`.

If there isn't a distributed precompiled assembly from which to inherit the exception classes, it is possible to adjust the default template-provided Web Part code from the WebPart template to include functionality such as writing custom Web Part errors to the event log using the `EventLog.WriteEntry` method of the `System.Diagnostics` namespace. That's particularly a superior practice for hosted environments because local listener log files for a custom Web Part that writes to the hosting assembly directory are typically inaccessible from outside. For example, you could use the following code in order to write log files to the location of where a Web Part assembly is located by using the `Assembly.GetExecutingAssembly` method of the `System.Reflection` namespace.

```
private static TextWriterTraceListener _listener;
private static Stream _logFile;
string directory = Path.GetDirectoryName(Assembly.GetExecutingAssembly().Location)
+ @"\LogFile_" + DateTime.Now.ToString("yyyyMMdd_HHmmss") + ".log";
_logFile = File.Create(directory);
_listener = new TextWriterTraceListener(_logFile);
Trace.Listeners.Add(_listener);
```

However, through the Web Event Viewer, MOSS provides the faculty, so all exceptions spawned from custom code can be viewed if using System.Diagnostics.EventLog. This is a very powerful standard for custom deployment options where control of the server is not possible. The Web Part project template can be extended to immediately provide some code to create a new event log source if one doesn't exist for the solution or to add `TraceLevel` information to an existing event log if the event source is found to exist (see Listing A-1).

Listing A-1: Modified WebPart1.cs with common exception-handling class

```
//References made by VSeWSS
using System;
using System.Runtime.InteropServices;
using System.Web.UI;
using System.Web.UI.WebControls.WebParts;
using System.Xml.Serialization;
using Microsoft.SharePoint;
using Microsoft.SharePoint.WebControls;
using Microsoft.SharePoint.WebPartPages;

// Added to facilitate example of writing to event log for WebPart
using System.Diagnostics;

namespace $safeitemname$
```

```csharp
{
    [Guid("$guid2$")]
    public class $safeitemname$ : System.Web.UI.WebControls.WebParts.WebPart
    {
        private static TraceSwitch traceSwitch;

        public $safeitemname$()
        {

            this.ExportMode = WebPartExportMode.All;
            traceSwitch = new TraceSwitch("MyWebPart ", "Tracing For My WebPart");
        }

        protected override void Render(HtmlTextWriter writer)
        {
            // TODO: add custom rendering code here.
            // writer.Write("Output HTML");
        }


        #region Corporate Event Log Standard For Exception Handling
        //===================================================================
        //Corporate standard exception handling classes
        //Corporate standard class to write errors to event log sources
         private static void WriteEventLog(TraceLevel TraceLevel, string Message)
    {
        EventLogEntryType eventType;
        switch (TraceLevel)
        {
            case TraceLevel.Error:
                eventType = EventLogEntryType.Error;
                break;

            case TraceLevel.Warning:
                eventType = EventLogEntryType.Warning;
                break;

            default:
                eventType = EventLogEntryType.Information;
                break;
        }
        if (!EventLog.SourceExists("WebPart1.cs"))
        {
            EventLog.CreateEventSource("WebPart1.cs", "Application");
        }
        EventLog logObject = new EventLog();
        logObject.Source = "WebPart1.cs";
        logObject.WriteEntry(Message, eventType);
    }

        //Helper class for writing errors to the event log
        internal static void exceptionWriteLine(DateTime time, TraceLevel
TraceLevel, string Message, string Category)
        {
```

```
                  int cLevel = (int)TraceLevel;
                  if ((cLevel <= 2) || (((TraceLevel)cLevel) <= traceSwitch.Level))
                  {
                      Trace.WriteLine(time.ToString() + " : " + Message, Category);
                  }
                  if ((cLevel != 4) && (((TraceLevel)cLevel) <= traceSwitch.Level))
                  {
                      WriteEventLog(TraceLevel, Category + ": " + Message);
                  }
              }

          //Property for trace level to set accessor
          internal static System.Diagnostics.TraceLevel TraceLevel
            {
              get
              {
                  return traceSwitch.Level;
              }
              set
              {
                  traceSwitch.Level = value;
              }
            }
      #endregion

        }
    }
```

WizardData

The `WizardData` element appears in Project and Item Templates that require some level of interaction before item or project creation, most frequently those that are derived from either a base object or assets that can provision a related event receiver. The `WizardExtension` elements that are used by VSeWSS rely on custom code from the `Microsoft.SharePoint.Tools.Wizards` assembly to build dialogs, which instantiate an explicit wizard interface by calling the specific a class name, such as `ListDefinitionProjectWizard` for a List Definition project. `WizardExtensions` and `WizardData` are common elements in templates where the content being leveraged within the template is subject to change based on user interaction. Take, for example, a SharePoint List Definition. The list that is going to be created can vary heavily based on the base List Definition that is used. In content-type-derived lists, the available content types used as a base content type will differ from project to project. Furthermore, both List Definitions and content types might also optionally leverage event receivers.

The Wizard Element contains the concept of Replacement Parameters, which will be found in other templates. Replacement Parameters allow dynamic substitution to make the project template more adaptable to project needs, so that predefined arguments can be consumed or pieces that have been custom developed can be leveraged. In essence, Replacement Parameters will allow VSeWSS project templates to be aware that the source files contain parameters, which are fundamentally placeholders for things like `$safeitemname$`, demonstrated in the WebPart template, that are going to be replaced when the project is created. For example, in the List Definition Project Template, a child type element `<ListDefinition Type>` exists within the `<ListDefinitions>` parent element, denoting the list type that is being created. For example, the document library List Definition looks like `<ListDefinition Type="DocumentLibrary" Name="Document`

`Library">`. Within this type declaration, there are the references to specific files that are going to be included within the project template file; if certain placeholders within the file are going to be subject to replacement, they are decorated with `ReplaceParameters="true"`. For instance, the list `schema.xml` file is included by the declaration `ProjectItem TargetFileName="schema.xml">ListDefinitions\ DocumentLibrary\schema.xml</ProjectItem>`. This is because within the `schema.xml` file in the VSeWSS List Definition template, you can see several variables denoted by the $ prefix and suffix, such as `Title="$projectname$"`, constituting something that will be replaced. Although the `WizardData` section is a fundamental segment of VSeWSS, it is typically not extended, since there are precompiled methods that are called from it.

Using VSeWSS to Build Site Definitions and Custom Modules

The VseWSS Site Definition Project Wizard enables you to build and deploy custom site templates for reuse within your SharePoint environment. This is a convenient way to produce a "starter kit" for your SharePoint community. For instance, if your company publishes books, you could define a site template that an acquisition editor could apply at the start of each new book project. The site could contain a document library to hold the chapters as they are submitted by various authors, a Wiki page for authors to share interesting information that they uncover during their research, a contact list specifying the book's team members, and a Task list used to create assignments for team members. Creating Site Definitions is the preferred way to create standardized, reusable site templates, as opposed to `.stp` files, for two major reasons. With Site Definitions, changes to the source files that build the template can be propagated through multiple sites that use the template, reflecting modifications throughout an environment with little effort. Furthermore, using Site Definitions saves server space and increases the performance of sites, since the pages of the site are not "customized" or "ghosted" and stored in the database; instead, they are served off the file system, decreasing database queries and increasing caching effectiveness.

With the introduction of Features into the MOSS framework, Site Definitions have become quite powerful, because they can easily incorporate existing Features without the need to create a complex ONET file. In previous versions of SharePoint, a Site Definition had to include the full details for all elements of the site even if similar elements were already present in other Site Definitions. Thus, if you examine the ONET configuration file produced by the Team Site and blank site project templates, you will find several Feature references instead of complex Feature Definition statements.

Differences Between Team Site Definition and Blank Site Definition Project

The main difference between a blank site project and a Team Site project is the set of Features and other elements specified in the ONET file. For example, the `<Configurations>` element for a Team Site project will contain several lists within the `<Lists>` element with their associated feature ID, type, title, and URL, whereas the blank site project will contain a self-terminating `<Lists/>`. Also, within the `<Modules>` element, there will not be associated list types, since there are no Web Parts provided to the `default.aspx` page by default, other than the image Web Part, which is prevalent across all standard SharePoint Site Definitions.

$Resources Strings and Custom .resx Files

Since WSSv3 has more robust support for localization than previous versions, the ONET.xml file contains numerous instances of $Resources tags, which refer to .NET resources. By supplying variations of the resources (typically strings), you will enable the Site Definition to be used in different locales. Specifying new resource files for a Site Definition is not required, and if the values that are provided in the core.resx file are sufficient, it is not necessary to construct new resource files. When making the decision whether or not to create a new resources file, examine the deployment scenario for your environment. If you are developing for a global deployment, and localized objects are of high importance, resource files are a powerful option to tailor objects to each particular locale.

Creating a .NET Resources File for a Site Definition

For the policy management Site Definition, create a policy.resx resources file to house a series of name/value pairs specific to the policy management site, which supports string localization for global deployments. This is done by specifying the parent data element and then by specifying the child value element, which then allows you to call the <value> by the resource alias. Once the policy resources file is defined, it can be called by placing the $Resources prefix before the resource file name (without the .resx extension), then specifying the data element. For example, $Resources:filename,dataname. The policy management site is going to integrate a few string changes to adjust the interface, specifically to change some of the navigation strings and the email alert footer. Therefore, specify new, friendly datanames with the <root> element in the resources files, with new string values that correspond to the localized text. The code below defines the name/value pairs that will be used for the policy document library navigation string, the sites navigation string, and a new footer outputting a disclaimer that will be used on the alerts sent from the Site Definition:

```
<root>
  <!-- Define new string alias for policy library nav bar -->
  <data name="policylibrary">
    <value>Policies</value>
  </data>
  <!-- Define new string alias for sites nav bar -->
  <data name="policysites">
    <value>Policy Workspaces</value>
  </data>
  <!-- Define new string alias for email alert footer -->
  <data name="policyalert">
    <value> These emails are from the Policy Management site. All information you
receive from this site is company confidential.</</value>
  </data>
</root>
```

Once this resources file has been created, it is necessary to store the .resx where SharePoint can locate it. All resource files are located in the 12 hive under the Resources folder, so that's the appropriate location in which to store the new policy management resource file as well.

In the ONET.xml file, it is now necessary to reference the new key pairs that were just created so that the standard core resources file is no longer referenced. The $Resource string elements can be adapted in order to modify how specified strings are called in the VSeWSS Site Definition file. The modifications to change the document library nav, site nav, and email alert elements will adjust to bind to the new data elements. In the ONET.xml file in the Site Definition project, it is necessary to change the resources from the values in the Old Resource Reference column to the New Resource Reference column for the new policy resources file to be utilized within the custom policy Site Definition (see the following table).

Old Resource Reference	New Resource Reference
`$Resources:core,category_Documents`	`$Resources:policy,policylibrary`
`$Resources:core,category_Sites`	`$Resources:policy,policysites`
`$Resources:ServerEmailFooter`	`$Resources:policy,policyalert`

One resource change of particular interest is the email footer resource. Since policy alerts will be tailored to your policy management text, it would be prudent to change the footer string output to more relevant text. You can find the `$Resources` element for the alert text within the `<ServerEmailFooter>` element in the `ONET.xml` file, located on the last line before the `</Project>` termination element. Altering this will append custom footer text to the policy alerts that users subscribe to on the site. For the policy management site, the values specified will inform users that the information they are receiving is specific to important, confidential policy documentation.

Including Custom Modules in Your Site Definition

It is common to include custom page instances or collections of page instances in your site using modules. The VSeWSS Module Item Template will generate the relevant module XML element code, and will reference a small sample document to aid you in developing custom modules. The Module Item Template is particularly helpful in circumstances where you want a custom `WebPartPage` instance to be included when a site is provisioned, but want a reference, not a library, to house the file instance. To include a custom document with your packaged Site Definition, you need to focus on the `<File>` element that contains the `Url` attribute, allowing you to point to the custom file that should be included. If a folder should hold the file instance after it is created following provisioning, you can optionally specify the `Url` attribute in the `<module>` element. You must ensure that the account calling the foreign document has Read access to it.

In the following code, a `policytraininginformation.aspx` file instance that contains policy training information is created when a new site is provisioned based on the policy Site Definition. Since the VSeWSS Module Item Template is being instantiated in a Site Definition project, the file instance reference can be established by modifying its location in the `Url` attribute in the `<file>` element, in this example relative to the site root.

```xml
<?xml version="1.0" encoding="utf-8"?>
<!-- _filecategory="Module" _filetype="File" _filename="module.xml"
_uniqueid="1fd39e42-6b6a-46dc-b140-c8e48e6e9e38" -->
<Elements xmlns="http://schemas.microsoft.com/sharepoint/">
  <Module Name="Module" Url="" Path="">
    <File Url="policytrainingmovie.aspx" />
  </Module>
</Elements>
```

Modifying the ONET.xml File

Since the `ONET.xml` file defines various aspects of the configuration of the site, it can be customized prior to deployment. For example, you might want to change or remove the SharePoint branding image that appears on Team and blank sites. This image is in a Web Part on the site's Home page, `default.aspx`, and can be found in the `Default <Modules>` element as the `<AllUsersWebPart>` with the typename `Microsoft.SharePoint.WebPartPages.ImageWebPart`. You can simply delete this Web Part, or you can specify a different image, which will adjust the `default.aspx` page when a new site is created based on this Site Definition.

Site Definition Event Handling

Site Definition projects also include a provisioning handler to catch several SharePoint events that fire during the deployment and activation of the Site Definition feature. The handler is a class that has the same name as the project, and this class is split between two files. The `SiteProvisioning.Internal.cs` file, which inherits from the `SPFeatureReceiver` base class, does the heavy lifting needed to get the site feature installed in the SharePoint environment. Normally, you shouldn't have to change anything in this file. The `SiteProvisioning.cs` file provides a stub that makes it easy for you to override the `onActivitated` method.

The `SiteProvisioning.Internal.cs` file is not usually modified, since the `SiteProvisioning.cs` file can instead consume methods for event capturing. The internal site-provisioning file, however, does have some interesting aspects that deserve attention. The actions can be broken down into two major categories; one manages the Feature handling (see the Events in SiteProvisioning.Internal table), and the other handles several restore activities (See the RestoreEvents in SiteProvisioning.Internal table).

Feature Events in SiteProvisioning.Internal

Synchronous/Asynchronous
FeatureDeactivating/FeatureActivated
FeatureUninstalling/FeatureInstalled

RestoreEvents in SiteProvisioning.Internal

Restore Web Properties
Restore CSS
Restore DataView WebParts Outside Zones
Restore DataView WebPart Inside Zones

All of these will have the `[SharePointPermission(SecurityAction.LinkDemand, ObjectModel = true)]` decoration. You have to consider the use of the `SharePointPermission` class (to communicate with the WSS object model) and the `LinkDemands` specification (to control sensitive operations) for security reasons.

To manage your own capturing of events, use the `onActivated` method provisioned in the `SiteProvisioning.cs` partial stub. Assume that it is desirable to change the site's title after the site has been provisioned to a passed string argument, such as "Policy Management Site" (see Listing A-2).

Listing A-2: Changing site title in the onActivated event

```
public void OnActivated(SPFeatureReceiverProperties properties)
    {
        SPSite proSharePointSiteCollection = (SPSite)properties.Feature.Parent
        SPWeb proSharePointSite = proSharePointSiteCollection.RootWeb;
        proSharePointSiteCollection.Title = "Policy Management Site";
        proSharePointSiteCollection.Update();
    }
```

You can see the returning of the site collection's root web, the current site that you are provisioning, and the changing of the site title property to a new string argument. Last, you can call the update method on the site to have the changes take effect.

It is also possible to provision new content when the onActivated event is triggered; for example, creating the policy library when the site provisioning occurs. For example, sometimes, it is advantageous to create a new document library using an event handler (see Listing A-3).

Listing A-3: Creating new content in the onActivated event

```
public void OnActivated(SPFeatureReceiverProperties properties)
    {
        SPSite proSharePointSiteCollection = (SPSite)properties.Feature.Parent;
        SPWeb proSharePointSite = proSharePointSiteCollection.RootWeb;
        SPListTemplate template = site.ListTemplates["Policy Library"];
        Guid docLibID = proSharePointSite.Lists.Add("PolicyLibrary", "Library for
Policies", template);
        SPList docLib = proSharePointSite.Lists[docLibID];
        docLib.Update();
    }
```

Using the SPWeb class to return the root web, you are defining getting a list template and using the Lists.Add method to provision a new Library for Policies document library. Finally, the code calls the Update method to update the changes to the site.

Using Embedded Solution Deployment to Provision the New Site Definition

Using the inherent SharePoint deployment options, you can package new SharePoint Site Definitions and all related items into a SharePoint solution file for automatic deployment to your SharePoint server or farm. Since solutions couple with SharePoint timer jobs in order to distribute new additions across a SharePoint farm, this process is generally automatic and the plumbing exists behind the scenes. The status can be tracked through the bottom-left status bar, just like the other publishing features in Visual Studio.

To get to the embedded solution deployment screen, you must open the project properties page within Visual Studio. On the project's properties page, select the SharePoint solution tab, which will bring you to the deployment screen; this provides a tree view of all the nodes branching to available deployment packages (see Figure A-4). For the Site Definition, there will be the Site Definition node, and for other items, such as the module that was created previously, a Feature node. Fortunately, the view that is provided is hierarchical in nature and is, therefore, easy to disseminate and follow. It is helpful to break down the nodes into parent/child elements to understand the attributes that are provided as well.

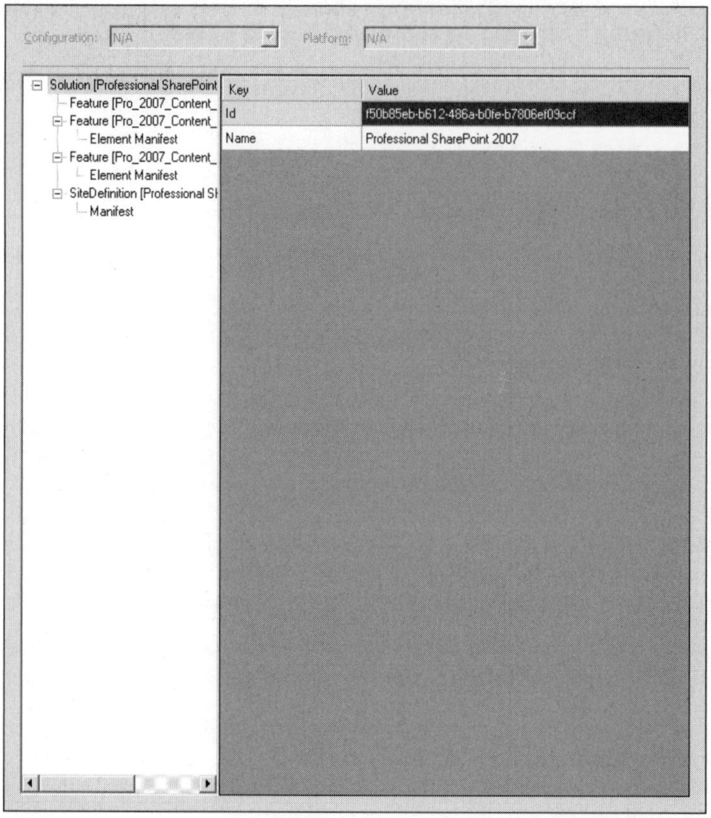

Figure A-4

Parent/Child Elements in an Embedded SharePoint Solution Deployment

There are the following elements available from this key/value DataGrid that allow you to structure some of the attributes of your SharePoint solution and its embedded content:

Parent Solution Key/Value Entries

Name	Description
ID	Field ID of the SharePoint solution file
Name	The name of the SharePoint solution file

SiteDefinition Key/Value Entries

Name	Description
Name	The name of the Site Definition
Language	The localization attributes (defaults to 1033 or English)

Manifest Key/Value Entries (Under Parent SiteDefinition)

Name	Description
TemplateID	Site Definition ID
Title	The Site Definition title
Description	The Site Definition description
ImageURL	The image displayed in the site creation screen
Display Category	The tab that the definition will appear under

Once Item Templates are added to the overall solution, as in the case with the small module, they are stapled into the menu as Features. The Features will have the following Key/Value entries. This same screen exists for all assets that are bound as features through embedded solution deployment.

Feature Key/Value Entries

Name	Description
FolderName	Feature folder's name
ID	Feature ID
Title	Feature title
Description	Description of the Feature
Version	The current version of the Feature
Scope	The tab that the definition will appear under
Hidden	Whether the feature is visible or not
DefaultResourceFile	The default .resx file of the feature

Continued

Name	Description
`RecieverAssembly` (Optional)	If you choose to instantiate an event receiver, the assembly the feature will use
`RecieverClass` (Optional)	If you choose to instantiate an event receiver, the default class the receiver will use

Attention to Detail Pays Off — Make Your Attributes Relevant!

Ensure that the attributes that are entered in Embedded SharePoint Solution Deployment key/value DataGrids are relevant and well formed, since some will be displayed for end user action. For Site Definition deployment, pay particular attention to the `DisplayCategory` in the `SiteDefinition` manifest, since this will create the tabs on the site creation screen, which has very little available real estate and will be heavily used by users.

Sometimes the `ReceiverAssembly` and `ReceiverClass` options will be grayed out in the `DataGrid`. When using the option to generate an event receiver for an item that uses the `RecieverAssembly` and `RecieverClass` attributes, you must choose an option within the wizards provided to generate the receiver or these options will not be selectable.

Structure of Deployed Assets

There are certain files that are built using VSeWSS with the embedded deployment options in which all the plumbing and related files are created by the extensions. (See the following table.) When using the Site Definitions Project Template, all requirements are generated with no interaction.

Files Generated By VSeWSS

Name	Description
`Setup.bat`	Batch file for deployment operations
`<SolutionName>.dll`	Assembly that builds all the embedded code, particularly that in the event receivers
`<SolutionName>.wsp`	SharePoint Solution file for deployment
`Solution\1033\xml/WebTemp<id>.xml`	New `webtemp` file to make the new site creation screen aware of the new Site Definition
`Solution\<SolutionName><id>\ default.aspx`	Default page of the Site Definition
`Solution\<SolutionName><id>\ elementManfiest.xml`	Builds a reference to its sister feature

Name	Description
`Solution\<SolutionName><id>\` `feature.xml`	Site Definition Feature
`Solution\<SolutionName><id>\xml\` `onet.xml`	`ONET.xml` to define the overall structure of the Site Definition
`Solution\<SolutionName><id>\xml\` `onet.xml`	`ONET.xml` to define the overall structure of the Site Definition
`Manifest.xml`	Defines the structure of the SharePoint solution file

Items that are added to the solution are deployed as Features, and therefore each will be given its relevant `Feature.xml` file, which references the attributes in the Feature Embedded SharePoint Solution Deployment key/value DataGrid (See the Feature Key/Value Entries table).

Debugging Using the Embedded Solution Deployment

By using the embedded deployment features, VSeWSS can be leveraged in order to debug the Site Definitions that are being created. This is a huge shift from previous versions of SharePoint in which Site Definitions were mostly constructed and debugged through trial and error.

This capability is particularly useful when developing event handlers like the `onActivated` example above. The debugging experience is just about the same as for any other .NET application. For instance, to step through the code, just set a breakpoint in the `onActivated` method. Previously, there was no easy way to do runtime debugging on Site Definition solutions, but now the close integration of SharePoint and VS2005 makes this pretty easy.

Using VSeWSS to Build Content Types

A content type is analogous to a class in object-oriented programming, and it's a major addition to SharePoint 2007. Content types allow the definition of a data diagram with associated metadata (columns), workflows, event receivers, and associated SharePoint listform pages. Although you can define content types directly on a SharePoint site via your browser, on the `ctypenew.aspx` page VSeWSS offers an Item Wizard that enables you to build and deploy more complex content types. (See Figure A-4.)

The first step is to define a parent, or base, for the new content type (see Figure A-5).

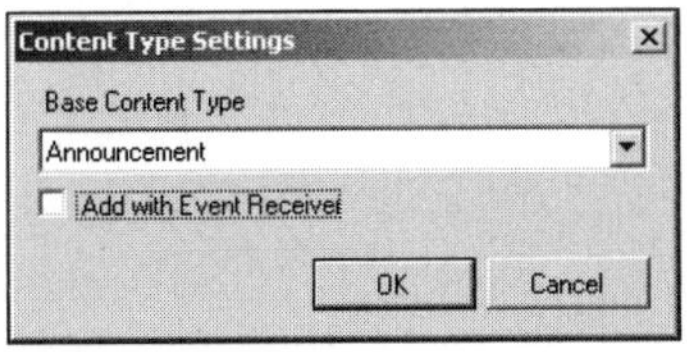

Figure A-5

The new content type will then inherit the base ancestral attributes of its parent, such as whether the content type is a list type or a library type. Here is a list of parent content types supported by VSeWSS:

- ❑ Announcement
- ❑ Contact
- ❑ Discussion
- ❑ Document
- ❑ Event
- ❑ Folder
- ❑ Issue
- ❑ Item
- ❑ Link
- ❑ Picture
- ❑ Task
- ❑ WikiDocument
- ❑ XMLDocument

Once the new content type is defined, it can be used as the parent for further derivations. This is handy, because you can then easily propagate attributes from parent to child in what OO programmers call an "inheritance tree." Furthermore, updates to parent content types can be propagated to derived child content types through update operations.

Building the Custom Content Type

When building a new content type, the VSeWSS Wizard creates two XML files: one to define the structure of the content type and the other to describe the default field type. These two files are related by the GUID that is specified within the child `<FieldRef>` element GUID that is in the `<FieldRefs>` parent element, which has the name `ProSharePointContentType.Fields.xml` in the following example (see Listing A-4).

Listing A-4: Default content type

```xml
<?xml version="1.0" encoding="utf-8"?>
<Elements xmlns="http://schemas.microsoft.com/sharepoint/">
  <!-- _filecategory="ContentType" _filetype="Schema" _filename="contenttype.xml"
_uniqueid="56ef1c27-ba63-4981-b9da-96f4ce299b52" -->
  <ContentType ID="0x0101008fde2958be9943828d6300c1151449f8"
      Name="ProSharePointContentType"
      Group="Development"
      Description="Developing Content Type"
      Version="0">
```

```
    <!-- This reference will lookup to the fields.xml document -->
    <FieldRefs>
      <FieldRef ID="{e8b0cc17-aa64-4061-9623-ca5f7c774e96}"
Name="ProSharePointContentTypeField" />
    </FieldRefs>
  </ContentType>
</Elements>
```

The field XML file that VSeWSS provisions is essentially a new column that is related to the content type being created. In the following piece of code (see Listing A-5), there is a boilerplate field type that can be used by the content type being created. There are two important elements to notice about this field type that VSeWSS provisions by default. The first is that by default VSeWSS will not make the field type hidden, so users with appropriate access will be allowed to make edits to this field type. The second is that the field is not marked as sealed, so updates to this field type through the SharePoint user interface (from `ChangeContentTypeOptionalSettings.aspx`) or object model operations will be allowed to propagate. If you want to prevent this throughout an enterprise, you should clone and customize the VSeWSS project templates so that the boilerplate XML files no longer have these attributes.

Listing A-5: Default field type

```xml
<?xml version="1.0" encoding="utf-8"?>
<Elements xmlns="http://schemas.microsoft.com/sharepoint/">
  <!-- _filecategory="ContentType" _filetype="File" _filename="fields.xml"
_uniqueid="b30ac938-2543-4159-9efd-6422eb42df33" -->
  <Field
    ID="{b30ac938-2543-4159-9efd-6422eb42df33}"
    Type="Text"
    Name="Content_Type1Field"
    DisplayName="Content Type1 Field"
    StaticName="Content_Type1Field"
    Hidden="FALSE"
    Required="FALSE"
    Sealed="FALSE"
    />
</Elements>
```

Building a Custom Content Type Using VSeWSS

The content type that the policy management site will use will have several custom fields defined that will appear in the available site columns' page after they are provisioned (see below table). Each of the fields that is being created will be referenced by the content type in the <FieldRefs> node (See Listing A-6) by using the ID and Name that is provided within the <Field> element of in `Policies.Field.xml` (see Listing A-7). When you define the content type using VSeWSS, it will generate the `contenttype.xml` and the `contenttype.fields.xml` file, already providing a sample field element that can be used as a boilerplate for further field integration.

Element Field (Column) Name	Field (Column) Type	Field Description
Policy ID	Number	Relevant Policy ID
Policy Name	Single Line of Text	Friendly Policy Title
Effective Policy Date	Date and Time	Date of Policy Enforcement

The following code defines the policy library content type with the ancestral attribute of the content type (0x0101, in this case, specifying a document library), the content type description attributes, the content type references to the three custom fields as defined by the `Policies.Field.xml` (see Listing A-7), and associated SharePoint listform pages for interacting with the policy library (see Listing A-6).

Listing A-6: Policies.xml (policies content type)

```
<?xml version="1.0" encoding="utf-8"?>
<Elements xmlns="http://schemas.microsoft.com/sharepoint/">
  <!--document library ancestral type 0x0101-->
  <ContentType  ID="0x0101005681071F88374fe0BFD45E7C0340C528"
        Name="PolicyLib"
        Group="Policy Content Type"
        Description="Documents for product"
        Version="0">
    <FieldRefs>
       <!--Policy ID-->
       <FieldRef ID="{78953994-21C2-4737-A7FA-E7FC6019CA74}" Name="PolicyID"
Required="TRUE" ShowInNewForm="TRUE" ShowInEditForm="TRUE"/>
       <!--Policy Name-->
       <FieldRef ID="{358E48C9-D527-4718-BA6F-438A6A12922A}" Name="PolicyName"
Required="TRUE" ShowInNewForm="TRUE" ShowInEditForm="TRUE"/>
       <!--Effective Policy Date-->
       <FieldRef ID="{3FB081E8-C903-48a6-A8E1-A2847082A40E}"
Name="EffectivePolicyDate" Required="TRUE" ShowInNewForm="TRUE"
ShowInEditForm="TRUE"/>
    </FieldRefs>
    <XmlDocuments>
       <XmlDocument NamespaceURI="http://schemas.microsoft.com/sharepoint/
v3/contenttype/forms">
         <FormTemplates xmlns="http://schemas.microsoft.com/sharepoint/
v3/contenttype/forms">
           <Display>DocumentLibraryForm</Display>
           <Edit>DocumentLibraryForm</Edit>
           <New>DocumentLibraryForm</New>
         </FormTemplates>
       </XmlDocument>
    </XmlDocuments>
  </ContentType>
</Elements>
```

When defining the new custom fields for the content type to consume, there are some fields that VSeWSS will give you by default and some fields that can be defined as optional attributes to the field element.

Name	Description
ID	Field ID to relate to `contenttype.xml` file
Type	The field type that the field (column) will use such as text, number, or choice
Name	Programmatic name used by the field to identify the reference
DisplayName	Friendly name of the content type field
StaticName	The static name of the content type field
Hidden	Whether the content type field is visible to users or not
Required	When using this field, if it is marked `true`, data must be entered when adding new items
Sealed	If set to `true`, this field can be overridden by update to its parent element

These are simply the fields that are required for the content type field to be acceptable to SharePoint. There are some other optional fields that can be used for things such as indicating that the schema of the content type field is being defined by SharePoint v3.

The following code defines the fields decorated with the relevant attributes (see the table above) that are going to be used by the policy content type, the most important being the ID and Name attributes, which correlate the field to the content type (see Listing A-7).

Listing A-7: Policies.Fields.xml

```xml
<?xml version="1.0" encoding="utf-8"?>
<Elements xmlns="http://schemas.microsoft.com/sharepoint/">
  <!-- Policy Field Types -->
  <Field ID="{78953994-21C2-4737-A7FA-E7FC6019CA74}"
      Name="PolicyID"
      SourceID="http://schemas.microsoft.com/sharepoint/v3"
      StaticName="PolicyID"
      Group="Policy Storage columns"
      Type="Number"
      Sealed="FALSE"
      ReadOnly="FALSE"
      Hidden="FALSE"
      DisplayName="Product ID"
      ColName="PolicyID">
  </Field>
  <Field ID="{358E48C9-D527-4718-BA6F-438A6A12922A}"
      Name="PolicyName"
      SourceID="http://schemas.microsoft.com/sharepoint/v3"
      StaticName="PolicyName"
      Group="Policy Storage columns"
      Type="Text"
      Sealed="FALSE"
```

```
            ReadOnly="FALSE"
            Hidden="FALSE"
            DisplayName="Policy Name"
            ColName="PolicyName">
    </Field>
    <Field ID="{3FB081E8-C903-48a6-A8E1-A2847082A40E}"
      Name="EffectivePolicyDate"
      SourceID="http://schemas.microsoft.com/sharepoint/v3"
      StaticName="EffectivePolicyDate"
      Group="Policy Storage columns"
      Type="Date and Time"
      Sealed="FALSE"
      ReadOnly="FALSE"
      Hidden="FALSE"
      DisplayName="Policy Effective Date"
      ColName="PolicyEffectiveDate">
    </Field>
  </Elements>
```

Event Handlers

The Content Type Wizard also offers the option to append an event receiver to the content type that you are creating. Adding an event receiver to the content type will add two new .cs files to the item folder: a class inheriting from the SPItemEventReceiver base class to handle item-level events, and an additional class inheriting from the SPListEventReceiver base class to handle list-level events. Within each of these receiver classes, there are the related overridden blank item or list event methods used to capture events as they occur or execute any wrapped logic within each event method. Whenever that specific event is triggered, the receiver class will be called and whatever methods are wrapped within the custom overrides will be triggered and executed. It is important that the same type of receiver architecture be used when appending event receivers to various other Item Templates in VSeWSS.

Event Handlers Provisioned By Default by VSeWSS

With the event handlers that you receive when you generate the receiver through the VSeWSS Wizard, you get both the synchronous events (events triggered before activity) and the asynchronous events (those that are handled after activity is triggered). The following table is a list of events that are overridden when using the VSeWSS table:

Synchronous/Asynchronous
ItemAdding/Item Added
ItemAttachmentAdding/ItemAttachment Added
ItemAttachmentDeleting/ItemAttachmentDeleted
ItemCheckingIn/ItemCheckedIn

Synchronous/Asynchronous
ItemCheckingOut/ItemCheckedOut
ItemDeleting/ItemDeleted
ItemFileMoving/ItemFileMoved
ItemUncheckingOut/ItemUncheckedOut
ItemUpdating/ItemUpdated

When you create a new content type and have VSeWSS provision the receiver for you, you will also get the ListEventReceiver.cs class, which will handle the list events, as opposed to the item event. The following table lists the item events that are overridden when using VSeWSS. This inherits from the SPListEventReceiver base class and has pre- and post-events.

Synchronous/Asynchronous
FieldAdding/FieldAdded
FieldDeleting/FieldDeleted
FieldUpdating/FieldUpdated

There is a series of event properties that can be used to customize the way that WSS interacts with the user to manage the overall user experience, and that only requires a brief set of custom code in order to populate. Specifically, for the policy management site, you want to make sure that relevant policy documents are not deleted from the policy library. In order to maintain an archive for legal purposes and business regulations, it is best to maintain records of all applicable standards. Therefore, modify the synchronous event before an item is actually deleted to display a message to users that they are about to delete a policy document (see Listing A-8). The code simply fires the pre-ItemDeleting event when a person attempts to delete a document, sending an error message with the cancel property set to true, preventing the actual deletion of the document from the policy library.

Listing A-8: ItemDeleting an event handler to display a message to the user

```
[SharePointPermission(SecurityAction.LinkDemand, ObjectModel = true)]
public override void ItemDeleting(SPItemEventProperties properties)
    {
    string policyDocName = properties.ListItem;
    string currentUser = properties.UserDisplayName;
    string listname = properties.ListName;
    properties.Cancel = true;
    properties.ErrorMessage = "Deleting {0} policy is not allowed {1} from the {2}";
    }
```

Using VSeWSS to Build List Definitions

VSeWSS allows innovative ways to manufacture List Definitions. You can create a new List Definition from scratch, also known as an explicit list, where only a list base type needs to be defined for VSeWSS to assimilate. You can also instantiate a new List Definition from a custom content type. If you instantiate a new list, you can consume the policy content type that was just created in order to build a new list, a very powerful feature for SharePoint development. When building a List Definition from a previously created content type, the content type you wish to base the list on is the only supplied argument (see Figure A-6).

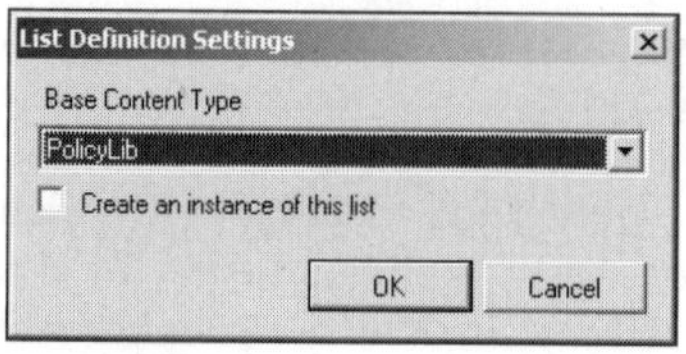

Figure A-6

The most important noticeable code difference between an explicit list and a List Definition based on a content type is located within the major definition file, schema.xml. The generated schema.xml file will define list information, such as fields and views, along with other granular list data. When building a new List Definition from an existing content type, under the <ContentTypes> parent element, in the <ContentTypeRef> child element, a reference is built into the content type GUID (see the following code).

```
<!- GUID defined with the custom content type generator from VSeWSS ->
<ContentType ID="0x010100966c882da1884476bbfff3e10bbedfbb" />

<!- Reference to custom content type GUID in new list definition ->
<ContentTypes>
      <ContentTypeRef ID="0x010100966c882da1884476bbfff3e10bbedfbb" />
</ContentTypes>
```

Also, the fields that are referenced by the list will be assimilated according to the content type that you are basing the List Definition on, so the columns made in the content type, along with any other custom assets, will be available when creating an instance of the list.

When creating an explicit list, or a list that is only defining a parent list type, the only argument you need to supply is the base List Definition (see Figure A-7).

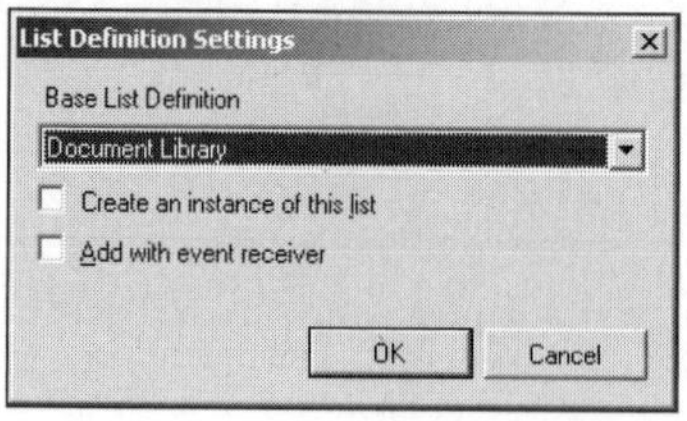

Figure A-7

Depending on the list or content type that is chosen as the base, different form pages will be generated. This is because the same files that exist in libraries don't exist in lists, such as the `WebFldr.aspx` and `Upload.aspx` files don't exist for lists, since they don't provide these facilities. Therefore, it is important to choose the base type that you wish to inherit from wisely.

The content type supplies this information to the list by using its ancestral attributes. For example, when you create a content type that is based on a document library, it will have a certain prefix. In the policy document content type, there exists `ID="0x0101005681071F88374fe0BFD45E7C0340C528"`. There are prefix numerals on this number that define it as being derived from a document library, specifically, `0x0101` means that it is derived from a document library. Lists of various types will supply different numeric prefixes.

Creating a Custom List Definition

The structure of a custom List Definition is defined in the `schema.xml` file provided by VSeWSS when you use the List Definition Template. The first element in the `schema.xml` file is `<metadata>`, which provides the blueprint for the list and the largest option for extensibility. The second element, which is absent from the VSeWSS-provided List Definition, is `<data>`. The `<data>` element is not frequently used, since it is solely meant to prepopulate the list with a set of values. The `<metadata>` element, however, allows some options for a high level of extendibility.

Within the `<metadata>` element, there are several `<View>` elements that can be tailored to a specific list interface. Within each of the `<View>` elements there are `WebPartZones` defined, where new Web Part can be added to the pages. This can be accomplished by adding a new `<WebPart>` element to the page and then adjusting the `WebPart` file through the use of a `CDATA` element, which allows the XML parser to ignore the text that is placed between the CDATA tags. The structure of the `CDATA` section should start with `<![CDATA[` and should terminate with `]]>"`. Following the declaration of the `CDATA` piece, you can locate a `.webpart` file that has been exported or pooled from the Web Part gallery at the root of the SharePoint site collection, and place it between these tags; it will be parsed out appropriately.

It is also possible to modify the various listform pages that are given by default with the List Definition Template to satisfy whatever predeployment customization needs you have. The options for this are very flexible; just ensure that the additions to the pages are well formed and that the ASP.NET 2.0 runtime engine can output them correctly.

Creating a New List Instance

When creating a new List Definition either from a content type or as an explicit list from a base type, you can also create a new instance of the list. When creating a new list instance, you are given a boilerplate `instance.xml` file. The `instance.xml` file is essentially a file that aids in the deployment of your new list by defining a Feature ID that will establish a deployment dependency (see the following code). This allows you to deploy the new list as a manageable Feature when using the embedded SharePoint solution deployment options.

```xml
<?xml version="1.0" encoding="utf-8"?>
<!-- _filecategory="ListInstance" _filetype="File" _filename="instance.xml"
_uniqueid="fccba0b8-cd3e-4bb3-a5b1-df2fe3894070" -->
<Elements xmlns="http://schemas.microsoft.com/sharepoint/">
  <ListInstance
```

```
        FeatureId="2c978926-a8e2-49b2-a01b-6fcc17175f72"
        TemplateType="100"
        Title="ProSharePointListDefinition"
        Url="Lists/ProSharePointListDefinition">
    </ListInstance>
</Elements>
```

Event Receivers

When generating a new list from VSeWSS, you are afforded the option to generate a receiver for the list. This option will generate the same receiver options used for the content type, with which you can granularly control event capturing for both list-level and item-level events that occur with the list. Therefore, the same type of overrides of event methods that apply to content types can be applied to list items. Thus, you can override the `ItemDeleting` event to cancel the event and then use the `ErrorMessage` property to display a message to the user that deleting item operations is not allowed (See Listing A-9).

Listing A-9: ItemDeleting event handler for lists

```
[SharePointPermission(SecurityAction.LinkDemand, ObjectModel = true)]
 public override void ItemDeleting(SPItemEventProperties properties)
    {
    properties.Cancel = true;
    properties.ErrorMessage = "Deleting list items is not allowed;
    }
```

Using VSeWSS to Build Web Parts

The VSeWSS Web Part Wizard enables you to quickly create SharePoint Web Parts that can inherit from the SharePoint `WebPart` base class or the ASP.NET 2.0 `WebPart` base class. It also offers quick deployment of Web Parts using a SharePoint feature manifest built into the embedded SharePoint Solution deployment.

There are several major tasks that are automated by using the SharePoint `WebPart` template:

1. Conventional reference establishment and base class inheritance.

2. Auto-packaging Web Parts into SharePoint solution files for deployment ease (easily the most useful feature).

3. Temporary key provisioning to sign assembly with a strong name (`Temporary.snk`), for Web Part deployment into the Global Assembly Cache (GAC) if Code Access Security (CAS) isn't a large concern. This key should be replaced by the enterprise key, which is password protected once the Web Part is pushed to production.

4. A generic render method to output embedded (child) HTML using `HtmlTextWriter`, since it allows a granular level of the child control output.

There are very specific references established for some very concrete purposes by using the WebPart project template. The first and most obvious are the SharePoint specific references, since they are required to work with the SharePoint object model. For example, there will be references made to the `Microsoft.SharePoint` DLL because Web Parts may need site objects (`SPSite`), web objects (`SPWeb`), and user (`SPUser`) objects. `Microsoft.SharePoint.Webcontrols` is referenced because it is needed for assets like `SPcontrol`. By putting these together, you can start to build intuitive Web Parts that will interact more with SharePoint, doing something as simple as getting the context of the current web with `TheCurWeb = SPControl.GetContextWeb(Context);` or as complex as getting a folder by passing in an argument that will define the source URL (see Listing A-10).

Listing A-10: Using SPWeb to get a folder by the source URL

```
public static SPFolder getFolderBySourceFileUrl(SPWeb webSite, string fileURL)
    {
        SPFolder folder = null;
        if (fileURL.Length > 0)
        {
            int urlNumeric = SPEncode.UrlEncodeAsUrl(webSite.Url).Length;
            int lengthNumeric = fileURL.Length;
            string urlString = fileURL.Substring(urlNumeric + 1, (lengthNumeric
- urlNumeric) - 1);
            string[] textArray = urlString.Replace("%20", " ").Split(new char[]
{ '/' });

            for (int i = 0; i < (textArray.Length - 1); i++)
            {
                if (i == 0)
                {
                    try
                    {
                        folder = webSite.Folders[textArray[i]];
                    }
                    catch
                    {
                        return null;
                    }
                }
                else
                {
                    try
                    {
                        folder = folder.SubFolders[textArray[i]];
                    }
                    catch
                    {
                        return null;
                    }
                }
            }
        }
        return folder;
    }
```

`using` statements will also be created for `System.Runtime.InteropServices` so that tasks such as controlling instance fields for structs, by defining struct `layouts` attributes, can be implemented, as well as marshaling in unmanaged code. There will also be a `using` statement for `System.Xml.Serialization`, since your WebPart properties will generally make use of an XMLelement to specify an accessor for the SharePoint property XmlElement(ElementName="MyElementName"), but this becomes increasingly important when working with CAML (Collaboration Application Markup Language), a specialized XML language. For example, assume that it is necessary to construct a method that will allow a sort order to be added to a CAML query (see Listing A-11). This requires heavy use of the XML reference, since XmlNode and Xmlattribute have to be leveraged.

Listing A-11: Adding a sort order to an existing CAML query

```
private static string AddSortOrderCAML(XmlDocument existingQuery, string
orderColumnName, bool Ascending)
    {
        XmlNode orderNode = existingQuery.CreateElement("OrderBy");
        XmlNode refNode = existingQuery.CreateElement("FieldRef");
        XmlAttribute nameAttribute = existingQuery.CreateAttribute("Name");
        nameAttribute.Value = orderColumnName;
        refNode.Attributes.Append(attribute1);
        nameAttribute = existingQuery.CreateAttribute("Ascending");
        nameAttribute.Value = Ascending.ToString().ToUpper();
        refNode.Attributes.Append(nameAttribute);
        orderNode.AppendChild(refNode);
        return (orderNode.OuterXml + existingQuery.OuterXml);
    }

// Utilize the new option by passing in the appropriate parameters
AddSortOrderCAML(XMLdocument, webpart.SortField, webpart.SortDir == "ASC")
```

The SharePoint WebPart Template will take care of providing the basis for the Web Part, establishing base class inheritance and necessary reference establishment, and providing a cryptographic key pair with which to sign the compilation. Therefore, you just need to add some methods to the project template in order to do something relevant, initialize whatever properties are required in the constructor that is generated by the template, and add the final output method to the overridden RenderContents or RenderWebPart output method. As an example, many of the documents that are going to be put in the policy management site will maintain document workspaces, so it may be helpful to provide users with a Web Part that shows them all the subsites that they have access to on the front page.

The first step is to build out a method that will include the relevant site icon related to the site, using the SPWeb.WebTemplateId and SPWeb.Configuration properties with an if statement (see Listing A-12).

Listing A-12: Get the icon of the site

```
private string GetSiteIcon(SPWeb myWeb)
{
    if (myWeb.WebTemplateId == 2)
    {
        return "/_layouts/images/mtgicon.gif";
    }
    if (myWeb.Configuration == 2)
    {
        return "/_layouts/images/docicon.gif";
    }
    return "/_layouts/images/stsicon.gif";
}
```

Second, the site title for the relevant site should be collected for the Web Part to display. This can be generated through a `GetSiteTitle` method, which returns a string by passing in the `SPWeb` object, then using the `SPWeb.Title` public property to return the title of the site (see Listing A-13).

Listing A-13: Get the site title

```
private string GetSiteTitle(SPWeb myWeb)
{
    string siteTitle = "<a href='" + SPEncode.HtmlEncode(myWeb.Url) + "' ";
    siteTitle = siteTitle + "title='" + SPEncode.HtmlEncode(myWeb.Title) + "'";
    return (siteTitle + ">"+ "</a>");
}        }
```

The main body of the Web Part uses the `GetDesignTimeHtml()` method from the `IDesignTimeHtmlProvider` interface in order to return the HTML that will be output (see Listing A-14). The benefits of using the `GetDesignTimeHtml` method are that it will also render the output correctly when the Web Part is opened in an editing interface, such as Microsoft Office SharePoint Designer, and it reduces the codebloat in the overridden `RenderWebPart` method, since it will just output `this.GetDesignTimeHtml()`. The returned sites will be collected by the `SPWeb.GetSubwebsForCurrentUser` method, which will get the subsites of which a user is a member.

Listing A-14: GetDesignTimeHtml() method

```
public string GetDesignTimeHtml()
    {
        string designTime = "";

        SPWeb currentWebContext = SPControl.GetContextWeb(this.Context);
        SPWebCollection webCollectionBucket =
currentWebContext.GetSubwebsForCurrentUser();
        SPSite currentSiteWrap = currentWebContext.Site;
        foreach (SPWeb primaryWeb in webCollectionBucket)
        {
            designTime = designTime + this.GetSiteIcon(primaryWeb);
            designTime = designTime + this.GetSiteTitle(primaryWeb);
        }

        return (designTime);
    }
```

Now that you have built the Web Part, you can use some of the inherent features of the VSeWSS and deploy it across a SharePoint single server or SharePoint farm by packaging it within a SharePoint solution that defines a Feature for the SharePoint Web Part. Using this option is much more attractive for a server farm because, when coupled with a SharePoint timer job, the Web Part will be made available across all front-end web servers on a scheduled basis. As opposed to legacy methods of packaging our Web Part into a `.cab` file that contains the instructions for deployments such as Safe Control entries, resource file exposure, and sister assembly references, the solution file will take care of the deployment for you by generating the appropriate SharePoint Feature. Depending on the scope element for which the Feature is targeted (such as farm, web application, or site collection), it will alter where the Web Part is available for use through the SharePoint environment. The Feature scope can be controlled from the `scope` attribute in the version-incrementable Feature file.

Leveraging the SharePoint Solution Generator

The SharePoint Solution Generator (SPSolGen.exe) is one of the most powerful tools included with VSeWSS and the only included stand-alone Windows application. It allows you to package preexisting site and List Definitions, customize the content, and deploy it at will across an enterprise with ease, using embedded Solution Generator files. Thus, the main purpose of the SharePoint Solution Generator is to target a previously created Site or List Definition, provide integration by manufacturing a Visual Studio Project file, and finally wrap it in a deployable package with the embedded solution generation that can easily be provisioned at will.

Using the SharePoint Solution Generator to Reverse Engineer an Existing Site

The first step in using SPSolGen to reverse engineer an existing site is to choose the site that you wish to reverse engineer (see Figure A-8). There are some site templates that are not supported, such as the default News or Report Center sites. It is best to plan on using the Solution Generator with strictly Team, blank, or meeting workspace sites.

It is possible to also manually enter the URL as the argument that is passed if you are familiar with the site that you wish to package back into a project file. Next, you must define where you wish to store the new project file that will be generated (only C# is supported). By default, this will point to a Site Definition directory in the user's Documents folder, but it's better to point this to the existing Visual Studio My Projects directory in order to keep all relevant development assets in one uniform location (see Figure A-9).

Figure A-8

After selecting the location, reversing the Site Definition back into a project file can occur. This allows you, as a developer, to extend the existing site with new features. There are specified sequences of events that will occur when this happens:

1. Copy base Site Definition.

2. Copy base site properties.

3. Update Site Definition.

4. Copy base List Definitions.

5. Update List Definitions.

6.   Generate provisioning code.

7.   Create Visual Studio project file.

8.   Copy base site properties.

9.   Update Site Definition.

After these events occur, the final result is an extendable project file that can be redeployed using the embedded SharePoint solution options (see Figure A-10).

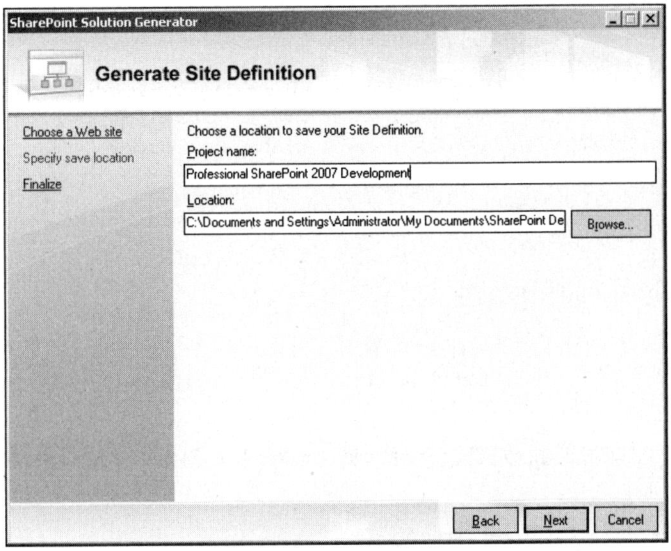

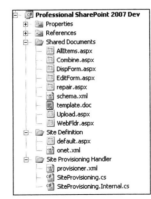

Figure A-9

Figure A-10

Using the SharePoint Solution Generator to Reverse an Existing List

You've seen how the Site Definition Generator can be used in order to reverse engineer an existing Site Definition into an extendable project file; the same process can be applied to lists, and the steps to get the unpackaged project file are very similar. The first step is to define the site where the list is housed. The options for doing this are the same as those for the Site Definition Generator. You can use the tree view provided to browse to the site or manually type in the URL of the location where the list you wish to pull down is housed. Second, once the site argument is passed, the List Definition for which the project is created must be selected (see Figure A-11).

Once the list argument has been selected, the project dump location must be specified (see Figure A-12).

Following this, a sequence of events occurs that generates the List Definition project for the list that was chosen in the previous step. The List Definition Generator sequence is:

1. Copy base List Definition.

2. Update List Definition.

3. Create Visual Studio project.

Following this, the selected List Definition will be available as a Visual Studio project and can be redeployed after customization, using the embedded solution deployment options (see Figure A-13).

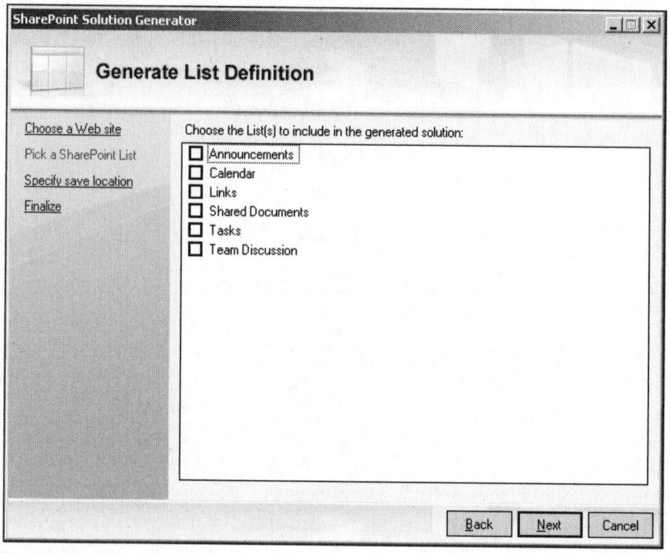

Figure A-11

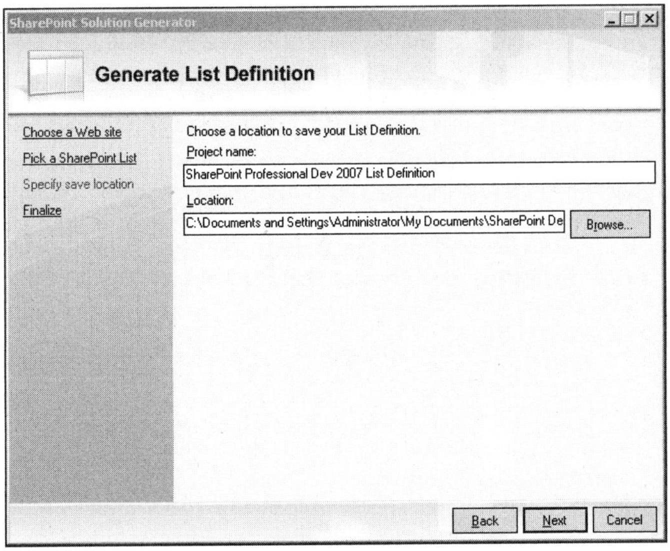

Figure A-12

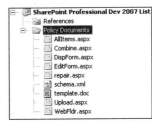

Figure A-13

Summary

VSeWSS is an efficient way for SharePoint developers to eliminate the redundant tasks that can sometimes make SharePoint development a tiresome effort. VSeWSS Visual Studio Project and Item Templates, such as the Site Definition, Content Type, List Definition, and Web Part, allow the creation of boilerplate code files that you can use to reduce framework integration code, allowing you to spend more time developing custom code. The embedded SharePoint solution deployment options support the familiar F5 runtime debugging and deployment scenario through the use of SharePoint Features and bundled SharePoint solutions. Using the embedded deployment functionality resolves two of the principal grievances in legacy SharePoint development: runtime debugging issues and the need for quick, easy deployment mechanisms that can be integrated directly into the development environment.

Appendix A: Using the Microsoft Visual Studio 2005 Extension

The VSeWSS templates can be extended by cloning the existing project templates to make new custom templates available from the Visual Studio interface. Doing so allows you to create SharePoint development templates that allow the implementation of coding standards, helper libraries/classes, and predefined coding attributes that can be distributed across an enterprise.

The SharePoint Solution Generator provides an easy way to take existing sites and lists within a live SharePoint environment and pull them back into an IDE that developers are familiar with by autogenerating the Visual Studio project file. Once site and List Definitions have been pulled back into Visual Studio, custom code can be added into them, and using the embedded solution mechanisms, they can be easily redistributed back into the environment using native, contemporary SharePoint functionality.

Index